Access Code to accompany

CENTRAL MICHIGAN UNIVERSITY

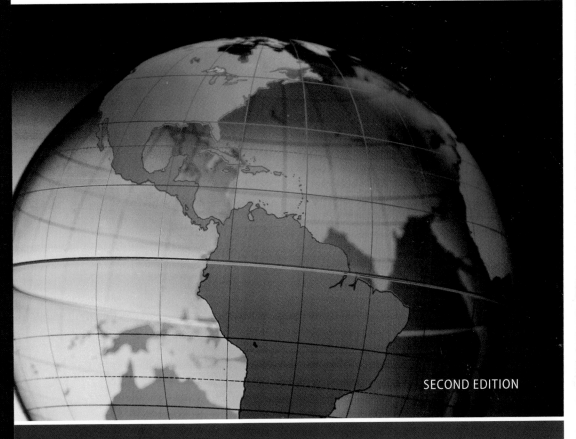

SECOND EDITION

MSA 604
Administration, Globalization and Multiculturalism

CENTRAL MICHIGAN UNIVERSITY

MASTER OF SCIENCE
IN ADMINISTRATION

Access Code to accompany

MSA 604
Administration, Globalization and Multiculturalism

Student Instructions:
The code below gives you access to course materials your instructor has assigned
and has required for your course.

Please follow the procedure listed below to log in to your online course and
access these assessment materials.

1. Confirm that you have an internet connection.

2. Log into your school's learning management system (Blackboard), **http://blackboard.cmich.edu**
   Use the **Global** ID and password issued to you by CMU soon after you registered for the course.
   If you do not know your Global ID and/or password, contact the CMU Help Desk by calling
   989-774-3662 or 800-950-1144 x. 3662.

3. Locate your class – **MSA 604**. Click the course to enter. If you find the course is listed but not
   accessible, it has not yet been made available by your instructor. Please contact your instructor to
   have the course made available to you.

4. When you click the course content icon for the first time, you will be prompted for a
   "Student Validation Key". Please use the key printed on this card.

This key grants you access to all course-related materials, including Partial eBook (First 2 Chapters)
published by McGraw-Hill and Harvard Business School Cases selected for use in this course.

If you have any key-related technical access issues, please visit:
www.mhhe.com/support

Student
Validation Key

ISBN-13: 978-0-697-79230-3 / ISBN-10: 0-697-79230-7

The Core Courses of the Master of Science in Administration Degree

The MSA degree from Central Michigan University is a comprehensive, interdisciplinary program that offers you a solid foundation in both the theory and application of administration. Every MSA graduate from CMU will share a common base in six core courses of administrative knowledge:

MSA 600 *Foundations of Research Methods in Administration*

An introduction to the research methods used in administration that will help you not only conduct meaningful research on problems affecting your organization but also interpret the results and implement change.

MSA 601 *Organizational Dynamics and Human Behavior*

How do all the aspects of an organization interact? This course describes various ways to understand, analyze, and direct behaviors in complex organizations.

MSA 602 *Financial Analysis, Planning and Control*

An important part of any administrator's job is understanding the overall financial health of their organization. This course explores the techniques and methods used from the initial analysis of the situation, to creating a plan, and its ultimate implementation.

MSA 603 *Strategic Planning for the Administrator*

Skills in long-term strategic organizational goals are in high demand whether you are in the private, public or non-profit sector. In this course, you'll learn the processes and approaches that can be used to analyze the internal and external forces that help or hinder your organization's overall strategy.

MSA 604 *Administration, Globalization and Multiculturalism*

Whether you are involved in a large international organization or a local business, you will encounter cultural issues. With this course, you'll learn how to successfully manage an environment of workplace diversity and multiculturalism.

MSA 699 *Applied Research Project in Administration*

Your MSA experience will culminate in a final research project on practical issues or problems facing administrators today. This project will combine all the theoretical, methodological, and applied knowledge you have gained from core and concentration course work with your own professional experience.

Acknowledgements

In total, from first idea to project completion, over fifty people have been involved in developing the revised MSA core courses and their associated customized textbooks. Each and every person involved in this project provided invaluable ideas, suggestions, and expertise. Without their contagious enthusiasm and continued dedication, our goal of providing CMU students with the best possible education in the study of Administration would not have been possible.

The MSA program staff acknowledges the contribution of each person involved in this project (faculty who provided course content ideas, curriculum and course developers, instructional designers for the online versions of the courses, and CMU staff who implemented the rollout of the core courses from a marketing, scheduling, advising, technology and overall program administration perspective). We sincerely thank you for your hard work and dedication to the MSA program, CMU, and most importantly our students.

brief CONTENTS

CONTENTS

CHAPTER 8
Nonverbal Language in Intercultural Communication   181

CHAPTER 9
Getting to Know Another Culture   209

CHAPTER 10
Intercultural Negotiation   239

An Introduction to Administration and Global Management

1

LEARNING OBJECTIVES

After completing this chapter, you should be able to:

 LO¹ Define the concepts of international business and international management.

 LO² Examine the dramatic growth and global impacts of international companies.

 LO³ Define and understand the strategic, marketing, and economic motives of firms seeking to expand internationally.

 LO⁴ Explain the strategic objectives and sources of competitive advantage for an international firm.

Trained Manpower and Low Cost Attract Global Giants

NEW DELHI: It has all the ingredients of a corporate blockbuster: a growing middle class, rising income levels and low production costs. That's the Indian market as seen by the global biggies from the world of car-making.

No wonder then that an increasing number of car manufacturers from across the world are making India—the second fastest growing car market in Asia after China—a hub for most of their manufacturing activities.

To name a few: Suzuki has decided to make India the only hub for making cost-effective small cars outside Japan. It is also Suzuki's R&D hub for developing new small cars.

The country is also the production and export base for Hyundai's Santro. Toyota is building a utility vehicle for the world market and India features in the small list of destinations where it will be produced. India has also been named the hub for Fiat's R&D activities.

Low production costs and a high number of trained manpower are the reasons behind this new-found fascination among global car makers. Also, the local laws in some European nations, like Italy and Greece, favor shipping cars from India over other Asian nations, with tax breaks.

This has helped South Korea's Hyundai Motor Corp. establish its Indian arm as the export hub for the compact car Santro. The made-in-India hatchback is today being sold in Greece, Germany and Italy, besides being sourced by Daimler Chrysler to be sold under its Dodge badge in Mexico.

"We have proved that India can become a cost-competitive base for producing technologically superior cars," said Hyundai Motor India (HMI) president BVR Subbu. Riding on this growing acceptance among global buyers, HMI drove home export earnings to the tune of Rs 1,000 crore (1,000 crore = 10 billion rupees) in the first eight months of 2004. That's not all. The firm is now gearing up to become the largest exporter of manufactured goods this calendar year in non-metallurgy and non-refinery sectors in India with an export earning of around Rs 1,500 crore (15 billion rupees).

Independent surveys by leading consultants also pointed out that India is fast emerging as the most-preferred sourcing base for global auto majors. U.S. auto executives have even picked India over China as the most popular business process outsourcing (BPO) destination as far as automotive activities are concerned. Even Nissan has last week procured the government nod to set up a subsidiary in India that will explore opportunities for sourcing low-cost components besides locally building cars. Above all, there's a burgeoning local population of professionals that can be targeted with soft loans. The industry is hopeful of selling 1 million units in the domestic market this fiscal. It's this captive industry that's working as an added bait for the global players.

As Maruti Udyog Managing Director Jagdish Khattar said: "There are about 40 million Indians who ride two-wheelers. I want them to upgrade to cars and that's what we are trying to achieve with our finance and exchange schemes." A recent ICRA study had also pointed out that the overall car segment in India is poised to grow at a compounded annual growth rate of 8 percent from 2004–2008, with compact and mid-range cars leading the growth. With an eye on this potential market, Suzuki has announced plans to invest Rs 6,000 crore in India over the next few years for setting up a new car-making venture.

With the Indian car market maturing, manufacturers are also experimenting with new vehicle types and segments that appeal to the new-age buyer. If 2003 was the year when manufacturers rolled out one SUV after the other, 2004 became the year of premium hatchbacks with Hyundai Getz, Ford Fusion and Indigo

Marina vying for buyer attention. "We want to play in the heart of volume segment and that's why we are looking at locally making a volume car here," said Aditya Vij, president, GM India.

They are also playing the 24x7 service card to pull customers to win over working couples. Car makers led by Maruti, Hyundai, GM and Fiat are also driving into the call centre market to offer a slew of support services like round-the-clock assistance in case of breakdowns and even for vehicle servicing. Hyundai has also announced an extended four-year warranty program on its big cars.

Source: Anand Byas, *Times of India*, November 21, 2004 (http://timesofindia.indiatimes.com/article-show/930106.cms).

DISCUSSION QUESTIONS

1. Why are foreign car companies making India a premium car market for car manufacturing?

2. Under what conditions will India serve as an export base for foreign cars made in India?

3. What are the competitive advantages of India in car manufacturing?

The International Management Setting

The world is becoming a smaller place. Look around you. The clothes you wear, the gadgets in the kitchen, the car you drive—all may be made in China, India, or Japan. Perhaps in your refrigerator you have Mexican tacos or Indian chicken curry. Now people can communicate with friends and business associates across the world through instant messaging simply by clicking the "send" button. Distance is measured not in miles or kilometers but in the time it takes to reach from one end of the world to another. Who is responsible for "shrinking" the world in which we live? This responsibility has been shouldered by the numerous small and large international companies, from different countries, that produce and market their wares worldwide.

Even though the world is becoming "smaller," significant political, legal, economic, and technological differences still distance us from our fellow inhabitants of Earth. In their quest to reach markets and customers in foreign countries, international companies have to navigate across the often turbulent international environment.

Consider an American company with, among other business units, sales offices in Buenos Aires, Toronto, and New York City, wholly owned manufacturing subsidiaries in Jakarta and Taipei, an equity joint venture in Shanghai, a research and development facility in Tel Aviv, and call service centers in Bangalore and Manila. In recent times, the economic collapse of Argentina, the political implosion of Indonesia, and the severe acute respiratory syndrome (SARS) scares in China, Taiwan, and Canada have exerted increased pressures, risks, and costs for that firm. Furthermore, the ongoing conflicts in the Middle East and southern Asia as well as the threat of terrorism aimed at Western targets worldwide have further increased risk and the cost of managing that risk for this company.

The excitement and opportunities of the new millennium have been accompanied by many new risks and associated costs of doing business internationally. This book is about the challenge of managing these risks of such international activities of international companies within the various international environments. Also, this book is about understanding and managing the tremendous amount of new opportunities internationally. Thus it is about the unique opportunities and problems that confront managers in international companies as they navigate through the extremely complex and ever-changing economic, political, legal, technological, and cultural environments of a world of increasingly interdependent nation-states. The choices that international managers make—plant location, products and services marketed in different countries or regions of the world, the mode used to penetrate foreign markets, the hiring of personnel to manage foreign operations, and so on—must take into account the limits imposed on such choices by the external environment, as well as the imperative to simultaneously adapt to local conditions and function efficiently on a global scale.

The need for international management arises with a firm's initial involvement in international operations by way of exports of its products, technology, or services to foreign markets. This need becomes even more critical when a company becomes involved in foreign direct investment. **Foreign direct investment (FDI)** is a long-term equity investment in a foreign affiliate or subsidiary; it gives the parent company (the investor) varying degrees of managerial control over the foreign operation, depending on the percentage of ownership by the parent company.[1] The more FDI that a company makes in a foreign affiliate, the greater the managerial control that it has over that foreign affiliate. FDI involves the establishment of facilities, buildings, plants, and equipment for the production of goods and/or services in a foreign country. And FDI is accompanied by the need to manage, market, and finance the foreign production. People manage enterprise functions like marketing, production, and finance. Managing the various enterprise functions abroad requires that managers in the parent company, as well as in every foreign affiliate, have the necessary skills and experience to manage the affairs of affiliates in countries whose political, cultural, economic, and financial environments may be very different from one another. It therefore follows that the greater a company's FDI, the greater will be its need for skilled international managers.

Figure 1.1 shows how international management can be discussed from a variety of perspectives. Section 1 represents the various macro-level environments where managers must effectively manage. Section 2 elaborates on strategic management issues. That is, what are the firm-level strategic considerations necessary to consider when expanding overseas? Section 3 focuses on the manager level and the need to effectively communicate, motivate, lead, and negotiate in order to manage internationally. Finally, Section 4 integrates serving the world's poor profitably and corporate social responsibility initiatives.

International management activities in a firm begin either when the firm's managers initiate the establishment of a foreign affiliate from the ground up, which is called a greenfield investment, or when it acquires an existing host-country firm. Furthermore, they continue as long as the parent company owns one or more functioning foreign affiliates.

FIGURE 1.1

Managing in the International Environment

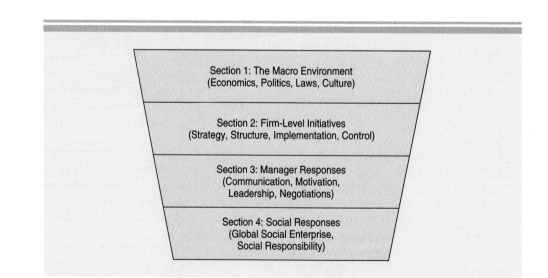

Section 1: The Macro Environment
(Economics, Politics, Laws, Culture)

Section 2: Firm-Level Initiatives
(Strategy, Structure, Implementation, Control)

Section 3: Manager Responses
(Communication, Motivation,
Leadership, Negotiations)

Section 4: Social Responses
(Global Social Enterprise,
Social Responsibility)

What Is International Business?

Besides their involvement in foreign acquisition and greenfield investments, international companies may be simultaneously involved in several other international business activities such as export, import, countertrade, licensing, and strategic alliances. Before delving into the distinctions of these various forms of international involvement, we should first understand what international business is. Several definitions of international business have been advanced through the years. The most basic definition is "all business transactions that involve two or more countries."[2] These business transactions or relationships may be conducted by private, nonprofit, or government organizations, as well as through a combination of the various organizations. In the case of private firms the transactions are for profit. Government-sponsored activities in international business may or may not have a profit orientation, and a nonprofit firm may be competing in an industry that has firms with profit motives.

Other definitions suggest that an international business is "a business whose activities involve the crossing of national boundaries"[3] or is "any commercial, industrial or professional endeavor involving two or more nations."[4] To Charles W. L. Hill, "an international business is any firm that engages in international trade and investment . . . all the firm has to do is export or import products from other countries."[5] Kolde and Hill say that "one cannot ignore the contrasts between domestic and international business, or in a more general phrase between uninational and multinational business. The primary distinction between the two lies in the environmental framework and the organizational and behavioral responses that flow from that framework."[6]

Taking the foregoing definitions of international business into account, we define **international business** as those business activities of private or public enterprises that involve the movement of resources across national boundaries. The resources that may be involved in the cross-national transfers include raw materials, semifinished and finished goods, services, capital, people, and technology. Specific services transferred may include functions such as accounting, consulting, legal counsel, and banking activities. Technology transferred may range from simple managerial and marketing know-how to higher level managerial and technical skills to ultimately high-end technological advancements.

What Is International Management?

The noted international management theorist and scholar Jean J. Boddewyn argues that a definition of international management must include an interpretation and "elaboration of the key terms *international* and *management* as well as of their *interaction*."[7] We also agree with him that the term international means "crossing borders and [applies] to processes intersected by national borders."[8] In very general terms, international management is the management of a firm's activities on an international scale. But before we define international management in specific terms, let us define management.

Management is defined in numerous ways. We would define management as the process aimed at accomplishing organizational objectives by (1) effectively coordinating the procurement, allocation, and utilization of the human, financial, intellectual, and physical resources of the organization and (2) maintaining the organization in a state of satisfactory, dynamic equilibrium within the environment—that is, the firm's strategies and operational plans are responsive to the demands and constraints embedded in the economic, political, legal, cultural, political, and competitive environment.

This definition of management has two basic premises. First, management is needed to coordinate the human, financial, intellectual, and physical resources and to integrate them into a unified whole. Without such coordination the resources would remain unrelated and disorganized and therefore inefficiently used. The second premise in the definition is that an organization lives in a dynamic environment that constantly affects its operations. To further complicate the manager's job, the various environments have different degrees of dynamism. "The multinational setting is more dynamic than the uninational (domestic) setting. This is due partly to the different rates of speed at which the various environmental parameters are changing in the different countries and in part to the nature of the parameters themselves."[9] For instance, some of the environmental factors, such as the distinct national cultures, evolve and converge over time. Others, like the political environments, have the ability to be radically changed through elections and revolutions. Furthermore, the financial environment, especially when one considers foreign exchange rates, is continually in a state of change. Note that "for domestic businesses, the external factors are relatively constant and homogeneous. Any changes that occur are gradual and generally do not lead to any sudden differentiation among the opportunities and constraints among different industries or types of enterprises."[10] However, with expansion abroad of a firm's operation, the environmental setting can no longer be called constant. Thus one managerial task is to effectively forecast the varying environmental forces that are likely to have a significant impact on the firm in the immediate and distant future and to determine the probable impact. Also, managers must respond to the environmental forecasts by designing appropriate strategies to ensure the survival and growth of the organization as it interacts with its dynamic environment.

On the basis of the preceding meaning of the term *international* and definition of *management*, we can now define **international management** as a process of accomplishing the global objectives of a firm by (1) effectively coordinating across national boundaries the procurement, allocation, and utilization of the human, financial, intellectual, and physical resources of the firm and (2) effectively charting the path toward the desired organizational goals by navigating the firm through a global environment that is not only dynamic but often very hostile to the firm's very survival. Note that our definition is focused on the *business firm* as the primary level and unit of analysis of international management, and it excludes the management of all international organizations such as the World Trade Organization, the International Labor Organization, and the United Nations. Focusing on the international business firm as an organization allows us to define the international management domain in terms of two central themes:

1. Why, when, and how does a business firm (as an organization) decide to "go international," including the expansion and reduction of such internalization?
2. Why, when, and how is its organizational behavior—a broad term covering mission, objectives, strategies, structures, staff, and processes [particularly decision making], internal and external transactions and relations, performance, impact, etc.—altered by internationalization?[11]

International Companies and Entry Modes

INTERNATIONAL COMPANIES

All firms, regardless of size, are affected by international competition. Specifically, any firm that has one or more foreign affiliates is involved in international management; it does not have to be a billion-dollar corporation. Even small and medium-sized firms can and do have international operations in several countries. Many international companies do not qualify for the exclusive list of the Fortune 500 or the BusinessWeek Global 1000 list of the largest international corporations. Even though they do not come close to Microsoft, Toyota, Wal-Mart, or Deutsche Bank in terms of total sales, gross profits, total assets, and similar measures of company size, they are still multinational companies. Many firms in Europe and Japan have also developed a multinational structure; and in the last 10 years or so, we have seen many government-owned enterprises that have become privatized and subsequently multinational. The 1960s laid the foundations for the massive growth of international companies. The growth of that decade far exceeded any achieved earlier by the United States or the other industrialized countries of the world. Since then, the growth in international business activities has been exponential, culminating during the last 10 years with the significant increase in privatization and deregulation in many industries and countries.

Although international enterprises are dissimilar in many respects—size of sales and profits, markets served, and location of affiliates abroad—they all have some common features. To begin, an **international company** is an enterprise that has operations in two or more countries. If it has operations in several countries, then it may have a network of wholly or partially (jointly with one or more foreign partners) owned producing and marketing foreign affiliates or subsidiaries. The foreign affiliates may be linked with the parent company and with each other by ties of common ownership and by a common global strategy to which each affiliate is responsive and committed. The parent company may control the foreign affiliates via resources that it allocates to each affiliate—capital, technology, trademarks, patents, and workforce—and through the right to approve each affiliate's long- and short-range plans and budgets.[12]

As pointed out earlier, there are many small- and medium-sized multinational companies. However, generally we are talking about a large corporation whose revenues, profits, and assets typically run into hundreds of millions of dollars. For example, the most profitable international company in 2007 was ExxonMobil with profits of $39.51 billion. In 2007, Wal-Mart Stores ranked number one in the world on the basis of sales, which approached $351 billion. In the same year, 30 companies accrued global revenues in excess of $100 billion. Table 1.1 lists the 15 largest international companies in terms of 2007 sales.

The top 100 international companies hold almost $5 trillion of assets outside their home countries. The economic power of these companies is evident in the fact that they are estimated to account for more than one-third of the combined outward FDI of their home countries. Because the largest international companies control such a large pool of assets, they exercise considerable influence over the home and host countries' output, economic policies, trade and technology flows, employment, and labor practices.

In 2005, the world's largest global (the terms *global* and *transnational* are used interchangeably) companies held 54.5 percent of their total assets in foreign countries and generated 56.5 percent of total sales from foreign countries. The foreign affiliates of these companies employed 8 million personnel, which amounted to 53.1 percent of their total employment. Global foreign direct investment in 2006 reached $1,306 billion, of which $857 billion flowed into the developed countries, as opposed to $379 billion to developing countries. This goes to show that the rich countries are getting the infusion of capital, technology, and knowledge that usually accompanies foreign direct investment, whereas the poorer countries do not enjoy such benefits from foreign direct investment. The world's gross domestic product (GDP) in 2006 amounted to almost $48.29 trillion, of which almost $4.8 trillion, or 11.5 percent, was accounted for by the production of foreign affiliates. The total world exports in 2006 amounted to $13.9 trillion, of which $4.7 trillion, or almost 34 percent, was generated by exports of foreign affiliates. In that same year, the total sales of foreign affiliates amounted to $25.2 trillion. Therefore, sales of goods and services produced by foreign affiliates are five times greater than their own exports and, not counting affiliates' exports, almost twice as large as total world exports. One could interpret this data to mean that local production by foreign affiliates to serve local markets has replaced exports to those markets.[13]

International companies have been growing in size at rates exceeding those of the economies of many countries. The size of the large international companies is often compared with that of countries' economies as an indicator of the power and influence of international companies in the world economy. Table 1.2 shows a comparison of the 100 largest country economies and global companies ranked by their GDP and total revenue respectively. This is a crude comparison as the domestic sales of foreign affiliates get included in the computation of a nation's GDP. Nevertheless, it is quite interesting to notice that Wal-Mart Stores (number 24), ExxonMobil (number 25), and Royal Dutch Shell (number 26) are "bigger" than 29 countries in the list. And of the 100 countries and companies in Table 1.2, there are 48 global companies.

TABLE 1.1

Largest International
Companies, by Sales

Source: Fortune Global 500, July
23, 2007.

Global Rank	Company	2007 Revenues ($ millions)
1	Wal-Mart Stores	$361,139.0
2	ExxonMobil	347,250.0
3	Royal Dutch Shell	318,845.0
4	BP	274,316.0
5	General Motors	207,349.0
6	Toyota Motor	204,746.4
7	Chevron	200,567.0
8	DaimlerChrysler	190,191.4
9	Conoco Phillips	172,451.0
10	Total	168,356.7
11	General Electric	168,307.0
12	Ford Motor	160,126.0
13	ING Group	158,274.3
14	Citigroup	146,777.0
15	AXA	139,738.1

FOREIGN MARKET ENTRY MODES

A company can achieve its international business aims through different forms of foreign market entry modes, such as:

- Exporting.
- Countertrade.
- Contract manufacturing.
- Licensing.
- Franchising.
- Turnkey projects.
- Nonequity strategic alliances.
- Equity-based ventures such as wholly owned subsidiaries and equity joint ventures.

Why Firms Seek to Engage in International Business

An international company may have several motivations for establishing various types of foreign operations. Let us examine some of the motivations for foreign operations that are illustrated in Figure 1.2 and grouped into three categories: market-seeking motives, cost-reduction motives, and strategic motives.

MARKET-SEEKING MOTIVES

Historically, companies have initially looked to overseas markets when their home market became saturated. In his landmark *product life cycle theory*, Vernon theorizes that firms will search foreign markets for product that has been standardized and has reached the maturity stage in its life cycle.[14] Because of social and regulatory pressures in the United

TABLE 1.2 How Large Are Global Companies in Comparison with Countries of the World?

Rank	Country/Company	GDP/Revenue ($ millions)	Rank	Country/Company	GDP/Revenue ($ millions)	Rank	Country/Company	GDP/Revenue ($ millions)
1	World	46,660,000	34	Greece	222,500	67	American International Group	113,194
2	European Union	13,620,000	35	Argentina	210,000	68	Hungary	113,100
3	United States	13,220,000	36	General Motors	207,349	69	United Arab Emirates	110,600
4	Japan	4,911,000	37	Toyota Motor	204,746	70	China National Petroleum	110,520
5	Germany	2,858,000	38	Ireland	202,900	71	BNP Paribas	109,214
6	China	2,512,000	39	Chevron	200,567	72	ENI	109,014
7	United Kingdom	2,341,000	40	South Africa	200,500	73	UBS	107,835
8	France	2,154,000	41	Thailand	196,600	74	Siemens	107,342
9	Italy	1,780,000	42	Finland	196,200	75	State Grid	107,186
10	Canada	1,089,000	43	Iran	194,800	76	Colombia	105,500
11	Spain	1,081,000	44	DaimlerChrysler	190,191	77	Assicurazioni Generali	101,811
12	India	796,100	45	Hong Kong	187,100	78	Chile	100,300
13	Korea, South	768,500	46	Portugal	176,600	79	J.P. Morgan Chase & Co.	99,973
14	Mexico	741,500	47	ConocoPhillips	172,451	80	Carrefour	99,015
15	Russia	733,000	48	Total	168,357	81	New Zealand	98,770
16	Australia	645,300	49	General Electric	168,307	82	Berkshire Hathaway	98,539
17	Brazil	620,700	50	Ford Motor	160,126	83	Philippines	98,480
18	Netherlands	612,700	51	ING Group	158,274	84	Pemex	97,469
19	Switzerland	386,800	52	Venezuela	147,900	85	Deutsche Bank	96,152
20	Sweden	371,500	53	Citigroup	146,777	86	Dexia Group	95,847
21	Belgium	367,800	54	AXA	139,738	87	Honda Motor	94,791
22	Turkey	358,200	55	Volkswagen	132,323	88	McKesson	93,574
23	Taiwan	353,900	56	Malaysia	131,800	89	Verizon Communications	93,221
24	Wal-Mart Stores	351,139	57	Sinopec	131,636	90	Algeria	92,220
25	ExxonMobil	347,254	58	Crédit Agricole	128,481	91	Nippon Telegraph Telephone	91,998
26	Royal Dutch Shell	318,845	59	Allianz	125,346	92	Hewlett-Packard	91,658
27	Austria	309,300	60	Pakistan	124,000	93	International Business Machines	91,424
28	Saudi Arabia	286,200	61	Israel	121,600	94	Valero Energy	91,051
29	BP	274,316	62	Singapore	121,500	95	Home Depot	90,837
30	Poland	265,400	63	Fortis	121,202	96	Nissan Motor	89,502
31	Indonesia	264,400	64	Czech Republic	118,900	97	Samsung Electronics	89,476
32	Norway	261,700	65	Bank of America Corp.	117,017	98	Credit Suisse	89,354
33	Denmark	256,300	66	HSBC Holdings	115,361	99	Hitachi	87,615
						100	Egypt	84,510

Source: Fortune Global 500, *Fortune*, July 23, 2007, and 2007 CIA *World Factbook*.

9

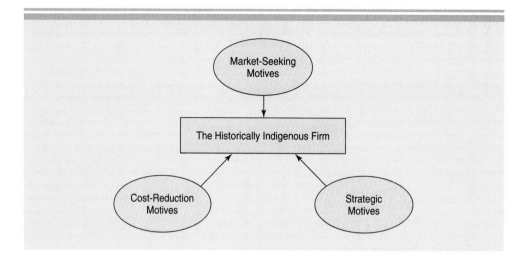

FIGURE 1.2

Motives to Go
International

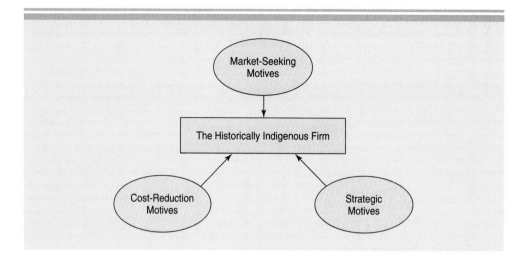

States that leveled off a once-growing market, the U.S. cigarette industry firms had to look to the foreign markets of eastern Europe and Asia to maintain sales volumes. Similarly, as revenue growth declined and the fast-food industry edged toward maturity in the United States, various fast-food firms like McDonald's and Pizza Hut expanded overseas to countries such as Russia, Japan, China, and India. Today, product life cycles in many industries have become very short because of next-generation technologies, so firms are seeking to penetrate overseas markets simultaneously with their respective home markets in order to recoup costs and make a profit before the next generation of technology comes to market.

Once firms have internationally expanded, many try to protect and maintain a market position abroad by establishing production facilities in foreign markets that had been served through exports. In this way companies bypass the threat of trade barriers such as the imposition of high tariffs or quotas. For instance, the so-called voluntary restrictions in 1980 on the export of Japanese automobiles to the United States was one factor that prompted Japanese auto companies like Toyota and Nissan to build car manufacturing plants in the United States. Toyota, Honda, and Nissan have established significant shares in the U.S. automobile market. Similarly, many U.S. and Japanese companies established plants in the 15-country European Union (EU) to circumvent potential trade barriers raised by the member countries against imports from non-EU countries. Over the years, through the efforts of the World Trade Organization (WTO), tariffs and quotas have been reduced dramatically.

The expectation of immense business opportunities in an integrated and unified market of the 27-nation European Union has brought an upsurge of both Japanese and American direct investment in Europe. As an example, for the past decade, Japanese banks and companies in the manufacturing sector have been continually investing, buying European companies, setting up manufacturing subsidiaries, and boosting sales forces throughout Europe. Japan's business activities in Europe intensified in 1990 when Japanese companies decided Europe was serious about market unification after 1992. The Japanese companies wanted a foothold in Europe before protectionism possibly kept them out. Japanese companies have responded by building new manufacturing plants and buying existing manufacturing capacity inside what could become a European fortress.

Historically, U.S. firms in many industries have been able to gain cost efficiencies and needed experience in their home market before venturing overseas. However, when a company's home market is not large enough to gain necessary cost efficiencies, that firm must look to international markets. The small size of the domestic market is the reason given by European companies that have developed international presences. Pharmaceuticals companies Hoffman–La Roche and Novartis (in 1996, in one of the largest corporate mergers in history, Ciba-Geigy and Sandoz merged to form Novartis), based in

Switzerland—a nation whose population is less than 8 million—could not have survived in their industry had they limited their business horizons to the Swiss market. These companies, and others like them in other European countries with small populations like Holland and Belgium, were forced to seek markets abroad, which eventually led to the creation of foreign manufacturing facilities in their major markets.

COST-REDUCTION MOTIVES

Companies venture overseas to lower factor costs. Intense competitive pressures and the resulting fall in profit margins serve as a powerful inducement for affected companies to seek cost-reduction measures. Firms therefore seek countries with low wages to shift manufacturing operations.[15]

Comparatively cheap labor is often the strongest incentive for companies to establish foreign operations.[16] For example, over the past two decades more than 2,000 maquiladoras have sprung up near the United States–Mexico border. These plants take advantage of cheap labor to assemble American-made components for reexport to the United States. Further inside Mexico, Japanese, German, and American automotive firms all have assembly facilities that ship final products to the United States and global markets. The economics of assembly in Mexico are favorable because jobs that are higher priced in the United States and fully "burdened" with benefits, Social Security, and so on, can be had in Mexico for a fraction of the cost.

In the 1950s and 1960s, many American companies had established not just assembly plants but fully integrated manufacturing plants in newly industrializing countries such as Taiwan and Singapore and the crown colony of Hong Kong. Even more foreign investment in manufacturing operations has flowed into Asia since then. Research indicates that "the high-wage differential between West Europe and Asia has been the most significant contribution to the restructuring of U.S. foreign direct investment (FDI) during 1981–2000."[17] As wages in Taiwan, Singapore, and Hong Kong rose in comparison to lesser developed Southeast Asian countries, the companies shifted their investment sights and moved to Malaysia, Thailand, and Indonesia. Most recently, even lower cost labor has been found in locales like southern China and Vietnam. During the 1990s and into the twenty-first century, Black & Decker, the U.S. power tools manufacturer, aggressively expanded production facilities for power drills throughout China, not to serve the Chinese market but rather to export to Europe. Automobile companies have engaged in several contracts with Indian suppliers for the supply of parts and components.

Another reason companies set up foreign plants is to eliminate or reduce high transportation costs, particularly if the ratio of the per-unit transportation expenditures to the per-unit selling price of the product is very high. For instance, if the product costs $10 to ship but it can be marketed for no more than $25 in the foreign market, all other things being nearly equal, the company may decide to produce it in the market to improve its competitiveness and profit margin. The trade-off for the company is giving up the economy-of-scale efficiencies of long production runs in one country in order to reduce transportation costs.

Costs can also be reduced for a firm through favorable host-government incentives and inducements. Local production often allows the company to take advantage of incentives that the host government may be offering to foreign companies that make direct investments in the country.[18] These incentives include reduced taxes for several years, free land, low-interest loans, and a guarantee of no labor strife. This was a principal motive for Intel to establish manufacturing operations in Costa Rica and for Mercedes, the German luxury car company, to build a manufacturing plant in Alabama.

Firms in industries with relatively high allocation of funds to research also look to overseas markets. Companies in pharmaceutical and high-technology industries that must spend large sums of money on research and development for new products and processes are compelled to look for ways to improve their sales volume in order to support their laboratories. If the domestic sales volume and exports do not raise the necessary cash flow, then strategically located manufacturing and sales affiliates are established abroad with the objective of attaining higher levels of sales volume and cash flow to support future research endeavors.

A factor that companies take into account in locating production plants is the comparative production costs in their major country markets. For example, a company that has major market positions in Japan, Germany, and the United States would be concerned about how costs are affected by the cross-exchange rates between the Japanese yen, the euro, and the U.S. dollar. If the yen were to rise significantly in value against the U.S. dollar and the euro, then exports to the United States and Germany of the company's Japanese-produced products could become relatively noncompetitive because of the rise of the yen-denominated Japanese wage rates and exports, especially if labor costs added significantly to the total product value. In such an event, the economics of production and distribution permitting, the company would gain if it could shift its production to either the United States or Germany. In fact, during the 1990s, when the yen appreciated against the U.S. dollar, Japanese auto companies used their U.S. plants to ship cars to Europe and even back to Japan! BMW and Mercedes, two of the major luxury carmakers of Germany, decided to commence manufacture of some models in the United States because of the highly noncompetitive labor rates in Germany largely due to the high value of the German mark. Global companies invest in favor of operational flexibility and in the ability to shift the sourcing of products and components from country to country. Global companies are therefore motivated to make major investments in operations and supply sites in their major country markets.

Firms have been known to move their operations to ecologically and environmentally friendly countries in order to reduce costs of adherence, both from the operations perspective and from the political perspective. Companies have been alleged to have moved their environmentally harmful operations to countries in Africa, Asia, and Latin America whose laws for environmental protection are less strict than those in the United States and therefore are considered ecologically and environmentally friendly to businesses. But companies do not have to migrate to developing countries to avoid environmental risks. A case in point is Germany's BASF, which moved its biotechnology research laboratory focusing on cancer and immune-system research from Germany—where it faced legal and political challenges from the environmentally conscious Green movement—to Cambridge, Massachusetts, which, according to BASF's director of biotechnology research, had more or less settled any controversies involving safety, animal rights, and the environment.[19]

STRATEGIC MOTIVES

Firms venture overseas for many long-term strategic reasons. Strategic decisions are those that are made to maintain or enhance the competitive position of a company in an industry or market. According to Hymer, who was the first to offer an explanation of why firms start production abroad, firms use foreign production as a means of transferring and taking advantage of the host country's specialized assets, knowledge, and capabilities, both tangible and intangible.[20] Firms also engage in foreign operations in several countries to diversify their strategic risk.[21] Both Caves and Dunning explain foreign production by firms as a means of taking advantage of their assets, knowledge, and capabilities that are superior to firms in the foreign markets.[22] A firm can accrue many distinct strategic advantages by producing a product in a foreign market. These include the ability to meet the demand for the product quickly, good public relations with customers and the host government, and improved service.

A firm may simply follow its major customers abroad. When the Japanese automakers Honda, Toyota, Nissan, Mazda, Subaru, and Isuzu established car manufacturing plants in the United States, their Japanese suppliers followed and set up their own plants in the United States. There are today more than 300 Japanese-owned parts suppliers in the United States, representing an investment in excess of $7 billion and employing more than 30,000 workers. Most of these supplier firms provide glass, brake systems, seats, air conditioners, heaters, filters, fuel pumps, and other components directly to the production plants. This pattern has been seen in the service industries as well. As major American corporations were expanding worldwide, they demanded better and more reliable services, including telecommunications services. Consequently, AT&T began the international expansion initiative of its communications line of business in the latter half of the 1980s, setting up overseas operations in five countries. AT&T now has major subsidiary locations in more than 50 countries.

The hardware line of business of AT&T, which was eventually spun off into a separate entity named Lucent, also made a big push overseas, mainly to satisfy the telecommunications needs of its large global customers, which had made their own push into overseas markets. Fearing that its major customers—the global companies—would turn to rival companies such as France's Alcatel, Italy's Italtel, IBM, and Japan's NEC if it did not operate advanced voice and data networks around the world, the company formed several joint ventures and strategic alliances around the globe.[23] Combined employment abroad for AT&T and Lucent jumped from a mere 50 people in 1983 to more than 50,000 today. Like AT&T, Federal Express followed the lead of its customers who increasingly wanted packages sent to Asia and Europe. Accordingly, with the aim of "keeping it purple"—the color of FedEx's planes and vans—the company set out to duplicate its business abroad.

Besides following their important customers, firms exhibit a *bandwagon effect*, venturing abroad to follow their major competitors.[24] This is especially true in an industry that is characterized by an oligopolistic rivalry. A competitor's inroads in certain foreign markets may translate to losing business in other markets. Years ago, fearing that they would eventually lose some of their U.S. business with Ford and General Motors if European tire manufacturers were able to sell to those auto manufacturers in Europe, U.S. tire manufacturers followed each and established plants in Europe to better service their major accounts. Similarly, Japanese tire manufacturers like Bridgestone have established manufacturing plants in the United States to serve Japanese carmakers. More recently, from the telecommunications service perspective, MCI followed AT&T to many overseas markets.

The competitive perspective is another strategically based motive for international expansion. If a company's competitor can make unencumbered profits in a specific host country, that competitor can use a portion of those profits to attack the firm in the firm's major markets. This is called *cross-subsidization*, that is, using profits generated in one market to compete in another market. Firms strategically look overseas to gain cross-subsidization possibilities as well as to block competitors from that advantage.[25]

Rapid expansion of a foreign market for the company's product and the desire to obtain a large market share in it before a major competitor can get in are other strong driving forces for companies to engage in foreign production. By being first into a new market, a firm may be able to obtain favorable deals with customers and suppliers. Furthermore, the firm may be able to secure the most efficient distribution channels and set both the strategic and technological agendas for the industry in that host country. This is an important reason for American and European companies wanting to enter the market in China.

The need for vertical integration is another strategic reason often responsible for the international expansion of operations. Companies are pushed into making direct investment abroad so that they can capture a source of supply or new markets for their products. For example, a company in the oil exploration and drilling business may integrate "downstream" by acquiring or building an oil refinery in a foreign country that has a market for its refined products. Conversely, a company that has strong distribution channels (e.g., gas stations) in a country but needs a steady source of supply of gasoline at predictable prices may integrate "upstream" and acquire an oil producer and refiner in another country.

Numerous companies have established operations abroad to exploit the strong brand name of their products. Realizing that they could not fully exploit their advantage by way of exports, they have set up plants in their major foreign markets. Examples of companies that have used this strategy are Coca-Cola, Pepsi-Cola, Budweiser, and Heineken. Scotch whiskey is now produced in India, replacing exports from abroad.

A global company may decide to locate its manufacturing plant in a country that is of strategic importance for the company's exports to a third country. For instance, Japanese companies have strictly observed the Arab boycott of Israel and therefore cannot export to Israel directly from Japan. However, Japanese plants in the United States can export their U.S.-made products to Israel, and this is exactly what Honda is doing. It is exporting Honda Civic sedans to Israel from its plant in Ohio. In the same vein, Northern Telecom Ltd. (Nortel), the Canadian telecommunications giant, has moved many of its manufacturing operations to the United States to gain the competitive edge that an American company can obtain in securing Japanese contracts. Nortel made this strategic move to the United States knowing that the Japanese would favor U.S. companies because of Japan's huge trade surplus with the United States.

As organizational knowledge is becoming a key competitive weapon, firms have recognized that scientific talent and brainpower are not the monopoly of any one country or group of countries. Thus international companies are establishing technological research and development centers around the world. Companies like IBM and Microsoft have established such centers in Japan and India respectively to tap into the "innovation culture" of those countries. Several global companies in a variety of knowledge-based industries such as biotechnology, pharmaceuticals, and electronics have set up such centers in the countries of the so-called Triad of Europe, the Pacific Basin (including Japan), and the United States. This strategy has paid rich dividends for Xerox, which has introduced 80 different office copier models in the United States that were engineered and built by its Japanese joint venture, Fuji-Xerox Company. Another example is Bangalore, India, which has become the global center for software development for major computer and software companies. The number-one global carmaker, General Motors, plans to invest $60 million in a technology center in Bangalore, India's technology hub. General Motors plans to hire 260 engineers, who will collaborate with the company's American and European research center through high-speed communication links. Most planes flying between Mumbai (Bombay), the major international gateway to India, and Bangalore are filled with U.S. technology executives looking to source business in this emerging Silicon Valley.[26] Similarly, firms in Malaysia have proactively marketed themselves to North American and European companies as the appropriate places to outsource their technology needs.

Paralleling financial planning thinking, firms have strategically ventured overseas to diversify their operations and, in effect, to hedge against the many environmental risks of doing business in one country. This strategy ranges from simply distribution and sales in multiple countries to rationalization of production across key countries. Regarding distribution and sales, firms relying solely on the Japanese market have been hurt due to the long-lasting recession in Japan. Firms with a portfolio of country businesses have somewhat hedged against such a recession. Likewise, firms try to balance the efficiencies of long production runs with the flexibility of being able to switch production should trouble arise in a certain country. For instance, auto parts are produced in many countries, including the United States, Japan, Argentina, Mexico, India, and Indonesia. Although the comparative costs in Argentina, Mexico, India, and Indonesia are lower than in the United States and Japan, the former countries are less stable than the latter. Mexico had a financial problem in the mid-1990s. From the late 1990s until today, Indonesia saw a combination of financial and political upheaval that put many foreign investments at risk. And most recently, Argentina's financial problems have bubbled over into increased instability of the market and workforce. Thus producing all of a firm's components in any one of these countries would have proved catastrophic to a firm.

In this section, we have introduced some of the many reasons why a firm may choose to "go international." However, it is important to remember that each company's decision should be based on a careful assessment of its own distinctive strengths (and weaknesses) and the potential for it to strengthen its overall competitive position by making the international move. In the next section, we look at one proposed framework for assessing such potential benefits.

Strategic Objectives and Sources of Competitive Advantage

Sumantra Ghoshal, in his seminal article "Global Strategy: An Organizing Framework,"[27] offered an excellent framework that explains the broad categories of objectives of a global firm and the sources for developing an international/global firm's competitive advantage. The framework is presented in Table 1.3.

As seen in Table 1.3, in its **global strategy,** a global firm pursues three categories of objectives: (1) achieving efficiency, (2) managing risks, and (3) innovating, learning, and adapting. The key is to create a firm's competitive advantage by developing and implementing strategies that optimize the firm's achievement of these three categories of objectives. This may require trade-offs to be made between the objectives because on occasion they may conflict. For example, the objective of achieving efficiency through economies of scale in production may conflict with the objective of minimizing risks emanating from economic or political conditions in a country where the plant is located.

Ghoshal identifies three sources through which a global firm may derive its competitive advantage: (1) national differences, (2) scale economies, and (3) scope economies. According to Ghoshal, the strategic task of managing globally is to use all three sources of competitive advantage to optimize efficiency, risk, and learning simultaneously in a worldwide business. The key to a successful global strategy is to manage the interactions between these different goals and means.[28]

ACHIEVING EFFICIENCY

If a firm is viewed as an input–output system, its overall efficiency is defined as a ratio of the value of all its outputs to the costs of all its inputs. A firm obtains the surplus resources needed to grow and prosper by maximizing this ratio. It may enhance the value of its products or services (outputs) by making them of higher quality than those of its competi-

TABLE 1.3   Global Strategy: An Organizing Framework

Strategic Objectives	Sources of Competitive Advantage		
	National Differences	**Scale Economies**	**Scope Economies**
Achieving efficiency in current operations	Benefiting from differences in factor costs (wages and cost of capital)	Expanding and exploiting potential scale economies in each activity	Sharing investments and costs across products, markets, and businesses
Managing risks	Managing different kinds of risks arising from market- or policy-induced changes in comparative advantage of different countries	Balancing scale with strategic and operational flexibility	Portfolio diversification of risks and creation of options and side-bets
Innovation, learning, and adapting	Learning from societal differences in organizational and managerial processes and systems	Benefiting from experience, cost reduction, and innovation	Sharing learning across organizational components in different products, markets, or businesses

Source: From Sumantra Ghoshal, "Global Strategy: An Organizing Framework," *Strategic Management Journal,* Vol. 8. Copyright © 1987 John Wiley & Sons Limited. Reproduced with permission.

tors, and at the same time it may lower the costs of inputs by obtaining low-cost factors of production such as labor and raw materials.[29] Different business functions—production, research and development, marketing, and so on—have different factor intensities. A firm could exploit *national differences* by locating a function in a country that has a comparative advantage in providing the factors required to perform it. Thus it could locate labor-intensive production in low-wage countries like Malaysia or Mexico and locate R & D activities in countries that have capable scientists who can do the work but who do not have to be paid high salaries. As an example, many American companies—Microsoft, Oracle, Hewlett-Packard, Novell, Motorola, and Texas Instruments—established centers for software development work in India, where personnel qualified to write innovative software are plentiful and can be employed for as little as $300 a month. Similarly, many U.S.-based companies have established service centers outside America in order to gain added cost efficiencies. For instance, when talking with a Compaq computer service representative, a customer is actually talking with a technical adviser in Ottawa, Canada. Service centers for various firms have been established in countries like Ireland, India, and the Philippines as well during the first part of the twenty-first century.

A firm could enjoy the benefits of *scale economies* like lower costs and higher quality resulting from specialization by designating one plant to serve as the sole producer of a component for use in the final assembly of a product. For example, a plant in the Philippines may make transmissions, another in Malaysia the steering mechanisms, and one in Thailand the engines. Each country would then do the final assembly of the complete automobile. Toyota Motor Company is rapidly moving in this direction. Practical Insight 1.1 illustrates steps taken by Dell Computer to take advantage of scale economies and proximity to key markets to reduce transportation costs.

The concept of *scope economies* is based on the notion that savings and cost reductions will accrue when two or more products can share the same asset, such as a production plant, distribution channel, brand name, or staff services (legal, public relations, etc.). A global company like Coca-Cola enjoys a competitive advantage because it is in a position to produce two or more products in one plant rather than two separate plants, market its products through common distribution channels, and share its world-famous brand name across a wide range of products.

MANAGING RISKS

A global company faces a number of different types of risk including economic, political, cultural, legal, and competitive. The nature and severity of such risks are not the same for all countries. A global company is in a position to manage such risks effectively by planning and implementing effective strategies aimed at diffusing risk.[30] For example, in a country that has high levels of unemployment, a global company could deflect restrictive and unfriendly governmental policies by sourcing products for world markets in that country, thus increasing much-needed employment opportunities for the local populace. An example of such a strategy is the transfer of significant amounts of car production to the United States by Japanese automakers like Toyota, Honda, and Nissan. One of the principal motivations behind this strategy was to minimize the growing anti-Japanese sentiment in the United States due to the alleged job losses caused by Japanese imports.

The benefits of scale economies must be weighed against their risks. A plant located in a country because of its low wages could lose its locational advantage if the wage rates in the country rise significantly because of economic development or appreciation of the country's currency. Global companies manage such risks by distributing production in more than one country even at the expense of benefits derived from lower scale economies. Japanese car companies have managed currency and wage-rate risks caused by rising wage rates in Japan and the much stronger Japanese yen compared to the U.S. dollar by exporting cars made in U.S.-based plants back to Japan. The flexibility afforded to Japanese car companies by having plants in both the United States and Japan was responsible for their effective management of risk.

Dell Computer's Supply Chain Extends Into China

Dell Computer's competitive advantage lies in its manufacturing acumen, an upstream activity in the value chain. Dell has dispersed its manufacturing operations to large manufacturing plants strategically located in various parts of the globe primarily to take advantage of scale economies and proximity to key markets to reduce transportation costs. Now Dell is making a big push to lower costs and prices across the board—especially in the two largest markets, Japan and China. In the past, most of the Dell computers that ended up in Japan were built at the company's giant facility in Malaysia. Now Dell is making PCs for the Japanese market at a factory in the southeastern Chinese city of Xiamen. The switch means Dell saves a third off its manufacturing and shipping costs—savings Dell can pass on to customers. Dell's market share in Japan jumped from 3.8% in 2000 to 5.8% in 2001, according to Gartner Group Inc. consultants, a surge that Dell execs attribute to better management and lower prices.

Source: Reprinted from Bruce Einhorn, Andrew Park, and Irene M. Kunii, "Will Dell Click in Asia? The PC Maker Is Going All Out to Win a Bigger Piece of the Pie," April 22, 2002 issue of *Business-Week* by special permission. Copyright © 2002 by The McGraw-Hill Companies, Inc.

INNOVATION AND LEARNING

A global company has a distinct advantage over its purely domestic competitor because of the multiple environments in which the global company operates. A company that has operations in many countries is exposed to a diversity of experiences and stimuli. Being in many countries allows it to develop a variety of capabilities.[31] A global company has opportunities to learn skills and acquire knowledge of a country, which can be transferred and applied in many other countries where it has operations.[32] For example, a company that has operations in Japan can learn about the very best aspects of the Japanese management system and adapt and use those that are most useful in its American or European operations. General Electric is marketing in India an ultrasound unit designed by Indian engineers, using technology developed in GE's Japanese operations.

Hewlett-Packard has continued pouring resources into the Asian region, opening a laboratory in Japan and new manufacturing facilities in Japan and Malaysia, while simultaneously beefing up its engineering, project management, and design capacity in Singapore. Such investments provide not only increased sales in the region but also skills and expertise in how to improve the production process, something that it lacks in the United States. Hewlett-Packard has learned process improvement techniques from its Asian operations and transferred the knowledge not only to its U.S. operations but also to operations worldwide.

Eli Lilly & Company, a global pharmaceutical corporation, and Ranbaxy Laboratories Limited, India's largest pharmaceutical company, have formed a path-breaking alliance to set up joint ventures in India and the United States. In the first phase, a state-of-the art research, development, and manufacturing facility is being set up in India to develop products for the U.S. market by undertaking chemical, pharmaceutical, and analytical research. Lilly's strategy apparently is to tap into the research capabilities of Indian scientists, and thereby to learn and develop innovative new products and processes. Moreover, the development of a new patented pharmaceutical product costs $800 million or more in the United States, but it may cost as little as $200 million in India.[33]

The framework we have discussed in this chapter is very useful in identifying possible sources of competitive advantage for an international company. However, the suggested strategies must be translated into operating decisions that can realize the broader goals. But before we take up the issue of strategy, we turn in the next section to a discussion of the environmental context within which the international firm must operate.

The Environment of International Management

A manager in an international company performs her or his managerial functions in an environment that is far more complex than that of her or his counterpart in a domestic company (see Figure 1.3). The international environment is the total world environment. However, it is also the sum total of the environments of every nation in which the company has its foreign affiliates. The environment within each nation consists of five dimensions: economic, political, legal, cultural, and technological. Table 1.4 lists the factors typically found in each of these environments.

FIGURE 1.3

The International Environment

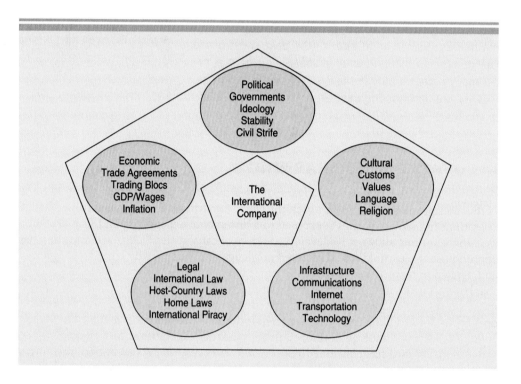

Economic Environment	Legal Environment
Economic system	Legal tradition
Level of economic development	Effectiveness of legal system
Population	Treaties with foreign nations
Gross national product	Patent trademark laws
Per capita income	Laws affecting business firms
Literacy level	**Cultural Environment**
Social infrastructure	Customs, norms, values, beliefs
Natural resources	Language
Climate	Attitudes
Membership in regional economic blocs (EU, NAFTA, LAFTA)	Motivations
Monetary and fiscal policies	Social institutions
Wage and salary levels	Status symbols
Nature of competition	Religious beliefs
Foreign exchange rates	**Technological Environment**
Currency convertibility	Inventions
Inflation	New-product development
Taxation system	New-process innovations
Interest rates	Internet capabilities
Political Environment	
Form of government	
Political ideology	
Stability of government	
Strength of opposition parties and groups	
Social unrest	
Political strife and insurgency	
Governmental attitude toward foreign firms	
Foreign policy	

TABLE 1.4

The International Environment

CHAPTER SUMMARY

This chapter provides an introduction to international management and to the world of the so-called international company. The nature of international business was explained first, and we saw that the need for international management and managers arises for many strategic and market reasons.

Although there are scores of small international companies, generally when one speaks about them, the reference is to the large multinationals. Increasingly, people are referring to these giant companies with operations throughout the world as international, multinational, and global companies. Because the other connotations are used more specifically in later chapters, we use the term *international companies* to define the entities with overseas sales and/or operations. International management and international companies are more or less like conjoined twins or the two sides of a coin. The growth of international companies has resulted from the astute management of these enterprises by international managers. And the management of these corporations epitomizes what international management is all about.

We saw something of the dimensions and drastic growth of multinational companies since the 1960s. We also examined the market-based, cost-based, and strategic motives a firm has to expand internationally. After this, we studied how global companies exploit economies of scale, economies of scope, and national differences to achieve their three generic objectives: (1) efficiency in current operations, (2) managing risks, and (3) innovation, learning, and adaptation. We concluded by introducing the nature and complexity of the international environment of international companies.

Key Terms and Concepts

cost-reduction motives for international expansion, *11*
foreign direct investment (FDI), *6*
global strategy, *15*
international business, *5*

international company, *7*
international management, *6*
market-seeking motives for international expansion, 8
strategic motives for international expansion, *12*

Critical Thinking and Discussion Questions

1. What is international business? How does it differ from international management?
2. Discuss the characteristics of multinational companies. What forces have contributed to their development and growth?
3. What are strategic, cost-based, and marketing-based company motives for expanding overseas?
4. Identify and explain the three categories of broad objectives of global companies. What strategic actions can a global company take in order to develop competitive advantage against its competitors?
5. Discuss the key differences between economies of scale and economies of scope.
6. Discuss how national differences can serve as a source of competitive advantage for a global company.

CLOSING CASE

Want to Be More Efficient, Spread Risk, and Learn and Innovate at the Same Time? Try Building a "World Car"

Japanese car companies like Toyota and the Honda Motor Company are pioneering the auto industry's truly global manufacturing system. The companies' aim is to perfect a car's design and production in one place and then churn out thousands of "world" cars each year that can be made in one place and sold worldwide. In an industry where the cost of tailoring car models to different markets can run into billions of dollars, the "world car" approach of Toyota and Honda—and which Ford is hoping to emulate—is targeted at sharply curtailing development costs, maximizing the use of assembly plants, and preserving the assembly line efficiencies that are a hallmark of the Japanese "lean" production system.

As for Honda, the goal is to create a "global base of complementary supply," says Roger Lambert, Honda's manager of corporate communications. "Japan can supply North America and Europe, North America can supply Japan and Europe, and Europe can supply Japan and the United States. So far, the first two are true. This means that you can more profitably utilize your production bases and talents."

The strategy of shipping components and fully assembled products from the U.S. to Europe and Japan couldn't have come at a more opportune time for the Japanese car companies, especially when political pressures are intense to reduce the Japanese trade surplus with the United States. The task was made easier due to

the strength of the Japanese yen, which has risen about 50 percent against the U.S. dollar. That has made production of cars in the United States cheaper, by some estimates, by $2,500 to $3,000 per car. That saving more than compensates for the transportation costs for a car overseas. For the first time, Toyota is creating a system that will give it the capability to manage the car production levels in Japan and the United States. It is moving toward a global manufacturing system that will enable it to enhance manufacturing efficiency by fine-tuning global production levels on a quarterly basis in response to economic conditions in different markets.

Source: Adapted from Paul Ingrassia, "Ford to Export Parts to Europe for a New Car," *The Wall Street Journal*, September 29, 1992, p. A5; Jane Perlez, "Toyota and Honda Create Global Production System," *The New York Times*, March 26, 1993, pp. A1, D2.

Case Discussion Questions

1. Discuss the strategies implemented by Toyota and Honda to achieve greater efficiency in car production.
2. How do the automobile companies plan to simultaneously manage risk and gain efficiencies?
3. Discuss how the car companies use national differences to gain a strategic advantage in the global car industry.

Notes

1. Richard E. Caves, "International Corporations: The Industrial Economics of Foreign Direct Investment," *Economica* 38, no. 141 (1971), pp. 1–27.
2. John D. Daniels and Lee H. Radebaugh, *International Business: Environment and Operations*, 6th ed. (Reading, MA: Addison-Wesley, 1992), p. 8.
3. Donald A. Ball and Wendell H. McCulloch Jr., *International Business: Introduction and Essentials*, 4th ed. (Homewood, IL: BPI/Irwin, 1990), p. 17.
4. Betty Jane Punett and David A. Ricks, *International Business* (Boston: PWS/Kent, 1992), p. 7.
5. Charles W. L. Hill, *International Business*, 4th ed. (New York: McGraw-Hill /Irwin, 2003), p. 29.
6. Endel J. Kolde and Richard E. Hill, "Conceptual and Normative Aspects of International Management," *Academy of Management Journal*, June 2001, p. 120.
7. Jean J. Boddewyn, "The Domain of International Management," *Journal of International Management* 5, no. 1 (Spring 1999), p. 5.

8. Ibid.

9. Ibid., p. 121.

10. Kolde and Hill, "Conceptual and Normative Aspects of International Management."

11. Boddewyn, "The Domain of International Management," p. 9.

12. Arvind V. Phatak, *International Management: Concepts and Cases* (Cincinnati: South-Western College Publishing, 1997), p. 3.

13. All statistics in this paragraph are from United Nations Conference on Trade and Development, *World Investment Report 2007* (Geneva: UNCTAD, 2007), chap. 1.

14. R. Vernon, "International Investment and International Trade in the Product Life Cycle," *Quarterly Journal of Economics* 80 (1965), pp. 190–207.

15. D. Sethi, S. E. Guisinger, S. E. Phelan, and D. M. Berg, "Trends in Foreign Direct Investment Flows: A Theoretical and Empirical Analysis," *Journal of International Business Studies* 34, no. 4 (2003), pp. 315–326.

16. Peter J. Buckley and Mark Casson, *The Economic Theory of the Multinational Enterprise* (London: St. Martin's Press, 1985).

17. Sethi, Guisinger, Phelan, and Berg, "Trends in Foreign Direct Investment Flows," p. 325.

18. Ibid., p. 319.

19. Ibid., p. 100.

20. S. H. Hymer, *The International Operations of National Firms: A Study of Direct Investment* (Cambridge, MA: MIT Press, 1960).

21. A. M. Rugman, *International Diversification and the Multinational Enterprise* (Lexington, MA: Lexington Books, 1979).

22. R. E. Caves, "Industrial Corporations: The Industrial Economics of Foreign Direct Investment," *Economica* 38 (1971), pp. 1–27; J. H. Dunning, "Toward an Eclectic Theory of International Production: Some Empirical Tests," *Journal of International Business Studies* 11, no. 1 (1980), pp. 9–31.

23. Roger Kashlak, former director for Italy for AT&T International, personal communication.

24. F. T. Knickerbocker, *Oligopolistic Reaction and the Multinational Enterprise* (Cambridge, MA: Harvard University Press, 1973).

25. Gary Hamel and C. K. Prahalad, "Do You Really Have a Global Strategy?" *Harvard Business Review* 63, no. 4 (1985), pp. 139–149.

26. Saritha Rai, "World Business Briefing, Asia: India: G. M. to Invest in Technology Center," *New York Times*, June 26, 2003, p. W1.

27. Sumantra Ghoshal, "Global Strategy: An Organizing Framework," *Strategic Management Journal* 8 (1987), pp. 425–440.

28. Ibid., p. 427.

29. Alan M. Rugman, *Inside the Multinationals: The Economics of International Markets* (New York: Columbia University Press, 1981).

30. Kent D. Miller, "A Framework for Integrated Risk Management in International Business," *Journal of International Business Studies* 23, no. 2 (1992), pp. 311–334.

31. Bruce Kogut and Sea-Jin Chang, "Technological Capabilities and Japanese Foreign Direct Investment in the United States," *Review of Economics and Statistics* 73 (1991), pp. 401–413.

32. John J. Dunning, "Multinational Enterprises and the Globalization of Innovative Capacity," *Research Policy* 23 (1994), pp. 67–68.

33. Comments made by G. P. Garnier to Arvind V. Phatak at the Greater Philadelphia Global Award of which Mr. Garnier was the awardee, June 12, 2003.

International Human Resources Management

2

LEARNING OBJECTIVES

After completing this chapter, you should be able to:

 LO¹ Understand the various approaches that multinational and global organizations undertake for managing and staffing subsidiaries in diverse parts of the world.

 LO² Distinguish between various functions of international human resources management.

 LO³ Identify the various strategies for selecting staff for foreign assignments.

 LO⁴ Explain how training programs prepare managers for overseas assignments.

 LO⁵ Understand the various schemes for compensation and benefits used by multinational and global organizations.

LO⁶ Identify the issues inherent in repatriation and explain why multinational and global companies need to address issues concerning managers returning from overseas assignments.

 LO⁷ Understand that labor relations practices differ in each country and explain how these differences affect multinational and global companies.

How to Avoid Culture Shock

The biggest hurdles to overcome when doing business internationally often have less to do with technology than with culture. "When we first went to Europe, we were shocked by the number of things that were different from the way we thought they were going to be," says Larry Schwartz, president of Hill Arts & Entertainment Systems Inc., a software VAR in Guilford, Conn. "The way they do business is just very different."

And each country has its own idiosyncrasies. For example, Schwartz had a difficult time cracking the German market because his company had first established a presence in England. "They saw us as English," he says, "which is even worse than being American."

When Schwartz finally did win German customers, he learned that the colors Americans find pleasing on a graphical user interface seemed ugly to the Germans.

"The Germans said, 'What are these?' They wanted garish colors, the brighter and bolder the better," he says. Schwartz realized why it's difficult for Americans to program for European customers. The English have one color preference, the Germans have another and the Italians look at color another way. "If you don't know the customs," Schwartz says, "you're just sunk."

Schwartz also made a gaffe during his first day of meetings in Munich by calling people by their first names, American style. "I was with one of my European people and I asked her why the Germans kept referring to each other by their last names, Herr This and Herr That, and she said that's what is expected in Germany." He adds that as an American, if you go in using first names at a meeting, from day one you've started alienating people.

Schwartz says the best thing to do is realize that business etiquette changes from country to country, and find local guides who can help you.

Don Howren, director of strategic alliances at Platinum Software Corp., Irvine, Calif., says his company has stepped on plenty of land mines while trying to expand into foreign markets. "We've done all the ugly American things you can come up with," he says. "But having good partnerships can help you dodge any issues that could hold you back."

Platinum tries to form partnerships with VARs and consultants in each new market. "There are a lot of things outside of the technical sphere that you have to deal with," Howren says. "Those are the greatest challenges for companies moving into those markets." For example, in the burgeoning Latin American market, Platinum is dealing constantly with a whole set of issues that are unique to those markets, such as hyperinflation and political situations.

American companies should also be aware that in some countries there is a cultural bias working against them before they even show up.

"I have found that the most difficult markets to break into are Germany and Japan," says Jennifer Meighan, an international business development consultant in San Francisco. "Both cultures are very tightly knit, very uniform and wary of American companies."

Some aspects of American business culture do have appeal in Europe, says Denise Sangster, president of Global Touch Inc., a channels consulting company in Berkeley, Calif.

"Europeans like nothing better than American-style service," Sangster says. "With some software companies in France, if you call during lunchtime with a question or a problem, they'll tell you to call back after lunch. So if you can provide them immediate support and service, they love you."

Also, European customers aren't accustomed to the "solution selling" approach that American software VARs espouse, but they appreciate it, Sangster says.

"If you can bring over that style of business, that approach of 'Let me help you solve your business problem,' which is not the normal way of doing things there, you'll have a tremendous opportunity," Sangster says. "You can win some very loyal and dedicated customers."

It can be tricky, though, to convince your European business partners, including VARs and distributors, to adopt your "solution sell" approach. "A lot of it has to do with your presentation," Sangster says. "There's a fine line between saying, 'Hey, look, we do things better, we're the best,' and saying, 'Let us show you a different way of looking at the same situation.' "

This kind of finesse is even more crucial in Asia, according to Bob Hoover, general manager of Asia/Pacific for Speedware Corp. in Toronto.

For example, forget about cold calling or making deals on the phone. Business is done in person, and introductions from mutual acquaintances or business contacts are often necessary, Hoover says. And it's important to build strong relationships before a deal is done, which means that compared to the West, business in Asia can seem to take forever.

"It took me 18 to 24 months to build ties there, work that would have taken about three months in the States," Hoover says.

The biggest mistake that U.S. companies make is to see Asia as a single entity. "Each country has a unique business culture," Hoover says. For example, in Japan and Korea, decisions are made by groups, so sales cycles are long—as much as three times longer than in the States. And Korean and Japanese companies tend to think strategically, with a long-term view.

In Taiwan, however, the business culture is built around small, family-owned companies. "Decisions are made very quickly. They tend to think tactically rather than strategically," Hoover says. "With Taiwanese customers you're always talking about new things, trying to keep them excited."

Hoover has a list of dos and don'ts that he gives to his sales reps when they move to Asia. Perhaps the biggest "don't" has to do with emotion. "You must never show emotion or lose your temper," Hoover says. "It's a sign of weakness. Customers will become very concerned about doing business with your company."

Americans should also avoid behaving in a way that is seen as stereotypically American: loud, fast-talking, slapping people on the back. Rather than trying to crack into Asian markets on your own, Hoover suggests hiring a well-connected consultant who can help you make connections. "This really can help you shorten the start-up period."

Source: Daniel Lyons, *VARBusiness,* June 15, 1995.

Discussion Questions

1. Discuss gaffes (mistakes) made when dealing with different cultures and their effects on management of companies.
2. How do you think the failure to understand cultural differences affects managing human resources?
3. What other insights can be gained from this case?

What Is International Human Resources Management?

International human resources management (IHRM) is concerned with the development of human resource capabilities to meet the diverse needs of various subsidiaries of multinational and global corporations. Management of human resources in multinational and global organizations differs greatly from that in domestic companies. Each multinational and global organization has a different approach for managing its employees. In most cases, how organizations find employees and pay, train, develop, and promote them varies in each subsidiary. These issues are complex, because they require a continuous link between corporate strategy and human resources management. National and cultural differences play important roles in the selection, compensation, training, development, placement, and promotion of employees.[1]

In this chapter, we discuss international human resources management. This field includes three major functions:

1. Management of human resources in global corporations, including issues of expatriation and repatriation.
2. Implementing corporate global strategy by adapting appropriate human resources management practices in different national, economic, and cultural environments.
3. Adopting labor relation practices in each subsidiary that match local requirements.

International human resources management is increasingly being recognized as a major determinant of success in the global environment. In the highly competitive global economy, where factors of production—capital, technology, raw material, and information—can be easily duplicated, the quality of human resources in the organization will be the sole source of competitive advantage.[2] Multinational and global corporations need to pay careful attention to this most critical resource, which, in its turn, can provide appropriate access to other resources needed for effective implementation of global strategy.

During the past decade, the number of multinational corporations engaged in business worldwide increased from 37,000 to more than 60,000. Foreign affiliates have increased from approximately 200,000 to more than 350,000. Foreign multinationals operating in the United States are employing more than 5 million Americans. About 80 percent of mid- to large-size U.S. multinationals have managers working in subsidiaries in other countries, and their numbers are increasing.[3] According to recent estimates by the National Foreign Trade Council, over 400,000 U.S. expatriates are working in different countries.

As multinational corporations from all countries are increasing, so too is the strategic pressure to select and staff overseas subsidiaries with the appropriate managers. The following sections discuss the critical issues associated with this strategic imperative.

MANAGING AND STAFFING SUBSIDIARIES

Multinational and global organizations take different approaches to managing and staffing subsidiaries. These approaches are linked with the company's overall strategy, and they reflect its human resources policies and practices. The four major approaches are as follows:[4]

1. **Ethnocentric staffing approach.** The company uses the approach developed in the home country, and the values, attitudes, practices, and priorities of headquarters determine the human resources policies and practices. Managers from the home country are preferred for leadership and other major positions in the subsidiary. Foreign staffing decisions are made in the headquarters.
2. **Polycentric staffing approach.** The company considers the needs of the local subsidiary when formulating human resources policies and practices. Individuals from host countries are selected for managerial positions; however, promotion of a manager from foreign subsidiaries to headquarters is rare. Human resources decisions, policies, and practices are developed at the local level.
3. **Regiocentric staffing approach.** The company considers the needs of an entire region when developing human resources policies and practices. Manag-

ers from the host country are often selected for managerial positions in their own countries, and some may be promoted to regional positions. Subsidiaries in a given region, such as Latin America, may develop a common set of human resources management policies that are uniquely applicable in the particular regional context.

4. **Geocentric (global) staffing approach.** The company's priority is the optimal use of all resources, including human resources, and local or regional considerations are not considered important for the success of the corporate strategy. Managers are selected and promoted on a global basis without regard to their country of origin or cultural background. HRM policies are developed at headquarters, and these policies are generally consistent across all subsidiaries.

Companies with ethnocentric or geocentric approaches generally have human resources policies and practices that are consistent globally. Those taking a polycentric or regiocentric approach vary their policies and practices depending on the local or regional culture and practices.

While international corporate strategy determines the choice of one of the four approaches, the following important factors should be considered in the ultimate selection of an IHRM approach:[5]

- **National concerns.** Subsidiaries have to function within the legal framework of the host country. For example, some countries require that an employee who is laid off must be given compensation at a certain percentage of his or her basic pay. Some countries restrict the number of employees the subsidiary may bring from outside the country. In these countries, the head and a few senior managers of the subsidiary may be from the headquarters or another country, but the majority of the managers and employees must be local. Laws governing occupational safety also vary a great deal from country to country and have to be incorporated into the formulation of international human resources management practices. In addition, political volatility inherent in some countries requires that global corporations provide appropriate measures for the physical well-being and safety of not only their expatriate managers but the local workforce as well.

- **Economic concerns.** The cost of living, such as housing, food, and other expenses, varies widely from country to country. This often poses significant economic concerns that must be addressed by the corporation as it formulates its international human resources management policies and practices.

- **Technological concerns.** Another concern, which is growing in importance, is the availability of skilled employees, especially for global service corporations, such as Citicorp and McKinsey & Company. As the use of highly sophisticated manufacturing technology and the need to produce high-quality products on a global scale increase, IHRM managers need to ensure that skilled employees are selected and developed in all of the subsidiaries. When the basic product must be modified to appeal to local or regional markets, a polycentric or regiocentric approach makes more sense.

- **Organizational concerns.** The stage of the internationalization of the company and the product life cycle are important determinants of the IHRM approach. For example, when a company first ventures into international business, it often adopts an ethnocentric approach, but as subsidiaries are added and managed by locals, a polycentric approach makes more sense. Later, growth, increased productivity, and cost control may cause the firm to adopt a regiocentric or geocentric approach. As operations become strictly global in nature, a complete geocentric IHRM policy is the best approach.

- **Cultural concerns.** The differences between the corporate and societal cultures of the headquarters and subsidiaries also influence the IHRM approach. If the corporate cultures are different, as is often the case for many European multinationals, it becomes necessary to adopt a polycentric or regiocentric approach. If the societal cultures are different, a polycentric or regiocentric approach may be more appropriate. For example, the cultural need for extended bereavement leave in many cultures, such as east Asian and Polynesian cultures, makes most U.S. and European HRM policies pertaining to such leave difficult to enforce. In some countries, the societal culture encourages the adoption of an ethnocentric HRM approach, as is the case with most Japanese multinationals.[6] For example, most Japanese multinationals hire only Japanese as senior managers, which is acceptable and expected in their culture. Furthermore, if the number and degree of cultural differences among the subsidiaries are of paramount significance, the adoption of a geocentric HRM policy will be difficult, regardless of its usefulness in implementing the overall corporate strategy.

The choice of an approach to IHRM is difficult, at best. A multinational or global corporation whose overall corporate strategy is reflected in its HRM practices will be more competitive in launching new products and services. We should, however, note that of all corporate functions, IHRM tends to be more reflective of local norms, customs, traditions, values, and practices.[7] While U.S. researchers emphasize the need for consistency between corporate-level strategy and adoption of IHRM policies of subsidiaries, European managers are less inclined to emphasize consistency in practice. European HRM managers are likely to closely follow guidelines from top management, and this gives them less control and strategic autonomy in running the HRM operations of subsidiaries, as compared to their American counterparts.

Major IHRM Functions

International human resources managers have the responsibility for the five functional human resource areas: recruitment and selection, performance evaluation, compensation and benefits, training and development, and labor relations. Management of expatriate workers is an additional function of IHRM. Table 2.1 summarizes the way that aspects of strategy influence IHRM.

RECRUITMENT AND SELECTION

Recruitment and selection are key processes through which a multinational or global corporation brings new employees into its network. *Recruitment* is the process of attracting a pool of qualified applicants for available positions. *Selection* is the process of choosing qualified applicants from the available candidates and ensuring that the skills, knowledge, and abilities of the selected employees match the requirements of the positions.

CLASSIFYING EMPLOYEES

Employees of multinational and global organizations are typically classified into three categories:

1. **Parent-country national (PCN).** The nationality of the employee is the same as that of the headquarters of the global organization. For example, a U.S. citizen working for a U.S. company, such as Microsoft, in Italy is a PCN.
2. **Host-country national (HCN).** The employee's nationality is the same as that of the subsidiary. For example, an Italian citizen working for a U.S. company, such as Microsoft, in Rome is an HCN.
3. **Third-country national (TCN).** The employee's nationality is neither that of the headquarters nor that of the local subsidiary. For example, an Italian citizen working for a U.S. company, such as Microsoft, in Brazil is a TCN.

TABLE 2.1   Strategic Approach, Organizational Concerns, and IHRM Approach

Aspects of the Enterprise	Orientation			
	Ethnocentric	**Polycentric**	**Regiocentric**	**Global**
Primary strategic orientation/stage	International	Multidomestic	Regional	Transnational
Perpetuation (recruiting, staffing, development)	People of home country developed for key positions everywhere in the world	People of local nationality developed for key positions in their own country	Regional people developed for key positions anywhere in the region	Best people everywhere in the world developed for key positions everywhere in the world
Complexity of organization	Complex in home country, simple in subsidiaries	Varied and independent	Highly interdependent on a regional basis	"Global web"; complex, independent, worldwide alliances/network
Authority; decision making	High in headquarters	Relatively low in headquarters	High regional headquarters and/or high collaboration among subsidiaries	Collaboration of headquarters and subsidiaries around the world
Evaluation and control	Home standards applied to people and performance	Determined locally	Determined regionally	Globally integrated
Rewards	High in headquarters; low in subsidiaries	Wide variation; can be high or low rewards for subsidiary performance	Rewards for contribution to regional objectives	Rewards to international and local executives for reaching local and worldwide objectives based on global company goals
Communication; information flow	High volume of orders, commands, advice to subsidiaries	Little to and from headquarters; little among subsidiaries	Little to and from corporate headquarters, but may be high to and from regional headquarters and among countries	Horizontal; network relations
Geographic identification	Nationality of owner	Nationality of host country	Regional company	Truly global company, but identifying with national interests ("glocal")

Source: D. A. Heenan and H. V. Perlmutter, *Multinational Organization Development*. Copyright © 1979. Used with permission of Pearson Education, Inc., Upper Saddle River, NJ 07458.

The classification of employees is important because it determines the adoption of the IHRM approach. While such classification helps us understand the general approach that characterizes most IHRM policies of multinational and global corporations, it is important to note that the classification scheme does not cover all possibilities. In many countries, classifications are related to seniority, compensation, and stage of career.

In multinational and global corporations, the staffing policy strongly affects the type of employee the company prefers. Companies with an ethnocentric orientation usually staff important positions with PCNs. Those adopting a polycentric orientation usually select HCNs for subsidiaries while PCNs manage headquarters. Those with regiocentric orientations staff positions with PCNs or with HCNs and TCNs from the region—the needs of the company and the product strategy determine the staffing. Those adopting a geocentric approach are likely to favor the selection of the most suitable person for the job, regardless of type.

It is important to consider the prevalent practices of the headquarters, as well as the practices and legal requirements of the countries in which the subsidiaries are located, as discussed earlier. In many countries, such in Mexico, it is common practice to recruit family members to work in the same subsidiary[8]—a practice that is strongly discouraged in the United States, United Kingdom, and western Europe. In some eastern European countries, such as Hungary, the need to reduce unemployment means that multinationals must obtain permission from the ministry of labor before hiring an expatriate.[9]

A balance must be struck between internal corporate consistency and sensitivity to local needs and practices. Different cultures emphasize different attributes in the selection process. Some cultures emphasize the need for universal criteria—what the person can do for the organization is more important than who the person is. Other cultures emphasize ascriptive criteria—who the person is, and his or her family background and connections, is more important than what he or she can do for the organization. The selection process in achievement-oriented countries, such as the United States, United Kingdom, Australia, and western European countries, highlights skills, knowledge, and abilities. While family or social connections might help, the emphasis is on hiring those who are best able to perform the job. In an ascriptive culture, age, gender, family background, and social connections are important, and the emphasis is on selecting someone whose personal characteristics fit the job. For example, in Japan and parts of Latin America, advertisements in newspapers might explicitly state that the company is looking for a young male within a specific age range for a job, while such specifications may be external to the job requirements. Such advertisements would be violations of the Fair Employment Practices Act in the United States. Many countries place few restrictions on recruitment, selection, or hiring, and an employer can ask any question or actively recruit candidates who fit certain personal characteristics.

Companies using a geocentric approach to IHRM have considerable difficulties in integrating the practices of various subsidiaries because the subsidiaries often vary from being heavily regulated by governments to having little regulation. One approach emphasizes the need for selecting applicants on the basis of not only ability and motivation but also the fit between the person and the organization, with selection modifications to suit cultural requirements.[10] This is important, for example, in some east Asian cultures such as Korea and Japan, where answering a question immediately is not seen as a positive attribute. The geocentric approach also highlights the development of a global system, based on achievement motivation, which may not be suitable in every country. Japanese managers feel that too much attention to qualifications and not enough on personal characteristics leads to selecting the wrong person for the company. The tendency in Japan is to recruit by emphasizing the fit with the entire company rather than with a specific job.

PERFORMANCE EVALUATION

Performance evaluation is the process of appraising employees' job performance. It is a systematic process, and in Western multinational organizations performance appraisals are usually done on a routine basis. Supervisors are required to discuss the results of appraisal with each employee.

Performance evaluation is often challenging, because it has two explicit purposes, which often conflict. The first is evaluative, while the second is developmental. Evaluative aspects of performance appraisal provide information for organizational decisions relating to compensation and advancement. Developmental aspects focus on feedback to help employees develop and improve their performance.

For international and global corporations, the complexity of performance evaluation increases because such organizations have the responsibility of developing systematic processes for the evaluation of employees from different countries who work in different locales. The need for developing consistent performance evaluations is often in conflict with the need to consider cultural factors. For example, in China, saving face is very important, and public criticism of an employee is counterproductive and may lead to turnover. This is also true in Mexico, where public criticism as a part of performance appraisal is avoided.[11] Developing a balanced performance review system for the Mexican situation requires an appreciation of Mexican culture, where tact and courtesy are key factors.

The organization's overall HRM strategy is the major determinant of the effectiveness of its performance evaluation system. A company with an ethnocentric approach designs appraisal systems that use the same techniques developed in headquarters, regardless of the need to incorporate some unique characteristics of each local subsidiary, such as national culture or legal issues. Some such companies translate their appraisal form into local languages. Multinational companies with polycentric or regiocentric approaches tend to be more sensitive to local conditions within each country or region. Those with a geocentric orientation use the same system of evaluating employees in various subsidiaries, but unlike ethnocentric organizations, the company develops universally applicable performance appraisal systems. Developing a global system of performance appraisal is time-consuming and requires a comprehensive consideration of many factors.

COMPENSATION AND BENEFITS

The compensation and benefit function of HRM is designed to develop uniform salary systems and other forms of remuneration, such as health insurance, pension funds, vacation, and sick pay. An international system of compensation is more difficult to develop, in that it must be concerned with the comparability across various subsidiaries located in various economic locales. The system must also be competitive, in order to attract and retain qualified employees. The salary structure of employees in different locations should reflect appropriate compensation schemes, taking into account local market conditions as well as consistency throughout the organization. Another concern is the overall cost of compensation to the multinational or global organization.[12]

Regardless of the approach to IHRM, compensation and benefit schemes reflect local market conditions. The availability of qualified local people to fill positions, the prevailing local wage rates, the use of expatriates, and various labor laws influence the level of compensation and benefits. If the supply of qualified applicants is limited, the wage rates typically rise. To lower such expenses, international HR managers may consider bringing in home-country or third-country nationals.

Typically, a global company attempts to develop a policy and apply it uniformly, offering salaries and benefits representing a specific market level. When the company emphasizes the quality of its products and employees, it often has a global policy to pay high wages everywhere to improve retention of quality employees. Another method is to pay high salaries in those countries where the company has its R&D operations but pay average wages elsewhere. Practical Insight 2.1, on page 34, illustrates the linkage between various cultures and distinct compensation and benefit requirements as reported in 2008.

TRAINING AND DEVELOPMENT

The training and development function involves planning for effective learning processes, organizational development, and career development. In the United States, there is a recognized field of HR called *human resource development (HRD)*. In global organizations, human resource development professionals are responsible for the training and development of employees located in subsidiaries around the world. They specialize in training employees for assignments abroad and in developing managers with a global mind-set, that is, managers who understand the complexities of managing in different countries.

The delivery of international training programs is either very centralized or decentralized.[13] A centralized approach originates at the headquarters, and corporate trainers travel to subsidiaries and adapt the program to local situations. This is an ethnocentric approach to training. In contrast, a geocentric approach allows the development of programs using inputs from both headquarters and subsidiary staff. Trainers are sent from headquarters or subsidiaries to any location where they are needed. In more polycentric approaches, the cultural backgrounds of the trainers and trainees tend to be similar. Subsidiary HR managers develop training materials and techniques for use in their own countries.

It is important to understand the learning process in order to implement effective training programs. Cultural differences in learning processes must be taken into account in developing training programs. An effective training program should focus on the specific needs of a subsidiary in a specific country and the cultural background of the trainees. In individualistic countries, the tendency is to emphasize learning mechanisms on an individual level; whereas in collectivistic countries, learning as a group is more effective. Similarly, where power distance is small, the relationship between the trainer and the trainee tends toward equality and challenging the trainer is acceptable. On the other hand, in countries where power distance is large, a trainer receives great respect and challenging the trainer in any way is not acceptable. Table 2.2 shows the impact of culture on training and development practices in four different parts of the world: The

TABLE 2.2 Impact of Culture on Training and Development Practices

	United States/ Canada	East Asia	Middle East/ North Africa	Latin America
HRD roles	Trainer and trainee as equals; trainees can and do challenge trainer; trainer can be informed and casual.	Trainees have great respect for trainer, who should behave, dress, and relate in a highly professional, formal manner.	Trainer highly respected; trainees want respect and friendly relationship; formality is important.	Preference for a decisive, clear, charismatic leader as trainer; trainees like to be identified with and loyal to a successful leader.
Analysis and design	Trainer determines objectives with input from trainees and their managers; trainees openly state needs and want to achieve success through learning.	Trainer should know what trainees need, admitting needs might represent loss of face to trainees.	Difficult to identify needs because it is improper to speak of other's faults; design must include time for socializing, relationship building, and prayers.	Difficult to get trainees to expose weaknesses and faults; design should include time for socializing.
Development and delivery	Programs should be practical and relevant, using a variety of methodologies with lecturing time limited.	Materials should be orderly, well organized, and unambiguous; trainees most accustomed to lecture, note taking, and limited questioning.	Need adequate opportunity for trainer and trainees to interact; rely on verbal rather than written demonstrations of knowledge acquired; avoid paper exercises and role playing.	Educational system relies on lecture and has more theoretical emphasis; training should be delivered in local language.
Administration and environment	Hold training in comfortable, economical location; trainee selection based on perceived needs of organization and individual.	Quality of program may be judged on the basis of quality of location and training materials; ceremonies with dignitaries, certificates, plaques, and speeches taken as signs of value of program.	The learning process should be permeated with flourishes and ceremonies; program should not be scheduled during Ramadan, the month of fasting.	Value and importance judged by location, which dignitaries invited for the ceremonies, and academic affiliation of trainer; time is flexible: beginning or ending at a certain time not important.

Source: Adapted from M. Marquardt and D. W. Engel, *Global Human Resource Development* (Prentice-Hall, 1993), pp. 25–32.

United States and Canada, east Asia, Middle East/north Africa, and Latin America. It also identifies the main differences among the regions, although the specifics of training practices may differ somewhat from country to country within each region.

LABOR RELATIONS

The labor relations function is designed to assist managers and workers determine their relationships within the workplace.[14] The concept and practice of labor relations vary greatly in different parts of the world. In the United States, labor relations practices generally are formal and confrontational and are governed by union contracts. In Japan, the relationship between management and unions is cooperative, and union leaders are determined by managers. In many countries, the government regulates labor relations. Therefore, a polycentric approach is generally more effective in managing this aspect of the HRM function. It has been suggested that even though labor relations are best addressed at the local or regional level, organizations should coordinate and develop labor relations policies uniformly across various subsidiaries.[15]

Although some unions are termed "international," most unions are organized at the local, company, regional (within country), or national level. Furthermore, some unions are in the process of developing regional (groups of nations) offices in various countries. These offices focus on issues that arise as a result of multiple-country trading blocks, such as the European Union, MERCOSUR, or NAFTA. In Europe, more than 50 industry-wide, cross-continent unions have emerged. Still, multinational and global companies have been slow to negotiate with them. An example of a worldwide union is the International Trade Union Confederation, which is the world's largest trade union. Formed in November 2006, it represents approximately 160 million workers worldwide and is represented in the majority of the countries in the world.

During the past 15 years, union membership has dropped significantly throughout the world. Still, in some countries and in some industries in those countries, powerful unions are a part of the business landscape. Table 2.3 illustrates the change in specific trade unions in Europe from 1993 to 2003.

Selecting Expatriates

Most research indicates that technical competence is the primary decision criteria used by global firms in selecting employees for overseas assignments.[16] (A person living in a foreign land is known as an **expatriate.**) Companies continue to endorse this practice, and other criteria that can have substantial effects on expatriates' adjustment and performance are not given enough attention.[17] This overemphasis on technical and job-related competence has guided the selection process because it is easier to measure these factors. Host-country organizations also prefer technically competent expatriates. However, cultural and national differences make expatriate adjustment difficult, and the ability to adapt to unfamiliar conditions is crucial.[18] Language skills and knowledge of the local area are straightforward criteria that could be incorporated, but what is not understood very well is that the factors that can ease adjustment to the new environment are generally less concrete.

CULTURE SHOCK

Culture shock—a state of anxiety and disorientation caused by exposure to a new culture—can be a significant barrier to the adjustment and performance of an expatriate. Differences in daily styles of interactions, including such things as whether to shake hands or not, when to present a gift, when and how to pay complements, cause difficulties in adjusting to the new environment. Coupled with this is the difference of familiar signs and ways of doing things, such as street signs, driving rules, and use of telephone and e-mail, that creates further problems for the expatriate.

The Right Perks

Global hiring means getting a handle on how different cultures view salaries, taxes, and benefits.

Brazilian supermodel Gisele Bundchen may be able to decide, as she did recently, that she would rather be paid in euros than once-mighty dollars. But for most mere mortals toiling away in cubicles around the globe, pay and benefits are a decidedly local affair. In Latin America, for instance, past financial crises mean employees aren't much interested in deferred compensation plans such as 401(k)s, which are common in the U.S. Why be rewarded in stocks and bonds that could collapse?

As expat packages decline and global growth requires attracting local talent, employers that ignore local quirks do so at their own risk. Peter D. Acker, a global rewards consultant for Hewitt Associates, reports that he sees companies extend their stock-option plans around the world, thinking everyone will love them. But local tax treatments for such options mean that's often not the case. Other companies, he says, have rolled out bonus plans in China that focus on individual performance, only to find that rewarding group achievements might have been a better cultural fit. Using data from benefits consulting firm Mercer, we compiled snapshots of pay and perks in 10 countries, including benefits ranging from company-owned ski chalets in France to bodyguards and bulletproof cars for top executives in Brazil:

India

Cost-of-living rank (Bangalore): 134

Salary, head of sales & marketing: $56,171

Salary, data-entry operator: $1,913

Projected average pay increase for 2008: 14.1%

Days off: 31

Local perk: CEOs might grumble about rising health-care costs for U.S. workers. But at least they don't have to pay for employees' aging parents, which is common for companies operating in India. Rosaline Chow Koo, Mercer's head of health and benefits consulting in Asia, says this is one reason health-care spending is rising swiftly: "It's growing so much faster than wages that it's become a hot issue."

Hong Kong

Cost-of-living rank: 5

Salary, head of sales & marketing: $149,905

Salary, data-entry operator: $16,139

Projected average pay increase for 2008: 3.8%

Days off: 26

Local perk: In recent years, Hong Kong workers have been asking for traditional Chinese medicine coverage as a supplement to regular health insurance. The plans, which cover everything from herbal therapies to fees for Chinese medicine practitioners, are offered by 55% of employers, says Mercer's Chow Koo.

Philippines

Cost-of-living rank (Manila): 137

Salary, head of sales & marketing: $95,286

Salary, data-entry operator: $6,829

Projected average pay increase for 2008: 7.4%

Days off: 19

Local perk: For years, many Filipinos received bags of rice as a benefit. Employers later converted the sacks to "rice allowances" paid in cash and now offer "flex" packages, where less tradition-minded workers can exchange the cash for perks such as free mobile phones.

China

Cost-of-living rank (Shanghai): 26

Salary, head of sales & marketing: $92,402

Salary, data-entry operator: $4,034

Projected average pay increase for 2008: 7.5%

Days off: 23

Local perk: Companies operating in China are required by the government to chip into a housing fund that's available to their Chinese employees, who also make contributions. When employees are ready to buy a home, they can draw from the funds to help. About 20% of multinationals currently chip in more to the housing fund than required, according to Mercer.

Japan

Cost-of-living rank (Tokyo): 4

Salary, head of sales & marketing: $148,899

Salary, data-entry operator: $30,933

Projected average pay increase for 2008: 2.5%

Days off: 35

Local perk: Japanese workers often receive "family allowances" (kazoku teiate) on top of their pay from employers, depending on the size of their family. Stemming from the country's tradition of lifetime employment, the stipends are most prevalent among native companies and range from about $100 to $300 a month. Some employers have been recasting them as incentives for workers to have kids in order to combat Japan's declining birthrate.

Mexico

Cost-of-living rank (Mexico City): 104

Salary, head of sales & marketing: $163,591

Salary, data-entry operator: $11,017

Projected average pay increase for 2008: 4.8%

Days off: 23

Local perk: Some companies having difficulty luring qualified expats to polluted Mexico City offer "pollution-escape trips," or all-expenses-paid getaways to the Pacific or Gulf coasts. One local holiday quirk: Mother's Day is on a weekday, and employees get a day or a half-day off to take Mom out to lunch, prompting massive traffic snarls.

Brazil

Cost-of-living rank (Rio de Janeiro): 64

Salary, head of sales & marketing: $208,691

Salary, data-entry operator: $11,829

Projected average pay increase for 2008: 5.0%

Days off: 40

Local perk: It's more of an essential safety precaution than a perk, but to foil kidnappers, top executives in Brazil are chauffeured in bulletproof cars and followed by bodyguards. (This benefit also shows up in Mexico.) "It's kind of a strange way to think about it," says Hewitt's Acker. "But if your executive is kidnapped for a month, your business really suffers."

USA

Cost-of-living rank (New York): 15

Salary, head of sales & marketing: $229,300

Salary, data-entry operator: $35,400

Projected average pay increase for 2008: 3.7%

Days off: 25

Local perk: To get a handle on those fat pay packages, U.S. CEOs commonly receive financial-planning benefits—averaging about $20,000 a year, reports executive pay consultants Pearl Meyer & Partners. The money helps pay their cadre of accountants, estate lawyers, and financial planners. The benefit is much rarer elsewhere. And unique to the U.S.'s litigious society, Mercer says, are group or prepaid legal services, which some companies offer employees. As with group health insurance, employees pay premiums to get free or discounted access to attorneys for needs such as wills, adoptions, or real estate transactions.

Russia

Cost-of-living rank (Moscow): 1

Salary, head of sales & marketing: $117,135

Salary, data-entry operator: $10,325

Projected average pay increase for 2008: 10.2%

Days off: 39

Local perk: Company-sponsored mortgages are seen as an attractive perk in Russia, where consumers have traditionally had less access to credit and where the cost of living is high. Companies who offer this perk secure the loans, says Hewitt's Acker, and in some cases, help employees pay more favorable rates. Corporate help for loans occurs in other emerging markets, such as India and Brazil.

France

Cost-of-living rank (Paris): 13

Salary, head of sales & marketing: $188,771

Salary, data-entry operator: $28,857

Projected average pay increase for 2008: 3.0%

Days off: 40

Local perk: As if the high number of days off were not enough, some French employers offer the use of company-owned ski chalets and beach houses to employees for a nominal fee. Such perks are also occasionally seen in Germany, says Charles Nelson, who leads Mercer's health and benefits practice in Britain and Ireland.

Data: Data are provided by Mercer, except where noted. Cost-of-living rank is based on Mercer's 2007 survey of the comparative cost of cities for expatriates. Salaries represent midpoint annual base salaries, using exchange rates from local currencies to U.S. dollars on Jan. 14. Days off combine minimum vacation days required by law and public or nationally recognized holidays for employees working five days a week after 10 years' service. China and the U.S. do not mandate vacation days nationally, but 15 days is common in the U.S. for employees with 10 years of service and 12 days is average in China, though numbers vary from city to city. Mercer notes that in Mexico, many companies supplement required public holidays with an additional 4 to 6 days.

Source: Jena McGregor, "The Right Perks," *BusinessWeek,* January 28, 2008, p. 42.

TABLE 2.3

European Trade Union Membership Figures, 1993–2003

Source: *European Industrial Relations Observatory*, May 21, 2004.

Country	1993	1998	2003	Change, 1993–2003 (%)
Austria	1,616,000	1,480,000	1,407,000	−12.9
Belgium	2,865,000	3,013,000	3,061,000	+6.8
Bulgaria	2,192,000	778,000	515,000	−76.5
Cyprus	159,000	167,000	175,000	+10.1
Denmark	2,116,000	2,170,000	2,151,000	+1.7
Estonia	—	—	93,000	—
Finland	2,069,000	2,084,000	2,122,000	+2.6
France	1,256,000	1,425,000	889,000	−320%
Germany	11,680,000	9,798,000	8,894,000	−23.9
Greece	721,000	656,000	639,000	−11.4
Hungary	—	—	936,000	—
Ireland	432,000	463,000	515,000	+19.2
Italy	10,594,000	10,763,000	11,266,000	+6.3
Latvia	nd	252,000	180,000	−28.6
Luxembourg	97,000	112,000	139,000	+43.3
Malta	74,000	82,000	87,000	+17.6
Netherlands	1,810,000	1,936,000	1,941,000	+7.2
Norway	1,325,000	1,489,000	1,498,000	+13.1
Poland	6,500,000	3,200,000	1,900,000	−70.8
Portugal	1,150,000	—	1,165,000	+1.3
Romania	—	—	4,399,000	—
Slovakia	1,583,000	854,000	576,000	−63.6
Slovenia	nd	nd	360,000	—
Spain	—	—	2,108,000	—
Sweden	3,712,000	3,562,000	3,446,000	−7.2
United Kingdom	8,804,000	7,852,000	7,751,000	−12.0

The effects of culture shock on adjustment can be shown as a U-shaped curve, as shown in Figure 2.1. Individuals who visit a country for a short time, such as tourists and others on short-term missions, do not go through the various degrees of adjustment. However, people who go to work or live abroad for a long period of time go through the phases of adjustment shown in the exhibit. The first phase, the *honeymoon*, begins with the initial contact with another culture, and a sense of optimism and euphoria are common. Expatriates live in pleasant surroundings and are welcomed by colleagues and other host-country nationals, who may arrange special welcome events and make them feel comfortable.

In the second stage, *culture shock*, difficulties in language, inadequate schooling for the children, lack of adequate housing, crowded buses and subways, differences in shopping habits, and other problems can create stress, unhappiness, and a dislike for the country. During this period, expatriates often seek others from their home country with whom they can compare experiences about their difficulties. They may try to escape through drinking

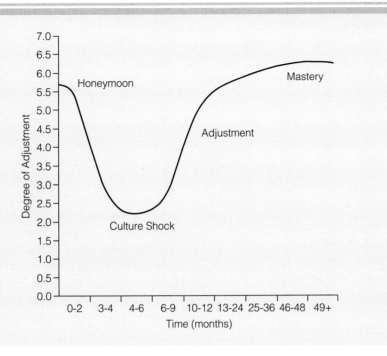

FIGURE 2.1

Effects of Culture Shock
on Adjustment

Source: From D. C. Thomas,
*Essentials of International
Management: A Cross-
Cultural Perspective.* Copyright
© 2002 by Sage Publications,
Inc. Reprinted by permission
of Sage Publications, Inc.

and socializing, as they experience a sense of powerlessness and alienation. Over time, these feeling may intensify in some expatriates and lead to depression and physical health problems. In addition, since the September 11, 2001, terrorist attacks on the World Trade Center and Pentagon, the incidences of terrorism are affecting placement of expatriates. Practical Insight 2.2 offers some tips for staying safe on foreign assignments. While there are no guarantees that the guidelines provided are foolproof, they will help.

In the third stage, *adjustment*, expatriates begin to develop new sets of skills that enable them to cope with their new environment. Anxiety and depression become less frequent, and expatriates begin to feel more positive about their new surroundings. Furthermore, the expatriate begins to become more productive at work and reverts back to being the confident manager who was selected for the overseas assignment.

In the fourth and last stage, *mastery*, expatriates know how to deal with the demands of their local environment and have learned enough about local customs and culture to feel "at home." Still, it is important for expatriates to continually realize that they will never know the entire culture as locals do and, thus, it is their responsibility to attain new knowledge and skills every day.

🌐 Managing Expatriates

Multinational and global organizations that make use of parent-country and third-country nationals must develop a process of handling the complexities of moving people outside their home countries. Employing expatriates may be linked with the global strategy, but it tends to be an expensive process most of the time. Careful managing of expatriate HRM is extremely important.

COST OF FAILURE

The cost of failure of the overseas assignments is much more than simply the cost of the executive's salary and transfer. Because of additional compensation, an expatriate stationed in an expensive city such as Tokyo, London, or Paris could cost a company up to $350,000 in the first year.[19] It is more cost-efficient to prevent a bad transfer than to have an expatriate return home because of difficulties in adjusting to foreign assignments.

Staying Safe on Foreign Assignments

Overseas travel has become an increasingly important part of conducting business in the era of globalization. This article outlines some of the precautions which human-resource specialists can take to help to protect their company employees who travel abroad.

Business Travelers Make Easy Targets

Increasing crime directed at business travelers abroad makes it more important than ever that human-resource specialists have a strategy for protecting company employees who travel overseas for the firm.

While companies see foreign trade as an exciting opportunity in the era of globalization, so too do some of the world's criminals.

Says Alan Stokes, of insurer CIGNA International: "Business travelers make easy targets. They often travel in unfamiliar territory, wear formal clothes, carry expensive laptop computers in readily-identifiable bags, use mobile telephones and wear watches which can cost more than a year's salary in less-privileged countries. All these factors combine to make them highly visible.

"Improved travel has made so many destinations accessible that business travelers can almost forget they are on foreign territory. The security of corporate-credit-card bookings, executive-club lounges and international hotel chains can cocoon them into a false sense of security. But believing they can go anywhere in the world and behave exactly as they do at home can make business travelers an easy target for anything from mugging to armed-car theft and even kidnap.

"The challenge for human-resource professionals is not only to ensure the personal safety of the individual, but also to ensure that their organization is not exposed to the business implications of losing the services of a key employee, of disruption to customer relationships or the loss of a contract, by preparing corporate travelers in advance."

Assets to Be Protected

"Companies generally send key personnel to conduct business overseas, so they should be seen as an asset to be protected."

Mr Stokes offers the following advice to human-resource specialists:

1. *Prepare the ground.* Make use of free pre-travel advice from the travel agent or insurance company. Do some homework on the destination. Check well in advance about inoculation and visa requirements. Find out about any dress codes and ask which taxi company to use on arrival at the destination. Make sure there is a contact number for the embassy and know if there are any areas of town which should be avoided.

2. *Check the insurance.* Make sure your company insurance covers the basics such as medical expenses, repatriation, personal injury and sickness for the area the executive is traveling to. Insurance bought with a travel ticket may be geared towards the needs of the holidaymaker. Business travelers need different support, such as cover for business equipment. Encourage the executive to carry the helpline number listed in the insurance documents, so that help is always at hand.

3. *Do not stand out from the crowd.* Avoid business luggage tickets. If the executive has a laptop computer, make sure he or she carries it in an ordinary holdall or briefcase. To the average thief, computer bags scream: "I have $2,000 of equipment on my shoulder."

If possible, the executive should travel in casual clothes. Expensive business clothes mark him or her as someone likely to be carrying valuable possessions and part of a larger, wealthy organization. Thieves target airports in the knowledge that business travelers will be carrying cash and credit cards. Keep credit cards on one's person and in separate places.

Thieves know which hotels are used by comparatively wealthy business travelers. If the executive feels like taking fresh air or sightseeing, he or she should ask the hotel staff where is safe to walk alone and which areas to avoid. Leave valuables such as jewellery and passport in the hotel safe, or keep them with money in a concealed money belt.

Take care when showing a gold or platinum credit card. Something which is taken for granted at home can also be a status symbol which clearly marks a person out as a target.

If the executive is to be met at an airport, ask the driver to use a code by which he or she can be recognized. Name and company on a card advertises the executive as a target to follow.

Such simple precautions can help to prevent a dream trip to an exotic foreign location from becoming a nightmare.

Source: *Human Resource Management International Digest,* May–June 1999.

Some managers fail because they are unhappy in their assignment. This is often due to the poor organizational support that promotes the feeling within the company that overseas assignments are not high-profile ones and do not lead to advancement.[20] It can also be due to the lack of family adjustment to the new culture.

COMPENSATION ISSUES

Sending home-country nationals abroad is expensive. Doing so costs one to two times more than keeping managers at home, and estimates indicate that it costs 10 times more than hiring a host-country national.[21] Until there is a global salary system, companies are generally forced to resort to one of two types of compensation systems.

1. **Headquarters salary system.** This system is based on the headquarters pay scale plus differentials. The salary for the same job at headquarters determines the base salary of the home-country national. The differential can be a positive addition to an expatriate's salary, or it can be a negative allowance to account for the extra benefits that might be associated with the particular overseas placement. When an expatriate is provided free housing and transportation and an equivalent sum is subtracted from his basic pay, the amount deducted is a negative allowance. Under the headquarters salary system, host-country nationals are entitled to neither the base salary nor the differentials of home-country nationals. Their salaries are based on local salary standards. Third-country nationals pose a unique compensation challenge. The company may treat them either as home- or host-country nationals, so inequities arise. The headquarters salary system is the more ethnocentric of the two compensation systems.

2. **Citizenship salary system.** The citizenship salary system solves the problem of what to do about the third-country nationals. The manager's salary is based on the standard for the country of his or her citizenship or native residence. An appropriate differential is then added, based on comparative factors between the two countries. This system works well as long as expatriates with similar positions do not come from countries with different salary scales. It is difficult to avoid this problem, however, and inequities arising from either compensation program are noticed by the managers.

Benefits In the United States, approximately 27 percent of compensation for home-country employees is benefits. Issues surrounding expatriate benefits are different from those affecting benefits of host-country employees. Expatriates need vacations to return home for extended visits. Multinational companies often pay airfare for home visits, emergency leave, illnesses, and a death in the expatriate's family. However, other questions must be dealt with on a country and case-by-case basis. For example, some benefits are taxable overseas but tax-deductible at home, and some countries provide government-sponsored social benefits, such as universal health care. The company must reach an agreement with either the government or the home-country manager about coverage for these necessities.

Allowances Multinational and global companies often pay allowances for cost of living, relocation expenses, housing, cars, and club memberships in the host country. In addition, education allowances for children are often expected, either to allow the children to attend private school in the host country or to allow them to be educated in the home country. Hardship allowances are often required to attract qualified individuals to less desirable locations, such as the Middle East or other less developed areas.

Incentives Only 20 percent of companies pay higher compensation to expatriates than to home-country managers. Instead, most offer a one-time lump-sum premium.[22]

Incentives are beginning to be phased out, because the manager sees the assignment as its own reward or as a step toward globalization.[23]

Taxes   Often multinational and global companies pay any extra tax burden. Taxes can be an extremely complex area in compensating expatriates. In some countries, expatriates' salary is taxable only when paid locally. In most countries, local authorities do not tax compensation based on a worldwide scheme. American companies prefer a tax equalization plan that allows the company to withhold the expatriate's U.S. tax liability and pay his or her local taxes. British companies, on the other hand, change their policy depending on the country in which the subsidiary is located. The tax equalization plan may create a situation in which the company pays taxes in multiple countries because taxes paid on behalf of an expatriate by the headquarters are also taxable locally. International compensation experts have suggested that companies with operations in many countries should adopt a policy of tax equalization. The company would gain in some countries and lose in others. However, if the scale of international operations is limited, it is best to leave the payment of local taxes to the expatriate and adjust other allowances in accordance with local standards.[24]

MANAGING DUAL-CAREER EXPATRIATES

A current critical strategic concern for multinational corporations is the consideration of attracting the right expatriates when their spouses also have careers, which are often not transferable overseas. The number of dual careers grew from 52 percent of all couples to 59 percent in the early 1990s, and the trend is on the rise. Over 50 percent of the expatriates being transferred abroad have spouses who worked before relocating.[25]

The dual-career expatriate couple has become a major concern of global companies, especially companies in which overseas experience can significantly advance one's career. In an interesting phenomenon, couples sustain their marriages by using the Internet and e-mail; this is becoming common as married men and women with careers take assignments in different parts of the world. Global companies must have sound policies to lessen the chances that a talented male or female manager will terminate employment because of the difficulties associated with separation from his or her spouse. Some of the suggestions for policies are:

- For transcontinental commuter marriages, providing for frequent visitation trips by the family or the expatriate to prevent the pain of separation from becoming too intense. One trip every two months is not unreasonable.
- Providing a generous allowance for long-distance telephone calls and other costs of communication. A phone conversation can ease the tension and loneliness of the expatriate and the family.
- Seeking employment opportunities for the spouse within the company or in the local area if the spouse is willing to quit his or her job in the home country to be with the married partner. The U.S. State Department has the practice of finding local jobs for spouses of employees sent abroad.
- Making connections with other global companies for employment of spouses. For example, the Hong Kong subsidiary of an international company, such as Proctor & Gamble, might be in a position to hire the spouse of an IBM expatriate manager working in Hong Kong.

REPATRIATION

Most overseas assignments last for five years. **Repatriation** is the term given to the return of the home-country manager. Managers return for a number of reasons:[26]

- The time of the overseas assignment is up.
- Children's education.
- Unhappy with the assignment.

- Family unhappiness.
- Failure—the expatriate does not meet stated objectives.

Readjustment problems occur when individuals arrive back after their overseas assignments. Tung found that the longer the assignment, the more problems with reabsorption.[27] Transition strategies are needed to retain these individuals and the experience they have acquired. One study showed:

- Three-fourths of expatriates felt they returned to a demotion,
- 60 percent felt they were unable to use their overseas experience because it was devalued by the organization.
- 60 percent believed that the company lacked any commitment to them on their return.[28]

The study also found that 25 percent of the expatriates left the organization within a year after their return.

Other readjustment problems are more personal, such as adjusting to lower pay and benefits after the overseas assignments. Some find difficulty in the housing market after they sold their house to go overseas. Children of expatriates may find that returning to public school is difficult after the smaller classes in private school. The change in the cultural lifestyle can affect those who transfer from cultural centers such as Paris or London or New York to less cosmopolitan areas in the home country.

Companies can prevent some of these problems by using transition strategies. One useful strategy is the use of repatriation agreements. These agreements define the company's responsibilities to the expatriate on his or her return, thereby providing the security often sought by managers on overseas assignments. Some companies have set up separate departments to deal with expatriates' special needs.[29] Another strategy used by some companies is the purchase of the manager's home until the foreign assignment is complete. This allows the expatriate to keep up with the generally increasing housing market while overseas. Some companies assign senior managers to be sponsors of expatriate managers.[30] These mentor programs maintain the individual's communication lines with headquarters, which is of crucial importance to expatriates on their return. Assigning expatriates to projects that are centered at the home office also enhances communication with headquarters. Practical Insight 2.3 illustrates the strategic importance of managing the expatriate's relocation to a new country.

International Human Resources Management and Competitive Advantage

In an era of globalization, when technology and capital flow freely across national and cultural boundaries, human resources take on new importance as critical strategic assets or factors of production that largely are not easily mobile. People resist permanent moves across cultures and boundaries, even if doing so means that they refuse better compensation and adequate living facilities. While political barriers to intercountry mobility have largely been removed, as in the case of integrated European Union countries, where free movement of labor is allowed, the actual size of the flow of talented people across national boundaries remains small. The main barriers are rooted in language differences, cultural preferences, and natural propensities to stay and work in the country of birth.

Intercountry competition in a global economy is likely to result in successes and failures of many large to medium-size organizations. One of the major ways failures can be averted and sustained competitive advantage maintained is by recruiting talented personnel from a global workforce who are able to manage technology and knowledge, motivate people in various worldwide subsidiaries, and exercise proper leadership and negotiating skills. Increasing the recruitment of women is one way to ensure continued success in the global workforce. Women are joining men as examples of successful global leaders and effective

Culture Shock in America?

Imagine you're embarking on your first foreign assignment. You had an outstanding academic career and are now in great demand in your field. After only a few years on the job, you're an undisputed star at your company. You've become so stellar, in fact, that with your ability to speak the international language of business-English, you're the obvious choice to be sent abroad. It's a developmental assignment, shall we say: five, maybe 10, years overseas. Then you'll return home with a skill set bulging with international savvy and your own personal spotlight on the world stage of business.

With confidence, you accept that exotic assignment abroad. Destination: the United States of America. But you soon discover that the Land of Opportunity is really the Land of "What's Your Social Security Number?" Without that nine-digit track record of your material viability, it doesn't matter where you came from or where you're going. You find yourself struggling to open accounts; to get an apartment, a phone, and electricity; and to figure out the bus route while you're waiting for a car loan to come through. You have somehow dropped into the Dead Zone; you're stuck in Culture Shock Purgatory.

It's ironic that this would be the case in a country with one of the world's most-traveled populations. Still, being sent to the United States on foreign assignment is not just a stressful business—it's a lonely one. From New Delhi to Cape Town to Minas Gerais, the observation is the same: Americans are friendly but hard to make friends with. We gregarious Americans don't truly bring international assignees into our lives, because we don't bring them into our homes after work.

What about corporate support? With rare exception, Corporate America is still focused more on making Americans' adventures abroad successful than on providing the same levels of support to those coming here on corporate assignments. This perspective will eventually come at great cost to any U.S. corporation with international ambitions, says Willa Hallowell, a partner with Brooklyn, N.Y.–based Cornelius Grove and Associates, a consultancy emphasizing cross-cultural support. You have to regard this person coming in as a business investment, and you therefore must guard that investment in every possible way. "If you don't, the mess you will have to clean up will be an even greater expense," Hallowell says. The costs associated with the mess include loss of productivity, the diminishment of the employee's self-confidence, the potential destruction of the employee's home life, and the corrosion of the company's reputation abroad.

"If things aren't going well, the returning employee will spread the seeds of discontent," Hallowell says. "Then, the next round of employees brought here will be prepared for problems, or they might choose to come here to look for another job."

The good news is that companies are moving toward seeking support services for their expatriates from all nations. "More and more companies are bringing expats to us," says Franchette Richards, until recently manager of Arthur Ander-sen's International Employment Solutions group. "We're helping them deal with visas and other immigration issues—financial obstacles, cultural differences. It's important for companies to realize that they must be consistent in the support of their expats, whether the employees are coming here or going outbound. An expat is an expat is an expat."

And no matter where they come from, expats share a critical concern: how well their spouses adjust to their new life. "It is the main reason why employees go home early," says Cornelius Grove, partner at Grove & Associates and an expert on the physiological effects of the stress of culture shock.

Most damaging to a spouse's accommodation: Under U.S. immigration laws, most spouses are not allowed to find jobs while they are "in country," so they are without the automatic social network that the office provides the employee.

Source: M. Finney, *Across the Board,* May 2000, p. 28.

expatriates. Still, despite such successes, many multinationals, particularly from collectivistic and developing economies, remain reluctant to employ women as senior-level managers in leadership roles. In addition, corporations avoid placement of women in cultures where they feel women are not accorded proper respect. While some of these assumptions might be true, research conducted in the human resource field shows that women are more effective than men as expatriate managers in parts of the world where relationship-oriented managers do much better.

CHAPTER SUMMARY

International human resources management is the process of managing human resources globally. An organization's corporate strategy drives the approach it takes to IHRM. The approach can influence implementation of major functions such as recruitment and selection, performance evaluation, compensation and benefits, training and development, and labor relations.

Multinational companies adopting a purely ethnocentric approach attempt to impose their home-country methods on their subsidiaries. Polycentric and regiocentric approaches tend to follow local practices more consistently. The geocentric or global approach develops practices for uniform worldwide use.

Management of expatriates is one of the major concerns of IHRM. Because expatriates function in dissimilar economic, political, and cultural environments and also need to function effectively in foreign work and living situations, they need special attention. It is important to motivate them in their assignments and upgrade their compensation and benefits to make foreign assignments attractive.

Approaches to IHRM are both converging and diverging worldwide. Large global corporations, such as Microsoft, IBM, Sony, Toyota, and Unilever, prefer uniform practices, whereas smaller companies prefer IHRM practices tailored to the local needs. International managers have the important responsibility of managing human resources in various countries and should upgrade their knowledge continuously in order to effectively implement corporate strategies.

Key Terms and Concepts

culture shock, *21*
ethnocentric staffing approach, *26*
expatriate, *33*
geocentric (global) staffing approach, *27*
international human resources management (IHRM), *25*

performance evaluation, *30*
polycentric staffing approach, *26*
regiocentric staffing approach, *26*
repatriation, *40*

Critical Thinking and Discussion Questions

1. What is international human resources management? Why is it more difficult to manage human resources on a worldwide basis than on a national basis?

2. What are the various functions of international human resources management? How does the process of recruitment and selection differ in international corporations compared to domestic corporations?

3. How does the process of performance appraisal differ in organizations that adopt a geocentric approach compared to the ones that adopt an ethnocentric approach?

4. When should an international corporation use universal compensation policies and practices? When should it use policies and practices tailored to local needs?

5. Explain the concept of culture shock. What is the role of the spouse of an expatriate in adjusting to foreign countries?

CLOSING CASE

Cracks in a Particularly Thick Glass Ceiling

Women in South Korea are slowly changing a corporate culture.

South Koreans are a bit conflicted about career women. Gender wasn't much of an issue in the selection of a female astronaut to fly this month on the country's first space mission. But when women are seeking workaday corporate jobs, some South Korean men still resist change. Outer space is one thing, but a woman in the next cubicle is something else.

For years, most educated women in South Korea who wanted to work could follow but one career path, which began and ended with teaching. The situation started to change after the 1998 Asian financial crisis. Thousands of men lost their jobs or took salary cuts, and their wives had to pick up the slack by starting businesses in their homes or seeking part-time work. A couple of years later, the government banned gender discrimination in the workplace and required businesses with more than 500 employees to set up child-care facilities. It also created a Gender Equality Ministry.

These days the government hires thousands of women (42% of its new employees last year), many for senior positions in the judiciary, international trade administration, and foreign service. Startups and foreign companies also employ (and promote) increasing numbers of Korean women. But at the top 400 companies, many of which are family-run conglomerates, it's hard for women to reach the upper ranks. In all, about 8% of working women hold managerial positions. (In the U.S. nearly 51% do.) "We have a long way to go," says Cho Jin Woo, director of the Gender Equality Ministry.

South Koreans are grappling with traditional attitudes about women, a hierarchical business culture, and the need to open up the workplace to compete globally. A senior manager at SK Holdings, which controls the giant mobile phone carrier SK Telecom, says he avoids hiring women because he believes they lack tenacity. When deadlines are tight, he says, "you need people prepared to put in long hours at the office." Park Myung Soon, a 39-year-old woman who is in charge of business development at the carrier, says, "Many men are preoccupied with the notion that women are a different species." To get ahead, Park says she had to achieve 120% of what her male colleagues did—as well as play basketball and drink with them after work. "Luckily, I like sports, and I like to drink," she says.

When Choi Dong Hee joined SK's research arm in 2005, she was the only woman there and had no major assignment until she created one. After conducting a yearlong study, Choi, 30, proposed changing the company's policy to allow subscribers to use any wireless portal. Her managers ignored her. She persisted. Finally, they agreed to let her brief the division head, who agreed to let her make her case to the company chairman. Choi worked on the presentation for three weeks straight, sometimes alone in the office overnight (to her boss's horror). In the end, the company did adopt the open policy she advocated. Now her managers are quick to say that women's perspectives can help SK better serve its customers.

Sonia Kim, who is in charge of TV marketing at Samsung Electronics, says her male colleagues rarely argue with the boss, even if they think he's wrong. Kim, though, persuaded her manager to let her develop a promotional campaign rather than rely on an ad agency she thought had lost its creative edge. Kim also says some of the men used to overturn decisions made during the day while out drinking after hours. Since she and other women at Samsung complained, Kim says, the practice has mostly stopped.

Source: Moon Ihlwain, "Cracks in a Particularly Thick Glass Ceiling," *BusinessWeek*, April 21, 2008, p. 58.

Case Discussion Questions

1. Should gender be a consideration when staffing local management positions?
2. Should gender be a consideration when selecting an expatriate for an overseas assignment?
3. Discuss what factors must be considered if a U.S. multinational corporation decides to staff a leadership position in South Korea with a woman.

Notes

1. P. J. Dowling, R. S. Schuler, and D. E. Welch, *International Dimensions of Human Resource Management,* 2nd ed. (Belmont, CA: Wadsworth, 1994).

2. J. L. Laabs, "HR Pioneers Explore the Road Less Traveled," *Personnel Journal,* February 1996, pp. 70–72, 74, 77–78.

3. J. S. Black and H. B. Gregersen, "The Right Way to Manage Expats," *Harvard Business Review,* March/April 1999, pp. 52–62.

4. B. S. Chakravarthy and H. V. Perlmuter, "Strategic Planning for a Global Business," *Columbia Journal of World Business* 20, no. 2 (1985), pp. 3–10; Dowling, Schuler, and Welch, *International Dimensions of Human Resource Management.*

5. C. D. Fisher, L. F. Schoenfeldt, and J. B. Shaw, *Human Resource Management,* 2nd ed. (Boston: Houghton Mifflin, 1993).

6. R. Tung, *The New Expatriates: Managing Human Resources Abroad* (Cambridge, MA: Ballinger, 1988).

7. P. M. Rosenweig and N. Nohria, "Influences on Human Resource Management Practices in Multinational Corporations," *Journal of International Business Studies* 25 (1994), pp. 229–251.

8. M. B. Teagarden, M. A. Von Glinow, M. C. Butler, and E. Drost, "The Best Practices Learning Curve: Human Resource Management in Mexico's Maquiladora Industry," in O. Shenkar, ed., *Global Perspectives of Human Resource Management* (Upper Saddle River, NJ: Prentice Hall, 1995).

9. D. C. Bangert and J. Poor, "Human Resource Management in Foreign Affiliates in Hungary," in Shenkar, *Global Perspectives of Human Resource Management.*

10. J. Artise, "Selection, Coaching, and Evaluation of Employees in International Subsidiaries," in Shenkar, *Global Perspectives of Human Resource Management.*

11. M. E. de Forest, "Thinking of a Plant in Mexico?" *Academy of Management Executive* 8 (1994), pp. 33–40.

12. Dowling, Schuler, and Welch, *International Dimensions of Human Resource Management.*

13. M. Marquardt and D. W. Engel, *Global Human Resource Development* (Upper Saddle River, NJ: Prentice Hall, 1993).

14. R. M. Hodgetts and F. Luthans, *International Management,* 2nd ed. (New York: McGraw-Hill, 1994).

15. Dowling, Schuler, and Welch, *International Dimensions of Human Resource Management.*

16. E. L. Miller, "The Job Satisfaction of Expatriate American Managers: A Function of Regional Location and Previous Work Experience," *Journal of International Business Studies* 6, no. 2 (1975), pp. 65–73; R. L. Tung, "Selection and Training of Personnel for Overseas Assignments," *Columbia Journal of World Business* 16 (1981), pp. 68–78.

17. A. Haselberger and L. K. Stroh, "Development and Selection of Multinational Expatriates," *Human Resource Development Quarterly* 3 (1992), pp. 287–293.

18. R. J. Stone, "Expatriate Selection and Failure," *Human Resource Planning* 29, no. 1 (1991), pp. 9–17; R. L. Tung, "American Expatriates Abroad: From Neophytes to Cosmopolitans," *Journal of World Business* 33, no. 2 (1998), pp. 125–144.

19. D. R. Briscoe, *International Human Resource Management.* (Upper Saddle River, NJ: Prentice Hall, 1995).

20. M. L. Kraimer, S. J. Wayne, and R. A. Jaworski, "Sources of Support and Expatriate Performance: The Mediating

Role of Expatriate Adjustment," *Personnel Psychology* 54 (2001), pp. 71–99.

21. C. Reynolds, "Expatriate Compensations in Historical Perspective," *Journal of World Business* 32, no. 2 (1997), p. 127.

22. R. B. Peterson, N. K. Napier, and W. Shul-Shim, "Expatriate Management: A Comparison of MNCs across Four Parent Countries," *Thunderbird International Business Review*, March–April 2000, p. 155.

23. G. W. Latta, "Expatriate Incentives: Beyond Tradition," *HR Focus*, March 1998, p. 24.

24. D. Young, "Fair Compensation for Expatriates," *Harvard Business Review* 51, no. 4 (1973), p. 119.

25. J. S. Lubin, "Companies Use Cross-Cultural Training to Help Their Employees Adjust Abroad," *Wall Street Journal*, August 4, 1992, p. B1.

26. I. Torbiorn, *Living Abroad* (New York: John Wiley & Sons, 1982), p. 41; Kraimer, Wayne, and Jaworski, "Sources of Support and Expatriate Performance"; Y. Zeira and M. Banai, "Attitudes of Host-Country Organization toward MNCs' Staffing Policies: A Cross-Country and Cross-Industry Analysis," *Management International Review* 21, no. 2 (1981), p. 34.

27. R. L. Tung, "Career Issues in International Assignments," *Academy of Management Executive*, August 1988, p. 242.

28. J. E. Abueva, "Return of the Native Executive," *New York Times*, May 17, 2000, p. C1.

29. Tung, "Career Issues in International Assignments," p. 243.

30. Ibid.

Strategic Human Resource Management in a Changing Environment

3

LEARNING OBJECTIVES

After completing this chapter, you should be able to:

 LO¹ Describe the field of human resource management (HRM) and its potential for creating and sustaining competitive advantage.

 LO² Describe discrepancies between actual HRM practices and recommendations for HRM practice based on scholarly research.

 LO³ Describe the major activities of HRM.

LO⁴ Explain important trends relevant to HRM, including the increasing globalization of the economy, changing technology, the role of regulations and lawsuits, the changing demographics of the workforce, and the growing body of research linking particular HRM practices to corporate performance.

 LO⁵ Emphasize the importance of measurement for effective and strategic HRM.

 LO⁶ Understand what is meant by competitive advantage, and what the four mechanisms are for offering and maintaining uniqueness.

Introduction

In the 2008 presidential campaign, the *Los Angeles Times* ran an assessment of the two major presidential candidates' fitness for office based on an analysis of their handwriting known as graphology. According to graphologist Paul Sassi, the fluidity of Barack Obama's signature is a sign of high intelligence, while its illegibility shows he is protecting his privacy. "He doesn't want you to know him too well." Another handwriting expert concluded: "The large letters in Obama's signature show that he is ambitious, self-confident, and views himself as a leader. . . . The fluid letter forms reveal that he can form a coalition, be diplomatic, and get along with both sides of the aisle." She added: "He's the type of guy who could tell you to go to hell and you'd enjoy the trip." Another graphologist concluded that John McCain is proud but has a volatile temper, that he is a very accommodating person and will go out of his way to compromise and even yield up his own will, and that he tends to gloss over details and leaves too much to others. The graphologist thought he might sign agreements contrary to American interests.[1]

When I shared theses assessments with undergraduate human resources classes, about 25 percent of students thought the evaluations were "dead on accurate," another 25 percent described the profiles as "mostly accurate," about 20 percent thought they were "completely inaccurate," and about 30 percent had no opinion at all on the accuracy of the profiles. Within the last group, however, about half the students expressed great skepticism about assessing someone's personality, intelligence, motivation, or anything else important using the person's handwriting. It is this group of students who are "dead-on accurate." Research clearly shows that handwriting is not a valid means of assessing anything important (except your handwriting!).

The assessment of presidential candidates is not the only application you will find of such invalid assessment methods. Inc. magazine, one of the most popular magazines for U.S. small business, ran a story extolling the benefits of using graphology to hire managers.[2] The article reported that the use of graphology was on the increase and that the method was very effective for selecting managers and salespersons. Sound research in human resource management (HRM) has determined that companies would do just about as well picking names out of a hat to make personnel decisions.

Skilled HRM specialists help organizations with all activities related to staffing and maintaining an effective workforce. Major HRM responsibilities include work design and job analysis, training and development, recruiting, compensation, team-building, performance management and appraisal, and worker health and safety issues, as well as identifying and developing valid methods for selecting staff.

The author once had a conversation with a business owner who had hired his 145-person sales staff based on graphology reports (at $75 per report) and the answer to a single question posed in an interview. When questioned about the validity of these methods, the business owner described one terrible salesman he had hired out of desperation in a tight labor market despite a graphologist's report that said the "small writing with little slant indicated he may be too introverted for sales work." This one example had stuck in his mind as "proof" of graphology's effectiveness. He lamented, "If only I had listened to the handwriting expert. I wasted a bundle training the guy!" Those of us who teach statistics refer to this type of "research" as a "man who statistic." When you discuss the overwhelming evidence showing that smoking causes cancer, someone might offer the counterargument that "I knew a man who smoked three packs a day and lived to be 90." An article in the *Washington Post* reported that the Pilot Pen Company's CEO Ronald Shaw was a big believer in graphology and would use it for all hiring decisions because the graphologist's profile based on his own handwriting showed he was "sincere and intelligent and had a lot of integrity."[3] While (apparently) flattery will get you somewhere, graphology will not get you accurate or valid assessments of personal characteristics related to job performance. Needless to say, this is not the way to do research on a procedure.

There are good ways to do research and good ways to assess the effects of programs, procedures, and activities of HRM. Sound measurement is a key to effective management. Remember the old adage: if it's not measured, it's not managed. Graphology has been the subject of sound research looking at how well it predicts performance. It doesn't. There are many methods that do accurately predict performance. Effective HRM means decision makers are aware of these methods and use them. Ineffective HRM means management is either unaware of what really works and/or doesn't use them.

Stanford University professor Jeffrey Pfeffer considers measurement to be one of the keys to competitive advantage. His book *Competitive Advantage Through People* cites measurement as one of the 16 HRM practices that contribute the most to competitive advantage.[4] Pfeffer's views were echoed and expanded in the popular text *The Balanced Scorecard* by Harvard professor Robert Kaplan and consultant David Norton.[5] Kaplan and Norton stress that "if companies are to survive and prosper in information age competition, they must use measurement and management systems derived from their strategies and capabilities" (p. 21). Their "balanced scorecard" emphasizes much more management attention to "leading indicators" of performance that predict the "lagging" financial performance measures. The "balance" reflects the need to measure short- and long-term objectives, financial and nonfinancial measures, lagging and leading indicators, and internal and external performance perspectives.

In their book *The Workforce Scorecard*, Professors Mark Huselid, Brian Becker, and Dick Beatty extend research on the "balanced scorecard" to a comprehensive management and measurement system to maximize workforce potential.[6] These authors show that the traditional financial performance measures such as return on equity, stock price, and return on investment, the "lagging indicators," can be predicted by the way companies conduct their HR. HR practices are the "leading indicators" that predict subsequent financial performance measures. Unfortunately, research indicates that only a small percentage of HRM programs or activities are subjected to analysis. The good news, however, is that the percentage is at least going up. Measurement is essential for American business in the 21st century!

One prophetic study defined the vision of human resource management for the 21st century. HRM activities must be (1) responsive to a highly competitive marketplace and global business structures, (2) closely linked to business strategic plans, (3) jointly conceived and implemented by line and HR managers, and (4) focused on quality, customer service, productivity, employee involvement, teamwork, and workforce flexibility.[7]

The status of HRM is improving relative to other potential sources of competitive advantage for an organization. Professor Pfeffer notes that "traditional sources of success (e.g., speed to market, financial, technological) can still provide competitive leverage, but to a lesser degree now than in the past, leaving organizational culture and capabilities, derived from how people are managed, as comparatively more vital."[8]

⊕ What Is Human Resource Management?

The human resources of an organization consist of all people who perform its activities. In a sense, all decisions that affect the workforce concern the organization's HRM function. Human resource management concerns the personnel policies and managerial practices and systems that influence the workforce. Regardless of the size—or existence—of a formal HRM or Personnel Department (many small businesses have no HRM department), the activities involved in HRM are pervasive throughout the organization. Line managers, for example, will spend more than 50 percent of their time involved in human resource activities such as hiring, evaluating, disciplining, and scheduling employees.

The effectiveness with which line management performs HRM functions with the tools, data, and processes provided by HRM specialists is the key to competitive advantage through HRM. This principle generalizes from very small businesses to the very largest global enterprises. Dr. James Spina, former head of executive development at the Tribune Company, really put things in perspective about the role of HRM. He said, "The HRM focus should always be maintaining and, ideally, expanding the customer base while maintaining and, ideally, maximizing profit. HRM has a whole lot to do with this focus regardless of the size of the business, or the products or services you are trying to sell."

Those individuals classified within an HRM functional unit provide important products and services for the organization. These products and services may include the provision of, or recommendation for, systems or processes that facilitate organizational restructuring, job design, personnel planning, recruitment, hiring, evaluating, training, developing, promoting, compensating, and terminating personnel. A major goal of this book is to provide information and experiences that will improve the student's future involvement and effectiveness in HRM activities.

While HR can create and sustain competitive advantage, some would argue that HR as it is practiced is often more a weakness than a strength. A recent survey found that only 40 percent of employees thought their companies were doing a good job retaining high-quality workers and only 41 percent thought performance evaluations were fair. A mere 58 percent of respondents reported their job training as favorable. A majority said they had few opportunities for advancement and they had little idea about how to advance in the first place. Only about half of those surveyed below the managerial level believed their companies took a genuine interest in their well-being.[9]

HRM AND CORPORATE PERFORMANCE

A growing body of research shows that progressive HRM practices can have a significant effect on corporate performance. Studies now document the relationship between specific HR practices and critical outcome measures such as corporate financial performance, productivity, product and service quality, and cost control. Many of the methods characterizing these so-called **high-performance work systems** (HPWS) have been researched and developed by the HRM academic community. Figure 3.1 presents a summary of this research.

HPWS comprises HR practices or characteristics designed to enhance employees' competencies and productivity so that employees can be a reliable source of competitive advantage. They have been called "coherent practices that enhance the skills of the workforce, participation in decision making, and motivation to put forth discretionary effort." Research shows that "firm competitiveness can be enhanced by high-performance work systems." A summary of this research found that one standard deviation of improved assessment on an HPWS measurement tool increased sales per employee in excess of $15,000, an 8 percent gain in labor productivity.[10]

Recall the critical remarks earlier about graphology, or handwriting analysis. Validated selection and promotion systems are related to higher productivity and reduced costs (see Figure 3.1). The term *validated* means that the method has actually been shown to predict something important. If you're using a method to select managers or sales personnel, a "validated" method is a method shown to actually predict managerial or sales success. While graphology is no way to assess personality attributes, there are highly valid methods and procedures for predicting future employee performance based on the assessed personal characteristics of job candidates.

Better training and development programs and team-based work configurations improve performance and job satisfaction and decrease employee turnover. Particular incentive and compensation systems also translate into higher productivity and performance. The fair treatment of employees results in higher job satisfaction, which in turn facilitates higher performance, lower employee turnover, reduced costs, and a lower likelihood of successful union organizing.

Greater demands are now being made on HRM practitioners to respond to contemporary trends in the business environment. Today, the most effective HRM functions are conceptualized in a business capacity, constantly focusing on the strategy of the organiza-

- Large number of highly qualified applicants for each strategic position.
- The use of validated selection and promotion models/procedures.
- Extensive training and development of new employees.
- The use of formal performance appraisal and management.
- The use of multisource (360 degree) performance appraisal and feedback.
- Linkage of merit increases to formal appraisal processes.
- Above-market compensation for key positions.
- High percentage of entire workforce included in incentive systems.
- High differential in pay between high and low performers.
- High percentage of workforce working in self-managed, project-based work teams.
- Low percentage of employees covered by union contract.
- High percentage of jobs filled from within.

FIGURE 3.1

Characteristics of High-Performance Work Systems (HPWS)

Source: Reprinted by permission of Harvard Business School Press. *The HR Scorecard*, by B. Becker and M. Ulrich (Boston: Harvard Business School Press, 2001).

tion and the core competencies of the organization. HRM specialists must show how they can make a difference for the company's bottom line. Costs and efficiencies are necessary criteria for evaluating recommendations from research in HRM.

Many corporate strategy specialists maintain that the key to sustained competitive advantage is building and sustaining core competencies within the organization and maintaining flexibility in order to react quickly to the changing global marketplace and the advances in technology. One primary role of HRM practitioners should be to facilitate this process.

HRM practitioners need to pay more attention to academic research. There is a great deal of carefully crafted academic research that is highly relevant to HRM practice. Figure 3.2 presents a few examples of discrepancies between the current state of HR practice and what the academic literature clearly recommends. One study reinforced this "knowledge gap."[11] HR professionals were given a 35-item test that assessed the extent of their HR knowledge. The test was scored on findings from academic research, which would likely be covered in any basic HR course like this one. Items were developed where there was little or no argument on the correct answer within the academic community. The average grade for the nearly 1,000 HR professionals was "D." On numerous items, over 50 percent of the HR professionals got the answer wrong!

Many HR activities such as payroll, recruitment, and pre-employment screening are now outsourced to organizations that specialize in these areas. The number of consulting organizations specializing in HR activities has increased substantially in the last 10 years. There are now Web-based HR products and services in almost every major functional area and full-service HR online department. An organization's HR specialist must have the necessary knowledge and skills to be able to identify the best and most cost-effective of these HR products and services for a particular situation.

HRM professionals should possess up-to-date knowledge about the relative effectiveness of the various programs and activities related to HR planning, training and development, compensation, performance management, selection, information systems, equal employment opportunity/diversity, labor relations, recruitment, and health and safety issues. HRM professionals also should be capable of conducting their own research to evaluate their programs and program alternatives. Unfortunately, recent evidence suggests that HR professionals adopt many programs based either on effective marketing from the plethora of vendors selling HR materials and programs or simply on what other companies are doing. While some consideration may be given to the leading-indicator research described in Figure 3.1, greater weight seems to be given to slick marketing programs and simply what others are doing. When "bottom-line" questions arise later on—as they inevitably do—HR departments are caught off guard because costly and relatively ineffective programs have been adopted. A careful study of programs with evaluative criteria linked

FIGURE 3.2 Sample of Discrepancies between Academic Research Findings and HRM Practices

Academic Research Findings	HRM Practice
RECRUITMENT	
Quantitative analysis of recruitment sources using yield ratios can facilitate efficiencies in recruitment.	Less than 15% calculate yield ratios. Less than 28% know how.
STAFFING	
Realistic job previews can reduce turnover.	Less than 20% of companies use RJPs in high-turnover jobs.
Weighted application blanks reduce turnover.	Less than 35% know what a WAB is; less than 5% use WABs.
Structured and behavioral interviews are more valid.	40% of companies use structured interviews. Less than 50% use behavioral interviews.
Use actuarial model of prediction with multiple valid measures.	Less than 5% use actuarial model.
Graphology is invalid and should not be used.	Use is on the increase in the United States.
PERFORMANCE APPRAISAL	
Do not use traits on rating forms.	More than 70% still use traits.
Train raters (for accuracy, observation bias).	Less than 30% train raters.
Make appraisal process important element of manager's job.	Less than 35% of managers are evaluated on performance appraisal.
COMPENSATION	
Merit-based systems should not be tied into a base salary.	More than 75% tie merit pay into base pay.
Gain sharing is an effective PFP system.	Less than 5% of companies use it where they could.

Source: H. J. Bernardin (2009), "A Survey of Human Resource Practices: Discrepancies Between Research and HRM Practice." Paper presented at the annual meeting of Applied Psychologists.

to strategic goals might reveal negligible or no impact. Again, if you don't measure it, you can't manage it. A large number of quantitative reviews, known as **meta-analyses**, are now available to help managers make more informed decisions about methods for such critical HR activities as staffing, recruiting, evaluating, and compensating.

Many HR professionals are not even trained to ask the right questions and conduct the appropriate study of a given HR program or activity. The author had a conversation with a VP of HR of a Fortune 500 company. He had a Big-Ten MBA and was convinced that one particular test was the best way to hire retail sales personnel. The basis for his position was conversations with other poorly informed HRM MBAs who were using the test. This is no way to evaluate a selection method. Another HR vice president for a retailer adopted an expensive computerized testing program that the publisher claimed would reduce employee turnover by 50 percent. The VP did not request the research that purported to document this effect and later admitted that although he ultimately made the decision to adopt the test, he was unqualified to assess the test's usefulness since he could not even ask fundamental measurement questions that should be the focus of any evaluation of such a product or service. In addition, although the retailer had been using the test for over two years, it apparently never occurred to him to evaluate the extent to which the test actually did reduce turnover in his organization. A Connecticut police department used an intelligence test to screen for officers but eliminated candidates if their scores were too high. Their argument was that highly intelligent officers would get bored and quit. They had no evidence to support their theory and conceded that their leaders (e. g., their Captains, even the Chief of Police) were all selected from within the organization. This kind of theory should be tested first and its unintended consequences carefully examined before implementation!

One of the great values of academic research is the objective evaluation of activities or programs using well-controlled experimental designs, which allow for unambiguous assessments of effects. For example, *Buros Mental Measurements Yearbook* is a reference source that publishes evaluations of tests written by qualified academics who have no vested interest in the tests themselves. Over 2,000 tests have been reviewed, and the reviews can be downloaded from the Buros Web site for $15 per test (http://buros.unl.edu/buros/jsp/search). Many HRM professionals who adopt tests do not know that this very useful text (and Web site) even exists.

The Domains of Human Resource Management

Figure 3.3 presents a listing of some of the most commonly performed activities by HRM professionals. These HRM activities fall under five major **domains**: (1) Organizational Design, (2) Staffing, (3) Performance Management and Appraisal, (4) Employee Training and Organizational Development, and (5) Reward Systems, Benefits, and Compliance.

Although the particular activities subsumed under these five domains are conceptually independent, in practice they are not. Nevertheless, many organizations pursue the various activities in a particular domain as if they had no implications for any of the other domains. For example, many organizations have reduced or eliminated health care benefits without due consideration of the impact of the new compensation package on staffing and employee retention. In addition, all domain activity must be weighed in the context of the new global environment and contemporary legal interpretations.

Acquiring human resource capability should begin with organizational design and analysis. **Organizational design** involves the arrangement of work tasks based on the interaction of people, technology, and the tasks to be performed in the context of the mission, goals, and strategic plan of the organization. HRM activities such as human resources planning, job and work analysis, organizational restructuring, job design, team building, computerization, and worker-machine interfaces also fall under this domain.

Organizational and work design issues are almost always the first ones that should be addressed whenever significant change is necessary because of changing economic conditions, new technologies, new opportunities, potential advantages, or serious internal problems. Design issues usually drive other HR domains such as selection, training, performance management, and compensation. Economic downturns can provide an opportunity for a more serious evaluation of the organization's strategy and its competitive position. But there are clearly effective and ineffective approaches to organizational design.

Corporate downsizing, outsourcing, and reengineering efforts often begin with human resources planning in the context of a strategic plan and an analysis of how the work is performed, how jobs and work units relate to one another, and, of course, cost analysis. These decisions can be critical for the long-term survival of a struggling company. Research shows that layoffs designed to derive a short-term "cost savings" may foster an increase in market value in the short run but that investors often lose all of this value plus considerably more.

Trends Enhancing the Importance of HRM

As we have said, there is an increasing realization that the manner in which organizations conduct their HR activities will help create and sustain a competitive advantage. The contemporary trends and challenges in the business environment necessitate that

FIGURE 3.3

Major Activities of
Human Resource
Management

ORGANIZATIONAL DESIGN

Human resource planning based on strategy
Job analysis/work analysis
Job design
Information systems
Downsizing/restructuring

STAFFING

Recruiting/interviewing/hiring
Affirmative action/diversity/EEO compliance
Promotion/transfer/separation
Outplacement services
Induction/orientation
Employee selection methods

PERFORMANCE MANAGEMENT AND APPRAISAL

Management appraisal/management by objectives/strategy execution
Productivity/enhancement programs
Customer-focused performance appraisal
Multirater systems (360°, 180°)
Rater training programs

EMPLOYEE TRAINING AND ORGANIZATIONAL DEVELOPMENT

Management/supervisory development
Career planning/development
Employee assistance/counseling programs
Attitude surveys
Training delivery options
Diversity programs

REWARD SYSTEMS, BENEFITS, AND COMPLIANCE

Safety programs/OSHA compliance
Health/medical services
Complaint/disciplinary procedures
Compensation administration
Insurance benefits administration
Unemployment compensation administration
Pension/profit-sharing plans
Labor relations/collective bargaining

even greater attention be given to the human resources of an organization. Let us examine these trends next and relate each to particular HRM activities. Figure 3.4 presents a summary of major current trends.

The most significant trend is the increasing globalization of the economy and a growing competitive work environment with a premium on product and service quality. One of the most important factors affecting globalization and the growth of transnational corporations is the goal of reducing the cost of production, labor costs being the most

FIGURE 3.4

Major Trends Affecting HRM

TREND 1: THE INCREASED GLOBALIZATION OF THE ECONOMY

Opportunity for global workforce and labor cost reduction

Increasing global competition for U.S. products and services

Opportunity for expansion that presents global challenges for HR

TREND 2: TECHNOLOGICAL CHANGES, CHALLENGES, AND OPPORTUNITIES

Great opportunities presented by Web-based systems

New threats: privacy, confidentiality, intellectual property

TREND 3: INCREASE IN LITIGATION AND REGULATION RELATED TO HRM

Federal, state, and municipal legislation and lawsuits on the increase

Wrongful discharge; negligent hiring, retention, referral

TREND 4: CHANGING CHARACTERISTICS OF THE WORKFORCE

Growing workforce diversity, which complicates HRM

Labor shortages/aging workforce/Millennials rising

significant for U.S. companies. But, market-seeking behavior is now as important a motivator of globalization as the search for low-cost productivity.

Another major trend is the unpredictable but inevitable power of technology to transform HRM. There is a need to be more flexible today because of the incredible pace of change in markets and technology. HRM can facilitate this flexibility. The growth and proliferation of lawsuits related to HR practice and changes in workforce characteristics also have had a big impact on HRM. So is the fact that many in the workforce are ill-equipped with the necessary knowledge, skills and abilities, and job requirements to do their jobs well.

TREND 1: THE INCREASED GLOBALIZATION OF THE ECONOMY

In his bestseller *The World Is Flat: A Brief History of the Twenty-First Century*, Thomas Friedman described the next phase of globalization.[12] An Indian software executive told him how the world's economic playing field is being leveled. So-called barriers to entry are being destroyed. A company (or even an individual) can compete (or collaborate) from almost anywhere in the world. Over 500,000 American tax returns were prepared in India in 2008. Says Jerry Rao, Indian entrepreneur, "Any activity where we can digitize and decompose the value chain, and move the work around, will get moved around. Some people will say, 'Yes, but you can't serve me a steak.' True, but I can take the reservation for your table sitting anywhere in the world." Rao's 2009 projects include a partnership with an Israeli company that can transmit MRI and CAT scans through the Internet so Americans can get a second opinion very quickly (and relatively cheaply). When you order a Big Mac at the McDonald's on Route 55 in Cape Girardeau, Missouri, the person taking the order is at a call center in India.

There is no question that the increasing globalization of most of the world's economies will affect HRM. It is predicted that most of the largest U.S. companies soon will employ more workers in countries other than the United States and the growth for most major corporations will derive from off-shore operations. With technological advances, one of the strongest trends is the development of a worldwide labor market for U.S. companies. In their quest for greater efficiencies and reduced costs, American companies can now look globally to get work done. While this opportunity stands to decrease the cost of labor, the process of HRM can be more complicated. Of course, U.S. workers will resist this trend through union and political activity. They haven't been very successful in manufacturing. The United States lost over 4 million manufacturing jobs from May 1998 to May 2008.

The rise in oil prices and the cost of transportation have recently caused a bit of "reverse globalization" in the form of some jobs returning to the United States. In 2000 when oil was $20 a barrel, it cost $3,000 to ship one container of furniture from Shanghai to New York. In 2008, the cost of the same container is $8,000. The long-suffering furniture manufacturing business in North Carolina is making a comeback. DESA, a company that makes heaters to keep football players warm, is moving all of its production back to Kentucky from China. Carrier Battery is coming back to Ohio. "Cheap labor in China doesn't help you when you gotta pay so much to bring the goods over," says economist Jeff Rubin.

Nevertheless, most U.S. companies still see great potential for labor cost reductions by looking overseas, with more emphasis on services these days. But outsourcing can bring many problems along with the cheap labor. It's been over 10 years since some of the biggest companies in the world, because of political and consumer pressure, began their efforts to eliminate the "sweatshop" labor conditions that were pervasive across Asia. Yet, worker abuse is well-documented in many Chinese factories that supply U.S. companies. Chinese companies providing goods and services for Wal-Mart, Disney, and Dell routinely shortchange their employees on wages, withhold health benefits, and expose their workers to dangerous machinery and harmful chemicals like lead and mercury. Wal-Mart, the world's biggest retailer, sourced over $9 billion worth of goods from China in 2007. In 2008, two nongovernmental organizations documented incidents of abuse and labor violations, including child labor, at 15 factories that produce or supply goods for Wal-Mart. "At Wal-Mart, Christmas ornaments are cheap, and so are the lives of the young workers in China who make them," the National Labor Committee report said.

Globalization creates greater competition and fosters more concern over productivity and cost control. The fiscal conditions of General Motors and Ford Motor Company are clear illustrations. One important reason for the recent increased interest in HRM is the perceived connection between HRM expertise and productivity. A growing portion of corporate America has come to the realization that competing in an increasingly global environment requires constant vigilance over productivity and customer satisfaction. A smaller but growing percentage of managers recognize the importance of human resources in dealing with these issues. Indeed, a great deal of the recent corporate downsizing can be linked to technological improvement and corresponding estimates of productivity improvements with HR interacting with the technological changes. Bank of America, American Express, Coca-Cola, and General Electric have successfully followed a formula of cutting personnel costs while investing in automated equipment and more efficient facilities. The recent plant closures by Ford and GM are examples of major cost cutting.

U.S. exports now generate about one in six American jobs, an increase of over 20 percent in just 10 years. McDonald's opened its first non-U.S. restaurant in Canada in 1967. By 2009 their total sales outside of the United States contributed over 50 percent of the operating income of the firm. Two-thirds of McDonald's new restaurants are now opened outside the United States each year. While McDonald's has moved more quickly than other U.S. firms, many other U.S. firms are now expanding rapidly in both new countries and new markets. The majority of new restaurants opened by Burger King and KFC are now in international markets. The majority of new stores opened by Wal-Mart are now opened outside the United States.

Another response to increasing global competition is restructuring/downsizing, as mentioned earlier. Coca-Cola, Ford, Sears, AT&T, CBS, DuPont, GM, Kodak, Xerox, and IBM are among the many corporate behemoths that have reduced their workforces by more than 10 percent in the last decade. Many HRM specialists are experts in organizational restructuring and change procedures. They have expertise in downsizing and outsourcing options that can reduce labor costs. They may also conduct vocational counseling for those who are displaced or assist in developing new staffing plans as a result of the restructuring.

As described in more detail in later chapters, HRM specialists are also asked to help in legal defenses against allegations of discrimination related to corporate downsizing. Ford recently settled two discrimination lawsuits related to downsizing efforts. In an attempt to compete more effectively against Geico and Progressive, Allstate Insurance converted all of its 15,200-member sales force to independent contractors. To continue as contractors, the agents had to sign a waiver that they would not sue Allstate for discrimination. The result was a costly age discrimination lawsuit brought against Allstate. The law can impose constraints on companies trying to cut costs through changes in labor policies. Recent Supreme Court decisions have increased the likelihood of lawsuits related to downsizing.

TREND 2: TECHNOLOGICAL CHANGES, CHALLENGES, AND OPPORTUNITIES

The second trend is the rate of change in technology. More organizations are now evaluating their human resources and labor costs in the context of available technologies, based on the theory that products and services can be delivered more effectively (and efficiently) through an optimal combination of people, software, and equipment, increasing productivity. Instead of speaking to a customer service representative at Bank of America to discuss your account, you can interact with an automated system via the Internet or an automated teller machine (ATM) or through an 800 number. The program is designed to handle almost any problem about which you might inquire. With the automated system, BOA is able to shed customer service representatives, thereby reducing labor costs. As more people use their automated services and ATMs, there is less need for supervision. Customers, as a result, pay less in service charges and may earn more interest on their money. As these automated systems evolve, customers ultimately could be more satisfied with the service, even though they are not dealing with an actual person. HRM specialists participate in the development and execution of user testing programs to assess the design of the automated interface.

Today, with the assistance of HR, more companies are evaluating the role of organizational structure, technology, and human resources with the goal of providing more and higher-quality products and services to the customer at a lower price. This pricing reduction is at least partially achieved by controlling the cost of labor while not losing the focus on meeting customer definitions of quality. Of course, the ultimate goal of for-profit organizations is to maximize profit margins while sustaining (or improving) perceived customer value. HR has a great deal to offer in this endeavor.

While the potential is there, HR specialists are often ignored. Technological advances and offshoring are of course related. A recent survey found that only 35 percent of respondents reported that HR was involved in the offshoring process from an early stage, although HR does typically play a major role in restructuring the organization's workforce as a result of offshoring. Says Jennifer Schramm, manager of workplace trends and forecasting at the Society of Human Resource Management (SHRM.org), "From training HR professionals from offshore sites in the home organization's corporate culture and policies, to developing strong channels of communication between global satellite offices, HR's involvement is crucial in effectively managing cross-border human capital. . . . HR's role in boosting productivity through human capital and workplace culture, even as the scope of the workplace extends across the globe and spans very different cultures, will continue to grow."[13]

Technology is revolutionizing many HRM activities. Most organizations now use software packages to aid all HR domains. Many HR activities and outcome data are tracked electronically, such as recruitment, turnover, performance appraisals, and training. Managers from different departments, states, or even countries can readily access the HR system and update employment files. Software packages are easily customized to fit a specific organization's HR activities.

Technology has also changed the speed with which HR communicates with employees. HR can draft and e-mail a companywide memo to all employees within a single hour. In addition, employees can instantly communicate with Human Resources. Many companies have created intranet sites. These Web sites provide employees with a variety of information, such as health care benefits, personnel policies, and proposed changes.

The advent of new technology has created a variety of concerns for management. Employee privacy and intellectual property rights are increasingly cited as major concerns. With computer attacks occurring worldwide, ensuring confidentiality of employee data is a growing concern, and the liability of an organization in the event of security breaches is still unclear.[14]

Protecting intellectual property is vital for all organizations, especially emerging technology and research and development organizations. As a result, organizations are developing electronic communication policies that clearly outline permitted electronic activities, uses of employer systems, and monitoring of employees' files such as e-mail. Many companies have banned cellular cameras and instant messaging because of the increased risk of intellectual property theft.

Although still rare, the following scenario is already here for some companies: A manager or supervisor gets authorization to hire someone. The manager goes into a "node" on the Internet and completes a job analysis for the new position that establishes critical information regarding the job, including the necessary knowledge, ability, skills, and other critical characteristics. The job description is then used to conduct a "key word" computer search of a potential applicant pool in order to match the requirement of the job with the standardized résumés in the database. Out pops a number of potential candidates for the job. The manager then immediately sends out the job vacancy announcement to all of the potential candidates in the database through electronic mail. Interested candidates respond back via e-mail. The manager then selects the "short list" of candidates to compete for the job based on a quantitative analysis of the resumes.

The same job analysis information could also be used to construct or retrieve job-related tests or questions for an employment interview. The manager might even have a Web camera and could conduct the testing and "face-to-face" interviewing of the candidates as soon as the contact is made (assuming the candidate also has access to a camera-based computer). This process of going from describing the job to actually interviewing candidates could take less than a day. HR is playing a key role in getting these systems up and running.

Some of the most successful high-tech companies today rely on the Internet for fast, convenient, and efficient recruiting of their core personnel. Even the CIA and the FBI do recruiting on the Internet (try www.odci.gov/cia if you'd like to be a spy).

TREND 3: INCREASE IN LITIGATION AND REGULATION RELATED TO HRM

In addition to the recent concerns over survival, changes in technology, and increases in global competition, another important trend affecting the status of HRM is the proliferation of regulations and lawsuits related to personnel decisions. As predicted by one cynical statistician, by the year 2010, there will be more lawyers in this country than people. While this is obviously a joke, there is no question that the proliferation and creativity of lawyers have helped to foster our highly litigious society. There is no sign of this activity letting up in the near term. In fact, federal lawsuits charging violations of labor laws have increased faster (up over 125 percent since 1991) than any other area of civil rights legislation. Jury awards have gotten much bigger in recent years. In 2008, 26 percent of judgments against companies related to HR were $1 million or more. In 1994, the percentage of such awards was only 7 percent. The elections of 2008 are likely to increase legislation, regulation and litigation related to HRM.

In general, HRM-related laws and regulations reflect societal responses to economic, social, technical or political issues. For example, the Civil Rights Act of 1964, which prohibits job discrimination on the basis of race, sex, color, religion, or national origin, was passed primarily in response to the great differences in economic outcomes for blacks compared to whites. The 2008 Genetic Information Nondiscrimination Act is designed to address concerns that job seekers or workers could be denied employment opportunities due to a predisposition for a genetic disorder. Other examples are the proliferation of state laws regarding corporate acquisitions and mergers, laws protecting AIDS victims and homosexuals from employment discrimination, and regulations regarding family leave benefits.

Organizations are bound by a plethora of federal, state, and local laws, regulations, executive orders, and rules that have an impact on virtually every type of personnel decision. There are health and safety regulations, laws regarding employee pensions and other compensation programs, plant closures, mergers and acquisitions, new immigration laws, and a growing number of equal opportunity laws and guidelines. Today's HRM professionals and line managers must be familiar with the ADEA, OFCCP, OSHA, EEOC, ADA, FLSA, GINA, NLRA, and ERISA—among many other acronyms. Each represents a major regulatory effort. There is every indication that regulation will increase in the years ahead in the form of new EEO legislation related to fair pay, union organizing, several orientation protection, and especially laws related to work and illegal immigrants. In 2007 alone, 1,562 bills related to illegal immigration were introduced nationwide at the state or local level and 240 were enacted in 46 states.[15] A 2008 federal government plan may force businesses to fire employees whose names don't match the Social Security database. Companies that receive "no match" letters from the Social Security Administration warning of a discrepancy are put on notice and given 90 days to deal with the discrepancy. If employers do not comply, they face stiff penalties.

Organizations spend considerable time and expense in order to comply with labor laws and regulations and/or to defend against allegations regarding violations. Line managers who do not understand the implications of their actions in the context of these laws can cost a company dearly. Line managers may also be personally liable. Employers and managers now face huge fines, the possible loss of business licenses, and even criminal prosecution because of violations of new laws related to employing illegal immigrants.

Sometimes companies learn the hard way about the complexities of labor laws. In 2008, drivers in FedEx's Ground division claimed to have been improperly classified as independent contractors. IBM recently settled a lawsuit brought on behalf of 32,000 technical and support workers for $65 million who claimed they were entitled to overtime pay. Citigroup/Salomon Smith Barney settled a similar suit for $98 million. Abercrombie and Fitch recently settled a race discrimination lawsuit for $40 million and now conducts its staffing under close court-imposed scrutiny. Texaco and Coca-Cola settled similar lawsuits for over $165 million each. Baker and McKenzie, the largest law firm in the United States, was assessed $3.5 million in punitive damages for sexual harassment committed by one partner at the firm. The EEOC settled a similar suit with Honda of America for $6 million. Westinghouse Electric Corporation agreed to a $35 million settlement in an age discrimination suit involving 4,000 employees affected by the company's reorganization. Ford recently agreed to a $10.6 million settlement in an age discrimination case. Morgan Stanley settled a sex discrimination case for $54 million. Wal-Mart remained mired in a massive sex discrimination lawsuit over pay and promotions as this book went to press.

TREND 4: CHANGING CHARACTERISTICS OF THE WORKFORCE

Several trends regarding the future of the American workforce underscore the challenges to and the importance of the human resource function. Compared to 10 years ago, American workers are more ethnically diverse, more educated, more cynical toward work and organizations, getting older, and, for a growing number, becoming less prepared to handle the challenges of work today. The composition of the workforce is changing drastically, and these changes are affecting HRM policies and practices.

Increasing diversity creates the need for more diverse HRM systems and practices and increases the probability of litigation. It is estimated that by 2010 only 15 percent of the U.S. workforce will be native-born white males.[16] A greater proportion of women and minorities have entered the workforce and are beginning to move into previously white male–dominated positions, including managers, lawyers, accountants, medical doctors, and professors. Nearly 90 percent of the growth in the U.S. workforce from 1995 to 2008 came from women, immigrants, African-Americans, and people of Hispanic or Asian origin. In addition, there are more dual-career couples in the labor force. The "typical" U.S. worker in the past was a male—often white—who was a member of a single-earner household. Fewer than 20 percent of today's employees fit this description. In May 2008, an estimated 11.6 percent of the U.S. population was foreign born. The rapid increase in the foreign-born population from 9.6 million in 1970 to 33 million in 2008 reflects the very high rate of international migration. About half of the youngest 100 million Americans are immigrants and their U.S.-born children.[17]

Two other trends will surely make HR more challenging: a growing rate of "Baby-Boomer" retirements and a growing rate of Generation Yers (or Millennials) entering the workforce. The retirement of the Boomer generation, those born between 1946 and 1964, is expected to create a shortage of skilled workers and perhaps affect economic output. It is estimated that by 2014 there will be almost 63 million Generation Y employees (people born between 1977 and 1994) in the workforce, while the number of Baby Boomers in the workplace will decline to less than 48 million. In one recent survey, a majority of companies already reported intergenerational conflict at work between these two generations. The effects of the economic turmoil that began in 2008 may have a big impact on Baby Boomer retirement plans.

By 2030, American 65 and older will make up about 20 percent of the total population of the country. This could involve horrendous costs in the form of social security and Medicare contributions. Fortunately, some experts predict that enough Baby Boomers will remain in the workforce to make up for any shortfall of workers and hopefully reduce a portion of the staggering projected government unfunded obligations. The economic turmoil that began in 2008 will probably facilitate this. Unfortunately, this might aggravate the generational conflict alluded to earlier. Because of the larger numbers of workers over the age of 40, age discrimination litigation is expected to increase; moreover, a 2008 Supreme Court age discrimination ruling changed the burden of proof needed to prove age discrimination and may increase the amount of litigation. Also, the workforce under the age of 40 is expected to acquire more family responsibilities. The Generation Xers, the "sandwich generation," those workers born between the Boomer generation and Generation Y, are be expected to juggle both child care and especially elder care demands as the Boomers live longer. This is a concern HRM must address in the coming years.

As a result of these changes in workforce composition, organizations are having to develop and implement programs on diversity, more flexible work schedules, better training programs, child and elder care arrangements, and career development strategies, so that work and nonwork responsibilities can be more easily integrated. Building and sustaining a quality workforce from this diversity is a great challenge for HR.

While increasing diversity translates into a greater probability of EEO legal actions, many experts also argue that the diversity of the workforce must match the population demographics or an organization is vulnerable to public criticism that can hurt the business and the society. It is little wonder that most large U.S. companies have as a goal increasing the diversity of their workforce. The diversity goals of corporations can have an impact on the less diverse but older part of the workforce, particularly in downsizing situations. Such scenarios create difficulties for corporations. But here's some good news: Regarding Generation Y, one recent study concluded that "They combine the teamwork ethic of the Boomers with the can-do attitude of the Veterans and the technological savvy of the Xers. At first glance, and even at second glance, Generation Next may be the ideal workforce—and ideal citizens."[18] The Baby-Boomers should be proud of their parenting!

Millennials are not only more racially and ethnically diverse than Boomers or Xers, they are also more comfortable working in a diverse environment. Although there isn't strong research on this subject to date, it is thus likely that the Millennial generation might help run things a little more smoothly as organizations get more and more diverse. Figure 3.5 presents a summary of the 75-million-strong Millennials.

SUMMARY OF TREND EFFECTS

All of these trends are having a profound effect on the way HR is conducted. The changing demographics and cultural diversity of the workforce, the increased number of lawsuits and regulations, and the growing demands on American workers in the context of a paramount need to improve U.S. productivity and establish a competitive edge all create a situation that will challenge HRM professionals and line management. Yet through better coordination with organizational planning and strategy, human resources can be used to create and sustain an organization's advantage in an increasingly competitive and challenging economy.

Being innovative and responsive to changing business environments requires great flexibility. The trend toward the "elastic" company is clearly affecting the HR function, too. As more companies focus on their core competencies—essentially, what they do best and what is the essence of their business—they outsource other work, use temporary or leased employees or independent contractors to perform services or work on specific projects even at the professional level, and replace personnel with new technology. These so-called "modular" companies such as Apple, Nike, and Dell Computers have been successful because they have reliable vendors and suppliers and, most important, hot products. HR consultants have been instrumental in helping companies discover their core competencies and then developing optimal work design and HR strategies. HR departments themselves are not exempt from this trend toward outsourcing. The result has been a proliferation of consulting firms that compete for HR-related projects and programs previously performed within the company. Consulting is now a thriving business for HRM.

Outsourcing trends along with a myriad of Internet, software, and consulting options have reduced the size of many HR departments and have the potential for making them more efficient and more effective. How lean can you get in HR? Nucor, a steel company with 6,000 employees, has an HR staff of four at its headquarters. Most of the HR work is farmed out to HR consultants. Some experts argue that the most efficient and perhaps most effective HRM departments select the best and least costly outside contractors for HRM products and services, make certain these products or services are being used properly, and then evaluate and adapt these products and services to make certain they are working effectively and efficiently.

This trend toward outsourcing some of the personnel function supports the thesis of many experts that the HRM functions must be very lean in structure so that companies can react quickly to the changing world. Many HRM departments now assess the need for any expense, personnel included, in the context of the primary functions of the organization and its competitive strategy. So, if companies can maintain a leaner and more cost-effective structure by outsourcing, where will that leave the HR department in the future? one recent survey found that 94 percent of large companies reported they were outsourcing at least one human resources activity. Most employers indicated that they plan to expand HR outsourcing to include training and development, payroll, recruiting, health care, and global mobility.

Keith Hammonds, executive editor of *Fast Company*, predicts companies will "farm out pretty much everything HR does. The happy rhetoric from the HR world says this is

FIGURE 3.5

Who Are the Millennials? (aka: GenY, GenWHY, Nexers, Boomlets, Netizens, GenNext)

Source: Adapted from Zemke, R., Rainess, C., and Filipezak, B. (2000). *Generations at Work.* (New York: AMACOM).

DEMOGRAPHICS

- Born between 1978 and 1995
- Baby Boomer kids
- Largest generation (75 million) after the Boomers
- 38 percent of Millennials identify themselves as "nonwhite"
- Well educated

CHARACTERISTICS

- Techno savvy
- Connected 24/7
- Independent
- Self-reliant
- Global/civic minded
- Green
- Diverse
- Entrepreneurial
- Life-style centered
- Less religious

DEFINING LIFE EXPERIENCES/EVENTS

- Most "hovered over" generation
- 9/11
- Wars in Iraq, Afganistan
- Corporate scandal and greed
- Emerging nations (China, India, South Korea)
- Immigration issues/growing diversity

AT WORK

- Adaptable/comfortable with change
- Impatient/demanding/efficient
- More interested in corporate social performance and responsibility
- Want to produce something that makes a difference
- Thrive on flexibility and space to explore
- Require an explanation
- Like feedback/guidance

all for the best: Outsourcing the administrative minutiae, after all, would allow human resources professionals to focus on more important stuff that's central to the business. You know, being strategic partners." Hammonds argues that most HR people are not equipped to take on this more important, strategic responsibility because they don't know enough about the business.

There is no question that intense and growing competition has placed greater pressure on organizations to be more adaptive and to carefully examine all of their costs. Edward Lawler, a prominent management author and consultant, states, "All staff departments are being asked to justify their cost structures on a competitive basis . . . head-count comparisons are being made by corporations to check the ratio of employees to members of the HR department." In *Human Resources Business Process Outsourcing*, Lawler and colleagues illustrate how outsourcing can be a very effective and efficient approach to HR and give HR managers new opportunities to make a more important contribution to a company's bottom-line and overall strategy. They present a template for analyzing an HR department's value, value added, and cost-to-serve.

Whether the organization is facing increasing international competition or simply more intense pressure to improve the bottom line, HR has a great opportunity to meet new and old challenges as a business partner. Lawler sees the most pressing need in the area of corporate strategy. "The HR function must become a partner in developing an organization's strategic plan, for human resources are a key consideration in determining strategies that are both practical and feasible."[19] This HR partnership must evolve out of the major activities of the HR function. A key to this partnership is good, strategic measurement.

The Importance of HRM Measurement in Strategy Execution

In their excellent book *The Workforce Scorecard: Managing Human Capital to Execute Strategy*, Professors Mark Huselid, Brian Becker, and Dick Beatty argue that of all the controllable factors that can affect organizational performance, a workforce that can execute strategy is the most critical and underperforming asset in most organizations.[20] Measurement is front and center in their prescription for a more effective workforce. They outline three challenges organizations must take on to maximize workforce potential in order to meet strategic objectives: (1) view the workforce in terms of contribution rather than cost; (2) use measurement as a tool for differentiating contributions to strategic impact; and (3) hold line and HR management responsible for getting the workforce to execute strategy.

Their measurement strategy calls for the development of a "workforce scorecard" that evolves from six general steps an organization needs to take. Figure 3.6 summarizes this process: (1) identify critical and carefully defined outcome measures that really matter; (2) translate the measures into specific actions and accountabilities; (3) give employees detailed descriptions of what is expected and how improvements can be facilitated; (4) identify high and low performing employees and establish differentiated incentive systems; (5) develop supporting HR management and measurement systems; and (6) specify the roles of leadership, the workforce, and HR in strategy execution (go to www.theworkforcescorecard.com for more detail).

Huselid, Becker, and Beatty propose three challenges for successful workforce measurement and management (see Figure 3.6). The "perspective" challenge asks whether management fully understands how workforce behaviors affect strategy execution. The "metrics" challenge asks whether they have identified and collected the right measures of success. Finally, the "execution" challenge asks whether managers have the access, capability, and motivation to use the measurement data to communicate strategy and monitor progress.

Human resource activities, practices, and research typically focus on a relatively small number of criteria or outcome measures. These measures can be fine-tuned on the quality of their measurement and the extent to which they are related to customer satisfaction and then long-term profitability and growth. Much of the research in HRM and many of the criteria used to assess management practices focus on employee satisfaction. Figure 3.7 presents a simple model that illustrates why there is (and should be) such a focus. Throughout the book, many studies will be referenced that establish some relationship between an HR practice or HR policy or employee characteristics (e.g., employee job satisfaction) and one or more "bottom-line" criteria such as corporate profit or customer satisfaction. For example, in an excellent study of the relationship between employee attitudes and corporate performance measures in almost 8,000 business units and 36 companies, strong and reliable correlations were found between unit-level employee job

FIGURE 3.6

Steps and Challenges for Developing a Workforce Scorecard

Source: Adapted from M. A. Huselid, B. E. Becker, and R. W. Beatty, *The Workforce Scorecard: Managing Human Capital to Execute Strategy* (Boston: Harvard Business School Press, 2005).

STEPS

1. Identify critical and carefully defined outcome measures related to strategic objectives.
2. Translate the measures into specific actions and accountabilities.
3. Develop and communicate detailed descriptions of what is expected. Determine how (or if) improvements can be facilitated.
4. Identify high and low performing employees. Establish differentiated incentive systems.
5. Develop supporting HR management and measurement systems of selection, formal performance appraisal, promotion, development, and termination practices.
6. Specify the roles of leadership, the workforce, and HR in strategy execution.

CHALLENGES

Perspective challenge—Does management fully understand how workforce behaviors affect strategy execution?

Metrics challenge—Has the organization identified and collected the right measures of success?

Execution challenge—Does management have access to the data and the motivation to use the data in decision making?

satisfaction and job engagement and critical business-unit outcomes, including profit. "Engagement" in this study had to do with, among other things, the level of employee satisfaction regarding working conditions, recognition and encouragement for good work, opportunities to perform well, and commitment to quality. The authors estimated that those business units in the top quartile on the job engagement scale had, on average, from $80,000 to $120,000 higher monthly revenues or sales.

Can HRM practices facilitate higher engagement? Absolutely! It is clear that changes in HRM practices that serve to increase employee satisfaction and engagement can increase critical business-unit outcomes.[21] Many HR experts now say that the emphasis in corporate America is no longer on "happy" workers who will stay with the company forever. Rather, the new mantra is to retain employees who are "productive" and "engaged." Pay and bonuses are thus more driven by performance measures instead of seniority.

FIGURE 3.7

The Chain of Relationships Linking Management Practices to Employee Satisfaction, Customer Satisfaction, and Long-Term Profitability and Growth

Source: W. Cascio, "From Business Partner to Driving Business Success: The Next Step in the Evolution of HR Management," *Human Resource Management 44* (2005), p. 162. Reprinted with permission of John Wiley & Sons.

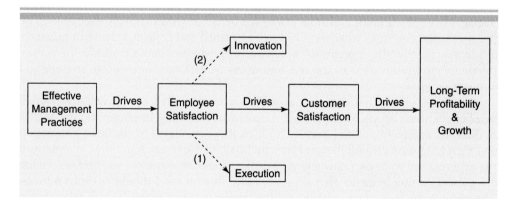

"It's an, 'If you give, you'll get' model," says David Ulrich, professor at the University of Michigan business school. "That's kind of the productive contract."[22]

Of course, many experts maintain that these simple "this for that" arrangements may have contributed to the trouble and demise of many U.S. corporations in 2008. Countrywide Financial rewarded its brokers for closing mortgages with questionable borrowers and its CEO Angelo Mozilo got over $10 million in bonuses in 2007, clearly connected to these bad mortgages. Borrowers began to default on the mortgages in droves in that same year, and the company was eventually swallowed up by Bank of America in 2008. Over 11,000 employees lost their jobs. Unfortunately, Countrywide is but one of many examples of companies rewarding employees for behaviors and outcomes that may be beneficial to these employees and their bosses in the short term but toxic for the company in the not too distant future. Corporate bankrupcies were at record levels in 2008. Some of the most costly (e.g., Lehman Brothers, Washington Mutual) can clearly be linked to deeply flawed "pay for performance" systems.

We should also be interested in how the various criteria relate to one another. A recent review showed a strong relationship between an employee attitudinal measure known as "organizational commitment" and both job performance and employee turnover. Employees with higher levels of "organizational commitment" were more likely to be better performers and also stay with the company longer. Obviously, managers will want to know how more "committed" or "engaged" employees can be found or developed. The author knows one CEO who was highly critical of academic research because it focused so much attention on variables like "engagement" and "commitment" or even "job satisfaction." He referred to these as "softies" and argued that they were not relevant to the "bottom line." In fact, an abundant literature now exists which documents that such "softies" are indeed strong predictors of bottom-line accounting and financial measures of organizational performance. A key to effective HR policy and practice is measuring such "softies" and understanding how they do relate to critical bottom-line measures like performance, costs, profit, and customer satisfaction.

Organizations should certainly strive to satisfy their employees with good pay, good supervision, and good, stimulating work. But the model presented in Figure 3.7 also helps keep measures of employee job satisfaction in perspective. Employee satisfaction is related to customer satisfaction. So is cost. Customers are particularly impressed with low cost. Wal-Mart does so well not because their employees are happy but because their products are on average 14 percent cheaper than their competitors'. The author would be a lot happier if his university salary was doubled! You'd probably be unhappy if your tuition was raised (again).

The key is linking measurement to strategic goals. "Thinking strategically means understanding whether the measurement system you are considering will provide you with the kinds of information that will help you manage the HR function strategically."[23] This linkage creates the connection between leading indicators and lagging indicators. Let us turn to illustrations of recent HRM activities directed at these criteria.

Frito-Lay had a problem with job vacancies in key positions, which they believed had a direct effect on sales. They instituted a training and development program through their HRM division to cross-train workers for several jobs in an effort to reduce downtime from employee vacancies and provide more opportunities for employees to move up. The down- time could be operationally defined in terms of dollars, and the training program saved the company $250,000 in the first year.

AMC Theaters developed a battery of applicant tests to identify individuals most likely to perform more effectively and to stay with the company longer. The reduction in turnover saved the company over a half million dollars in five years. Blockbuster Video tried an applicant test that purported to help reduce employee theft and developed a new performance management system for all employees. They estimated savings at $750,000. Owens-Corning Fiberglas trained all of its managers in statistical quality analysis as a part of their total quality management program. Trainees were made accountable for improving the quality at Owens-Corning and the program worked. Reduction of rejected materials saved over a million dollars. John Hancock Insurance installed a new managerial pay-for-performance system in order to increase regional sales and decrease employee turnover. J. Walter Thompson developed a new incentive system to promote creative advertising ideas from its consumer research and accounting units. RJR Nabisco replaced a fixed-rate commission with a new compensation system for its advertisers, which linked ad agency compensation to the success of the campaign. Concerned about the quality of one managerial level, Office Depot developed a managerial assessment center to select their district managers. They then determined the extent to which the quality of management improved as a function of the new screening method.

Turnover is a serious problem for many service industries and especially fastfood. Many consultants just write it off as part of the business. David Brandon, CEO of Domino's Pizza, did a study inside Domino's, the results of which surprised his top management team.[24] He found that the most important factor related to the success (or failure) of any individual store was not marketing, or packaging, or neighborhood demographics. It was the quality of the store manager. Store managers had a great deal to do with employee turnover, and turnover had a great deal to do with store profit. Domino's calculated that it costs the company $2,500 each time an hourly employee quits and $20,000 each time a store manager quits. Mr. Brandon focused on reducing the 158 percent turnover rate among all employees. Domino's implemented a new and more valid test for selecting managers and hourly personnel, installed new computerized systems for tracking and monitoring employee performance and output, and developed a much more focused pay-for-performance system for all managers. As of 2008, the program was a great success by all counts. Turnover was way down, store profit was up, and the stock price was doing well in an otherwise very difficult market. Brandon clearly showed how important HRM is to the bottom line. Attracting and keeping good employees, measuring and monitoring performance, and rewarding strategically important outcomes are all keys. Obviously, all of this has to translate into good (and cheap) pizza. Long-term profitability and growth are driven by customer satisfaction, and that's mainly a function of the quality and cost of the products and services. Research clearly shows HRM practice and employee satisfaction are in the "chain of relationships."

In the past, HRM interventions were rarely linked to financial measures or cost figures in order to show a reliable financial benefit. This inability to link such HRM practices to the "big picture" might explain why personnel departments in the past have had so little clout. While marketing departments were reporting the bottom-line impact of a new marketing strategy in terms of market share or sales volume, personnel could only show that absenteeism or turnover was reduced by some percentage, rarely assessing the relationship between these reductions and a specific financial benefit. Stanford professor Jeffrey Pfeffer summed it up: "In a world in which financial results are measured, a failure to measure human resource policy and practice implementation dooms this to second-class status, oversight neglect, and potential failure. The feedback from the measurements is essential to refine and further develop implementation ideas as well as to learn how well the practices are actually achieving their intended results."[25]

Developing clear criteria linked to strategic goals is critical for managerial success and should be a major driver of HR policy. Some experts argue that HR specialists should "quarterback" the development and administration of a "management by measurement" system, ensuring all functional business units are subscribing to the guidelines for sound, strategic measurement. Allowing business units to develop and administer "leading indicator" measures can result in the measurement of criteria more closely linked to making that unit (and particular managers) look good rather than the strategic goals of the unit. By contrast HR can help with sound measurement.

But what is sound measurement? One HR executive laid the groundwork with this definition: "The most effective employees are those who provide the highest possible quantity and quality of a product or service at the lowest cost and in the most timely fashion, with a maximum of positive impact on co-workers, organizational units, and the client/customer population." This statement of effectiveness also applies to particular HR programs, products, and services and all functional business units. In evaluating an outsourced recruiting effort, an HR VP provided the following criterion for evaluation: "Give me a large pool of highly qualified candidates, give me this list as quickly as possible, and don't charge me much when you're doing it." The details of the measurement system (e.g., the quantity and quality of products/services) must be linked to strategic goals. These measurement details are critical. As stated earlier, many of the problems at companies in crisis in 2008 and 2009 have been attributed to faulty incentive systems that met short-term goals and created long-term disasters.

The most effective organizations get down to specifics about all important criteria, and these are directly linked to key objectives or desired outcomes for the organization. This prescription applies to HR as for any other business function. Wayne Keegan, VP of HR for toymaker ERTL in Dyersville, Iowa, clearly represented the bottom line for HR: "HR managers should strive to quantify all facets of HR to determine what works and what doesn't."[26]

What works and doesn't work should focus on the "big picture." The most effective organizations are driven by measurement strategies perhaps conceptualized by HR specialists and applied to HR functions but, more important, applied throughout the workforce. HR can (and should) help senior management develop and focus on key workforce measures that derive from organizational strategy. The most effective organizations develop a set of "top tier" measurement tools that reflect and integrate the company's strategic goals. As Mark Huselid and his colleagues put it, "There should be no gap between what is measured and what is managed." Linking workforce success at the individual and unit level to the most critical business outcomes is a key to competitive advantage. Linking these outcomes to long-term measures of success is the key to long-term advantage and survival.

Competitive Advantage[27]

Competitive advantage refers to the ability of an organization to formulate strategies that place it in a favorable position relative to other companies in the industry. Two major principles describe the extent to which a business has a competitive advantage. These two principles are perceived customer value and uniqueness.

CUSTOMER VALUE

Competitive advantage occurs if customers perceive that they receive more value from their transaction with an organization than from its competitors. Ensuring that customers receive value from transacting with a business requires that all employees be focused on understanding customer needs and expectations. This can occur if customer data are used in the designing of products or service processes and customer value is used as the major criterion of interest. Some companies conduct value chain analysis that is designed to assess the amount of added value produced by each position, program, activity, and unit in the organization. The value chain analysis can be used to refocus the organization on its core competencies and the requirements of the customer base.

Customers not only perceive but actually realize value from Wal-Mart in the form of price. The products and services are available in convenient stores and average prices are 14 percent lower than its competitors. While there are many reasons Wal-Mart can price goods lower than competitors (e.g., economies of scale, price control pressures on suppliers, technology on products bought and sold, cheaper imports), low labor cost is certainly one factor. Sales clerks earn less at Wal-Mart compared to unionized workers doing essentially the same work for competitors. Health care benefits are estimated to be 15 percent less than coverage for workers within the same industry.

Wal-Mart's strategy to be a price leader and its obsession with cost control have the potential for trouble. The company has been mired in various labor-related lawsuits in recent years, all of which may be related to controlling costs. They paid a huge fine in 2005 for contracting with a company that employed illegal aliens, have been sued numerous times for violating labor laws, including firing people for union organizing efforts, and have been found guilty of violating the Fair Labor Standards Act regarding overtime. While they are the largest employer in the United States, the proportional rate of complaints related to their HR practices is high.

Value to Abercrombie and Fitch is related to creating and sustaining an image for its young customers. A&F went for an all-American look and it certainly worked. They are the largest teen retailer in the United States with over 600 stores and over a billion dollars in revenues. Their clothes are certainly not cheaper than competitors'. A&F is clearly promoting image as a part of its definition of value. But just like Wal-Mart's cost control/price strategy, A&F's "image" strategy created big trouble for the company. In a discrimination lawsuit settled for $40 million, A&F was accused of favoring white job applicants and employees. A&F agreed to change some of its marketing strategy as a part of the settlement.

CUSTOMER VALUE AND CORPORATE SOCIAL RESPONSIBILITY (CSR)

The notion of customer value is more complicated than it may seem to the uninitiated. Many customers seek out products and services at least to some extent as a function of the reputation of the organization selling the product or service in matters not directly related to the cost or quality of the particular product or service. One of the reasons companies (and politicians) wrap themselves around the Olympics every four years is they believe that the basic sense of American pride and excellence that goes with the Olympics tends to rub off onto the company. Research in marketing shows that perceptions of product quality are positively affected by affiliation with the Olympics and Olympic heroes such as Michael Phelps. Thus, at least the theory is that customer value is affected by this connection.

Likewise, the reputation of a company's environmental policies affects the decision making of a growing number of consumers. Concerns about global warming, the price of gasoline, and air pollution have prompted many companies to offer incentives to employees to encourage them to buy fuel-efficient vehicles that emit less carbon dioxide. As the companies go "Green," they report improvements in employee retention and increases in job applications, two HR metrics that have been linked to subsequent improvements in the bottom line.

Most companies with a connection to manufacturing facilities abroad are very concerned about pitiful labor conditions and child labor issues at these international facilities. When Kathy Lee Gifford was accused of exploiting child labor in Honduran clothing plants, some consumers avoided her line of clothing. Nike was accused by the chairman of the Made in the USA Foundation of using child labor in Indonesia to make its athletic shoes. Nike's business was affected to the extent that consumers consider these allegations when they buy sneakers. Jesse Jackson launched a boycott against Mitsubishi to "encourage" the company to put more women and minorities in executive positions.

American companies spend millions and hire thousands of foreign plant auditors to inspect off-shore plants, and there is no doubt worker conditions have improved since the 1990s. But many bad factories remain and Asian suppliers regularly outsource to other suppliers, who may in turn outsource to yet another operation, creating a supply chain that is difficult to follow.

Some companies obviously believe that their reputation for corporate social and environmental responsibility figures into the complicated calculation of value. There is evidence that companies are under increasing pressure to behave in a socially responsible manner. While there are a variety of definitions of corporate social/environmental performance (CSP), there is debate over the extent to which (or whether) a positive image of CSP is related to corporate financial performance. Two excellent studies on this subject provide compelling data that CSP does indeed affect the bottom line and investor behavior. The results suggest that "corporate virtue in the form of social responsibility and, to a lesser extent, environmental responsibility is likely to pay off."[28] Perhaps Wal-Mart already knew this. Have you noticed the many ads on TV informing the public about their many good deeds and how nice they are to their employees and their environment?

CSP has spawned socially responsible investing, or SRI, which enables investors to buy into companies with favorable CSP reputations. Mutual funds such as Calvert World Values, AXA Enterprise Global, and Henderson GlobalCare Growth invest only in companies that pass CSP muster. It is estimated that one out of every eight dollars invested by professional money managers is invested based on corporate CSP.[29] So, who are these socially responsible companies that dominate SRI? Among the well-known companies most likely to be part of an SRI mutual fund are Canon, Toyota and Sony (Japan), British Petroleum (UK), Nokia (Finland), SAP (Germany), and in the United States, Bank of America, Cisco Systems, Coca-Cola, Johnson & Johnson, Microsoft, and Procter and Gamble.

There is a related and growing "corporate sustainability movement." "Sustainability" has to do with a company's ability to make a profit while not sacrificing the resources of its people, the community, and the planet. Many executives now claim sustainability can improve the company's financial performance. A 2007 survey of executives indicated that the greatest benefits of sustainability programs are improving public opinion, improving customer relations, and attracting and retaining talent. Over 75 percent of the participating executives anticipated more investment in environmental programs.[30]

Many college students are now involved in tracking the manufacturing process for their school paraphernalia. The United Students Against Sweatshops (USASNET.org) is an organization of students from over 200 universities affiliated with the Worker's Rights Consortium. The WRC conducts investigations of manufacturing plants, issues reports, and initiates boycotts against certain university products such as hats or T-shirts if plants do not meet its standards for wages and safety. This movement is growing and has already had some major successes.

Many consumers use "Newman's Own" products (as in the late actor Paul Newman) not only because they like the products but because all profits are donated to "educational and charitable purposes." (Go to newmansown.com.) Sure, Newman's Sockarooni spaghetti sauce is tasty. But does the taste account for all of the customer value when the sauce typically costs more than other sauces? Customer value can be complicated. Jesse Jackson and Burger King were well aware of this when Burger King agreed to special financing and support for minority-owned franchises. Most people do not live and die for a Whopper. Consumers' knowledge regarding Burger King's policy toward minorities could affect their fast-food decision.

So, an organization's CSR and CSP reputation regarding its corporate ethics, environmental positions, pro-family policies, or affirmative action/diversity practices can go into the "customer value" assessment. For years, Dow Chemical in Midland, Michigan, had a negative reputation on college campuses because of its production of napalm, a chemical agent used in the Vietnam war. Dow had a terrible time recruiting chemists and other vital professionals because of this one product. Dow launched a public relations campaign to enhance its reputation. They focused their advertising on the many agricultural products that they produced and marketed. The result was a profound improvement in Dow's ability to recruit on college campuses. Obviously, Dow's ability to recruit and retain the best chemists was vital to their competitiveness.

While consumers undoubtedly place greater weight on the quality of the product or service, there is no question that "customer value" can also include intangible variables such as corporate responsibility, environmental impacts, diversity policies, and being on the right side of political issues. Activist consumer groups, by calling attention to corporate greed, may foster more social responsibility by simply affecting the complicated variable of the customer value equation. There is also evidence that Gen Y Americans are more sensitive to CSR and CSP issues, especially environmental concerns, and that this Millennial generation is more likely to buy from (and invest in) companies with strong CSP reputations and more inclined to work for such companies.

One hot issue related to the complicated equation of "customer value" is the way a company treats its employees. The reputation of a company regarding how it treats its employees can also affect the size of the pool of candidates for any job within the organization. Organizations work hard to make the list of the "most admired" companies for which to work because it does help attract more qualified workers. Google, the most admired company on *Fortune* magazine's list in 2008, received almost 800,000 applicants for the 3,100 positions it filled in 2007. Recall that the ratio of the number of qualified applicants to the number of key positions is a "high-performance work system characteristic" and is thus related to corporate financial success (see again Figure 3.1).

At SAS, a North Carolina computer software company with over 10,000 employees, it all started with free M&Ms every Wednesday. The SAS HR strategy is clearly designed to attract the best programmers and to keep the SAS workforce happy. The strategy has worked. They sold over a billion dollars of analytical software to retailers like Victoria's Secret and the U.S. military in 2008 alone. SAS has never had a losing year and has never laid off a single employee! Says Jim Goodnight, the founder of the company, "If employees are happy, they make the customers happy. If they make the customers happy, they make me happy." SAS is always ranked high in *Fortune* magazine's list of best companies to work for (they ranked 29th in 2008; go to Fortune.com or SAS.com for their current rank). SAS offers a myriad of benefits you don't find at many companies. They have a Work/Life Center made up of social workers who help SAS employees solve life's problems like elder care and college selection for SAS kids. They'll even have someone pick up and deliver your dry cleaning! Says Jeff Chambers, director of HR, "We do all these things because it makes good business sense," saving staff time. SAS claims a turnover rate differential of 5 percent at SAS versus 20 percent at competitors (true even in the heat of the 90s' dot-com craze!). That savings in turnover at SAS is estimated at $60–70 million annually. While some companies treat employees as costs or necessities, Jim Goodnight regards his SAS employees as the best investments he ever made. "Ninety-five percent of my assets drive out the front gate every evening. It's my job to bring them back." Google has adopted this HR philosophy with record-low turnover rates as a consequence.

There is hard and growing evidence that treating employees well will translate into better financial performance. One study found that positive employee relations served as an "intangible and enduring asset and . . . a source of sustained competitive advantage at the firm level."[31] The study found that companies that made the "100 Best Companies to Work for in America" list had much more positive employee attitudes toward work and a significant financial performance advantage over competitors. The advantage is self-sustaining. Once companies make the list, the quality and quantity of their applicants for key positions go up and thus the quality of their new hires improves! Among the companies that have been on the list for years are Starbucks, Whole Foods, Cisco Systems, JM Family Enterprises, J.M. Smucker, Nordstrom, and Ernst and Young. Perceived customer value is the principle source of competitive advantage. While it mainly derives from the actual product or service, it derives indirectly from an organization's reputation.

MAINTAINING UNIQUENESS

The second principle of competitive advantage derives from offering a product or service that your competitor cannot easily imitate or copy. For example, if you open a restaurant and serve hamburgers, and a competitor moves in next to you and also serves hamburgers that taste, cost, and are prepared just like yours, unless you quickly offer something unique in your restaurant, you may lose a large part of your business to your competitor. Your restaurant needs to have something that is unique to continue to attract customers. Competitive advantage comes to a business when it adds value to customers through some form of uniqueness. The author of this book works in Boca Raton, Florida, one of the great resort areas of the world (and a golfer's paradise). This location enables his university to attract (and retain) top faculty from around the world—clearly a competitive (and unique) advantage.

Apple has a great history for being unique. consider the Apple strategy for the original iPod. Says Apple VP Phillip Schiller, the iPod development was about how many songs it holds, how quickly songs can be transferred, and how good the sound is in the context of the design. These were the essential questions the customer was asking regarding MP3 players. The uniform whiteness, even the headphones, certainly contributed to the product's iconic (and unique) status. But as one devoted iPod owner put it, "If it didn't load up fast, store a lot and, above all, sound good, I probably would have stuck with my Walkman for a while longer." Apple's latest iPhone is even more sensitive to customer demands and projected to be more profitable than any of the other products in the iPod line of music players, even though the price tag is about half of the original iPhone. Because of lower component costs, profit margins for the new iPhone should exceed the 50 percent level achieved by the original Apple iPod and the first iPhone.[32] Apple products have succeeded in maintaining their uniqueness.

SOURCES OF UNIQUENESS

The key to any business's sustained competitive advantage is to ensure that uniqueness lasts over time. Three traditional mechanisms exist to offer customers uniqueness. A fourth is often a necessary condition to take advantage of one (or more) of the other three. The four mechanisms for offering uniqueness are described below and summarized in Figure 3.8. First, **financial or economic capability** derives from an advantage related to costs; when a business is able to produce or provide a good or service more cheaply than competitiors. If in your hamburger restaurant, you have received a financial gift from family or friends to build the restaurant, without repayment of the gift, you may be able to charge less for your product than a competitor who borrowed money from a bank or financial institution. Your cheaper-priced hamburger would then become a source of uniqueness that customers value. Toyota and Honda do not have anywhere near the "legacy" costs that Ford, GM, and Chrysler have (pension and health care commitments to retirees). This is a huge financial advantage.

The question of what is unique about a product or service is almost always asked and answered in the context of the usually overriding "cost" question. Wal-Mart's source of uniqueness is rather simple: They have what we want and it's cheaper (on average, about 14 percent)! For most people and for almost any product or service, the assessment of the product or service is done in the context of price or cost, at both a relative and an absolute level.

The second source of uniqueness comes from having **strategic or product capability**. That is, a business needs to offer a product or service that differentiates it from other products or services. The iPod is a clear example. One early reviewer of the iPod took a look at the $400 initial price tag and suggested that the name might be an acronym for "Idiots Price Our Devices"! But despite its pricey introduction, the iPod overwhelmed the other MP3 players and acquired what pop star Moby referred to as an "insidious revolutionary quality . . . it becomes a part of your life so quickly that you can't remember what it was like beforehand." Apple has had the same success with the iPhone. Now that's uniqueness! In the hamburger wars, fast-food restaurants have attempted to offer unique products and services to attract customers. Salad bars, taco bars, kiddie meals, and $30 breakfasts with giant rodents named Mickey and Minnie are all examples of restaurants attempting to make their product unique and appealing to customers. The possession of a patent for a critical drug is an advantage for a pharmaceutical company.

A third source of uniqueness for a business is a **technological or operational capability**. That is, a business can have a distinctive way of building or delivering its product or service. In the hamburger restaurant, the different methods of preparing the hamburgers may distinguish restaurants from each other (broiled versus flame-grilled). Customers

FIGURE 3.8

The Four Mechanisms
for Offering and
Maintaining Uniqueness

- FINANCIAL OR ECONOMIC CAPABILITY DERIVES FROM AN ADVANTAGE
  RELATED TO COSTS

   WHEN A BUSINESS IS ABLE TO PRODUCE OR PROVIDE A GOOD OR SERVICE
   MORE CHEAPLY THAN COMPETITORS

   EXAMPLES: WAL-MART, BANK OF AMERICA

- STRATEGIC OR PRODUCT CAPABILITY

   A BUSINESS OFFERS A PRODUCT OR SERVICE THAT DIFFERENTIATES IT
   FROM OTHER PRODUCTS OR SERVICES.

   EXAMPLES: McDONALD'S, APPLE, GOOGLE, ROCKSTAR GAMES

- TECHNOLOGICAL OR OPERATIONAL CAPABILITY

   A DISTINCTIVE WAY OF BUILDING OR DELIVERING A PRODUCT OR SERVICE

   EXAMPLES: GOOGLE, EBAY, CISCO SYSTEMS, MICROSOFT, MICROPOSITE

- ORGANIZATIONAL CAPABILITY

   ABILITY TO MANAGE ORGANIZATIONAL SYSTEMS AND PEOPLE THAT
   MATCHES CUSTOMER AND STRATEGIC NEEDS

   ***EXAMPLES: GOOGLE, SAS, WHOLE FOODS, JM FAMILY ENTERPRISES,
   PUBLIX SUPER MARKETS***

may prefer one technological (cooking) process over another, and thus continue to patronize one restaurant. In more complex businesses, technological capability may include research and development, engineering, computer systems and/or software, and manufacturing facilities. Microsoft has thrived in this area by getting consumers to purchase and get comfortable with one of their products so they are more attracted to future products related to their technological capability. Google is a great example of unique technological and operational capability. Another example is Michigan-based Microposite that introduced a patented, state-of-the-art form of siding in 2008.

A fourth source of uniqueness aiding a company in seeking competitive advantage is **organizational capability**. Organizational capability represents the business's ability to manage organizational systems and people in order to match customer and strategic needs. In a complex, dynamic, uncertain, and turbulent environment (e.g., changing customers, technology, suppliers, relevant laws and regulations), organizational capability derives from the organization's flexibility, adaptiveness, and responsiveness. In a restaurant, organizational capability may be derived from having employees who ensure that when customers enter the restaurant, their customer requirements, their needs, are better met than when the customers go to a competitor's restaurant. That is, employees will want to ensure that customers are served promptly and pleasantly, and that the food is well prepared.

The implications for human resource management should be clear. HR systems need to be put in place that maximize organizational capability and exploit all other potential sources of uniqueness. Organizations with serious problems on the organizational capability side of the ledger can fail to exploit other potential sources of competitive advantage. The cultural problems after the merger of Chrysler and Daimler-Benz are a good illustration of this interaction. Despite a solid financial situation and unique technological advantages the company never gained synergy as DaimlerChrysler and eventually split up in 2006.

With increased globalization and the need for strategic alliances, organizational capability is a key to sustained competitive advantage as companies expand their businesses around the world. Take McDonald's as one example of a successful global expansion with a need for strategic alliances. McDonald's has restaurants in over 115 countries, and expansion to some areas of the world poses special challenges. Their marketing determined that they could sell the Big Macs in Saudi Arabia. Here's the line-up for the Saudi Big Mac: two all beef patties from Spain, the special sauce from the United States, lettuce from Holland, cheese from New Zealand, pickles from the United States, onions and sesame seeds from Mexico, the bun from Saudi wheat, sugar and oil from Brazil, and the packaging from Germany. Organizational capability enables McDonald's to pull this integration off, and the result is a highly popular and profitable product. Globalization will necessitate more of these challenging arrangements. HR will have a lot to do with success through enhanced organizational capability, as HR systems help determine how smart people are recruited, hired, trained, motivated, treated, evaluated, paid, and integrated into the organization.

Research shows that organizational capability influenced by particular HR activities is a reliable predictor of corporate financial performance. HR activities and processes such as those characterizing "leading indicator" high-performance work systems illustrate organizational capability as a source of competitive advantage. The ability to attract and retain individuals with the skills to establish and maintain potential sources of uniqueness should be a key metric in any "management by measurement" system.

CHAPTER SUMMARY

Human resource management is to some extent concerned with any organizational decision that has an impact on the workforce or the potential workforce. The trends underscore the importance of HR to meet the challenges of the 21st century. While there is typically a human resource or personnel department in medium-sized to large corporations, line management is still primarily responsible for the application of HRM policies and practices. There are critical competencies for general management and HRM professionals. An organization needs both competent personnel trained in HRM and motivated managers who recognize the importance of HRM activities and will apply the best procedures in the recommended manner. HR managers are more likely to convince line managers of the value of HR programs by focusing on "leading indicator" measurements, which can be linked to the lagging financial indicators that are more clearly understood by management. Personnel/HR functions are often perceived by line managers to be out of step with the real bottom-line outcome measures for the organization. Therefore, the most effective human resource departments are those in which HRM policy and activities are established and measured in the context of the mission and strategic objectives of the organization. HRM should assist management in the difficult task of integrating and coordinating the interests of the various organizational constituencies, with the ultimate aim being to enhance the organization's competitive position by focusing on meeting or exceeding customer requirements and expanding the customer base.

Competitive advantage is the key to success for most businesses. To attain competitive advantage, businesses need to add (and sustain) value for customers and offer uniqueness. Four capabilities provide a business's uniqueness: financial, strategic or product, technological or operational, and organizational. To sustain competitive advantage, organizational capability should be emphasized, ideally in the context of the other sources of uniqueness. Organizational capability derives from a business's HRM practices.

The view of HRM outlined in this chapter provides a foundation for integrating HRM activities into the organization's mission and goals. HRM professionals should be actively involved in building more competitive organizations through the HRM domains. One necessary competency for both line managers and HRM professionals is an understanding of the growing impact of globalization in HR policy and practice.

Key Terms and Concepts

domain, *53*

financial or economic capability, *71*

high-performance work systems, *50*

meta-analysis, *52*

organizational capability, *72*

organizational design, *53*

strategic or product capability, *71*

technological or operational capability, *71*

Critical Thinking and Discussion Questions

1. Describe the changing status of HRM. What factors have led to these changes?

2. How do productivity concerns influence organizational policies and procedures regarding HRM activities?

3. Describe the major HRM activities conducted in an organization. Provide an example of each from an organization with which you are familiar.

4. What impact should the composition of the workforce have on HRM practices or activities? What future trends do you see that will influence HRM activities? Why is the growing cultural diversity of the workforce a management challenge?

5. Why is the support of line management critical to the effective functioning of HRM practices in an organization? Provide some suggestions to ensure that this support is maintained.

6. Why does the number of qualified applicants for each strategic position relate to corporate effectiveness? How can HRM enhance this applicant pool?

7. What are the sources of uniqueness that can aid a company seeking competitive advantage?

8. Explain how Ford and GM have a competitive disadvantage related to financial capability. How does Wal-Mart have an advantage?

Diversity Management

LEARNING OBJECTIVES

After completing this chapter, you should be able to:

 LO¹ Describe some of the forces that are contributing to the increase in diversity of labor forces in many countries.

 LO² Define diversity and understand how it can influence workplace productivity.

 LO³ Explain how diversity issues are affecting Japan, the European Union, and the United States.

 LO⁴ Identify the advantages that organizations receive from having successful diversity management programs.

LO⁵ Understand the main characteristics of a multicultural organization.

Global Diversity: Knowledge Is Power

Brigitta Hochstrasser, vice president of marketing and sales for a large Swiss food products company, is responsible for staffing the new sales and distribution center in Los Angeles, California. After placing various job advertisements in the local newspapers, radio, and Internet, she flew to Los Angeles to begin the interviewing. To her surprise, most of the candidates for the open positions were very diverse in nature, including male and female Russians, Japanese, Koreans, Vietnamese, Armenians, Mexicans, Guatemalans, Salvadorans, and African-Americans.

Hochstrasser is no stranger to interviewing and hiring candidates from diverse backgrounds. In her native country of Switzerland, the population is a rich mixture of cultural and ethnic backgrounds: 65 percent German, 18 percent French, 10 percent Italian, and 7 percent Romansch and other.

The Swiss found that it was important to learn more about the candidates' backgrounds and perspectives to assist them in making better hiring decisions. By doing some research, she was able to learn more about her diverse candidates and also decided this would be good information for students, global managers, and others to know.

What race are Hispanics (or Latinos)? The correct answer is they can be Caucasian, black, native, or some combination. Hispanic refers not only to a race but also to an origin or an ethnicity. There are many Hispanic segments in Los Angeles—Mexicans, Guatemalans, Salvadorans, and others who are different in their indigenous ancestry, origins, accents, and many other characteristics.

What is Confucianism? Confucianism is the major religious influence on Chinese, Japanese, Korean, and Vietnamese cultures. It emphasizes response to authority, especially to parents and teachers; hard work; discipline and the ability to delay gratification; harmony in relationships; and the importance of the group over individual needs.

Does the term African-American apply to all blacks? No. Black Americans came from cultures others than just those in Africa, including the Caribbean, Central America, and South America. Just as in the general population, there is great variety in lifestyle, career choice, educational level attained, and value systems across segments of the over 36 million black American (including African and other cultural backgrounds) population.

After she completes the Los Angeles hiring, Hochstrasser will fill similar assignments in France and India. She thinks to herself how important it's becoming to develop a style and pattern of behavior that appeals to and reaches all segments of the diverse recruits that she encounters. By relating better to these job candidates, Hochstrasser hopes this relationship building will generate enthusiasm for the company. She believes that a diverse set of employees will go a long way to dealing with the mix of diverse customers, suppliers, food inspectors, and the other important stakeholders that share in the success of his enterprise.

Sources: *CIA World Factbook* (http://www.cia.gov/cia/publications/factbook/); Lynette Clemetson, "Hispanics Now Largest Minority, Census Shows," *New York Times,* January 22, 2003; and John Naisbitt, *Global Paradox* (New York: Morrow, 1994), pp. 227–35.

As the opening vignette illustrates, labor forces in Los Angeles and in many other cities and countries in the world are becoming much more diverse than was the case several decades ago. There are a variety of reasons for this increase in labor force diversity, including globalization, sociopolitical events, immigration, and population trends. Here are some examples to illustrate the impact these forces are exerting on diversity.

- *From now until 2010, women, Asians, and Hispanics are projected to enter the U.S. labor force at a higher rate than white non-Hispanics.*[1] Added to this is the fact that with the aging of the baby-boom generation (born between 1946 and 1964), the percentage of employees age 55 and older is expected to increase from 13 to 20 percent by 2020.[2]

- *France and Germany have between 400,000 and 1.5 million illegal immigrants.* In 2001, France received 47,000 asylum applications (mostly from Chinese and Turks). In that same year, Germany received 90,000 asylum petitions.

- *In the Philippines, a traditional and conservative society, women are entering the workforce at a higher rate than ever before not only as employees, but also as entrepreneurs.* Economic necessity and opportunity are driving many women to enter the workforce and/or create businesses.[3]

- *Changing geopolitical landscapes, economic downturns, and regional conflicts are creating large-scale immigration movements between countries.* Turmoil in the Middle East, the demise of the Soviet Union, unification of the German Democratic Republic (East) and German Federal Republic (West), Chinese government crackdown on protesters in Tiananmen Square, fighting in Croatia and Serbia, and economic crises in countries like Argentina and Russia all lead to immigration. In the United States, Hispanics are now the largest minority group with a population of 37 million as of 2001.[4] This is nearly equal to the combined populations of Venezuela (24 million) and Chile (15.4 million); and it represents over one-third the population of Mexico (103 million).[5]

These trends show that workforce diversity is an important topic for global managers to understand. Not only will managers need to know how to organize, motivate, and lead "domestically diverse employees" of different gender, race, ethnic, religious, age, and racial backgrounds, but managers will also need to know how to relate effectively to key customers, joint-venture managers and employees, vendors, and government officials located around the globe. For these reasons, global managers should develop an effective approach to diversity management.

Diversity: An Introduction

Diversity refers to a vast array of physical and cultural variation that constitutes the spectrum of human differences. The six primary dimensions of diversity include age, ethnicity, gender, physical attributes, race, and sexual/affectional orientation. These core elements of diversity have a lifelong impact on behavior and attitudes. Secondary forms of diversity—the differences that people acquire, discard, or modify throughout their lives—can be changed. Secondary dimensions of diversity include educational background, marital status, religious belief, health disabilities, and work experience.[6]

Valuing diversity from an organizational and leadership perspective means understanding and accepting differences in core and secondary diversity dimensions in others. An increasingly important goal in a changing society is to understand that all individuals are different and to appreciate these differences.[7] From an international business perspective, the more global managers know and understand their diverse stakeholders, the more effective and productive they will be. Table 4.1 illustrates the extent to which countries are diverse in terms of ethnicity, religions, and languages.

TABLE 4.1

Diversity around the World

Sources: *CIA World Factbook*; J.L. Price and W.G. Barron, *Profiles of General Demographic Characteristics: 2000 Census of Population and Housing—United States* (Washington, DC: U.S. Department of Commerce, May 2001).

Country	Ethnic Groups	Religions	Languages
Germany	German 91.5%, Turkish 2.4%, Other 6.1% (comprised mostly of Serbo-Croatian, Italian, Russian, Greek, Polish, and Spanish)	Protestant 34%, Roman Catholic 34%, Muslim 3.7%, Other 28.3%	German
India	Indo-Aryan 72%, Dravidian 25%, and Other 3%	Hindu 81.3%, Muslim 12%, Christian 2.3%, Sikh 1.9%, Other 2.5% (includes Buddhist, Jain, and Parsi)	English for national, political, and commercial communication; Hindi is the national language and primary tongue of 30 percent of the people; 14 other official languages are spoken (Bengali, Telugu, Marathi, Tamil, Urdu, etc.)
Brazil	White (includes Portuguese, German, Italian, Spanish, Polish) 55%, mixed white and black 38%, black 6%, and Other (includes Japanese, Arab, and Amerindian) 1%	Roman Catholic (nominal) 80%	Portuguese (official), Spanish, English, and French
China	Han Chinese 91.9%, Other (Zhuang, Uygur, Hui, Yi, Tibetan, Miao, Manchu, Mongol, Buyi, Korean) 8.1%	Taoist, Buddhist, Muslim 1–2%, Christian 3–4% (note: officially atheist)	Mandarin (Putonghua, based on Beijing dialect), Yue (Cantonese), Wu (Shanghaiese), Minbei (Fuzhou), Minnan (Hokkien-Taiwanese), Xiang, Gan, Hakka dialects, and others
South Africa	Black 75.2%, white 13.6%, colored 8.6%, and Indian 2.6%	Christian 68%, Muslim 2%, Hindu 1.5%, and indigenous beliefs and animist 28.5%	11 official languages, including Afrikaans, English, Ndebele, Pedi, Sotho, Swazi, Tsonga, Tswana, Venda, Xhosa, and Zulu
Canada	British Isles origin 28%, French origin 23%, other European 15%, Amerindian 2%, Other (mostly Asian, African, Arab) 6%, and mixed background 26%	Roman Catholic 46%, Protestant 36%, Other 18%	English 59.3% (official), French 23.2% (official), and Other 17.5%

🌐 Global Perspectives on Diversity

Japan, the European Union, and the United States have very different views of diversity.

JAPAN

As one of the most homogenous societies in the world, being considered Japanese requires an individual to be born to Japanese parents, to look Japanese, to speak the Japanese language, and to behave like Japanese.[8] These considerations have led to a population that is 99 percent Japanese, with the remaining 1 percent being Korean, Chinese, Brazilian, or Filipino. Due to several years of low birthrates and an aging workforce, the Japanese exclusionary stance toward *gaijin* (foreigners) is beginning to be challenged. For example, Japan has liberalized its immigration laws allowing Brazilians of Japanese descent (and their spouses) to migrate to Japan on temporary work visas. Reflecting the cultural diversity of the 254,000 Brazilians in Japan, there are now 41 Brazilian schools, two Brazilian television stations, and four Brazilian weekly newspapers.[9] This more encouraging stance toward guest workers is expected to continue as Japan grapples with its labor shortage.

Another diversity-related issue, women in managerial and leadership positions, is gaining attention. Japanese women who enter the workforce often take positions of "office lady," meaning that they will be labeled as clerical workers with little to no promotability. These individuals often wear uniforms and perform jobs that include photocopying, serving tea, and creating a "pleasant atmosphere" in the office. These women can be high school or college educated, and it is expected that after being married for a few years, they will drop out of the workforce to raise children and provide a suitable home environment for their working spouses.[10]

Better career opportunities are slowly beginning to become available for women in Japan. For example, the percentage of women in management positions has grown in the past 10 years, from 6.0 to 8.9 percent of all managers. This is still disproportionate to the percentage of women in the workforce (40.6 percent).[11]

In 1986, an equal employment law was passed to encourage fair and equitable treatment for women in terms of recruitment, hiring decisions, and promotions. In addition, the law prohibited illegal discrimination against women in new employee training, retirement, and dismissal, and lifted the ban on overtime for women working in "professional positions" such as doctors, engineers, and so on. This law has paved the way for a two-tiered career track system, one for women with traditional aspirations and one for women who want equivalent career opportunities as their male counterparts.[12]

These diversity issues in Japan hold implications for global managers. For example, foreign managers operating out of companies in Japan might be able to attract talented Japanese female managers and employees if they offer more opportunities for equal treatment and career advancement. Also, Japanese expatriate managers will need to make adjustments in their policies and management style when working in subsidiaries located in host countries with diverse cultures. If not, they may place their companies at risk of lawsuits and damage public relations with future employees and customers in the host country. One example of this is the discrimination lawsuits filed against Mitsubishi Motor Manufacturing of America in the United States. In 1998, the automobile manufacturer agreed to a record $34 million deal to settle claims that 350 women were sexually harassed on the factory floor at one of the plants. Also in that same year, the company agreed to pay $3 million to settle the complaints of 87 people who alleged they were not hired because of their disabilities.[13] To combat some of these problems, Mitsubishi asked former U.S. Secretary of Labor Lynn Martin to conduct a third-party review of all the company's workplace policies and procedures, including those related to sexual harassment, discrimination, and diversity.[14]

Thus, the development and implementation of diversity management programs that are appropriate for a given host country can improve relations with the public in general, and employees, customers, and vendors in particular. The goodwill that is created can help a global organization gain and sustain competitive advantage in the markets in which it operates.

EUROPEAN UNION

Historically, the European Union nations have provided generous protection and benefits to pregnant women and parents of infants, but have been less proactive in developing broad-based antidiscrimination legislation. To create a unified effort against workplace discrimination, the European Union is attempting to establish minimum standards. The Directorate-General for Employment and Social Affairs has issued a three-part strategy that forms the basis for future legislative action:[15]

1. Directive implementing equal treatment irrespective of racial and ethnic origin.
2. Directive establishing a framework for equal treatment in employment and occupation (covers discrimination on grounds of religion and belief, disability, age, and sexual orientation).
3. Community Action Program controlling the spending required to support development of new legislation in the member states and acceding countries.

The member states of the European Union will have to modify their existing legislation to make these into national law. In addition to this pan-European legislation, the EU is also taking steps and establishing programs to enhance women's participation in European business.[16] For example, WOMENCRAFT involves 25 women-managed or -owned small and medium-size businesses from all over Europe whose goal is to encourage technological research among member firms. The project is being run by Beta Technology, a center of excellence for innovation, which specializes in technology transfer, technology funding, and consulting. Another project, ProWomEn has been launched by the European Commission to promote women entrepreneurs. This project's main goal is to create a strong network of high-potential individuals from the member countries to discuss and exchange regional policies and actions to promote the creation of start-ups by women. Specific objectives of the ProWomEm project include:

- Build awareness among regional decision makers as to the importance of promoting women entrepreneurs.
- Collect and distribute supporting tools for women entrepreneurs, including case studies and best practice models.
- Set up regional networks for women entrepreneurs that include discussion and initiation of pilot projects.
- Develop ways to change education and training systems to create a culture of entrepreneurship for women, specifically focusing on the development of valuable life skills for women.

UNITED STATES

By 2010, most of the new entrants into the civilian labor force in the United States will be individuals age 55 and older, Asians, Hispanics, blacks, and women.[17] In an attempt to ensure that all individuals have an equal chance for employment without concern for race, color, religion, sex, age, disability, or national origin, the U.S. government passed a series of **equal employment opportunity laws** over the past 40 years. A sample of major U.S. EEO laws and regulations can be found in Table 4.2.

Although some progress has been made, sex discrimination in employment in the United States continues to be a problem. Though accounting for approximately 50 percent of the U.S. workforce, women occupy about 30 percent of all salaried managerial positions, 20 percent of middle-manager positions, and 5 percent of executive jobs. Contributing to this problem is occupational segregation, in which at least 75 percent of workers in an occupation are male or female. Seven of the 10 most common jobs for women

TABLE 4.2

Sample of Equal
Employment
Opportunity Laws
in the United
States

Source: Adapted from
John M. Ivancevich, *Human Resource Management, 8th ed.* (New York:
McGraw-Hill/Irwin,
2001), pp. 73–90.

Name of the Act	Stipulations
Equal Pay Act (1963)	Requires that men and women performing substantially equal work receive equal pay.
Title VII of Civil Rights Act (1964)	Prohibits illegal discrimination based on race, color, religion, sex, or national origin.
Executive Order 11246 (1965)	Requires federal contractors and subcontractors with contracts greater than $10,000 to implement affirmative action in hiring women and minorities.
Age Discrimination in Employment Act (1967)	Prohibits discrimination in employment against individuals 40 years of age and older.
Americans with Disabilities (1990)	Prohibits discrimination against individuals with Act disabilities who can perform the essential functions of a job.

are sex-segregated and are characterized by low pay, low status, and short career ladders: secretaries, cashiers, registered nurses, nursing aides/orderlies/assistants, elementary school teachers, and servers.[18] Laws such as the Civil Rights Act of 1964 and the Equal Pay Act of 1963 were developed to help deal with some of these issues.

To combat the overt and subtle barriers to advancement faced by women in the U.S. workplace, a combination of individual and organizational strategies should be developed. Individual strategies that women can follow to break the **glass ceiling** include:[19]

- Exceed performance expectations on a consistent basis.
- Develop a style with which male managers are comfortable.
- Find difficult or challenging assignments.
- Identify influential mentors.

As a complement to these individual strategies, companies can be proactive in helping employees receive fair and equal treatment. The accompanying Global Focus discusses what some companies are doing to help employees break through the glass ceiling.

Signed by Lyndon B. Johnson in 1965, **Executive Order 11246** created affirmative action as a way to deal with some of the barriers to advancement for minorities. **Affirmative action** is a proactive, intervention-based approach that organizations follow to increase the participation of historically underrepresented groups in the workforce. Though its intent is to achieve fair employment for everyone in the United States, affirmative action has suffered from negative perceptions and poor implementation. Negative perceptions surrounding affirmative action are illustrated by the following statements:[20]

- Affirmative action has created a "spoils system" in which people who have not experienced discrimination are reaping benefits at the direct expense of white males.[21]
- Lower hiring and performance standards have been applied to minorities.[22]
- Minorities have achieved their professional goals and no longer need affirmative action. To illustrate this is not the case, women make about 77 percent of men's earnings, and African-Americans and Hispanics held 11.3 percent and 10.9 percent, respectively, of all managerial and professional jobs in 2001.

Add to these the perception that affirmative action hires are selected on the basis of irrelevant workplace characteristics,[23] and one can conclude that the future of affirmative action is in question. In contrast, the successor of affirmative action, diversity management, has been portrayed as a critical component to the survival of global organizations. Some have argued that a more inclusive approach to embracing diversity is needed to enhance overall U.S. competitiveness vis-à-vis other economic powers.[24]

What Can Companies Do to Break the Glass Ceiling?

Global organizations can take a variety of steps to help their female employees advance within the company. First, place more women on boards of directors; this will signal to lower-level female employees that capable women are recognized and rewarded with the firm. Second, hold senior management accountable for identifying and promoting women into line and general management positions. Third, institute a support program to assist working women; this can include flexible work arrangements and child care vouchers. Fourth, facilitate networking and mentoring relationships with senior successful individuals within the company. Last, understand and appreciate that men and women may take varied approaches to management issues.

Several companies have made strides in creating a friendly work environment for their female and minority employees. Deloitte & Touche is attempting to facilitate advancement of all its employees by using task forces, focus groups, and questionnaires to gather data on problems causing the glass ceiling; creating awareness of how gender attitudes affect the work environment; encouraging accountability through reviews of promotion rates and assignment decisions; and promoting development opportunities for all employees. In 1993, the company established "The Initiative for the Retention and Advancement of Women" to identify and develop female leaders. The programs in the initiative focused on the following concepts:

- Men and women as colleagues.
- Enhanced career opportunities for women.
- Balance between work and personal life.
- Diversity goals built into business planning and HR processes.
- Communication of these changes to all employees.

How successful has this program been? Overall, the initiative has produced some strong results. Currently, about 13 percent of the partners and directors are women (growing at about 30 percent per year), and more than 90 women have key leadership positions. Turnover has decreased 25 percent and the company has been ranked in Fortune's Best 100 Places to Work list for three years. Additionally, it has been ranked on the Working Mother's list and has received Workforce's Optimas award.

Other notable efforts have been made by Corning, American Airlines, and DuPont. At Corning, the CEO and top executives attend a gender training program that is followed up by a three-year program that directs managers to incorporate what they learned into daily working life. The company also sponsors quality improvement teams that focus on issues confronted by blacks and women, and organizes mandatory seminars to reinforce its policies against racial bias and gender discrimination. American Airlines has issued a directive that mandates that all corporate officers submit detailed, cross-functional development plans for all high-potential women in middle-management jobs and above. DuPont uses a rotation process that moves men and women through at least two or three functions before reaching top management positions.

Sources: Douglas M. McCracken, "Winning the Talent War for Women: Sometimes It Takes a Revolution," *Harvard Business Review*, November–December 2000, pp. 159–67; Charlene M. Solomon, "Cracks in the Glass Ceiling," *Workforce* 79, (September 2000), pp. 86–94; and Alison Eyring and Bette Ann Stead, "Shattering the Glass Ceiling: Some Successful Corporate Practices," *Journal of Business Ethics* 17 (February 1998), pp. 245–51.

Diversity Management

Global legislative efforts to deal with discrimination in the workplace are an important step to creating a more inclusive workplace. In addition, organizations have considerable incentive to not only follow the laws that prohibit discrimination, but also to voluntarily design and implement **diversity management** programs that lead to greater inclusion of all types of individuals into informal social networks and formal company programs.[25] Making all types of employees feel included and an important part of the organization can contribute to several positive organizational outcomes. For example, Cox and Blake argue that an organization's ability to attract, retain, and motivate individuals from diverse backgrounds (age, gender, ethnicity, etc.) helps it achieve and sustain competitive advantage in a variety of key areas:[26]

1. Cost savings: In many companies, turnover and absenteeism rates are higher while job satisfaction levels are lower among women and minorities. Diversity management initiatives such as flexible work scheduling, mentoring, and equal access to training and development opportunities will help an organization retain these valuable human resources, especially in times of labor shortages.

2. Resource acquisition: Competitive advantage in human resources can come from hiring and retaining top talent from different demographic groups. Companies are increasingly turning to creative ads that focus on diversity:[27]

    -   Pitney Bowes—"We're interested in Genius . . . not Genes . . . Genius is diverse."
    -   Prudential—"At Prudential, diversity has its rewards."
    -   Morgan Stanley—"Diversity. It's not an obligation—It's an opportunity."
    -   Bristol-Myers Squibb—". . . we believe that diversity is the cornerstone of a high performance organization . . ."

    Diversity recruitment efforts are boosted when a company earns a spot on a public listing such as Fortune's 50 Best Companies for Minorities.[28] In 2002, the large mortgage company Fannie Mae earned the top spot for the first time thanks largely to its many powerful minority executives. Rounding out the top five are Sempra Energy, fast-food company Advantica (Denny's parent and 2001's No. 1 winner), Baby Bell SBC Communications, and McDonald's.

3. Marketing: Having a workforce that is representative of an organization's customers and other stakeholders can add value in a variety of ways. First, global managers who are from the country or region in which operations are located are able to communicate with and understand the needs and preferences of the host-country customers. Possessing the appropriate intercultural communication skills is important for managing culturally diverse relationships with customers.[29] The same holds true for marketing to customers and consumers that are part of a subculture within the same country. Early in the 21st century, African-Americans, Asians, and Hispanics are expected to account for 25 percent of the U.S. consumer base and are projected to have annual spending power of approximately $650 billion.[30] Some organizations are proactively marketing to these subcultures. For example, Avon Corporation made major improvements in its profitability in inner-city markets in the United States by giving its black and Hispanic managers much more authority over these markets. Another example is *People* magazine, which markets its Spanish-language version, *People en español*, to over 400,000 subscribers in the United States. Advertising revenues for the magazine in 2002 were estimated at $24.3 million, or about 25 percent of the $98 million Hispanic magazine advertising market.[31]

4. Creativity and problem solving: Research supports the idea that diverse teams tend to generate ideas and solutions to problems that are more creative and innovative compared to those produced by homogenous teams.[32] Although too much diversity can lead to a decrease in team cohesiveness, companies that foster diversity and openness internally may do better in attracting talented, creative people who can collaborate and produce innovative ideas and solutions.[33] In addition, the global nature of business today increasingly requires people to collaborate in teams that cross cultural and geographic boundaries. These teams are in a unique position to create competitive advantage by forging different ideas, pools of knowledge, and approaches to work.[34]

5. <u>System flexibility</u>: A successfully managed diversity program enhances organizational flexibility, or the ability to react to changes in the environment faster and at less cost. Women tend to have a higher tolerance for ambiguity than men, which has been linked to their ability to excel in performing complex and ambiguous tasks.[35] In addition, research on bilingual versus monolingual subcultures from several countries indicates that bilingual individuals have higher levels of divergent thinking and cognitive flexibility.[36] In countries such as Canada, the hiring and inclusion of bilingual (French and English) employees in organizations will provide openness and adaptability, both important characteristics for global organizations that are fighting for success and competitive advantage.

MONOLITHIC, PLURAL, AND MULTICULTURAL ORGANIZATIONS

Cox classified organizations based on the extent of their diversity initiative implementation.[37] **Monolithic organizations** are in the early stages of developing a diversity management orientation. Women and ethnic minority men tend to be segregated into low-status jobs, reflecting a low degree of integration and inclusiveness into the organizational structure. Ethnocentrism leads to little to no adoption of minority-culture norms by majority group members. An example of this would be Honda Motors in Japan in which most of the manager and higher-status positions are occupied by members of the majority, Japanese men. The women and Brazilian employees (of Japanese heritage) are not treated with the same respect as the Japanese male employees.

Some of the potential problems associated with this unequal treatment is that monolithic organizations lose out on reaping the benefits of high-performing minority employees who are blocked from higher-level positions within the organization. Because of blocked career paths, many of these companies will end up with higher costs due to employee turnover, and subsequent replacement and training expenditures. Research has shown that Japanese companies that utilize only Japanese expatriates in high-level positions in overseas subsidiaries tend to experience more international human resource management problems than do U.S. and European firms.[38]

Compared with the monolithic organization, the **plural organization** has a more heterogeneous membership and will take steps to be more inclusive of persons who are different from the majority group. Such steps can include giving preference to minority-culture groups in hiring and promotion decisions, as well as training all managers and supervisors on equal employment opportunity issues. These initiatives create organizations characterized by the integration of minorities into informal networks and reductions in discrimination and prejudicial attitudes. However, similar to the monolithic organization, plural organizations expect minority members to assimilate and adjust to the majority culture and behavioral norms. Thus, some of the same problems (albeit less severe) that can impact monolithic organizations can be found in plural organizations.

Multicultural organizations not only contain different cultural groups but also value the diversity that these groups bring to the table. Full integration is achieved in terms of including minorities in informal networks. Discrimination is minimized in employment decisions, and the diversity is used to gain competitive advantage in the marketplace. Steps that organizations can take to become more inclusive and accepting of diverse groups while simultaneously creating a motivated workforce include:[39]

- Training and orientation programs. Organizations can build employee awareness of diversity issues and provide the necessary skills to work effectively with diverse stakeholders. McDonnell Douglas has a program titled "Woman-wise and Business Savvy" that focuses on gender differences in work-related behaviors.
- Language training. For companies that hire individuals whose native tongue is different from that of the headquarters' language, language training is critical to ensure good communications. Motorola provides English as a second language classes at company expense on company time.

- Mentoring and access to senior management. Global organizations are encouraging diverse employees to seek out mentors who can help guide them regarding the organization's politics and unspoken rules. Also, some firms are establishing minority advisory groups that have direct access to high-level executives. At Equitable Life Assurance, groups of blacks, women, and Hispanics meet with the CEO to make suggestions on how to improve the organizational climate.

DIVERSITY IN MULTICULTURAL AND VIRTUAL TEAMS

In contrast to homogenous teams in which members are very similar in terms of cultural background, heterogeneous teams are those in which members hail from different cultures.[40] An example of a homogenous team would be when a group of five Chinese managers moves from Shanghai to Tokyo to launch a new joint venture with their Japanese partner. In contrast, members of the MERCOSUR free trade area make up a heterogeneous team in that they represent such diverse cultural backgrounds as Argentina, Brazil, Paraguay, and Uruguay.[41] In today's Internet-based environment, many teams operate in a virtual manner, whereby members are dispersed across different geographical and cultural boundaries. The advantages and disadvantages of multicultural teams are discussed in the accompanying Global Focus.

Special care needs to be taken when managing virtual teams whose members are from countries with distinct cultures and languages. Such team members can find communication and building trust more challenging.[42] Cultural nuances that might be detected in face-to-face meetings may go unnoticed during a teleconference or Webcast. As a result, virtual team members may experience misunderstandings and miscommunications while working on important projects. To decrease the risk of such problems, team members should be brought together for face-to-face meetings and cross-cultural training sessions in the early stages of the team process.

As companies such as GE, AT&T, Pfizer, Motorola, Shell Oil, and Sun Microsystems continue to experiment with and use virtual teams across their global businesses, such practices will become more common in organizations of all types and sizes.[43]

When working with culturally diverse teams, some steps can be taken to improve their effectiveness. One researcher has made the following suggestions:[44]

1. Use task-related selection. The primary selection criteria for team selection should be their task-related abilities and track record.
2. Recognize differences. Teams and team leaders should not ignore or minimize differences, but rather should accept team members' unique insights and contributions to the group.
3. Establish a vision or subordinate goal. To help team members overcome individual differences, direct their energies and attention to achieving important goals that benefit the entire group.
4. Create mutual respect. This can be done by selecting team members of similar ability, making prior accomplishments and task-related skills known to all team members, and minimizing the use of stereotypes and ethnocentrism.
5. Give feedback. Since heterogeneous teams can take longer in reaching agreements, managers should provide the team with feedback regarding the team's process and productivity. Also, suggestions for improvement and team-building training should be offered to enhance team functioning.

CREATING A SUCCESSFUL CLIMATE FOR DIVERSITY

A global organization can control several factors to bring about positive outcomes from diversity initiatives. These factors include CEO leadership and support as well as modification of accountability, development, and recruitment practices.[45]

Advantages and Disadvantages of Multicultural Teams

MAJOR ADVANTAGES

1. *More creativity.* Cultural diversity among team members can lead to increased creativity due to a wider range of ideas and perspectives, and less influence of groupthink.

2. *Increased quality of output.* Diverse ideas and perspectives can lead to better problem identification, more alternatives, and better decision making.

3. *Enhanced exploration of problems.* As multicultural team members discuss their unique points of view, others are forced to concentrate more on the issues at hand in order to defend their positions. This enhanced concentration can lead to more thorough problem solving.

MAJOR DISADVANTAGES

1. *Lack of trust between team members.* This can be caused by lower interpersonal attractiveness, inaccurate stereotyping, and less cross-cultural conversation.

2. *Miscommunication.* Less accurate and slower speech, coupled with translation difficulties, can lead to misunderstandings among diverse team members.

3. *Lack of cohesion.* Problems with trust and miscommunication can lead to a lack of cohesion among team members. When teams suffer from low cohesion, this can lead to the inability to validate ideas, agree when necessary, and take action when appropriate.

Source: Adapted from Nancy J. Adler, *International Dimensions of Organizational Behavior,* 4th ed. (Cincinnati: South-Western, 2002), p. 143.

CEO Leadership and Ongoing Support

CEOs have the power to instill in the organizational culture that valuing differences makes sense both from a perspective of justice and improving the bottom line. At Xerox, CEOs have consistently viewed diversity management in terms of social responsibility and sound business practice. The company was one of the first to use caucus groups (discussion and advocacy groups representing ethnicity, sexual orientation, gender, and race) to advance the interests of minority employees through direct dialogue with top management.[46]

Accountability, Development, and Recruitment Practices

Ann Morrison conducted a large-scale study of diversity practices used by 16 organizations that had successful diversity management programs.[47] The results indicated three sets of practices contribute to successful diversity management: accountability, development, and recruitment practices.

- *Accountability practices* refer to managers' responsibility to treat diverse employees in a fair manner. Morrison's research found the most important practices to be top management's personal intervention, internal advocacy groups, emphasis on equal employment opportunity statistics, inclusion of diversity in performance evaluation goals and ratings, and inclusion of diversity in promotion decisions.

- *Development practices* focus on preparing diverse employees for greater responsibility and advancement. Key practices include diversity training programs, networks and support groups, development programs for all high-potential managers, informal networking activities, and job rotation.

- *Recruitment activities* attempt to attract job applicants from all levels and groups who are willing to work hard and seek challenging assignments. The study reported these best practices: targeted recruitment of nonmanagers; key outside hires; extensive public exposure on diversity (affirmative action); corporate image as liberal, progressive, or benevolent; and partnerships with educational institutions.

IMPLICATIONS FOR GLOBAL AND TRANSNATIONAL ORGANIZATIONS

As globalization continues, organizations will continue to expand into new international markets. This expansion will bring the organizations into more direct contact with diverse sets of host-country employees and alliance partners, customers, suppliers, government officials, and union representatives. These individuals will be characterized by a variety of ages, religions, ethnicities, languages, and skin colors. To establish and maintain productive relationships with these stakeholders, global and transnational managers will need to have empathy and develop a thorough understanding of how to relate to these individuals.

In addition, many organizations are shifting to a team-based work environment. Driven by the need to enhance quality and promote innovation, organizations are helping diverse teams understand and accept one another in the name of higher productivity and group cohesion. For example, the employees at Corning Glass are organized into approximately 3,000 teams; the goal is to achieve higher quality through cooperation and team member involvement and commitment.[48]

Globalization and the movement toward team-based work are occurring in the midst of changing labor markets.[49] As discussed earlier, Japan, the European Union, and the United States as well as other countries and regions of the world are experiencing increases in the amount of gender, ethnic, and age diversity in their workforces. Combine this with the projected labor shortages that are occurring in many countries, and we can expect that organizations that successfully integrate valuing diversity into their organizational cultures will be an employer of choice for many new entrants into the workforce for years to come. Because the majority of the new entrants in the United States, for example, will be women, Hispanics, and blacks, then the organizations that value diversity will be in the best position to attract and retain these valuable employees.

Key Terms and Concepts

affirmative action, *81*

Confucianism, *76*

diversity, *77*

diversity management, *82*

EEO laws, *80*

Executive Order 11246, *81*

glass ceiling, *81*

monolithic organization, *84*

multicultural organization, *84*

plural organization, *84*

Critical Thinking and Discussion Questions

1. Assume you are working on a virtual team and teammates are from countries with very diverse cultural heritages. What are some diversity-related issues your team will need to confront to function effectively? What language will the team communicate in? To what extent will written e-mails and communications be used?

2. What are some of the influences affecting the labor force in Japan? How is it changing? Be sure to include in your answer information about women and ethnic minorities.

3. In your opinion, which of the equal employment opportunity laws in the United States has had the most impact on creating a more diverse workforce? Explain.

4. Should labor shortages in countries such as the United States, Germany, and Japan influence immigration policy? Explain.

5. What is the glass ceiling and how can it be broken by individuals and organizations?

6. This chapter has argued that successful diversity management is a source of competitive advantage for global and transnational organizations. Provide two examples of how a company such as Nestlé or Fiat can use diversity to their advantage.

7. Provide two advantages and two disadvantages of using multicultural teams. How can the disadvantages be mitigated or decreased?

8. Why do you think there are still barriers to advancement for many women, minorities, and the disabled? Explain.

9. Beyond the cost savings that can be realized due to lower absenteeism and turnover rates, identify and describe three additional benefits associated with making all types of individuals feel included and valued in a global organization.

10. Think about the organizations (companies, federal and state agencies, schools, etc.) with which you have had contact. Identify the one that appeared to be the most diverse in terms of gender, race, ethnicity, and so on. Then, identify the organization that seemed to be the least diverse. Can you think of any reasons to explain the differences?

Notes

1. Howard N. Fullerton, Jr., and Mitra Toossi, "Labor Force Projections to 2010: Steady Growth and Changing Composition," *Bureau of Labor Statistics Monthly Labor Review*, (November 2001), pp. 1–4.

2. Mitra Toossi, "A Century of Change: The U.S. Labor Force, 1950–2050," *Bureau of Labor Statistics Monthly Labor Review*, (May 2002), pp. 15–28.

3. Rene Mallari, "Toughing It Out," *Asian Business* 38 (March 2002), pp. 30–31.

4. Lynette Clemetson, "Hispanics Now Largest Minority, Census Shows," *New York Times*, (January 22, 2003), p. A1.

5. CIA World Factbook found on the Web at www.ciafact book.com.

6. James L. Gibson, James H. Donnelly, Jr., John M. Ivancevich, and Robert Konopaske, *Organizations: Behavior, Structure, Processes*, 11th ed. (New York: McGraw-Hill/Irwin, 2003), p. 47.

7. Mark A. Williams, Mark W. Williams, and Donald O. Clifton, *The 10 Lenses: Your Guide to Living and Working in a Multicultural World* (New York: Capital Books, 2001).

8. John C. Condon, *With Respect to the Japanese: A Guide for Americans* (Yarmouth, ME: Intercultural Press, 1984).

9. James Brooke, "Sons and Daughters of Japan, Back from Brazil," *New York Times,* (November 27, 2001), p. A4.

10. John P. Fernandez and Mary Barr, *The Diversity Advantage: How American Business Can Out-Perform Japanese and European Companies in the Global Marketplace* (New York: Lexington, 1993).

11. Jean R. Renshaw, "Kimono in the Boardroom: The Invisible Evolution of Japanese Women Managers," (New York and Oxford: Oxford University Press, 1999).

12. Fernandez and Barr, *Diversity Advantage*.

13. Christopher Thorne, "Black Workers Sue Mitsubishi," *ABC News Corporation* (www.abcnews.com), (February 20, 2003); Jean P. Kamp, Steven J. Levine, and Reginald Welch, "EEOC Scores Major Victory in Mitsubishi Lawsuit," *The U.S. Equal Employment Opportunity Commission* (www.eeoc.gov/press/1-21-98.html), (January 21, 1998).

14. Jennifer J. Laabs, "Lynn Martin to Review Mitsubishi's Policies in Wake of Sexual-Harassment Charges," *Personnel Journal* 75, (July 1996), pp. 12–15.

15. Board Europe, "Embracing Diversity," (www.conference-board.org/publications/ boardeurope/diversity.cfm), November–December 2002.

16. Sarah Clothier, "Cracking the Glass Ceiling in Europe," *The British Journal of Administrative Management* 24, (March/April 2001), pp. 21–32.

17. Fullerton and Toossi, "Labor Force Projections."

18. Myrtle P. Bell, Mary E. McLaughlin, and Jennifer M. Sequeira, "Discrimination, Harassment, and the Glass Ceiling: Women Executives as Change Agents," *Journal of Business Ethics* 37 (2002), pp. 65–76; C.E. Bose and R.B. Whaley, "Sex Segregation in the U.S. Labor Force," in *Gender Mosaics: Social Perspectives* ed. D. Vannoy (Los Angeles: Roxbury Publishing, 2001), pp. 228–48; B. Reskin, "Sex Segregation in the Workforce," in *Workplace/Women's Place*, ed. D. Dunn (Los Angeles: Roxbury Publishing, 1997), pp. 69–73; and E.A. Fagenson and J.J. Jackson, "The Status of Women Managers in the United States," *International Studies of Management and Organizations* 23 (1993), pp. 93–112.

19. B.R. Ragins, B. Townsend, and M. Mattis, "Gender Gap in the Executive Suite: CEOs and Female Executives Report on Breaking the Glass Ceiling," *The Academy of Management Executive*, (1998), pp. 28–42.

20. Jacqueline A. Gilbert, Bette Ann Stead, and John M. Ivancevich, "Diversity Management: A New Organizational Paradigm," *Journal of Business Ethics* 21 (1999), pp. 61–76.

21. R.K. Robinson, "Affirmative Action Plans in the 1990s: A Double-Edged Sword?" *Public Personnel Management* 21 (1992), pp. 261–72.

22. L.W. Wynter, "Diversity Is All Talk, No Affirmative Action," *The Wall Street Journal,* (December 21, 1994), p. B1.

23. M.E. Heilman, M.C. Simon, and D.P. Repper, "Intentionally Favored, Unintentionally Harmed? The Impact of Sex Based Preferential Selection on Self-Perceptions and Self-Evaluations," *Journal of Applied Psychology* 72 (1987), pp. 62–68.

24. Fernandez and Barr, *Diversity Advantage*.

25. Gilbert et al., "Diversity Management."

26. Taylor H. Cox and Stacy Blake, "Managing Cultural Diversity: Implications for Organizational Competitiveness," *The Academy of Management Executive* 5 (August 1991), pp. 45–57.

27. Ruth E. Thaler-Carter, "Diversify Your Recruitment Advertising," *HRMagazine* 46 (June 2001), pp. 92–100.

28. Fortune Magazine's 50 Best Companies for Minorities (www.fortune.com), July 8, 2002.

29. Victoria D. Bush, Gregory M. Rose, Faye Gilbert, and Thomas N. Ingram, "Managing Culturally Diverse Buyer-Seller Relationships: The Role of Intercultural Disposition and Adaptive Selling in Developing Intercultural Communication Competence," *Academy of Marketing Science Journal* 29, (Fall 2001), pp. 391–404.

30. Gilbert et al., "Diversity Management."

31. Christina Hoag, "People Leads Stack in Market for Hispanic Magazine Ads," Wilmington, North Carolina, *Star-News,* (February 23, 2003), p. E1.

32. William B. Johnston, "Global Work Force 2000: The New World Labor Market," In *Differences That Work: Organizational Excellence Through Diversity*, ed. Mary C. Gentile, (Cambridge, MA: Harvard Business Review, 1994).

33. Richard Florida, Robert Cushing, and Gary Gates, "When Social Capital Stifles Innovation," *Harvard Business Review* 80 (August 2002), pp. 20–26.

34. Martha L. Maznevski and Joseph J. DiStefano, "Global Leaders Are Team Players: Developing Global Leaders through Membership on Global Teams," *Human Resource Management* 39 (Summer/Fall 2000), pp. 195–208.

35. Naomi G. Rotter and Agnes N. O'Connell, "The Relationships Among Sex-Role Orientation, Cognitive Complexity, and Tolerance for Ambiguity," *Sex Roles* 8 (1982), pp. 1209–20.

36. Wallace Lambert, "The Effects of Bilingualism on the Individual: Cognitive and Sociocultural Consequences," in *Bilingualism: Psychological, Social, and Educational Implications*, ed. Peter A. Hurnbey, (New York: Academic Press, 1977), pp. 15–27.

37. Taylor Cox, Jr., "The Multicultural Organization," *The Academy of Management Executive* 5 (May 1991), pp. 34–48.

38. Kopp Rochelle, "International Human Resource Policies and Practices in Japanese, European, and United States Multinationals," *Human Resource Management* 33 (1994), pp. 581–99.

39. Cox, "Multicultural Organization."

40. R.C. Ziller, "Homogeneity and Heterogeneity of Group Membership," in *Experimental Social Psychology*, ed. C.G. McClintock (New York: Holt, Rinehart and Winston, 1972), pp. 385–411.

41. Charles W.L. Hill, *International Business: Competing in the Global Marketplace*, 4th ed. (New York: McGraw-Hill/Irwin, 2003) p. 259.

42. Richard Benson-Armer and Tsun-yan Hsieh, "Teamwork Across Time and Space," *The McKinsey Quarterly,* (November 4, 1997), pp. 18–27, Julekha Dash, "Think of People When Planning Virtual Teams," *Computerworld,* (February 2001), pp. 34–36.

43. Dash, "Think of People When Planning Virtual Teams."

44. Nancy J. Adler, *International Dimensions of Organizational Behavior,* 4th ed. (Cincinnati: South-Western, 2002), p. 74.

45. Ann M. Morrison, *The New Leaders: Guidelines on Leadership Diversity in America* (San Francisco: Jossey-Bass, 1992).

46. Gilbert et al., "Diversity Management."

47. Morrison, *New Leaders.*

48. B. Duhaime, "Who Needs a Boss?" *Fortune,* May 7, 1990, pp. 52–60.

49. Susan E. Jackson and Associates, *Diversity in the Workplace: Human Resource Initiatives* (New York: Guilford Press, 1992), p. 19.

Surviving in a Multicultural World

5

LEARNING OBJECTIVES [TO COME]

After completing this chapter, you should be able to:

LO¹ Understand how to survive and manage in a multicultural world

LO² Able to cope and manage organization with cultural differences

LO³ Deal with global changes taking place in intercultural settings

Introduction

Everybody looks at the world from behind the windows of a cultural home, and everybody prefers to act as if people from other countries have something special about them (a national character) but home is normal. Unfortunately there is no normal position in cultural matters. This is an uncomfortable message, as uncomfortable as Galileo Galilei's claim in the seventeenth century that the Earth is not the center of the universe.

Culture has been described through the metaphor of *mental software*—a usually unconscious conditioning that leaves individual considerable freedom to think, feel , and act but within the constraints of what his or her social environment offers in terms of possible thoughts, feelings, and actions. These constraints are present in all spheres of life, and in order to understand them, human life should be seen as an integrated whole.

Cultural programming starts in the environment in which a young child grows up—usually a family of some kind. It continues at school, and what happens in schools can only be understood if one knows what happens before and after school. It continues at work. Workers' behavior is an extension of behavior acquired at school and in the family. Managers' behavior is an extension of the managers' school and family experiences as well as a mirror image of the behavior of the managed. Politics and the relationships between citizens and authorities are extensions of relationships in the family, at school, and at work, and in their turn they affect these other spheres of life. Religious beliefs, secular ideologies, and scientific theories are extensions of mental software demonstrated in the family at school, at work, and in government relations, and they reinforce the dominant patterns of thinking, feeling, and acting in the other spheres.

Cultural programs differ from one group or category of people to another in ways that are rarely acknowledged and often misunderstood. The cultural category to which most of the book has been devoted is the nation-state; some attention has been given to differences according to social class, gender, generation, work organization, and occupation. Every nation has a considerable moral investment in its own dominant mental software, which explains the common hesitation to make cultural differences discussable. The origins of the differences from one nation to another and sometimes between ethnic, religious, or linguistic subgroups within nations, are hidden in history. In some cases causal explanations are possible; in many other cases one should assume that a small difference arose many centuries ago, and that in being transferred from generation to generation, this small difference grew into the large difference it is today.

The main cultural differences between nations lie in values. Systematic differences exist with regard to values about power and inequality, with regard to the relationship between the individual and the group, with regard to the emotional and social roles expected from men or women, with respect to ways of dealing with uncertainties in life, and with respect to whether one is mainly preoccupied with the future or with the past and present.

The Moral Issue

Some people wonder whether the advocated consciousness of the limits of one's own value system does not lead to moral laxity. A call for *cultural relativism*: the recognition that, as a famous French anthropologist expressed it, "one culture has no absolute criteria for judging the activities of another culture as 'low' or 'noble.'" But this is no call for dropping values together. As a matter of fact, this entire book shows that no human being can escape from using value standards all the time. Successful intercultural encounters presuppose that the partners believe in their own values. If not, they have become alienated persons, lacking a sense of identity. A sense of identity provides the feeling of security from which one can encounter other cultures with an open mind.

The principle of surviving in a multicultural world is that one does not need to think, feel, and act in the same way in order to agree on practical issues and to cooperate. For example, the value differences among employees in different countries working for IBM have been shown to be quite considerable. Nevertheless, IBM employees the world over have cooperated in reasonable harmony toward practical goals. There is nothing unique about IBM employees in this respect; other people can and do cooperate across national borders, too. The fact that organizational cultures are relatively superficial and value-free phenomena, is precisely the reason why international organizations can exist and be composed of different nationals, each with its own different national values.

People from cultures very dissimilar on the national culture dimensions of power distance, individualism, masculinity, uncertainty avoidance, and long-term orientation can cooperate fruitfully. Yet people from some cultures will cooperate more easily than others with foreigners. The most problematic are nations and groups within nations that score very high on uncertainty avoidance and thus feel that what is different is dangerous. Also problematic is the cooperation with nations and groups scoring very high on power distance, because such cooperation depends on the whims of powerful individuals. In a work kept together by intercultural cooperation, such cultural groups will certainly not be forerunners. They may have to be left alone for some time until they discover they have no other choice but to join.

Cultural Convergence and Divergence

Research about the development of cultural values has shown repeatedly that there is little evidence of international convergence over time, except an increase of individualism for countries having become wealthier. Value differences between nations described by authors centuries ago are still present today, in spite of continued close contacts. For the next few hundred years at least, countries will remain culturally diverse.

Not only will cultural diversity between countries remain with us, but it even looks like differences within countries are increasing. Ethnic groups arrive at a new consciousness of their identity as ask for a political recognition of this fact. Of course, these ethnic differences have always been there. What has changed is the intensity of contact between groups, which has confirmed group members in their own identities. Also, the spread of information (by international media) on how people live elsewhere in the world ahs affected minorities, who compare their situation to the lives of others whom they suppose to be better off. World news media also spread information of suffering and strife much wider than ever before. Pogroms, uprisings, and violent repression are no new inventions, but in the past relatively few people beyond those directly involved would know about them; now they are visible on TV screens around the world. This has the effect of increasing anxiety, particularly in uncertainty avoiding cultures.

Educating for Intercultural Understanding: Suggestions for Parents

In this and the three following sections, some of the conclusions will be translated into practical advice. Such advice is unavoidable subjective, for which we beg the reader's tolerance.

The basic skill for surviving in a multicultural works, as this book has argued, is understanding first one's own cultural values (and that is why one needs a cultural identity of one's own) and next the cultural values of the others with whom one has to cooperate. As parents, we have more influence on creating multicultural understanding in future world citizens than in any other role. Values are mainly acquired during the first ten years of a child's life. They are absorbed by observation and imitation of adults and older children rather than by indoctrination. The way parents live their own culture provides the child with his or her cultural identity. The way parents talk about and behave toward persons and groups from other cultures determines the degree to which the child's mind will be opened or closed for cross-cultural understanding.

Growing up in a bicultural environment (for example, having parents from different nationalities, living abroad during childhood, or going to a foreign school) can be an asset to a child. Whether such biculturality really is an asset or instead becomes a liability depends on the parents' ability to cope with the bicultural situation themselves. Having foreign friends, hearing different languages spoken, traveling with parents who awake the children's interests in things foreign are definite assets. Learning at least one other language—whatever other language—is a unique ingredient of education for multicultural understanding. This supposes, of course, that the teaching of the other language is effective: a lot of language classes in schools are a waste of time. The stress should be on full immersion whereby suing the foreign language becomes indispensable for practical purposes. Becoming really bi- or multilingual is one of the advantages of children belonging to a minority or to a small nation. It is more difficult for those belonging to a big nation.

Coping with Cultural Difference: Suggestions for Managers

There are many ways in which cultural values affect the practices and theories of organizations. Culturally a manager is the follower of his or her followers: she or he has to meet the subordinates on these subordinates' cultural ground. There is some free choice in managerial behavior, but the cultural constraints are much tighter than most of the management literature admits.

The work situation is basically a highly suitable laboratory for intercultural cooperation, as the problems are practical and results are visible to everybody. Yet managers, workers, and worker representatives are rarely in the front ranks for promoting intercultural understanding. Narrow economic interest viewpoints tend to prevail on all sides. An exception is maybe the increasing use of expatriate manager training. When managers are sent abroad, their organizations more and more offer opportunities for some cross-cultural training or briefing. Managers chronically underestimate cultural factors in the case of mergers and acquisitions.

Experiments with intercultural diversity in the workplace are easier to start in public than in private organizations, as the former by definition have greater responsibility to society. They are also easier in service organizations than in manufacturing, especially in those service organizations having a culturally diverse clientele. The ideal organization from an intercultural point of view, in our opinion, is one in which members can fully use their skills, even those deriving from their cultural identity—be these artistic, social, linguistic, temperamental, or other.

Spreading Multicultural Understanding: Suggestions for the Media

Media people—journalists, reporters, and radio and TV producers—play a uniquely important role in creating multicultural understanding, or misunderstanding. The battle for survival in a multicultural world will to a large extent be fought in the media. Media people are human: they have cultural values of their own. With regard to other cultures, their position is ambiguous. On the one hand, they cater to a public and their success depends on the extent to which they write or speak what the public wants to read or hear. On the other hand, they are in a position to direct people's attention—to create an image of reality that to many people becomes reality itself. A member of the public has to be pretty sophisticated to critically scrutinize the beliefs about other cultures reflected in television shows, radio programs, and newspapers.

The consciousness that people in other parts of one's society, and people in other societies, think, feel, and act on the basis of other but not necessarily evil value assumptions may or may not be recognized by media people and reflected in their productions. Simple information of the public can avoid big misunderstandings. There undoubtedly exist reporters who only want simple black-and-white messages or even have a vested interest in showing who are the good guys and who are the bad ones. For those with a greater sense of responsibility, there still is a big untapped potential for spreading understanding about differences in cultural values and practices. For example, using the television eye to compare similar aspects of daily behavior in different countries can be extremely powerful and is still too seldom done.

A problem particular to small countries like our own, the Netherlands, is that both TV and newspapers buy materials from larger countries with out stressing the different cultural contexts in which these materials were produced. An example is newspaper articles reporting on survey research about rends in society. The material used is most frequently from the United States, and the implicit assumption of the editor responsible is that the conclusions are valid for the Netherlands as well. If one realizes the large distance between the two societies on the masculinity-feminity dimension, which affects many societal phenomena, Dutch readers should at least be cautioned when interpreting U.S. data. The funny thing is that no Dutch journalist would dream of producing Japanese or German statistics with the tacit assumption that these apply in the Netherlands.

🌐 Global Challenges Call for Intercultural Cooperation

The word *surviving* in the title of this chapter is no exaggeration. Humankind today is threatened by a number of disasters that have all been manmade: they are disasters of culture rather than the disasters of nature to which our ancestors were regularly exposed.

Their common cause is that man has become both too numerous and too clever for the limited size of our globe. But while we are clever about technology and getting more so each day, we are still naïve about ourselves. Our mental software is not adapted to the environment we created in recent centuries. The only way toward survival is getting to understand ourselves better as social beings, so that we may control our technological cleverness and not use it in destructive ways. This demands concerted action on issues for which, unfortunately, different cultural values make people disagree rather than agree.

A number of value-laden world problems have been signaled in this book. There are the economic problems: international economic cooperation versus competition and the distribution of wealth and poverty across and within countries. There are the technology-induced problems. In the past, whenever a new technology had been invented, it could also be applied. This is no longer the case, and decisions have to be made whether some of the things humans can make should be made and, if so, subject to which precautions. Such decisions should be agreed upon on a world scale, and if countries, groups, or persons do not respect the decisions or the precautions, they should be forced to do so. Examples are certain uses of nuclear energy both for peaceful and aggressive purposes, certain chemical processes and products, certain applications of informatics and certain applications of genetic manipulation. An example of the latter is influencing whether a baby to be born will be a boy or girl. In some cultures the desirability of having boys over girls is very strong. In view of both ethical and demographic considerations, should this technology be allowed to spread? If so, where and under what conditions, and if not, can one stop it?

The combination of world population growth, economic development, and technological developments affects the world ecosystem in ways that are only very partly known. Uncontrolled tree cutting in many parts of the world destroys forests; acid rain threatens other forests. The problem of the reduction of the ozone layer is known, but its seriousness is not. Long-term climate changes resulting from the greenhouse effect of increase emission of CO_2 and other gases are evident; they have a built-in delay of decades, so that even if we were to stop emitting now, the greenhouse effect will increase for a long time. Coping with these problems requires worldwide research and political decision making in areas in which both perceived national interest and cultural values are in conflict. Decisions about sacrifices made today for benefits to be reaped by the next generation have to be made by politicians whose main concern is with being reelected next year or surviving a power struggle tomorrow. In addition, the sacrifices may lie in other parts of the world than the main benefactors. The greenhouse effect can be reduced if the tropical countries preserve their rain forests. These countries are mainly poor, and their governments want the revenue of selling their hardwoods. Can they be compensated for leaving intact what remains of their rain forests?

The trends depicted are threats to humankind as a whole. They represent the common enemy of the future. A common enemy has always been the most effective way of making leaders and groups with conflicting values and interest cooperate. Maybe these threats will become so imminent as to force us to achieve a global intercultural cooperation that has never existed.

Much will depend on the acquisition of intercultural cooperation skills as part of the mental software of politicians. Former U.S. diplomat Glen Fisher in his book *Mindsets* has written about the relationship between economics, culture, and politics:

> An interdisciplinary approach to international economic processes hardly exists. Most important, routine applications of conventional economic analysis cannot tolerate "irrational" behavior. But, from a cross-national and cross-cultural perspective, there is a real question as to what is rational and what irrational; both are very relative terms and very much culture bound; one person's irrationality might turn out to be another's orderly and predictable behavior….Despite the frequent assertion that sentimentality and pursuit of economic interest don't mix, economic systems are in fact ethical systems. Whether by law and regulation or by custom, some economic activities are sanctioned while others are not. And what is sanctioned differs from culture to culture.

Both what is "rational" and what is "ethical" depend on cultural value positions. In politics value positions are further confounded by perceived interests. There is a strong tendency international politics to use different ethical standards toward other countries than toward one's own.

A case study that should encourage modesty about ethics in politics is the international drug trade. Western countries for decades have been involved in a virtual war to prevent the importation of drugs. Not so long ago, from 1839 to 1842, a Western country (Britain) fought an opium war with Imperial China. The Chinese emperor took the position Western governments are taking now, trying to keep drugs out of his country. The British, however, had strong economic interests in a Chinese market for the opium they imported from India, and through an active sales promotion they got large numbers of Chinese addicted. The British won the war, and in the peace treaty they not only got the right to continue importing opium but they also acquire Hong Kong Island as a permanent foothold on the Chinese coast. The return of Honk Kong to China in 1997 in a way was a belated victory of the Chinese in their war against drugs.

From a values point of view it is difficult to defend the position that the trade in arms is less unethical than the trade in drugs. One difference is that in the drugs traffic the poor countries tend to be the sellers, in the arms traffic the rich countries. The latter have made more money on selling arms the Third World countries than they spent on development assistance to these countries. Of course, in this case the buyers and the sellers are both to blame, but the rich countries are in a better position to break the vicious circle.

Reducing the trade in arms would reduce civil wars, terrorism, and murder. It would improve the chances of respect for human rights in the world, as these arms are often used to crush human rights. While it is unrealistic to expect all countries of the world to become Western-style democracies, a more feasible goal is to strive for more respect fro human rights even in autocratically led states.

The Universal Declaration of Human Rights adopted in 1948 is based on universalist, individualist Western values that clearly are not shared by the political leaders nor by the populations of all other parts of the world. On the other hand, the Declaration is a fact, and international organizations as well as individuals will undoubtedly continue to signal infringements, regardless of the country in which these take place. No government is powerful enough to silence, for example, Amnesty International. All but the most ruthless governments try to maintain an appearance of international respectability. The fact that the world has become one scene leads to the public being informed about more suffering than ever before, but it also offers more opportunities to act against this suffering.

On the global scene, many of us see the same plays in terms of world news, sports events, and marketing messages. But we do not get together to discuss the play. If we inhabit a global village, it only consists of a theater and a marketplace. We need houses, sanctuaries, and other places to meet and talk in out global village.

In London in the fall of 2003, Ger Jan sat in a pub with four students from four continents. An Indian and a man from Ghana were arguing whether and how they could help their respective countries. The Indian pressed the other to admit that if he could only spare one pound a day for education children in his home country, that would make a difference. But the Ghanaian said that giving money only made things worse and that, for the time being, educating himself was the only thing he could do. They got pretty heated and did not agree, but they did listen to one another, and they left as friends. In the global village we need many more pubs like that one.

Globalization

6

LEARNING OBJECTIVES

After completing this chapter, you should be able to:

 LO¹ Understand what is meant by the term *globalization*.

 LO² Be familiar with the main drivers of globalization.

LO³ Appreciate the changing nature of the global economy.

 LO⁴ Understand the main arguments in the debate over the impact of globalization.

LO⁵ Appreciate how the process of globalization is creating opportunities and challenges for business managers.

Introduction

Over the last three decades a fundamental shift has been occurring in the world economy. We have been moving away from a world in which national economies were relatively self-contained entities, isolated from each other by barriers to cross-border trade and investment; by distance, time zones, and language; and by national differences in government regulation, culture, and business systems. And we are moving toward a world in which barriers to cross-border trade and investment are declining; perceived distance is shrinking due to advances in transportation and telecommunications technology; material culture is starting to look similar the world over; and national economies are merging into an interdependent, integrated global economic system. The process by which this is occurring is commonly referred to as *globalization*.

In today's interdependent global economy, an American might drive to work in a car designed in Germany that was assembled in Mexico by Ford from components made in the United States and Japan that were fabricated from Korean steel and Malaysian rubber. She may have filled the car with gasoline at a BP service station owned by a British multinational company. The gasoline could have been made from oil pumped out of a well off the coast of Africa by a French oil company that transported it to the United States in a ship owned by a Greek shipping line. While driving to work, the American might talk to her stockbroker on a Nokia cell phone that was designed in Finland and assembled in Texas using chip sets produced in Taiwan that were designed by Indian engineers working for Texas Instruments. She could tell the stockbroker to purchase shares in Deutsche Telekom, a German telecommunications firm that was transformed from a former state-owned monopoly into a global company by an energetic Israeli CEO. She may turn on the car radio, which was made in Malaysia by a Japanese firm, to hear a popular hip-hop song composed by a Swede and sung by a group of Danes in English who signed a record contract with a French music company to promote their record in America. The driver might pull into a drive-through coffee shop run by a Korean immigrant and order a "single, tall, nonfat latte" and chocolate-covered biscotti. The coffee beans came from Brazil and the chocolate from Peru, while the biscotti was made locally using an old Italian recipe. After the song ends, a news announcer might inform the American listener that antiglobalization protests at a meeting of the World Economic Forum in Davos, Switzerland, have turned violent. One protester has been killed. The announcer then turns to the next item, a story about how financial crisis that started in the United States banking sector may trigger a global recession and is sending stock markets down all over the world.

This is the world in which we live. It is a world where the volume of goods, services, and investment crossing national borders has expanded faster than world output for more than half a century. It is a world where over $4 trillion in foreign exchange transactions are made every day, where more than $15 trillion of goods and $3.7 trillion of services are sold across national borders.[2] It is a world in which international institutions such as the World Trade Organization and gatherings of leaders from the world's most powerful economies have repeatedly called for even lower barriers to cross-border trade and investment. It is a world where the symbols of material and popular culture are increasingly global: from Coca-Cola and Starbucks to Sony PlayStations, Nokia cell phones, MTV shows, Disney films, IKEA stores, and Apple iPods and iPhones. It is a world in which products are made from inputs that come from all over the world. It is a world in which a financial crisis in America can trigger a global economic recession, which is exactly what occurred in 2008 and 2009. It is also a world in which vigorous and vocal groups protest against globalization, which they blame for a list of ills, from unemployment in developed nations to environmental degradation and the Americanization of popular culture. And yes, these protests have on occasion turned violent.

For businesses, this process has produced many opportunities. Firms can expand their revenues by selling around the world and/or reduce their costs by producing in nations where key inputs, including labor, are cheap. The global expansion of enterprises has been facilitated by favorable political and economic trends. Since the collapse of communism at the end of the 1980s, the pendulum of public policy in nation after nation has swung toward the free market end of the economic spectrum. Regulatory and administrative barriers to doing business in foreign nations have come down, while those nations have often transformed their economies, privatizing state-owned enterprises, deregulating markets, increasing competition, and welcoming investment by foreign businesses. This has allowed businesses both large and small, from both advanced nations and developing nations, to expand internationally.

What is now starting to happen in the health care industry exemplifies the changes now taking place. Health care has long been thought to be immune from the effects of globalization, but this is now no longer true. Medical tourism is becoming a significant business, with Americans in particular traveling to places like India and Singapore to have surgical procedures performed because the costs of surgery are lower and the quality of care often comparable to what they would receive in the United States. Obviously this creates opportunities for health care providers in India and Singapore to grow their businesses, for U.S. insurance companies to lower their costs by agreeing to pay for treatment in accredited hospitals overseas, and for health brokers in the United States, who make money by arranging for U.S. citizens to have treatment overseas. The trend also clearly benefits some health care consumers.

At the same time, globalization has created new threats for businesses accustomed to dominating their domestic markets. Foreign companies have entered many formerly protected industries in developing nations, increasing competition and driving down prices. For three decades, U.S. automobile companies have been battling foreign enterprises, as Japanese, European, and now Korean companies have taken business from them. General Motors has seen its U.S. market share decline from more than 50 percent to around 20 percent, while Japan's Toyota has surpassed first Ford, and now GM, to become the largest automobile company in the world.

As globalization unfolds, it is transforming industries and creating anxiety among those who believed their jobs were protected from foreign competition. Historically, while many workers in manufacturing industries worried about the impact foreign competition might have on their jobs, workers in service industries felt more secure. Now this too is changing. Advances in technology, lower transportation costs, and the rise of skilled workers in developing countries imply that many services no longer need to be performed where they are delivered, as the example of health care clearly indicates (see the Opening Case). For example, accounting work is being outsourced from America to India. In 2005, some 400,000 individual tax returns were compiled in India. Indian accountants, trained in U.S. tax rules, perform work for U.S. accounting firms.[3] They access individual tax returns stored on computers in the United States, perform routine calculations, and save their work so that it can be inspected by a U.S. accountant, who then bills clients. As the best-selling author Thomas Friedman has argued, the world is becoming flat.[4] People living in developed nations no longer have the playing field tilted in their favor. Increasingly, enterprising individuals based in India, China, or Brazil have the same opportunities to better themselves as those living in Western Europe, the United States, or Canada.

What is Globalization?

Globalization refers to the shift toward a more integrated and interdependent world economy. Globalization has several facets, including the globalization of markets and the globalization of production.

THE GLOBALIZATION OF MARKETS

The **globalization of markets** refers to the merging of historically distinct and separate national markets into one huge global marketplace. Falling barriers to cross-border trade have made it easier to sell internationally. It has been argued for some time that the tastes and preferences of consumers in different nations are beginning to converge on some global norm, thereby helping to create a global market.[5] Consumer products such as Citigroup credit cards, Coca-Cola soft drinks, Sony PlayStation video games, McDonald's hamburgers, Starbucks coffee, and IKEA furniture are frequently held up as prototypical examples of this trend. Firms such as those just cited are more than just benefactors of this trend; they are also facilitators of it. By offering the same basic product worldwide, they help to create a global market.

A company does not have to be the size of these multinational giants to facilitate, and benefit from, the globalization of markets. In the United States, for example, nearly 90 percent of firms that export are small businesses employing less than 100 people, and their share of total U.S. exports has grown steadily over the last decade to now exceed 20 percent.[6] Firms with fewer than 500 employees account for 97 percent of all U.S. exporters and almost 30 percent of all exports by value.[7] Typical of these is Hytech, a New York–based manufacturer of solar panels that generates 40 percent of its $3 million in annual sales from exports to five countries, or B&S Aircraft Alloys, another New York company whose exports account for 40 percent of its $8 million annual revenues.[8] The situation is similar in several other nations. In Germany, for example, which is the world's largest exporter, a staggering 98 percent of small and midsized companies have exposure to international markets, either via exports or international production.[9]

Despite the global prevalence of Citigroup credit cards, McDonald's hamburgers, Starbucks coffee, and IKEA stores, it is important not to push too far the view that national markets are giving way to the global market. Significant differences still exist among national markets along many relevant dimensions, including consumer tastes and preferences, distribution channels, culturally embedded value systems, business systems, and legal regulations. These differences frequently require companies to customize marketing strategies, product features, and operating practices to best match conditions in a particular country.

The most global markets currently are not markets for consumer products—where national differences in tastes and preferences are still often important enough to act as a brake on globalization—but markets for industrial goods and materials that serve a universal need the world over. These include the markets for commodities such as aluminum, oil, and wheat; for industrial products such as microprocessors, DRAMs (computer memory chips), and commercial jet aircraft; for computer software; and for financial assets from U.S. Treasury bills to eurobonds and futures on the Nikkei index or the Mexican peso.

In many global markets, the same firms frequently confront each other as competitors in nation after nation. Coca-Cola's rivalry with PepsiCo is a global one, as are the rivalries between Ford and Toyota, Boeing and Airbus, Caterpillar and Komatsu in earthmoving equipment, General Electric and Rolls Royce in aero engines, and Sony, Nintendo, and Microsoft in video games. If a firm moves into a nation not currently served by its rivals, many of those rivals are sure to follow to prevent their competitor from gaining an advantage.[10] As firms follow each other around the world, they bring with them many of the assets that served them well in other national markets—including their products, operating strategies, marketing strategies, and brand names—creating some homogeneity across markets. Thus, greater uniformity replaces diversity. In an increasing number of industries, it is no longer meaningful to talk about

Beijing, China: Chinese shoppers walk through Beijing's main downtown shopping promenade past a Kentucky Fried Chicken (KFC) franchise. KFC is one of the most successful international businesses in China due to its adaptation and appeal to the Chinese market.

"the German market," "the American market," "the Brazilian market," or "the Japanese market"; for many firms there is only the global market.

THE GLOBALIZATION OF PRODUCTION

The **globalization of production** refers to sourcing goods and services from locations around the globe to take advantage of national differences in the cost and quality of **factors of production** (such as labor, energy, land, and capital). By using global sourcing, companies hope to lower their overall cost structure or improve the quality or functionality of their product offering, thereby allowing them to compete more effectively. Consider the Boeing's 777, a commercial jet airliner. Eight Japanese suppliers make parts for the fuselage, doors, and wings; a supplier in Singapore makes the doors for the nose landing gear; three suppliers in Italy manufacture wing flaps; and so on.[11] In total, foreign companies build about 30 percent of the 777, by value. For its most recent jet airliner, the 787, Boeing has pushed this trend even further, with some 65 percent of the total value of the aircraft scheduled to be outsourced to foreign companies, 35 percent of which will go to three major Japanese companies.[12]

Part of Boeing's rationale for outsourcing so much production to foreign suppliers is that these suppliers are the best in the world at their particular activity. A global web of suppliers yields a better final product, which enhances the chances of Boeing winning a greater share of total orders for aircraft than its global rival Airbus Industrie. Boeing also outsources some production to foreign countries to increase the chance that it will win significant orders from airlines based in that country. For another example of a global web of activities, consider the example of Vizio profiled in the Management Focus feature.

Early outsourcing efforts were primarily confined to manufacturing activities, such as those undertaken by Boeing and Vizio; increasingly, however, companies are taking advantage of modern communications technology, particularly the Internet, to outsource service activities to low-cost producers in other nations. As described in the opening discussion of health care, the Internet has allowed hospitals to outsource some

Boeing's new global product, the 787, rolls out.

MANAGEMENT FOCUS

Vizio and the Market for Flat Panel TVs

They begin as glass panels that are manufactured in high-tech fabrication centers in South Korean, Taiwan, and Japan. Operating sophisticated tooling in environments that must be kept absolutely clean, these factories produce sheets of glass twice as large as king size beds to exacting specifications. From there, the glass panels travel to Mexican plants located alongside the U.S. border. There they are cut to size, combined with electronic components shipped in from Asia and the United States, assembled into finished TVs, and loaded onto trucks bound for retail stores in the United States. It's a huge business. U.S. consumers spend over $35 billion a year on flat panel TVs.

The underlying technology for flat panel displays was invented in the United States in the late 1960s by RCA. But after RCA and rivals Westinghouse and Xerox opted not to pursue the technology, the Japanese company Sharp made aggressive investments in flat panel displays. By the early 1990s Sharp was selling the first flat panel screens, but as the Japanese economy plunged into a decade-long recession, investment leadership shifted to South Korean companies such as Samsung. Then the 1997 Asian crisis hit Korea hard, and Taiwanese companies seized leadership. Today, Chinese companies are starting to elbow their way into the flat panel display manufacturing business.

As production for flat panel displays migrates its way around the globe to low cost locations, there are clear winners and losers. U.S. consumers, who have benefited from the falling prices of flat panel TVs and are snapping them up. Efficient manufacturers have taken advantage of globally dispersed supply chains to make and sell low-cost, high-quality flat panel TVs. Foremost among these

has been the California-based company, Vizio. Founded by a Taiwanese immigrant, in just six years sales of Vizio flat panel TVs ballooned from nothing to over $2 billion in 2008, and in early 2009, the company was the largest provider to the United States market with a 21.7 percent share. Vizio, however, has less than 100 employees. They focus on final product design, sales, and customer service. Vizio outsources most of its engineering work, all of its manufacturing and much of its logistics. For each of its models, Vizio assembles a team of supplier partners strung across the globe. Its 42-inch flat panel TV, for example, contains a panel from South Korea, electronic components from China, and processors from the United States, and it is assembled in Mexico. Vizio's managers scour the globe continually for the cheapest manufacturers of flat panel displays and electronic components. They sell most of their TVs to large discount retailers such as Costco and Sam's Club. Good order visibility from retailers, coupled with tight management of global logistics, allows Vizio to turn over its inventory every three weeks, twice as fast as many of its competitors, which is a major source of cost saving in a business where prices are falling continually.

On the other hand, the shift to flat panel TVs has caused pain in certain sectors of the economy, such as those firms that make traditional cathode ray TVs in high-cost locations. In 2006, for example, Japanese electronics manufacturers Sanyo laid off 300 employees at its U.S. factory, and Hitachi closed its TV manufacturing plant in South Carolina, laying off 200 employees. Both Sony and Hitachi of course both make still make TVs, but they are flat panel TVs assembled in Mexico from components manufactured in Asia.[13]

radiology work to India, where images from MRI scans and the like are read at night while U.S. physicians sleep and the results are ready for them in the morning. Many software companies, including IBM, now use Indian engineers to perform maintenance functions on software designed in the United States. The time difference allows Indian engineers to run debugging tests on software written in the United States when U.S. engineers sleep, transmitting the corrected code back to the United States over secure Internet connections so it is ready for U.S. engineers to work on the following day. Dispersing value-creation activities in this way can compress the time and lower the costs required to develop new software programs. Other companies, from computer makers to banks, are outsourcing customer service functions, such as customer call centers, to developing nations where labor is cheaper. In another example from health care, in 2008 some 34,000 Filipinos were employed in the business of transcribing American medical files (such as audio files from doctors seeking approval from insurance companies for performing a procedure). More generally, some estimates suggest that the outsourcing of many administrative procedures in health care, such as customer service and claims processing, could reduce health care costs in America by as much as $70 billion.[14]

Robert Reich, who served as secretary of labor in the Clinton administration, has argued that as a consequence of the trend exemplified by companies such as Boeing, IBM, and Vizio, in many cases it is becoming irrelevant to talk about American products, Japanese products, German products, or Korean products. Increasingly, according to Reich, outsourcing productive activities to different suppliers results in the creation of products that are global in nature, that is, "global products."[15] But as with the globalization of markets, companies must be careful not to push the globalization of production too far. Substantial impediments still make it difficult for firms to achieve the optimal dispersion of their productive activities to locations around the globe. These impediments include formal and informal barriers to trade between countries, barriers to foreign direct investment, transportation costs, and issues associated with economic and political risk. For example, government regulations ultimately limit the ability of hospitals to outsource the process of interpreting MRI scans to developing nations where radiologists are cheaper.

Nevertheless, the globalization of markets and production will continue. Modern firms are important actors in this trend, their very actions fostering increased globalization. These firms, however, are merely responding in an efficient manner to changing conditions in their operating environment—as well they should.

The Emergence of Global Institutions

As markets globalize and an increasing proportion of business activity transcends national borders, institutions are needed to help manage, regulate, and police the global marketplace, and to promote the establishment of multinational treaties to govern the global business system. Over the past half century, a number of important global institutions have been created to help perform these functions, including the **General Agreement on Tariffs and Trade (GATT)** and its successor, the World Trade Organization (WTO); the International Monetary Fund (IMF) and its sister institution, the World Bank; and the United Nations (UN). All these institutions were created by voluntary agreement between individual nation-states, and their functions are enshrined in international treaties.

The **World Trade Organization** (like the GATT before it) is primarily responsible for policing the world trading system and making sure nation-states adhere to the rules laid down in trade treaties signed by WTO member states. As of 2009, 153 nations that collectively accounted for 97 percent of world trade were WTO members, thereby giving the organization enormous scope and influence. The WTO is also responsible for facilitating the establishment of additional multinational agreements between WTO member states. Over its entire history, and that of the GATT before it, the WTO has promoted lowering barriers to cross-border trade and investment. In doing so, the WTO has been the instrument of its member states, which have sought to create a more open global business system unencumbered by barriers to trade and investment between countries. Without an institution such as the WTO, it is unlikely that the globalization of markets and production could have proceeded as far as it has. However, as we shall see in this chapter and in Chapter 6 when we look closely at the WTO, critics charge that the organization is usurping the national sovereignty of individual nation-states.

The **International Monetary Fund** and the **World Bank** were both created in 1944 by 44 nations that met at Bretton Woods, New Hampshire. The IMF was established to maintain order in the international monetary system; the World Bank was set up to promote economic development. In the 65 years since their creation, both institutions have emerged as significant players in the global economy. The World Bank is the less controversial of the two sister institutions. It has focused on making low-interest loans to cash-strapped governments in poor nations that wish to undertake significant infrastructure investments (such as building dams or roads).

The IMF is often seen as the lender of last resort to nation-states whose economies are in turmoil and currencies are losing value against those of other nations. During the past two decades, for example, the IMF has lent money to the governments of troubled states, including Argentina, Indonesia, Mexico, Russia, South Korea, Thailand, and Turkey. More recently, the IMF has taken a very proactive role in helping countries to cope with some of the effects of the 2008–2009 global financial crises. IMF loans come with strings attached, however; in return for loans, the IMF requires nation-states to adopt specific economic policies aimed at returning their troubled economies to stability and growth. These requirements have sparked controversy. Some critics charge that the IMF's policy recommendations are often inappropriate; others maintain that by telling national governments what economic policies they must adopt, the IMF, like the WTO, is usurping the sovereignty of nation-states.

The **United Nations** was established October 24, 1945, by 51 countries committed to preserving peace through international cooperation and collective security. Today nearly every nation in the world belongs to the United Nations; membership now totals 191 countries. When states become members of the United Nations, they agree to accept the obligations of the UN Charter, an international treaty that establishes basic principles of international relations. According to the charter, the UN has four purposes: to maintain international peace and security, to develop friendly relations among nations, to cooperate in solving international problems and in promoting respect for human rights, and to be a center for harmonizing the actions of

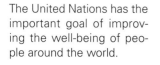

The United Nations has the important goal of improving the well-being of people around the world.

nations. Although the UN is perhaps best known for its peace-keeping role, one of the organization's central mandates is the promotion of higher standards of living, full employment, and conditions of economic and social progress and development—all issues that are central to the creation of a vibrant global economy. As much as 70 percent of the work of the UN system is devoted to accomplishing this mandate. To do so, the UN works closely with other international institutions such as the World Bank. Guiding the work is the belief that eradicating poverty and improving the well-being of people everywhere are necessary steps in creating conditions for lasting world peace.[16]

Another institution that has been in the news of late is the **G20**. Established in 1999, the G20 comprises the finance ministers and central bank governors of the 19 largest economies in the world, plus representatives from the European Union and the European Central Bank. Originally established to formulate a coordinated policy response to financial crises in developing nations, in 2008 and 2009, G20 became the forum through which major nations attempted to launch a coordinated policy response to the global financial crisis that started in American and then rapidly spread around the world, ushering in the first serious global economic recession since 1981.

Drivers of Globalization

Two macro factors underlie the trend toward greater globalization.[17] The first is the decline in barriers to the free flow of goods, services, and capital that has occurred since the end of World War II. The second factor is technological change, particularly the dramatic developments in recent years in communication, information processing, and transportation technologies.

DECLINING TRADE AND INVESTMENT BARRIERS

During the 1920s and 30s many of the world's nation-states erected formidable barriers to international trade and foreign direct investment. **International trade** occurs when a firm exports goods or services to consumers in another country. **Foreign direct investment (FDI)** occurs when a firm invests resources in business activities outside its home country. Many of the barriers to international trade took the form of high tariffs on imports of manufactured goods. The typical aim of such tariffs was to protect domestic industries from foreign competition. One consequence, however, was "beggar thy neighbor" retaliatory trade policies, with countries progressively raising trade barriers against each other. Ultimately, this depressed world demand and contributed to the Great Depression of the 1930s.

Having learned from this experience, the advanced industrial nations of the West committed themselves after World War II to removing barriers to the free flow of goods, services, and capital between nations.[18] This goal was enshrined in the General Agreement on Tariffs and Trade. Under the umbrella of GATT, eight rounds of negotiations among member states (now numbering 153) have worked to lower barriers to the free flow of goods and services. The most recent round of negotiations to be completed, known as the Uruguay Round, were finalized in December 1993. The Uruguay Round further reduced trade barriers; extended GATT to cover services as well as manufactured goods; provided enhanced protection for patents, trademarks, and copyrights; and established the World Trade Organization to police the international trading system.[19] Table 6.1 summarizes the impact of GATT agreements on average tariff rates for manufactured goods. As can be seen, average tariff rates have fallen significantly since 1950 and now stand at about 4 percent.

In late 2001, the WTO launched a new round of talks aimed at further liberalizing the global trade and investment framework. For this meeting, it picked the remote location of Doha in the Persian Gulf state of Qatar. At Doha, the member states of the WTO

TABLE 6.1

Average Tariff Rates on
Manufactured Products
as Percent of Value

Source: 1913–90 data are from
"Who Wants to Be a Giant?" *The
Economist: A Survey of the Multi-
nationals*, June 24, 1995, pp. 3–4.
Copyright © The Economist
Books, Ltd. The 2008 data are
from World Trade Organization,
2009 World Trade Report
(Geneva: WTO, 2009).

	1913	1950	1990	2008
France		21%	18%	5.9%	3.9%
Germany	20	26	5.9	3.9	3.9%
Italy	18	25	5.9	3.9	3.9%
Japan	30	—	5.3	2.3	3.9%
Holland	5	11	5.9	3.9	3.9%
Sweden	20	9	4.4	3.9	3.9%
Great Britain	—	23	5.9	3.9	3.9%
United States	44	14	4.8	3.2	3.9%

staked out an agenda. The talks were scheduled to last three years, although as of 2009 they are effectively stalled due to opposition from several key nations. The Doha agenda includes cutting tariffs on industrial goods, services, and agricultural products; phasing out subsidies to agricultural producers; reducing barriers to cross-border investment; and limiting the use of antidumping laws. If the Doha talks are ever completed, the biggest gain may come from discussion on agricultural products; average agricultural tariff rates are still about 40 percent, and rich nations spend some $300 billion a year in subsidies to support their farm sectors. The world's poorer nations have the most to gain from any reduction in agricultural tariffs and subsidies; such reforms would give them access to the markets of the developed world.[20]

In addition to reducing trade barriers, many countries have also been progressively removing restrictions to foreign direct investment. According to the United Nations, some 90 percent of the 2,5424 changes made worldwide between 1992 and 2007 in the laws governing foreign direct investment created a more favorable environment for FDI.[21]

Such trends have been driving both the globalization of markets and the globalization of production. Lowering barriers to international trade enables firms to view the world, rather than a single country, as their market. Lowering trade and investment barriers also allows firms to base production at the optimal location for that activity. Thus, a firm might design a product in one country, produce component parts in two other countries, assemble the product in yet another country, and then export the finished product around the world.

According to WTO data, the volume of world merchandise trade has grown faster than the world economy since 1950 (see Figure 6.1).[22] From 1970 to 2008, the volume of world merchandise trade expanded more than 30 fold, outstripping the expansion of world production, which grew close to 10 times in real terms. (World merchandise trade includes trade in manufactured goods, agricultural goods, and mining products, but *not* services). What Figure 6.1 does not show is that since the mid-1980s the value of international trade in services has also grown robustly. Trade in services now accounts for around 20 percent of the value of all international trade. Increasingly, international trade in services has been driven by advances in communications, which allow corporations to outsource service activities to different locations around the globe (see the opening case). Thus, as noted earlier, many corporations in the developed world outsource customer service functions, from software maintenance activities to customer call centers, to developing nations where labor costs are lower.

The data summarized in Figure 6.1 imply several things. First, more firms are doing what Boeing does with the 777 and 787: dispersing parts of their production process to different locations around the globe to drive down production costs and increase product quality. Second, the economies of the world's nation-states are becoming more intertwined. As trade expands, nations are becoming increasingly dependent on each other for important goods and services. Third, the world has become significantly wealthier since 1950, and the implication is that rising trade is the engine that has helped to pull the global economy along.

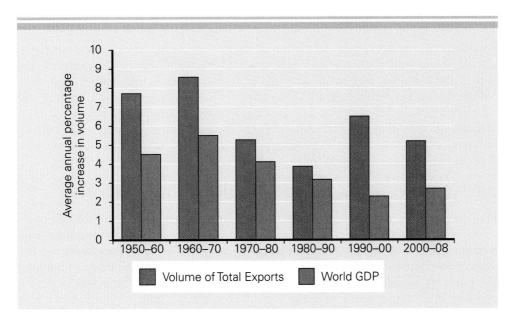

FIGURE 6.1

Average Annual Percentage Growth in volume of Exports and World GDP, 1950–2008

Source: Constructed by the author from World Trade Organization, *World Trade Statistics 2008.*

Evidence also suggests that foreign direct investment is playing an increasing role in the global economy as firms increase their cross-border investments. The average yearly outflow of FDI increased from $25 billion in 1975 to $1.4 trillion in 2000. It fell back in the early 2000s, but by 2007 FDI flows were a record $1.8 trillion (however, FDI outflows did contract to $1.4 trillion in the wake of the 2008 global financial crisis, and are forecasted to fall further in 2009, as corporations retrench in the face of weak global demand conditions).[23] Over this period, the flow of FDI accelerated faster than the growth in world trade and world output. For example, between 1992 and 2008, the total flow of FDI from all countries increased more than eightfold while world trade by value grew by some 160 percent and world output by around 47 percent.[24] As a result of the strong FDI flow, by 2007 the global stock of FDI exceeded $15 trillion. At least 79,000 parent companies had 790,000 affiliates in foreign markets that collectively employed more than 82 million people abroad and generated value accounting for about 11 percent of global GDP. The foreign affiliates of multinationals had an estimated $31 trillion in global sales, higher than the value of global exports of goods and services, which stood at close to $19.5 trillion.[25]

The globalization of markets and production and the resulting growth of world trade, foreign direct investment, and imports all imply that firms are finding their home markets under attack from foreign competitors. This is true in Japan, where U.S. companies such as Kodak and Procter & Gamble are expanding their presence. It is true in the United States, where Japanese automobile firms have taken market share away from General Motors and Ford. And it is true in Europe, where the once-dominant Dutch company Philips has seen its market share in the consumer electronics industry taken by Japan's JVC, Matsushita, and Sony, and Korea's Samsung and LG. The growing integration of the world economy into a single, huge marketplace is increasing the intensity of competition in a range of manufacturing and service industries.

However, declining barriers to cross-border trade and investment cannot be taken for granted. Demands for "protection" from foreign competitors are still often heard in countries around the world, including the United States. Although a return to the restrictive trade policies of the 1920s and 30s is unlikely, it is not clear whether the political majority in the industrialized world favors further reductions in trade barriers. Indeed, the global financial crisis of 2008–2009, and the associated drop in global output that occurred, led to more calls for trade barriers to protect jobs at home. If trade barriers decline no further, at least for the time being, the financial crisis will put a brake upon the globalization of both markets and production.

THE ROLE OF TECHNOLOGICAL CHANGE

Lowering trade barriers made globalization of markets and production a theoretical possibility. Technological change has made it a tangible reality. Since the end of World War II, the world has seen major advances in communication, information processing, and transportation technology, including the explosive emergence of the Internet and World Wide Web. Telecommunications is creating a global audience. Transportation is creating a global village. From Buenos Aires to Boston, and from Birmingham to Beijing, ordinary people are watching MTV, they're wearing blue jeans, and they're listening to iPods as they commute to work.

MICROPROCESSORS AND TELECOMMUNICATIONS

Perhaps the single most important innovation has been development of the microprocessor, which enabled the explosive growth of high-power, low-cost computing, vastly increasing the amount of information that can be processed by individuals and firms. The microprocessor also underlies many recent advances in telecommunications technology. Over the past 30 years, developments in satellite, optical fiber, and wireless technologies, and now the Internet and the World Wide Web (WWW) have revolutionized global communications. These technologies rely on the microprocessor to encode, transmit, and decode the vast amount of information that flows along these electronic highways. The cost of microprocessors continues to fall, while their power increases (a phenomenon known as **Moore's Law**, which predicts that the power of microprocessor technology doubles and its cost of production falls in half every 18 months).[26] As this happens, the cost of global communications plummets, which lowers the costs of coordinating and controlling a global organization. Thus, between 1930 and 1990, the cost of a three-minute phone call between New York and London fell from $244.65 to $3.32.[27] By 1998, it had plunged to just 36 cents for consumers, and much lower rates were available for businesses.[28] Indeed, by using the Internet, the cost of an international phone call is rapidly plummeting toward just a few cents per minute.

The Internet and World Wide Web

The rapid growth of the World Wide Web is the latest expression of this development. In 1990, fewer than 1 million users were connected to the Internet. By 1995, the figure had risen to 50 million. By May 2009 the Internet had 1.6 billion users.[29] The WWW has developed into the information backbone of the global economy. In the United States alone, e-commerce retail sales reached $133 billion in 2008, up from almost nothing in 1998.[30] Viewed globally, the Web is emerging as an equalizer. It rolls back some of the constraints of location, scale, and time zones.[31] The Web makes it much easier for buyers and sellers to find each other, wherever they may be located and whatever their size. It allows businesses, both small and large, to expand their global presence at a lower cost than ever before.

Transportation Technology

In addition to developments in communication technology, several major innovations in transportation technology have occurred since World War II. In economic terms, the most important are probably the development of commercial jet aircraft and superfreighters and the introduction of containerization, which simplifies transshipment from one mode of transport to another. The advent of commercial jet travel, by reducing the time needed to get from one location to another, has effectively shrunk the globe. In terms of travel time, New York is now "closer" to Tokyo than it was to Philadelphia in the Colonial days.

Containerization has revolutionized the transportation business, significantly lowering the costs of shipping goods over long distances. Before the advent of containerization, moving goods from one mode of transport to another was very labor intensive, lengthy, and costly. It could take days and several hundred longshoremen to unload a ship and reload goods onto trucks and trains. With the advent of widespread containerization in the 1970s and 1980s, the whole process can now be executed by a handful of long-shoremen in a couple of days. Since 1980, the world's containership fleet has more than quadrupled, reflecting in part the growing volume of international trade and in part the switch to this mode of transportation. As a result of the efficiency gains associated with containerization, transportation costs have plummeted, making it much more economical to ship goods around the globe, thereby helping to drive the globalization of markets and production. Between 1920 and 1990, the average ocean freight and port charges per ton of U.S. export and import cargo fell from $95 to $29 (in 1990 dollars).[32] The cost of shipping freight per ton-mile on railroads in the United States fell from 3.04 cents in 1985 to 2.3 cents in 2000, largely as a result of efficiency gains from the widespread use of containers.[33] An increased share of cargo now goes by air. Between 1955 and 1999, average air transportation revenue per ton-kilometer fell by more than 80 percent.[34] Reflecting the falling cost of airfreight, by the early 2000s air shipments accounted for 28 percent of the value of U.S. trade, up from 7 percent in 1965.[35]

Implications for the Globalization of Production

As transportation costs associated with the globalization of production declined, dispersal of production to geographically separate locations became more economical. As a result of the technological innovations discussed above, the real costs of information processing and communication have fallen dramatically in the past two decades. These developments make it possible for a firm to create and then manage a globally dispersed production system, further facilitating the globalization of production. A worldwide communications network has become essential for many international businesses. For example, Dell uses the Internet to coordinate and control a globally dispersed production system to such an extent that it holds only three days' worth of inventory at its assembly locations. Dell's Internet-based system records orders for computer equipment as customers submit them via the company's Web site, then immediately transmits the resulting orders for components to various suppliers around the world, which have a real-time look at Dell's order flow and can adjust their production schedules accordingly. Given the low cost of airfreight, Dell can use air transportation to speed up the delivery of critical components to meet unanticipated demand shifts without delaying the shipment of final product to consumers. Dell also has used modern communications technology to outsource its customer service operations to India. When U.S. customers call Dell with a service inquiry, they are routed to Bangalore in India, where English-speaking service personnel handle the call.

The Internet has been a major force facilitating international trade in services. It is the Web that allows hospitals in Chicago to send MRI scans to India for analysis, accounting offices in San Francisco to outsource routine tax preparation work to accountants living in the Philippines, and software testers in India to debug code written by developers in Redmond, Washington, the headquarters of Microsoft. We are probably still in the early stages of this development. As Moore's Law continues to advance and telecommunications bandwidth continues to increase, almost any work processes that can be digitalized will be, and this will allow that work to be performed wherever in the world it is most efficient and effective to do so.

The development of commercial jet aircraft has also helped knit together the worldwide operations of many international businesses. Using jet travel, an American manager need spend a day at most traveling to his or her firm's European or Asian operations. This enables the manager to oversee a globally dispersed production system.

Implications for the Globalization of Markets

In addition to the globalization of production, technological innovations have also facilitated the globalization of markets. Low-cost global communications networks such as the World Wide Web are helping to create electronic global marketplaces. As noted above, low-cost transportation has made it more economical to ship products around the world, thereby helping to create global markets. For example, due to the tumbling costs of shipping goods by air, roses grown in Ecuador can be cut and sold in New York two days later while they are still fresh. This has given rise to an industry in Ecuador that did not exist 20 years ago and now supplies a global market for roses. In addition, low-cost jet travel has resulted in the mass movement of people between countries. This has reduced the cultural distance between countries and is bringing about some convergence of consumer tastes and preferences. At the same time, global communication networks and global media are creating a worldwide culture. Many countries now receive U.S. television networks such as CNN, MTV, and HBO, and people watch Hollywood films the world over. In any society, the media are primary conveyors of culture; as global media develop, we must expect the evolution of something akin to a global culture. A logical result of this evolution is the emergence of global markets for consumer products. The first signs of this are already apparent. It is now as easy to find a McDonald's restaurant in Tokyo as it is in New York, to buy an iPod in Rio as it is in Berlin, and to buy Gap jeans in Paris as it is in San Francisco.

Despite these trends, we must be careful not to overemphasize their importance. While modern communication and transportation technologies are ushering in the "global village," significant national differences remain in culture, consumer preferences, and business practices. A firm that ignores differences between countries does so at its peril.

The Changing Demographics of the Global Economy

Hand in hand with the trend toward globalization has been a fairly dramatic change in the demographics of the global economy over the past 30 years. As late as the 1960s, the global economy reflected four facts. The first was U.S. dominance in the world economy and world trade. The second was U.S. dominance in world foreign direct investment. Related to the first two points, the third fact was the dominance of large, multinational U.S. firms on the international business scene. The fourth was that roughly half the globe—the centrally planned economies of the Communist world—were off-limits to Western international businesses. As will be explained below, all four of these qualities either have changed or are now changing rapidly.

THE CHANGING WORLD OUTPUT AND WORLD TRADE PICTURE

In the early 1960s, the United States was still by far the world's dominant industrial power. In 1963 the United States accounted for 40.3 percent of world economic activity, measured by gross domestic product (GDP). By 2008, the United States accounted for 20.7 percent of world GDP, still the world's largest industrial power but down significantly in relative size since the 1960s (see Table 6.2). Nor was the United States the only developed nation to see its relative standing slip. The same occurred to Germany, France, and the United Kingdom, all nations that were among the first to industrialize. This change in the U.S. position was not an absolute decline, since the U.S. economy grew at a robust average annual rate of more than 3 percent from 1963 to 2008 (the economies of Germany, France, and the United Kingdom also grew during this time). Rather, it was a relative decline, reflecting the faster economic growth of several other economies, particularly in Asia. For example, as Table 6.2 shows, from 1963 to 2008, China's share of world GDP increased from a trivial amount to 11.4 percent. Other countries that markedly increased their share of world output included Japan, Thailand, Malaysia, Taiwan, and South Korea (note that GDP data in Table 6.2 are based on purchasing power parity figures, which adjust the value of GDP to reflect the cost of living in various economies).

By the end of the 1980s, the U.S. position as the world's leading exporter was threatened. Over the past 30 years, U.S. dominance in export markets has waned as Japan,

Country	Share of World Output, 1963	Share of World GDP, 2008	Share of World Exports, 2008
United States	40.3%	20.7%	9.3%
Germany	9.7	4.2	8.7
France	6.3	3.1	3.8
Italy	3.4	2.6	3.4
United Kingdom	6.5	3.2	3.9
Canada	3.0	1.9	2.7
Japan	5.5	6.4	4.5
China	NA	11.4	8.4

TABLE 6.2

The Changing Demographics of World GDP and Trade

Sources: IMF, *World Economic Outlook*, April 2009. Data for 1963 are from N. Hood and J. Young, *The Economics of the Multinational Enterprise* (New York: Longman, 1973). The GDP data are based on purchasing power parity figures, which adjust the value of GDP to reflect the cost of living in various economies.

Germany, and a number of newly industrialized countries such as South Korea and China have taken a larger share of world exports. During the 1960s, the United States routinely accounted for 20 percent of world exports of manufactured goods. But as Table 6.2 shows, the U.S. share of world exports of goods and services had slipped to 9.3 percent by 2008. Despite the fall, the United States still remained the world's largest exporter, ahead of Germany, Japan, France, and the fast-rising economic power, China. If China's rapid rise continues, however, it could soon overtake the United States as the world's largest economy and largest exporter.

As emerging economies such as China, India, and Brazil continue to grow, a further relative decline in the share of world output and world exports accounted for by the United States and other long-established developed nations seems likely. By itself, this is not bad. The relative decline of the United States reflects the growing economic development and industrialization of the world economy, as opposed to any absolute decline in the health of the U.S. economy, which by many measures is stronger than ever.

Most forecasts now predict a rapid rise in the share of world output accounted for by developing nations such as China, India, Indonesia, Thailand, South Korea, Mexico, and Brazil, and a commensurate decline in the share enjoyed by rich industrialized countries such as Great Britain, Germany, Japan, and the United States. If current trends continue, the Chinese economy could ultimately be larger than that of the United States on a purchasing power parity basis, while the economy of India will approach that of Germany. The World Bank has estimated that today's developing nations may account for more than 60 percent of world economic activity by 2020, while today's rich nations, which currently account for more than 55 percent of world economic activity, may account for only about 38 percent. Forecasts are not always correct, but these suggest that a shift in the economic geography of the world is now under way, although the magnitude of that shift is not totally evident. For international businesses, the implications of this changing economic geography are clear: Many of tomorrow's economic opportunities may be found in the developing nations of the world, and many of tomorrow's most capable competitors will probably also emerge from these regions. A case in point has been the dramatic expansion of India's software sector, which is profiled in the Country Focus.

THE CHANGING FOREIGN DIRECT INVESTMENT PICTURE

Reflecting the dominance of the United States in the global economy, U.S. firms accounted for 66.3 percent of worldwide foreign direct investment flows in the 1960s. British firms were second, accounting for 10.5 percent, while Japanese firms were a distant eighth, with only 2 percent. The dominance of U.S. firms was so great that books

India's Software Sector

Some 25 years ago a number of small software enterprises were established in Bangalore, India. Typical of these enterprises was Infosys Technologies, which was started by seven Indian entrepreneurs with about $1,000 between them. Infosys now has annual revenues of $22 billion and some 60,000 employees, but it is just one of over a hundred software companies clustered around Bangalore, which has become the epicenter of India's fast growing information technology sector. From a standing start in the mid 1980s, by 2008–2009 this sector was generating revenues of $60 billion. Combined software services, hardware sales, and business process outsourcing exports were expected to hit $47 billion, a 16 percent growth rate despite a sharp global economic slowdown during 2008–2009. India had also emerged as home to some of the fastest growing software service companies on the planet, including Infosys, Wipro, Tata Consultancy Services, and HCL Technologies.

The growth of the Indian software sector is based on four factors. First, the country has an abundant supply of engineering talent. Every year Indian universities graduate some 400,000 engineers. Second, labor costs in India are low. The cost to hire an Indian graduate is roughly 12 percent of the cost of hiring an American graduate. Third, many Indians are fluent in English, which makes coordination between Western firms and India easier. Fourth, due to time differences, Indians can work while Americans sleep. This means, for example, that software code written in America during the day can be tested in India and at night shipped back via the Internet to America in time for the start of work the following day. In other words, by utilizing Indian labor and the Internet, software enterprises can create global software development factories that are working 24 hours a day.

Initially Indian software enterprises focused on the low end of the software industry, supplying basic software development and testing services to Western firms. But as the industry has grown in size and sophistication, Indian firms have moved up market. Today the leading Indian companies compete directly with the likes of IBM and EDS for large software development projects, business process outsourcing contracts, and information technology consulting services. These markets are booming. Estimates suggest that global spending on information technology outsourcing will rise from $193 billion in 2004 to over $250 billion by 2010, with Indian enterprises capturing a larger slice of the pie. One response of Western firms to this emerging competitive threat has been to invest in India to garner the same kind of economic advantages that Indian firms enjoy. IBM, for example, has invested $2 billion in its Indian operations, and now has 53,000 employees located there, more than in any other country except America. In 2007 it announced plans to invest another $6 billion over the next few years in India. Microsoft too has made major investments in India, including an R&D center in Hyderabad which employees 900 people. The center was located there specifically to tap into talented Indian engineers who did not want to move to the United States.[36]

were written about the economic threat posed to Europe by U.S. corporations.[37] Several European governments, most notably France, talked of limiting inward investment by U.S. firms.

However, as the barriers to the free flow of goods, services, and capital fell, and as other countries increased their shares of world output, non-U.S. firms increasingly began to invest across national borders. The motivation for much of this foreign direct investment by non-U.S. firms was the desire to disperse production activities to optimal locations and to build a direct presence in major foreign markets. Thus, beginning in the 1970s, European and Japanese firms began to shift labor-intensive manufacturing operations from their home markets to developing nations where labor costs were lower. In addition, many Japanese firms invested in North America and Europe—often as a hedge against unfavorable currency movements and the possible imposition of trade barriers. For example, Toyota, the Japanese automobile company, rapidly increased its investment in automobile production facilities in the United States and Europe during the late 1980s and early 1990s. Toyota executives believed that an increasingly strong Japanese yen would price Japanese automobile exports out of foreign markets; therefore, production in the most important foreign markets, as opposed to exports from Japan, made sense. Toyota also undertook these investments to head off growing political pressures in the United States and Europe to restrict Japanese automobile exports into those markets.

One consequence of these developments is illustrated in Figure 6.2, which shows how the stock of foreign direct investment by the world's six most important national sources—the United States, the United Kingdom, Germany, the Netherlands, France, and Japan—changed between 1980 and 2007. (The **stock of foreign direct investment** refers to the total cumulative value of foreign investments.) Figure 6.2 also shows the stock accounted for by firms from developing economies. The share of the total stock accounted for by U.S. firms declined from about 38 percent in 1980 to 17.9 percent in 2007. Meanwhile, the shares accounted for by France and the world's developing nations increased markedly. The rise in the share of FDI stock accounted for by developing nations reflects a growing trend for firms from these countries to invest outside their borders. In 2007, firms based in developing nations accounted for 14.7 percent of the stock of foreign direct investment, up from only 1.1 percent in 1980. Firms based in Hong Kong, South Korea, Singapore, Taiwan, India and mainland China accounted for much of this investment.

Figure 6.3 illustrates two other important trends—the sustained growth in cross-border flows of foreign direct investment that occurred during the 1990s and the importance of developing nations as the destination of foreign direct investment. Throughout the 1990s, the amount of investment directed at both developed and developing nations increased dramatically, a trend that reflects the increasing internationalization of business corporations. A surge in foreign direct investment from 1998 to 2000 was followed by a slump from 2001 to 2003 associated with a slowdown in global economic activity after the collapse of the financial bubble of the late 1990s and 2000. However, the growth of foreign direct investment resumed in 2004 and continued through 2007, when it hit record levels, only

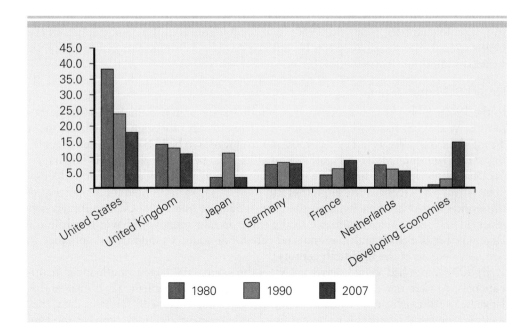

FIGURE 6.2

Percentage Share of Total FDI Stock, 1980–2007

Source: UNCTAD, *World Investment Report, 2008* (United Nations, Geneva).

FIGURE 6.3

FDI Inflows, 1988–2008

Source: UNCTAD, *World Investment Report, 2008* (United Nations, Geneva). UNCTAD Press release, "Global Foreign Investment Now in Decline," January 19, 2009.

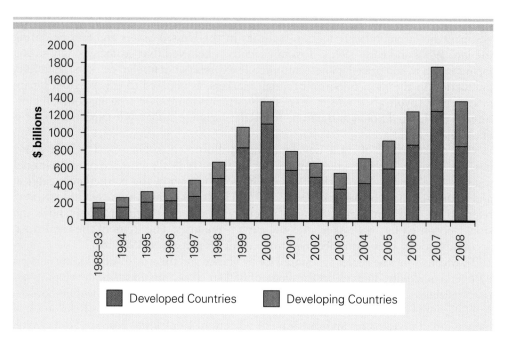

to slow down again in 2008 as the global financial crisis took hold. Among developing nations, the largest recipient of foreign direct investment has been China, which from 2004 to 2008 received $60 to $90 billion a year in inflows. The sustained flow of foreign investment into developing nations is an important stimulus for economic growth in those countries, which bodes well for the future of countries such as China, Mexico, and Brazil, all leading beneficiaries of this trend.

The Changing Nature of the Multinational Enterprise

A **multinational enterprise** (MNE) is any business that has productive activities in two or more countries. Since the 1960s, two notable trends in the demographics of the multinational enterprise have been (1) the rise of non-U.S. multinationals and (2) the growth of mini-multinationals.

Non-U.S. Multinationals

In the 1960s, global business activity was dominated by large U.S. multinational corporations. With U.S. firms accounting for about two-thirds of foreign direct investment during the 1960s, one would expect most multinationals to be U.S. enterprises. According to the data summarized in Figure 6.4, in 1973, 48.5 percent of the world's 260 largest multinationals were U.S. firms. The second-largest source country was the United Kingdom, with 18.8 percent of the largest multinationals. Japan accounted for 3.5 percent of the world's largest multinationals at the time. The large number of U.S. multinationals reflected U.S. economic dominance in the three decades after World War II, while the large number of British multinationals reflected that country's industrial dominance in the early decades of the twentieth century.

By 2006 things had shifted significantly. Of the world's 100 largest nonfinancial multinationals, 24 were now U.S. enterprises; 13 were French; 12, German; 12, British; and 9, Japanese.[38] Although the 1973 data are not strictly comparable with the later data, they illustrate the trend (the 1973 figures are based on the largest 260 firms, whereas the later

FIGURE 6.4

National Origin of Largest Multinational Enterprises, 1973 and 2006

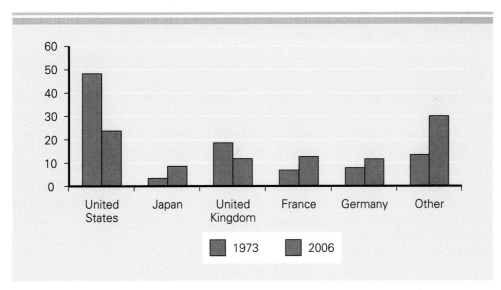

figures are based on the largest 100 multinationals). The globalization of the world economy has resulted in a relative decline in the dominance of U.S. firms in the global marketplace.

According to UN data, the ranks of the world's largest 100 multinationals are still dominated by firms from developed economies.[39] However, seven firms from developing economies had entered the UN's list of the 100 largest multinationals by 2006. The largest was Hutchison Whampoa of Hong Kong, China, which ranked 20.[40] The growth in the number of multinationals from developing economies is evident when we look at smaller firms. By 2005, the largest 50 multinationals from developing economies had foreign sales of $323 billion out of total sales of $738 billion and employed 1.1 million people outside of their home countries. Some 64 percent of the largest 100 multinationals from developing nations came from Hong King, Taiwan, Singapore, and mainland China. Other nations with multiple entries on the list included South Korea, Brazil, Mexico, and Malaysia. We can reasonably expect more growth of new multinational enterprises from the world's developing nations. Firms from developing nations can be expected to emerge as important competitors in global markets, further shifting the axis of the world economy away from North America and Western Europe and threatening the long dominance of Western companies. One such rising competitor, Hisense, one of China's premier manufacturers of consumer appliances and telecommunications equipment, is profiled in the accompanying Management Focus.

The Rise of Mini-Multinationals

Another trend in international business has been the growth of medium-size and small multinationals (mini-multinationals).[41] When people think of international businesses, they tend to think of firms such as Exxon, General Motors, Ford, Fuji, Kodak, Matsushita, Procter & Gamble, Sony, and Unilever—large, complex multinational corporations with operations that span the globe. Although most international trade and investment is still conducted by large firms, many medium-size and small businesses are becoming increasingly involved in international trade and investment. We have already noted how the rise of the Internet is lowering the barriers that small firms face in building international sales.

For another example, consider Lubricating Systems, Inc., of Kent, Washington. Lubricating Systems, which manufactures lubricating fluids for machine tools, employs 25 people and generates sales of $6.5 million. It's hardly a large, complex multinational, yet more than $2 million of the company's sales are generated by exports to a score of countries, including Japan, Israel, and the United Arab Emirates. Lubricating Systems

China's Hisense—An Emerging Multinational

Hisense is rapidly emerging as one of China's leading multinationals. Like many other Chinese corporations, Hisense traces its origins back to a state-owned manufacturer, in this case Qingdao No. 2 Radio Factory, which was established in 1969 with just 10 employees. In the 1970s the state-owned factory diversified into the manufacture of TV sets, and by the 1980s it was one of China's leading manufacturers of color TVs, making sets designed by Matsushita under license. In 1992 a 35-year-old engineer named Zhou Houjian was appointed head of the enterprise. In 1994 the shackles of state ownership were relaxed when the Hisense Company Ltd was established, with Zhou as CEO (he is now Chairman of the Board).

Under Zhou's leadership, Hisense entered a period of rapid growth, product diversification, and global expansion. By 2007 the company had sales of $6.2 billion and had emerged as one of China's premier makers of TV sets (with an 11 percent share of the domestic market), air conditioners, refrigerators, personal computers, and telecommunications equipment. In 2007, Hisense sold around 10 million TV sets, 3 million air conditioners, 4 million CDMA wireless phones, 6 million refrigerators, and 1 million personal computers. International sales accounted for $490 million, or more than 15 percent of total revenue. The company had established overseas manufacturing subsidiaries in Algeria, Hungary, Iran, Pakistan, and South Africa, and it was growing rapidly in developing markets where it was taking share away from long-established consumer electronics and appliance makers.

Hisense's ambitions are grand. It seeks to become a global enterprise with a world class consumer brand. It aims to increase revenue to over $12 billion in 2010, a goal that may be attainable following the 2006 acquisition of its troubled Chinese rival, Kelon. What is different about Hisense is that although it is without question a low-cost manufacturer, it believes its core strength is not in low-cost manufacturing, but in rapid product innovation. The company believes that the only way to gain leadership in the highly competitive markets in which it competes is to continuously launch advanced, high-quality and competitively priced products. To this end, Hisense established its first R&D center in China in the mid-1990s. This was followed by a South African R&D center in 1997 and a European R&D center in 2007. The company also has plans for an R&D center in the United States. In 2006 these R&D centers filed for some 534 patents.

Hisense's technological prowess is evident in its digital TV business. It introduced set-top boxes in 1999, making it possible to browse the Internet from a TV. In 2002, Hisense introduced its first interactive digital TV set, and in 2005 it developed China's first core digital processing chip for digital TVs, breaking the country's reliance on foreign chip makers for this core technology. In 2006, Hisense launched an innovative line of multimedia TV sets that integrated digital high definition technology, network technology, and flat panel displays.[42]

also has set up a joint venture with a German company to serve the European market.[43] Consider also Lixi, Inc., a small U.S. manufacturer of industrial X-ray equipment; 70 percent of Lixi's $4.5 million in revenues comes from exports to Japan.[44] Or take G. W. Barth, a manufacturer of cocoa-bean roasting machinery based in Ludwigsburg, Germany. Employing just 65 people, this small company has captured 70 percent of the global market for cocoa-bean roasting machines.[45] International business is conducted not just by large firms but also by medium-size and small enterprises.

THE CHANGING WORLD ORDER

Between 1989 and 1991 a series of democratic revolutions swept the Communist world. In country after country throughout Eastern Europe and eventually in the Soviet Union itself, Communist Party governments collapsed. The Soviet Union receded into history, having been replaced by 15 independent republics. Czechoslovakia divided itself into two states, while Yugoslavia dissolved into a bloody civil war, now thankfully over, among its five successor states.

Many of the former Communist nations of Europe and Asia seem to share a commitment to democratic politics and free market economics. If this continues, the opportunities for international businesses are significant. For half a century, these countries were essentially closed to Western international businesses. Now they present a host of export and investment opportunities. Just how this will play out over the next 10 to 20 years is difficult to say. The economies of many of the former Communist states are still relatively undeveloped, and their continued commitment to democracy and free market economics cannot be taken for granted. Disturbing signs of growing unrest and totalitarian tendencies continue to be seen in several Eastern European and Central Asian states, including Russia, which has shown signs of shifting back toward greater state involvement in economic activity and authoritarian government.[46] Thus, the risks involved in doing business in such countries are high, but so may be the returns.

In addition to these changes, quieter revolutions have been occurring in China, other states in South East Asia, and Latin America. Their implications for international businesses may be just as profound as the collapse of communism in Eastern Europe. China suppressed its own pro-democracy movement in the bloody Tiananmen Square massacre of 1989. Despite this, China continues to move progressively toward greater free market reforms. If what is occurring in China continues for two more decades, China may move from Third World to industrial superpower status even more rapidly than Japan did. If China's gross domestic product (GDP) per capita grows by an average of 6 to 7 percent, which is slower than the 8 percent growth rate achieved during the last decade, then by 2020 this nation of 1.273 billion people could boast an average income per capita of about $13,000, roughly equivalent to that of Spain's today.

The potential consequences for international business are enormous. On the one hand, with more than 1 billion people, China represents a huge and largely untapped market. Reflecting this, between 1983 and 2008, annual foreign direct investment in China increased from less than $2 billion to $90 billion annually. On the other hand, China's new firms are proving to be very capable competitors, and they could take global market share away from Western and Japanese enterprises (for example, see the Management Focus about Hisense). Thus, the changes in China are creating both opportunities and threats for established international businesses.

As for Latin America, both democracy and free market reforms have been evident there too. For decades, most Latin American countries were ruled by dictators, many of whom seemed to view Western international businesses as instruments of imperialist domination. Accordingly, they restricted direct investment by foreign firms. In addition, the poorly managed economies of Latin America were characterized by low growth, high debt, and hyperinflation—all of which discouraged investment by international businesses. In the last two decades much of this had changed. Throughout most of Latin America, debt and inflation are down, governments have sold state-owned enterprises to private investors, foreign investment is welcomed, and the region's economies have expanded. Brazil, Mexico, and Chile have led the way here. These changes have increased the attractiveness of Latin America, both as a market for exports and as a site for foreign direct investment. At the same time, given the long history of economic mismanagement in Latin America, there is no guarantee that these favorable trends will continue. Indeed, in Bolivia, Ecuador, and most notable Venezuela there have been shifts back toward greater state involvement in industry in the last few years, and foreign investment is now less welcome than it was during the 1990s. In these nations, the government has seized control of oil and gas fields from foreign investors and has limited the rights of foreign energy companies to extract oil and gas from their nations. Thus, as in the case of Eastern Europe, substantial opportunities are accompanied by substantial risks.

THE GLOBAL ECONOMY OF THE TWENTY-FIRST CENTURY

As discussed, the past quarter-century has seen rapid changes in the global economy. Barriers to the free flow of goods, services, and capital have been coming down. The volume of cross-border trade and investment has been growing more rapidly than global output, indicating that national economies are becoming more closely integrated into a single, interdependent, global economic system. As their economies advance, more nations are joining the ranks of the developed world. A generation ago, South Korea and Taiwan were viewed as second-tier developing nations. Now they boast large economies, and their firms are major players in many global industries, from shipbuilding and steel to electronics and chemicals. The move toward a global economy has been further strengthened by the widespread adoption of liberal economic policies by countries that had firmly opposed them for two generations or more. Thus, in keeping with the normative prescriptions of liberal economic ideology, in country after country we have seen state-owned businesses privatized, widespread deregulation adopted, markets opened to more competition, and commitment increased to removing barriers to cross-border trade and investment. This suggests that over the next few decades, countries such as the Czech Republic, Mexico, Poland, Brazil, China, India, and South Africa may build powerful market-oriented economies. In short, current trends indicate that the world is moving toward an economic system that is more favorable for international business.

But it is always hazardous to use established trends to predict the future. The world may be moving toward a more global economic system, but globalization is not inevitable. Countries may pull back from the recent commitment to liberal economic ideology if their experiences do not match their expectations. There are clear signs, for example, of a retreat from liberal economic ideology in Russia. If Russia's hesitation were to become more permanent and widespread, the liberal vision of a more prosperous global economy based on free market principles might not occur as quickly as many hope. Clearly, this would be a tougher world for international businesses.

Also, greater globalization brings with it risks of its own. This was starkly demonstrated in 1997 and 1998 when a financial crisis in Thailand spread first to other East Asian nations and then in 1998 to Russia and Brazil. Ultimately, the crisis threatened to plunge the economies of the developed world, including the United States, into a recession. Even from a purely economic perspective, globalization is not all good. The opportunities for doing business in a global economy may be significantly enhanced, but as we saw in 1997–98, the risks associated with global financial contagion are also greater. Indeed, during 2007 and 2008 a crisis that started in the financial sector of America, where banks had been too liberal in their lending policies to home owners, swept around the world and plunged the global economy into its deepest recession since the early 1980s, illustrating once more that in an interconnected world a severe crisis in one region can impact the entire globe. Still, firms can exploit the opportunities associated with globalization, while at the same time reducing the risks through appropriate hedging strategies.

The Globalization Debate

Is the shift toward a more integrated and interdependent global economy a good thing? Many influential economists, politicians, and business leaders seem to think so.[47] They argue that falling barriers to international trade and investment are the twin engines driving the global economy toward greater prosperity. They say increased international trade and cross-border investment will result in lower prices for goods and services. They believe that globalization stimulates economic growth, raises the incomes of consumers, and helps to create jobs in all countries that participate in the global trading system. There are good theoretical reasons for believing that declining barriers to international trade and investment do stimulate economic growth, create jobs, and raise income levels. Empirical evidence lends support to the predictions of this theory. However, despite the existence of a compelling body of theory and evidence, globalization has its critics.[48] Some of these critics have become increasingly vocal and active, taking to the streets to demonstrate their opposition to globalization. Here we look at the nature of protests against globalization and briefly review the main themes of the debate concerning the merits of globalization.

ANTIGLOBALIZATION PROTESTS

Street demonstrations against globalization date to December 1999, when more than 40,000 protesters blocked the streets of Seattle in an attempt to shut down a World Trade Organization meeting being held in the city. The demonstrators were protesting against a wide range of issues, including job losses in industries under attack from foreign competitors, downward pressure on the wage rates of unskilled workers, environmental degradation, and the cultural imperialism of global media and multinational enterprises, which was seen as being dominated by what some protesters called the "culturally impoverished" interests and values of the United States. All of these ills, the demonstrators claimed, could be laid at the feet of globalization. The World Trade Organization was meeting to try to launch a new round of talks to cut barriers to cross-border trade and investment. As such, it was seen as a promoter of globalization and a target for the antiglobalization protesters. The protests turned violent, transforming the normally placid streets of Seattle into a running battle between "anarchists" and Seattle's bemused and poorly prepared police department. Pictures of brick-throwing protesters and armored police wielding their batons were duly recorded by the global media, which then circulated the images around the world. Meanwhile, the World Trade Organization meeting failed to reach agreement, and although the protests outside the meeting halls had little to do with that failure, the impression took hold that the demonstrators had succeeded in derailing the meetings.

Emboldened by the experience in Seattle, antiglobalization protesters now turn up at almost every major meeting of a global institution. Smaller-scale protests have occurred in several countries, such as France, where antiglobalization activists destroyed a McDonald's restaurant in August 1999 to protest the impoverishment of French culture

Demonstrators at the WTO meeting in Seattle in December 1999 began looting and rioting in the city's downtown area.

by American imperialism (see the Country Focus, "Protesting Globalization in France," for details). While violent protests may give the antiglobalization effort a bad name, it is clear from the scale of the demonstrations that support for the cause goes beyond a core of anarchists. Large segments of the population in many countries believe that globalization has detrimental effects on living standards and the environment, and the media have often fed on this fear. For example, CNN news anchor Lou Dobbs moderates TV shows that are highly critical of the trend by American companies to take advantage of globalization and "export jobs" overseas. As the world slipped into a recession in 2008, Dobbs stepped up his antiglobalization rhetoric.

Both theory and evidence suggest that many of these fears are exaggerated, but this may not have been communicated clearly and both politicians and businesspeople need to do more to counter these fears. Many protests against globalization are tapping into a general sense of loss at the passing of a world in which barriers of time and distance, and vast differences in economic institutions, political institutions, and the level of development of different nations, produced a world rich in the diversity of human cultures. This world is now passing into history. However, while the rich citizens of the developed world may have the luxury of mourning the fact that they can now see McDonald's restaurants and Starbucks coffeehouses on their vacations to exotic locations such as Thailand, fewer complaints are heard from the citizens of those countries, who welcome the higher living standards that progress brings.

GLOBALIZATION, JOBS, AND INCOME

One concern frequently voiced by globalization opponents is that falling barriers to international trade destroy manufacturing jobs in wealthy advanced economies such as the United States and Western Europe. The critics argue that falling trade barriers allow firms to move manufacturing activities to countries where wage rates are much lower.[49] Indeed, due to the entry of China, India, and states from Eastern Europe into the global trading system, along with global population growth, estimates suggest that the pool of global labor may have quadrupled between 1985 and 2005, with most of the increase taking place after 1990.[50] Other things being equal, one might conclude that this enormous expansion in the global labor force, when coupled with expanding international trade, would have depressed wages in developed nations.

This fear is supported by anecdotes. For example, D. L. Bartlett and J. B. Steele, two journalists for the *Philadelphia Inquirer* who gained notoriety for their attacks on free trade, cite the case of Harwood Industries, a U.S. clothing manufacturer that closed its U.S. operations, where it paid workers $9 per hour, and shifted manufacturing to Honduras, where textile workers receive 48 cents per hour.[51] Because of moves such as this, argue Bartlett and Steele, the wage rates of poorer Americans have fallen significantly over the past quarter of a century.

In the last few years, the same fears have been applied to services, which have increasingly been outsourced to nations with lower labor costs. The popular feeling is that when corporations such as Dell, IBM, or Citigroup outsource service activities to lower-cost foreign suppliers—as all three have done—they are "exporting jobs" to low-wage nations and contributing to higher unemployment and lower living standards in their home nations (in this case, the United States). Some lawmakers in the United States have responded by calling for legal barriers to job outsourcing.

Supporters of globalization reply that critics of these trends miss the essential point about free trade—the benefits outweigh the costs.[52] They argue that free trade will result in countries specializing in the production of those goods and services that they can produce most efficiently, while importing goods and services that they cannot produce as efficiently. When a country embraces free trade, there is always some dislocation—lost textile jobs at Harwood Industries, or lost call center jobs at Dell—but the whole economy is better off as a result. According to this view, it makes little sense for the United States to produce textiles at home when they can be produced at a lower cost in

Protesting Globalization in France

One night in August 1999, 10 men under the leadership of local sheep farmer and rural activist Jose Bove crept into the town of Millau in central France and vandalized a McDonald's restaurant under construction, causing an estimated $150,000 damage. These were no ordinary vandals, however, at least according to their supporters, for the "symbolic dismantling" of the McDonald's outlet had noble aims, or so it was claimed. The attack was initially presented as a protest against unfair American trade policies. The European Union had banned imports of hormone-treated beef from the United States, primarily because of fears that it might lead to health problems (although EU scientists had concluded there was no evidence of this). After a careful review, the World Trade Organization stated that the EU ban was not allowed under trading rules the European Union and United States were party to, and that the European Union would have to lift the ban or face retaliation. The European Union refused to comply, so the U.S. government imposed a 100 percent tariff on imports of certain EU products, including French staples such as foie gras, mustard, and Roquefort cheese. On farms near Millau, Bove and others raised sheep whose milk was used to make Roquefort. They felt incensed by the American tariff and decided to vent their frustrations on McDonald's.

Bove and his compatriots were arrested and charged. They quickly became a focus of the antiglobalization movement in France that was protesting everything from a loss of national sovereignty and "unfair" trade policies that were trying to force hormone-treated beef on French consumers, to the invasion of French culture by alien American values, so aptly symbolized by McDonald's. Lionel Jospin, France's prime minister, called the cause of Jose Bove "just." Allowed to remain free pending his trial, Bove traveled to Seattle in December to protest against the World Trade Organization, where he was feted as a hero of the antiglobalization movement. In France, Bove's July 2000 trial drew some 40,000 supporters to the small town of Millau, where they camped outside the courthouse and waited for the verdict. Bove was found guilty and sentenced to three months in jail, far less than the maximum possible sentence of five years. His supporters wore T-shirts claiming, "The world is not merchandise, and neither am I."

About the same time in the Languedoc region of France, California winemaker Robert Mondavi had reached agreement with the mayor and council of the village of Aniane and regional authorities to turn 125 acres of wooded hillside belonging to the village into a vineyard. Mondavi planned to invest $7 million in the project and hoped to produce top-quality wine that would sell in Europe and the United States for $60 a bottle. However, local environmentalists objected to the plan, which they claimed would destroy the area's unique ecological heritage. Jose Bove, basking in sudden fame, offered his support to the opponents, and the protests started. In May 2001, the Socialist mayor who had approved the project was defeated in local elections in which the Mondavi project had become the major issue. He was replaced by a Communist, Manuel Diaz, who denounced the project as a capitalist plot designed to enrich wealthy U.S. shareholders at the cost of his villagers and the environment. Following Diaz's victory, Mondavi announced he would pull out of the project. A spokesman noted, "It's a huge waste, but there are clearly personal and political interests at play here that go way beyond us."

So are the French opposed to foreign investment? The experiences of McDonald's and Mondavi seem to suggest so, as does the associated news coverage, but look closer and a different reality seems to emerge. McDonald's has more than 800 restaurants in France and continues to do very well there. In fact, France is one of the most profitable markets for McDonald's. France has long been one of the most favored locations for inward foreign direct investment, receiving over $450 billion of foreign investment between 2006 and 2008, more than any other European nation with the exception of Britain. American companies have always accounted for a significant percentage of this investment. Moreover, French enterprises have also been significant foreign investors; some 1,100 French multinationals account for around 8 percent of the global stock of foreign direct investment.[53]

Honduras or China (which, unlike Honduras, is a major source of U.S. textile imports). Importing textiles from China leads to lower prices for clothes in the United States, which enables consumers to spend more of their money on other items. At the same time, the increased income generated in China from textile exports increases income levels in that country, which helps the Chinese to purchase more products produced in the United States, such as pharmaceuticals from Amgen, Boeing jets, Intel-based computers, Microsoft software, and Cisco routers.

The same argument can be made to support the outsourcing of services to low-wage countries. By outsourcing its customer service call centers to India, Dell can reduce its cost structure, and thereby its prices for PCs. U.S. consumers benefit from this development. As prices for PCs fall, Americans can spend more of their money on other goods and services. Moreover, the increase in income levels in India allows Indians to purchase more U.S. goods and services, which helps to create jobs in the United States. In this manner, supporters of globalization argue that free trade benefits *all* countries that adhere to a free trade regime.

Critics of globalization must demonstrate three points to prove their argument. First, the share of national income labor receives, as opposed to the share the owners of capital (e.g. stockholders and bondholders) receive, should have declined in advanced nations as a result of downward pressure on wage rates. Second, even though labor's share of the economic pie may have declined, this does not mean lower living standards if the size of the total pie has increased sufficiently to offset the decline in labor's share—in other words, if economic growth and rising living standards in advanced economies make up for labor's smaller portion (this is the position argued by supporters of globalization). Third, the decline in labor's share of national income must be due to moving production to low-wage countries, as opposed to improvement in production technology and productivity.

So what do the data say? Several recent studies shed light on these questions.[54] First, the data do suggest that over the last two decades the share of labor in national income has declined. The decline in share is much more pronounced in Europe and Japan (about 10 percentage points) than in the United States and the United Kingdom (where it is 3–4 percentage points). However, detailed analysis suggests that the share of national income enjoyed by *skilled labor* has actually *increased*, suggesting that the fall in labor's share has been due to a fall in the share taken by *unskilled labor*. A study of long-term trends in income distribution in the United States concluded, for example, that

> Nationwide, from the late 1970s to the late 1990s, the average income of the lowest-income families fell by over 6 percent after adjustment for inflation, and the average real income of the middle fifth of families grew by about 5 percent. By contrast, the average real income of the highest-income fifth of families increased by over 30 percent.[55]

Another study suggested that the earnings gap between workers in skilled and unskilled sectors has widened by 25 percent over the last two decades.[56] In sum, it is unskilled labor in developed nations that has seen its share of national income decline over the last two decades.

However, this does not mean that the *living standards* of unskilled workers in developed nations have declined. It is possible that economic growth in developed nations has offset the fall in the share of national income enjoyed by unskilled workers, raising their living standards. In fact, there is evidence to suggest that real labor compensation has expanded in most developed nations since the 1980s, including the United States. A study by the Organization for Economic Cooperation and Development, whose members include the 20 richest economies in the world, noted that while the gap between the poorest and richest segments of society in some OECD countries had widened, this trend was by no means universal.[57] Contrary to the results of the study cited above, the OECD study found that while income inequality increased from the mid-1970s to the mid-1980s in the United States, it did not widen further in the next decade. The report also notes that in almost all countries, real income levels rose over the 20-year period the study considered, including the incomes of the poorest segment of most OECD societies. To add to the mixed research results, a 2002 U.S. study that included data from 1990 to 2000 concluded that during those years, falling unemployment rates brought gains to low-wage workers and fairly broad-based wage growth, especially in the latter half of the 1990s. The income of the worst-paid 10 percent of the population actually rose twice as fast as that of the average worker during 1998–2000.[58] If such trends continued—and they may not have—the argument that globalization leads to growing income inequality may lose some of its punch.

As noted earlier, globalization critics argue that the decline in unskilled wage rates is due to the migration of low-wage manufacturing jobs offshore and a corresponding reduction in demand for unskilled workers. However, supporters of globalization see a more complex picture. They maintain that the apparent decline in real wage rates of unskilled workers owes far more to a technology-induced shift within advanced economies away from jobs where the only qualification was a willingness to turn up for work every day and toward jobs that require significant education and skills. They point out that many advanced economies report a shortage of highly skilled workers and an excess supply of unskilled workers. Thus, growing income inequality is a result of the wages for skilled workers being bid up by the labor market and the wages for unskilled workers being discounted. In fact, evidence suggests that technological change has had a bigger impact than globalization on the declining share of national income enjoyed by labor.[59] This indicates that the solution to the problem of stagnant incomes among the unskilled is not to be found in limiting free trade and globalization, but in increasing society's investment in education to reduce the supply of unskilled workers.[60]

Finally, it is worth noting that the wage gap between developing and developed nations is closing as developing nations experience rapid economic growth. For example, one estimate suggests that wages in China will approach Western levels in about 30 years.[61] To the extent that this is the case, any migration of unskilled jobs to low-wage countries is a temporary phenomenon representing a structural adjustment on the way to a more tightly integrated global economy.

GLOBALIZATION, LABOR POLICIES, AND THE ENVIRONMENT

A second source of concern is that free trade encourages firms from advanced nations to move manufacturing facilities to less-developed countries that lack adequate regulations to protect labor and the environment from abuse by the unscrupulous.[62] Globalization critics often argue that adhering to labor and environmental regulations significantly increases costs and puts manufacturing enterprises that follow such rules at a competitive disadvantage in the global marketplace vis-à-vis firms based in developing nations that do not have to comply with these regulations. Firms deal with this cost disadvantage, the theory goes, by moving their production facilities to nations that do not have such burdensome regulations or that fail to enforce the regulations they have.

If this were the case, one might expect free trade to lead to an increase in pollution and result in firms from advanced nations exploiting the labor of less developed nations.[63] Opponents of the 1994 formation of the North American Free Trade Agreement (NAFTA) between Canada, Mexico, and the United States repeatedly used this argument. They painted a picture of U.S. manufacturing firms moving to Mexico in droves so that they would be free to pollute the environment, employ child labor, and ignore workplace safety and health issues, all in the name of higher profits.[64]

Supporters of free trade and greater globalization express doubts about this scenario. They argue that tougher environmental regulations and stricter labor standards go hand in hand with economic progress.[65] In general, as countries get richer, they enact tougher environmental and labor regulations.[66] Because free trade enables developing countries to increase their economic growth rates and become richer, this should lead to tougher environmental and labor laws. In this view, the critics of free trade have got it backward—free trade does not lead to more pollution and labor exploitation, it leads

FIGURE 6.5

Income Levels and
Environmental Pollution

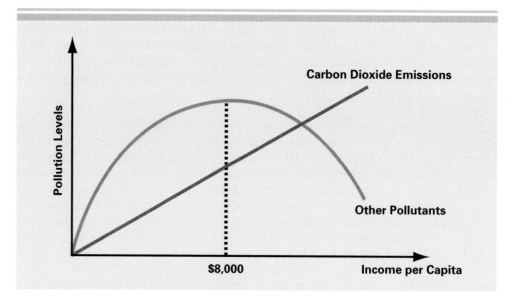

to less. By creating wealth and incentives for enterprises to produce technological innovations, the free market system and free trade could make it easier for the world to
cope with pollution and population growth. Indeed, while pollution levels are rising in
the world's poorer countries, they have been falling in developed nations. In the United
States, for example, the concentration of carbon monoxide and sulphur dioxide pollutants in the atmosphere decreased by 60 percent between 1978 and 1997, while lead
concentrations decreased by 98 percent—and these reductions have occurred against a
background of sustained economic expansion.[67]

A number of econometric studies have found consistent evidence of a hump-shaped
relationship between income levels and pollution levels (see Figure 6.5).[68] As an economy grows and income levels rise, initially pollution levels also rise. However, past some
point, rising income levels lead to demands for greater environmental protection, and
pollution levels then fall. A seminal study by Grossman and Krueger found that the turning point generally occurs before per capita income levels reach $8,000.[69]

While the hump-shaped relationship depicted in Figure 6.5 seems to hold across
a wide range of pollutants—from sulphur dioxide to lead concentrations and water
quality—carbon dioxide emissions are an important exception, rising steadily with
higher income levels. Given that increased atmospheric carbon dioxide concentrations
are a cause of global warming, this should be of serious concern. The solution to the
problem, however, is probably not to roll back the trade liberalization efforts that have
fostered economic growth and globalization, but to get the nations of the world to agree
to tougher standards on limiting carbon emissions. Although UN-sponsored talks have
had this as a central aim since the 1992 Earth Summit in Rio de Janeiro, there has been
little success in moving toward the ambitious goals for reducing carbon emissions laid
down there and subsequent talks in Kyoto, Japan, in part because the largest emitter of
carbon dioxide, the United States, has refused to sign global agreements that it claims
would unreasonably retard economic growth. In addition, the United States, whose
carbon emissions are increasing at an alarming rate, has so far shown little appetite to
adopt tighter pollution controls.

Notwithstanding this, supporters of free trade point out that it is possible to tie free
trade agreements to the implementation of tougher environmental and labor laws in
less-developed countries. NAFTA, for example, was passed only after side agreements
had been negotiated that committed Mexico to tougher enforcement of environmental

protection regulations. Thus, supporters of free trade argue that factories based in Mexico are now cleaner than they would have been without the passage of NAFTA.[70]

They also argue that business firms are not the amoral organizations that critics suggest. While there may be some rotten apples, most business enterprises are staffed by managers who are committed to behave in an ethical manner and would be unlikely to move production offshore just so they could pump more pollution into the atmosphere or exploit labor. Furthermore, the relationship between pollution, labor exploitation, and production costs may not be as suggested by critics. In general, a well-treated labor force is productive, and it is productivity rather than base wage rates that often has the greatest influence on costs. The vision of greedy managers who shift production to low-wage countries to exploit their labor force may be misplaced.

GLOBALIZATION AND NATIONAL SOVEREIGNTY

Another concern voiced by critics of globalization is that today's increasingly interdependent global economy shifts economic power away from national governments and toward supranational organizations such as the World Trade Organization, the European Union, and the United Nations. As a result, critics claim, unelected bureaucrats now impose policies on the democratically elected governments of nation-states, thereby undermining the sovereignty of those states and limiting the nation's ability to control its own destiny.[71]

The World Trade Organization is a favorite target of those who attack the headlong rush toward a global economy. As noted earlier, the WTO was founded in 1994 to police the world trading system established by the General Agreement on Tariffs and Trade. The WTO arbitrates trade disputes between the 150 states that are signatories to the GATT. The arbitration panel can issue a ruling instructing a member state to change trade policies that violate GATT regulations. If the violator refuses to comply with the ruling, the WTO allows other states to impose appropriate trade sanctions on the transgressor. As a result, according to the prominent critic, U.S. environmentalist, consumer rights advocate, and sometime presidential candidate Ralph Nader,

> Under the new system, many decisions that affect billions of people are no longer made by local or national governments but instead, if challenged by any WTO member nation, would be deferred to a group of unelected bureaucrats sitting behind closed doors in Geneva (which is where the headquarters of the WTO are located). The bureaucrats can decide whether or not people in California can prevent the destruction of the last virgin forests or determine if carcinogenic pesticides can be banned from their foods; or whether European countries have the right to ban dangerous biotech hormones in meat. . . . At risk is the very basis of democracy and accountable decision making.[72]

In contrast to Nader, many economists and politicians maintain that the power of supranational organizations such as the WTO is limited to what nation-states collectively agree to grant. They argue that bodies such as the United Nations and the WTO exist to serve the collective interests of member states, not to subvert those interests. Supporters of supranational organizations point out that the power of these bodies rests largely on their ability to persuade member states to follow a certain action. If these bodies fail to serve the collective interests of member states, those states will withdraw their support and the supranational organization will quickly collapse. In this view, real power still resides with individual nation-states, not supranational organizations.

GLOBALIZATION AND THE WORLD'S POOR

Critics of globalization argue that despite the supposed benefits associated with free trade and investment, over the past hundred years or so the gap between the rich and poor nations of the world has gotten wider. In 1870, the average income per capita in the world's 17 richest nations was 2.4 times that of all other countries. In 1990, the same group was 4.5 times as rich as the rest.[73] While recent history has shown that some of the world's poorer nations are capable of rapid periods of economic growth—witness the transformation that has occurred in some Southeast Asian nations such as South Korea, Thailand, and Malaysia—strong forces for stagnation appear to exist in the world's poorest nations. A quarter of the countries with a GDP per capita of less than $1,000 in 1960 had growth rates of less than zero from 1960 to 1995, and a third had growth rates of less than 0.05 percent.[74] Critics argue that if globalization is such a positive development, this divergence between the rich and poor should not have occurred.

Although the reasons for economic stagnation vary, several factors stand out, none of which have anything to do with free trade or globalization.[75] Many of the world's poorest countries have suffered from totalitarian governments, economic policies that destroyed wealth rather than facilitated its creation, endemic corruption, scant protection for property rights, and war. Such factors help explain why countries such as Afghanistan, Cambodia, Cuba, Haiti, Iraq, Libya, Nigeria, Sudan, Vietnam, and Zaire have failed to improve the economic lot of their citizens during recent decades. A complicating factor is the rapidly expanding populations in many of these countries. Without a major change in government, population growth may exacerbate their problems. Promoters of free trade argue that the best way for these countries to improve their lot is to lower their barriers to free trade and investment and to implement economic policies based on free market economics.[76]

Many of the world's poorer nations are being held back by large debt burdens. Of particular concern are the 40 or so "highly indebted poorer countries" (HIPCs), which are home to some 700 million people. Among these countries, the average government debt burden has been has high as 85 percent of the value of the economy, as measured by gross domestic product, and the annual costs of serving government debt consumed 15 percent of the country's export earnings.[77] Servicing such a heavy debt load leaves the governments of these countries with little left to invest in important public infrastructure projects, such as education, health care, roads, and power. The result is that the HIPCs are trapped in a cycle of poverty and debt that inhibits economic development. Free trade alone, some argue, is a necessary but not sufficient prerequisite to help these countries bootstrap themselves out of poverty. Instead, large-scale debt relief is needed for the world's poorest nations to give them the opportunity to restructure their economies and start the long climb toward prosperity. Supporters of debt relief also argue that new democratic governments in poor nations should not be forced to honor debts that were incurred and mismanaged long ago by their corrupt and dictatorial predecessors.

U2's Bono has actively lobbied to have the unpayable debt of poor countries written off.

In the late 1990s, a debt relief movement began to gain ground among the political establishment in the world's richer nations.[78] Fueled by high-profile endorsements from Irish rock star Bono (who has been a tireless and increasingly effective advocate for debt relief), Pope John Paul II, the Dalai Lama, and influential Harvard economist Jeffrey Sachs, the debt relief movement was instrumental in persuading the United States to enact legislation in 2000 that provided $435 million in debt relief for HIPCs. More important perhaps, the United States also backed an IMF plan to sell some of its gold reserves and use the proceeds to help with debt relief. The IMF and World Bank have now picked up the banner and have embarked on a systematic debt relief program.

For such a program to have a lasting effect, however, debt relief must be matched by wise investment in public projects that boost economic growth (such as education) and by the adoption of economic policies that facilitate investment and trade. The rich nations of the world also can help by reducing barriers to importing products from the world's poorer nations, particularly tariffs on imports of agricultural products and textiles. High tariff barriers and other impediments to trade make it difficult for poor countries to export more of their agricultural production. The World Trade Organization has estimated that if the developed nations of the world eradicated subsidies to their agricultural producers and removed tariff barriers to trade in agriculture, they would raise global economic welfare by $128 billion, with $30 billion of that going to developing nations, many of which are highly indebted. The faster growth associated with expanded trade in agriculture could reduce the number of people living in poverty by as much as 13 percent by 2015, according to the WTO.[79]

Managing in the Global Marketplace

There are many challenges of managing in an international business. An **international business** is any firm that engages in international trade or investment. A firm does not have to become a multinational enterprise, investing directly in operations in other countries, to engage in international business, although multinational enterprises are international businesses. All a firm has to do is export or import products from other countries. As the world shifts toward a truly integrated global economy, more firms, both large and small, are becoming international businesses. What does this shift toward a global economy mean for managers within an international business?

As their organizations increasingly engage in cross-border trade and investment, managers need to recognize that the task of managing an international business differs from that of managing a purely domestic business in many ways. At the most fundamental level, the differences arise from the simple fact that countries are different. Countries differ in their cultures, political systems, economic systems, legal systems, and levels of economic development. Despite all the talk about the emerging global village, and despite the trend toward globalization of markets and production, many of these differences are very profound and enduring.

Differences between countries require that an international business vary its practices country by country. Marketing a product in Brazil may require a different approach from marketing the product in Germany; managing U.S. workers might require different skills than managing Japanese workers; maintaining close relations with a particular level of government may be very important in Mexico and irrelevant in Great Britain; the business strategy pursued in Canada might not work in South Korea; and so on. Managers in an international business must not only be sensitive to these differences; they must also adopt the appropriate policies and strategies for coping with them.

A further way in which international business differs from domestic business is the greater complexity of managing an international business. In addition to the problems that arise from the differences between countries, a manager in an international business is confronted with a range of other issues that the manager in a domestic business never confronts. The managers of an international business must decide where in the world to site production activities to minimize costs and to maximize value added. They must decide whether it is ethical to adhere to the lower labor and environmental standards found in many less-developed nations. Then they must decide how best to coordinate and control globally dispersed production activities (which, is not a trivial problem). The managers in an international business also must decide which foreign markets to enter and which to avoid. They must choose the appropriate mode for entering a particular foreign country. Is it best to export the product to the foreign country? Should the firm allow a local company to produce its product under license in that country? Should the firm enter into a joint venture with a local firm to produce its product in that country? Or should the firm set up a wholly owned subsidiary to serve the market in that country? As we shall see, the choice of entry mode is critical because it has major implications for the long-term health of the firm.

Conducting business transactions across national borders requires understanding the rules governing the international trading and investment system. Managers in an international business must also deal with government restrictions on international trade and investment. They must find ways to work within the limits imposed by specific governmental interventions. Even though many governments are nominally committed to free trade, they often intervene to regulate cross-border trade and investment. Managers within international businesses must develop strategies and policies for dealing with such interventions.

Cross-border transactions also require that money be converted from the firm's home currency into a foreign currency and vice versa. Because currency exchange rates vary in response to changing economic conditions, managers in an international business must develop policies for dealing with exchange rate movements. A firm that adopts a wrong policy can lose large amounts of money, whereas one that adopts the right policy can increase the profitability of its international transactions.

In sum, managing an international business is different from managing a purely domestic business for at least four reasons: (1) countries are different, (2) the range of problems a manager confronts in an international business is wider and the problems themselves more complex than those a manager confronts in a domestic business, (3) an international business must find ways to work within the limits imposed by government intervention in the international trade and investment system, and (4) international transactions involve converting money into different currencies.

CHAPTER SUMMARY

This chapter shows how the world economy is becoming more global and reviews the main drivers of globalization, arguing that they seem to be thrusting nation-states toward a more tightly integrated global economy. We looked at how the nature of international business is changing in response to the changing global economy; we discussed some concerns raised by rapid globalization; and we reviewed implications of rapid globalization for individual managers. The chapter made the following points:

1. Over the past two decades, we have witnessed the globalization of markets and production.

2. The globalization of markets implies that national markets are merging into one huge marketplace. However, it is important not to push this view too far.

3. The globalization of production implies that firms are basing individual productive activities at the optimal world locations for the particular activities. As a consequence, it is increasingly irrelevant to talk about American products, Japanese products, or German products, since they are being replaced by "global" products.

4. Two factors seem to underlie the trend toward globalization: declining trade barriers and changes in communication, information, and transportation technologies.

5. Since the end of World War II, barriers to the free flow of goods, services, and capital have been lowered significantly. More than anything else, this has facilitated the trend toward the globalization of production and has enabled firms to view the world as a single market.

6. As a consequence of the globalization of production and markets, in the last decade world trade has grown faster than world output, foreign direct investment has surged, imports have penetrated more deeply into the world's industrial nations, and competitive pressures have increased in industry after industry.

7. The development of the microprocessor and related developments in communication and information processing technology have helped firms link their worldwide operations into sophisticated information networks. Jet air travel, by shrinking travel time, has also helped to link the worldwide operations of international businesses. These changes have enabled firms to achieve tight coordination of their worldwide operations and to view the world as a single market.

8. In the 1960s, the U.S. economy was dominant in the world, U.S. firms accounted for most of the foreign direct investment in the world economy, U.S. firms dominated the list of large multinationals, and roughly half the world—the centrally planned economies of the Communist world—was closed to Western businesses.

9. By the mid-1990s, the U.S. share of world output had been cut in half, with Western European and Southeast Asian economies accounting for

major shares. The U.S. share of worldwide foreign direct investment had also fallen by about two-thirds. U.S. multinationals were now facing competition from a large number of Japanese and European multinationals. In addition, mini-multinationals emerged.

10. One of the most dramatic developments of the past 20 years has been the collapse of communism in Eastern Europe, which has created enormous long-run opportunities for international businesses. In addition, the move toward free market economies in China and Latin America is creating opportunities (and threats) for Western international businesses.

11. The benefits and costs of the emerging global economy are being hotly debated among businesspeople, economists, and politicians. The debate focuses on the impact of globalization on jobs, wages, the environment, working conditions, and national sovereignty.

12. Managing an international business is different from managing a domestic business for at least four reasons: (*a*) countries are different, (*b*) the range of problems a manager confronts in an international business is wider and the problems themselves more complex than those a manager in a domestic business confronts, (*c*) managers in an international business must find ways to work within the limits imposed by governments' intervention in the international trade and investment system, and (*d*) international transactions involve converting money into different currencies.

Key Terms and Concepts

factors of production, *103*

foreign direct investment (FDI), *107*

G20, *107*

General Agreement on Tariffs and Trade (GATT), *105*

globalization, *102*

globalization of markets, *102*

globalization of production, *103*

international business, *129*

International Monetary Fund, *106*

International trade, *107*

Moore's Law, *110*

multinational enterprise, *116*

stock of foreign direct investment, *115*

United Nations, *106*

World Bank, *106*

World Trade Organization, *105*

Critical Thinking and Discussion Questions

1. Describe the shifts in the world economy over the past 30 years. What are the implications of these shifts for international businesses based in Great Britain? North America? Hong Kong?

2. "The study of international business is fine if you are going to work in a large multinational enterprise, but it has no relevance for individuals who are going to work in small firms." Evaluate this statement.

3. How have changes in technology contributed to the globalization of markets and production? Would the globalization of production and markets have been possible without these technological changes?

4. "Ultimately, the study of international business is no different from the study of domestic business. Thus, there is no point in having a separate course on international business." Evaluate this statement.

5. How does the Internet and the associated World Wide Web affect international business activity and the globalization of the world economy?

6. If current trends continue, China may be the world's largest economy by 2020. Discuss the possible implications of such a development for (*a*) the world trading system, (*b*) the world monetary system, (*c*) the business strategy of today's European and U.S.-based global corporations, and (*d*) global commodity prices.

7. Reread the Management Focus on Vizio and answer the following questions:
   a. Why is the manufacturing of flat panel TVs migrating to different locations around the world?
   b. Who benefits from the globalization of the flat panel display industry? Who are the losers?
   c. What would happen if the U.S. government required that flat panel displays sold in the United States had to also be made in the United States? On balance, would this be a good or a bad thing?
   d. What does the example of Vizio tell you about the future of production in an increasingly integrated global economy? What does it tell you about the strategies that enterprises must adopt in order to thrive in highly competitive global markets?

Research Task globalEDGE globaledge.msu.edu

Globalization

Use the globalEDGE™ site to complete the following exercises:

Exercise 1

Your company has developed a new product that has universal appeal across countries and cultures. In fact, it is expected to achieve high penetration rates in all the countries where it is introduced, regardless of the average income of the local populace. Considering the costs of the product launch, the management team has decided to introduce the product initially only in countries that have a sizeable population base. You are required to prepare a preliminary report about the top 10 countries in terms of population size. A member of management has indicated that a resource called the "World Population Data Sheet" may be useful for the report. Since growth opportunities are another major concern, the average population growth rates should be listed also for management's consideration.

Exercise 2

You are working for a company that is considering investing in a foreign country. Investing in countries with different traditions is an important element of your company's long-term strategic goals. As such, management has requested a report regarding the attractiveness of alternative countries based on the potential return of FDI. Accordingly, the ranking of the top 25 countries in terms of FDI attractiveness is a crucial ingredient for your report. A colleague mentioned a potentially useful tool called the "FDI Confidence Index," which is updated periodically. Find this index and provide additional information regarding how the index is constructed.

CLOSING CASE

Globalization at General Electric

General Electric, the company that Thomas Edison founded, and now the largest industrial conglomerate in America, produces a wide array of goods and services, from medical equipment, power generators, jet engines, and home appliances, to financial services and even television broadcasting (GE owns NBC, one of America's big three network broadcasters). This giant company with revenues of close to $180 billion is no stranger to international business. GE has been operating and selling overseas for decades. During the tenure of legendary CEO Jack Welch, GE's main goal was to be number 1 or 2 *globally* in every business in which it participated. To further this goal, Welch sanctioned an aggressive and often opportunistic foreign direct investment strategy. GE took advantage of economic weakness in Europe from 1989 to1995 to invest $17.5 billion in the region, half of which was used to acquire some 50 companies. When the Mexican *peso* collapsed in value in 1995, GE took advantage of the economic uncertainty to purchase companies throughout in Latin America. And when Asian slipped into a major economic crisis in 1997–1998 due to turmoil in the Asian currency markets, Welch urged his managers to view it as a buying opportunity. In Japan alone, the company spent $15 billion on acquisition in just six months. As a result, by the end of Welch's tenure in 2001, GE earned over 40 percent of its revenues from international sales, up from 20 percent in 1985.

Welch's GE, however, was still very much an American company doing business abroad. Under the leadership of his successor, Jeffery Immelt, GE seems to be intent on becoming a true *global* company. For one thing, international revenues continue to grow faster than domestic revenues, passing 50 percent of the total in 2007. This expansion is increasingly being powered by the dynamic economies of Asia, particularly India and China. GE now sells more wide-bodied jet engines to India than in the Untied States, and GE is a major beneficiary of the huge infrastructure investments now taking place in China as that country invests rapidly in airports, railways, and power stations. By 2012, analysts estimate that GE will be generating 55 to 60 percent of its business internationally.

To reflect the shifting center of gravity, Immelt has made some major changes in the way GE is organized and operates. Until recently, all of GE's major businesses had head offices in the United States and were tightly controlled from the center. Then in 2004, GE moved the head office of its health care business from the United States to London, the home of Amersham, a company GE had just bought. Next, GE relocated the headquarters for the unit that sells equipment to oil and gas companies to Florence, Italy. And in 2008, the company moved the headquarters for GE Money to London. Moreover, it gave country managers more power. Why is GE doing this? The company believes that to succeed internationally, it must be close to its customers. Moving GE Money to London, for example, was prompted by a desire to be closer to customers in Europe and Asia. Executives at GE Health Care like London because it allows easier flights to anywhere in the world.

GE has also shifted research overseas. Since 2004 it has opened R&D centers in Munich, Germany; Shanghai, China; and Bangalore, India. The belief is that by locating in those economies where it is growing rapidly, GE can better design equipment that is best suited to local needs. For example, GE Health Care makes MRI scanners that cost $1.5 million each, but its Chinese research center is designing MRI scanners that can be priced for $500,000 and are more likely to gain sales in the developing world.

GE is also rapidly internationalizing its senior management. Once viewed as a company that preferred to hire managers from the Midwest because of their strong work ethic, foreign accents are now frequently heard among the higher ranks. Country managers, who in the past were often American expatriates, increasingly come from the regions in where they work. GE has found that local nationals are invaluable when trying to sell to local companies and governments, where a deep understanding of local language and culture is often critical. In China, for example, the government is a large customer, and working closely with government bureaucrats requires a cultural sensitivity that is difficult for outsiders to gain. In addition to the internationalization of their management ranks, GE's American managers are increasingly traveling overseas for management training and company events. In 2008, in a highly symbolic gesture, GE Transportation, which is based in Erie, Pennsylvania, moved its annual sales meeting to Sorrento, Italy from Florida. "It was time that the Americans learnt to deal with jet lag," according to the head of the unit.[80]

Case Discussion Questions

1. Why do you think GE has invested so aggressively in foreign expansion? What opportunities is it trying to exploit?
2. What is GE trying to achieve by moving some of the headquarters of its global businesses to foreign locations? How might such moves benefit the company? Do these moves benefit the United States?
3. What is the goal behind trying to "internationalize" the senior management ranks at GE? What do you think it means to "internationalize" these ranks?
4. What does the GE example tell you about the nature of true global businesses?

Notes

1. Sources: G. Colvin, "Think Your Job Can't Be Sent to India?" *Fortune*, December 13, 2004, p. 80; A. Pollack, "Who's Reading Your X-Ray," *The New York Times*, November 16, 2003, pp. 1, 9; "Sun, Sand and Scalpels," *The Economist*, March 10, 2007, p. 6; "Operating Profit," *The Economist*, August 16, 2008, pp 74–76; and R. Bailey, "Hips Abroad," *Reason*, May 2009, p. 14.
2. Trade statistics from World Trade Organization, trade statistics database, accessed May 12, 2009, at http://stat.wto.org/ Home/WSDBHome.aspx. Foreign Exchange statistics from Bank for International Settlements at http://www.bis.org/index.htm.
3. Thomas L. Friedman, *The World Is Flat* (New York: Farrar, Straus and Giroux, 2005).

4. Ibid.

5. T. Levitt, "The Globalization of Markets," *Harvard Business Review*, May–June 1983, pp. 92–102.

6. U.S. Department of Commerce, "A Profile of U.S. Exporting Companies, 2000–2001," February 2003; report available at www.census.gov/ foreign-trade/aip/index. html#profile.

7. Ibid.

8. C. M. Draffen, "Going Global: Export Market Proves Profitable for Region's Small Businesses," *Newsday*, March 19, 2001, p. C18.

9. B. Benoit and R. Milne, "Germany's Best Kept Secret, How Its Exporters Are Betting the World," *Financial Times*, May 19, 2006, p. 11.

10. See F. T. Knickerbocker, *Oligopolistic Reaction and Multinational Enterprise* (Boston: Harvard Business School Press, 1973); and R. E. Caves, "Japanese Investment in the U.S.: Lessons for the Economic Analysis of Foreign Investment," *The World Economy* 16 (1993), pp. 279–300.

11. I. Metthee, "Playing a Large Part," *Seattle Post-Intelligencer*, April 9, 1994, p. 13.

12. D. Pritchard, "Are Federal Tax Laws and State Subsidies for Boeing 7E7 Selling America Short?" *Aviation Week*, April 12, 2004, pp. 74–75.

13. D.J. Lynch. "Flat Panel TVs Display Effects of Globalization," *USA Today*, May 8, 2007, pp. 1B and 2B; P. Engardio and E. Woyke, "Flat Panels, Thin Margins," *Business Week*, February 26, 2007, p. 50; B. Womack, "Flat TV Seller Vizio Hits $600 Million in Sales, Growing," *Orange County Business Journal*, September 4, 2007, pp. 1, 64; and E.Taub, "Vizio's Flat Panel Display Sales Are Anything But Flat," *New York Times Online*, May 12, 2009.

14. "Operating Profit," *The Economist*, August 16, 2008, pp. 74–76.

15. R. B. Reich, *The Work of Nations* (New York: A. A. Knopf, 1991).

16. United Nations, "The UN in Brief," www.un.org/Overview/brief.html.

17. J. A. Frankel, "Globalization of the Economy," National Bureau of Economic Research, working paper no. 7858, 2000.

18. J. Bhagwati, *Protectionism* (Cambridge, MA: MIT Press, 1989).

19. F. Williams, "Trade Round Like This May Never Be Seen Again," *Financial Times*, April 15, 1994, p. 8.

20. W. Vieth, "Major Concessions Lead to Success for WTO Talks," *Los Angeles Times*, November 14, 2001, p. A1; and "Seeds Sown for Future Growth," *The Economist*, November 17, 2001, pp. 65–66.

21. Ibid.

22. World Trade Organization, International Trade Trends and Statistics, 2007 (Geneva: WTO, 2007).

23. United Nations, *World Investment Report, 2008*; and "Global Foreign Direct Investment Now in Decline," UN Conference on Trade and Development, press release, January 19, 2009.

24. World Trade Organization, *International Trade Statistics, 2007* (Geneva: WTO, 2007); and United Nations, *World Investment Report, 2007*.

25. United Nations, *World Investment Report, 2008*.

26. Moore's Law is named after Intel founder Gordon Moore.

27. Frankel, "Globalization of the Economy."

28. J. G. Fernald and V. Greenfield, "The Fall and Rise of the Global Economy," *Chicago Fed Letters*, April 2001, pp. 1–4.

29. Data compiled from various sources and listed at http://www.internetworldstats.com/stats.htm.

30. Accessed May 15, 2009, at http://www.census.gov/mrts/www/ecomm.html.

31. For a counterpoint, see "Geography and the Net: Putting It in Its Place," *The Economist*, August 11, 2001, pp. 18–20.

32. Frankel, "Globalization of the Economy."

33. Data from Bureau of Transportation Statistics, 2001.

34. Fernald and Greenfield, "The Fall and Rise of the Global Economy."

35. Data located at www.bts.gov/publications/us_international_trade_and_freight_transportation_trends/2003/index.html.

36. "America's Pain, India's Gain: Outsourcing," *The Economist*, January 11, 2003, p. 59; "The World Is Our Oyster," *The Economist*, October 7, 2006, pp. 9–10. Anonymous, "IBM and Globalization: Hungry Tiger, Dancing Elephant", *The Economist*, April 7th, 2007, pp. 67–69.

37. N. Hood and J. Young, *The Economics of the Multinational Enterprise* (New York, Longman, 1973).

38. United Nations, *World Investment Report, 2008*.

39. Ibid.

40. Ibid.

41. S. Chetty, "Explosive International Growth and Problems of Success among Small and Medium Sized Firms," *International Small Business Journal*, February 2003, pp. 5–28.

42. Harold L. Sirkin, "Someone May Be Gaining on Us," *Barron's*, February 5, 2007, p. 53; "Hisense Plans to Grab More International Sales," *Sino Cast China IT Watch*, November 30, 2006; "Hisense's Wonder Chip," *Financial Times Information Limited – Asian Intelligence Wire*, October 30, 2006; and Hisense's Web site, accessed June 14, 2007, at http://www.hisense.com/en/index.jsp.

43. R. A. Mosbacher, "Opening Up Export Doors for Smaller Firms," *Seattle Times*, July 24, 1991, p. A7.

44. "Small Companies Learn How to Sell to the Japanese," *Seattle Times*, March 19, 1992.

45. Holstein, "Why Johann Can Export, but Johnny Can't."

46. N. Buckley and A. Ostrovsky, "Back to Business—How Putin's Allies Are Turning Russia into a Corporate State," *Financial Times*, June 19, 2006, p. 11.

47. J. E. Stiglitz, *Globalization and Its Discontents* (New York: W. W. Norton, 2003); J. Bhagwati, *In Defense of Globaliza-*

tion (New York: Oxford University Press, 2004); and Friedman, *The World Is Flat.*

48. See, for example, Ravi Batra, *The Myth of Free Trade* (New York: Touchstone Books, 1993); William Greider, *One World, Ready or Not: The Manic Logic of Global Capitalism* (New York: Simon and Schuster, 1997); and D. Radrik, *Has Globalization Gone Too Far?* (Washington, DC: Institution for International Economics, 1997).

49. James Goldsmith, "The Winners and the Losers," in *The Case against the Global Economy*, eds. J. Mander and E. Goldsmith (San Francisco: Sierra Club, 1996); and Lou Dobbs, *Exporting America* (New York: Time Warner Books, 2004).

50. For an excellent summary see "The Globalization of Labor," Chapter 5 in IMF, *World Economic Outlook 2007*, April 2007. Also see R. Freeman, "Labor Market Imbalances," Harvard University Working Paper, accessed June 14, 2007 at http://www.bos.frb.org/economic/conf/conf51/papers/freeman.pdf.

51. D. L. Bartlett and J. B. Steele, "America: Who Stole the Dream," *Philadelphia Inquirer*, September 9, 1996.

52. For example, see Paul Krugman, *Pop Internationalism* (Cambridge, MA: MIT Press, 1996).

53. Sources: "Behind the Bluster," *The Economist*, May 26, 2001; "The French Farmers' Anti-global Hero," *The Economist*, July 8, 2000; C. Trueheart, "France's Golden Arch Enemy?" *Toronto Star*, July 1, 2000; J. Henley, "Grapes of Wrath Scare Off U.S. Firm," *The Economist*, May 18, 2001, p. 11; and United Nations, *World Investment Report, 2006* (New York and Geneva: United Nations, 2006).

54. For example, see B. Milanovic and L. Squire, "Does Tariff Liberalization Increase Wage Inequality?" *National Bureau of Economic Research*, working paper no. 11046, January 2005; and B. Milanovic, "Can We Discern the Effect of Globalization on Income Distribution?" *World Bank Economic Review*, 19, 2005, pp. 21–44. Also see the summary in "The Globalization of Labor."

55. Jared Bernstein, Elizabeth C. McNichol, Lawrence Mishel, and Robert Zahradnik, "Pulling Apart: A State by State Analysis of Income Trends," *Economic Policy Institute*, January 2000.

56. See "The Globalization of Labor."

57. M. Forster and M. Pearson, "Income Distribution and Poverty in the OECD Area," *OECD Economic Studies 34* (2002).

58. Bernstein et al., "Pulling Apart."

59. See "The Globalization of Labor."

60. See Krugman, *Pop Internationalism*; and D. Belman and T. M. Lee, "International Trade and the Performance of U.S. Labor Markets," in *U.S. Trade Policy and Global Growth*, ed. R. A. Blecker (New York: Economic Policy Institute, 1996).

61. R. Freeman, "Labor Market Imbalances."

62. E. Goldsmith, "Global Trade and the Environment," in *The Case against the Global Economy*, eds. J. Mander and E. Goldsmith (San Francisco: Sierra Club, 1996).

63. P. Choate, *Jobs at Risk: Vulnerable U.S. Industries and Jobs under NAFTA* (Washington, DC: Manufacturing Policy Project, 1993).

64. Ibid.

65. B. Lomborg, *The Skeptical Environmentalist* (Cambridge: Cambridge University Press, 2001).

66. H. Nordstrom and S. Vaughan, Trade and the Environment, World Trade Organization Special Studies No. 4 (Geneva: WTO, 1999).

67. Figures are from "Freedom's Journey: A Survey of the 20th Century. Our Durable Planet," *The Economist*, September 11, 1999, p. 30.

68. For an exhaustive review of the empirical literature, see B. R. Copeland and M. Scott Taylor, "Trade, Growth and the Environment," *Journal of Economic Literature*, March 2004, pp. 7–77.

69. G. M. Grossman and A. B. Krueger, "Economic Growth and the Environment," *Quarterly Journal of Economics* 110 (1995), pp. 353–78.

70. Krugman, *Pop Internationalism.*

71. R. Kuttner, "Managed Trade and Economic Sovereignty," in *U.S. Trade Policy and Global Growth*, ed. R. A. Blecker (New York: Economic Policy Institute, 1996).

72. Ralph Nader and Lori Wallach, "GATT, NAFTA, and the Subversion of the Democratic Process," in *U.S. Trade Policy and Global Growth*, ed. R. A. Blecker (New York: Economic Policy Institute, 1996), pp. 93–94.

73. Lant Pritchett, "Divergence, Big Time," *Journal of Economic Perspectives* 11, no. 3 (Summer 1997), pp. 3–18.

74. Ibid.

75. W. Easterly, "How Did Heavily Indebted Poor Countries Become Heavily Indebted?" *World Development*, October 2002, pp. 1677–96; and J. Sachs, *The End of Poverty* (New York, Penguin Books, 2006).

76. See D. Ben-David, H. Nordstrom, and L. A. Winters, "Trade, Income Disparity and Poverty", *World Trade Organization Special Studies No. 5* (Geneva: WTO, 1999).

77. William Easterly, "Debt Relief," *Foreign Policy*, November–December 2001, pp. 20–26.

78. Jeffrey Sachs, "Sachs on Development: Helping the World's Poorest," *The Economist*, August 14, 1999, pp. 17–20.

79. World Trade Organization, *Annual Report 2003* (Geneva: WTO, 2004).

80. C. H. Deutsch, "At Home in the World," *The New York Times*, February 14, 2008, pp. C1, C4; V.J. Racanelli, GE's Moment", *Barron's*, June 4, 2007, pp. 25–29; "General Electric: The Immelt Way," *Business Week*, September 11, 2006, p. 30; and F. Guerrera, "GE Money Moves its HQ to London," *Financial Times*, February 8, 2008, p. 18.

Is Economic Globalization Good for Humankind?

YES: Paul A. Gigot, from "Foreword" and **Guy Sorman,** from "Globalization Is Making the World a Better Place," (2008). http://www.heritage.org/index/PDF/2008/Index2008_Foreword.pdf; http://www.heritage.org/ index/PDF/2008/Index2008_Chap3.pdf

NO: Branco Milanovic, from "Why Globalization Is in Trouble—Parts 1 and 2," (August 31, 2006). http:// yaleglobal .yale.edu/display.article?id=8073

ISSUE SUMMARY

YES: Arguing that globalization is good for humankind are Paul Gigot and Guy Sorman. They outline seven ways in which globalization has positively impacted life and what needs to be done to further its advancement.

NO: Branko Milanovic, an economist with both the Carnegie Endowment for International Peace and the World Bank, is against globalization. He addresses several reasons for his views while emphasizing the incompatibility of globalization with the ages-old ethnic and religious traditions and values that characterize much of the world.

According to a leading international business textbook, globalization is "the inexorable integration of markets, nation-states, and technologies . . . in a way that is enabling individuals, corporations, and nation-states to reach around the world farther, faster, deeper, and cheaper than ever before" (Ricky W. Griffin and Michael W. Pustay, *International Business*, 6th ed., Prentice Hall, 2010). Globalism is a phenomenon that has its roots in the rebuilding of Europe and Asia in the aftermath of World War II. As a measure of how powerful a phenomenon it has become, consider that the volume of international trade has increased over 3000 percent since 1960! Most of this tremendous growth has occurred in the TRIAD, a free-trade market consisting of three regional trading blocs: Western Europe in its current form as the European Union, North America, and Asia (including Australia). Increasingly, however, the developing nations of the world are contributing to the expansion in world trade. Foreign investment has grown at staggering rates as well: over three times faster than the world output of goods. In the early part of the twenty-first century, it is not a stretch to say that virtually all businesses in industrialized nations are impacted to some degree by globalization.

It seems pretty clear that globalization will continue to grow as a dominant force in international relations among countries, particularly as more Second and Third World countries open their borders to international trade and investment. What may be less clear, however,

is whether or not this is a positive development. In other words, as we ask in this topic, is economic globalization good for humankind?

Like many of the topics in this book, globalization invokes strong arguments and strong emotions from supporters on each side. Those that believe globalization is a beneficial force for humans have a plethora of reasons for their view. From an economic perspective, the spread of free trade and free markets across the globe has liberated hundreds of millions from poverty over the past 40 years. Studies on economic freedom consistently show that countries that embrace globalization are more economically free and, as a direct result, enjoy higher per capita wealth than countries that are more isolated economically. Supporters also note that the growth in globalization has been accompanied by a growth in democracy as well. Along with these two benefits, globalization enhances the cultures of those countries that embrace it. Guy Sorman, one of the authors of the "yes" article in this debate, points out: "Through popular culture, people from different backgrounds and nations discover one another, and their 'otherness' suddenly disappears." Increases in cultural tolerance and openness to different worldviews is part-and-parcel of globalization. A tangentially related benefit involves the spread of respect for the rights of women and minorities around the globe. Discrimination is incompatible with freedom and democracy, and the spread of globalization brings pressure to bear on governments to recognize and protect the rights of all their citizens.

Detractors of globalization also raise several important points. Echoing anti-outsourcing advocates, they argue that globalization results in a loss of jobs due to competition with low-wage countries. Indeed, the major economic force driving the tremendous growth of the Indian and Chinese economies over the past 15 years is their competitive advantage in access to cheap labor. Many anti-globalization supporters argue that corporations are becoming too powerful politically and economically and believe that the search for overseas profits markets is the primary cause. Opponents also raise concerns over

national safety and security issues. As the globe continues to shrink and the ease and speed of information exchange continues to increase, the likelihood of cyberattacks and the theft of sensitive military, technological, and economic information is assumed to increase. The threat of terrorism has grown dramatically in the past 30 years due in large part, say the globalization critics, to the spread of globalization driven by the United States and other western, First-World civilizations. And, as the recent Swine Flu outbreak reminds us, the threat of a worldwide health pandemic grows larger the more integrated the world becomes.

YES

Paul A. Gigot and Guy Sorman

Foreword[1]

I don't know who first used the word "globalization," but he was probably no friend of capitalism. The word is bureaucratic and implies that the world economy is subject to the control of some vast, nefarious force beyond human influence. The reality is that the world economy is enjoying its strongest run of prosperity in 40 years thanks to the greater ability of billions of individuals to make free choices in their own self-interest. The *Index of Economic Freedom* has been encouraging this trend for 14 years, and at the end of 2007, we can happily say it continues.

The world economy extended its multiyear run of 5 percent or so annual GDP growth this year, notwithstanding an American slowdown due mainly to the housing correction. As I write this, the U.S. economy seems to have survived the August credit crunch related to the collapse of the sub-prime mortgage market. The summer squall showed once again how interrelated financial markets have become, with sub-prime losses popping up around the world and even causing an old-fashioned bank run at Northern Rock in the United Kingdom.

The episode is naturally leading to soul-searching about the stability of this brave new world of global finance—including the spread of asset securitization, the rise of hedge funds, and an explosion in derivatives. This introspection ought to be healthy. The sub-prime fiasco has, at the very least, exposed the need for more careful vetting by investors, but regulators and

bankers are also sure to examine the rules for transparency and capital requirements to prevent the spread of problems throughout the financial system. The event also shows the need for more careful driving by America's Federal Reserve, whose easy-money policy in the first half of this decade was the root cause of the housing boom and bust. The good news is that, at least so far, there hasn't been a regulatory overreaction that could stymie growth.

The irony of the year has been the shifting economic policy trends in America and France, of all places. The U.S. political debate is moving in a negative direction as "fairness" and income redistribution replace growth as the policy lodestar and proposals for tax increases proliferate. The Bush tax cuts of 2003 were crucial to kicking the economy out of its post-9/11, post-dot.com doldrums. But they expire after 2010 and are in serious jeopardy. The free-trade agenda has also stalled as bilateral pacts with Latin America and South Korea face heavy going on Capitol Hill. The 2008 election will be as much a referendum on economic policy as on foreign policy.

Perhaps the rest of the world will have to teach America a policy lesson or two. As the *Index* shows, Europe overall has moved in a freer direction this decade. This is due in large part to reform in the former Eastern Europe, as well as to the policy competition caused by the success of the euro. With capital and people free to move and governments no longer able to inflate their way out of fiscal difficulty, the trend has been toward lower tax rates and labor market liberalization.

Miracle of miracles, even France has been mugged by this reality. Nicolas Sarkozy made the revival of the French economy a main theme of his successful cam-

---

1   From *Index of Economic Freedom*, 2008, pp. ix–x, 35–38. Copyright © 2008 by Heritage Foundation. Reprinted by permission.

paign for president, and he has followed with proposals for what he called "a new social contract founded on work, merit and equal opportunity." We should all hope he succeeds—not merely to compensate for any slowdown in America, but for its own sake to help Europe break away from its self-imposed sense of diminished expectations. In any event, this policy churning in Europe shows how the ability to move capital freely across borders imposes a price on bad government decisions.

The larger point is that if we step back from the daily turmoil, we can see that we live in a remarkable era of prosperity and spreading freedom. Hundreds of millions of people are being lifted out of poverty around the world as global trade and investment expand and countries like India and China liberalize parts of their economies. The International Monetary Fund reported in early 2007 that every country in the world, save for a couple of small dictatorships, was growing. This prosperity can itself create discontent due to the rapidity of change, and it certainly poses a challenge to political leaders who are obliged to explain and manage its consequences. The *Index of Economic Freedom* exists to help in that explanation, and we hope readers continue to find it a source of comparative policy wisdom.

Globalization Is Making the World a Better Place

What we call "globalization," one of the most powerful and positive forces ever to have arisen in the history of mankind, is redefining civilization as we know it. This is one of my hypotheses. To be more specific, I will try to describe what globalization is, its impact on world peace, and the freedom it brings from want, fear, and misery.

Globalization has six major characteristics: economic development, democracy, cultural enrichment, political and cultural norms, information, and internationalization of the rule of law.

Economic Development

Usually, globalization is described in terms of intensified commercial and trade exchanges, but it is about more than just trade, stock exchanges, and currencies. It is about people. What is significant today is that through globalization many nations are converging toward enhanced welfare.

This convergence is exemplified by the 800 million people who, in the past 30 years, have left poverty and misery behind. They have greater access to health care, schooling, and information. They have more choices, and their children will have even more choices. The absolutely remarkable part is that it happened not by accident but through a combination of good economic policy, technology, and management.

Of course, not all nations are following this path, but since the fall of the Berlin Wall, more and more are coming closer. Only Africa's nations have yet to join, but who would have hoped and predicted 30 years ago that China and India, with such rapidity and efficiency, would pull their people out of misery? There is no reason why Africa, when its turn comes, will not do the same. Convergence should be a source of hope for us all.

Democracy

In general, since 1989, the best system to improve the welfare of all people—not only economically, but also in terms of access to equality and freedom—appears to be democracy, the new international norm. As more and more countries turn democratic or converge toward democratic norms, respect for other cultures increases.

Democracy has guaranteed welfare far better than any dictatorship ever could. Even enlightened despots cannot bring the kind of safety democracy is bringing. Sometimes a trade-off between economic allotment and democracy occurs. Sometimes the economy grows more slowly because of democracy. Let it be that way. Democracy brings values that are as important for the welfare of the human being as [the] economy is.

After all, as history shows, the chance of international war diminishes step by step any time a country moves from tyranny to democracy, as democracies do not war against one other. That more and more nations are turning democratic improves everyone's way of life.

Cultural Enrichment

Critics of globalization frequently charge that it results in an "Americanization of culture" and concomitant loss of identity and local cultural values. I would propose a more optimistic view, and that is that globalization leads to never-ending exchange of ideas, especially through popular culture, since it affects the greatest number of people.

Through popular culture, people from different backgrounds and nations discover one another, and their "otherness" suddenly disappears. For example, a popular Korean television sitcom now popular in Japan has shown its Japanese viewers that, like them, Koreans fall in love, feel despair, and harbor the same hopes and fears for themselves and for their children. This sitcom has transformed the image Japanese have of the Korean nation more profoundly than any number of diplomatic efforts and demonstrates that globalization can erode prejudices that have existed between neighboring countries for centuries.

Furthermore, this process of better understanding allows us to keep our identity and add new identities. The Koreans absorb a bit of the American culture, a bit of the French, a bit of other European societies. Perhaps they have become a different sort of Korean, but they remain Korean nonetheless. It is quite the illusion to think you can lose your identity. And it goes both ways. When you look at the success of cultural exports out of Korea—this so-called new wave through music, television, movies, and art—Korea becomes part of the identity of other people.

Now, as a Frenchman, I am a bit Korean myself. This is how globalization works. We do not lose our identity. We enter into the world that I call the world of multi-identity, and that is progress, not loss.

Political and Cultural Norms

One of the most significant transformations in terms of welfare for the people in the globalized world is the increased respect given to the rights of women and minorities. In many nations, to be a woman or to belong to a minority has not been easy. In the past 30 years, however, women and minorities everywhere have become better informed and have learned that the repression they suffered until very recently is not typical in a modern democracy.

Let us consider India, where a strong caste system historically has subjugated women and untouchables. Thanks to the globalization of democratic norms, these minorities are better protected; through various affirmative action policies, they can access the better jobs that traditionally were forbidden to them. This transformation has positive consequences for them, of course, and also creates better outcomes for their children's welfare and education. We are entering into a better world because of their improved status, thanks to the cultural and democratic exchanges generated by globalization.

Information

Through legacy media and, more and more, through the Internet and cellular phones, everyone today, even in authoritarian countries, is better informed. For one year, I lived in the poorest part of China, and I remember well how a farmer, in the most remote village, knew exactly what was happening not only in the next village, but also in Beijing and New York because of the Internet and his cellular phone. No government can stop information now. People know today that, as they say, "knowledge is power."

Now let us imagine if the genocide in Darfur had happened 20 or 30 years ago. The Darfur population would have been annihilated by the Sudanese government, and no one would have known. Today we all know about the genocide. The reason why the international community has been forced to intervene is because of the flood of information. Knowledge is proving to be the best protection for oppressed minorities and, thus, one of the most vital aspects of globalization.

Internationalization of the Rule of Law

Internationalization of rule of law, of course, has limitations. The institutions in charge of this emerging rule of law, whether the United Nations or the World Trade Organization, are criticized. They are not completely legitimate. They are certainly not perfectly democratic, but you cannot build a democratic organization with non-democratic governments. It becomes a trade-off.

In spite of all the weaknesses of international organizations, the emergence of a real international rule of law replaces the pure barbarism that existed before, which had consisted of the most powerful against the weak. Even though globalization cannot suppress war, it is remarkably efficient at containing war. If you examine the kinds of wars we have today, compared to the history of mankind, the number of victims and number of nations involved are very few. We are all safer because of both this emerging rule of law and the flow of information provided by globalization.

Invented by Entrepreneurs

We also need to remember that globalization is not some historical accident but has been devised and built by those who wanted it. Diplomats did not invent it. Entrepreneurs did.

Let us look at Europe. After World War II, the Europeans discovered that they had been their own worst enemies. For 1,000 years, we were fighting each other. Why? We do not remember very well. Every 30 years, we went to war. The French killed the Germans. The Germans killed the French. When you try to explain this history to your children, they cannot understand. Diplomats and politicians from the 18th century onward unsuccessfully made plans to avoid this kind of civil war within Europe.

Then, in the 1940s, a businessman came along named Jean Monnet. His business was to sell cognac in the United States, and he was very good at it. The idea Jean Monnet had was that perhaps the unification process of Europe should not be started by diplomats. Maybe it should be started by business people. He proceeded to build the European Union on a foundation of commerce. He started with coal and steel in 1950, and it was through the liberation of that trade that he conceived the unification of Europe, which has played a crucial role in the globalization process.

Monnet's guiding principle was that commercial and financial ties would lead to political unification. The true basis of European solidarity has come through trade. Through this method, all of the benefits of globalization have been made possible, because free trade has been at the root level. An attack on free trade is an attack on both globalization and the welfare of the peoples of the world, so we must be very cautious when we discuss trade, as it is the essential key allowing the rest to happen.

None of this is to imply that trade is easy. In the case of Europe, it was made easier because all of the governments were democratic. It is much more complicated to build free trade with non-democratic governments, but because globalization starts with the construction of this materialistic solidarity, ideals must come afterwards.

Two Threats to Globalization

Perhaps what I have presented so far is too optimistic a picture of globalization, but I believe we have good reason to be upbeat. However, there are two threats to globalization that may be taken too lightly today.

Global epidemics.   In terms of health care, we are more and more able to cope with the current illnesses of the world. Though Africa still poses a problem, through global efforts it will be possible in the years to come to reduce the major epidemics there: AIDS and malaria.

But new epidemics are threatening the world. If we remember what happened in China some years ago with the SARS epidemic, which was very short, and then the avian flu threat in 2005, you understand that there are new threats somewhere out there and that the modern world is not really prepared. One of the consequences of globalization is that people travel more, which means that viruses travel more and adapt.

Therefore, I think globalization should require the international community to develop ever more sophisticated systems to detect and cure the new epidemics that have been a negative consequence of globalization.

Terrorism.   Although wars these days are more limited, new forms of warfare have emerged, which we call terrorism. Terrorism today can seem like a distant menace somewhere between the United States and the Middle East. Because of the global progress of the rule of law, however, violent groups know that it is no longer possible to wage war in the traditional way; therefore, people driven by ideological passions are increasingly tempted by terrorist methods as a way of implementing their agenda.

Those are the true negative aspects of globalization: epidemics and terrorism. Regretfully, we are too focused on the traditional problems like free trade. We are not focused enough on the future threats.

I wish globalization were more popular, but it is our fault if it is not. Perhaps we should use different words. "Globalization" is ugly. We should find a better word, and we should try to explain to the media and students that we are entering into a new civilization of welfare, progress, and happiness, because if they do not understand the beauty of globalization, they will not stand up for it when it is threatened.

NO

Branko Milanovic

Why Globalization Is in Trouble—Parts 1 and 2

Part I[2]

Washington: Historically, the dominant power tends to support globalization as a way to increase the ambit of its influence, expand trade and gain economic advantage, co-opt new citizens and possibly show the advantages of its own pax. This was the case with the Roman, British and now American-led globalizations. But recently, the rich West—which saw globalization as a prelude to "the end of history"—is having second thoughts.

2 From *YaleGlobal Online* by Branko Milanovic, August 29, 2006 and August 31, 2006. Copyright © 2006 by YaleGlobal Online. Reprinted by permission of Yale Center for the Study of Globalization and the author.

Two fears drive this unease with globalization: The first is a fear of job loss due to competition from low-wage countries. The second is the fear of ethnic and cultural dilution due to increased immigration.

The cause of the first fear is a fast reemergence on the world stage of China and India. For students of history, the rise of China and India is not a surprise. The two countries are just recapturing the ground lost during the 19th and most of the 20th century. Before the Industrial Revolution, China's and India's combined output accounted for one half of the world's total. Now, after a quarter-century of China's spectacular growth, and more than a decade of India's growth acceleration, the two countries contribute less than a fifth of total world output. Although their share is, in the long-term historical sense, still below what it used to be, it has nevertheless increased dramatically compared to where it was 30 years ago. The rise of the two Asian giants, reflected in their dynamic trade, large Chinese export surpluses and India's role as an outsourcing center and a potential leader in information technology, has made the West wonder whether it can compete with such hardworking, cheap, plentiful and yet relatively skilled labor.

While the fear of job loss is driven by fast economic growth of the two giants, the fear of immigration is, ironically, caused by the slow economic growth of the rest of the developing world. The people who try to reach the shores of Europe or cross from Mexico into the US come from the countries that have disastrously fallen behind Western Europe and the US during the last quarter century. In 1980, Mexico's real per-capita income, adjusted for the differential price level between Mexico and the US, was a third of that in the US. Today, the ratio is almost 4.5 to 1. The poor Africans who land daily on beaches of the Spanish Canary Islands come from the countries that have seen no economic growth in 50 years. Take Ghana, a country often touted as an African success case: Around its independence, in 1957, its income was one half of Spain's; today, it is one tenth.

Immigration puts a similar pressure on low- or medium-skilled jobs in the West as do cheap imports from China and outsourcing to India. And indeed, wages of low- and medium-skilled workers in the rich countries have failed to keep pace with incomes of educated workers at the top of the pyramid. While the median US real wage has not risen in real terms over the last 25 years, real wages of the top 1 percent have more than doubled. The richest 1 percent of Americans today controls almost 20 percent of total US income, a proportion higher than at any time since the Roaring Twenties. The U-turn of inequality—a sharp increase that started during the Thatcher-Reagan era, after a long decline—has affected, to a varying extent, all Western countries.

But at stake is something more profound than a threat to jobs and stagnant wages in a few "exposed" sectors. After all, the West is no stranger to structural change. Ricardo in his "Principles" written in 1815 discusses labor dislocation "occasioned" by the introduction of machinery. The Western countries handled the decline of powerful industries like coal, textile and steel. Economists have never been sympathetic to the protection arguments of sunset industries: In an expanding economy, structural change is necessary and inevitable; jobs lost in one industry will reappear as new jobs in another industry.

The difference now is that the twin challenge undermines the consensus upon which the West's welfare state was built since World War II. To understand why, recall that the Western welfare states rest on two building blocks: those of ethnic and social solidarity. The first building block implies that one is willing to be taxed if

certain that aid will flow to somebody who is ethnically or culturally similar. But once large stocks of immigrants with different, and not easily adaptable, social norms, arrive, that certainly is no longer. More immigrants will strain the already-tattered solidarity among citizens of rich European countries.

The second building block of the welfare state is class solidarity. For it to exist, there must be relatively similar economic conditions between classes so that one can reasonably expect that for social transfers paid out of his pocket today, he may be compensated—if the need arose—by a similar benefit in the future. If, for example, unemployment rates are relatively equal across skill levels, then the highly skilled will pay for unemployment benefits; but if unemployment rates are different, the highly skilled may opt out. As the income divide widens in the West between the rich and the highly educated who have done well, and the middle classes and the unskilled who are merely scraping by, the second building block on which welfare capitalism was built crumbles. Economic inequality also translates into a cultural divide. "Ethnic" migrants who fill the rungs of low-paid workers are not the only ones economically and culturally different from today's Western elites; the elites are also growing more different from their own poorer ethnic brethren.

So far reaching, these developments require an entirely new social contract, a redefinition of capitalism no less. Such fundamental changes are not easy to come by when the threat is subtle, continuous, incremental and far from dramatic in a daily sense. Difficult decisions can be postponed, and neither politicians nor the electorate have an appetite for change. A battle of attrition regarding who would bear the costs of adjustment ensues, and this is at the heart of Europe's present immobilism.

Why is the development of "new capitalism" and rethinking of the old social contract so much more difficult for Europe than for the US? First, for an obvious reason, because Europe's welfare state is much more extensive, more embedded in ordinary life, and its dismantlement is more socially disruptive. Second, because a low population growth—or in many countries, a decline—necessitates continuing large immigration. But, and this is the crux of the matter, Europe struggles more in absorbing immigrants than the US. Historically, of course, Europe was not a society of immigrants. Europeans were happy to receive foreign workers as long as they would do low-paying jobs and stay out of the way. This quasi-apartheid solution preserved immigrants' culture, which then, most famously in the Netherlands, was found to clash with some European values. Immigrants, more so their daughters and sons, were not happy to remain in subaltern jobs. And while Europe was good about welcoming them to its soccer and basketball teams, it was more stingy when it came allowing them to direct operating rooms or boardrooms.

The bottom line is that Europe needs no less than a social revolution: replacement of its welfare state, and acceptance that Germans, French or Italians of tomorrow will be much darker in their skin color, composed of individuals of various religions, and in many respects indeed a different people. As fusion of Frankish ethnicity and Latin culture created France, a similar Christiano-Islamic and Afro-European fusion may create new European nations, perhaps with a different outlook on life and social norms. No society can accomplish such epochal transformation quickly and painlessly.

Part II

Washington: In the rich world globalization had driven the wedge between social classes, while in the poor world, the main divide is between countries: those that adjusted to globalization and, in many areas, prospered and those that adjusted badly and, in many cases, collapsed.

Indeed the Third World was never a bloc the way that that the first and second worlds were. But it was united by its opposition to colonialism and dislike for being used as a battlefield of the two then-dominant ideologies. As the Second World collapsed and globalization took off, the latter rationale evaporated, and a few countries, most notably India and China, accelerated their growth rates significantly, enjoying the fruits of freer trade and larger capital flows. And although these two countries adapted well to globalization, there is little doubt that their newfound relative prosperity opened many new fissure lines. Inequality between coastal and inland provinces, as well as between urban and rural areas, skyrocketed in China. So did, and perhaps by even more, inequality between Southern Indian states, where the hub cities of Mumbai, Chennai and Bangalore are located, and the slow-growing Northeast. For China, which still may face political transition to democracy, widening inequality between different parts of the country, could have disastrous consequences.

But another large group of Third World countries, from Latin America to Africa to former Communist countries, experienced a quarter century of decline or stagnation punctuated by civil wars, international conflicts and the plight of AIDS. While between 1980 and 2002, the rich countries grew, on average, by almost 2 percent per capita annually, the poorest 40 countries in the world had a combined growth rate of zero. For large swaths of Africa where about 200 million people live, the income level today is less than it was during the US presidency of John F. Kennedy.

For these countries the promised benefits of globalization never arrived. The vaunted Washington con-

sensus policies brought no improvement for the masses, but rather a deterioration in the living conditions as key social services became privatized and more costly as was the case, for example, with water privatizations in Cochabamba, Bolivia, and Trinidad, electricity privatization in Argentina and Chad. They were often taken over by foreigners, and to add insult to injury, Western pundits arrived by jets, stayed in luxury hotels and hailed obvious worsening of economic and social conditions as a step toward better lives and international integration. For many people in Latin America and Africa, globalization appeared as new, more attractive label put on the old imperialism, or worse as a form of re-colonization. The left-wing reaction sweeping Latin America, from Mexico to Argentina, is a direct consequence of the fault lines opened by policies that were often designed to benefit Wall Street, not the people in the streets of Lima or Caracas.

Other Third World states—particularly those at the frontline of the battle between communism and capitalism, with ethnic animosities encouraged during the Cold War, efforts by Washington and Moscow to get the upper hand in the conflict—exploded in civil wars and social anomies. That part of the world associates globalization with disappointment (because Washington consensus never delivered), resentment (because others got ahead) and poverty, disease and war. In several sub-Saharan African countries, life expectancy at the turn of the 21st century is not only where it was in Europe almost two centuries ago but is getting worse. In Zimbabwe, between 1995 and 2003, life expectancy declined by 11 years to reach only 39 years.

Ideologies which proposed some economic betterment and offered self-respect to many people in Africa (from Kwame Nkrumah's African socialism to Julius Nyerere's "cooperative economy") and parts of the former Communist bloc (Tito's "labor management") all collapsed and have given way to self-serving oligarchies that justified their policies, not by calling on their own citizens, but by publishing excerpts from reports written by the World Bank and the International Monetary Fund.

In the Third World as a whole, globalization, at best, produced what Tocqueville, with a touch of aristocratic disdain, called a government of the commercially-minded middle classes, "a government without virtue and without greatness"; at worst, it produced governments of plutocrats or elites unconcerned about their own populations. Globalization thus appeared in the poorest and weakest countries at its roughest.

Perhaps the greatest casualty of the money-grubbing global capitalism was loss of self-respect among those who have failed economically—and they are preponderantly located in the poorest countries. The desperate African masses who want to flee their own countries leave not only because incomes are low and prospects bleak, but also because of a lack of confidence that either they or their governments, no matter who is in power, can change life for the better. This despondency and loss of self-respect is indeed a product of globalization. In the past one could feel slighted by fortune for having been born in a poor country, yet have as compensation a belief that other qualities mattered, that one's country offered the world something valuable, a different ideology, a different way of life. But none of that survives today.

The problem was, strangely, noticed by Friedrich Hayek. Market outcomes, Hayek argued, must not be presented as ethically just or unjust because the market is ethically neutral. But to buttress the case for global capitalism, its proponents insist in an almost Calvinist fashion that economic success is not only good in a purely material sense, but reveals some moral superiority. Thus winners are made to feel not only richer but morally superior, and the converse: The losers feel poor and are supposed to be ashamed of their failure. Many people do, but understandably not all take gladly to such judgment.

An interesting coincidence of interests emerges between the desperate masses and the rich in advanced countries. The latter, educated and with considerable property "interests," are, economically, often in favor of greater Third World competitiveness and migration since, either as investors abroad or consumers of cheap labor services at home, they benefit from low-wage labor. This unlikely coincidence of interest lends some superficial justification to the claims of George Bush and Tony Blair that the opponents of free-trade pacts work against the interests of the poor. The problem that the president and the prime minister fail to acknowledge, or perhaps even to realize, is that many of the policies urged by their governments on poor countries in the last two decades have indeed brought people to their current point of desperation.

Sandwiched between this unlikely "coalition" of the global top and the global bottom, are globalization's losers: the lower and middle classes in the West, and those in the "failed" states, not yet sufficiently desperate to board the boats to Europe or cross the US border at night. They too lost in terms of their national sovereignty and personal income. They may not gladly accept, though, that they are morally inferior. At first sight, they do not seem likely to derail globalization because their power is limited. Yet in a more interdependent world with an easy access to deadly weapons, politics of global resentment may find many followers.

POSTSCRIPT

Is Economic Globalization Good for Humankind?

According to Freedom House, a non-partisan think tank that monitors the progress of freedom and democracy around the world, the rise in globalization and free trade over the past 35 years has been accompanied by an increase in the percentage of countries whose population enjoys civil and political freedom. Since 1972, the share of those countries where these rights are denied has dropped from 47% to 34%, whereas the share of those countries enjoying these rights has increased from 34% to 46%. Freedom House also reports that the most economically open—that is, receptive to the idea of globalization—are three times more likely to enjoy full civil and political liberties than are economically closed countries. Further, numerous studies indicate that nations that are receptive to free trade grow faster and have higher levels of per capita income than nations that resist economic openness.

Facts such as these seem to provide considerable support for the pro-globalization stance. But keep in mind that an integral aspect of Branko Milanovic's argument is that a country's national and cultural identity will be swept away in the wake of rapid economic growth. And in case you think his fears are unfounded, consider the existence of the European Union. There is strength in size, and joining a unified collection of European nations allows each country to better compete in the global marketplace. However, membership in the EU has come at a price: Member countries have to agree to dissolve their currency and adopt a new, single currency, the euro. Across Europe, the history and cultural identity of many countries is intimately tied to its currency, and the decision to disband it for economic reasons was the source of much social unrest. Many critics of the EU fear that this is merely an early example of the destructive effects globalization—in the form of the EU—has on the national sovereignty of those countries that embrace it.

Suggested Readings

Arch Puddington, "Findings of *Freedom in the World 2008*—Freedom in Retreat: Is the Tide Turning?" Freedom House.org (2008). http://www .freedomhouse.org/template.cfm?page=130&year=2008

Investor's Business Daily, "The Backlash Against Globalization," *Investor's Business Daily Editorial* (July 23, 2007). http://www.ibdeditorials.com/IBDArticles.aspx?id=270083115591444

Gennady Stoylarov, "Globalization: Extending the Market and Human Well-Being," *The Freeman* (vol. 59, no. 3, April 2009).

Christine Elsaeßer, "Strength in Numbers for Globalization's Critics," *Deutch Welle* (September 5, 2007). http://www.dw-world.de/dw/article/ 0,2144,2473215,00.html

Andrew Nikiforuk, *Pandemonium: How Globalization and Trade Are Putting the World at Risk*, (University of Queensland Press, 2007).

Martin Wolf, "Remarks at a National Center for Policy Analysis Conference in London," National Center for Policy Analysis (May 2006). http://www .ncpa.org/sub/dpd/index.php?Article_ID=3386

Differences in Culture

7

LEARNING OBJECTIVES

After completing this chapter, you should be able to:

 LO¹ Know what is meant by the culture of a society.

 LO² Identify the forces that lead to differences in social culture.

 LO³ Identify the business and economic implications of differences in culture.

 LO⁴ Understand how differences in social culture influence values in the workplace.

LO⁵ Develop an appreciation for the economic and business implications of cultural change.

McDonald's in India

In many ways, McDonald's Corporation has written the book on global expansion. Every day, on average, somewhere around the world four new McDonald's restaurants are opened. The company has some 30,000 restaurants in more than 120 countries that collectively served close to 50 million customers each day.

One of the latest additions to McDonald's list of countries hosting the famous golden arches is India, where McDonald's started to establish restaurants in the late 1990s. Although India is a poor nation, the large and relatively prosperous middle class, estimated to number around 200 million, attracted McDonald's. India, however, offered McDonald's unique challenges. For thousands of years, India's Hindu culture has revered the cow. Hindu scriptures state that the cow is a gift of the gods to the human race. The cow represents the Divine Mother that sustains all human beings. Cows give birth to bulls that are harnessed to pull plows, cow milk is highly valued and used to produce yogurt and ghee (a form of butter), cow urine has a unique place in traditional Hindu medicine, and cow dung is used as fuel. Some 300 million of these animals roam India, untethered, revered as sacred providers. They are everywhere, ambling down roads, grazing in rubbish dumps, and resting in temples—everywhere, that is, except on your plate, for Hindus do not eat the meat of the sacred cow.

McDonald's is the world's largest user of beef. Since its founding in 1955, countless animals have died to produce Big Macs. How can a company whose fortunes are built upon beef enter a country where the consumption of beef is a grave sin? Use pork instead? However, there are some 140 million Muslims in India, and Muslims don't eat pork. This leaves chicken and mutton. McDonald's responded to this cultural food dilemma by creating an Indian version of its Big Mac—the "Maharaja Mac"—which is made from mutton. Other additions to the menu conform to local sensibilities such as the "McAloo Tikki Burger," which is made from chicken. All foods are strictly segregated into vegetarian and nonvegetarian lines to conform with preferences in a country where many Hindus are vegetarian. According to the head of McDonald's Indian operations, "We had to reinvent ourselves for the Indian palate." Indeed, 75 percent of the menu in McDonald's in India is Indianized.

For a while, this seemed to work. Then in 2001 McDonald's was blindsided by a class-action lawsuit brought against it in the United States by three Indian businessmen living in Seattle. The businessmen were all vegetarians and two of them were Hindus, and they sued McDonald's for "fraudulently concealing" the existence of beef in McDonald's French fries! McDonald's had said it used only 100 percent vegetable oil to make French fries, but the company soon admitted that it used a "minuscule" amount of beef extract in the oil. McDonald's settled the suit for $10 million and issued an apology, which read, "McDonald's sincerely apologizes to Hindus, vegetarians, and others for failing to provide the kind of information they needed to make informed dietary decisions at our U.S. restaurants." Going forward, the company pledged to do a better job of labeling the ingredients of its food and to find a substitute for the beef extract used in its oil.

However, news travels fast in the global society of the twenty-first century, and the revelation that McDonald's used beef extract in its oil was enough to bring Hindu nationalists onto the streets in Delhi, where they vandalized one McDonald's restaurant, causing $45,000 in damage; shouted slogans outside of another; picketed the company's headquarters; and called on India's prime minister to close McDonald's stores in the country. McDonald's Indian franchise holders quickly issued denials that they used oil that contained beef extract, and Hindu extremists responded by stating they would submit McDonald's oil to laboratory tests to see if they could detect beef extract.

The negative publicity seemed to have little impact on McDonald's long-term plans in India, however. The company continued to open restaurants, and by 2008 had over 136 restaurants in the country with plans to triple the number of restaurants by 2011. When asked why they frequented McDonald's restaurants, Indian customers noted that their children enjoyed the "American" experience, the food was of a consistent quality, and the toilets were always clean![1]

🌐 Introduction

As McDonald's has long known, international business is different from domestic business because countries are different. As detailed in the Opening Case, to succeed in India, McDonald's has had to customize its offering to the tastes and preferences of a Hindu culture that venerates the cow, will not eat beef, and has a large vegetarian population. National differences in political, economic, and legal systems can influence the benefits, costs, and risks associated with doing business in different countries. In this chapter, we will explore how differences in culture across and within countries can affect international business.

Several themes run through this chapter. The first theme is that business success in a variety of countries requires cross-cultural literacy. By **cross-cultural literacy**, we mean an understanding of how cultural differences across and within nations can affect the way business is practiced. In these days of global communications, rapid transportation, and worldwide markets, when the era of the global village seems just around the corner, it is easy to forget just how different various cultures really are. Underneath the veneer of modernism, deep cultural differences often remain. Westerners in general, and Americans in particular, are quick to conclude that because people from other parts of the world also wear blue jeans, listen to Western popular music, eat at McDonald's, and drink Coca-Cola, they also accept the basic tenets of Western (or American) culture. However, this is not true. For example, take the Chinese. Increasingly, they are embracing the material products of modern society. Anyone who has visited Shanghai cannot fail to be struck by how modern the city seems, with its skyscrapers, department stores, and freeways. Yet beneath the veneer of Western modernism, long-standing cultural traditions rooted in a 2,000-year-old ideology continue to have an important influence on the way business is transacted in China. For example, in China, *guanxi*, or a network of social relationships with others backed by reciprocal obligations, are central to getting business done. Firms that lack sufficient *guanxi* may find themselves at a disadvantage when doing business in China. The lesson: to succeed in China you have to play by Chinese rules, just as McDonald's found that to succeed in India you have to play by Indian rules. More generally, in this chapter, we shall argue that it is important for foreign businesses to gain an understanding of the culture that prevails in those countries where they do business, and that success requires a foreign enterprise to adapt to the culture of its host country.[2]

Another theme developed in this chapter is that a relationship may exist between culture and the cost of doing business in a country or region. Different cultures are more or less supportive of the capitalist mode of production and may increase or lower the costs of doing business. For example, some observers have argued that cultural factors lowered the costs of doing business in Japan and helped to explain Japan's rapid economic ascent during the 1960s, 70s, and 80s.[3] Similarly, cultural factors can sometimes raise the costs of doing business. Historically, class divisions were an important aspect of British culture, and for a long time, firms operating in Great Britain found it difficult to achieve cooperation between management and labor. Class divisions led to a high level of industrial disputes in that country during the 1960s and 1970s and raised the costs of doing business relative to the costs in countries such as Switzerland, Norway, Germany, or Japan, where class conflict was historically less prevalent.

The British example, however, brings us to another theme we will explore in this chapter. Culture is not static. It can and does evolve, although the rate at which culture can change is the subject of some dispute. Important aspects of British culture have changed significantly over the past 20 years, and this is reflected in weaker class distinctions and a lower level of industrial disputes. Between 1995 and 2005, the number of days lost per 1,000 workers due to strikes in the United Kingdom was on average 28 each year, significantly less than in the United States (33 each year), Ireland (81), and Canada (168).[4] Finally, it is important to note that multinational enterprises can themselves be engines of cultural change. In India, for example, McDonald's and other Western fast food companies may help to change the dining culture of that nation, drawing them away from traditional restaurants and towards fast food outlets.

What Is Culture?

Scholars have never been able to agree on a simple definition of *culture*. In the 1870s, the anthropologist Edward Tylor defined culture as "that complex whole which includes knowledge, belief, art, morals, law, custom, and other capabilities acquired by man as a member of society."[5] Since then hundreds of other definitions have been offered. Geert Hofstede, an expert on cross-cultural differences and management, defined culture as "the collective programming of the mind which distinguishes the members of one human group from another. . . . Culture, in this sense, includes systems of values; and values are among the building blocks of culture."[6] Another definition of culture comes from sociologists Zvi Namenwirth and Robert Weber, who see culture as a system of ideas and argue that these ideas constitute a design for living.[7]

Here we follow both Hofstede and Namenwirth and Weber by viewing **culture** as a system of values and norms that are shared among a group of people and that when taken together constitute a design for living. By **values** we mean abstract ideas about what a group believes to be good, right, and desirable. Put differently, values are shared assumptions about how things ought to be.[8] By **norms** we mean the social rules and guidelines that prescribe appropriate behavior in particular situations. We shall use the term *society* to refer to a group of people who share a common set of values and norms. While a society may be equivalent to a country, some countries harbor several societies (i.e., they support multiple cultures), and some societies embrace more than one country.

VALUES AND NORMS

Values form the bedrock of a culture. They provide the context within which a society's norms are established and justified. They may include a society's attitudes toward such concepts as individual freedom, democracy, truth, justice, honesty, loyalty, social obligations, collective responsibility, the role of women, love, sex, marriage, and so on. Values are not just abstract concepts; they are invested with considerable emotional significance. People argue, fight, and even die over values such as freedom. Values also often are reflected in the political and economic systems of a society. As we saw in Chapter 2, democratic free market capitalism is a reflection of a philosophical value system that emphasizes individual freedom.

Norms are the social rules that govern people's actions toward one another. Norms can be subdivided further into two major categories: folkways and mores. **Folkways** are the routine conventions of everyday life. Generally, folkways are actions of little moral significance. Rather, they are social conventions concerning things such as the appropriate dress code in a particular situation, good social manners, eating with the correct utensils, neighborly behavior, and the like. Although folkways define the way people are expected to behave, violation of them is not normally a serious matter. People who violate folkways may be thought of as eccentric or ill-mannered, but they are not usually considered to be evil or bad. In many countries, foreigners may initially be excused for violating folkways.

A good example of folkways concerns attitudes toward time in different countries. People are keenly aware of the passage of time in the United States and Northern European cultures such as Germany and Britain. Businesspeople are very conscious about scheduling their time and are quickly irritated when their time is wasted because a business associate is late for a meeting or they are kept waiting. They talk about time as though it were money, as something that can be spent, saved, wasted, and lost.[9] Alternatively, in Arab, Latin, and Mediterranean cultures, time has a more elastic character. Keeping to a schedule is viewed as less important than finishing an interaction with people. For example, an American businesswoman might feel slighted if she is kept waiting for 30 minutes outside the office of a Latin American executive before a meeting; but the Latin American may simply be completing an interaction with an associate and view the information gathered from this as more important than sticking to a rigid schedule. The Latin American executive intends no disrespect, but due to a mutual misunderstanding about the importance of time, the American may see things differently. Similarly, Saudi attitudes to time have been shaped by their nomadic Bedouin heritage, in which precise time played no real role and arriving somewhere tomorrow might mean next week. Like Latin Americans, many Saudis are unlikely to understand the American obsession with precise time and schedules, and Americans need to adjust their expectations accordingly.

Understanding rituals and symbolic behaviors are essential to doing business in foreign countries.

Folkways include rituals and symbolic behavior. Rituals and symbols are the most visible manifestations of a culture and constitute the outward expression of deeper values. For example, upon meeting a foreign business executive, a Japanese executive will hold his business card in both hands and bow while presenting the card to the foreigner.[10] This ritual behavior is loaded with deep cultural symbolism. The card specifies the rank of the Japanese executive, which is a very important piece of information in a hierarchical society such as Japan (Japanese often have business cards with Japanese printed on one side, and English printed on the other). The bow is a sign of respect, and the deeper the angle of the bow, the greater the reverence one person shows for the other. The person receiving the card is expected to examine it carefully, which is a way of returning respect and acknowledging the card giver's position in the hierarchy. The foreigner is also expected to bow when taking the card, and to return the greeting by presenting the Japanese executive with his own card, similarly bowing in the process. To not do so, and to fail to read the card that he has been given, instead casually placing it in his jacket, violates this important folkway and is considered rude.

Mores are norms that are seen as central to the functioning of a society and its social life. They have much greater significance than folkways. Accordingly, violating mores can bring serious retribution. Mores include such factors as indictments against theft, adultery, incest, and cannibalism. In many societies, certain mores have been enacted into law. Thus, all advanced societies have laws against theft, incest, and cannibalism. However, there are also many differences between cultures. In America, for example, drinking alcohol is widely accepted, whereas in Saudi Arabia the consumption of alcohol is viewed as violating important social mores and is punishable by imprisonment (as some Western citizens working in Saudi Arabia have discovered).

CULTURE, SOCIETY, AND THE NATION-STATE

We have defined a society as a group of people that share a common set of values and norms; that is, people who are bound together by a common culture. There is not a strict one-to-one correspondence between a society and a nation-state. Nation-states are political creations. They may contain a single culture or several cultures. While the French nation can be thought of as the political embodiment of French culture, the nation of Canada has at least three cultures—an Anglo culture, a French-speaking "Quebecois" culture, and a Native American culture. Similarly, many African nations have important cultural differences between tribal groups, as exhibited in the early 1990s when Rwanda dissolved into a bloody civil war between two tribes, the Tutsis and Hutus. Africa is not alone in this regard. India is composed of many distinct cultural groups. During the first Gulf War, the prevailing view presented to Western audiences was that Iraq was a homogenous Arab nation. However, since then we have learned that several different societies exist within Iraq, each with its own culture. The Kurds in the north do not view themselves as Arabs and have their own distinct history and traditions. There are two Arab societies: the Shiites in the South and the Sunnis who populate the middle of the country and who ruled Iraq under the regime of Saddam Hussein (the terms *Shiites* and *Sunnis* refer to different sects within the religion of Islam). Among the southern Sunnis is another distinct society of 500,000 Marsh Arabs who live at the confluence of the Tigris and Euphrates rivers, pursuing a way of life that dates back 5,000 years.[11]

At the other end of the scale are cultures that embrace several nations. Several scholars argue that we can speak of an Islamic society or culture that the citizens of many different nations in the Middle East, Asia, and Africa share. This view of expansive cultures that embrace several nations underpins Samuel Huntington's view of a world that is fragmented into different civilizations, including Western, Islamic, and Sinic (Chinese).[12]

To complicate things further, it is also possible to talk about culture at different levels. It is reasonable to talk about "American society" and "American culture," but there are several societies within America, each with its own culture. One can talk about African American culture, Cajun culture, Chinese American culture, Hispanic culture, Indian culture, Irish American culture, and Southern culture. The relationship between culture and country is often ambiguous. Even if a country can be characterized as having a single homogenous culture, often that national culture is a mosaic of subcultures.

THE DETERMINANTS OF CULTURE

The values and norms of a culture do not emerge fully formed. They are the evolutionary product of a number of factors, including the prevailing political and economic philosophies, the social structure of a society, and the dominant religion, language, and education (see Figure 7.1). Such philosophies clearly influence the value systems of a society. For example, the values found in Communist North Korea toward freedom, justice, and individual achievement are clearly different from the values found in the United States, precisely because each society operates according to different political and economic philosophies. Here we will discuss the influence of social structure, religion, language, and education. The chain of causation runs both ways. While factors such as social structure and religion clearly influence the values and norms of a society, the values and norms of a society can influence social structure and religion.

FIGURE 7.1

The Determinants of Culture

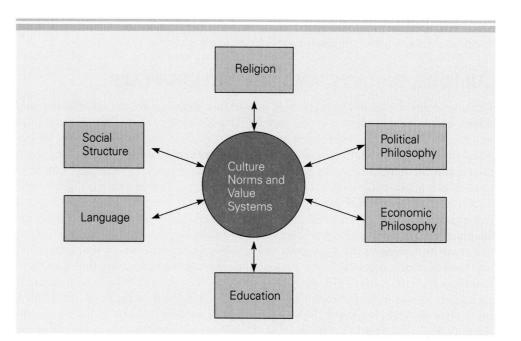

Social Structure

A society's **social structure** refers to its basic social organization. Although social structure consists of many different aspects, two dimensions are particularly important when explaining differences between cultures. The first is the degree to which the basic unit of social organization is the individual, as opposed to the group. In general, Western societies tend to emphasize the primacy of the individual, whereas groups tend to figure much larger in many other societies. The second dimension is the degree to which a society is stratified into classes or castes. Some societies are characterized by a relatively high degree of social stratification and relatively low mobility between strata (e.g., Indian); other societies are characterized by a low degree of social stratification and high mobility between strata (e.g., American).

INDIVIDUALS AND GROUPS

A **group** is an association of two or more individuals who have a shared sense of identity and who interact with each other in structured ways on the basis of a common set of expectations about each other's behavior.[13] Human social life is group life. Individuals are involved in families, work groups, social groups, recreational groups, and so on. However, while groups are found in all societies, societies differ according to the degree to which the group is viewed as the primary means of social organization.[14] In some societies, individual attributes and achievements are viewed as being more important than group membership; in others the reverse is true.

The Individual

Iindividualism is more than just an abstract political philosophy. In many Western societies, the individual is the basic building block of social organization. This viewpoint is reflected not just in the political and economic organization of society but also in the way people perceive themselves and relate to each other in social and business settings. The value systems of many Western societies, for example, emphasize individual achievement. The social standing of individuals is not so much a function of whom they work for as of their individual performance in whatever work setting they choose.

The emphasis on individual performance in many Western societies has both beneficial and harmful aspects. In the United States, the emphasis on individual performance finds expression in an admiration of rugged individualism and entrepreneurship. One benefit of this is the high level of entrepreneurial activity in the United States and other Western societies. In the United States, entrepreneurial individuals have repeatedly created new products and new ways of doing business (e.g., personal computers, photocopiers, computer software, biotechnology, supermarkets, and discount retail stores). One can argue that the dynamism of the U.S. economy owes much to the philosophy of individualism.

Individualism also finds expression in a high degree of managerial mobility between companies, which is not always a good thing. Although moving from company to company may be good for individual managers who are trying to build impressive résumés, it is not necessarily good for American companies. The lack of loyalty and commitment to an individual company, and the tendency to move on for a better offer, can result in managers who have good general skills but lack the knowledge, experience, and network of interpersonal contacts that come from years of working within the same company. An effective manager draws on company-specific experience, knowledge, and a network of contacts to find solutions to current problems, and American companies may suffer if their managers lack these attributes. One positive aspect of high managerial mobility is that executives are exposed to different ways of doing business. The ability to compare business practices helps U.S. executives identify how good practices and techniques developed in one firm might be profitably applied to other firms.

The emphasis on individualism may also make it difficult to build teams within an organization to perform collective tasks. If individuals are always competing with each other on the basis of individual performance, it may be difficult for them to cooperate. A study of U.S. competitiveness by the Massachusetts Institute of Technology suggested that U.S. firms are being hurt in the global economy by a failure to achieve cooperation both within a company (e.g., between functions or between management and labor) and between companies (e.g., between a firm and its suppliers). Given the emphasis on individualism in the American value system, this failure is not surprising.[15] The emphasis on individualism in the United States, while helping to create a dynamic entrepreneurial economy, may raise the costs of doing business due to its adverse impact on managerial stability and cooperation.

The Group

In contrast to the Western emphasis on the individual, the group is the primary unit of social organization in many other societies. For example, in Japan, the social status of an individual is determined as much by the standing of the group to which he or she belongs as by his or her individual performance.[16] In traditional Japanese society, the group was the family or village to which an individual belonged. Today, the group has frequently come to be associated with the work team or business organization to which an individual belongs. In a now-classic study of Japanese society, Nakane noted how this expresses itself in everyday life:

> When a Japanese faces the outside (confronts another person) and affixes some position to himself socially he is inclined to give precedence to institution over kind of occupation. Rather than saying, "I am a typesetter" or "I am a filing clerk," he is likely to say, "I am from B Publishing Group" or "I belong to S company."[17]

Nakane goes on to observe that the primacy of the group to which an individual belongs often evolves into a deeply emotional attachment in which identification with the group becomes all-important in one's life. One central value of Japanese culture is the importance attached to group membership. This may have beneficial implications for business firms. Strong identification with the group is argued to create pressures for mutual self-help and collective action. If the worth of an individual is closely linked to the achievements of the group (e.g., firm), as Nakane maintains is the case in Japan, this creates a strong incentive for individual members of the group to work together for the common good. Some argue that the success of Japanese enterprises in the global economy has been based partly on their ability to achieve close cooperation between individuals within a company and between companies. This has found expression in the widespread diffusion of self-managing work teams within Japanese organizations, the close cooperation among different functions within Japanese companies (e.g., among manufacturing, marketing, and R&D), and the cooperation between a company and its suppliers on issues such as design, quality control, and inventory reduction.[18] In all of these cases, cooperation is driven by the need to improve the performance of the group (i.e., the business firm).

The primacy of the value of group identification also discourages managers and workers from moving from company to company. Lifetime employment in a particular company was long the norm in certain sectors of the Japanese economy (estimates suggest that between 20 and 40 percent of all Japanese employees have formal or informal lifetime employment guarantees). Over the years, managers and workers build up knowledge, experience, and a network of interpersonal business contacts. All these things can help managers perform their jobs more effectively and achieve cooperation with others.

However, the primacy of the group is not always beneficial. Just as U.S. society is characterized by a great deal of dynamism and entrepreneurship, reflecting the primacy of values associated with individualism, some argue that Japanese society is characterized by a corresponding lack of dynamism and entrepreneurship. Although the long-run consequences are unclear, the United States could continue to create more new industries than Japan and continue to be more successful at pioneering radically new products and new ways of doing business.

SOCIAL STRATIFICATION

All societies are stratified on a hierarchical basis into social categories—that is, into **social strata**. These strata are typically defined on the basis of characteristics such as family background, occupation, and income. Individuals are born into a particular stratum. They become a member of the social category to which their parents belong. Individuals born into a stratum toward the top of the social hierarchy tend to have better life chances than those born into a stratum toward the bottom of the hierarchy. They are likely to have better education, health, standard of living, and work opportunities. Although all societies are stratified to some degree, they differ in two related ways. First, they differ from each other with regard to the degree of mobility between social strata; second, they differ with regard to the significance attached to social strata in business contexts.

Social Mobility

The term **social mobility** refers to the extent to which individuals can move out of the strata into which they are born. Social mobility varies significantly from society to society. The most rigid system of stratification is a caste system. A **caste system** is a closed system of stratification in which social position is determined by the family into which a person is born, and change in that position is usually not possible during an individual's lifetime. Often a caste position carries with it a specific occupation. Members of one caste might be shoemakers, members of another might be butchers, and so on. These occupations are embedded in the caste and passed down through the family to succeeding generations. Although the number of societies with caste systems diminished rapidly during the twentieth century, one partial example still remains. India has four main castes and several thousand subcastes. Even though the caste system was officially abolished in 1949, two years after India became independent, it is still a force in rural Indian society where occupation and marital opportunities are still partly related to caste (for more details, see the Country Focus feature on the caste system in India today).[19]

A **class system** is a less rigid form of social stratification in which social mobility is possible. It is a form of open stratification in which the position a person has by birth can be changed through his or her own achievements or luck. Individuals born into a class at the bottom of the hierarchy can work their way up; conversely, individuals born into a class at the top of the hierarchy can slip down.

While many societies have class systems, social mobility within a class system varies from society to society. For example, some sociologists have argued that Britain has a more rigid class structure than certain other Western societies, such as the United States.[20] Historically, British society was divided into three main classes: the upper class, which was made up of individuals whose families for generations had wealth, prestige, and occasionally power; the middle class, whose members were involved in professional, managerial, and clerical occupations; and the working class, whose members earned their living from manual occupations. The middle class was further subdivided into the upper-middle class, whose members were involved in important managerial occupations and the prestigious professions (e.g., lawyers, accountants, doctors), and the lower-middle class, whose members were involved in clerical work (e.g., bank tellers) and the less prestigious professions (e.g., schoolteachers).

The British class system exhibited significant divergence between the life chances of members of different classes. The upper and upper-middle classes typically sent their children to a select group of private schools, where they wouldn't mix with lower-class children and where they picked up many of the speech accents and social norms that marked them as being from the higher strata of society. These same private schools also had close ties with the most prestigious universities, such as Oxford and Cambridge. Until fairly recently, Oxford and Cambridge guaranteed a certain number of places for the graduates of these private schools. Having been to a prestigious university, the offspring of the upper and upper-middle classes then had an excellent chance of being offered a

Breaking India's Caste System

Modern-day India is a country of dramatic contrasts. Its information technology sector is among the most vibrant in the world, with companies like Infosys and Wipro emerging as powerful global players. India's caste system, long an impediment to social mobility, is a fading memory among the educated urban middle class Indians who make up the majority of employees in the high-tech economy. However, the same is not true in rural India where 70 percent of the population still resides. There caste remains a pervasive influence. In 1950, the national constitution reserved 22.5 percent of jobs for people from the lower castes, or *dalits* (also known as "untouchables") and for tribal people. In 1990, an additional 27 percent of jobs were set aside for what were called "other backward castes." Some Indian states set higher quotas, including Tamil Nadu, which reserves 69 percent of government jobs for lower castes and other needy groups. Despite these long-standing policies, anecdotal and hard evidence suggests that castes still play an important role in daily life.

For example, a young female engineer at Infosys who grew up in a small rural village and is a *dalits* recounts how she never entered the house of a *Brahmin,* India's elite priestly caste, even though half the residents of her village were *Brahmins.* When a *dalit* was hired to cook at the school in her native village, *Brahmins* withdrew their children from the school. The engineer herself is the beneficiary of a charitable training scheme for *dalit* university

leavers that Infosys launched in 2006. Her caste is among the poorest in India, with some 91 percent making less than $100 a month, compared to 65 percent of *Brahmins* who earn more than that amount.

To try to correct this historic inequality, politicians have talked for years about extending the employment quota system to private enterprises. The government has told private companies to hire more *dalits* and members of tribal communities and warned that "strong measures" will be taken if companies do not comply. Private employers are resisting attempts to impose quotas, arguing with some justification that people who are guaranteed a job by a quota system are unlikely to work very hard. At the same time, progressive employers realize that they need to do something to correct the inequalities and that, moreover, unless India taps into the lower castes, it may not be able to find the employees required to staff rapidly growing high-technology enterprises. Thus the Confederation of Indian Industry recently introduced a package of *dalit*-friendly measures, including scholarships for bright lower caste children. Building on this approach, Infosys is leading the way among high tech enterprises. The company provides special training to low-caste engineering graduates who have failed to get a job in industry after graduation. While the training does not promise employment, so far almost all graduates who completed the seven-month training program have found jobs with Infosys and other enterprises.[21]

prestigious job in companies, banks, brokerage firms, and law firms run by members of the upper and upper-middle classes.

In contrast, the members of the British working and lower-middle classes typically went to state schools. The majority left at 16, and those who went on to higher education found it more difficult to get accepted at the best universities. When they did, they found that their lower-class accent and lack of social skills marked them as being from a lower social stratum, which made it more difficult for them to get access to the most prestigious jobs.

Because of this, the class system in Britain perpetuated itself from generation to generation, and mobility was limited. Although upward mobility was possible, it could not normally be achieved in one generation. While an individual from a working-class background may have established an income level that was consistent with membership in the upper-middle class, he or she may not have been accepted as such by others of that class due to accent and background. However, by sending his or her offspring to the "right kind of school," the individual could ensure that his or her children were accepted.

According to many commentators, modern British society is now rapidly leaving this class structure behind and moving toward a classless society. However, sociologists continue to dispute this finding and present evidence that this is not the case. For example, one study reported that state schools in the London suburb of Islington, which has a population of 175,000, had only 79 candidates for university, while one prestigious private school alone, Eton, sent more than that number to Oxford and Cambridge.[22] This, according to the study's authors, implies that "money still begets money." They argue that a good school means a good university, a good university means a good job, and merit has only a limited chance of elbowing its way into this tight little circle.

The class system in the United States is less pronounced than in Britain and mobility is greater. Like Britain, the United States has its own upper, middle, and working classes. However, class membership is determined to a much greater degree by individual economic achievements, as opposed to background and schooling. Thus, an individual can, by his or her own economic achievement, move smoothly from the working class to the upper class in a lifetime. Successful individuals from humble origins are highly respected in American society.

Another society where class divisions have historically been of some importance has been China, where there has been a long-standing difference between the life chances of the rural peasantry and urban dwellers. Ironically, this historic division was strengthened during the high point of Communist rule because of a rigid system of household registration that restricted most Chinese to the place of their birth for their lifetime. Bound to collective farming, peasants were cut off from many urban privileges—compulsory education, quality schools, health care, public housing, varieties of foodstuffs, to name only a few—and they largely lived in poverty. Social mobility was thus very limited. This system crumbled following reforms of the late 1970s and early 1980s, and as a consequence, migrant peasant laborers have flooded into China's cities looking for work. Sociologists now hypothesize that a new class system is emerging in China based less on the rural-urban divide and more on urban occupation.[23]

Significance

From a business perspective, the stratification of a society is significant if it affects the operation of business organizations. In American society, the high degree of social mobility and the extreme emphasis on individualism limit the impact of class background on business operations. The same is true in Japan, where most of the population perceives itself to be middle class. In a country such as Great Britain, however, the relative lack of class mobility and the differences between classes have resulted in the emergence of class consciousness. **Class consciousness** refers to a condition where people tend to perceive themselves in terms of their class background, and this shapes their relationships with members of other classes.

Class consciousness has been played out in British society in the traditional hostility between upper-middle-class managers and their working-class employees. Mutual antagonism and lack of respect historically made it difficult to achieve cooperation between management and labor in many British companies and resulted in a relatively high level of industrial disputes. However, as noted earlier, the last two decades have seen a dramatic reduction in industrial disputes, which bolsters the arguments of those who claim that the country is moving toward a classless society (the level of industrial disputes in the United Kingdom is now lower than in the United States). Alternatively, as previously noted, class consciousness may be reemerging in urban China, and it may ultimately prove to be significant there.

An antagonistic relationship between management and labor classes, and the resulting lack of cooperation and high level of industrial disruption, tend to raise the costs of production in countries characterized by significant class divisions. In turn, higher costs can make it more difficult for companies based in such countries to establish a competitive advantage in the global economy.

Religious and Ethical Systems

Religion may be defined as a system of shared beliefs and rituals that are concerned with the realm of the sacred.[24] **Ethical systems** refer to a set of moral principles, or values, that are used to guide and shape behavior. Most of the world's ethical systems are the product of religions. Thus, we can talk about Christian ethics and Islamic ethics. However, there is a major exception to the principle that ethical systems are grounded in religion. Confucianism and Confucian ethics influence behavior and shape culture in parts of Asia, yet it is incorrect to characterize Confucianism as a religion.

The relationship among religion, ethics, and society is subtle and complex. Among the thousands of religions in the world today, four dominate in terms of numbers of adherents: Christianity with 1.7 billion adherents, Islam with around 1 billion adherents, Hinduism with 750 million adherents (primarily in India), and Buddhism with 350 million adherents (see Map 7.1). Although many other religions have an important influence in certain parts of the modern world (for example, Judaism, which has 18 million adherents), their numbers pale in comparison with these dominant religions (however, as the precursor of both Christianity and Islam, Judaism has an indirect influence that goes beyond its numbers). We will review these four religions, along with Confucianism, focusing on their business implications. Some scholars have argued that the most important business implications of religion center on the extent to which different religions shape attitudes toward work and entrepreneurship and the degree to which the religious ethics affect the costs of doing business in a country.

It is hazardous to make sweeping generalizations about the nature of the relationship between religion and ethical systems and business practice. While some scholars argue that there is a relationship between religious and ethical systems and business practice in a society, in a world where nations with Catholic, Protestant, Muslim, Hindu, and Buddhist majorities all show evidence of entrepreneurial activity and sustainable economic growth, it is important to view such proposed relationships with a degree of skepticism. The proposed relationships may exist, but their impact is probably small compared to the impact of economic policy. Alternatively, research by economists Robert Barro and Rachel McCleary does suggest that strong religious beliefs, and particularly beliefs in heaven, hell, and an afterlife, have a positive impact on economic growth rates, irrespective of the particular religion in question.[25] Barro and McCleary looked at religious beliefs and economic growth rates in 59 countries during the 1980s and 1990s. Their conjecture was that higher religious beliefs stimulate economic growth because they help to sustain aspects of individual behavior that lead to higher productivity.

CHRISTIANITY

Christianity is the most widely practiced religion in the world. Approximately 20 percent of the world's people identify themselves as Christians. The vast majority of Christians live in Europe and the Americas, although their numbers are growing rapidly in Africa. Christianity grew out of Judaism. Like Judaism, it is a monotheistic religion (monotheism is the belief in one god). A religious division in the eleventh century led to the establishment of two major Christian organizations—the Roman Catholic Church and the Orthodox Church. Today, the Roman Catholic Church accounts for more than half of all Christians, most of whom are found in southern Europe and Latin America. The Orthodox Church, while less influential, is still of major importance in several countries (e.g., Greece and Russia). In the sixteenth century, the Reformation led to a further split with Rome; the result was Protestantism. The nonconformist nature of Protestantism has facilitated the emergence of numerous denominations under the Protestant umbrella (e.g., Baptist, Methodist, Calvinist).

Economic Implications of Christianity: The Protestant Work Ethic

Several sociologists have argued that of the main branches of Christianity—Catholic, Orthodox, and Protestant—the latter has the most important economic implications. In

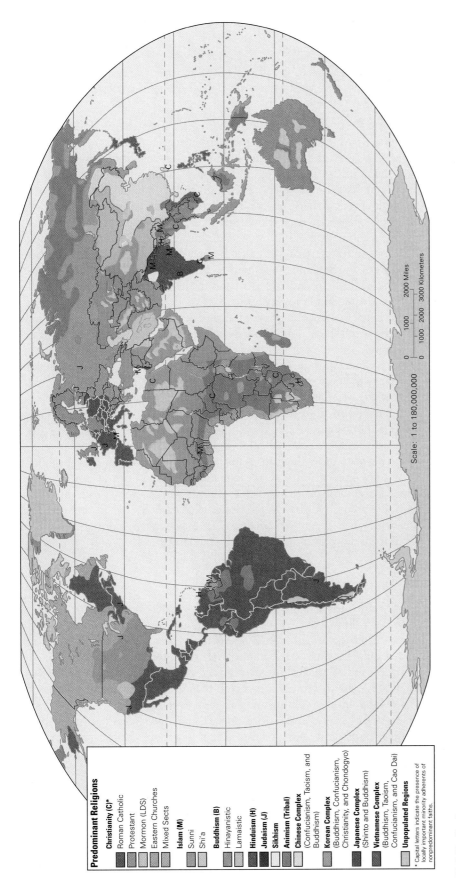

Predominant Religions

Christianity (C)*
- Roman Catholic
- Protestant
- Mormon (LDS)
- Eastern Churches
- Mixed Sects

Islam (M)
- Sunni
- Shi'a

Buddhism (B)
- Hinayanistic
- Lamaistic

Hinduism (H)

Judaism (J)

Sikhism

Animism (Tribal)

Chinese Complex
(Confucianism, Taoism, and Buddhism)

Korean Complex
(Buddhism, Confucianism, Christianity, and Chondogyo)

Japanese Complex
(Shinto and Buddhism)

Vietnamese Complex
(Buddhism, Taoism, Confucianism, and Cao Dai)

Unpopulated Regions

* Capital letters indicate the presence of locally important minority adherents of nonpredominant faiths.

Scale: 1 to 180,000,000

0   1000   2000 Miles

0   1000   2000   3000 Kilometers

MAP 7.1

World Religions

John L. Allen, *Student Atlas of World Geography*, 8th ed. (New York: McGraw-Hill, 2007).

1904, a German sociologist, Max Weber, made a connection between Protestant ethics and "the spirit of capitalism" that has since become famous.[26] Weber noted that capitalism emerged in Western Europe, where

> business leaders and owners of capital, as well as the higher grades of skilled labor, and even more the higher technically and commercially trained personnel of modern enterprises, are overwhelmingly Protestant.[27]

Weber theorized that there was a relationship between Protestantism and the emergence of modern capitalism. He argued that Protestant ethics emphasize the importance of hard work and wealth creation (for the glory of God) and frugality (abstinence from worldly pleasures). According to Weber, this kind of value system was needed to facilitate the development of capitalism. Protestants worked hard and systematically to accumulate wealth. However, their ascetic beliefs suggested that rather than consuming this wealth by indulging in worldly pleasures, they should invest it in the expansion of capitalist enterprises. Thus, the combination of hard work and the accumulation of capital, which could be used to finance investment and expansion, paved the way for the development of capitalism in Western Europe and subsequently in the United States. In contrast, Weber argued that the Catholic promise of salvation in the next world, rather than this world, did not foster the same kind of work ethic.

Protestantism also may have encouraged capitalism's development in another way. By breaking away from the hierarchical domination of religious and social life that characterized the Catholic Church for much of its history, Protestantism gave individuals significantly more freedom to develop their own relationship with God. The right to freedom of worship was central to the nonconformist nature of early Protestantism. This emphasis on individual religious freedom may have paved the way for the subsequent emphasis on individual economic and political freedoms and the development of individualism as an economic and political philosophy. A philosophy like this forms the bedrock on which entrepreneurial free market capitalism is based. Building on this, some scholars claim there is a connection between individualism, as inspired by Protestantism, and the extent of entrepreneurial activity in a nation.[28] Again, one must be careful not to generalize too much from this historical-sociological view. While nations with a strong Protestant tradition such as Britain, Germany, and the United States were early leaders in the industrial revolution, nations with Catholic or Orthodox majorities show significant and sustained entrepreneurial activity and economic growth in the modern world.

ISLAM

With around 1 billion adherents, Islam is the second-largest of the world's major religions. Islam dates back to 610 AD when the prophet Muhammad began spreading the word, although the Muslim calendar begins in 622 AD when, to escape growing opposition, Muhammad left Mecca for the oasis settlement of Yathrib, later known as Madina. Adherents of Islam are referred to as Muslims. Muslims constitute a majority in more than 35 countries and inhabit a nearly contiguous stretch of land from the northwest coast of Africa, through the Middle East, to China and Malaysia in the Far East.

Islam has roots in both Judaism and Christianity (Islam views Jesus Christ as one of God's prophets). Like Christianity and Judaism, Islam is a monotheistic religion. The central principle of Islam is that there is but the one true omnipotent God. Islam requires unconditional acceptance of the uniqueness, power, and authority of God and the understanding that the objective of life is to fulfill the dictates of his will in the hope of admission to paradise. According to Islam, worldly gain and temporal power are an illusion. Those who pursue riches on earth may gain them, but those who forgo worldly ambitions to seek the favor of Allah may gain the greater treasure—entry into paradise. Other major principles of Islam include (1) honoring and respecting parents, (2) respecting the rights of others, (3) being generous but not a squanderer, (4) avoiding killing except for justifiable causes, (5) not committing adultery, (6) dealing justly and equitably with others, (7)

Despite the rise of radical Islamic fundamentalism, the vast majority of the Muslim population supports peace.

being of pure heart and mind, (8) safeguarding the possessions of orphans, and (9) being humble and unpretentious.[29] Obvious parallels exist with many of the central principles of both Judaism and Christianity.

Islam is an all-embracing way of life governing the totality of a Muslim's being.[30] As God's surrogate in this world, a Muslim is not a totally free agent but is circumscribed by religious principles—by a code of conduct for interpersonal relations—in social and economic activities. Religion is paramount in all areas of life. The Muslim lives in a social structure that is shaped by Islamic values and norms of moral conduct. The ritual nature of everyday life in a Muslim country is striking to a Western visitor. Among other things, orthodox Muslim ritual requires prayer five times a day (business meetings may be put on hold while the Muslim participants engage in their daily prayer ritual), requires that women should be dressed in a certain manner, and forbids the consumption of pork and alcohol.

Islamic Fundamentalism

The past three decades have witnessed the growth of a social movement often referred to as Islamic fundamentalism.[31] In the West, Islamic fundamentalism is associated in the media with militants, terrorists, and violent upheavals, such as the bloody conflict occurring in Algeria, the killing of foreign tourists in Egypt, and the September 11, 2001, attacks on the World Trade Center and Pentagon in the United States. This characterization is misleading. Just as Christian fundamentalists are motivated by sincere and deeply held religious values firmly rooted in their faith, so are Islamic fundamentalists. The violence that the Western media associates with Islamic fundamentalism is perpetrated by a small minority of radical "fundamentalists" who have hijacked the religion to further their own political and violent ends. (Some Christian "fundamentalists" have done exactly the same, including Jim Jones and David Koresh.) The vast majority of Muslims point out that Islam teaches peace, justice, and tolerance, not violence and intolerance, and that Islam explicitly repudiates the violence that a radical minority practices.

The rise of fundamentalism has no one cause. In part, it is a response to the social pressures created in traditional Islamic societies by the move toward modernization and by the influence of Western ideas, such as liberal democracy, materialism, equal rights for women, and attitudes toward sex, marriage, and alcohol. In many Muslim countries, modernization has been accompanied by a growing gap between a rich urban minority and an impoverished urban and rural majority. For the impoverished majority, modernization has offered little in the way of tangible economic progress, while threatening the traditional value system. Thus, for a Muslim who cherishes his or her traditions and feels that his or her identity is jeopardized by the encroachment of alien Western values, Islamic fundamentalism has become a cultural anchor.

Fundamentalists demand commitment to traditional religious beliefs and rituals. The result has been a marked increase in the use of symbolic gestures that confirm Islamic values. In areas where fundamentalism is strong, women have resumed wearing floor-length, long-sleeved dresses and covering their hair; religious studies have increased in universities; the publication of religious tracts has increased; and public religious orations have risen.[32] Also, the sentiments of some fundamentalist groups are often anti-Western. Rightly or wrongly, Western influence is blamed for a range of social ills, and many fundamentalists' actions are directed against Western governments, cultural symbols, businesses, and even individuals.

In several Muslim countries, fundamentalists have gained political power and have used this to try to make Islamic law (as set down in the Koran, the bible of Islam) the law of the land. There are good grounds for this in Islam. Islam makes no distinction between church and state. It is not just a religion; Islam is also the source of law, a guide to statecraft, and an arbiter of social behavior. Muslims believe that every human endeavor is within the purview of the faith—and this includes political activity—because the only purpose of any activity is to do God's will.[33] (Some Christian fundamentalists also share this view.) Muslim fundamentalists have been most successful in Iran, where a fundamentalist party has held power since 1979, but they also have had an influence in many other countries, such as Algeria, Afghanistan (where the Taliban established an extreme fundamentalist state until removed by the U.S.-led coalition in 2002), Egypt, Pakistan, the Sudan, and Saudi Arabia.

Economic Implications of Islam

The Koran establishes some explicit economic principles, many of which are pro–free enterprise.[34] The Koran speaks approvingly of free enterprise and of earning legitimate profit through trade and commerce (the prophet Mohammed was once a trader). The protection of the right to private property is also embedded within Islam, although Islam asserts that all property is a favor from Allah (God), who created and so owns everything. Those who hold property are regarded as trustees rather than owners in the Western sense of the word. As trustees they are entitled to receive profits from the property but are admonished to use it in a righteous, socially beneficial, and prudent manner. This reflects Islam's concern with social justice. Islam is critical of those who earn profit through the exploitation of others. In the Islamic view of the world, humans are part of a collective in which the wealthy and successful have obligations to help the disadvantaged. Put simply, in Muslim countries, it is fine to earn a profit, so long as that profit is justly earned and not based on the exploitation of others for one's own advantage. It also helps if those making profits undertake charitable acts to help the poor. Furthermore, Islam stresses the importance of living up to contractual obligations, of keeping one's word, and of abstaining from deception. For a closer look at how Islam, capitalism, and globalization can coexist, see the next country focus feature on the region around Kayseri in Central Turkey.

Given the Islamic proclivity to favor market-based systems, Muslim countries are likely to be receptive to international businesses as long as those businesses behave in a manner that is consistent with Islamic ethics. Businesses that are perceived as making an unjust profit through the exploitation of others, by deception, or by breaking contractual obligations are unlikely to be welcomed in an Islamic country. In addition, in Islamic countries where fundamentalism is on the rise, hostility toward Western-owned businesses is likely to increase.

One economic principle of Islam prohibits the payment or receipt of interest, which is considered usury. This is not just a matter of theology; in several Islamic states, it is also becoming a matter of law. The Koran clearly condemns interest, which is called *riba* in Arabic, as exploitative and unjust. For many years, banks operating in Islamic countries conveniently ignored this condemnation, but starting about 30 years ago with the establishment of an Islamic bank in Egypt, Islamic banks started to open in predominantly Muslim countries. By 2008, more than 200 Islamic financial institutions world-

Islamic Capitalism in Turkey

For years now Turkey has been lobbying the European Union to allow it to join the free trade block as a member state. If the EU says yes, it will be the first Muslim state in the Union. Many critics in the EU worry that Islam and Western style capitalism do not mix well, and that as a consequence, allowing Turkey into the EU would be a mistake. However, a close look at what is going on in Turkey suggests that this view may be misplaced. Consider the area around the city of Kayseri in central Turkey. Many dismiss this poor, largely agricultural region of Turkey as a non-European backwater, far removed from the secular bustle of Istanbul. It is a region where traditional Islamic values hold sway. And yet, it is also a region that has produced so many thriving Muslim enterprises that it is sometimes called the "Anatolian Tiger." Businesses based here include large food manufacturers, textile companies, furniture manufacturers, and engineering enterprises, many of which export a substantial percentage of their production.

Local business leaders attribute the success of companies in the region to an entrepreneurial spirit that they say is part of Islam. They point out that the Prophet Muhammad, who was himself a trader, preached merchant honor and commanded that 90 percent of a Muslim's life be devoted to work in order to put food on the table. Outside observers have gone further, arguing that what is occurring around Kayseri is an example of Islamic Calvinism, a fusion of traditional Islamic values and the work ethic often associated with Protestantism in general, and Calvinism in particular.

Within Kayseri, the influence of Islam is plain to see. Many companies set aside rooms and time for 15-minute prayer breaks. Most of the older businessmen have been to Mecca on the Haji, the pilgrimage that all Muslims are meant to make at least once in a lifetime. Few of the cafés and restaurants in Kayseri serve alcohol, and most women wear a headscarf.

At the Kayseri sugar factory, one of the most profitable in the region, a senior manager claims that Islam has played a large part in improving the profitability of the enterprise. For a long time the factory bought most of its sugar beets from a single monopoly supplier, who charged a high price. But because Islam preaches equal opportunity in business, managers at the sugar factory decided that the Islamic thing to do was to diversify the supply base and encourage small producers to sell beets to them. Today the factory buys sugar beets from 20,000 small growers. Competition between them has lowered prices and boosted the factory's profitability. The same manager also noted that "If you are not a good Muslim, don't pray five times a day and don't have a wife who wears a headscarf, it can be difficult to do business here."

However, not everyone agrees that Islam is the driving force behind the region's success. Saffet Arslan, the managing director of Ipek, the largest furniture producer in the region (which exports to more than 30 countries) claims that another force is at work—globalization! According to Mr. Arslan, over the last three decades local Muslims who once eschewed making money in favor of focusing on religion are now making business a priority. They see the Western world, and Western capitalism, as a model, not Islam, and because of globalization and the opportunities associated with it, they want to become successful. At the same time, Mr. Arslan is a practicing Muslim who has built a mosque in the basement of Ipec's headquarters building so that people can pray while at work.

If there is a weakness in the Islamic model of business that is emerging in places like Kayseri, some say it can be found in traditional attitudes towards the role of women in the workplace, and the low level of female employment in the region. According to a report by the European Stability Initiative, the same group that holds up the Kayseri region as an example of Islamic Calvinism, the low participation of women in the local workforce is the Achilles heel of the economy and may stymie the attempts of the region to catch up with the countries of the European Union.[35]

wide managed more than $700 billion in assets.[36] Even conventional banks are entering the market—both Citigroup and HSBC, two of the world's largest financial institutions, now offer Islamic financial services. While only Iran and the Sudan enforce Islamic banking conventions, in an increasing number of countries customers can choose between conventional banks and Islamic banks.

Conventional banks make a profit on the spread between the interest rate they have to pay to depositors and the higher interest rate they charge borrowers. Because Islamic banks cannot pay or charge interest, they must find a different way of making money. Islamic banks have experimented with two different banking methods—the *mudarabah* and the *murabaha*.[37]

A *mudarabah* contract is similar to a profit-sharing scheme. Under *mudarabah*, when an Islamic bank lends money to a business, rather than charging that business interest on the loan, it takes a share in the profits that are derived from the investment. Similarly, when a business (or individual) deposits money at an Islamic bank in a savings account, the deposit is treated as an equity investment in whatever activity the bank uses the capital for. Thus, the depositor receives a share in the profit from the bank's investment (as opposed to interest payments) according to an agreed-on ratio. Some Muslims claim this is a more efficient system than the Western banking system, since it encourages both long-term savings and long-term investment. However, there is no hard evidence of this, and many believe that a *mudarabah* system is less efficient than a conventional Western banking system.

The second Islamic banking method, the *murabaha* contract, is the most widely used among the world's Islamic banks, primarily because it is the easiest to implement. In a *murabaha* contract, when a firm wishes to purchase something using a loan—let's say a piece of equipment that costs $1,000—the firm tells the bank after having negotiated the price with the equipment manufacturer. The bank then buys the equipment for $1,000, and the borrower buys it back from the bank at some later date for, say, $1,100, a price that includes a $100 markup for the bank. A cynic might point out that such a markup is functionally equivalent to an interest payment, and it is the similarity between this method and conventional banking that makes it so much easier to adopt.

HINDUISM

Hinduism has approximately 750 million adherents, most of them on the Indian subcontinent. Hinduism began in the Indus Valley in India more than 4,000 years ago, making it the world's oldest major religion. Unlike Christianity and Islam, its founding is not linked to a particular person. Nor does it have an officially sanctioned sacred book such as the Bible or the Koran. Hindus believe that a moral force in society requires the acceptance of certain responsibilities, called *dharma*. Hindus believe in reincarnation, or rebirth into a different body, after death. Hindus also believe in *karma*, the spiritual progression of each person's soul. A person's karma is affected by the way he or she lives. The moral state of an individual's karma determines the challenges he or she will face in the next life. By perfecting the soul in each new life, Hindus believe that an individual can eventually achieve *nirvana*, a state of complete spiritual perfection that renders reincarnation no longer necessary. Many Hindus believe that the way to achieve nirvana is to lead a severe ascetic lifestyle of material and physical self-denial, devoting life to a spiritual rather than material quest.

The unique challenge that the Hindu culture's reverence for the cow created for McDonald's when it entered India in the 1990s (devout Hindus do not eat beef and many are vegetarians) is discussed in the chapter opening case.

Economic Implications of Hinduism

Max Weber, famous for expounding on the Protestant work ethic, also argued that the ascetic principles embedded in Hinduism do not encourage the kind of entrepreneurial activity in pursuit of wealth creation that we find in Protestantism.[38] According to Weber, traditional Hindu values emphasize that individuals should be judged not by their material achievements but by their spiritual achievements. Hindus perceive the pursuit of material well-being as making the attainment of nirvana more difficult. Given the emphasis on an ascetic lifestyle, Weber thought that devout Hindus would be less likely to engage in entrepreneurial activity than devout Protestants.

Mahatma Gandhi, the famous Indian nationalist and spiritual leader, was certainly the embodiment of Hindu asceticism. It has been argued that the values of Hindu asceticism and self-reliance that Gandhi advocated had a negative impact on the economic development of postindependence India.[39] But one must be careful not to read too much into Weber's arguments. Modern India is a very dynamic entrepreneurial society, and millions of hard-working entrepreneurs form the economic backbone of the country's rapidly growing economy.

Historically, Hinduism also supported India's caste system. The concept of mobility between castes within an individual's lifetime makes no sense to traditional Hindus. Hindus see mobility between castes as something that is achieved through spiritual progression and reincarnation. An individual can be reborn into a higher caste in his or her next life if he or she achieves spiritual development in this life. Although the caste system has been abolished in India, it still casts a long shadow over Indian life according to many observers. In so far as the caste system limits individuals' opportunities to adopt positions of responsibility and influence in society, the economic consequences of this religious belief are somewhat negative. For example, within a business organization, the most able individuals may find their route to the higher levels of the organization blocked simply because they come from a lower caste. By the same token, individuals may get promoted to higher positions within a firm as much because of their caste background as because of their ability.

BUDDHISM

Buddhism was founded in India in the sixth century BC by Siddhartha Gautama, an Indian prince who renounced his wealth to pursue an ascetic lifestyle and spiritual perfection. Siddhartha achieved nirvana but decided to remain on earth to teach his followers how they too could achieve this state of spiritual enlightenment. Siddhartha became known as the Buddha (which means "the awakened one"). Today, Buddhism has 350 million followers, most of whom are found in Central and Southeast Asia, China, Korea, and Japan. According to Buddhism, suffering originates in people's desires for pleasure. Cessation of suffering can be achieved by following a path for transformation. Siddhartha offered the Noble Eightfold Path as a route for transformation. This emphasizes right seeing, thinking, speech, action, living, effort, mindfulness, and meditation. Unlike Hinduism, Buddhism does not support the caste system. Nor does Buddhism advocate the kind of extreme ascetic behavior that Hinduism encourages. Nevertheless, like Hindus, Buddhists stress the afterlife and spiritual achievement rather than involvement in this world.

Economic Implications of Buddhism

The emphasis on creating wealth that is embedded in Protestantism is not found in Buddhism. Thus, in Buddhist societies, we do not see the same kind of historical-cultural stress on entrepreneurial behavior that Weber claimed could be found in the Protestant West. But unlike Hinduism, the lack of support for the caste system and extreme ascetic behavior suggests that a Buddhist society may represent a more fertile ground for entrepreneurial activity than a Hindu culture.

CONFUCIANISM

Confucianism was founded in the fifth century BC by K'ung-Fu-tzu, more generally known as Confucius. For more than 2,000 years until the 1949 Communist revolution, Confucianism was the official ethical system of China. While observance of Confucian ethics has been weakened in China since 1949, more than 200 million people still follow the teachings of Confucius, principally in China, Korea, and Japan. Confucianism teaches the importance of attaining personal salvation through right action. Although not a religion, Confucian ideology has become deeply embedded in the culture of these countries over the centuries, and through that, has an impact on the lives of many millions more. Confucianism is built around a comprehensive ethical code that sets down guidelines for relationships with others. High moral and ethical conduct and loyalty to others are central to Confucianism. Unlike religions, Confucianism is not concerned with the supernatural and has little to say about the concept of a supreme being or an afterlife.

Economic Implications of Confucianism

Some scholars maintain that Confucianism may have economic implications as profound as those Weber argued were to be found in Protestantism, although they are of a different nature.[40] This basic thesis proposes that the influence of Confucian ethics on the culture of China, Japan, South Korea, and Taiwan, by lowering the costs of doing business in those countries, may help explain their economic success. In this regard, three values central to the Confucian system of ethics are of particular interest: loyalty, reciprocal obligations, and honesty in dealings with others.

In Confucian thought, loyalty to one's superiors is regarded as a sacred duty—an absolute obligation. In modern organizations based in Confucian cultures, the loyalty that binds employees to the heads of their organization can reduce the conflict between management and labor that we find in more class-conscious societies. Cooperation between management and labor can be achieved at a lower cost in a culture where the virtue of loyalty is emphasized in the value systems.

However, in a Confucian culture, loyalty to one's superiors, such as a worker's loyalty to management, is not blind loyalty. The concept of reciprocal obligations is important. Confucian ethics stress that superiors are obliged to reward the loyalty of their subordinates by bestowing blessings on them. If these "blessings" are not forthcoming, then neither will be the loyalty. This Confucian ethic is central to the Chinese concept of *guanxi*, which refers to relationship networks supported by reciprocal obligations.[41] *Guanxi* means relationships, although in business settings it can be better understood as connections. Today, Chinese will often cultivate a *guanxiwang*, or "relationship network," for help. Reciprocal obligations are the glue that holds such networks together. If those obligations are not met—if favors done are not paid back or reciprocated—the reputation of the transgressor is tarnished and the person will be less able to draw on his or her *guanxiwang* for help in the future. Thus, the implicit threat of social sanctions is often sufficient to ensure that favors are repaid, obligations are met, and relationships are honored. In a society that lacks a rule-based legal tradition, and thus legal ways of redressing wrongs such as violations of business agreements, *guanxi* is an important mechanism for building long-term business relationships and getting business done in China. For an example of the importance of *guanxi*, read the Management Focus on DMG-Shanghai.

A third concept found in Confucian ethics is the importance attached to honesty. Confucian thinkers emphasize that, although dishonest behavior may yield short-term benefits for the transgressor, dishonesty does not pay in the long run. The importance attached to honesty has major economic implications. When companies can trust each other not to break contractual obligations, the costs of doing business are lowered. Expensive lawyers are not needed to resolve contract disputes. In a Confucian society, people may be less hesitant to commit substantial resources to cooperative ventures than in a society where honesty is less pervasive. When companies adhere to Confucian ethics, they can trust each other not to violate the terms of cooperative agreements. Thus, the costs of achieving cooperation between companies may be lower in societies such as Japan relative to societies where trust is less pervasive.

For example, it has been argued that the close ties between the automobile companies and their component parts suppliers in Japan are facilitated by a combination of trust and reciprocal obligations. These close ties allow the auto companies and their suppliers to work together on a range of issues, including inventory reduction, quality control, and design. The competitive advantage of Japanese auto companies such as Toyota may in part be explained by such factors.[42] Similarly, the combination of trust and reciprocal obligations is central to the workings and persistence of *guanxi* networks in China. Someone seeking and receiving help through a *guanxi* network is then obligated to return the favor and faces social sanctions if he or she does not reciprocate that obligation when called upon to do

DMG-Shanghai

Back in 1993, New Yorker Dan Mintz moved to China as a freelance film director with no contacts, no advertising experience, and no Mandarin. By 2006, the company he subsequently founded in China, DMG, had emerged as one of China's fastest-growing advertising agencies with a client list that includes Budweiser, Unilever, Sony, Nabisco, Audi, Volkswagen, China Mobile, and dozens of other Chinese brands. Mintz attributes his success in part to what the Chinese call *guanxi*.

Guanxi literally means relationships, although in business settings it can be better understood as connections. *Guanxi* has its roots in the Confucian philosophy of valuing social hierarchy and reciprocal obligations. Confucian ideology has a 2,000-year-old history in China. Confucianism stresses the importance of relationships, both within the family and between master and servant. Confucian ideology teaches that people are not created equal. In Confucian thought, loyalty and obligations to one's superiors (or to family) is regarded as a sacred duty, but at the same time, this loyalty has its price. Social superiors are obligated to reward the loyalty of their social inferiors by bestowing "blessings" upon them; thus, the obligations are reciprocal.

Today, Chinese will often cultivate a *guanxiwang*, or "relationship network," for help. Reciprocal obligations are the glue that holds such networks together. If those obligations are not met—if favors done are not paid back or reciprocated—the reputation of the transgressor is tarnished, and he or she will be less able to draw on his or her *guanxiwang* for help in the future. Thus, the implicit threat of social sanctions is often sufficient to ensure that favors are repaid, obligations are met, and relationships are honored. In a society that lacks a strong rule-based legal tradition, and thus legal ways of redressing wrongs such as violations of business agreements, *guanxi* is an important mechanism for building long-term business relationships and getting business done in China. According to tacit acknowledgment, if you have the right *guanxi*, legal rules can be broken, or at least bent.

Mintz, who is now fluent in Mandarin, cultivated his *guanxiwang* by going into business with two young Chinese who had connections, Bing Wu and Peter Xiao. Bing Wu, who works on the production side of the business, was a former national gymnastics champion, which translates into prestige and access to business and government officials. Peter Xiao comes from a military family with major political connections. Together, these three have been able to open doors that long-established Western advertising agencies have not. They have done it in large part by leveraging the contacts of Wu and Xiao, and by backing up their connections with what the Chinese call *Shi li*, the ability to do good work.

A case in point was DMG's campaign for Volkswagen, which helped the German company to become ubiquitous in China. The ads used traditional Chinese characters, which had been banned by Chairman Mao during the cultural revolution in favor of simplified versions. To get permission to use the characters in film and print ads—a first in modern China—the trio had to draw on high-level government contacts in Beijing. They won over officials by arguing that the old characters should be thought of not as "characters," but as art. Later, they shot TV spots for the ad on Shanghai's famous Bund, a congested boulevard that runs along the waterfront of the old city. Drawing again on government contacts, they were able to shut down the Bund to make the shoot. Steven Spielberg had been able to close down only a portion of the street when he filmed *Empire of the Sun* there in 1986. DMG has also filmed inside Beijing's Forbidden City, even though it is against the law to do so. Using his contacts, Mintz persuaded the government to lift the law for 24 hours. As Mintz has noted, "We don't stop when we come across regulations. There are restrictions everywhere you go. You have to know how get around them and get things done."[43]

so. If the person does not return the favor, his or her reputation will be tarnished and he or she will be unable to draw on the resources of the network in the future. It is claimed that these relationship-based networks can be more important in helping to enforce agreements between businesses than the Chinese legal system. Some claim that *guanxi* networks are, in fact, a substitute for the legal system.[44]

Language

One obvious way in which countries differ is language. By language, we mean both the spoken and the unspoken means of communication. Language is one of the defining characteristics of a culture.

SPOKEN LANGUAGE

Language does far more than just enable people to communicate with each other. The nature of a language also structures the way we perceive the world. The language of a society can direct the attention of its members to certain features of the world rather than others. The classic illustration of this phenomenon is that whereas the English language has but one word for snow, the language of the Inuit (Eskimos) lacks a general term for it. Instead, because distinguishing different forms of snow is so important in the lives of the Inuit, they have 24 words that describe different types of snow (e.g., powder snow, falling snow, wet snow, drifting snow).[45]

Because language shapes the way people perceive the world, it also helps define culture. Countries with more than one language often have more than one culture. Canada has an English-speaking culture and a French-speaking culture. Tensions between the two can run quite high, with a substantial proportion of the French-speaking minority demanding independence from a Canada "dominated by English speakers." The same phenomenon can be observed in many other countries. Belgium is divided into Flemish and French speakers, and tensions between the two groups exist; in Spain, a Basque-speaking minority with its own distinctive culture has been agitating for independence from the Spanish-speaking majority for decades; on the Mediterranean island of Cyprus, the culturally diverse Greek- and Turkish-speaking populations of the island engaged in open conflict in the 1970s, and the island is now partitioned into two parts. While it does not necessarily follow that language differences create differences in culture and, therefore, separatist pressures (e.g., witness the harmony in Switzerland, where four languages are spoken), there certainly seems to be a tendency in this direction.[46]

Chinese is the mother tongue of the largest number of people, followed by English and Hindi, which is spoken in India. However, the most widely spoken language in the world is English, followed by French, Spanish, and Chinese (i.e., many people speak English as a second language). English is increasingly becoming the language of international business. When a Japanese and a German businessperson get together to do business, it is almost certain that they will communicate in English. However, although English is widely used, learning the local language yields considerable advantages. Most people prefer to converse in their own language, and being able to speak the local language can build rapport, which may be very important for a business deal. International businesses that do not understand the local language can make major blunders through improper translation. For example, the Sunbeam Corporation used the English words for its "Mist-Stick" mist-producing hair curling iron when it entered the German market, only to discover after an expensive advertising campaign that *mist* means excrement in German. General Motors was troubled by the lack of enthusiasm among Puerto Rican dealers for its new Chevrolet Nova. When literally translated into Spanish, *nova* means star. However, when spoken it sounds like "no va," which in Spanish means "it doesn't go." General Motors changed the name of the car to Caribe.[47]

Language is primary to establishing quality business relationships.

UNSPOKEN LANGUAGE

Unspoken language refers to nonverbal communication. We all communicate with each other by a host of nonverbal cues. Raising the eyebrows, for example, is a sign of recognition in most cultures, while a smile is a sign of joy. Many nonverbal cues, however, are culturally bound. A failure to understand the nonverbal cues of another culture can lead to a communication failure. For example, making a circle with the thumb and the forefinger is a friendly gesture in the United States, but it is a vulgar sexual invitation in Greece and Turkey. Similarly, while most Americans and Europeans use the thumbs-up gesture to indicate that "it's all right," in Greece the gesture is obscene.

Another aspect of nonverbal communication is personal space, which is the comfortable amount of distance between you and someone you are talking with. In the United States, the customary distance apart adopted by parties in a business discussion is five to eight feet. In Latin America, it is three to five feet. Consequently, many North Americans unconsciously feel that Latin Americans are invading their personal space and can be seen backing away from them during a conversation. Indeed, the American may feel that the Latin is being aggressive and pushy. In turn, the Latin American may interpret such backing away as aloofness. The result can be a regrettable lack of rapport between two businesspeople from different cultures.

Education

Formal education plays a key role in a society. Formal education is the medium through which individuals learn many of the language, conceptual, and mathematical skills that are indispensable in a modern society. Formal education also supplements the family's role in socializing the young into the values and norms of a society. Values and norms are taught both directly and indirectly. Schools generally teach basic facts about the social and political nature of a society. They also focus on the fundamental obligations of citizenship. Cultural norms are also taught indirectly at school. Respect for others, obedience to authority, honesty, neatness, being on time, and so on are all part of the "hidden curriculum" of schools. The use of a grading system also teaches children the value of personal achievement and competition.[48]

From an international business perspective, one important aspect of education is its role as a determinant of national competitive advantage.[49] The availability of a pool of skilled and educated workers seems to be a major determinant of the likely economic success of a country. In analyzing the competitive success of Japan since 1945, for example, Michael Porter notes that after the war, Japan had almost nothing except for a pool of skilled and educated human resources.

> With a long tradition of respect for education that borders on reverence, Japan possessed a large pool of literate, educated, and increasingly skilled human resources. . . . Japan has benefited from a large pool of trained engineers. Japanese universities graduate many more engineers per capita than in the United States. . . . A first-rate primary and secondary education system in Japan operates based on high standards and emphasizes math and science. Primary and secondary education is highly competitive. . . . Japanese education provides most students all over Japan with a sound education for later education and training. A Japanese high school graduate knows as much about math as most American college graduates.[50]

Porter's point is that Japan's excellent education system is an important factor explaining the country's postwar economic success. Not only is a good education system a determinant of national competitive advantage, but it is also an important factor guiding the location choices of international businesses. The recent trend to outsource information technology jobs to India, for example, is partly due to the presence of significant numbers of trained engineers in India, which in turn is a result of the Indian education system. By the same token, it would make little sense to base production facilities that require highly skilled labor in a country where the education system was so poor that a skilled labor pool wasn't available, no matter how attractive the country might seem on other dimensions. It might make sense to base production operations that require only unskilled labor in such a country.

The general education level of a country is also a good index of the kind of products that might sell in a country and of the type of promotional material that should be used. For example, a country where more than 70 percent of the population is illiterate is unlikely to be a good market for popular books. Promotional material containing written descriptions of mass-marketed products is unlikely to have an effect in a country where almost three-quarters of the population cannot read. It is far better to use pictorial promotions in such circumstances.

Culture and the Workplace

Of considerable importance for an international business with operations in different countries is how a society's culture affects the values found in the workplace. Management process and practices may need to vary according to culturally determined work-related values. For example, if the cultures of the United States and France result in different work-related values, an international business with operations in both countries should vary its management process and practices to account for these differences.

Probably the most famous study of how culture relates to values in the workplace was undertaken by Geert Hofstede.[51] As part of his job as a psychologist working for IBM, Hofstede collected data on employee attitudes and values for more than 100,000 individuals from 1967 to 1973. These data enabled him to compare dimensions of culture across 40 countries. Hofstede isolated four dimensions that he claimed summarized different cultures—power distance, uncertainty avoidance, individualism versus collectivism, and masculinity versus femininity.

Hofstede's **power distance** dimension focused on how a society deals with the fact that people are unequal in physical and intellectual capabilities. According to Hofstede, high power distance cultures were found in countries that let inequalities grow over time into inequalities of power and wealth. Low power distance cultures were found in societies that tried to play down such inequalities as much as possible.

Hofstede's **uncertainty avoidance** dimension measured the extent to which different cultures socialize their members into accepting ambiguous situations and tolerating uncertainty. Members of high uncertainty avoidance cultures placed a premium on job security, career patterns, retirement benefits, and so on. They also had a strong need for rules and regulations; the manager was expected to issue clear instructions, and subordinates' initiatives were tightly controlled. Lower uncertainty avoidance cultures were characterized by a greater readiness to take risks and less emotional resistance to change.

The **individualism versus collectivism** dimension focused on the relationship between the individual and his or her fellows. In individualistic societies, the ties between individuals were loose and individual achievement and freedom were highly valued. In societies where collectivism was emphasized, the ties between individuals were tight. In such societies, people were born into collectives, such as extended families, and everyone was supposed to look after the interest of his or her collective.

Hofstede's **masculinity versus femininity** dimension looked at the relationship between gender and work roles. In masculine cultures, sex roles were sharply differentiated and traditional "masculine values," such as achievement and the effective exercise of power, determined cultural ideals. In feminine cultures, sex roles were less sharply distinguished, and little differentiation was made between men and women in the same job.

TABLE 7.1

Work-Related Values for
20 Selected Countries

	Power Distance	Uncertainty Avoidance	Individualism	Masculinity
Argentina	49	86	46	56
Australia	36	51	90	61
Brazil	69	76	38	49
Canada	39	48	80	52
Denmark	18	23	74	16
France	68	86	71	43
Germany (F.R.)	35	65	67	66
Great Britain	35	35	89	66
India	77	40	48	56
Indonesia	78	48	14	46
Israel	13	81	54	47
Japan	54	92	46	95
Mexico	81	82	30	69
Netherlands	38	53	80	14
Panama	95	86	11	44
Spain	57	86	51	42
Sweden	31	29	71	5
Thailand	64	64	20	34
Turkey	66	85	37	45
United States	40	46	91	62

Hofstede created an index score for each of these four dimensions that ranged from 0 to 100 and gave high scores for high individualism, high power distance, high uncertainty avoidance, and high masculinity. He averaged the score for all employees from a given country. Table 7.1 summarizes these data for 20 selected countries. Western nations such as the United States, Canada, and Britain scored high on the individualism scale and low on the power distance scale. At the other extreme were a group of Latin American and Asian countries that emphasize collectivism over individualism and score high on the power distance scale. Table 7.1 also reveals that Japan's culture had strong uncertainty avoidance and high masculinity. This characterization fits the standard stereotype of Japan as a country that is male dominant and where uncertainty avoidance exhibits itself in the institution of lifetime employment. Sweden and Denmark stand out as countries that had both low uncertainty avoidance and low masculinity (high emphasis on "feminine" values).

Hofstede's results are interesting for what they tell us in a very general way about differences between cultures. Many of Hofstede's findings are consistent with standard Western stereotypes about cultural differences. For example, many people believe Americans are more individualistic and egalitarian than the Japanese (they have a lower power distance), who in turn are more individualistic and egalitarian than Mexicans. Similarly, many might agree that Latin countries such as Mexico place a higher emphasis on masculine value—they are machismo cultures—than the Nordic countries of Denmark and Sweden.

However, one should be careful about reading too much into Hofstede's research. It has been criticized on a number of points.[52] First, Hofstede assumes there is a one-to-one correspondence between culture and the nation-state, but as we saw earlier, many countries have more than one culture. Hofstede's results do not capture this distinction. Second, the research may have been culturally bound. The research team was composed of Europeans and Americans. The questions they asked of IBM employees and their analysis of the answers may have been shaped by their own cultural biases and concerns. So it is not surprising that Hofstede's results confirm Western stereotypes because it was Westerners who undertook the research.

Third, Hofstede's informants worked not only within a single industry, the computer industry, but also within one company, IBM. At the time, IBM was renowned for its own strong corporate culture and employee selection procedures, making it possible that the employees' values were different in important respects from the values of the cultures from which those employees came. Also, Hofstede's sample excluded certain social classes (such as unskilled manual workers). A final caution is that Hofstede's work is now beginning to look dated. Cultures do not stand still; they evolve, albeit slowly. What was a reasonable characterization in the 1960s and 1970s may not be so today.

Still, just as it should not be accepted without question, Hofstede's work should not be dismissed either. It represents a starting point for managers trying to figure out how cultures differ and what that might mean for management practices. Also, several other scholars have found strong evidence that differences in culture affect values and practices in the workplace, and Hofstede's basic results have been replicated using more diverse samples of individuals in different settings.[53] Still, managers should use the results with caution, for they are not necessarily accurate.

Hofstede subsequently expanded his original research to include a fifth dimension that he argued captured additional cultural differences not brought out in his earlier work.[54] He referred to this dimension as "Confucian dynamism" (sometimes called *long-term orientation*). According to Hofstede, **Confucian dynamism** captures attitudes toward time, persistence, ordering by status, protection of face, respect for tradition, and reciprocation of gifts and favors. The label refers to the derivation of these "values" in Confucian teachings. As might be expected, East Asian countries such as Japan, Hong Kong, and Thailand scored high on Confucian dynamism, while nations such as the United States and Canada scored low. Hofstede and his associates went on to argue that their evidence suggested that nations with higher economic growth rates scored high on Confucian dynamism and low on individualism—the implication being that Confucianism is good for growth. However, subsequent studies have shown that this finding does not hold up under more sophisticated statistical analysis.[55] During the past decade, countries with high individualism and low Confucian dynamics such as the United States have attained high growth rates, while some Confucian cultures such as Japan have had stagnant economic growth. In reality, while culture might influence the economic success of a nation, it is just one of many factors, and while its importance should not be ignored, it should not be overstated either. Factors such as economic, political, and legal systems are probably more important than culture in explaining differential economic growth rates over time.

Cultural Change

Culture is not a constant; it evolves over time.[56] Changes in value systems can be slow and painful for a society. In the 1960s, for example, American values toward the role of women, love, sex, and marriage underwent significant changes. Much of the social turmoil of that time reflected these changes. Change, however, does occur and can often be quite profound. For example, at the beginning of the 1960s, the idea that women might hold senior management positions in major corporations was not widely accepted. Many scoffed at the idea. Today, it is a reality, and few in the mainstream of American society question the development or the capability of women in the business world. American culture has changed (although it is still more difficult for women to gain senior management positions than men). Similarly, the value systems of many ex-communist states, such as Russia, are undergoing significant changes as those countries move away from values that emphasize collectivism and toward those that emphasize individualism. While social turmoil is an inevitable outcome of such a shift, the shift will still probably occur.

Similarly, some claim that a major cultural shift has been occurring in Japan, with a move toward greater individualism.[57] The model Japanese office worker, or "salaryman," is characterized as being loyal to his boss and the organization to the point of giving up evenings, weekends, and vacations to serve the organization, which is the collective of which the employee is a member. However, a new generation of office workers does not seem to fit this model. An individual from the new generation is likely to be more direct than the traditional Japanese. He acts more like a Westerner, a *gaijian*. He does not live for the company and will move on if he gets the offer of a better job. He is not keen on overtime, especially if he has a date. He has his own plans for his free time, and they may not include drinking or playing golf with the boss.[58]

Several studies have suggested that economic advancement and globalization may be important factors in societal change.[59] For example, there is evidence that economic progress is accompanied by a shift in values away from collectivism and toward individualism.[60] Thus, as Japan has become richer, the cultural emphasis on collectivism has declined and greater individualism is being witnessed. One reason for this shift may be that richer societies exhibit less need for social and material support structures built on collectives, whether the collective is the extended family or the paternalistic company. People are better able to take care of their own needs. As a result, the importance attached to collectivism declines, while greater economic freedoms lead to an increase in opportunities for expressing individualism.

The culture of societies may also change as they become richer because economic progress affects a number of other factors, which in turn influence culture. For example, increased urbanization and improvements in the quality and availability of education are both a function of economic progress, and both can lead to declining emphasis on the traditional values associated with poor rural societies. A 25-year study of values in 78 countries, known as the World Values Survey, coordinated by the University of Michigan's Institute for Social Research, has documented how values change. The study linked these changes in values to changes in a country's level of economic development.[61] According to this research, as countries get richer, a shift occurs away from "traditional values" linked to religion, family, and country, and toward "secular rational" values. Traditionalists say religion is important in their lives. They have a strong sense of national pride; they also think that children should be taught to obey and that the first duty of a child is to make his or her parents proud. They say abortion, euthanasia, divorce, and suicide are never justified. At the other end of this spectrum are secular rational values.

Another category in the World Values Survey is quality of life attributes. At one end of this spectrum are "survival values," the values people hold when the struggle for survival is of paramount importance. These values tend to stress that economic and physical security are more important than self-expression. People who cannot take food or safety for granted tend to be xenophobic, are wary of political activity, have authoritarian tendencies, and believe that men make better political leaders than women. "Self-expression" or "well-being" values stress the importance of diversity, belonging, and participation in political processes.

As countries get richer, there seems to be a shift from "traditional" to "secular rational" values, and from "survival values" to "well-being" values. The shift, however, takes time, primarily because individuals are socialized into a set of values when they are young and find it difficult to change as they grow older. Substantial changes in values are linked to generations, with younger people typically being in the vanguard of a significant change in values.

With regard to globalization, some have argued that advances in transportation and communication technologies, the dramatic increase in trade that we have witnessed since World War II, and the rise of global corporations such as Hitachi, Disney, Microsoft, and Levi Strauss, whose products and operations can be found around the globe, are creating conditions for the merging of cultures.[62] With McDonald's hamburgers in China, The Gap in India, iPods in South Africa, and MTV everywhere helping to foster a ubiquitous youth culture, some argue that less cultural variation will be available. At the same time, one must not ignore important countertrends, such as the shift toward Islamic fundamentalism in several countries; the separatist movement in Quebec, Canada; or the continuing ethnic strains and separatist movements in Russia. Such countertrends in many ways are a reaction to the pressures for cultural convergence. In an increasingly modern and materialistic world, some societies are trying to reemphasize their cultural roots and uniqueness. Cultural change is not unidirectional, with national cultures converging toward some homogenous global entity. Also, while some elements of culture change quite rapidly—particularly the use of material symbols—other elements change slowly if at all. Thus, just because people the world over wear blue jeans and eat at McDonald's, one should not assume that they have also adopted American values—for more often than not, they have not.

IMPLICATIONS FOR MANAGERS

International business is different from national business because countries and societies are different. In this chapter, we have seen just how different societies can be. Societies differ because their cultures vary. Their cultures vary because of profound differences in social structure, religion, language, education, economic philosophy, and political philosophy. Three important implications for international business flow from these differences. The first is the need to develop cross-cultural literacy. Businesspeople need not only to appreciate that cultural differences exist but also to appreciate what such differences mean for international business. A second implication centers on the connection between culture and national competitive advantage. A third implication looks at the connection between culture and ethics in decision making. In this section, we will explore the first two of these issues in depth.

CROSS-CULTURAL LITERACY

One of the biggest dangers confronting a company that goes abroad for the first time is the danger of being ill-informed. International businesses that are ill-informed about the practices of another culture are likely to fail. Doing business in different cultures requires adaptation to conform with the value systems and norms of that culture. Adaptation can embrace all aspects of an international firm's operations in a foreign country. The way in which deals are negotiated, the appropriate incentive pay systems for salespeople, the structure of the organization, the name of a product, the tenor of relations between management and labor, the manner in which the product is promoted, and so on, are all sensitive to cultural differences. What works in one culture might not work in another.

To combat the danger of being ill-informed, international businesses should consider employing local citizens to help them do business in a particular culture. They must also ensure that home-country executives are cosmopolitan enough to understand how differences in culture affect the practice of international business. Transferring executives overseas at regular intervals to expose them to different cultures will help build a cadre of cosmopolitan executives. An international business must also be constantly on guard against the dangers of *ethnocentric behavior.* **Ethnocentrism** is a belief in the superiority of one's own ethnic group or culture. Hand in hand with ethnocentrism goes a disregard or contempt for the culture of other countries. Unfortunately, ethnocentrism is all too prevalent; many Americans are guilty of it, as are many French people, Japanese people, British people, and so on. Ugly as it is, ethnocentrism is a fact of life, one that international businesses must be on guard against.

Simple examples illustrate how important cross-cultural literacy can be. Anthropologist Edward T. Hall has described how Americans, who tend to be informal in nature, react strongly to being corrected or reprimanded in public.[63] This can cause problems in Germany, where a cultural tendency toward correcting strangers can shock and offend most Americans. For their part, Germans can be a bit taken aback by the tendency of Americans to call everyone by their first name. This is uncomfortable enough among executives of the same rank, but it can be seen as insulting when a young and junior American executive addresses an older and more senior German manager by his first name without having been invited to do so. Hall concludes it can take a long time to get on a first-name basis with a German; if you rush the process you will be perceived as overfriendly and rude, and that may not be good for business.

Hall also notes that cultural differences in attitudes toward time can cause a myriad of problems. He notes that in the United States, giving a person a deadline is a way of increasing the urgency or relative importance of a task. However, in the Middle East, giving a deadline can have exactly the opposite effect. The American who insists an Arab business associate make his mind up in a hurry is likely to be perceived as overly demanding and exerting undue pressure. The result may be exactly the opposite of what the American intended, with the Arab slowing down as a reaction to the American's arrogance and rudeness. For his part, the American may believe that an Arab associate is being rude if he shows up late to a meeting because he met a friend in the street and stopped to talk. The American, of course, is very concerned about time and scheduling. But for the Arab, who lives in a society where social networks are a major source of information and maintaining relationships is important, finishing the discussion with a friend is more important than adhering to a strict schedule. Indeed, the Arab may be puzzled as to why the American attaches so much importance to time and schedule.

CULTURE AND COMPETITIVE ADVANTAGE

One theme that continually surfaces in this chapter is the relationship between culture and national competitive advantage. Put simply, the value systems and norms of a country influence the costs of doing business in that country. The costs of doing business in a country influence the ability of firms to establish a competitive advantage in the global marketplace. We have seen how attitudes toward cooperation between management and labor, work, and paying interest are influenced by social structure and religion. It can be argued that the class-based conflict between workers and management in class-conscious societies, when it leads to industrial disruption, raises the costs of doing business in that society. Similarly, we have seen how some sociologists have argued that the ascetic "other-worldly" ethics of Hinduism may not be as supportive of capitalism as the ethics embedded in Protestantism and Confucianism. Also, Islamic laws banning interest payments may raise the costs of doing business by constraining a country's banking system.

Japan presents an interesting case study of how culture can influence competitive advantage. Some scholars have argued that the culture of modern Japan lowers the costs of doing business relative to the costs in most Western nations. Japan's emphasis on group affiliation, loyalty, reciprocal obligations, honesty, and education all boost the competitiveness of Japanese companies. The emphasis on group affiliation and loyalty encourages individuals to identify strongly with the companies in which they work. This tends to foster an ethic of hard work and cooperation between management and labor "for the good of the company." Similarly, reciprocal obligations and honesty help foster an atmosphere of trust between companies and their suppliers. This encourages them to enter into long-term relationships with each other to work on inventory reduction, quality control, and design—all of which have been shown to improve an organization's competitiveness. This level of cooperation has often been lacking in the West, where the relationship between a company and its suppliers tends to be a short-term one structured around competitive bidding rather than one based on long-term mutual commitments. In addition, the availability of a pool of highly skilled labor, particularly engineers, has helped Japanese enterprises develop cost-reducing process innovations that have boosted their productivity.[64] Thus, cultural factors may help explain the competitive advantage enjoyed by many Japanese businesses in the global marketplace. The rise of Japan as an economic power during the second half of the twentieth century may be in part attributed to the economic consequences of its culture.

It also has been argued that the Japanese culture is less supportive of entrepreneurial activity than, say, American society. In many ways, entrepreneurial activity is a product of an individualistic mind-set, not a classic characteristic of the Japanese. This may explain why American enterprises, rather than Japanese corporations, dominate industries where entrepreneurship and innovation are highly valued, such as computer software and biotechnology. Of course, obvious and significant exceptions to this generalization exist. Masayoshi Son recognized the potential of software far faster than any of Japan's corporate giants; set up his company, Softbank, in 1981; and has since built it into Japan's top software distributor. Similarly, dynamic entrepreneurial individuals established major Japanese companies such as Sony and Matsushita. But these examples may be the exceptions that prove the rule, for as yet there has been no surge in entrepreneurial high-technology enterprises in Japan equivalent to what has occurred in the United States.

For the international business, the connection between culture and competitive advantage is important for two reasons. First, the connection suggests which countries are likely to produce the most viable competitors. For example, one might argue that U.S. enterprises are likely to see continued growth in aggressive, cost-efficient competitors from those Pacific Rim nations where a combination of free market economics, Confucian ideology, group-oriented social structures, and advanced education systems can all be found (e.g., South Korea, Taiwan, Japan, and, increasingly, China).

Second, the connection between culture and competitive advantage has important implications for the choice of countries in which to locate production facilities and do business. Consider a hypothetical case when a company has to choose between two countries, A and B, for locating a production facility. Both countries are characterized by low labor costs and good access to world markets. Both countries are of roughly the same size (in terms of population) and both are at a similar stage of economic development. In country A, the education system is undeveloped, the society is characterized by a marked stratification between the upper and lower classes, and there are six major linguistic groups. In country B, the education system is well developed, social stratification is lacking, group identification is valued by the culture, and there is only one linguistic group. Which country makes the best investment site?

Country B probably does. In country A, conflict between management and labor, and between different language groups, can be expected to lead to social and industrial disruption, thereby raising the costs of doing business.[65] The lack of a good education system also can be expected to work against the attainment of business goals.

The same kind of comparison could be made for an international business trying to decide where to push its products, country A or B. Again, country B would be the logical choice because cultural factors suggest that in the long run, country B is the nation most likely to achieve the greatest level of economic growth.

But as important as culture is, it is probably less important than economic, political, and legal systems in explaining differential economic growth between nations. Cultural differences are significant, but we should not overemphasize their importance in the economic sphere. For example, earlier we noted that Max Weber argued that the ascetic principles embedded in Hinduism do not encourage entrepreneurial activity. While this is an interesting academic thesis, recent years have seen an increase in entrepreneurial activity in India, particularly in the information technology sector where India is rapidly becoming an important global player. The ascetic principles of Hinduism and caste-based social stratification have apparently not held back entrepreneurial activity in this sector.

CHAPTER SUMMARY

We have looked at the nature of social culture and studied some implications for business practice. The chapter made the following points:

1. Culture is a complex whole that includes knowledge, beliefs, art, morals, law, customs, and other capabilities people acquire as members of society.

2. Values and norms are the central components of a culture. Values are abstract ideals about what a society believes to be good, right, and desirable. Norms are social rules and guidelines that prescribe appropriate behavior in particular situations.

3. Values and norms are influenced by political and economic philosophy, social structure, religion, language, and education.

4. The social structure of a society refers to its basic social organization. Two main dimensions along which social structures differ are the individual—group dimension and the stratification dimension.

5. In some societies, the individual is the basic building block of social organization. These societies emphasize individual achievements above all else. In other societies, the group is the basic building block of social organization. These societies emphasize group membership and group achievements above all else.

6. All societies are stratified into different classes. Class-conscious societies are characterized by low social mobility and a high degree of stratification. Less class-conscious societies are characterized by high social mobility and a low degree of stratification.

7. Religion may be defined as a system of shared beliefs and rituals that is concerned with the realm of the sacred. Ethical systems refer to a set of moral principles, or values, that are used to guide and shape behavior. The world's major religions are Christianity, Islam, Hinduism, and Buddhism. Although not a religion, Confucianism has an impact on behavior as profound as that of many religions. The value systems of different religious and ethical systems have different implications for business practice.

8. Language is one defining characteristic of a culture. It has both spoken and unspoken dimensions. In countries with more than one spoken language, we tend to find more than one culture.

9. Formal education is the medium through which individuals learn skills and are socialized into the values and norms of a society. Education plays an important role in the determination of national competitive advantage.

10. Geert Hofstede studied how culture relates to values in the workplace. He isolated four dimensions that he claimed summarized different cultures: power distance, uncertainty avoidance, individualism versus collectivism, and masculinity versus femininity.

11. Culture is not a constant; it evolves. Economic progress and globalization seem to be two important engines of cultural change.

12. One danger confronting a company that goes abroad for the first time is being ill-informed. To develop cross-cultural literacy, international businesses need to employ host-country nationals, build a cadre of cosmopolitan executives, and guard against the dangers of ethnocentric behavior.

13. The value systems and norms of a country can affect the costs of doing business in that country.

Key Terms and Concepts

caste system, *153*

class consciousness, *155*

class system, *153*

Confucian dynamism, *169*

cross-cultural literacy, *147*

culture, *148*

ethical systems, *156*

ethnocentrism, *173*

folkways, *148*

group, *151*

individualism versus collectivism, *168*

masculinity versus femininity, *168*

mores, *149*

norms, *148*

power distance, *168*

religion, *156*

social mobility, *153*

social strata, *153*

social structure, *151*

society, *148*

uncertainty avoidance, *168*

values, *148*

Critical Thinking and Discussion Questions

1. Outline why the culture of a country might influence the costs of doing business in that country. Illustrate your answer with examples.

2. Do you think that business practices in an Islamic country are likely to differ from business practices in the United States? If so, how?

3. What are the implications for international business of differences in the dominant religion or ethical system of a country?

4. Choose two countries that appear to be culturally diverse. Compare the cultures of those countries and then indicate how cultural differences influence (a) the costs of doing business in each country, (b) the likely future economic development of that country, and (c) business practices.

5. Reread the Country Focus on Islamic Capitalism in Turkey. Then answer the following questions:
   a. Can you see anything in the values of Islam that is hostile to business?
   b. What does the experience of the region around Kayseri teach us about the relationship between Islam and business?
   c. What are the implications of Islamic values towards business for the participation of a country like Turkey in the global economy?

6. Reread the Management Focus on DMG-Shanghai and answer the follow questions:
   a. Why do you think that it is so important to cultivate *guanxi* and *guanxiwang* in China?
   b. What does the experience of DMG tell us about the way things work in China? What would likely happen to a business that obeyed all the rules and regulations, rather than trying to find a way around them as Dan Mintz apparently does?
   c. What are the ethical issues that might arise when drawing upon *guanxiwang* to get things done in China? What does this suggest about the limits of using *guanxiwang* for a Western business committed to high ethical standards?

Research Task ⊘ globalEDGE | globaledge.msu.edu
Differences in Culture

Use the globalEDGE™ site to complete the following exercises:

Exercise 1

You are preparing for a business trip to Brazil where you will need to interact extensively with local professionals. Therefore, you should consider collecting information regarding local culture and business habits prior to your departure. A colleague from Latin America recommends you visit the *Centre for Intercultural Learning* and read through the country insights provided for Brazil. Prepare a short description of the most striking cultural characteristics that may effect business interactions in this country.

Exercise 2

Typically, cultural factors drive the differences in business etiquette encountered during international business travel. In fact, Asian cultures exhibit significant differences in business etiquette when compared to Western cultures. For example, in Thailand it is considered offensive to show the sole of the shoe or foot to another. Prior to leaving for your first business trip to Asia, a colleague informed you that a guide to business etiquette around the world may help you. Using the globalEDGE Web site, find five tips regarding business etiquette in the Asian country of your choice.

CLOSING CASE

Wal-Mart's Foreign Expansion

Wal-Mart, the world's largest retailer, has built its success on a strategy of everyday low prices, and highly efficient operations, logistics, and information systems that keeps inventory to a minimum and ensures against both overstocking and understocking. The company employs some 2.1 million people, operates 4,200 stores in the United States and 3,600 in the rest of the world, and generates sales of almost $400 billion (as of fiscal 2008). Approximately $91 billion of these sales were generated in 15 nations outside of the United States. Facing a slowdown in growth in the United States, Wal-Mart began its international expansion in the early 1990s when it entered Mexico, teaming up in a joint venture with Cifra, Mexico's largest retailer, to open a series of supercenters that sell both groceries and general merchandise.

Initially the retailer hit some headwinds in Mexico. It quickly discovered that shopping habits were different. Most people preferred to buy fresh produce at local stores, particularly items like meat, tortillas and pan dulce which didn't keep well overnight (many Mexicans lacked large refrigerators). Many consumers also lacked cars, and did not buy in large volumes as consumers in the United States did. Wal-Mart adjusted its strategy to meet the local conditions, hiring local managers who understood Mexican culture, letting those managers control merchandising strategy, building smaller stores that people could walk to, and offering more fresh produce. At the same time, the company believed that it could gradually change the shopping culture in Mexico, educating consumers by showing them the benefits of its American merchandising culture. After all, Wal-Mart's managers reasoned, people once shopped at small stores in the United States, but starting in the 1950s they increasingly gravitated towards large stores like Wal-Mart. As it built up its distribution systems in Mexico, Wal-Mart was able to lower its own costs, and it passed these on to Mexican consumers in the form of lower prices. The customization, persistence, and low prices paid off. Mexicans started to change their shopping habits. Today Wal-Mart is Mexico's largest retailer and the country is widely considered to be the company's most successful foreign venture.

Next Wal-Mart expanded into a number of developed nations, including Britain, Germany and South Korea. There its experiences have been less successful. In all three countries it found itself going head to head against well-established local rivals who had nicely matched their offerings to local shopping habits and consumer preferences. Moreover, consumers in all three countries seemed to have a preference for higher quality merchandise and were not as attracted to Wal-Mart's discount strategy as consumers in the United States and Mexico. After years of losses, Wal-Mart pulled out of Germany and South Korea in 2006. At the same time, it continued to look for retailing opportunities elsewhere, particularly in developing nations where it lacked strong local competitors, where it could gradually alter the shopping culture to its advantage, and where its low price strategy was appealing.

Recently, the centerpiece of its international expansion efforts has been China. Wal-Mart opened its first store in China in 1996, but initially expanded very slowly, and by 2006 had only 66 stores. What Wal-Mart discovered, however, was that the Chinese were bargain hunters, and open to the low price strategy and wide selection offered at Wal-Mart stores. Indeed, in terms of their shopping habits, the emerging Chinese middle class seemed more like Americans than Europeans. But to succeed in China, Wal-Mart also found it had to adapt its merchandising and operations strategy to mesh with Chinese culture. One of the things that Wal-Mart has learned is that Chinese consumers insist that food must be freshly harvested, or even killed in front of them. Wal-Mart initially offended Chinese consumers by trying to sell them dead fish, as well as meat packed in Styrofoam and cellophane. Shoppers turned their noses up at what they saw as old merchandise. So Wal-Mart began to display the meat uncovered, installed fish tanks into which shoppers could plunge fishing nets to pull out their evening meal, and began selling live turtles for turtle soup. Sales soared.

Wal-Mart has also learned that in China, success requires it to embrace unions. Whereas in the United States Wal-Mart has vigorously resisted unionization, it came to the realization that in China unions don't bargain for labor contracts. Instead, they are an arm of the state, providing funding for the Communist Party and (in the government's view) securing social order. In mid-2006 Wal-Mart broke with its long standing antagonism to unions and agreed to allow unions in its Chinese stores. Many believe this set the stage for Wal-Mart's most recent move, the purchase in December 2006 of a 35 percent stake in the Trust-Mart chain, which has 101 hypermarkets in 34 cities across China. Now Wal-Mart has proclaimed that China lies at the center of its growth strategy. By early 2009 Wal-Mart had some 243 stores in the country, and despite the global economic slowdown, the company insists that it will continue to open new stores in China at a "double digit rate."[66]

Case Discussion Questions

1. Do you think Wal-Mart could translate its merchandising strategy wholesale to another country and succeed? If not, why not?

2. Why do you think Wal-Mart was successful in Mexico?

3. Why do you think Wal-Mart failed in South Korea and Germany? What are the differences between these countries and Mexico?

4. What must Wal-Mart do to succeed in China? Is it on track?

5. To what extent can a company like Wal-Mart change the culture of the nation where it is doing business?

Notes

1. Luke Harding, "Give Me a Big Mac—But Hold the Beef," *The Guardian*, December 28, 2000, p. 24; Luke Harding, "Indian McAnger," *The Guardian*, May 7, 2001, p. 1; A. Dhillon, "India Has No Beef with Fast Food Chains," *Financial Times*, March 23, 2002, p. 3; "McDonald's Plans More Outlets in India," *Associated Press Worldstream*, December 24, 2004; D. Dutta, "The Perishable Food Chain in India," *Just Food*, September 2005, pp. 22–29; R. Verma, "Branded Foods in India," *Just Food*, November 2007, pp. 14–17; and M. Hughlett, "Overseas Sales Surging for McDonald's Amid U.S. Slowdown," *Chicago Tribune*, September 14, 2008, p. 1.

2. Mary Yoko Brannen, "When Micky Loses Face: Recontextualization, Semantic Fit, and the Semiotics of Foreignness," *Academy of Management Review*, 2004, pp. 593–616.

3. See R. Dore, *Taking Japan Seriously* (Stanford, CA: Stanford University Press, 1987).

4. Data come from J. Monger, "International Comparison of Labor Disputes in 2004," *Labor Market Trends*, April 2006, pp. 117–128.

5. E. B. Tylor, *Primitive Culture* (London: Murray, 1871).

6. Geert Hofstede, *Culture's Consequences: International Differences in Work-Related Values* (Beverly Hills, CA: Sage Publications, 1984), p. 21.

7. J. Z. Namenwirth and R. B. Weber, *Dynamics of Culture* (Boston: Allen & Unwin, 1987), p. 8.

8. R. Mead, *International Management: Cross-Cultural Dimensions* (Oxford: Blackwell Business, 1994), p. 7.

9. Edward T. Hall and M. R. Hall, *Understanding Cultural Differences* (Yarmouth, ME: Intercultural Press, 1990).

10. Edward T. Hall and M. R. Hall, *Hidden Differences: Doing Business with the Japanese* (New York: Doubleday, 1987).

11. "Iraq: Down but Not Out," *The Economist*, April 8, 1995, pp. 21–23.

12. S. P. Huntington, *The Clash of Civilizations* (New York: Simon & Schuster, 1996).

13. M. Thompson, R. Ellis, and A. Wildavsky, *Cultural Theory* (Boulder, CO: Westview Press, 1990).

14. M. Douglas, *In the Active Voice* (London: Routledge, 1982), pp. 183–254.

15. M. L. Dertouzos, R. K. Lester, and R. M. Solow, *Made in America* (Cambridge, MA: MIT Press, 1989).

16. C. Nakane, *Japanese Society* (Berkeley: University of California Press, 1970).

17. Ibid.

18. For details, see M. Aoki, *Information, Incentives, and Bargaining in the Japanese Economy* (Cambridge: Cambridge University Press, 1988); and Dertouzos et al., *Made in America*.

19. E. Luce. *The Strange Rise of Modern India.* (Boston: Little Brown, 2006); and D. Pick and K. Dayaram, "Modernity and Tradition in the Global Era: The Re-invention of Caste in India," *International Journal of Sociology and Social Policy*, 2006, pp. 284–301.

20. For an excellent historical treatment of the evolution of the English class system, see E. P. Thompson, *The Making of the English Working Class* (London: Vintage Books, 1966). See also R. Miliband, *The State in Capitalist Society* (New York: Basic Books, 1969), especially Chapter 2. For more recent studies of class in British societies, see Stephen Brook, *Class: Knowing Your Place in Modern Britain* (London: Victor Gollancz, 1997); A. Adonis and S. Pollard, *A Class Act: The Myth of Britain's Classless Society* (London: Hamish Hamilton, 1997); and J. Gerteis and M. Savage, "The Salience of Class in Britain and America: A Comparative Analysis," *British Journal of Sociology*, June 1998.

21. "With Reservations: Business and Caste in India," *The Economist*, October 6, 2007, pp. 81–83; and Eric Bellman, "Reversal of Fortune Isolates India's Brahmins," *The Wall Street Journal*, December 24, 2007, p. 4.

22. Adonis and Pollard, *A Class Act*.

23. Y. Bian, "Chinese Social Stratification and Social Mobility," *Annual Review of Sociology* 28 (2002), pp. 91–117.

24. N. Goodman, *An Introduction to Sociology* (New York: HarperCollins, 1991).

25. R. J. Barro and R. McCleary, "Religion and Economic Growth across Countries," *American Sociological Review*, October 2003, pp. 760–82.

26. M. Weber, *The Protestant Ethic and the Spirit of Capitalism* (New York: Charles Scribner's Sons, 1958, original 1904–

1905). For an excellent review of Weber's work, see A. Giddens, *Capitalism and Modern Social Theory* (Cambridge: Cambridge University Press, 1971).

27. Weber, *The Protestant Ethic and the Spirit of Capitalism*, p. 35.

28. A. S. Thomas and S. L. Mueller, "The Case for Comparative Entrepreneurship," *Journal of International Business Studies* 31, no. 2 (2000), pp. 287–302; and S. A. Shane, "Why Do Some Societies Invent More than Others?" *Journal of Business Venturing* 7 (1992), pp. 29–46.

29. See S. M. Abbasi, K. W. Hollman, and J. H. Murrey, "Islamic Economics: Foundations and Practices," *International Journal of Social Economics* 16, no. 5 (1990), pp. 5–17; and R. H. Dekmejian, *Islam in Revolution: Fundamentalism in the Arab World* (Syracuse, NY: Syracuse University Press, 1995).

30. T. W. Lippman, *Understanding Islam* (New York: Meridian Books, 1995).

31. Dekmejian, *Islam in Revolution*.

32. M. K. Nydell, *Understanding Arabs* (Yarmouth, ME: Intercultural Press, 1987).

33. Lippman, *Understanding Islam*.

34. The material in this section is based largely on Abbasi et al., "Islamic Economics."

35. D. Bilefsky, "Turks Knock on Europe's Door with Evidence That Islam and Capitalism Can Coexist," *New York Times*, August 27, 2006, p. 4; and European Stability Imitative, *Islamic Calvinists*, September 19, 2005. Archived at www.esiweb.org.

36. "Islamic Finance: Calling the Faithful," *The Economist*, December 9, 2006, pp. 77–78; and "Savings and Souls," *The Economist*, September 6, 2008, pp. 81–83.

37. "Forced Devotion," *The Economist*, February 17, 2001, pp. 76–77.

38. For details of Weber's work and views, see Giddens, *Capitalism and Modern Social Theory*.

39. See, for example, the views expressed in "A Survey of India: The Tiger Steps Out," *The Economist*, January 21, 1995.

40. See R. Dore, *Taking Japan Seriously*; and C. W. L. Hill, "Transaction Cost Economizing as a Source of Comparative Advantage: The Case of Japan," *Organization Science* 6 (1995).

41. C. C. Chen, Y. R. Chen, and K. Xin, "Guanxi Practices and Trust in Management," *Organization Science* 15, no. 2 (March–April 2004), pp. 200–10.

42. See Aoki, *Information, Incentives, and Bargaining*; and J. P. Womack, D. T. Jones, and D. Roos, *The Machine That Changed the World* (New York: Rawson Associates, 1990).

43. Sources: J. Bryan, "The Mintz Dynasty," *Fast Company*, April 2006, pp. 56–62; and M. Graser, "Featured Player," *Variety*, October 18, 2004, p. 6.

44. For examples of this line of thinking, see M. W. Peng and P. S. Heath, "The Growth of the Firm in Planned Economies in Transition," *Academy of Management Review* 21 (1996), pp. 492–528; M. W. Peng, *Business Strategies in*

Transition Economies (Thousand Oaks, CA: Sage, 2000); and M. W. Peng and Y. Luo, "Managerial Ties and Firm Performance in a Transition Economy," *Academy of Management Journal*, June 2000, pp. 486–501.

45. This hypothesis dates back to two anthropologists, Edward Sapir and Benjamin Lee Whorf. See E. Sapir, "The Status of Linguistics as a Science," *Language* 5 (1929), pp. 207–14; and B. L. Whorf, *Language, Thought, and Reality* (Cambridge, MA: MIT Press, 1956).

46. The tendency has been documented empirically. See A. Annett, "Social Fractionalization, Political Instability, and the Size of Government," *IMF Staff Papers* 48 (2001), pp. 561–92.

47. D. A. Ricks, *Big Business Blunders: Mistakes in Multinational Marketing* (Homewood, IL: Dow Jones-Irwin, 1983).

48. Goodman, *An Introduction to Sociology.*

49. M. E. Porter, *The Competitive Advantage of Nations* (New York: Free Press, 1990).

50. Ibid., pp. 395–97.

51. G. Hofstede, "The Cultural Relativity of Organizational Practices and Theories," *Journal of International Business Studies*, Fall 1983, pp. 75–89; and G. Hofstede, *Cultures and Organizations: Software of the Mind* (New York: McGraw-Hill, 1997).

52. For a more detailed critique, see R. Mead, *International Management: Cross-Cultural Dimensions* (Oxford: Blackwell, 1994), pp. 73–75.

53. For example, see W. J. Bigoness and G. L. Blakely, "A Cross-National Study of Managerial Values," *Journal of International Business Studies*, December 1996, p. 739; D. H. Ralston, D. H. Holt, R. H. Terpstra, and Y. Kai-Cheng, "The Impact of National Culture and Economic Ideology on Managerial Work Values," *Journal of International Business Studies* 28, no. 1 (1997), pp. 177–208; P. B. Smith, M. F. Peterson, and Z. Ming Wang, "The Manager as a Mediator of Alternative Meanings," *Journal of International Business Studies* 27, no. 1 (1996), pp. 115–37; and L. Tang and P. E. Koves, "A Framework to Update Hofstede's Cultural Value Indices," *Journal of International Business Studies* 39 (2008), pp. 1045–63.

54. G. Hofstede and M. H. Bond, "The Confucius Connection," *Organizational Dynamics* 16, no. 4 (1988), pp. 5–12; and G. Hofstede, *Culture's Consequences: Comparing Values, Behaviors, Institutions and Organizations across Nations* (Thousand Oaks, CA: Sage, 2001).

55. R. S. Yeh and J. J. Lawerence, "Individualism and Confucian Dynamism," *Journal of International Business Studies* 26, no. 3 (1995), pp. 655–66.

56. For evidence of this, see R. Inglehart. "Globalization and Postmodern Values," *The Washington Quarterly*, Winter 2000, pp. 215–28.

57. Mead, *International Management*, Chapter 17.

58. "Free, Young, and Japanese," *The Economist*, December 21, 1991.

59. Namenwirth and Weber, *Dynamics of Culture*; and Inglehart, "Globalization and Postmodern Values."

60. G. Hofstede, "National Cultures in Four Dimensions," *International Studies of Management and Organization* 13, no. 1, pp. 46–74; and L. Tang and P. E. Koves, "A Framework to Update Hofstede's Cultural Value Indices," *Journal of International Business Studies* 39 (2008), 39, pp. 1045–1063.

61. See Inglehart, "Globalization and Postmodern-Values." For updates, go to http://wvs.isr.umich.edu/index.html.

62. Hofstede, "National Cultures in Four Dimensions."

63. Hall and Hall, *Understanding Cultural Differences.*

64. See Aoki, Information, *Incentives, and Bargaining*; Dertouzos et al., *Made in America*; and Porter, *The Competitive Advantage of Nations*, pp. 395–97.

65. For empirical work supporting such a view, see Annett, "Social Fractionalization, Political Instability, and the Size of Government."

66. J. Lyons, "In Mexico Wal-Mart Is Defying Its Critics," *The Wall Street Journal*, March 5, 2007, page A1. A9; K. Norton, "The Great Wal Mart of China," *Newsweek*, October 30, 2006, pp. 50–51. E. Rigby, "Smooth Supply in High Demand," *Financial Times*, February 14, 2007, p. 10; and M. Fong, "Retailers Still Expanding in China," *The Wall Street Journal*, January 22, 2009, pp. B1, B4.

Nonverbal Language in Intercultural Communication

LEARNING OBJECTIVES

After completing this chapter, you should be able to:

 LO¹ Understand the role of nonverbal communication in intercultural business communication.

 LO² Discuss the impact of paralanguage on sending and receiving messages.

LO³ Identify the major components of nonverbal communication.

 LO⁴ Evaluate the relationship between verbal and nonverbal signals.

Rana Zarvi from Lebanon has been working for a Swedish firm for several months. When she arrived in January, she did not think she would last very long; the short days and the cold winter made her wonder how anyone could live in such an environment. But now that summer has arrived, she is getting used to the climate and her surroundings. She likes her work, and her colleagues are friendly, but she has no real feel for them. What do they think? How do they live? What do they do in their free time? What are their hobbies? In her previous job in Beirut, for example, she would socialize with her co-workers after hours. She knew about their families, and in the office there was an easygoing camaraderie. Rana misses the enthusiastic greetings with co-workers and the hugs with the other female employees. In Stockholm, her co-workers are friendly but more distant. Rana is used to speaking with her whole body, using her arms to emphasize her points, and showing her emotions through her facial expressions. Increasingly, she is wondering how she is doing. Her boss, Arne Gustafson, seems to appreciate her work, but sometimes she has doubts. He never just comes out and says, "Great job!" Yesterday he called her into his office to set the agenda of an upcoming negotiation session with managers from Malaysia. Rana knows that the firm faces tough competition and a joint venture with the Malaysian firm would help open the Asian market. Arne discussed the negotiation strategy and gave her several assignments for the negotiation. He was all business, correct but without emotion. Rana is wondering: Is he confident that this Malaysian negotiation will go well? Does he have any doubts? What does he think is going to happen? Is she doing her part? His words sound confident, but during her time in Sweden she has found that she has not been very successful at reading the thoughts and emotions of her co-workers.

How often have we listened to someone speak and wondered what the speaker really was saying? We may agree intuitively with the words, but in the back of our minds we feel that there is more to the message than the words. We may even come to the conclusion that the speaker means the opposite of what she says. We may base our judgment on an evaluation of tone, intonation, emphasis, facial expressions, gestures and hand movements, distance, and eye contact—in short, on nonverbal signals, or the silent language.[1]

Although nonverbal signals tend to enhance and support language, they can minimize or even contradict a verbal message. For example, the phrase "I would love to meet with you and discuss this issue in more detail" can take on different meanings depending on the nonverbal signals accompanying the words, such as the following:

- A smile while pulling out a calendar will support the words.
- Going on to the next topic without pausing after the statement may indicate that the speaker is not serious and is not interested in meeting, at least not now.
- A frown and a search for something on the desk while uttering the words may contradict the message altogether.

Some researchers maintain that in face-to-face communication up to 93 percent of an oral message is communicated nonverbally and that the nonverbal elements are a much better indicator of the true meaning than the actual words are.

Yet the true meaning and the interpretation depend on a variety of factors. As we will see in this chapter, people from different cultures attach different meanings to nonverbal signals. As one example, in Western cultures eye contact can signify honesty, whereas in Asian cultures it may indicate rudeness.

The interpretation of nonverbal signals is complicated further by the fact that within a culture not all people use the same signals. Men and women often use different nonverbal language. Men in Western cultures tend to be more outspoken than women are; however, with women asserting their rights more, women's communication is changing.[2] People from different social classes within a culture also may use nonverbal signals differently.

People from the upper classes or people in leading positions may be more assertive and outspoken in many cultures when they are communicating with people from lower classes and in lower positions.[3]

Nonverbal communication is influenced by a number of factors, including

- Cultural background
- Socioeconomic background
- Education
- Gender
- Age
- Personal preferences and idiosyncrasies

All these factors complicate the interpretation of the nonverbal aspects of communication.

Needless to say, valid generalizations are difficult to make and always must be reevaluated and seen in the context of the situation. For example, in a Western cultural setting crossing one's arms may be interpreted as being defensive, rejecting the other person, or being closed-minded. However, it is also possible that the nonverbal signal simply means that the speaker is cold. The isolated symbol may not carry any deeper meaning. It is only one contributor to communication. To get the whole meaning, one must look at all the signals together.

Other nonverbal symbols are interesting but not that important. For example, when Europeans use their fingers in counting to five, they start with the thumb and go in sequence to the little finger. Americans, in contrast, start with the index finger, go on to the little finger, and count the thumb last.[4] Although this difference is interesting, it does not influence the meaning of what is being said. A German manager who works in Dallas needs to sort out which signals are important and which ones are not.

You may wonder why we are concerned at all with nonverbal communication if its interpretation is so difficult. The point is that nonverbal communication, because it varies so much and because it carries so much meaning, needs close attention so that we can decode and get our messages across more effectively. In this chapter, we examine nonverbal language in several cultures, but bear in mind that these are generalizations; although the descriptions are true generally for a culture, there are many variations within a culture. As you learn more about a culture and meet more people from that culture, you need to adapt and adjust your interpretation of nonverbal language signals.

What exactly is nonverbal language? Although researchers agree that nonverbal communication refers to nonworded language, they use a variety of definitions that can be divided into two major categories:

- Nonverbal or nonworded communication includes *all* communication beyond the spoken or written word. It includes aspects such as the language of friendship and material possessions, as well as the nonverbal aspects of written communication, like weight and color of paper, format, typeface, and binding.
- Nonverbal communication consisting only of nonverbal language using the body, including paralanguage.

    In this chapter, we will specifically examine

- Paralanguage
    - Vocal qualifiers
    - Vocalization
- Nonverbal conventions in face-to-face communication
    - Eye contact
    - Facial expressions
    - Gestures

- Timing in spoken exchange
- Touching
- Language of space
- Appearance
- Silence

Paralanguage

Paralanguage lies between verbal and nonverbal communication. It involves sounds but not words. The *uhs*, *ahas*, and *uhms* we use in our conversation are examples of paralanguage. Researchers divide paralanguage into three categories: voice quality, vocal qualifiers, and vocalization.[5] Voice quality seems to be more of an individual than a cultural characteristic, and so we will examine vocal qualifiers and vocalization.

VOCAL QUALIFIERS

The term *vocal qualifiers* refers to volume, pitch, and the overall intonation or "melody" of the spoken word. For example, does the speaker raise or lower his voice at the end of a sentence? Does the speaker vary the speed of what she says, or does she speak very evenly? Does the speaker vary the volume between loud and soft; in other words, does he speak softly or does he shout? Vocal qualifiers differ from culture to culture. For example, a non-Japanese person listening to a Japanese man can get the impression that the Japanese speaker "spits" words out in clusters. A cluster comes very fast, followed by a slight pause before the next cluster emerges. Japanese women, by comparison, may seem to speak more evenly.

In English as it is spoken in the United States, a speaker raises the pitch at the end of a question, signifying a nonverbal question mark. If the rise in pitch is accompanied by a pause, the listener interprets this to mean that the speaker is waiting for an answer. However, if the speaker asks a question without the pitch going up, he may not expect or want an answer. The speaker may be asking a rhetorical question and then be ready to make the next point. A speaker who has finished expressing an idea typically lowers her pitch, signifying that she is done. Someone else can speak now.

Vocal qualifiers provide important signals in turn taking in a conversation. If everyone in the group is used to the same signals, the conversation can flow and speakers seem to take their turns almost automatically. The rhythm of the conversation feels natural. In contrast, if people use different intonation patterns, interlocutors may feel that the conversation is strained, that one side is trying to dominate or is not contributing to the discussion.

Ending sentences with a high pitch in American English may indicate self-doubt and uncertainty. In French, in contrast, sentences tend to end on a higher pitch than they do in German or English. A French speaker may be very certain of what she is saying, yet given the cultural background of the United States or Germany, a listener may have a different impression.

VOCALIZATION

All cultures use nonword noises such as "ahem," "um," "er," sucking in one's breath, and clicking one's tongue. These noises may be used as connectors between ideas; they also may be used to indicate that someone is ready to say something or that more time is needed to think things over. Generally, the interpretation of these noises does not present a major hurdle in intercultural communication. The frequency of their use, however, varies from culture to culture.[6]

Related to the nonword vocalizers are fillers. For example, in English, "okay" and "you know" often are used as fillers. The words have a meaning, but a speaker who uses them does not attach that specific meaning to them. The words simply build a bridge to what the speaker says next. The use of *hai* (literally translated *yes*) in Japanese serves the same function. Most Japanese use *hai* as a filler without a particular meaning. It serves as a lubricant for the flow of the speech. In intercultural communication, people must be aware of the appropriate frequency and meaning of fillers.

Nonverbal Business Conventions in Face-to-Face Encounters

Nonverbal messages can be broken down into subcategories. Although this makes the discussion easier, we must be careful not to assume that speakers use nonverbal signals in isolation. In most cases, speakers use many different signals at the same time. We may move our hands, nod with our heads, smile, and keep close eye contact, all at the same time. The nonverbal messages that give listeners the most trouble are those which accompany words. It's the tone of voice, the look on someone's face, or the lack of eye contact that makes you wonder if you are understood. As we discuss nonverbal conventions in face-to-face encounters, we will start with the nonverbal signals that most closely accompany the verbal message and go on to those which are not connected with words, such as the use of space, appearance, and silence.

To some extent, we are able to manipulate the signals consciously: We may smile because that is expected of us even though we may not feel like smiling. In many cases, however, we send nonverbal signals without being aware of doing so. Those signals, the experts agree, are a reflection of our true feelings and reactions. One of the goals in intercultural communication is to interpret *all* nonverbal signals.

EYE CONTACT

In most cultures, superiors are freer to look at subordinates than the other way around. Eye contact, therefore, also is related to power and perceived power. If Alberto looks directly at his employee John, he indicates that he has a right to do so. If John lowers his eyes when Alberto looks at him, he may be indicating that he accepts his subordinate position. Of course, eye contact is only one aspect of showing power. Traditionally, men can look more at women than women can look at men. In the United States, for example, "ogling," looking at the other sex, may be interpreted as a form of sexual harassment and may even have legal consequences. Eye contact, as a result, is becoming complicated in that culture. European women sometimes comment that men from the United States are cold and don't know how to flirt, the innocent game of looking and establishing eye contact. At the same time, women from the United States who visit Southern European countries are often uncomfortable when men look at them. The looking is interpreted as offensive staring.

Rules governing eye contact are different in different cultures, and that difference can make people feel uncomfortable without being aware of why they are uncomfortable. In the United States, it is customary to look at the speaker's mouth when listening but make intermittent eye contact with the eyes of a listener when speaking. In China, it is the opposite: A speaker rivets the listener with sustained, unbroken eye contact, but a listener does not make eye contact or look at the speaker's face consistently.

Since several cultures consider the eye to be "the window of the soul," eye contact or its lack is interpreted to have special meaning. In these cultures, eye contact is related to honesty. In other cultures, eye contact is seen as an invasion of privacy.

Eye Contact as a Sign of Honesty

"He couldn't even look me in the eye" is a common phrase that in Western cultures indicates that the speaker had something to hide. In North American and Northern European cultures, eye contact shows openness, trustworthiness, and integrity. One doesn't have anything to hide. If a woman from the United States looks directly at someone, she allows that person to see her eyes and decide whether she is trustworthy. Someone who does not make eye contact is considered shifty and makes the listener suspicious. In that case, the defenses go up and one becomes more careful. People from all cultures carry their cultural attitudes toward eye contact with them, and like most aspects of nonverbal behavior, eye contact does not travel easily across cultural boundaries. In most cases, we don't consciously think of eye contact; we do it subconsciously. As a result, habits relating to eye contact are difficult to change.

Arab cultures, even more than Western cultures, use very intense eye contact and concentrate on eye movement to read real intentions. The feeling is that the eye does not lie. To see the eye more clearly, Arabs move closer, and that makes non-Arabs uncomfortable. This links eye contact to the use of space. As we will see throughout this chapter, nonverbal communication signals are linked.

A person from Japan, for example, would feel uncomfortable both with the intense eye contact and with the close physical proximity. That person will feel even more uncomfortable if the Arab, in addition to making close eye contact and standing very close to the listener, touches the listener. In this case, the Arab is sending three very strong nonverbal signals, all of which run counter to what is acceptable nonverbal behavior in Japan.

In many cases an Arab speaker may not want to disclose his innermost feelings, yet because of the culture, he cannot refuse eye contact. Therefore, he may look for other means to protect his feelings and intentions. Some people say that the former Palestinian leader Yasser Arafat, for example, always used to wear sunglasses so that the people he was talking to could not follow the movement of his eyes. They argued that the sunglasses were an attempt to hide his true intentions and motives.

Eye Contact as a Sign of Invasion of Privacy

To look someone in the eye in Japan is to invade that person's space. It is rude. When samurai held power, a strict code of behavior was enforced regarding who could look at whom and for how long one could look, and one violated those codes at one's peril.[7] This has carried over into modern society. The Japanese may sit close together in an office, but they seldom look each other in the eye.

The Japanese feel uncomfortable with direct eye contact, and they want to avoid it. In addition, not looking someone in the eye preserves that person's private space or bubble. In a crowded country, the preservation of privacy by any means is considered important. When greeting someone, one bows and looks past the other person. If you do not want to acknowledge a person at all—for example, if you are concentrating on something important and don't want to lose your focus—you may simply look down as you walk past the other person. What could be seen as a slight or insult in Western countries would simply be a signal that you do not want to be interrupted. The degree of American eye contact would be considered staring and rude in the Japanese environment. Even on the crowded subways and trains, nobody makes eye contact. People look past each other. As we will discuss in greater detail later in the chapter, during negotiation the Japanese may look down past their counterparts. In fact, they may even close their eyes, which can be very disconcerting to American negotiators who are used to looking at the people across the negotiation table.

FACIAL EXPRESSIONS

Words often are accompanied by distinct facial expressions. In many cultures, when people are surprised, they may open their eyes widely and also open their mouths. When they like something, their eyes may beam and they may smile. When they are angry, they may frown and narrow their eyes. Although many facial expressions carry similar meanings in a variety of cultures, the frequency and intensity of their use may vary. Latin and Arab cultures use more intense facial expressions, whereas East Asian cultures use more subdued facial expressions.

Smiling

People in all cultures smile at times; however, the meaning of a smile may vary. Depending on the culture, it can indicate joy and amusement, but it also can indicate embarrassment.

In an attempt to appear open and friendly, people in the United States smile a lot. Everyone smiles at everyone. To those in other cultures, the American smile often appears insincere and frozen. Why, for example, should a waitress smile? Restaurants in the United States go to great lengths in training to ensure that all employees use the appropriate smile. Americans are surprised and puzzled that the rest of the world does not seem to share the American emphasis on the smile. McDonald's, for example, had a hard time teaching waitresses in Moscow the importance of the smile and the proper type of smile.

In Japan, people don't smile the way people from the United States do. One does not show feelings freely and force one's emotions on anybody else. Men don't smile in public, and women are not supposed to show their teeth when they smile. To guarantee that the teeth are hidden, Japanese women tend to put a hand in front of their mouths when laughing. The women who greet customers in banks and stores with a deep bow do not really smile by U.S. standards. They look pleasant, but they don't really smile at the customer the way an American would.

Germans smile, but not nearly as much as people in the United States do. They will say bluntly, "Life is severe, and there is very little to smile about." Germans are very reserved, but for reasons different from those of the Japanese. The Japanese don't want to intrude; the Germans recognize that the world is not necessarily a pleasant place. Life is doing one's duty, and duty does not necessarily lend itself to smiling. Wal-Mart wanted to lighten up the poor service in German stores (Germans frequently say that Germany is a *Service Wüste*, literally meaning a desert as far as service is concerned) by insisting that personnel greet shoppers and smile at them. The Germans, while moaning about unfriendly service, were not impressed by the efforts. They saw the smiling employees as manipulative and insincere.

Koreans consider it inappropriate for adults to smile in public. Smiling at strangers is something the mentally retarded do or children do before they are trained properly. In addition, for Koreans, as for the members of many other cultures in East Asia, a smile often is an expression not of pleasure but of embarrassment. When a person from the United States or Europe might blush with embarrassment or become defensive, an Asian might smile. To avoid serious misunderstandings, people who engage in intercultural communication should be able to interpret a smile appropriately.

Related to the smile is the laugh. Americans can have a very deeply felt belly laugh that comes from the deepest emotions. In Arabic and Latin cultures, the laugh often is accompanied by expressive gestures such as arm waving and touching. The Japanese seldom laugh that way except among intimates. A laugh is not necessarily an expression of joy and happiness. Like a smile, a laugh often is an expression of being uncomfortable, nervous, and embarrassed.

Showing Anger

The expression of anger also varies from culture to culture in terms of both intensity and type of expression. In addition, cultural values dictate who can show anger. For example, negotiators from Korea are expected to behave with dignity and maintain face so as not to violate the emphasis on formality and courtesy. As Korean society has become more industrialized, younger businesspeople may behave less traditionally, but the influence of tradition is still strong.[8] Generally, older people, men, and people in authority may show anger more readily than do younger people, women, and subordinates. The boss may get angry at the subordinate, but the subordinate is well advised not to react in kind. The result is that the interpretation and the display of anger are influenced by culture.

One of the milder forms of showing anger in Western cultures, for example, is frowning. Depending on the context, frowning can indicate anger, doubt, questioning of authority, suspicion, or disagreement. In cultures in which the open expression of one's feeling is not appreciated, frowning may be much more subdued. The Japanese, for example, avert the gaze to hide anger; showing anger openly even through frowning is considered inappropriate in business contexts and may result in loss of face.

Another way to show anger is to shout and gesture. As we mentioned earlier, nonverbal communication signals often are combined. Germans, Canadians, Arabs, and Latins often raise their voices when angry. The Japanese seldom raise their voices when angry. Instead, anger may be shown by sucking in one's breath rather than letting it out with a scream. When Germans are angry, their faces may get red and they may shout, but typically they are still fairly correct in the way they address the opponent. Many would still call the opponent "*Sie*" (the formal address for "you") even if they throw all sorts of epithets at him.

Some cultures use intense and expressive gesturing to show anger. People from the Middle East accompany their verbal tirades with big gestures. The whole body is involved in showing anger and outrage as if to illustrate that the entire person is affected. Showing anger means not just a battle of words but a battle of one's entire existence.

Research in Korean companies has revealed the surprising fact that Korean managers often show anger toward subordinates not only with verbal criticism but also with nonverbal acts of violence—even throwing coffee on a subordinate or causing physical injury![9] This is surprising behavior because it is so different from what is known of Asian attention to face and harmony. It also shows that people in cultures in the same geographic area may act very differently.

Asian cultures tend to restrict the range of facial expressions by Western standards. As a result, anger is not expressed openly in work environments in many Asian cultures. People from Asian cultures are able to read the message of the subdued nonverbal facial communication of anger, but people from Western cultures tend to have a hard time deciphering the code. Compared with Japanese culture, facial expressions in Arabic cultures tend to overstate feelings such as anger. From the facial expression, an outsider may find it hard to determine how angry a person from the Middle East really is. Nonverbal and verbal communication in Arabic cultures tends towards greater expressiveness and emotion. Eloquence is valued in Arabic cultures, and how one says something is as important as what one says. Arabic speakers repeat ideas, phrases, and words to show sincerity about what they are saying, and sometimes to show authenticity of authority. Outsiders may easily interpret the show of emotion as anger.[10] The point is that people from the same culture have no trouble reading the message. The problem comes when people cross cultural boundaries and enter a different system of communicating through facial expressions and gestures.

GESTURES

Head Movements

In most cultures, nodding one's head is seen as agreeing. Shaking one's head is seen as rejecting, although Bulgarians do the opposite—they shake their heads when agreeing. In southern India, moving one's head from side to side is not a negation. Even in this area where most cultures agree, there is some disagreement.

A speaker may nod her head to affirm what she is saying and emphasize the verbal message. The listener may nod to signal understanding and approval. Nodding can be a signal that the listener understands and that the speaker can continue with the discussion.

A lowered head in Western culture can signify defeat or uncertainty. In Asian cultures, lowering one's head may represent accepting one's place in the hierarchy, but it also may be an indication of intent listening. Japanese managers, for example, frequently lower their heads and close their eyes during negotiations. Americans see this as a lack of interest or even disrespect; for the Japanese, this may merely be natural listening behavior. In contrast, tilting the head upward in Western cultures is interpreted as being arrogant, as is illustrated in the expression "His nose was in the air."

One of the authors videotaped students making oral presentations in English and in their native languages to see if the nonverbal codes differed in the same speaker. These presentations seemed to indicate that nonverbal codes learned with a specific language did not transfer to another language. For example, an Iranian student, when speaking Farsi, put his hands behind his back in a gesture of respect, straightened his back, and spoke with his chin up, making eye contact only with the professor, the authority figure. When the same student gave his presentation in English, he looked like an ordinary American student, keeping one hand in his pocket, occasionally shifting his weight from one foot to the other, and maintaining eye contact with everyone in the room.

It would be interesting to see the extent to which the change in body movements was a conscious effort to fit into American culture and the extent to which it was a subconscious connection of English with a certain set of nonverbal signals.

Arm Movements

Arm movements take up space and thus enlarge the size of the speaker. A speaker who uses big arm movements can intimidate the listener and appear more powerful. In most cultures, men tend to use larger gestures than women do.

When a businessman from the United States wants to emphasize a point in a discussion, he may pound his fist on the table and underline his statements with staccato drumming of the table. Businesswomen in the United States in the same situation use far fewer arm and hand movements. However, compared with Japanese women, American women use very expressive arm movements.

Japanese men use far fewer arm movements than do both men and women from the United States. Personal space in Japan is limited, and big arm movements could invade someone's private space. In addition, big gestures draw attention to the speaker and single him out from the group, thereby threatening the harmony of the group. Someone from a more openly expressive culture may interpret the subdued arm and body movements of a Japanese person as submissive or timid. A non-Japanese negotiator may even think that the Japanese businessperson is not interested and does not care about the discussion. Yet by Japanese standards this person may be quite expressive. People who are used to expressive gestures often have difficulty recognizing and interpreting subdued gestures. They may be so busy talking with their arms that they don't hear the body language of the other person. The person from the subdued culture, however, may be overwhelmed by the gestures that he too has difficulty understanding. The gestures seem to scream at him.

Arab men use their arms even more than men from the United States do. Gestures and waving of the arms accompany almost every spoken word and seem to embrace a wide space. Arm movements can signal happiness but also anger (see the earlier discussion in the "Showing Anger" section of this chapter). The expansive gestures run parallel to the hyperbole in the spoken language. The exaggeration and repetition help establish credibility and seriousness. In the process of waving his arms, an Arab may touch the listener occasionally. For Arabs, words do not seem to be sufficient to express thoughts. The nonverbal signals do not just accompany the spoken word; they are an integral part of the verbal message.[11]

English is used frequently in international business, but many businesspeople speak English as a foreign language. Do those businesspeople synchronize their nonverbal communication with English nonverbals or with nonverbals from their native culture? If they synchronize it with English nonverbal signals, which nonverbal patterns do they use? Those of Great Britain, the United States, Australia, New Zealand, or India? Unless a businessperson is fluent linguistically and culturally, she probably will combine English with nonverbals from her own culture.

Posture

The way we sit, stand, and walk sends a nonverbal message. In Western culture, standing tall conveys confidence. A confident person stands erect with the shoulders back and the head up. The posture signals, "I am not afraid of anything." The appropriate posture is related to a person's status in society. For example, a manager may stand erect when talking to subordinates, but the subordinates may drop their shoulders when talking to the manager. In traditional societies, the person lower in the hierarchy may be expected to prostate himself in front of the tribal chief or village elder to show respect. Although this form of showing respect and submission is not practiced in intercultural business communication, an international manager needs to know what is acceptable posture in a given culture.

Although in most business situations people sit on chairs, in many Arab cultures men conduct business while sitting on the floor. In traditional Japanese businesses, people also may sit on the floor. The Japanese style of sitting with the legs tucked under can be very taxing for outsiders who are not used to that posture. In after-hours entertaining, the Japanese like to challenge Westerners to sit in the Japanese pose.

In many cultures, women with middle-class and upper-class backgrounds are supposed to sit with their legs and ankles together and their arms close to their bodies. Women are to be modest and take up little space. When women sit in an easy chair, they seem to "borrow" the space; men, in contrast, seem to "own" the space. In Western cultures, this has changed to quite an extent over the last two decades, and young women often are as relaxed as men are while sitting. When Western women do business in more traditional societies, such as Japan and India, they need to adapt the way they sit and stand to avoid giving offense.

The way we use our bodies when communicating indicates how we perceive our power, authority, and position in relation to the person with whom we are communicating. If the other person comes from the same culture, she can read the signals fairly accurately. If the other person is from another culture, she may have difficulties. She may interpret the lack of body language as rejection or the expressive body language as threatening when the speaker was simply using his or her own cultural style.

TIMING IN SPOKEN EXCHANGES

A conversation is verbal exchange between people. Although the words are obviously important, the timing of the exchange also carries a significant nonverbal message. To examine the timing of nonverbal communication, we must answer several questions:

- Who initiates the communication?
- What are the patterns of frequency of exchange?
- What is acceptable behavior for interrupting the speaker?
- What are the patterns for terminating the exchange?

In their own culture, people know what the typical patterns for verbal interaction are. For an outsider, the timing issue becomes more complex because it is related closely to issues of gender, status, and hierarchy. In many cultures, men initiate verbal exchanges more frequently than women do, older people are more likely to start the exchange than younger people are, people with authority are more likely to initiate communication than are subordinates, and this behavior is carried into the office.

Questions 2 and 3 are connected. Whoever interrupts also controls the exchange. Again, in most cultures the patterns are similar, but Japan is an exception: Interrupting others is not acceptable. In cultures in which interrupting the speaker is acceptable, businessmen tend to interrupt businesswomen more often than the other way around. Older people interrupt younger people more often, and people in power positions interrupt subordinates. Although anyone can end the communication, frequently men, older people, and people in positions of authority are the ones who control the termination.

The roles that gender, age, and authority play in the timing of communication in all cultures might suggest that culture-based differences in timing are small, yet the differences are significant. For example, even though research has shown that in the United States men tend to dominate the timing of communication,[12] American women are much more assertive and outspoken in business and in public than Saudi and Japanese women are.

The following examples illustrate the timing behavior in three different environments:

- An environment that emphasizes equality
- An environment that emphasizes seniority and hierarchy
- An environment that emphasizes the role of men

These areas overlap; the Japanese, for example, value seniority, but life is dominated by men. In Saudi Arabia, women are almost banished from public life but seniority plays a role in the lives of both men and women.

Emphasis on Equal Status

For most people in the United States, a discussion is a give-and-take procedure in which people take turns speaking. The speaker gives clues indicating when he expects the other side to come in, when to wait, and when to be silent. The listener also sends signals indicating when he wants to get in. These signals are internalized, and most people don't think much about them unless the reality clashes with their expectations. One of the signals an American may use to indicate readiness for a reply is to lower the voice, pause at the end of a phrase or sentence, gesture for a response, or look expectantly at the other person. A person from another culture who is used to different rules for turn-taking may misinterpret the signals or even miss the signals that it is appropriate to enter the conversation.

Women and young people in the United States have become more assertive and outspoken over the last few years and increasingly influence and even control the timing of communication. Many companies proclaim open-door policies and strive to empower employees in an effort to tap the creativity of their workers. They encourage subordinates to initiate communication with supervisors and express their ideas more openly. As a result, employees have gained some control over the timing of both verbal and nonverbal communication.

Emphasis on Seniority and Hierarchy

The timing in a Japanese conversation is dominated by the person with seniority, who also typically is higher in the hierarchy. A younger person will wait to be addressed and avoid eye contact while being addressed and while speaking. For a non-Japanese person, the timing of a Japanese interchange is difficult to follow because much of the conversation is nonverbal and the nonverbal signals are difficult for outsiders to decipher. The timing signals are more subtle than those in the United States, almost imperceptible. The verbal duel, common in Western culture, is frowned upon.

Emphasis on the Role of Men

In contrast to Japan, Arabic cultures are more verbally oriented. People enjoy the lively exchange of ideas. At first glance, one may get the impression that everyone can interrupt everyone and jump into the conversation. Yet older men clearly dominate the exchange and timing. Although many people, including younger ones, may speak, a few older men control the process. Women in many Arab countries do not speak in public, and in business settings women are seldom participants. The timing of communication typically is controlled by men. Women appear to be more reactive than proactive participants.

TOUCHING

In many international business settings, the handshake has become an accepted touch between businesspeople when they first meet, replacing or complementing traditional greeting rituals. But the type of handshake varies widely (see Figure 8.1). Germans and Americans prefer a firm handshake, which is seen as a symbol of strength and character.

The French generally have a much softer handshake. They may feel uncomfortable with the grip of a German, and a German may wonder about the limp handshake of a French person. Middle Easterners and men from many Latin cultures may put the free hand on the forearm of the person with whom they are shaking hands. As a result, the distance to the other person diminishes. The Japanese, who are used to bowing, may shake hands with foreign business partners but keep the arm firmly extended to maintain a greater distance. In addition, they may bow slightly and thereby combine the Japanese and Western greeting rituals. German men traditionally also bow when shaking someone's hand. The German bow, however, differs significantly from the Japanese bow.

The handshake with the bow illustrates that greeting rituals in many cases combine different types of nonverbal communication. As was mentioned earlier, the German and Japanese bows differ (see Figure 8.2). The Japanese bow from the hip with a straight back. Men keep their arms at their sides with the hands extended at the sides of the upper legs. Japanese women when bowing put their hands on the front of their thighs. During the bowing the neck remains straight. In German bowing, by comparison, the hips remain straight; the bow comes out of a lowering of the head. The German bow is called a *Diener*. This means it is a bow to, and a recognition of, authority. The word *Diener* means "servant," and so with the bow the German says "at your service." Older Germans may still do a *Diener*, but most people today just give a slight nod of the head. The bow does not fit with notions of democracy and equality. Former Chancellor Helmut Kohl was criticized by a number of people and magazines because he did a *Diener* when greeting the first President Bush. The gesture was seen by many Germans as unacceptably servile.

In Argentina, when women meet work associates or friends, they stretch forward so that their right cheek is touching the other person's right cheek and perhaps kiss the air below the other person's right ear. Women do this when meeting men or women; men do this only when meeting women. Not to perform this greeting ritual is to appear cold, unfriendly, and even angry. In Lebanon, men typically kiss the right cheek, the left cheek, and perhaps the right cheek again of other men. In Estonia, however, cheek kissing is not approved of. Estonians expect a firm handshake upon meeting and again when taking leave of someone.

The German culture uses the handshake more frequently than does almost any other culture. In fact, this form of touch is the acceptable and expected form of touch in virtually every situation, whether meeting a stranger or greeting a family member. Not following the custom is viewed negatively.

In Germany, shaking hands is an accepted and expected greeting ritual; however, Germans seldom embrace. Hugging, even among family members, is rarer than it is in France and in Latin cultures. The handshake establishes touch, but at arm's length, whereas an embrace represents too much invasion of the personal bubble.

Increasingly, German managers who are working internationally go through training programs to become familiar and comfortable with different greeting rituals. At first glance, a German manager may expect a manager from Slovakia, a country in central Europe, to exhibit similar behavior patterns. After all, the countries are very close. Yet, managers from Slovakia, while formal during the first meeting, typically become less

FIGURE 8.1

The Handshake

Country or Region	Type of Handshake
United States	Firm handshake
France	Soft handshake
Germany	Firm handshake, for men, traditionally accompanied by a slight bow
Japan	Handshake with arm firmly extended, accompanied by bow
Middle East	Handshake and free hand placed on forearm of other person

Ulrike Schumacher, a German student, worked as an au pair girl with an English family for a summer. She had a very good experience and improved her English tremendously. The host family welcomed her and was rather generous. In many ways, she was part of the family. However, she thought it strange that throughout her stay she never once shook hands with the family, neither at the beginning nor at the end of her stay. She became accustomed to the lack of touch, though, and did not think much about it; she adapted. When she returned to Germany, her family members were gathered and eager to hear about her experiences. As Ulrike entered the living room where everyone was congregated, she said, *"Guten Abend, schön wieder daheim zu sein"* (Good evening, nice to be back home again) and nodded to the group. Afterward, her parents criticized Ulrike for being distant and uppity in not going around the room and shaking everyone's hand.

formal in the second meeting. They touch each other and even embrace. In their view, the German formality is considered cold and impersonal.[13]

The Māori of New Zealand, in contrast, expect touching as part of the greeting ritual. Māori businesspeople may feel left out of business meetings if the traditional greeting, the *hongi*, or pressing of noses, and the *karanga*, or formal cry of welcome, are not performed. They serve a similar function to handshaking in German society, setting everyone at ease. It would be unthinkable for a Māori function not to begin with both *hongi* and *karanga*, however many non-Māori are present.

People from low-context cultures tend to feel crowded by people from high-context cultures, and people from high-context cultures feel left out and rejected by people from low-context cultures. People come with certain expectations that frame their behavior, and when those expectations are not met, they feel confused, resentful, or excluded. All people from all cultures bring their unique cultural baggage with them. However, as people learn more about another culture, they adjust their expectations. They become

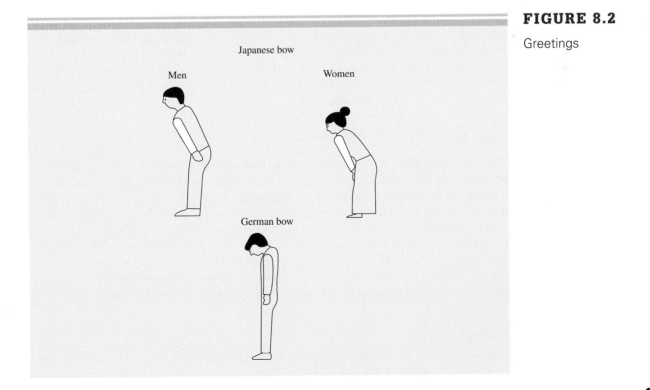

FIGURE 8.2

Greetings

more sophisticated and adjust their behavior according to the context and their degree of awareness of that context.

A Bolivian and a Dutchman who meet for the first time to do business will both be dissatisfied unless they understand each other's touching behavior. The Bolivian comes from a culture that is close, where people touch each other frequently while speaking. He will approach his Dutch counterpart with this background and act accordingly. The Dutchman comes from a much more reserved culture where people are more distant and cold. He too will bring his background to the meeting and act accordingly. If they want to work together, they need to come to terms with these differences.

How do we know what the "right" distance is and what acceptable touch is? As in childhood, we learn by observation in individual situations. Books can help, but lists of dos and don'ts, while providing some initial guidelines, do not give the underlying reasons for individual differences, variations, and changes.

Touching behavior can, and does, change as people adapt to new cultural environments. Sometimes they very consciously decide to change to fit in. When Vittorio Sanchez goes to Chicago on business, he refrains from touching the businessmen he meets because he knows that businesspeople in the United States touch each other less frequently than Latins do. In other cases, the adaptation occurs more at the intuitive level, at which people are not necessarily consciously aware of changes in their touching behavior. Urs Luder, a businessman from Switzerland, has noticed that his past few visits to Abu Dhabi have been much more pleasant. He is not as tense and nervous as before, and the atmosphere is more relaxed. His hosts seem more pleasant. What Urs may not be aware of is that his nonverbal behavior has changed. He does not avoid being touched by the people he talks to, and he approaches people more openly and feels comfortable putting his hand on someone's arm.

If we understand that touching is natural to some cultures, we will be less offended if someone touches us. By the same token, if the other person knows that we need our space, he or she will allow us more room and breathing space.

Above all, we need to keep things in perspective and not get offended each time we deal with someone who has a different relationship to space. Men in Africa hold hands with other men while walking down the street. Men in the Middle East kiss the cheeks of other men in greeting. Russian men embrace in a bear hug. Doing business with people from other cultures may mean setting aside ideas about touching learned in one's culture. During a television interview, the late Egyptian president Anwar Sadat, in the excitement of the discussion, slapped the former British prime minister, Margaret Thatcher, on the knee. Most people think of Mrs. Thatcher as properly British and fairly distant, but she was not offended. She correctly interpreted the gesture as acceptable in the Egyptian culture.

THE LANGUAGE OF SPACE

The language of space is powerful. How close can we get to people; how distant should we be? Most of us never think about space; we intuitively know what the right distance is. Our use of space in communication is an excellent illustration that culture is learned and not inborn. Though our parents may have given us some verbal instruction on space, we have learned most of our behavior by means of observation. We simply do what is "right."

Arabs learn the same way, and so do Japanese, Mexicans, Russians, and the members of all other cultures. The problem is that the acceptable use of space varies widely among cultures. What feels right for us may be totally offensive to someone else. Space in many ways becomes an extension of us, and we feel uncomfortable with people who play by different rules.

Private Space

In many cultures, the private space is sacred, and people feel violated if someone invades that personal bubble. In the United States, that bubble is about the length of an arm, and we talk about arm's-length relationships, meaning that we keep someone at a distance and don't allow that person into our personal sphere. That bubble is a little bit smaller in France, but larger in the Netherlands and Germany. It is even larger in Japan, but much smaller in Latin countries and the Middle East (see Figure 8.3). The size of the private space also is influenced by social status, gender, age, and level of authority, further complicating the interpretation of space in communication. Our attitude toward space reflects our attitude toward privacy. If we understand how people arrange their personal space at home, we will gain insight into the way they communicate through space at work.

Northern Europeans cherish their privacy and arrange their dwellings accordingly. Property boundaries are marked carefully, and everyone ensures that they are not violated. Fences and hedges separate gardens. Traditionally, a German house had a fence around the front yard with a gate that was closed and in many cases locked. Over the last two decades, the front gate increasingly has been left open, and today it usually is removed altogether. As more and more Germans acquired automobiles, dealing with the gate became inconvenient.

In Germany, elaborate laws detail rules on the use of the garden. Fences must be on the property line, and their height is regulated. In a country that is crowded and where sunlight is cherished, the fence must be low enough that it does not hinder the growth of vegetables in the neighbor's garden. Trees must be planted at a prescribed distance from the lot line so that they don't shade the neighbor's property. Germans send a strong signal that they don't want anyone to invade their space. If necessary, legal regulations will enforce the cultural predisposition toward privacy.

In a German house, the emphasis on privacy also is obvious. For example, all rooms have doors with locks, and the doors are closed and often locked. It would be inconsiderate to enter someone's room without first knocking on the door and waiting for an invitation to come in. In the common areas, one may enter without knocking, but the doors are still closed. As more and more houses have gotten central heat, the doors to the common living area now tend to remain open, but bedroom and bathroom doors are always closed.

In contrast to Germany, houses in the United States may have fences or hedges surrounding the backyard, but the front yards are wide open and inviting. Doors tend to be open, an invitation to come in. If someone wants to be alone, the door may be closed.

In Japan, privacy is defined altogether differently than it is in the United States and Germany. Japan is a crowded country, and space is costly; therefore, houses and apartments are smaller. Yet within this crowdedness the Japanese are able to create a private sphere. The private bubble and the personal space are more a creation of the mind than an actual entity. Americans connect privacy with physical space, whereas Japanese people connect privacy with mental space.

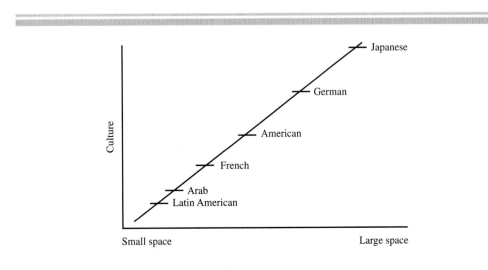

FIGURE 8.3

Personal Space in Several Cultures

When Mr. Schubert came home from work, he would have to get out of the car, unlock the gate and open it, unlock the garage door and open it, get back into the car, and drive the car into the garage. Then he would have to lock both the garage door and the front gate. This process became too inconvenient; hence, the changing custom.

The Swiss deal with lack of space and the desire for privacy by creating elaborate rules. Many apartment complexes in big Swiss cities, for example, prescribe how late one can take a bath, flush the toilet, or use the washing machine.

Middle Eastern and Latin cultures also reflect their attitudes toward privacy and personal space in the way they arrange their houses. A house in the Middle East traditionally has few or no windows to the street; all the windows open into an inner courtyard. The family is protected from the outside world by walling itself off in a realm of privacy. Within the house, however, personal space for the individual is often limited; family togetherness is emphasized. To remove oneself physically and insist on one's own space is not acceptable and is not easily tolerated. Individuals are first and foremost part of a family, and the living arrangement emphasizes that concept. Within the family space, men's and women's areas are separated in Islamic homes. In many ways, men and women dwell in the same compound but live separate lives in separate quarters. Uzbeks emphasize family as well. When an Uzbek man marries, his parents traditionally add a room to the compound. The couple has one private room; the rest of life is shared with the family.

Office Space

Our attitudes toward private space also are carried over into our attitudes toward office space. Generally, cultures that value a big personal space value large and private offices. In cultures in which personal distance is smaller, the size of the office is not as crucial. Japan does not quite fit into this pattern. The Japanese prefer a larger interpersonal distance, yet they seldom have private offices. We must keep in mind, however, that the Japanese, as was mentioned earlier, do not so much emphasize actual physical distance to attain privacy as they emphasize mental distance. In addition, the emphasis on group orientation in Japan carries more weight than does any consideration for privacy. The whole issue of office space in the case of Japan is influenced by other cultural values and considerations.

The following examples illustrate the idea that the arrangement of office space is a reflection of underlying cultural values.

In the United States, the size of an office and its location are indicative of a businessperson's success, importance, power, and status within the hierarchy. In a country where many offices do not have windows, windows are a status symbol. Top managers have their offices on top floors with plenty of windows. In a Midwestern university, for example, offices are assigned by seniority, and a goal of every professor is ultimately to have one of the rare outside offices with a window.

In addition to size and location, the furnishings signify the level of importance. A Midwestern insurance firm in the United States has three grades of wastebaskets. The kinds of desks, desk lamps, artwork, and plants employees can have in their workspaces are dictated by status and level of importance.

The French are horrified when they look at typical American offices with their artificial light because both in France and in Germany every employee is entitled to a workplace with natural light. They are puzzled how human beings can work and concentrate in offices without natural light. Schools in Germany, by law, must have windows large enough

Two German women living with an Iraqi family for a summer had to see a doctor; one had an ear infection, and the other suffered from laryngitis. The family contacted a specialist, and the son of the host family accompanied the two women to interpret for them. The doctor had a long line of patients waiting outside the office, all of whom had applied for work at the Baghdad airport and needed vision and hearing examinations. The Germans and their friend were whisked past the line of people and taken directly into the office. The doctor, who had studied in Europe, was delighted to see them and interrupted the examination of a patient to serve tea to the new arrivals. He invited them to sit down and then finished the examination of the man. Next he examined the German women and gave them each a shot of penicillin. He asked them to stay longer and visit with him. During that time he continued his examination of the other patients, and nobody seemed offended.

This scene would be unthinkable in North America or Europe. It is important to keep in mind that the patients were there for a routine check of vision and hearing and did not have to undress or discuss personal matters; even so, a Western patient would expect total attention from the doctor and resent having other people sitting in the examination room. Yet this is acceptable behavior in the Middle East.

that the square footage of the windows equals at least two-thirds of the square footage of the room. American schools without windows look like prisons to Europeans.

Office size and furnishings are important in Europe also. A manager who has a private office with a *Vorzimmer* (outer office) and a secretary is important, and everyone knows it. As in private houses, German office doors are closed. It would be unthinkable to barge into an office without first knocking at the doors, both the boss's and the secretary's, and waiting for "*Herein*" (come in). An office is a private workplace that one does not enter uninvited.

French offices tend to reflect the cultural value of centralization. Just as France is centralized, with every major road converging on Paris, offices are spatially organized around the manager who is at the center. The manager is the controller and observer of everything going on in the office. Currently, most companies are headquartered in Paris. The top managers control all activities at headquarters, and headquarters in Paris controls all company activities across France. Most French people agree that anyone who wants to get ahead in this environment must move to Paris. Ambitious people are petrified at the idea of being "banished" to the provinces. The centralized office arrangement reflects the historical developments and realities of France.

Office space in the Middle East and in Latin America can be quite different. Big multinationals in the Middle East and high-technology oil firms have a more Western approach to office space, but the attitude in smaller and midsize Arab firms is quite different.

The office is a meeting place. A businessperson thinks nothing of having several different persons in the office at the same time and doing business with them simultaneously. Westerners, who may be offended by the informality and lack of privacy and total attention, may have a hard time coping, but an Arab businessman sees nothing wrong with the arrangement.

Offices in the Middle East tend to be crowded. Importance is not necessarily reflected in the size and location of the office, and the typical American status perks may be meaningless. That does not mean, however, that there are no symbols to indicate the level of importance. Since in many ways status is conveyed by the importance and number of connections one has, a manager who has many visitors and receives many phone calls during your visit may show his importance that way. Where an American manager may ask her assistant to hold all calls while she is meeting with a potential client, a manager in Saudi Arabia may make sure that a lot of calls come in while he meets with a future business partner.

Japanese offices also reflect cultural values. In Japan, the individual is expected to fit into the group and respect group goals and norms. Harmony is an overriding principle. As a result, private offices in Japan are rare and are reserved for upper managers; even then, depending on the firm, managers may sit or work in the same area with their employees. A typical office arrangement has file cabinets along the outside walls of the office. The employees sit in groups at large tables in the center of the room (see Figure 8.4). In many cases, these are regular tables rather than desks with drawers, and everything is out in the open. The employees are facing each other, with the leader of the group seated at the head of the table. Unless the nature of the business requires a phone, individual employees typically do not have phones at their workstations. Although Japanese businesses have undergone a number of changes, the traditional office arrangement has remained the same.

The Japanese believe that this arrangement emphasizes the importance of the group and the need to work together. When an employee needs to discuss something with a co-worker from the same table or from another table in the room, he or she goes to one of the tables near the file cabinets to avoid disturbing the rest of the group.

From the Western viewpoint, with its emphasis on individuality and privacy, this arrangement seems oppressive. With everyone watching, one can't even use the phone without the rest of the group listening. And of course private phone conversations, such as calling the children when they get home from school and making social arrangements with friends, are out of the question. Many Westerners would resent this arrangement, seeing it as a lack of trust.

Another typical arrangement in a Japanese office is to have everyone sit at individual tables or desks facing in the same direction. Sometimes the manager sits in the front of the room, facing the employees, but in many cases the manager sits in the back, behind the employees (see Figure 8.5). Again, businesspeople from the United States or Canada would be uncomfortable with this arrangement and would feel as though someone were looking over their shoulders the whole time they were working. The Japanese, who are accustomed to the group watching and to being expected to follow norms, have far fewer problems with this arrangement. At work, the employee is first and foremost a member of the team rather than an individual with individual rights to privacy and territory.

FIGURE 8.4

Japanese Office Layout

Fred Brunell, a French manager, is visiting Ayub Rabah in his office in Amman, Jordan. They intend to discuss possible joint-venture opportunities. They are still in the beginning stages and are trying to get to know each other and determine relative status, position, and power to negotiate. While Fred Brunell sits in the office, Ayub Rabah receives several phone calls, including one from a friend in the government office for foreign investment to arrange an evening together and another from an old school friend who is a banker. The banker is discussing some financial arrangement. The phone conversations are personal and illustrate that Ayub Rabah is well connected and has clout. Fred Brunell is impressed by the prospect of working with someone who can get things moving. In a culture in which connections are important, Ayub Rabah has shown that he is somebody. He has sent important signals to Fred Brunell, but it is up to Fred to interpret those signals in the context of doing business in Jordan.

FIGURE 8.5

Japanese Office Layout

Manager

If a Japanese manager has a private office, it often has windows to the large common work area, where the manager can look out at the employees but the employees also can look into the manager's office.

The Japanese office layout sends a strong symbolic message: "We are in this together." The welfare of the whole is more important than are the concerns of individuals. Although behind the scenes there may be quite a bit of maneuvering for individual recognition, on the surface harmony rules and everyone works for the common good.

As a result, the furnishings in Japanese offices are not as important as they are in U.S. offices. Even in big companies the office decor usually looks rather modest by Western standards. Businesspeople from the United States, used to more lavish furnishings, may misinterpret the signals and question the importance or profitability of the Japanese business they are dealing with.

Furnishings also may signal political clout. A private business school in Tashkent, Uzbekistan, has rundown facilities. The school, an offshoot of a public university, is housed on two floors of the university. The two floors are in terrible shape. Holes in the walls, lack of paint, dingy lighting, and a broken heating system are all the result of years of neglect. Yet this business school is the most innovative in the country. Politicians send their children there because they know they will get a Western education. Employers in Uzbekistan and foreign firms like to hire the graduates. The manager of the Eurasia Foundation in Uzbekistan offered to provide the money for an updating of the facility, but the director of the school declined. She would have liked a better facility, but she figured it was not worth the price. She was convinced that as soon as the two floors were renovated, the university would all of a sudden find that it really needed that space. However, it would happily provide space on other floors, which of course were in bad shape as well. Because furnishings in Uzbekistan indicate power, the university probably would claim the two floors for itself if they were to be refurbished. In this case, furnishing and surroundings show power, but the power structure makes it dangerous to show the power through better facilities.

Public Space

The way people arrange and use public spaces also reflects their cultural attitude toward space and privacy. Businesspeople from the United States who go to Japan or China often comment on how crowded the cities are and state that there just is not enough breathing space. That may be true by U.S. standards, but the Japanese and Chinese may interpret the conditions differently. Two people from different cultures may look at the same space yet come to different conclusions, as the following example illustrates.

Numerous articles have illustrated the prime example of crowdedness in Japan: rush hour on the subway in Tokyo. They usually show a picture of a person whose job it is to push people into the train so that the doors can close. This phenomenon has been exaggerated greatly in the American press, however. In 2003, it seems there were still some pushers at Shinjuku station, but only during rush hour.[14] When looking at these pictures one wonders how the throngs of people fit the cultural emphasis on personal distance and private space. How do the Japanese cope with that? Many Japanese do not like the crowded conditions, and increasingly people are moving from Tokyo back to their hometowns to have more space.

Most Japanese people have found a way to cope with the overcrowded public space of the subway system. In this environment, filled with people pushing and shoving one another, the Japanese riders become islands. Each is alone as long as he does not acknowledge any of the other people; the others do not really exist in his space. As was pointed out earlier, space becomes a psychological phenomenon. The Chinese deal with crowded public spaces in a similar fashion.

People from the United States carry their idea of individuality over into public spaces. They consider it their right to walk and play on the grass in the park. After all, it is their park; their taxes paid for it. Government buildings in the United States are open to the public. Anyone can go into the Capitol in Washington or the various state capitols. In no other

Aki Hayashi, a Japanese visiting professor at a university in Illinois, was going to a convention in New Orleans, about 800 miles (1,200 kilometers) away. His American colleagues were all flying, but he was going to take the train. He wanted to see something of the country. Brian Ober, one of his American friends, warned him that the train would be very crowded and that he would not like it at all. Mr. Ober was very surprised when Professor Hayashi told him that his compartment on the train had been very nice and spacious.

country is the residence of the president open to the public. Access has become tighter since the September 11, 2001, terrorist attacks, but Americans still see it as their right to have access to public buildings. A manager from Poland had the opportunity to visit U.S. President Abraham Lincoln's mid–19th century house and the new Lincoln museum in Springfield, Illinois. He was quite impressed and appreciated the building's historical significance. However, it was the visit to the United States Capitol in Washington that really excited him. The fact he could go to the galleries of the Senate and House of Representatives, that he could observe the Senate in action was absolutely amazing to him. In the United States, the right to access is considered important. In contrast, Schloss Bellevue in Berlin, 10 Downing Street in London, and the Elysee Palace in Paris are all closed to the public. Ordinary citizens are not allowed entry into the new Shanghai city hall. It is where the mayor and vice mayors, as well as all the key officials for the city, work. Ordinary people have no business there and are turned away by security officers

The Germans organize their public spaces in the same way they organize their private lives. *Alles muss seine Ordnung haben* (Everything must have its order). Order is an overriding concern, and detailed provisions are made to guarantee that order. Germans tend to not have problems with this control because they grew up with an emphasis on order. As a result, parks tend to be clean and neat; the grass is not trampled down. This order is achieved through the use of numerous signs; *Betreten des Rasens verboten* (It is forbidden to step on the grass) is typical and is enforced strictly. For most Germans, there is nothing wrong with the content or tone of the rules, most of which are issued as clear orders in a negative tone. The emphasis is on clarity rather than friendliness. However, during the last decade the universal acceptance of the tight regulation of public spaces began breaking down. One of the side effects has been more litter in parks and plazas. This change in behavior indicates that the nonverbal language of space can change over time. The study of nonverbal communication therefore must be an ongoing activity.

Germans tend to be very aggressive in crowds. The British queue (line up) at the bus stop, in stores, and at theaters. Theatergoers in London, for example, follow strict unwritten rules on queuing to get tickets; it is expected that everyone will follow the unwritten honor system. Germans, in contrast, form throngs and push and shove without any order at all, and they are surprised at the voluntary order of the British. One evening during rush hour, two friends—a German and an Englishman—wanted to take the Tube (subway) in London. As they approached the station, they encountered a long line of people waiting to buy tickets. As the Englishman turned toward the end of the line, the German said, "Waiting in line is going to take forever; let's just get to the front." The Englishman was horrified and explained that such a move was absolutely unthinkable and could not be done. The German, in turn, was amazed at how fast the orderly line moved; waiting in line did not take so long after all.

The Japanese tend to be even more disciplined than the British. The Japanese wait in marked spaces on the train platform in rows of three. People who want to wait for their next train because they figure that the current one is too crowded will wait in the same formation in a line right next to the people who want to take the immediate train. Once that train has departed, they will move over.

A German woman who had lived in the United States for many years was visiting her hometown and took her two young children to a *Schulfest*, a school carnival. When her children wanted to ride the merry-go-round, they waited on the side till the merry-go-round came to a stop. Even though they had been in front of the other children, they were swept aside and did not get on. The same scene repeated itself several times. German parents were saving places for other children or were pushing their own children on. Finally, the visitor used her elbows too and got her children on the ride.

Generally, people from Northern Europe prefer a larger physical space and therefore stand farther apart in waiting lines. People from Latin countries, in contrast, have a smaller physical space and stand closer. Seeing space in lines at EuroDisney, Latin visitors frequently try to fill in the spaces left by people from Northern Europe. This annoys the Northern Europeans.[15]

In public spaces, Germans also emphasize their rights. Individuals are expected to protect and insist on their rights. Children must be prepared for a rough and cruel world; therefore, they must practice insisting on their rights from an early age.

In the United States, this scenario would have been entirely different. First of all, all the children would have waited in an orderly line. Everyone would have taken one turn and would have been expected to get off after one ride. If a child wanted another ride, he would have had to go to the end of the line again. Everyone would have understood that the procedure had to be fair to everyone and not be based on bullying.

As conditions in big cities become more crowded, traditional etiquette and rules of acceptable verbal and nonverbal communication behavior may face major challenges. The pushing and shoving on Japanese subways, as was pointed out earlier, does not fit the traditional value of personal distance and harmony. Japan is not the only country that must deal with a breakdown of traditional behaviors. In Mexico City, for example, the subways are overcrowded with commuters on weekdays during rush hour and with families on weekends. Traditionally, unrelated Mexican men and women do not mix in public. In particular, unmarried women are protected by their families to preserve their virtue. In this traditional environment, men are seen as protectors of women, and women are expected to behave modestly and shy away from public places.

In modern Mexico, many women (young and old, married and single) have jobs. They must get to and from work on their own without any chaperon or male protector. In the past, young women moving about on their own were suspected of dishonorable behavior. Men knew that such women did not require the same courteous treatment they extended to their own sisters. Today, the lines are blurred, and many men do not know how to behave. In this case, the changing social environment has had a profound influence on nonverbal communication. During rush hour, many female riders were being molested by men in overcrowded subway cars. The solution was to separate women and men on the subway during rush hour. Now men are not allowed into cars reserved for women, and women who go into the men's cars do so at their own risk. The crowded conditions encouraged nonverbal behavior that was not acceptable in normal circumstances. As the environment of a culture changes, society must reevaluate its standards of nonverbal communication and develop safeguards to protect those standards.

Behavior in public spaces is carried over into offices and business practices. One cannot separate general cultural behavior from business behavior. The two go together. The way we approach people and the way we deal with space and issues of privacy have deep cultural roots. We may not agree with or like what others do. That is not the issue; the point is that we must understand what the others are doing and why they are doing it.

APPEARANCE

The way we dress also communicates. Dressing according to custom and expectations shows respect for form and establishes a foundation for future dealings. Subtle aspects of dress can let people know where one is from.

When one is examining appearance in intercultural communication, one must ask a number of questions, such as

- What is appropriate business dress for men and women in a particular culture?
- What is the difference in attire when doing business in one's own culture and doing business with another culture?
- What degree of importance is attached to one's attire?
- What are the penalties for inappropriate attire?

In some ways, business dress for men is universal around the world, yet there are differences. The suit, the dress shirt, and the tie are generally acceptable, but the styles may vary widely. Europeans tend to wear suits that are more tailored and youthful looking than those worn by businessmen in the United States. The severe business suit, sometimes described as the IBM look, is rare in Europe today. The Japanese, in contrast, remain conservative. They tend to wear either gray or dark blue suits with white shirts. Japanese young people tend to wear T-shirts and jeans. They may have long hair in a variety of colors. On the outside, they look very similar to young people in North America or Europe. Yet, when interviewing season starts, these very same people become conservative overnight. They dye their hair black, get traditional haircuts and wear the traditional interview uniform. Arabs may wear Western suits, but when doing business in Arab countries, they usually wear traditional dress, the white flowing robe and the headdress.

In Southeast Asia, the European business suit, with its origin in cool and cloudy England, is giving way to a new uniform: slacks and a short-sleeve shirt worn outside the pants with a collar and an attached belt. However, when a businessman from that part of the world travels to the United States or Japan for business, he will wear a conservative business suit.

For women, dress is more complicated. Businesswomen from the United States tend to wear suits. Even though the suits have softer lines and are less masculine, and even though dresses have become more acceptable, business dress for American women in managerial positions is still more severe than it is in Western Europe.

A German student, after finishing her MBA in the United States and looking for a job in her native country, discovered very quickly that her American business suit was totally inappropriate for interviews. It was too severe and too conservative. No young businesswomen were wearing that kind of suit. A short skirt with a stylish blouse was the norm.

IN FOCUS

Two professors from the United States were sitting in the office for foreign trade in Poland, waiting for an appointment. A businessman entered and sat down, obviously also waiting for an appointment. Without having spoken to the newcomer or having heard him speak, the two professors looked at each other and agreed: another American. How did they know? The button-down collar, the style of the suit, and the wing-tip shoes were clear signals. They were right; he was American.

A group of professors from the United States attending a four-week seminar in Taipei were moaning about the heat and the lack of air-conditioning. The seminar leader, a Chinese woman professor, at first did not say anything; she simply assumed that everyone agreed on what appropriate dress was for the seminar lectures and company visits. When some of the professors started showing up in shorts and T-shirts, she asked them to dress up, meaning suit, shirt, and tie. The Americans immediately tried to negotiate down the expected level of formality. As a Chinese woman, she felt very uncomfortable telling the mostly male group what to do, but finally she had to be direct. The group was to visit Chiang Kai-shek's tomb, and there could be no compromise. She ordered suit, dress shirt, and tie, and the Americans finally gave in.

French female students who return to France from the United States make the same comment. They too find that French businesswomen dress more femininely than their American counterparts. These returning students feel uncomfortable in the typical American business dress; however, they also point out that although women in French or German businesses tend to dress more fashionably, very few are in managerial positions. That, of course, is another question, a matter of tactics, perhaps. If women want to succeed in business, they have to dress and look the part.

In Japan, women often work as office ladies who serve tea and greet customers. They do not have to worry about what to wear; the company provides them with a uniform, usually a conservative suit with a blouse, white gloves, and a hat. However, as more women enter management training programs at Japanese firms, they may change their appearance to indicate the different status.

In most cultures, dress also identifies a person as belonging to a specific group and having a certain status. Dress can offend, but it also can protect. With the growing number of assaults on foreigners in Germany, the Japanese issued a dress code for after-business hours for all Japanese employees in that country. Immediately, all Japanese had to wear dark conservative suits with white shirts, ties, and dress shoes at *all* times to establish them as businesspeople and distinguish them from other Asians who might be in the country illegally and involved in illegal dealings. The business dress, it was assumed, would identify a person as doing business in Germany rather than wanting to immigrate illegally.

With the growing emphasis on comfort and leisure-time activities, attitudes toward appearance and dress are changing in many cultures. In many cases, young people around the world have more in common with young people from other cultures than with the older generation of their own culture when it comes to dress. Jeans, tennis shoes, and sweatshirts are taking the place of formal business attire.

A few years ago, Germans were very conservative in their dress both in business and in their private lives. It was expected that one would dress up for the office and on Sundays. Every German man, from age 14 on, owned a black suit to be worn at weddings, funerals, and other important occasions. During final examinations in the *Gymnasium* (high school) and the university, both men and women were expected to wear black suits to acknowledge the importance of the occasion. Much of that has changed. The young people are very informal, and many go to interviews in casual dress. Although older Germans may bemoan casual dress as a sign of lack of respect and the general decline and downfall of behavioral norms, young people are enjoying the more relaxed attire.

If a person from a more casual culture with an emphasis on comfort does business with someone older from a conservative and formal culture, dress can become a serious issue.

SILENCE

Many people connect communicating with doing something verbally, nonverbally, or both. Communication means action such as encoding a message, decoding a message, sending a message, and sending feedback. At first glance, silence does not indicate action, yet communication through silence plays an important role in all cultures. The importance of silence as a communication tool, and the interpretation of silence varies from culture to culture, but all cultures use silence at times to get a point across.

Differences in the use of silence can be best examined by looking at high-context and low-context cultures.

Silence in Low-Context Cultures

In low-context cultures in which ideas are encoded explicitly into words, silence often is interpreted as the absence of communication. It is *downtime*. Silence means that the act of actively worded communication has stopped.

Yet even in low-context cultures, silence is not necessarily without meaning. When someone is silent after being asked a question, the silence is an answer. The English phrase "The silence was deafening" describes this interpretation. When someone falls silent in conversation, another person may ask, "What's wrong?" The silence communicates a message. It may indicate that the receiver of the message did not hear the message, is angry at the message, needs time to think, or is embarrassed. Usually, low-context cultures view silence as communication gone wrong. To them it indicates that a rupture has occurred in the communication process.

Phrases such as *Reden ist Silber; Schweigen ist Gold* (speaking is silver; being silent is gold) seem to contradict the view of silence as being negative; however, when given a choice, people in low-context cultures tend to choose speaking over being silent. Silence is ambiguous; it must be interpreted, and the interpretation of silence is more difficult than the interpretation of words. Silence does not fit with a low-context culture's emphasis on precision and clarity.

For this reason, people in low-context cultures generally are uncomfortable with silence. They often feel responsible for starting a conversation or keeping it going, even with strangers. Passengers on a train that makes an unscheduled stop in the countryside, for example, may start a conversation because they feel uncomfortable just sitting there.

Silence in High-Context Cultures

High-context cultures have a different attitude toward the use of silence. Perhaps the most obvious example is Japan, although other Asian countries share the Japanese attitude about silence. The Japanese believe that silence is preferable to conversation. It is through silence that one can discover the truth inside oneself. Contemplation and meditation take place in silence. Buddha taught that words make truth untrue, and there is a view in Japanese society that words contaminate understanding. Reading another person's inner core, a kind of communication without words, can take place only in silence. Speech distracts people from true understanding. This attitude toward, and the use of, silence can become a serious stumbling block in the progress of negotiations between businesspeople from Japan and the United States. Most of the discussion in Japanese negotiations is in groups, and much is said through silence, facial expressions, and body gestures among the Japanese team.

Silence to the Japanese is not empty. Whereas Westerners typically view silence as gaps in conversation, the Japanese believe that silence is part of conversation. In a crowded country, silence evokes space; a person can be in his or her own realm through silence even when surrounded by others. Japanese speakers are comfortable with silence in communication and do not hurry to fill it up with speech. In fact, they may use silence as a very powerful communication tool.

CHAPTER SUMMARY

This chapter examined the major aspects of nonverbal signals in intercultural communication. Much of what people say in all cultures is said without words or in addition to words. In many cases, the nonverbal symbols support the spoken word, but they also can contradict what is being said.

Paralanguage lies between verbal and nonverbal communication, as in the following:

- *Vocal qualifiers.* The term refers to volume, pitch, and intonation. Different cultures use different vocal qualifiers.
- *Nonverbal business conventions* in face-to-face encounters.
- *Eye contact.* Conventions relating to eye contact are related to position in the hierarchy. Eye contact has implications for perceptions of honesty and the importance of privacy.
- *Facial expressions.* Facial expressions have different meanings in different cultures. A smile can express friendliness or embarrassment. A frown can be an indication of anger or doubt.
- *Gestures.* Head movements, arm movements, and posture communicate a message to the other side.
- *Timing in spoken exchanges.* Timing behavior reflects the importance of equality, hierarchy, and gender relationships.

- *Touching.* Cultures have different conventions for touching in social and business situations. Touching typically is related to status, gender, and seniority.
- *The language of space.* We communicate through our use of private, office, and public space.
- *Appearance.* Dress sends signals relating to respect.
- *Silence.* High-context and low-context cultures differ in their interpretation of silence. In high-context cultures, silence frequently is seen as an absence of communication, whereas in high-context cultures silence is an important communication channel.

The interpretation of the nonverbal language is complicated by the fact that different groups within a culture often use different nonverbal signals. To be successful in interpreting the nonverbal language of a culture, you need to go beyond memorizing the dos and don'ts of touching, using space, making eye contact, and using facial expressions and gestures. To be successful in reading the nonverbal symbols, you must understand the cultural values that give rise to a specific nonverbal language.

Notes

1. Edward T. Hall, "The Silent Language in Overseas Business," *Harvard Business Review*, 38, no. 3 (1960), pp. 87–95.

2. Deborah Tannen, *Communicating from 9 to 5* (New York: William Morrow and Company, 1994).

3. Kate Fox, *Watching the English: The Hidden Rules of English Behavior* (London: Hodder & Stroughton, 2004).

4. David Victor, *International Business Communication* (New York: HarperCollins, 1992).

5. Ibid.

6. Ibid.

7. Ruth Benedikt, *The Crysanthemum and the Sword* (Cleveland: Meridian Books, 1967).

8. Yong-Jin Song, Claudia L. Hale, and Nagesh Rao, "The South Korean Chief Negotiator: Balancing Traditional Values and Contemporary Business Practices," *International Journal of Cross Cultural Management*, 5, no. 3 (2005), pp. 313–328.

9. In-ah Ha, unpublished paper presented at the IAIR inaugural conference, Kent State University, April 1999.

10. For a more detailed discussion see: Margaret K. Omar Nydell, (2002), *Understanding Arabs*, 3rd ed. (Yarmouth, ME: Intercultural Press, 2002); K. Versteegh, *Landmarks in Linguistic Thought III: The Arabic Tradition* (New York: Routledge, 1997).

11. Nydell, 2002.

12. Deborah Tannen, *You Just Don't Understand* (New York: Ballantine Books, 1992).

13. Andreas Unger, "Auf Tuchfuehlung Gehen," *Die Zeit*, no. 48 (November 24, 2005), p. 86.

14. http://home.comcast.net/~subwaymark/trips/Japan/Trip2003-5.htm.

15. Susan C. Schneider and Jean-Louis Barsoux, *Managing Across Cultures* (Harlow, UK: Pearson Education Limited, 1997).

Getting to Know Another Culture

LEARNING OBJECTIVES

After completing this chapter, you should be able to:

 Able to identify sources of information about another culture.

 Understand how different people reason.

LO³ Evaluate the human dominance with cultural differences.

Juan Marin is meeting with Lei Peng about a business deal. Marin wants to open a Chinese restaurant in Mexico City and is working out a joint-venture agreement with Lei who has several successful restaurants in Hong Kong and Los Angeles, California. But Marin is discovering a number of things that surprise him about his would-be partner as they negotiate the details, meeting face to face at last in Los Angeles.

Lei has just mentioned that Juan should construct a fish tank in the entrance to his restaurant. "Why?" Juan asks. "We're not just serving fish, apart from a few dishes. But people will see the fish and think it's a fish restaurant."

"You need fish," Lei asserts. "You need that because it means good profit!" He explains that in Chinese the phrase "to have fish" (*yo yu*) sounds like the phrase "to have profit after expenses," and for that reason Juan must have a fish tank. Juan is amazed that the Chinese man thinks he should go to the expense of placing a large fish tank at the front door of his restaurant simply on the basis of the sound of the Chinese word for *fish*.

While he and Lei continue their discussion, Juan notices several times that people are interrupting them to bring Lei a telephone, provide tea, or ask for answers to quick questions. Juan doesn't really mind; he understands that these are signs of how important and busy Lei is.

Juan is a little hungry, though, since it's three o'clock in the afternoon and time for his large meal of the day. Lei seems unaware of the hour, and although someone provides tea for them, there is no mention of dinner. Juan thinks he'd better clarify the hours during which the restaurant will operate in Mexico. Lei simply says, "No problem. The Chinese staff I'll get for you will work whenever you tell them." Juan wonders about that. What if a relative needs some help at home? After all, Juan himself arrived at their meeting just before 2 p.m., although he had meant to come at 1 p.m. as agreed. His son had asked him to bring a special video game back from the U.S. to Mexico, and the traffic between the store and the meeting was heavy, causing Juan to be late. Lei didn't show any emotion, so Juan couldn't tell if he was angry. Family matters always take priority, as the Chinese must agree. But maybe the Chinese restaurant isn't such a good idea for his family business interests. How will he explain the fish tank?

For his part, Lei Peng is surprised at Juan Marin's behavior in person. How serious is he about this restaurant venture? He was an hour late for their first meeting! And although it's the middle of the afternoon, he keeps suggesting they go out for a meal to a nice Mexican restaurant he knows. As if Lei weren't an owner of restaurants in Los Angeles! How odd his associate is. Is it a good idea to open a restaurant in Mexico City?

Understanding another culture is an ongoing experience that can last a lifetime. However, sometimes businesspeople have only a short time to prepare to do business in another country. How can a brief amount of time best be spent to yield the greatest understanding?

Asking Questions

The approach in this book is to identify certain questions to ask about cultures in order to gain the most useful level of understanding. It is derived from work done in the early 1960s by Kluckhohn and Strodtbeck and developed further by the more recent interculturalists, Condon and Yousef.[1] The answers to these questions help businesspeople understand why their foreign counterparts think, believe, and act as they do. The questions don't cover every aspect of life lived in another culture. For example, behavior related to bringing up children is not included since it seldom impinges upon business. Courtship and marriage customs, kinship systems, types of music and dance, and many other aspects of life lie outside the world of business. We are interested in how culture affects business, so we will focus on questions that pertain to the world of work.

Business cultures exist wholly within the larger culture of a society. Nothing occurs in the business culture that does not occur in the general society of which it is a part. But business cultures do not include everything from the general culture; they select only what is useful for conducting business transactions. Terpstra and David in *The Cultural Environment of International Business* give an example from India.[2] Two forms of paternalistic leadership exist in India: one that is benevolent, and one that is autocratic. Indian business culture typically uses only the autocratic form of leadership. Thus, for business purposes, one needs to know what the business culture includes, not everything in the general culture.

THEORIES ABOUT UNDERSTANDING AN UNFAMILIAR CULTURE

This chapter outlines a values orientation. Many scholars have used this approach, since values generate attitudes and behavior. Perhaps the most significant study about culture was conducted by Geert Hofstede, a Dutch researcher who gathered data from 116,000 respondents to a questionnaire distributed in 53 countries.[3] The participants in the study were all managers for IBM (that, of course, raises questions about reliability and validity). Hofstede was interested in finding out if national cultures could be compared along the same dimensions, and he approached this study from the viewpoint of a Western male in the 1960s. The research originally identified four dimensions along which country cultures differ.

- Individualism versus collectivism
- Power distance
- Uncertainty avoidance versus uncertainty tolerance
- Masculinity versus femininity

Among these dimensions, the first is the most widely researched. Individualistic cultures are those that emphasize individual achievements and rights, including the individual's right to make decisions for himself or herself; collectivistic cultures emphasize the group's achievements and rights, including the group's right to make decisions for the individual.

Power distance is the degree to which less-powerful members of an organization tolerate unequal distribution of power, say, between managers and employees. Uncertainty avoidance is the tendency to behave so as to arrange things in a way that minimizes unforeseen consequences; uncertainty tolerance results in behavior that is less concerned with unforeseen consequences. Masculinity, according to Hofstede, is a way to characterize cultures that value assertiveness, competitiveness, and material success, while femininity characterizes cultural preferences for collaboration, nurturing, and harmony. Hofstede's work often is cited by international business and intercultural communication scholars. Later, Michael Bond, a Canadian working and living in Hong Kong, developed a way to assess cultural values based on a survey instrument written by Asians, not Westerners. This resulted in a fifth cultural dimension reported by Bond and Hofstede as long-term orientation.[4] It includes values that can be called "future-looking," such as perseverance, thrift, observing a hierarchy of status in relationships, and having a sense of shame. Short-term orientation, looking more to the past, includes protecting one's "face," respecting tradition, maintaining personal steadiness, and reciprocating favors and gifts.

Another Dutch interculturalist, Fons Trompenaars, developed seven cultural dimensions.[5] They include universalism versus particularism, individualism versus collectivism (Hofstede's and other scholars' influence), neutral versus emotional, specific versus diffuse, and achievement versus ascription. To these dimensions Trompenaars added attitudes toward time and the environment. Meanwhile, other scholars were developing cultural values by which to compare cultures. André Laurent looked at European managers and came up with four parameters for understanding how culture affects relationships of power: the perception of organizations as political systems, authority systems, role formulation systems, and hierarchical relationship systems.[6] Shalom Schwartz developed a values survey in the 1990s based on theories that tried to account for some of the biases that may have affected earlier studies, notably Hofstede's.

These brief descriptions of well-known studies indicate that there are many ways to approach understanding a culture. We synthesize these studies into the following Five Categories of questions that focus on values in a culture, allowing you to compare cultures by assessing how each of the questions can be answered for different cultures. Questions about a culture that need to be asked for business fall into these five categories:

- Thinking and Knowing
- Doing and Achieving
- The Big Picture
- The Self
- Social Organization

WHERE CAN INFORMATION ABOUT CULTURES BE FOUND?

Anyone can ask the questions that follow, but of whom? The obvious place to start is to ask people who are members of the culture you want to understand. A logical source is someone who comes from a background similar to yours (economic, educational, family), or someone who has had similar experiences or holds the same kind of job. You can gain insight this way since people can identify to some degree the value orientations of their own cultures. For instance, if someone asked you whether members of your culture learn by probing and questioning or by mastering and memorizing a body of knowledge, you probably would give an answer that would concur with those of others in your culture (or those who study your culture).

But some of the questions are not easy for people to discuss because they have never considered them. For instance, most people don't know whether they think in a linear pattern or in a cluster pattern. In fact, *the members of a culture are not necessarily the best authorities on that culture.*

That may surprise you, but culture is embedded deep in the unconscious part of the mind. As Edward Hall pointed out in *Beyond Culture*, the closer something is to seeming true, the less aware we probably are of its cultural origin.[7] People's own culture seems normal to them; it seems just the way things are. One way of asking questions is to notice that another culture goes about something differently from the way you expect.

Another good source may be someone who has spent considerable time in that culture but is not a native member of it. Someone who has lived in the other culture has had exposure to the differences between his or her own culture and the culture you want to understand. You may be able to learn from a nonnative about cultural priorities that a native of that culture simply takes for granted.

But asking questions is a general approach that includes inquiring into a culture's priorities by finding out what is important to its members, and it involves more than simply asking questions of people. For example, you can inquire by reading fiction written by authors in the culture you want to understand. By reading how characters act and interact and why, you will learn something about what is important to that culture, what its priorities are. For example, you can learn how Japanese culture views the public expression of emotion, the relative status of older people compared with younger people, the importance of not causing someone to lose face, and the difference between outward public action and private opinion by reading modern short stories in translation. You also can watch Japanese movies and see what people's behavior looks like—their nonverbal

One particular television commercial [for a Lexus] shows the car being driven down a country lane. It stops, and a woman in *kimono* and a man in a suit emerge. As they walk around the car, the camera shows a close-up shot of a green leaf that has fallen on the windshield. There are drops of moisture on the leaf and the window; birds are heard in the background. The man and the woman walk up next to a potter who is holding a recently fired bowl. The three gaze in silence at the bowl. The potter throws the bowl to the ground .It breaks. The couple get back in the car and drive away.[8]

communication—when they behave in Japanese ways, and how they sound when they speak the Japanese language.

Another way to pursue your inquiries is to find out what people of a culture say about themselves. Countries publish nonfiction books in translation that describe their institutions, history, beliefs, practices, and goals for the future. Even travel guides contain insights.

Cultures also define themselves less directly in communications that are nevertheless revealing. For example, television commercials offer insights into cultural priorities—not so much in the products they advertise as in the values implied by the appeals the commercials make to the viewers. Whereas peer group membership (doing the "in thing") is the central appeal in certain breakfast cereal advertisements to young married couples in the United States, family membership is the central appeal in advertisements for the same product in Mexico.

The Japanese television commercial offers a contrast.

The message is that only perfection is good enough for the master craftsman (the product's slogan in English is "the pursuit of perfection"). It is communicated without words in the Japanese ad.

Print ads also reflect cultural values. One Southeast Asian country has advertised its airlines for years by showing attractive young women attentively serving male customers. In North America and Europe this approach has offended many who see in it the evaluation of women as objects of sexual interest whose role is to attend to the physical comfort of men. To members of Islamic cultures, the Asian women in the commercials display an availability to strange men that devout Muslim women are taught to reject. As the case that opens this chapter shows, symbols also convey cultural values.

Other sources of information about cultures include studies by anthropologists who research cultures in the field, going to live among the members of the culture they want to understand. They are trained to observe and report their observations. As a result, their accounts are more objective and less anecdotal than are those of other visitors. But even the casual, anecdotal tales of travelers often can add to your understanding.

ARE GENERALIZATIONS PRODUCTIVE OR PERILOUS?

Before we launch into the cultural priorities, a brief rationale about generalizing is necessary. The following discussions about cultural priorities generalize out of necessity. It can be useful to learn that *in general* members of a culture view something in a certain way, but it is also true that in any culture individuals have their own priorities that may deviate from those of the general culture. Thus, each specific case you encounter has to be the subject of fresh inquiry and fresh testing of the validity of the priority you expect in order to avoid fixed, inflexible mental categories. *Individual episodes can always be found to contradict generalizations about a culture.*

In addition to individual differences, there are also cultural paradoxes. Cultures are seldom a strict either-or in every instance for all people. For example, members of the

Several years ago one of the authors invited a young nurse, recently arrived for a work-study year from Beijing, home for dinner. Since her hosts knew that the Chinese have a strong orientation toward form and politeness in social situations, they expected to have to urge the young woman repeatedly to help herself to the dinner dishes. In China, refusal of proffered food is considered polite, and further refusal is even more polite. Some intercultural trainers advise Western hosts to offer *three* times so that Chinese guests can politely refuse twice and then reluctantly be persuaded the third time. However, the young woman's first words as she came through the door were, "Oh, I'm so hungry; I hope you don't mind if I eat a lot!" Contrary to the cultural generalization, she didn't hesitate at all to help herself to the food and didn't need to be urged.

But generalizations are not therefore meaningless. It could be useful to know that typically in China—as in Jordan, for example—a guest will twice refuse food out of politeness.

United States culture are individualistic, but the group is important as well. Americans join groups very easily, and the local Welcome Wagon is just one example of making people feel comfortable in the group. The young woman from Beijing may have been paying her hosts the compliment of treating them like family, in which formal politeness is not appropriate and can make family members feel they are being treated as strangers.

General insights you form about a culture from asking about cultural priorities will always need to be revised and reexamined in specific contexts. Key factors include how much previous knowledge the others have about your culture, how much time both parties have spent in each other's cultural environment, and what the dominant influences of prior encounters were. Former soldiers from various nations who fought in armed conflicts in previous decades and who now want to do business together will have to consider how much they really know about each other and what their war experiences can tell them that might prove useful for business.

The pursuit of answers to questions about cultural priorities is an ongoing process. You can continue to learn about other cultures and your own culture for as long as you continue to pose questions. The cultural priorities this chapter discusses are all related to business communication, but they do not include all the ways to view cultures. The five categories of questions are just the first step to get you started in intercultural communication fluency.

Finally, each of the questions to pose of a culture should be thought of as a continuum, with the first characteristic at one pole and the other at the opposite pole. You can position the culture you are considering at any point between the two poles, wherever it seems appropriate in light of your level of knowledge of that culture. Thus, for the question "Are results important or are relationships important?" if you are asked to locate United States culture somewhere between those two poles, where would you put it? Right in the middle? Slightly toward the results end? Strongly toward the results end? Draw on your own experience and understanding to formulate an answer. This is the way to consider each question in the Five Categories. Then, as you learn more about a culture, you can continue to ask and continue to adjust where you would locate the culture.

Category 1: Thinking and Knowing

DOES KNOWING COME FROM CONCEPTS OR EXPERIENCE?

How do people know things? The answers vary from culture to culture. Some people know because they have experienced for themselves what a thing means. Few of us would argue that knowing how to bargain prices for cold-rolled steel is acquired by anything other than experience. However, since few of us have done that, we know *about* doing it from reading about bargaining and the market and past prices. Our information is secondhand, but in English-speaking cultures most people accept the validity (if still second best) of knowledge that is acquired from a reliable source—books, training programs on bargaining—rather than from firsthand experience.

In some cultures, however, firsthand experience alone legitimately constitutes what is known. All else is hearsay. This is particularly true in cultures that have no written language, but it also can be identified in cultures that emphasize personal vision. The vision of the individual prophet or priest or shaman constitutes knowledge that is undoubted by the visionary himself or herself. Followers often believe also that the visionary knows what they cannot know. Reading or hearing about a vision is not the same as experiencing it. Visionaries play powerful roles and enjoy high status in many cultures. Corporations cannot assume that all their employees, associates, partners, and subsidiaries share the same definition of *to know*.

Seniority often accompanies long years of experience, which leads to knowledge. In some cultures, older members are considered wise. In Thailand, for instance, elders are presumed to "know" what is necessary and true even though they may not be on top of cutting-edge technological research. In cultures in which age and status go together, younger members don't challenge the truth of what seniors say.

Knowing by intuition is another kind of experience. Or consider meditation. In some cultures in which Daoism, Buddhism, and Hinduism are the dominant religions, knowledge of the true nature of things comes from meditation, which isn't quite the same as intuition. Buddha taught that each person has truth within; meditation is a way to reach that inner knowing and allow it to be recognized. Accordingly, Buddhists believe that knowledge gained from study or listening isn't as valuable as knowledge that comes from meditation. Only by emptying the mind of sensory stimuli and concerns and finally of thought, can one experience true understanding.

The notion of *knowledge* in European cultures often calls to mind a traditional body of abstract concepts, philosophies, and arguments reaching back to the classical works of Greece and Rome. Knowledge sometimes seems rather solemn, dusty, and remote. Perhaps that is why we have a number of other terms for the activity *to know: grasp, comprehend, understand, ken, perceive*. There are even more terms for a person who knows, or is *in the know: smart, knowledgeable, savvy, perceptive, clever, astute*. Another key term is *learned*. This leads to the next question we can ask of a culture.

DOES LEARNING COME FROM ASKING QUESTIONS OR MASTERING RECEIVED WISDOM?

What does it mean to learn? Cultures have a variety of answers. People learn how to learn when they are very young, first at home before they go to school and then later at school. Those early learning patterns are followed with little change throughout people's lives. In North America, learning is a process that involves asking questions. This book is by one United States–Canadian citizen who is a New Zealand resident and one United States resident of Northern European descent. In the cultures from which we write, asking questions opens the door to understanding. Therefore, the process we present for learning about cultures is one that involves asking questions.

In the United States, from kindergarten through graduate seminars, students who ask questions are rewarded. They bask in their teachers' approval and often receive higher grades than their unquestioning peers. Teachers tend to find question-askers intelligent. In commerce, industry, and medicine, legends are told about heroes who asked, "What if we do it this way?" and "Why not?" Stephen Wozniak and Steve Jobs, the computer whiz kids who began their company in a garage, asked why computers couldn't be fun to use by someone who had no technical background, and they thereby created the Apple Computer Corpora-

Physicists are busy trying to identify the ultimate minute particle of creation, a "God particle" used to fashion everything in the known universe.[9] It has been elusive and the search has been intense, but some physicists believe that tiny vibrating particles of energy in strands or strings are the basic building blocks that underlie everything in the universe. It is known as string theory and has been the subject of intense debate for several decades. The Western tradition of learning since ancient Greece has followed this process to knowledge: dissect, deconstruct, and atomize until you identify the smallest component and can relate each building block to each other building block. Then you have mastered the understanding of something. Then you know it.

tion. The hero in your own organization, whoever he or she may be, asked a question, and by the light of that question went forward to illuminate previously unlit territory.

Many leaders in United States businesses believe—with a fervor that the 18th-century Age of Enlightenment would have approved—in the candlepower of question- asking. They believe that when they have answers to questions, they know.

In many cultures, knowing does not involve laying something open and examining its components minutely. Quite the opposite. Knowing involves seeing the connections and links between something and everything else. Knowing something means being able to fit it into the universal scheme of things. A prominent Chinese scientist once described the difference between Western and Chinese approaches to knowing. He used the disease AIDS as an example and pointed out that in the West medical researchers were diligently trying to isolate the virus that causes the disease. But in China researchers were trying to find ways to strengthen the body's immune system. One method looks at the most elemental unit of the disease, while the other looks at its place in the context of what the disease does.

In many cultures in Asia, Latin America, and Southern Europe, learning does not come from asking questions. Learning means receiving and taking in what is given by teachers. Some teachers may speak through written texts. Teachers *know*; their role is to pass knowledge on to learners so that the learners also will know. In China, Japan, Korea, Thailand, Hong Kong, Vietnam, Malaysia, Cambodia, and Indonesia—among other places—the teacher in the classroom is an unassailable authority. The textbook and the teacher do not disagree. What teachers deliver to the student is true knowledge and is not to be doubted. Although sometimes students ask questions for clarification, they do not question the authenticity or reliability of the knowledge they are given. Their role is to master it.

Frequently that means committing knowledge to memory so that they can reconstruct it when called upon to do so, as in an exam. Reproducing exactly what was delivered is the best possible demonstration a student can give of really having learned.

Culture defines what it means to know and to learn. This basic fact is important for any organization that plans to—or already does—operate with personnel from many cultures. Most organizations have training programs for employees and expect their workers to continue to learn new things as technology and the organization's needs change. The need to learn is unavoidable when an organization engages a multicultural workforce or engages in global activities for the first time.

DOES KNOWLEDGE HAVE LIMITS?

Can everything be known eventually? In cultures with highly developed research economies, some people assume that with enough science, the right theories, and the best equipment, eventually the physical world will be known. Probes into space, into the seas, into the atom, into human behavior—all these will yield final answers one day. This is a view often held by nonscientists who have faith in what science can achieve. But many people who aren't engaged in science hold a different view, believing that scientific inquiry into the physical world will never reveal everything.

Are some things unknowable? In Western Christian cultures, following a separation between the sacred and the secular that began hundreds of years ago, the spiritual truths generally have been held to be knowable through *faith*: If you believe, you can know. When scientific findings and faith are in conflict, science has little effect on the beliefs of the faithful. Scientific analyses of the Shroud of Turin, which some Christians believe bears the imprint of Christ's body, have had little effect on belief or unbelief.[10] Attempts to explain the Star of Bethlehem, which biblical accounts say shone at the birth of Christ, by means of astronomical computer programs run backward in time, have had little effect on belief. For those Christians, knowing in spiritual terms involves a different approach from knowing in material terms.

Other cultures find this approach to knowing very strange and schizophrenic; for them there is no separation between sacred and secular. For many Hindus in India, for example, all human undertakings and all episodes of nature—in fact, all things—are embraced by the spiritual. Believers visit temples daily, sometimes three or four times a day. Businesspeople obtain blessings for ventures, and new work premises are blessed before they are occupied. No separation is made between material life and spiritual life; all life is seamlessly part of the real, unseen but felt realm of the divine. All of life is sacred. Any foreign organization that wishes to do business in India has to accept this view of knowing.

For many cultures, some things are too ineffable—too sacred and inexpressible— to be known by any means. The ineffable may be delineated to a greater extent by the persons who are assigned that role—priests, shamans, wise women—than by ordinary businesspeople. When this is true in cultures in which such knowledge is valued, these people enjoy a high status.

HOW DO PEOPLE REASON?

How people know is closely related to how people reason. Patterns of reasoning also vary from culture to culture. Patterns in the mind map a person's life experiences. (The converse is also true: Experiences verify patterns of the mind.) The map affects how a person frames communication about life.

The patterns are processes learned from birth; they are culturally determined. We suppose that all normal human babies are capable of any of the thought patterns ever used in the whole history of human existence, but babies learn to pattern their thinking after the patterns their world shows them. If they are fortunate enough to have more than one culture in their socialization process, they will learn more patterns than their monocultural counterparts will. It is remarkable to watch someone moving from one culture into another and discern the difference in an individual's patterns of thought that the cultural change brings.

Perhaps the most typical pattern of thinking for members of Western cultures involves cause and effect. To speak of *reasons* in English is to speak of causes, of reasons why. In fact, a *reasonable* person is one who sees relationships of cause and effect between things. *Why* questions in Western cultures inevitably invoke explanations of causes: Why has the market share shrunk for widgets in Malaysia? Why are productivity figures up for March? Why is the chief accountant not at work today? (Because Widgets Inc., our competitor, launched a marketing campaign last month. Because the new equipment was running without problems in March. Because her husband is in surgery.)

Cause-and-effect thinking is linear. We could draw a straight line from cause to effect, with an arrowhead at the results end. Many sentences in English employ this pattern. Consider that last one: The subject is *sentences*, and it has some descriptors around it (*many, in English*); *employ* is what the sentences do; *this pattern* is the outcome, or the result of the activity of the verb. The subject does the activity. That's how the sentence unfolds, and that's the linear pattern of what actually happens, not just what the sentence describes.

Westerners think that cause-and-effect patterns are logical and that *logical* means cause and effect, the pattern Westerners call the Aristotelian syllogism. So deeply embedded is this notion that it is assumed to be universal. But as experts in intercultural understanding warn, it isn't.

> The syllogistic reasoning of Aristotle . . . is not a universal phenomenon; it has been a part of the Anglo-European tradition for such a long time that speakers of English tend to assume that it is a natural phenomenon of the human mind, rather than an invention of the human mind.[11]

What a blow Western minds suffer when they discover that *logical* means something very different to non-Western people! For example, Chinese people often use a pattern of logic that contrasts elements: An A must have a B, hot implies cold, and so forth. When this pattern of thinking is communicated, the form that results is parallelism by contrasts or a sequence of antitheses that nevertheless are not mutually exclusive. Contradictory opposites co-exist. Arabic reasoning often begins with an assertion that then is restated and repeated so that the accumulated weight of repetition demonstrates its truth.[12]

The key in Asian patterns of thinking is linkage. Links are always being sought to show the wholeness of life, even when that whole embraces contradiction. The importance of the fish tank to Lei Peng in the case that opens this chapter shows a linkage of ideas because of the sounds of the words that represent those ideas: fish and profit. Events are likened to other, larger events that occurred in the past. Businesses in China use this linkage pattern in negotiations. For example, a meeting between negotiating companies is related to momentous encounters between nations in distant historical accounts. This kind of historical reference often figures in the early, informal stages of negotiation: the toast by a Chinese host to the foreign guests.[13] It often sails past Western guests, who do not recognize in a historical reference any substantive link to the business at hand. The unity of human experience with the whole of life is the fundamental philosophical basis for the thinking patterns that can be identified in Chinese business communication.

The point for business communication is that Asian businesspeople tend to look at the links between things and the relationships that give things meaning by providing a context. Western businesspeople, however, tend to consider issues in isolation. For example, a Westerner trying to establish joint-venture guidelines in Japan may look at professional credentials only in relation to hiring personnel. The Japanese look at credentials, but also at the character of employees, their seniority, their past service, perhaps their family members' service, and certainly who the candidates' contacts are—a large tissue of interrelated factors that form a context for hiring and wages. The fish-tank images recalled by Japanese and United States observers bear out this difference between focusing on the individual and focusing on the individual in context.

Roderick McLeod, an entrepreneur in China more than 20 years ago, made this prediction:

> I believe that the subject of patterns of thinking, explored in all its daunting depths and complexities, holds a promise of a "quantum leap" in cross-cultural understanding and communication.[15]

His projection still holds true today. Richard Nisbett has engaged in an exploration of the differences in the ways Westerners and Asians reason. Westerners, according to Nisbett, going back to the classical Greeks, consider the perceivable world as made up of objects. The reasoning method by which objects are grouped into categories entails identifying attributes that objects have in common. Individuals that have fur, for instance, can be classed together into a group. Asians, in contrast, reason that objects that influence one another belong in a group. An example is "spring," "east," "wood," "wind," and "green," all of which influence each other. Both Westerners and Asians focus on the relationships of things, but Westerners look at the relationship of individual to group, whereas Asians look at the relationship of part to whole.[16]

The Chinese *yin-yang* symbol used in many Asian countries and displayed on the Korean flag (see Figure 9.1), expresses the way opposites contain something of each other.

Yin is negative, cold, downward and inward, dark, and night; it is also feminine. *Yang* is positive, hot, upward and outward, light, and day; it is also masculine. The *yin* and the *yang* interact. Where one grows, the other contracts, but they make up a whole. Neither can exist without the other.

Furthermore, each has an element of the other within it. As the *yin* grows larger, so does the *yang* element within it, and vice versa.

Yin and *yang* can offer a perspective for understanding technological growth and development in Asia.[14] Urban development, telecommunications, and fast transportation systems bring people into contact: This is a *yang* aspect of technology. Family structure is threatened by urban growth as people leave their villages and migrate to urban centers: This is a *yin* aspect of development and technology.

These patterns of thinking are generated by culture. People in European cultures believe that objects cannot belong in two contradictory categories at the same time; they must be one or the other. In Russia, as in Asian countries, thinking patterns embrace contradictions rather than oppose them. Extremes and contradictions delight Russians, who do not seek to reconcile them but to see them exist together in a pattern.[17]

Category 2: Doing and Achieving

IS DOING IMPORTANT OR IS BEING IMPORTANT?

The existential view of some cultures calls for valuing the present moment and celebrating being. One worker expressed an existential view by saying that he regards work as a blessing; you work hard at whatever your work is. But you don't continue to set yourself new challenges or imagine new activity beyond the blessing you have been given. This is hard for the activity-oriented to understand. It looks like shirking.

In contrast, to the celebrators of existence, a great deal of activity in *doing* cultures looks pointless. Where are people going in such a hurry? What have they left behind? What is the meaning of so much activity? *Being* cultures value stillness, collectedness, and serenity. Many visitors to Western cultures are amazed by the pace of life, especially in

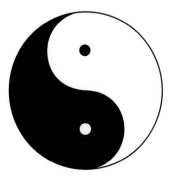

FIGURE 9.1

The Yin-Yang Symbol

cities: so many activities crammed into a short time, requiring so much speed to fit them all in. Such crowded agendas seem to leave little room for simply *being.*

According to Condon and Yousef, Clifford Clarke (as foreign student adviser at Stanford) first observed the correlation between cultures in which activity is valued—almost for its own sake at times—and in which silence is of little value.[18] Members of *doing* cultures view silence as a waste, a time when "nothing is doing." However, members of cultures that value *being* also often value silence. In silence the present moment can best be appreciated and experienced. A foreign businessperson in Japan who is unaware of the importance of silence in that culture may rush to fill silence with words.

Obviously, great potential for conflict exists when co-workers have opposing views about doing versus being. The potential is increased when neither side understands that the other side may feel sure of the rightness of its view. The most obvious arena for conflict is negotiations. Both sides have goals for the outcome, but low-context cultures—which emphasize results—generate more concretely framed goals. Negotiators from high-context cultures have expectations for the outcomes that are less specific and more relationship-oriented.

ARE TASKS DONE SEQUENTIALLY OR SIMULTANEOUSLY?

Even when many cultures value activity, they may regard *doing* differently. In some cultures, the sequential performance of tasks is considered normal behavior, whereas in others, simultaneous performance is normal.

People may have personal styles and preferences for getting work done—that is, within a sequential-task culture, individuals may prefer a flexibility that allows them to do more than one thing at a time. (They may be called "disorganized" by others in that culture.) In general, however, workers in sequential-task cultures know at the start of the day what they will do during the segments of the day: morning, lunch hour, afternoon, and divisions thereof. When unexpected tasks arise, others that had been scheduled are rescheduled. The essence of *time management* is organizing and sequencing tasks, a notion that seems peculiar to members of other cultures.

In contrast, although a simultaneous-task performer knows in general what the tasks in a given day will be, the day has a fluidity that allows for more and less important tasks that take more or less time, and the performer assumes that many tasks will be attacked simultaneously. (The question of time and how it is valued is discussed in detail later in this chapter under the heading "The Big Picture.")

Simultaneity is extremely useful when people and relationships between people are valued highly: You can spend all the time you want or need with a person when you are at the same time giving some attention to other (valued) persons. This leads to the next question to pose of a culture concerning doing and achieving.

DO RESULTS OR RELATIONSHIPS TAKE PRIORITY?

Results cultures regard ends as more significant than the means used to achieve those ends. The United States is where Management by Objectives (MBO) had its origin; that isn't surprising when one considers the dominance of cause-and-effect thinking in United States culture. The basis of MBO is that you identify your goals and then work out a strategy to achieve them. Along the way, you measure how close you have come. That's how you know you're making progress.

Goals-oriented societies place a very high value on making progress, which naturally leads to methods by which to measure progress. Measurements that seem logical to Americans may not seem so logical to others, however. The French (among others) often marvel at the American penchant for statistics and measurements of qualities they consider intangible. ("How satisfied are you with your present superior: 10 percent, 25

A Canadian sales representative from British Columbia to Venezuela goes to the office of a shipping company to arrange for the ongoing shipment of an order in transit from Quebec to another country. She is on time for her appointment but has to wait while the shipping agent serves a number of customers who are already in the office. When the Canadian's turn finally comes, she explains what she needs, and the agent begins filling out the documentation for the shipment and discussing prices. At the same time the agent takes a phone call, responds to a question from a co-worker about schedules, and directs the faxing of a message about something else—in effect working on three other projects besides the Canadian's. This is efficient activity in the Venezuelan agent's culture.

To the Canadian, however, this is unfocused activity that is not nearly as efficient as it would be—particularly from her point of view—if the agent simply dealt exclusively with her during her scheduled appointment.

In Canada, businesspeople typically write appointments and activities into the day's agenda every day. They then work sequentially through the agenda until they have completed each task, or until the day is over.

percent, 50 percent, 75 percent, or 90 percent?" "On a score from one to five, how well do you think you are performing in your job?")

The emphasis on measurement has led to an enormous preoccupation by business with figures of productivity and cost, which in turn has led to the high status and power accorded to accountants. Not all cultures feel the need to identify goals and work toward them. One reason is that the goals that matter to many cultures include nurturing close relationships with co-workers. Even if the proposed sale falls through, the relationship has been strengthened by the contact made in the effort to close a sale.

In countries where power is concentrated at the top levels of organizations and is wielded according to personal favor, a healthy and strong relationship with the powerful one is a primary goal of every endeavor. This is evident, for example, in former (and current) communist countries. Having good access to the party secretary or a member in good standing of the party was a conduit to effecting desired outcomes. The immediate goal for a floor supervisor in a textile factory in former Soviet Georgia may have been a new apartment, but the ongoing goal of every interaction was to nurture a good relationship with the party secretary in the factory.

Relationships are the basis for much of the business conducted in Asia. In places where relationships are so highly valued, business is done only with people who have entered into a relationship with you and whose organization has connections to your organization. In fact, in the high-context cultures of Asia, business preferably is transacted face to face.

In China, for five decades after the beginning of the communist rule, every government-based work unit had a travel allocation in its budget from the government so that representatives could travel and meet with suppliers, buyers, associates, and related organizations (those reporting to the same ministry in Beijing). Similarly, many work units had hotels on the premises to receive visitors from within and outside China. Business correspondence was minimal; business was transacted face to face. The preference for face-to-face communication is still strong today. Relationship building is the key activity.

When there is a strong relationship, specific outcomes can be worked out. Contracts can be written and signed because relationships exist that will ensure their performance. The ends flow from the means. No wonder relationship-oriented cultures value the means to an end more than the end itself. Furthermore, if success eludes you this time, you can always try again if the relationship is intact.

Finally, people don't necessarily agree about what signifies an achievement. You may assume that all businesspeople equate achievement with profit, but that assumption is not always correct. Furthermore, even when people agree that making money is their goal, they may have very different ideas about what it means to have money—what it is worth.

For instance, in Brazil wealth is important because it can buy an elite car, a spacious apartment in a desirable area, servants, memberships in private clubs, travel, exclusive brands of liquor, clothing, personal entertainment equipment, and entertainment for friends.

When graduate students in Shanghai were asked in 1985 to describe *wealth*, they all agreed that it meant having money in your own pocket; they also agreed with the statement "If you have 10,000 yuan in your pocket, you're rich because you can buy the best banquet for all your friends!" Today, the same people may indeed be buying banquets along with homes, cars, and consumer goods. Economic growth of an average 8.5 percent in China since the mid-1980s has fueled huge leaps in prosperity for many. Consumerism is rampant in China today, driven in large part by the willingness and ability of parents to spend money on their one child. Still, people value being able to buy banquets for family and friends.

This dimension of results versus relationships corresponds in part to Hofstede's dimension of individualism versus collectivism. Individualist cultures are performance-oriented and emphasize personal achievement and winning the competition. Collectivist cultures are relationship-oriented and emphasize supportive networks and collaboration.

IS UNCERTAINTY AVOIDED OR TOLERATED?

Uncertainty—the inability to be sure about exactly what the future will hold for oneself and one's business environment—exists in all cultures and, Hofstede points out, in all organizations as well. Some people react to uncertainty with greater levels of anxiety than others. An employee who is averse to uncertainty will want to know what the prospects are for job advancement, based on what criteria, at the recommendation of whom, at which times of the year. Employees who calculate carefully and minutely what the effect is on a retirement income of working an extra month before retiring and base their decision to retire on that information are probably uncertainty-averse. They strive to protect themselves from the unknown. By comparison, an employee who tolerates uncertainty may be willing to transfer to a different geographic location at short notice or leave a place of employment before lining up the next job. Such employees are more open to accepting the unexpected. What Hofstede showed is that like some individuals, some cultures react with greater anxiety than others. As a broad generalization, *being* cultures tend to be more uncertainty-tolerant, while goal-oriented *doing* cultures tend to be more uncertainty-averse. Doing cultures have a Plan A, and then a backup Plan B, and often even a Plan C "just in case" the first two fall through.

Two members of an organization who come from different cultures and have to work together—say, a production manager and a supervisor—who do not agree about whether to avoid or tolerate uncertainty may have a hard time understanding each other. If the person from the avoiding culture wants more guidelines about how to deal with uncertainty, and if that person is a subordinate, then the subordinate's relationship with the boss may suffer from distrust and diminished respect. The uncertainty avoider may not understand that a different attitude toward uncertainty lies behind what appears to be simply an irresponsible approach on the part of a superior who is supposed to be responsible. The uncertainty tolerator, the boss, may identify the subordinate as anxious for no good reason—simply a worrier—rather than someone with a different attitude toward uncertainty.

Uncertainty is not the same thing as risk. Risk involves a specific potential loss, but uncertainty does not involve a specifically identifiable loss. Risk in business is an everyday fact; risk in business that involves multicultural and multinational contact is even more inevitable. The risk may be social ostracization, economic loss, or a legal liability. Businesses must consider risks in all business transactions. Businesspeople from various cultures approach risk differently, but all organizations want to minimize risk.

Hong Kong may be the place where practices to ensure good luck and avoid bad luck are most often observed. For example, a desk in a business office may display a jade carving of a stylized bat (the flying rodent); the word for bat sounds like the word for prosperity, and the jade carving is a conscious invocation of luck that brings prosperity. (Luck means material wealth to the pragmatic Hong Kongese.) Fortune-tellers abound, and businesses consult them about making business decisions.

Feng shui (literally "wind water") is the ancient practice of geomancy—aligning sites and buildings in harmony with the earth's energy forces so that locations will be propitious. Its expert interpreters typically are called in when buildings are oriented on construction sites. Owners of restaurants, hotels, and retail businesses also call in *feng shui* experts when trade slumps. The experts' recommendations often include repositioning the manager's desk or hanging mirrors to deflect the flow of disharmonious influences into the building or partially screening the entrance to prevent money from running out the door. *Feng shui* is not always a guarantee of luck, however. A Chinese-American–owned business in California was poised to purchase a property adjacent to it when the property came up for sale and the business had an investor willing to loan the $1.2 million price. However, when a *feng shui* master expressed strong negative opinions about the purchase, the company did not complete the purchase. Instead, an Armenian businessman bought the land. Within 18 months the value had soared to $3 million, and the hapless Chinese-American business owners were deeply chagrined. They needed the property but now lacked the funds to buy it.

Some numbers are lucky in Hong Kong, such as eight (which sounds like the word for prosperity), seven, and three. The government raises extra money by auctioning off auspicious-number license plates, and in recent years one man paid $5 million HK (U.S.$641,000) for a car license plate with a string of lucky number eights. By contrast, the number four is unlucky since it is pronounced like the word for death. Hotels and office buildings do not have a number four, and observers say subway passengers are reluctant to pass through gate 44 even during rush hour. Phone numbers and street addresses with a four in them are also regarded as unlucky by many.

IS LUCK AN ESSENTIAL FACTOR OR AN IRRELEVANCE?

Luck is one way to deal with one's anxiety about the unknown. Cultures vary in the importance they attach to the influence of an unseen power over events. Is luck (fortune, fate) responsible for success? Or is success the responsibility of the human engineers of it? Not surprisingly, in cultures that think in cause-and-effect patterns and that value results, *planning*—not luck—is the key to success. Westerners are fond of sayings that present this view: "We are the architects of our own destiny."

Planning appears to equal control. If you plan carefully and omit no detail, you may ensure the outcome. Control means calculating the variables so that nothing unexpected can intervene between cause (means) and effect (ends). Attending carefully to the details resembles an orientation toward rules, as is discussed in the next section; they are both attempts to shape outcomes by controlling variables.

As anyone who has carefully laid plans knows, however, the unexpected has a way of ambushing you. Even some Westerners think that Western rationalism, which is our heritage from Aristotle through Voltaire to modern technocrats, has traveled too far from human experience. The discounting of fate and the belief in human planning and engineering seem foolish to some Western thinkers.

Western cultures, which have tended to discount the role of fate since the Enlightenment of the 18th century, nevertheless number millions of horoscope readers. This perhaps is because, in spite of technology and planning and control mechanisms, life frequently persists in not being orderly. People whose cultures acknowledge the role of luck in human affairs view the attempt to control life through planning as merely an illusory and pointless activity.

In the United States, observances to ward off bad luck also affect business. Office buildings frequently do not have a 13th floor, for example, and some airplanes have no aisle numbered 13. Then there are the pyramid letters that supposedly bring good luck to the person who doesn't break the chain (throw the letter away) and bad luck to the scoffer who fails to send the letter on to more people. (While few executives admit to playing along, nevertheless their names often crop up on the lists of senders of the chain letters, with comments about not needing any more bad luck.)[21]

Although few in the United States (and in other English-speaking cultures as well as Europe) are unaware of "unlucky 13," not many know it comes from the Last Supper in Christian teaching, at which 13 were present, including Jesus' betrayer. Jesus was crucified on Friday, and so "Friday the 13th" was thought to be especially unlucky in Europe in past centuries.

In Taiwan, the Ghost month (the seventh in the lunar calendar) is traditionally not a time of good luck for making an important decision such as a new business venture. Rather than risk a business loss, some people figure that they might as well wait until the (lucky) eighth month to make decisions. After all, although it may be superstitious nonsense, one never knows. Fate is unpredictable. Good luck comes, according to the Chinese, when invoked by homonyms, such as the fish in the opening case of this chapter. To "have fish" sounds exactly like "to have prosperity."

Filipino fatalism is summed up in the phrase *bahala na*, which in Tagalog roughly means "accept what comes and bear it with hope and patience"; success in a business venture may well be attributed to fate rather than effort.[19] In Thailand, *mai pen rai* means "Never mind; it's fate, and you are not responsible." In Chinese, *mei guanxi* has a similar meaning. It literally translates as "no connection" and suggests that the addressee isn't responsible for the inexplicable whims of fate.

In India, fate is widely credited for events. It is preordained and can be known by studying the stars and the procession of the planets. Many companies in India have their own astrologers who practice the 5,000-year-old *jyotish*, or astrology. Businesses consult with astrologers when they recruit new employees to ascertain whether they are lucky. After all, if employees have no luck as individuals, how can they be lucky for the organization?

Wearing specific precious and semiprecious stones can counteract the planetary influence and mediate fate somewhat; many Indians wear specific stones for the purpose of just such intervention.[20] In Turkey, businesspeople often wear a blue-bead amulet for good luck and more specifically, for warding off the evil eye's bad luck.

In Mexico, the unexpected working of fate is well known. A supplier may promise delivery on Thursday, for example, knowing all the indications are that Thursday will not be possible since he has a full agenda of promised orders for Thursday. But the supplier may consider that perhaps one of the previously scheduled orders will be canceled, or perhaps the driver of the delivery truck won't come to work that day, making all deliveries impossible, or perhaps it will rain too heavily for delivery, or perhaps the company placing the new order will change it, which could alter the delivery day. Fate is always a possible factor. A Mexican student may sigh over a failed exam, "It was my destiny, I guess."

It's important to recognize that an attitude of "Oh, well, might as well play it safe . . . you never know" in the United States can be an earnest belief in another culture. In cultures in which luck is acknowledged to play a role in business, people who discount luck may not only insult the luck seekers but can also risk being thought negligent or even endangering the business.

In the Beijing airport in the late 1990s, an amazing sight greeted the visitor. Check-in took place at portable booths; airline personnel came to a booth with a sign that declared it was open, about one hour before departure. Once passengers had all been checked in, the airline employee took down the sign and moved the booth to a less prominent position. Behind the booths was the luggage belt. It stood about a meter high, was about two-thirds of a meter wide, and was always moving. Behind the belt were the offices for the airlines personnel. Clearly, many people used these rooms. There was much coming and going, laughter, cups of tea being carried in and out, and so forth. When employees wished to leave the office area and come out to speak to passengers on the other side of the luggage belt and the booths, they climbed up onto the belt and straddled it to jump down on the other side! They could have gone around the belt, but that would have taken them perhaps ten meters out of their way. No doubt they had been cautioned about the physical danger of crossing directly over the moving belt, but expediency won over rules.

ARE RULES TO BE FOLLOWED OR BENT?

This cultural dimension is closely related to uncertainty avoidance versus uncertainty tolerance and to luck. Having rules and following them—and making sure others follow them too—is a way of diminishing anxiety about the uncertain. However, whether rules are followed also has to do with what is important in a society: Is neat, predictable behavior by everyone preferable? Or is having the flexibility to meet human needs preferable? In all societies, conflicts arise between what the rules state ought to be done and what is convenient or helpful to individuals.

For example, take the simple act of crossing the street. In strongly rules-adhering societies, pedestrians may not cross anywhere they like. They must use crosswalks that are marked; they must wait until a signal indicates they may walk (perhaps a white-lit figure walking, a traffic sign used throughout the world). When the signal changes to a blinking red hand, they must hurry to finish crossing and must not begin to cross at this point. When the red hand is unblinking, they must remain on the side of the street. In London, the corners of some intersections have railings so that pedestrians cannot cross exactly at the corner but must use a designated crosswalk several feet away. In Canadian cities, pedestrians are ticketed for jaywalking. But in rules-bending societies—Mexico is one—people cross whenever they perceive a break in motor (or bicycle) traffic and wherever it is convenient for them to cross. Although they have been told that the rule is to cross at a designated crosswalk only when the signal indicates they may, they cross where and when it suits them. Rules-oriented cultures are puzzled by this seemingly cavalier attitude toward safety. In the United States, for example, the Occupational Safety and Health Administration (OSHA) would get after the company for not cracking down on the behavior in the following example.

Category 3: the Big Picture

This category of cultural priorities encompasses the big things cultures deal with: the questions every society has to answer. Why are we here? What is the significance of life? Where did we come from? What do we go to, after this life?

The ways in which cultures answer these questions correspond to many of the beliefs and attitudes we can identify with a particular culture. The answers to these questions also enable us to understand the motivations for behaviors that belong to a specific culture.

Religion is a *belief system* that informs the attitudes and behaviors of members of a culture, even of those who do not actively practice the religion. When you are learning about an unfamiliar culture, studying the religion(s) is a lengthy and demanding undertaking. It's like studying Russian so that you can read the street signs—a worthwhile endeavor but not the first thing you need to know to begin doing business in Russia. Religions or belief systems come from cultural values and also contribute to cultural values. You can benefit from understanding the world's belief systems, but you can benefit for purposes of business from understanding the cultural priorities of your business contacts.

DO HUMANS DOMINATE NATURE OR DOES NATURE DOMINATE HUMANS?

Nature is the natural environment and natural phenomena that envelop human endeavors. At one extreme, humans view nature as an inexhaustible resource. The assumption is—or, at any rate, was— that the land is there to sustain life, especially human life. The Book of Genesis in the Bible proclaims that after God made man:

> God said, "Behold, I have given you every plant yielding seed which is upon the face of all the earth, and every tree with seed in its fruit; you shall have them for food. And to every beast of the earth, and to every bird of the air, and to everything that creeps upon the earth, everything that has the breath of life, I have given every green plant for food." And it was so.[22]

However, archaeologists have shown that ancient cultures, for example those around the Mediterranean and Aegean seas, cultivated land for crops in ways that ultimately exhausted the soil, and deforestation caused its erosion. Nevertheless, the assumption that the earth and all that flourishes in it is for us to use as a God-given right has persisted into this century. Only in this generation, and particularly in the last several decades, has the argument for environmental protection been put forward seriously as public policy, even though the concept of stewardship of the created universe is present in Genesis. Simultaneously, the assumption that the earth is an inexhaustible source of sustenance is part of the Judeo-Christian tradition, and part of Islam, also.

In religions such as Hinduism, Daoism, and Buddhism, as well as earlier animistic religions that endow certain trees and rocks and rivers with spirits, nature plays a different role. But what role? Japanese culture, which reflects the value orientations of Buddhism and Shintoism more than other religions, views nature as a source of aesthetic appreciation. Nature is observed; it is contemplated and meditated upon just like a painting or an object of sculptural art, and it is shaped into art in forms such as *bonsai*—trees that have been carefully pruned to grow in miniature. Wilderness, unadulterated nature, plays virtually no role in modern Japan. For example, boatloads of Japanese citizens organized protests against a dam in the Nagara River, but not to protect the river. Rather, it was to protest the intrusion of a large concrete structure in the carefully cultivated scenery. (It was also to protest the impact on the fishing industry since the dam would prevent trout from spawning.) However, Japan has pledged the largest amount of money of any nation for environmental protection worldwide. The Kyoto Treaty of protocols calling on the nations of the world to agree to protect the global environment was presented to the world in Japan.

In India, some Hindu sects, such as the Bishois, do not allow the cutting down of any trees or the slaughter of animals. This is extreme reverence for nature, which has precedence over human activities. However, piety does not always mean protection of the environment in that country. The pollution of India's rivers has been an enormous problem for the environmental protection ministry. It is particularly tricky when the river is the sacred Ganges with its freight of untreated waste and the ashes and remains of cremated people from the funeral pyres on its banks.

The Daoists in traditional China held that the Way, the *dao*, meant becoming one with nature and its life energy. Chinese gardens represent mountains, streams, and caves, all places where spirits dwell that are sources of meditative serenity in escaping from the pressures of the world. Nature dominates human activity in that view. But in modern China, traditional gardens are state-owned and constantly crowded with Chinese visitors who litter. One of the most renowned natural beauty spots in China, the Three Gorges of the Yangzi River, has been flooded by a great dam built to provide electricity for the major cities downriver from it, including the enormous city of Shanghai. Over a million people have been relocated from their homes along the river, and the project has been decried by the international community. The traditional value of nature has given way to the need for hydroelectric power.

Among cultures whose priority is dominating nature, technology often is invoked. Technology is concerned with the relationship of people to their natural environment.[23] All cultures develop tools for survival in their immediate environment. Very old and very new cultures share this human endeavor; creating tools is something all cultures have always done and will do. It has been called a particularly human activity; certainly only humans can create tools by pondering imaginatively upon other tools.

Members of cultures with advanced tool-making capabilities often assume their culture is superior to others with less advanced technology. This is not a basis on which to assess a whole culture; it is only one priority. Present-day technology is not necessarily the most sophisticated ever known; some processes used by ancient civilizations, like mummification of corpses in the Egypt of the pharaohs, and the firing of certain ceramic glazes in China, cannot be reproduced exactly today. Technology, the relationship of people to their natural environment, is often tempered and influenced by other cultural priorities.

More and more technology has produced more and more resistance to technology in cultures that wish to protect nature rather than dominate it. New Zealand has strict controls on genetically modified agricultural processes and products. Genetic modifications to crops may make them resistant to parasites, or they may make an organism dangerous to local species.

The *butterfly theory* suggests that a butterfly moving its wings on one branch in one place can ultimately be a factor in whether a hurricane blows in another place. Whether the hypothesis can be demonstrated satisfactorily or not, the fragility of the world's ecosystem is of greater concern than ever before. Scientists warn about holes developing in the ozone layer and about global warming. Governments and businesses worldwide—not just countries that possess the most technology—are addressing that concern with policies to protect the environment. But even though space photography and sophisticated measurements of contamination and other sources of information have changed our scientific understanding, nevertheless the cultural priorities about nature as dominated or indomitable change slowly.

In places where nature is endowed with spiritual life, such as certain mountains or rivers, human activity appears to believers to be too insignificant to have a lasting impact on transcendental nature. Thus, most cultures have a plurality of complex attitudes from different value orientations toward nature.

That means that businesses have to contend with complex attitudes toward nature. A foreign firm may identify an ideal site for a joint-venture manufacturing plant on a river, but the site may be revered by local citizens as a spot of natural beauty or spiritual significance. Who wins—the sacred or the secular—will depend on the priorities of the culture. That brings us to the next question to ask of a culture.

ARE DIVINE POWERS OR HUMANS AT THE CENTER OF EVENTS?

Who controls the outcomes of activity? Of business? Of life and death? In many cultures today, deities exist in a sphere of influence that is apart from the secular world.

Businesspeople may pray regularly to a God they revere but base their business decisions on factors that appear not to be divinely inspired. Devout individuals may indeed act on private divine guidance but probably will not publicly explain their actions that way. This is generally the case in societies that follow a stated policy of separation of public affairs and private belief. Religious spokespersons in those cultures are respected but not relied on for decisions. Questions of ethics may be referred to them, but the decisions rest with those whose responsibility it is to make the decision: organizations' chief executive officers (CEOs) or managing directors, union presidents, newspaper publishers, directors of government programs, and so forth. Even in societies in which human activity is accountable for outcomes, such as Great Britain, Poland, Hungary, Austria, and Greece, to name a few, public reference to a deity in the carrying on of human activity varies greatly. Canadians, for example, are bemused by the frequency with which leaders in the United States refer to God.

Some cultures see little or no separation between secular life and sacred life. All human activity, including business, comes within the all-embracing circle of the divine. A deity is at the center of every occurrence. In Madras, India, a businessman goes to the temple several times a day and has his company truck blessed each morning before work begins. In Bangkok, Thailand, a businesswoman offers food to Buddhist monks early in the morning before opening up her shop, and she may stop at a street shrine later in the day to pray. In Ankara, Turkey, the day begins with prayers to Allah, and prayers follow at intervals throughout the day in response to the muezzin's call. India, Thailand, and Turkey are all secular states and guarantee freedom of religion for all, but the practices of the faith of the majority have an impact on all affairs.

Of course, some nations historically have been theocracies whose governments followed the principles and regulations of a religion in conducting their activities. A modern example is Iran. Yet the tendency to see divine power at the center of human endeavor is widespread.

Let's examine some of the major world religions.

Hinduism is one of the world's oldest religions. It includes the idea of the world as a great system of hierarchies, with the purest at the top. Living things are reborn in cycle after cycle of death and rebirth until at last they reach *nirvana*, a state of eternal peace and bliss. In hierarchies of people, called *castes*, the purest are the *Brahmin* priests. They are not necessarily also the most powerful, and this can confuse businesspeople from Western cultures. Each caste carries its own *dharma*, or duties, and members of each caste are encoded with aptitudes for certain work.[24] People traditionally are expected to live according to the expectations of their caste. This has had an effect on ambition and social mobility. Further, it means that individuals have specific careers in which they enjoy mobility and others that are closed to them. The caste system has been declared illegal as a basis for hiring and promoting, but its priorities still exist in Indian culture.

Hinduism has a dynamism that is the result of its embracing many ancient beliefs and rituals and also embracing newer religions such as Buddhism. This means that Hinduism has remarkable diversity. Hindus in western India do not worship the same god or observe the same holy days as do Hindus in eastern India. Although most Hindus do not eat beef and venerate cows because souls can be incarnated in animals as well as in humans, the Tantric (mystical) tradition is an exception. Basic beliefs in one part of the country are rejected in another part. Hinduism has been called the most accommodating of religions and also has been charged with resisting change.

For many Hindus, the belief system is a way of life. But educated Indians are likely to separate work and the rest of life, often as a result of Western influence. A businessperson who is a foreigner will have to learn what people's beliefs are in the specific area of India. Gentle questioning will reveal how willing an Indian is to speak about religious issues and the impact of caste on professional life.

Buddhism began in India in the 6th century B.C. with a prince, Siddhartha Gautama. The prince led a sheltered life of wealth and luxury until one day he met a beggar, an old man, and one who was dead. His eyes were opened to the harshness of life, and he left his home to ponder the meaning of suffering. He became enlightened after meditating under a sacred *boda* tree and subsequently taught what he had come to understand.

His Four Noble Truths are as follows:

- To exist is to suffer.
- Suffering is caused by desire, which is never satisfied completely.
- Suffering stops when desire ceases.
- The Noble Eightfold Path is the way to end desire and thus suffering.

Buddhism offers passive resistance to suffering, when viewed from action-oriented thinkers. Desire and ambition are positive in many Western cultures, not the cause of suffering.

The Eightfold Path outlines ethical behavior that avoids evil and violence and contemplates the transitoriness of the body. Meditation is the complete concentration of the mind on a single thought to achieve freedom from desire and finally freedom from sensation.

Buddhism was originally a reformation movement within Hinduism. It interprets one of the ideas of Hinduism, *karma,* to mean the inevitable result of behavior in an ethical cause-and-effect sequence. Good deeds generate good karma; bad deeds generate bad karma. Good karma and bad karma are the results one experiences not only in this life but in subsequent lives as well. Gautama taught that the end of the cycle of rebirths is *nibbana,* similar to the Hindu nirvana, except that it is a state of nothingness beyond creation. Individuals merge themselves with it in a final nonbeing. That is ultimately the end of suffering.

Buddhism has two great subdivisions: Theravada and Mahayana. Theravada ("teaching of the elders") Buddhism is based on scripture, and believers do not practice any other religion mixed in with Buddhism. It tends to be prevalent in South and Southeast Asia. Countries that practice Theravada Buddhism include Sri Lanka, Cambodia, Thailand, Laos, Burma, and Vietnam.

Mahayana Buddhists generally live in East Asia. *Mahayana* means "the greater vehicle," meaning that Gautama intended his teachings to include other ways as well. These people observe other religions along with Buddhism. Mahayana Buddhism is found in China, Nepal, Mongolia, Korea, and Japan. In China, Buddhist priests often share their temples with Daoist priests. In Korea, Buddhism and Confucianism are practiced together. In Japan, Zen Buddhism and Shintoism are both practiced by most people, but they worship in Buddhist temples and in Shinto shrines—not in the same temple. In Taiwan, Buddhism includes observances from Daoism, Confucianism, and animism.

In some Buddhist cultures, such as Thailand's Theravada Buddhism, strict observances have an impact on business life. Men become monks for some period of their lives, usually before entering the workforce. Women must never come in physical contact with monks or their robes but daily offer rice and other food to gain merit. Monks may be influential in decisions that affect local businesses in areas such as labor and wages, locations for new businesses, and markets. Theravada Buddhism emphasizes learning not to desire things, and this can be contrary to a market economy. Yet many countries with Buddhist followers—Thailand, Taiwan, Japan, and South Korea—became economic dynamos in the early 1990s.

Hinduism and Buddhism are both polytheistic religions—that is, more than one god is worshipped—although the emphasis on specific deities varies from one geographic region to another. In contrast, three other major world religions are monotheistic; worshippers pray to only one god.

Judaism is the religion of the Jews. It began before 1200 B.C. and is the basis or context for the development of both Christianity and Islam. The Christian Bible contains the 39 "books" or separate writings, called the Old Testament, that make up Judaism's sacred scripture. Most of those 39 books were written originally in Hebrew. The first five books together are called the Torah. Another important document is the Talmud, made up of the Mishna (which deals with the legal component of the Jewish oral tradition) and the Gemara (a commentary on the Mishna by Jewish scholars over the centuries). Both written and oral texts are the basis of the practice of Judaism. Practice means following the rules and holy laws.

Most Jews share certain beliefs. Among these are beliefs in

- One God
- God's concern for humans
- The concern that one person should show for another
- The covenant, an agreement between God and the people of Israel expressed through God's laws for the proper use of the universe
- Belief in the world to come or in the Messiah or the Messianic Age.
  Jews who participate in religious observances also share
- Jewish practices
- Jewish holy days and the Jewish calendar

Finally, those who in any way identify themselves as Jews share the long chain of tradition that is the history of the Jewish people.

Judaism today is divided into four modern religious movements represented by synagogue membership: Orthodox, Reform, Conservative, and Reconstructionist. A small percentage of Jews identify with more conservative movements (such as Hasidism) that had their origins in 18th-century Europe. A large percentage of Jews worldwide identify themselves as Jewish even though they belong to no movement; some of them join synagogues from time to time, but others prefer to remain "secular" for ideological reasons. Mixed among both secular and synagogue- based Jews, there are others who center their Jewish identity on Zionism, the movement to create and sustain a Jewish homeland in Israel.

No matter what beliefs a Jew subscribes to, there is a sense of solidarity among Jews that is born of the recognition that Jews share a common history, heritage, language, and culture. They also feel themselves to be a community. The Talmud expressed its recognition of this commonality in a positive statement, "All Jews are responsible one for another." This captures the Jewish value called *Klal Yisrael*, the "Community of Israel."

Christianity is the faith of a plurality of the world's population—2 billion in the year 2000—but Christians are divided into several major branches: Catholicism, Protestantism, and Orthodoxism. Roman Catholics are the largest body. They emphasize the authority of the Roman Catholic Church in a centralized, hierarchical system. Jesus, the Son of God as well as the Son of Man, born of a woman, Mary, is held to be the advocate for the individual with God. Apart from this advocacy (or that of his Mother) and observation of the sacramental rites of the Church, there is no salvation. Priests carry out the sacraments. Protestants differ from Catholics in that they hold that Jesus alone is the mediator by grace, and that individuals must have direct and personal access to Jesus.

Christians believe in one God. Jesus is claimed by believers to have been God incarnate in a historical person who was an itinerant teacher in Judea, Sumaria, and Galilee (present-day Israel). He spoke about God as Father and about himself as the Son of God. Jesus was born during the Roman occupation of the area and was put to death by the Roman powers with the cooperation of the local governor and religious leaders. His death was not the end, however; after three days in a tomb, according to Biblical accounts, Jesus appeared and walked among people who knew him, then was taken up into heaven. He claimed to have eternal life and furthermore to offer eternal life to believers. The resurrection of Jesus is what Christians celebrate at Easter, the holiest event of the Christian year. Christianity is based on the teachings of Jesus and of interpreters of those teachings.

The Catholic Church, centered in Rome, historically had large economic interests but discouraged its priests from involvement in business. Individuals in religious orders usually renounce personal economic and business endeavors. The Protestant Reformation emphasized the lack of distinction between religious and secular life, and thus the way was opened for the merging of the pursuit of financial goals with spiritual goals.

The concept of predestination, which is prominent in some Protestant sects, holds that the elect or chosen individuals are the ones who receive the gift of grace. Some historians see the linkage of material prosperity to the elect as a visible sign of God's blessing, as the linkage that made the development of capitalism possible and even pious. Wealth came to be taken as a sign of God's approval and blessing. If God's approval rested on you, you worked hard and became wealthy. Wealth wasn't to be spent on self-indulgence, however. Along with the notion of gaining riches went the notion of not spending wealth but rather saving and investing it—in other words, creating capital. Capitalism grew in that environment.

Orthodox Christianity refers to the branches of the Christian movement that developed early in the Middle East and in Eastern Europe and Russia, whereas to the west, Catholicism had its center in Rome. Orthodox Christianity has three branches. Orthodoxy is distinguished by a traditional and highly formalized order of worship called the Divine Liturgy. Emphasis in Orthodoxy today remains on the priesthood, which is considered to have continued in an unbroken tradition from the earliest apostles who were the disciples of Jesus.

Islam has approximately as many adherents as Hinduism and Buddhism combined.[25] Muslims live in countries all over the world, and Islam is the dominant religion in 19 nations. Islam began with the prophet Mohammed, who in about 610 started to receive revelations from God dictated by the Archangel Gabriel. He delivered the revelations to Arabs in Mecca through preaching, and later he preached in Medina. (His withdrawal from Mecca to Medina is called the *hegira*.) Many of the revelations or *suras* (chapters) were memorized by professional reciters. Mohammed was illiterate, but the *suras* eventually were written down in the language in which Mohammed had received them: Arabic. The collection of written revelations is the *Qur'an*, which represents the revealed word of God to Muslims; God is the author. Islam spread rapidly through military conquest for 200 years. Part of its appeal, besides the imperative of the sword, was and continues to be its undiscriminating and equal embrace of members of all races and ethnicities. It is the fastest growing religion in the United States.

Islam means "to submit," and *Muslim* means "submitting" or "obeying." A believer submits to the word of God as it was transmitted through the Prophet Mohammed. In Muslim countries perhaps the most common phrase is *Inshallah*, meaning "the will of God be done." A fundamental belief in Islam is that everything, good or bad, proceeds from the will of God. Islam affects every aspect of daily life through the *Sharia*, legal and religious precepts that cover the totality of religious, political, social, domestic, and private life. Iran and Libya follow the Sharia in their courts of law.

Islam is practiced differently in different countries. For example, Muslims in Indonesia, Malaysia, Turkey, Egypt, Saudi Arabia, and Tunisia differ from one another in some behaviors while remaining obedient to the precepts of the *Qur'an*. Recent international events have made Islam more than ever a subject of discussion, study, and articles in the popular press. There is an increased need for understanding the distinctions among Muslim communities throughout the world and for accuracy of information.

The Five Pillars of Islam are

- *Shahadah*, or the profession of the faith. This is summed up in the creed: "There is no god but God, and Mohammed is his prophet."
- Salah, or worship. Islam requires prayer five times a day. Worshippers face Mecca, the holy city, and pray in Arabic. The most important prayer time is noon on Friday, when males are required to attend the mosque.
- Zakat, or alms giving. Mohammed was an orphan, and Muslims are urged to give generously to the poor.
- Sawm, or fasting. The month of Ramadan, the ninth month of the Muslim calendar, entails 30 days of fasting from sunrise to sunset.
- Haj, or pilgrimage. Every adult who can afford it is required to visit Mecca once. Pilgrimage occurs during the 12th month of the Muslim calendar.

Some Western business practices are contrary to the precepts of Islam. Islamic countries continue to sort out behavior that is consonant with Islamic principles but also in keeping with profitable business. For example, Muslims are not supposed to charge interest or pay interest on loans. By receiving guaranteed interest, an individual gets a reward without working for it, and that is prohibited.[26] A return on the deposit is acceptable only if the individual works for the return, or if the profit or loss is shared with all depositors. This has given rise to Islamic banking, in which profit and loss sharing replaces interest earning and speculation. Another different business practice concerns insurance. Since the will of Allah is omnipotent, Muslims who carry insurance policies risk being accused of lack of devotion or even defiance of Allah's will. In Western countries, Muslims' daily prayers may be at odds with business schedules; in Muslim countries, Westerners are often out of step with the prayer schedules.

Just as Buddhism and Christianity have branches, so does Islam: Sunni and Shia. Their difference is based on their attitudes toward the rightful heir to Mohammed's power. Sunnis—who won a majority of followers—claimed it should be disciples, and Shiites claimed it should be a nephew of Mohammed. Shiites are dominant in Iran and eastern Iraq and are a powerful minority in other countries. They are for reviving fundamental principles of Islam and against compromising Islam with modern cultures.

The role of religion in people's lives is something businesspeople need to know about. Most cultures have some procedure for young people to learn about their family's religion. Children in Catholic homes have their first communion at about seven years of age. Protestant children in mainline denominations are accepted as members into a church as teenagers (in some Protestant churches adult members are received upon baptism). Jewish offspring have bar mitzvahs and bat mitzvahs at the age of religious responsibility, usually thirteen. In Thailand, every male is expected to spend some time as a Buddhist monk, usually for six months to two years, after completing his education and before getting married and establishing a family.

One way religion affects people's lives is in the special days of observance or celebration. Business travelers need to be aware of religious holidays in other cultures. Friday is Muslims' holy day; Saturday is the Sabbath of Jews. Sunday, the holy day of Christians, may mean that stores and places of business are closed. Ramadan, the ninth month of the Islamic year, is a month of fasting from sunrise to sunset—not the time to invite a business colleague to lunch.

The new year begins for Buddhists on the first new moon of the lunar year, any time from late January to mid-February, and usually involves several days' closure of businesses. (But Thailand, the most Buddhist nation in the world, also celebrates the new year in April.) In China, the Buddhist lunar new year has been replaced by Spring Festival, which takes place at the same time, the first new moon of the first month of the lunar calendar. The festival in China is a national holiday that usually lasts a week, when many factories close down and the transportation systems are overloaded with travelers. Obviously, a business visitor to another country needs to find out when that nation's holidays are and when people will be available to meet in order to plan an effective visit.

Businesspeople also need to be very careful not to make assumptions based on stereotypes about other religions. Whether welcoming a new employee or investigating the possibility of a business operation abroad, businesspeople need to keep their minds open and their inquiries gentle.

HOW IS TIME UNDERSTOOD, MEASURED, AND KEPT?

Another value orientation that has to do with *big* questions concerns a culture's view of time. Traditional cultures think of time as cyclical. The rhythms of nature and the cosmos dictate this view: Day yields to night, which in turn yields to day again; rain follows dry periods that come after rain; the time to plant leads to the time to nurture, then the time to harvest and the time plants die. Everything follows a pattern of birth, life, death, and renewal—even daily activity, after which the weary body sleeps and wakes refreshed. Within the cyclical framework, events that occur take as long as they take; their duration is dictated by their essential nature. This view is common among agrarian cultures whose

"Time is money." "Save time." "Spend time." "Use time wisely; don't waste time." "Make time." "Take your time." These are some of the phrases we commonly use that underscore the value of time as something to be bought and sold. Employees sell their time to an organization and are paid for their time. Lawyers and consultants of all stripes bill clients for their time. Workers talk about doing something on the company's time versus doing it on one's own "free" time. Telecommuting employees who work at home using a computer modem say "my time is my own," suggesting that they "own" their work schedules and can work when they please, not only when the organization's doors are open to the public. The opposite case is an employee whose hours are "owned" by the organization.

members are closely attuned to the rhythms of cultivation. The corn will be ripe when it has finished ripening, in its own time. It is also persistent in cultures that value human interaction and relationships.

Monastic life in the Middle Ages often is credited with the development of a notion of time as modern European and American cultures know it. The monks needed to regulate their prayers as a community. If everyone woke up later one day and earlier the next, the community's prayer life would be undisciplined and other activities would be erratic. Monasteries began ringing bells to maintain a scheduled, ordered life. An idea took shape: to measure something abstract, intangible, and defined however you wanted to define it, called *time*. Time could be given an identity and then segmented into component parts. Monks gave the segments names, such as *none* (noon, the fifth canonical hour and mid-afternoon prayer) and *compline* (the seventh and last of the canonical hours and evening prayer).

European monks weren't the only ones to try to measure time; Mayan priests had been doing it in Mexico, Guatemala, and Belize for a thousand years. Measuring instruments became more precise as navigational needs grew in Europe and as astronomy developed. By the 18th century, the instruments used to measure time and the movement of planets seemed able to reveal the secrets of the clockwork universe, and time became a commodity.

What does it mean to be "on time"? The definition of punctuality varies from culture to culture. The cultural priority of time has close links to another priority: relationships versus results. When people are important and the nurturing of relationships matters, the time necessary for nurturing activities is flexible.

You may have an appointment in Puerto Rico for 10:30 in the morning; you may be the second appointment on the other person's agenda, and you can still be waiting at 11:30. Everybody is so important that no meeting can be rushed for the sake of a schedule that is imposed arbitrarily. In São Paulo, Brazil traffic snarls often delay people from arriving on time at meetings, and although an apology is expected, lateness is not considered an insult. Both Puerto Rico and Brazil have strong orientations toward building relationships to do business effectively.

In results-oriented cultures, adherence to schedules is much more important. In Israel, for example, promptness is a basic courtesy as well as an indication of seriousness about work. In Russia, time is not related to cost or profits, and punctuality—being "on time"— is an alien concept: "Russians are notoriously not on time, and they think nothing of arriving long after the appointed hour, which is not considered as being late."[27]

What does effective use of time mean? As we discussed earlier, results-oriented cultures tend to use a cause-and-effect pattern to understand something and use planning to control uncertainty. These cultures also have a linear view of time; after all, a cause-and-effect sequence unfolds in time from the generation of something to its results. People who view time as a highway progressing from the past into the future also tend to believe that the past is background and preparation for the present. They think the present will be the basis for the future. Time is used effectively when goals can be accomplished speedily. They are very different from people who see cyclical patterns that repeat themselves.

People who view time as linear, and as divisible into chunks that have a market value, measure time in relatively short periods: minutes, hours, and days. In cultures in which time is expansive, measurements are in weeks and months, as in Russia, where patience has a high priority.

Time can be monochronic (one-dimensional time) or polychronic (multidimensional time).[28] Monochronic time is linear. People are expected to arrive at work on time and work for a certain number of hours at certain activities. Then, after resting for an appointed period, they are expected to resume work activities. In some monochronic organizations, being even a few minutes off schedule is not acceptable.

In polychronic cultures, time is an open-ended resource that is not to be constrained. Context sets the pace and rhythm, not the clock. Events take as long as they need to take; communication does not have to conclude according to the clock or arrive at a closure of the business at hand. Different activities have different clocks. The idea of monochronic or polychronic time can be related to a previously examined cultural dimension: whether tasks are done serially or sequentially. Monochronic cultures do one thing at a time. Polychronic cultures have several time-schemes running simultaneously; people in these cultures can be observed doing more than one thing at a time to accommodate more than one clock. Modern multitasking is also doing several things at the same time, and is talked about primarily in monochronic cultures. It occurs because of the value of efficiency and timesaving—the idea of being able to manage time effectively. This isn't the same as a polychronic approach, where doing more than one thing at a time occurs because that is how activities unfold. Polychronicity isn't planned and managed.

IS CHANGE POSITIVE OR NEGATIVE?

The culture of the United States thinks of change as desirable and positive. At the nation's founding, the *new* was thought to be better than the old. In advertising slogans today, new means *better* products and services. Change means moving forward in linear time toward ever more desirable achievements. The business culture of the United States puts a high priority on the accomplishment of goals, the accumulation of wealth, the efficient use of time to do this, and a positivism that claims that tomorrow will be better than today just as today is better than yesterday. When change has a high priority, the members of a culture express optimism about the future.

Traditionally, agrarian cultures typically view change in the opposite way. Since people who live on the land cannot move away and take their land with them, they tend to develop stable, static communities. They see the cycles of planting and harvest, rain and sun, day and night at a very close view. They also think of change as negative. It means disruption to the established patterns of life. They believe that yesterday was better than today and tomorrow will be worse than today. Products that call themselves *new* are not to be trusted.

Russians, for example, view change as negative. Russians expect things to be bad in the present and worse in the future, and in part this is a posture that enables them to face change and uncertainty stoically. There is justification for pessimism. After all, historically the "best and brightest have traditionally been banished. In Old Russia, independent thinkers were exiled to Siberia . . . Stalin's purges of the 1930s further decimated the intelligentsia, and today many of Russia's best are being lost through emigration."[29] Endurance is one of Russian culture's top priorities.

Clearly, the priority involving change has a close connection with an earlier one: uncertainty avoidance. Change always involves uncertainty about what will result, and cultures that view change negatively are typically keen to avoid uncertainty. The old ways are best; the familiar is trustworthy even when it is known to have faults. Yesterday is often endowed with a golden glow and thought of as superior to today; the past may come again one day if things stabilize, and we may even return to the old ways. Cyclical views of time are consistent with anti-change cultures.

Cultures that are conscious of their long histories cannot easily understand severing connections to the past or wanting to do so. Businesspeople from younger cultures such as the United States or Australia are often impatient with the clinging to old ways that they observe in other cultures. They operate with cause-and-effect logic and see that to accomplish a particular goal (an orientation they value highly) new ways (or products or procedures) are helpful. They cannot understand why others balk at adopting something new.

IS DEATH THE END OF LIFE OR PART OF LIFE?

The final priority we'll consider in this chapter for posing questions of a culture involves final things. Some cultures view death as the end of life, a quenching of the light. It is dreaded. Some cultures view death as another phase in life, a necessary step in the pattern of life. It is accepted.

Hindus believe in reincarnation, and in India's burning *ghats* bodies are cremated and sent on their journey toward another birth. People are reincarnated over and over in a cycle that can't be numbered. Your status in life is the result of how you lived a former life, and your present life will affect the next life. When a loved one dies, the loss is mourned just as it would be in Copenhagen or Cairo, but the mourners know the soul will be born again. In Russia, death is familiar; it is fought and welcomed, in a contradictory attitude. A former American foreign service officer quotes a modern Russian poet's response to his question about what Americans should know to understand Russians better:

> In our cold winter each opening of the door is a repetition of dying. Russians do not fear death because every day is a struggle. It is a pity to die, and a pity not to die.

> —Mark Davydov[30]

Death is not such an enemy as it is in the West.

In Holland, death is sometimes embraced by appointment, since doctors may legally assist terminally ill patients in dying. This enables patients to die with dignity rather than dying in slow stages with increased discomfort and perceived humiliation. There is a relationship between this death by appointment and control over the unknown; uncertainty avoidance and a preference for planning and doing correlate with this approach to death.

Many cultures have religious beliefs that teach death is the only way to join the gods or God. In Islam, life after death is freedom from obstacles to the enjoyment of God's gifts. A Muslim's heaven is experienced through the senses. A Christian also looks forward to heaven after death, to joy and an absence of pain, but the Christian heaven is less clearly defined than is the Islamic heaven. Attitudes toward dying vary widely among members of Christian cultures and among members of Islamic cultures.

Funerals also mean different things in different cultures. In Nigeria funerals are very important. Unless you are dying yourself, you are expected to attend. It is thought that the deceased will reward you for your presence. In the Māori culture of New Zealand, funerals involve a three-day observance (*tangi*). Employers recognize the need for relatives to be absent from work for this occasion. Family members sit around the departed loved one and receive visits of condolence from relatives and friends in the community. People tell stories, pray, and sing while shedding tears together. After three days the body is buried, and the community has had its relationship bonds affirmed by the experience of shared grieving.

Funerals are dreaded in Asian cultures, where even the suggestion of death or funerals is considered rude. That's why you should never give a clock or watch to a Taiwanese as a gift (a reminder of the inevitable end of one's life span) or a bell (rung in funeral ceremonies) or white flowers (white is the color of mourning). You must even avoid using the word *death*. In Hong Kong recently, many people were upset when clairvoyants charged that ghosts of dead children had appeared in TV commercials. Reminders of death are impolite at best and unlucky at worst. In Japan, it is intolerably rude to stick your chopsticks straight up in a bowl because then they resemble the incense burned at funerals.

Some take a proactive position toward death, however. In Singapore, as in other Chinese cultures, funeral objects such as televisions, cars, and money made of paper are burned to accompany the deceased into the world of the dead and to ensure a comfortable existence in the next world. In China, expensive tombs have been created, some for living people who have not yet been able to use them.

Businesspeople need to be aware of the cultural priority put on death and the observances that attend it. The expectations for how the mourning friends and relatives will act differ from culture to culture.

In many cultures, mourners wear a black armband or black clothing to signal to others that they are grieving the loss of someone and should be treated with respect. The color of mourning traditionally in China is white, however, as it is in India. (Brides in those cultures traditionally wear red.) Mourning is signaled with a white armband or rosette in some countries, and with white flowers.

Special observances besides the funeral service may include a wake or a special feast where mourners come together to solidify new social relationships without the departed one. This is true in such divergent cultures as Catholic Ireland, with its wakes, and Buddhist Taiwan. These two different cultures share characteristics common to high-context cultures, however, where the meaning of the individual is derived from the network of relationships into which an individual life is woven.

CHAPTER SUMMARY

This chapter introduced the approach of asking questions in order to understand cultures.

Asking questions involves identifying where information can be found. Answers may be general, and to be useful, they need to be generalized. Questions can be posed in five categories; the first three are Thinking and Knowing, Doing and Achieving, and the Big Picture.

The first category of questions is Thinking and Knowing, which covers the following dimensions:

- *Does knowing come from concepts or experience?* Some people truly know something only when experience has taught them; without experience, they merely know *about* something. For others, knowing comes from conceptual understanding.

- *Does learning come from asking questions or mastering received wisdom?* In many cultures, the acknowledged authority gives knowledge, and one knows when one has mastered what the textbook or teacher says. In other cultures, going beyond what one has been given is how one truly knows something.

- *Does knowledge have limits?* In some cultures, not everything is knowable. Other cultures have the idea that everything can be known if the key is found.

- *How do people reason?* Western cultures use a cause-and-effect pattern of thinking. Other cultures use different patterns. The balance of complementary opposites, as illustrated in the yin-yang symbol, is one example.

The second category of questions covers Doing and Achieving—how people understand their actions at work.

- *Is doing important or is being important?*
- *Are tasks done sequentially or simultaneously?* Some cultures view one who works efficiently as one who accomplishes several things at once. Other cultures value a one-thing-at-a-time approach as the most efficient.
- *Do results or relationships take priority?* Relationship-oriented cultures tend to be collec-

tivistic. The relationships that connect people in networks are more significant than the tasks people accomplish. Results-oriented cultures value the outcomes of actions, especially measurable outcomes, as what matters at work and in life.

- *Is uncertainty avoided or tolerated?* People who are uncomfortable with uncertainty tend to stay with their employers and follow established procedures at work. People who are able to tolerate uncertainty with lower levels of anxiety may attempt new things in their professional lives.

- *Is luck an essential factor or an irrelevance?* Luck or fate or destiny plays a large role in cultures in which people recognize that their role in achieving success has less effect than do forces outside themselves. In other cultures, outcomes are not left to luck but are considered to be largely controllable by human effort.

- *Are rules to be followed or bent?* In places where relationships are primary and power distances are great, rules may be bent to serve those more important values. In places where results matter, rules are viewed as important to facilitate results.

The last category in this chapter is The Big Picture. This section deals with the "big" questions cultures answer:

- *Do humans dominate nature or does nature dominate humans?*

- *Are divine powers or humans at the center of events?* Belief in divine beings underlies the values, behaviors, and attitudes of many people of different cultures. Two major polytheistic religions are Hinduism and Buddhism. Three other major world religions—Judaism, Christianity, and Islam—share roots and a belief in one deity.

- *How is time understood, measured, and kept?* Cultures differ in attitudes toward time and how it should be observed. Some view time as cyclical, whereas others view it as an unrolling continuous line. Some cultures treasure time as a commodity; others use it as the flexible medium in which activities take place.

- *Is change positive or negative?* New may not be positively received in traditional cultures. Old may not be a word of approval in cultures that embrace change.

- *Is death the end of life or part of life?* How death is viewed and how that view affects business varies from culture to culture.

Key Terms and Concepts

Hinduism, *228*
Buddhism, *229*
Judaism, *229*

Christianity, *230*
Islam, *231*
role of religion, *232*

Notes

1. Florence Kluckhohn and Fred Strodtbeck, *Variations in Value Orientations* (Evanston, IL: Row, Peterson, 1961); John C. Condon and Fathi Yousef, *An Introduction to Intercultural Communication* (New York: Macmillan, 1974).

2. Vern Terpstra and Kenneth David, *The Cultural Environment of International Business,* 3rd ed. (Cincinnati: South-Western, 1991), p. 13.

3. Geert Hofstede, *Culture's Consequences,* abridged ed. (Beverly Hills: Sage, 1984).

4. Geert Hofstede, *Cultures and Organizations* (New York: McGraw-Hill, 1991).

5. Fons Trompenaars, *Riding the Waves of Culture* (Burr Ridge, IL: Irwin, 1994).

6. Andre Laurent, "The Cultural Diversity of Western Conceptions of Management," *International Studies of Management and Organization,* 13, no. 1–2 (1983), pp. 75–96.

7. Edward T. Hall, *Beyond Culture* (New York: Anchor Press/ Doubleday, 1976).

8. Sheila Ramsay, "To Hear One and Understand Ten: Nonverbal Behavior in Japan." In *Intercultural Communication: A Reader,* 4th ed., Larry A. Samovar and Richard E. Porter, eds. (Belmont, CA: Wadsworth, 1985), p. 311.

9. Leon Lederman and Dick Teresi, *The God Particle: If the Universe Is the Answer, What Is the Question?* (New York: Houghton-Mifflin, 1993).

10. Ed Schwortz, www.shroud.com, retrieved on July 24, 2006.

11. Robert B. Kaplan, "Writing in a Multilingual/Multicultural Context: What's Contrastive about Contrastive Rhetoric?" *The Writing Instructor,* 10, no. 7 (1990), p. 10.

12. Barbara Johnstone, *Repetition in Arabic Discourse* (Philadelphia: John Benjamins, 1991).

13. Linda Beamer, "Toasts: Rhetoric and Ritual in Business Negotiation in Confucian Cultures," *Business Forum* (Winter 1994), pp. 22–25.

14. Colin E. Tweddell and Linda Amy Kimball, *Introduction to the Peoples and Cultures of Asia* (Englewood Cliffs, NJ: Prentice-Hall, 1985), pp. 319–320.

15. Roderick McLeod, *China Inc.: How to do Business with the Chinese* (New York: Bantam Books, 1988), p. 72.

16. Richard Nisbett, *The Geography of Thought* (New York: Free Press, 2003).

17. Yale Richmond, *From Nyet to Da: Understanding the Russians* (Yarmouth, ME: Intercultural Press, 1992), p. 45.

18. Condon and Yousef, p. 137.

19. *Culturgrams,* Vol. II (Provo, UT: Brigham Young University, 1984).

20. Margaret Lyons, "Australia: Jyotek Sets Up Local Office," *Business Review Weekly,* 21 (June 1991), p. 46.

21. Mike Clowes, "Superstition Extends Yet to Top Levels," *Pensions & Investments,* 15 (April 1991), p. 14.

22. Genesis 1:29–30, rev. ed.

23. Terpstra and David, p. 136.

24. Ibid., p. 83.

25. A. L. M. Abdul Gafoor, "Islamic Banking." In *Interest-Free Commercial Banking* (1995), http://users.bart.nl/abdul/ chap4.html, retrieved on June 7, 2003.

26. The following discussion is adapted from Terpstra and David, pp. 89–94.

27. Richmond, p. 122.

28. Edward T. Hall, *The Silent Language* (New York: Doubleday, 1959).

29. Richmond, p. 43.

30. Ibid., p. 40.

Intercultural Negotiation

LEARNING OBJECTIVES

After completing this chapter, you should be able to:

 LO¹ Understand how knowledge of culture helps in negotiation.

LO² Understand the role of a member of negotiating team and how to succeed in negotiation.

 LO³ Negotiate with other culture.

Two Canadians representing Canwall, a manufacturer of wallpaper printing equipment, went to a town north of Shanghai in the province of Jiangsu, China, to negotiate a sale to a new wallpaper production company. Charlie Burton, the president of Canwall, was traveling with his Marketing Director, Phil Raines. The company had never before sold its equipment outside Canada, and the two Canadians were delighted with the warm reception they enjoyed in China.

This wasn't the first meeting between the Canadian company and the Chinese wallpaper factory. The manager of the Chinese company, Mr. Li, had been a member of a delegation to Canada. He had met with one of Canwall's senior salespersons and the director of manufacturing. Subsequently, a trade representative from Canada had been in China representing Canwall's interests to the Chinese manager. After those meetings and numerous letters and faxes, Canwall's top people were now ready to negotiate the sale.

The day they arrived they were met at the airport in Shanghai by Manager Li himself, and transported in a chauffer-driven car 90 miles to the town. Their accommodation was in a newly built hotel. A few hours after their arrival they were treated to a 12-course banquet given by their host, with several high-level municipal officials present. This red-carpet treatment made them feel optimistic about the sale.

The next day, they were taken to see the sights nearby: a large port for container ships and several factories that indicated the prosperity of the region. They were eager to begin discussing the sale, but after lunch they were given time to rest. In the late afternoon, one of the manager's English-speaking employees came by with news that they would be taken to see a local dance company's performance that night.

On the third day, they finally sat down to meetings. Progress seemed very slow, with each side giving generalizations about itself that seemed to the Canadians to be unrelated to the sale. They used an interpreter supplied by the Chinese, who was eager to please them, so the Canadians felt comfortable with her, but translation slowed down communication.

The Chinese also spent a lot of time talking about the Canadian trade agent who had been in their town earlier and asking about him. Burton wasn't able to tell them much about that person since he had never met him.

When the Canadians at last were able to make the presentation they had prepared, they were surprised at the number of people who showed up: ten Chinese faced them across the table. The Canadians were a bit disconcerted when several people at different times answered mobile phone calls, without leaving the room and without apologies. Still, the Chinese frequently nodded and smiled and said "yes." Burton and Raines had prepared sales data and showed, effectively they thought, that within five years the factory could double its current production. At the end of the day, the jubilant Canadians returned to their hotel rooms confident they had sold the equipment.

The next day, they were asked to explain once again things they thought had been covered already to a Chinese team with four new faces in it. They were confused about who their negotiating counterparts really were. Their jubilation began to evaporate. They were asked to explain the technology in minute detail. Neither Burton nor Raines had been involved in the engineering of the high-tech component that was the heart of the equipment. After doing the best they could, they returned to the hotel exhausted.

Their interpreter also seemed to be unfamiliar with technological terms, since she and the interpreter for the factory spent some time discussing the terms between themselves. Because the Canadians' interpreter was a woman, they had to meet with her in the hotel lobby to discuss their plan for the next day. The two tired men would have preferred to sit in their room while they talked with her, rather than in the noisy lobby where they were the object of curiosity, but she requested they remain in a public place because as a woman she could not meet with them in their room.

The next day one member of the first-day Chinese team pointed out discrepancies between what they had said and what the manufacturing director, an engineer, had told them in Canada. Burton and Raines were chagrined. The Chinese were reproachful about the discrepancies, as if the Canadians had been caught out. At lunch, the two Canadians quickly faxed Canada for specifications and explanations. The afternoon session was uncomfortable, although everyone was polite. Burton and Raines were a bit unsettled when a middle-aged woman suddenly burst into the negotiating room and whispered in the ear of one of the key Chinese speakers, who immediately got up and left the room. The Canadians expected some explanation for the emergency, but none ever came.

The Canadians didn't receive some of the documentation they needed by fax until the following day, because of the time difference. Discussions resumed with the same questions being asked yet again. It all went very slowly. The Chinese appreciated the high quality of the Canadian product but worried they wouldn't be able to fix the equipment if it broke down. They suggested—delicately, to avoid implying that they *expected* breakdowns—that perhaps the Canadians could give them some help with maintenance training. The Canadians pointed out the expense and difficulty of keeping someone in their city for several weeks or months and expressed confidence that there wouldn't be any problems the manual didn't cover. They confidently asserted that Chinese would be able to look after the equipment just fine.

Finally, the technical discussions gave way to the issue central to most business negotiations: price. This proved to be the most difficult of all. The Chinese began by asking for a 20-percent price discount. The Canadians thought this was simply an outrageous negotiating ploy; they stuck to their price, which they knew to be fair, and offered a 3-percent discount on the printing cylinders.

Although Burton and Raines had heard that negotiations took time in China, they had thought a week would be ample. Now time was running out, and they were due in Beijing in two days. The Canadians began to ask pointed questions about what the Chinese were unhappy with and where they needed to go over issues again. During the last two sessions, the Canadians tried to get the Chinese to focus on the unresolved points, but the Chinese seemed reluctant to do so.

Things were still unresolved when the farewell banquet was held the following noon. The question of price seemed near solution, but not the method of payment. That was the final, apparently insurmountable hurdle, since the Chinese couldn't guarantee the payment schedule; it seemed tied to deadlines and requirements of the municipal officials. Nevertheless, Manager Li smiled and spoke of mutual cooperation for the future, and past Chinese–Canadian relations, and the great amount he and his factory could learn from the Canadians. They signed an expanded version of the letter of intent that had been signed nine months earlier in Canada. The Canadians left disappointed but with expressions on both sides of willingness to continue to discuss the sale by mail and fax.

The Canadians were stunned to learn two weeks later that the factory had decided to buy from a Japanese equipment manufacturer. They knew their product was good and their price was fair. What had happened to derail their sale?

Negotiating is a special communication task. It occurs when two or more parties have common interests and therefore have a reason to work together, but who also have conflicts about their goals and how to accomplish them. Negotiation is the communication that takes place in order to reach agreement about how to handle both common and conflicting interests between two or more parties. Negotiation always has an element of persuasion in it.

Negotiating "how-to" books abound. Some authorities on negotiation claim cultural difference is only one of many factors and may boil down to being "simply differences in style and language."[1] But this view assumes that negotiating *skills* are value-free and are the same around the world, like the rules of chess for opening moves, middle game, and endgame.

One interculturalist has this to say about negotiation:

> In the USA several books have appeared on the art of negotiation; it is a popular theme for training courses. Negotiations have even been simulated in computer programs, which use a mathematical theory of games to calculate the optimal choice in a negotiation situation. These approaches are largely irrelevant.[2]

This critical view comes from the author's observation that the books and simulation games are based on the assumption that both sides have the values of the United States. Raymond Cohen refers to the "instrumental and manipulative" style of negotiators from the United States.[3]

Not only does this view mistakenly discount the role of culture in framing the priorities of negotiators, it also overlooks what happens when people from different cultures interact. The *interaction* produces an intercultural communication situation that is the product of both cultures and of the personalities of both teams, which we call *transactional culture*.

Culture tells negotiators what is important, and enables them to assign meaning to the other side's communication and guess at their motives. Cultural intelligence (CQ) enables negotiators to behave appropriately to the members of the other culture. Therefore, to negotiate effectively, intercultural negotiators not only need special communication skills, they also need to understand both their own and the other team's culture. They need to be able to switch from behavior they use in their own culture to the behavior that will be most appropriate for another culture.

WHAT *REALLY* HAPPENED WITH CANWALL IN CHINA?

What happened with Canwall in China was a combination of cultural factors that worked against the Canadians, some within their control and some outside their control. Here are a few of the reasons for the outcome of this episode.

Chinese Emphasis on Relationships

First, the Chinese felt they had already formed a relationship with the Canadian firm because they earlier had formed a relationship with the trade representative. But Burton and Raines, who came to negotiate the sale, were new to them and didn't seem to know the trade agent very well. The trade representative had actually been an agent who represented a number of Canadian light industry manufacturers, not a Canwall employee. The Chinese also had developed a relationship with a salesperson and the director of manufacturing of Canwall. They were disconcerted by having to develop new relationships from the beginning, all over again. But the Canadians typically used lower-level people for preliminary discussions where technical details were ironed out and then sent in their top-level people to sign the contract.

Canadian Expectations about Time and Efficiency

The two Canadians had expected a much faster pace of negotiating and had not expected to spend so much time eating, resting, and sight-seeing. After all, their product was familiar to the Chinese, and it was a good product, fairly priced. They had looked forward to ironing out any wrinkles about payment and schedules and concluding the sale in three or four days. In fact, Charlie Burton had worried they'd have time on their hands after the contract was signed. The Chinese, however, wanted to get to know these two men they hadn't previously met. Also, Manager Li had to make sure the Communist party secretary of the municipality would support his purchase from overseas; the party secretary and other government party officials had to be kept informed and also had to get to know these new Canwall people.

Differences in Negotiating Style

The Chinese began with generalities about their factory and the local government's successes. This was done to create a context for the negotiation at hand, but it seemed inconsequential to Burton and Raines. On the other hand, the Canadian presentation of specific data, moving to generalized projections, seemed rushed and incomplete to the Chinese.

The Chinese spent a long time on the technical specifications of the equipment partly because they wanted to learn how it was made and partly because they wanted to be sure they were being given accurate information. When Burton fudged a bit on the details (with which he was unfamiliar), the Chinese suspected he was trying to deceive them. It took a lot of time to undo the loss of trust and to verify the true information with the faxed documents. The Chinese were painfully conscious of being perceived to be lagging behind in the latest technology, and their sense of national honor made them determined to show China's technological savvy.

Once the negotiations were well under way, the Canadians focused on points of contention that remained unresolved; the Chinese preferred to focus on what had already been agreed. The Canadians found the Chinese slow and unwilling to be specific about the outstanding problems; the Chinese found the Canadians assertive and too absorbed with the negative, unresolved conflicts.

Differences in Ranking Issues to Be Negotiated

Price   The Chinese had determined that the Canadians were more advanced in their technology and wealthier in their resources. Furthermore, sensible price negotiations meant getting a good price. The Canadians should be more generous in their terms since they were dealing with a less-developed country. Negotiations between Chinese and foreign companies routinely involved asking for price concessions and getting them. Li's purchase costs were market-driven, not state-determined as in earlier decades, but Li was not very experienced at costing out his expenses or profit. He was not able to rely absolutely on the stability of his financing arrangements. So his inflated opening price gave him a comfortable margin.

During negotiations, the Chinese had also reminded the Canadians that other manufacturers—notably the Japanese—could undercut the Canadian price; however, the Canadians responded, with some chagrin, that their industry was not subsidized by their government in the way Japanese industries were. They were touchy about that fact (and their bargaining position as a consequence of it) within the global field of competitors.

Payment Schedule   The issue of the payment schedule was thorny. The Chinese manager wanted some leeway so he could make the most of his capital. He was wary about being taken advantage of.

Attitudes toward the Relationship   The Chinese also welcomed a chance to form a relationship that they could pursue further. For them, the relationship was still "on" even if in a dormant period. They were well aware of the high quality of the Canadian equipment but were happy to do business with the lowest-priced supplier of quality equipment. The Canadians, for their part, felt that when they lost the sale, they had lost their chance in China, after spending considerable time and money to chase it. For them the deal was dead.

Factors that Determined the Deal

The week after the Canadians left, a Japanese manufacturer's representative made his third visit to Manager Li's operation. He was authorized to offer a lower price on the equipment than the Canadians; his price on pattern-printing cylinders was higher, however. He also offered to have a company employee stay in the town for four months and train Chinese employees in the maintenance of the equipment. The Chinese manager felt this was a better deal, although he also looked forward to future negotiations with the Canadians. The Chinese party secretary, who also had his own personal agenda to consider, sent up to the provincial government a report on the manager's decision to buy the Japanese equipment at the lower price. This enhanced his personal standing as a shrewd negotiator. He didn't mention the higher price of the pattern cylinders.

Pattern cylinders were the costliest part of the equipment. Since Li wanted his firm to produce more than one pattern, his expense in the end was no lower than it would have been with the Canadian product. (Subsequently, Li felt he had not negotiated well with the Japanese because the pattern cylinders had to be replaced more frequently than originally planned.)

As for the maintenance issue, the Japanese firm was happy to supply someone to teach the Chinese how to maintain and troubleshoot the equipment. They planned to keep this trainer in China in order to learn about other market possibilities. Of course, the distance from Jiangsu to Japan is about one-fifteenth the distance to the Canwall head office. The Japanese employee could go home frequently, whereas for a Canadian such travel would be very costly.

HOW KNOWLEDGE OF CULTURE CAN HELP

This case illustrates a number of negotiation strategy differences and expectations at work. All interactions with other cultures are more likely to succeed when you know something about the other culture's strategy differences and expectations. You have to identify cultural factors, consider the best way to organize and structure the negotiation communication and how best to persuade, take into account the nonverbal and behavioral signals involved, and considered the way decisions are made, information is collected, and problems are solved in the other culture. The negotiation communication task requires knowledge about the company and the industry, about the culture, about processes for decision making, about communication preferences, and the ability to enact this knowledge. Good negotiators are people with high CQs.

For instance, the Canadians could have kept in mind that the Chinese value **relationships** as much as results. They are disconcerted when people they have entered into relationships with suddenly disappear, like the agent they mistakenly thought was closely tied to Canwall. The Chinese expect to spend **time** developing the links that knit individuals into webs of relationships. Guests are treated to sight-seeing jaunts and special dinners and entertainment in order to give the Chinese a chance to share some experiences with them and chat informally. They want to cultivate a sense of friendship and, with it, obligation. Then they will pursue their goals by appealing to the **obligation** of friendship.

Relationships need a context in which to flourish, so the Chinese spent time giving background information and reminding the Canadians of historical China–Canada ties. Their value of **harmony** in group interactions means they prefer to focus on the things that already have been agreed upon rather than on conflicts that remain unresolved. They are careful to **avoid displays of anger** or express criticism that might cause **loss of face** for the other side. However, they are masterful at using **shame,** which only works when one side can be alleged to be guilty of misconduct that jeopardizes negotiations. Pointing out the inconsistencies in the specifications was a way of causing the Canadians shame and thereby moving the Canadians to a weaker negotiating position. (The Canadians, however, missed this maneuver, so it didn't produce shame or concessions.)

In negotiations, the Chinese often dwell at length on technical details. They want to understand the technology; they also want to be sure they are being told the same thing each time. Since in general the Chinese do **not use question asking as a primary**

learning method the way Westerners do, they often ask questions in order to verify the accuracy of what they have been told, as much as to find out something they have not understood. Asking questions is also a way to get to know someone, to develop an understanding of someone, and build a relationship.

The Chinese **perform tasks simultaneously;** a mobile telephone call may be taken by someone on the negotiating team (since Chinese mobile phones are rarely turned off) who disappears and then reappears without explanation. The Canadians viewed this as a most unusual interruption—either a sign of their low status in the eyes of the Chinese or, more probably, an indication of an emergency of grave importance—but that is because Canadians tend to do tasks sequentially, devoting their entire attention to only one thing at a time.

The Chinese have a **preference for form** in negotiations or, in other words, for following a specific protocol. This usually means that the opening discussion will be very formally conducted. The host side will first describe themselves—who they are and what they do—with many statistics. Then they will expect the guests (in this case, the Canadians) to do the same. None of this has any real relevance to the issue being negotiated, but this form is important. The preference for form and correct manner—which preserves the harmony mentioned earlier—provides the context within which the negotiations will take place.

The most important person on the negotiating team from the Chinese perspective is the one who is most **senior in age;** this is a key, along with membership in the Chinese Communist party, to the **hierarchy** of the Chinese workplace. The key persons on the Chinese team may not be much in evidence during the negotiations. It will also be how the Chinese view your negotiating team.

Since **access to authority is mediated** in Chinese culture, the real decision-swaying power may not be identifiable to a foreigner. The company doing the negotiating with Canwall was government-operated, and the municipal party officials, while not determining the purchase of the wallpaper printing equipment, nevertheless were involved because their goodwill could be crucial to Manager Li. The people with the authority to make decisions—the manager, the powerful municipal officials, and the most powerful people in the factory—were no doubt all Communist party members. Their network of obligations would also have played a role. When the company is privately operated, there are also stakeholders whose approvals count.

Interdependence characterizes Chinese social organization, and the members of the Chinese team are conscious of representing a larger collective. The employees of the company, from the manager down, could spend their entire working lives in that factory. The county officials may never change jobs either. Their work colleagues are also their neighbors; many are even relatives. Even after retirement, employees are still associated with their workplace, which may provide housing, access to food and other products, health care, and many other services.

Since the Chinese value relationships and can accept failure in specific undertakings as long as the relationships are intact, they can **tolerate uncertainty** about outcomes. If success doesn't come this time, it may come the next. As long as the relationship has not been ruptured, there is always a chance for future cooperation. The Canadians viewed the loss of the sale as the end of their dealings with this factory.

Awareness of these cultural priorities can help Burton and Raines prepare for their next Chinese sale. Neither side is right or wrong; just different. But as sellers in this case, the Canadians probably need to develop more understanding of cultural priorities than the Chinese.

This chapter will now address the factors in negotiations. They include expectations for outcomes, the makeup of the team, the physical context of the negotiation, communication, and style of negotiating. A discussion of the phases of negotiation follows the factors.

Factors in Negotiation

The remainder of this chapter looks at negotiating with these aspects in mind:

- Expectations for negotiation outcomes
- Team members: makeup and motivation
- Physical factors
- Communication and negotiating style

The aim of this discussion is to show how culture affects negotiations. A number of books on *how to* negotiate exist in your own culture. Primarily, since this is a book about communication, we'll concentrate on the fourth item. But we'll examine all four aspects of negotiating, beginning with expectations for what the negotiations will accomplish.

EXPECTATIONS FOR OUTCOMES

Different Goals

Different sides of the negotiating table often seem to be after very different things. This may appear to be the result of shrewd negotiating tactics—and maybe it is—in which a side doesn't disclose openly what its goals are. You may decide the other team is craftily hiding what it wants behind some other, seemingly unimportant aims. But another reason for this obliqueness may simply be that they want something different from what you think they want. People from different cultures often are looking for different outcomes. As far as possible, you need to identify ahead of time what the probable goals of the other side are.

For example, in the case of the Chinese–Canadian negotiation, the Chinese had four goals: (1) to buy the best quality they could find at the very best world price, (2) to develop an ongoing relationship with Canwall, and (3) to learn as much as they could about Canwall's new technology. Had the contract been signed, the Chinese also would have expected (4) exclusive access to the Canadian equipment. The Canadians understood only the first of the Chinese negotiation goals. The second goal may drive the opening encounters with high-context cultures.

As high-context negotiators, the Chinese were concerned with getting a sense of the people they were dealing with.

Fairness and Advantage

As the case shows, the Chinese were interested in developing a relationship. Negotiating teams from India, Korea, Japan, Thailand, and Singapore—as well as teams from African, Middle Eastern, Latin American, and southern European cultures—usually are, too. A relationship, implies to most Asians a willingness to incur indebtedness. This may help explain the tendency among countries on the lower end of the technology scale, as illustrated in the opening case, to believe the wealthier, more advanced side should give proportionately *more* than the less advanced, less wealthy country. The less advanced team will thus be indebted to the other party in the relationship. The payback date, however, may be far into the future, since the collectivist view of relationships is that they extend for generations. The Philippines and Indonesia are among the countries today that are looking to bridge the digital divide.

North Americans and Europeans are not usually happy with an agreement that gives one side greater advantage than the other. They are accustomed to thinking of a "fair" settlement as one that evenhandedly splits advantage between the two parties. But obviously the 50–50 ideal is not shared among all cultures. As some researchers point out, the use of the English term *fair play* does not seem to be translatable into some other languages; if the term does not exist, it is likely the identical concept does not exist either.[4]

Negotiation Outcomes: Winning, Losing, and Reaching a Stalemate

Competition cultures, especially those that put a strong priority on achievement, doing, accomplishing goals through planning and taking control, and national or family honor (powerful in Middle Eastern and Korean companies, for example), look upon negotiations as situations to *win*.

Winning means not having to make concessions beyond the reserve point—the bargaining limit established by a negotiating team before the negotiations begin—in order to gain the team's objectives. Winning can also mean you have achieved an agreement in which the other side gives up more than you do.

In order to "win," a team may have to give up some wished-for things. *Compromise* is a standard expectation in bargaining and negotiation in many Western countries. The notion of fairness in these cultures means both sides have to give a bit, and the bits are equal. A good end is achieved when the compromises made by each side are about the same size. However, you may need to be careful about using the word *compromise*:

> In some cultures, such as Iran, the term *compromise* has moral connotations and implies a corrupt betrayal of principle. So it has to be kept out of your vocabulary.[5]

Russians do not view compromise as a fair and equitable conceding of position by each side:

> Russians regard compromise as a sign of weakness, a retreat from a correct and morally justified position. Russians, therefore, are great "sitters," prepared to wait out their opposite numbers in the expectation that time and Russian patience will produce more concessions from the impatient Americans.[6]

Win–Lose

To some negotiators, however, winning means more than getting everything at the terms desired; it means beating down the other party so that it has to go past its reserve point. This may involve price or schedule or marketing terms, or any of a host of issues. Or winning may mean making a small compromise but demanding a large compromise from the other side. In other words, in this outcome winning means that the other side also has to *lose*. This is sometimes called *zero-sum* negotiation.

Win–Win

Cooperation cultures—usually collectivist cultures that value relationships that are ongoing between organizations and last longer than the lifetimes of those at the negotiating table—often prefer outcomes that emphasize the advantages gained by both sides. In other words, the objectives are win–win or *non-zero-sum*. When both sides win, nobody loses face or is shamed.

The difference between a win–win outcome and compromise lies in a negotiator's focus. If the negotiator primarily thinks of his or her own team's outcome, the attitude will probably be to expect compromise: what we will gain in return for what we will have to give up. The focus is on our loss as well as our gain. If the negotiator looks at *both* his or her own team and the other team, then the attitude will probably be to expect each side to gain. The focus is on mutual gain. One of these three modes is usually what a negotiator expects: compromise, win–lose, or win–win.

Stalemate

However, negotiators sometimes have to accept a stalemate when no agreement can be reached. In this outcome, the negotiating parties walk away from the table without any agreement. Nobody enters into trade negotiations with this goal in mind. It represents a failure of the negotiation. Negotiators usually expect movement toward agreement. Occasionally, one side gains everything without giving up anything, and the other side simply agrees. In this case, rather than a failed negotiation, no negotiation has taken place. This is a simple agreement without conflicting interests. "Without common interests there is nothing to negotiate for, and without conflict there is nothing to negotiate about."[7]

Finally, fundamental advice about expectations for the outcomes of negotiation is to make sure what you are negotiating is negotiable.[8] It may *not* be negotiable because the party negotiating with you doesn't have the power or access to grant what you want, or because it doesn't exist, or because what you want simply cannot be bought or obtained.

MEMBERS OF THE NEGOTIATING TEAM

Negotiators fit one of two basic descriptors: strategic or synergistic.[9] A **strategic negotiator** is out to win and sees the process as something to be won through cleverness, competitiveness, and even deceit. This negotiator is suspicious of, and hostile toward, the other side. The style is confrontational. A **synergistic negotiator** wants to avoid confrontation and is cooperative rather than competitive. This negotiator focuses on common interests but allows opposing interests to exist even beyond the point at which agreement is possible. The style is trusting and friendly.

Members with High Status

Negotiators frequently are chosen because they are high-status members of the organization. Their presence on the team indicates the organization is serious about concluding negotiations successfully. In the case example, Canwall's president— the highest-status person in that company—led the negotiating team to China. Many firms follow the practice of having lower-level negotiators do the groundwork and then sending in top-level people to close the deal. Considerable "face" can be gained by the top-level people when a negotiation reaches a successful conclusion, but having the lower-level workers involved is also useful. A manager of a Japanese–Chinese joint venture in Shanghai told one of the authors that high-level executives and politicians had initiated that joint venture, following the successful outcome of negotiations, with great fanfare. But it was low-level employees who had to make it work. He said their valuable contributions were not solicited during the negotiation process, at a time when potential problems and conflicts could have been addressed, and their pictures were not in the news!

Including high-status members on the negotiating team is usually meant to communicate to the other team the importance of the negotiations to the organization. It can get in the way of smooth negotiating, however, unless the high-status persons are also well informed about the history of past meetings between representatives of the two negotiating sides. The top executive must be thoroughly briefed about people, interests, and previous discussions, because the other side will expect that he or she has been involved all along. In addition to information, the high-status member needs to have the same communication skills necessary for intercultural interaction that the other team members need. Status isn't enough.

The presence of a high-level person on the team also signals the authority to make a binding agreement. But some companies delegate that authority to other team members when a high-status person is not part of the team. Negotiators from the United States, for example, value efficiency—achieving goals with the smallest expenditure of time and money—more than status. Consequently, they view as wasteful the practice of sending a team to negotiate that has to keep going back to higher authorities at home for decisions. They want their negotiating team to be able to conclude an agreement on the spot. Koreans, with their value of respect for seniority, want their older and higher-status authorities to exercise their judgment about agreements. If the senior person is in Korea and the negotiations take place in another country, time has to be allowed for the senior person to be reached and the progress of the talks discussed.

Members with Special Expertise

Some negotiators become members of a team because of their specialized expertise. For example, a person with technical or technological knowledge may be very important, or an expert in financing with accurate cost figures may be able to make the difference between success and failure in Kuwait. Someone with marketing expertise in a specialized product or legal experience in a particular country can make or break negotiations. For example, one person's experience with Japan's import regulations governing agricultural products and health inspections enabled a German company to negotiate an agreement for the sale of sausages to Japan. The expertise may consist of knowledge of the culture and values of the other side. Richard Welzel, a German-Canadian broker of food-processing equipment, was able to negotiate a purchase of secondhand German-made stainless steel machinery in Bulgaria because he understood the quality of the machinery.

The Translator

One of the most important people on the team is the translator. Many negotiating teams choose not to take their own translator but instead to depend on the host country to supply a translator. This is usually a mistake. Obviously, a translator's first loyalty is to his or her employer. The Chinese who supplied the translator to the Canadians in the Canwell case could have asked the translator for daily reports on what the Canadians said when they were alone with her. This would have given the Chinese a great advantage in the negotiations. Similarly, a Chinese team in another country would be wise to bring its own translator.

Having your own translator means you have an ear to hear what the other team says in side conversations and comments among themselves. English-speaking teams frequently rely on the widespread use of English around the globe; they assume it is possible to negotiate in English—and cheaper—if they don't have to take a translator with them. But they miss out. They don't understand what the other team is saying when its members converse in their own language. When the English-speaking team has a side conversation, however, the other team's translator and English-speaking members can understand what is being said.

Another benefit of having your own translator is the translations by the other side's translator can be heard and understood by yours. This means errors or omissions—which are frequently unintentional—can be corrected immediately. Translation is extremely hard work and doesn't stop just because the formal session is over. At social gatherings, the translators work just as hard as they do at the meeting table. It is understandable that a tired translator may misunderstand or mistranslate. A second translator offers a check against errors.

Occasionally, a translator's mistranslation is used by a member of a negotiating team to display knowledge of the language of the other side. This is done at the expense of the translator's face. A Vice Premier in China whose English was excellent corrected his young female translator's use of *could* instead of *should*—among other corrections—to illustrate his excellent command of English to his audience of foreigners. Why would he do this? Because he was receiving the guests on behalf of the Chinese government, and his words were being officially recorded—in Chinese. His translator was a person of very much lower status than the Vice Premier, so she had much less face to lose and gained collective face from his excellent English. He made the point about his accomplished use of English, and the guests were duly impressed.

Translation errors are mines waiting to explode around unsuspecting negotiators. Simple mistakes in translation can cause days of delay while a misunderstanding is identified and cleared up. One key to preventing errors is not only to have your own translator but also to have a translator who is familiar with the vocabulary of the business. Someone with a degree in language studies may have read bookshelves of literature in the other language but lack technical vocabulary. In fact, the translator needs to have a technical vocabulary in *both* languages.

Another factor in the selection of a translator is *specific* language skills. Many foreign firms negotiating in China take with them a Chinese person who lives in the firm's country and works for the firm. This can be excellent, provided the language spoken by the Chinese employee is the language spoken in the area of China where negotiations will take place. China is a country of many regional dialects. Many foreign firms use the services of trading companies in Hong Kong, where the language of more than 90 percent of the people is Cantonese. In China, the official language is Mandarin. The two spoken languages are mutually unintelligible. A Cantonese translator in Beijing cannot translate spoken Mandarin, and a northern Chinese cannot translate the Cantonese spoken in Hong Kong or Canton province. The Chinese also, like people in many countries around the world, practice regional snobbery about accents. A translator who speaks Mandarin with a strong Cantonese accent will not be as highly regarded in Beijing as a translator who speaks with a north China accent.

China, like India and many other countries, is a land of multiple dialects. The regional language in the case study example would have been Shanghai dialect, but in addition, the factory town has its own dialect. That means even if the Canadians from Canwall had brought their own Mandarin-speaking translator—even if they had found one who also spoke Shanghai dialect—the opposite team could possibly have exchanged comments in its local dialect that would not have been understood by the Canadian translator. Similarly, in India the regional dialect (and there are over 600 of them) may not be known to your translator. This means the microphone—your translator—for eavesdropping on the other team's side conversations is closed off.

You can make your translator's job easier, if you speak in very straightforward language. Consider, for example, the difficulty in translating the warning uttered by a spokesperson for a nongovernment international aid organization who said the United States should continue its involvement in rebuilding the social institutions in a country that had been at war "or else the line will not be drawn in the sand and we'll be back in the soup again."[10]

Makeup of the Other Side's Team

Analysis of the other team is very important. With a bit of application of what you have learned about a culture from the questions you have posed, you can see the cultural priorities that generate communication behavior at the negotiating table.

Kuwaiti culture encourages competitiveness among organizations. Women are not usually part of negotiating teams. Achieving goals for the sake of the group's honor—or often the royal al-Sabah family's honor—is very important, although the will of Allah may intervene. Goals may be long-term, and Kuwaitis are patient. The society is hierarchical, with members of the ruling family in key positions. Access to authority is mediated. Form and protocol are important, and negotiations may have a ceremonial aspect. Courtesy and patience are characteristic of Kuwaitis' interaction with others, since acceptance in the group is an important part of their Bedouin heritage. Language may be used flamboyantly and with an eloquence that is valued for its own sake, beyond or beside the meaning of the words. The way Kuwaitis understand and think about issues is to take several levels into account rather than move in a mental linear path. The chess-playing characteristic of some negotiations is renowned. The display of emotion is typical.

Once you have gathered responses to the culture questions and have considered the rules of engagement, a picture of the Kuwaiti negotiator emerges. He will be educated and skilled, a member of the ruling family or valued by it, with a strong expectation that negotiation will involve a need for cleverness on his part in order to win. Suspicion and hostility will probably not be evident because he will display Kuwaiti politeness and Bedouin hospitality. His love of verbal play and the importance of emotion in communication may make the Kuwaiti negotiator's wording of messages seem theatrical to a low-context communicator who shuns ambiguity and strives for directness and simplicity. He will probably possess technological expertise and expect to be given accurate and complete information. His religion, Islam, will frame his thinking and communicating acts, and he may quote the *Qur'an* as a guide for his behavior. He will be patient and will be ready to spend months negotiating. Finally, he will value a personal relationship with the negotiator on the other side of the table.

Members' Decision-Making Authority

You will want to consider as far as possible the question of how much authority rests with the negotiating team to conclude an agreement. In hierarchical cultures, the ultimate authority may lie with someone who is never present at the negotiating table. Where hierarchy and consensus both characterize a culture, the most influential person may be present at some meetings but may not be introduced in a way that suggests the power that person wields.

In Japanese negotiations, for example, the senior member of the group may not appear at all—or even any—meetings. He (nearly always it's a man) will receive regular and detailed reports, however, of all that is said during the negotiations, and he will direct his team members to proceed in a certain way. No agreement will be reached without his approval. No hint will be given by team members that an agreement could exist until they have had a chance to discuss things with him. If the senior authority is not physically present as a member of the negotiating team, he may be in a hotel room or office nearby. Or he may be in another city or country. In that case, obviously consultation with him will take more time than if he were present. On the other hand, the team members you are negotiating with may have full power to commit their organization to an agreement.

Team Members' Status

Members of the other team, like yours, may be chosen because of their status. In addition to high status within the organization, sometimes being in a special relationship to someone in power is a reason for inclusion on a team. The relatively young and inexperienced nephew of the president, for example, may have a place on a negotiating team mainly because his uncle owns the company. But this may not simply be nepotism. This may make good business sense: it may be that a family member can be trusted best to look after the interests of the family in reaching a certain agreement. If the family rules the country, as in some Middle Eastern nations, then the family's interests coincide with national interests, and family members play key roles in foreign negotiations.

We've already seen that family loyalties can motivate negotiators, and so can company loyalties or national loyalties. The desire to win through the use of clever strategies can motivate negotiators. The wish to develop a relationship that will continue and will allow for indebtedness and favors is a motivator. The value of harmony in human interactions, along with avoidance of confrontation, can motivate negotiators to reach agreement rather than continue to hold discussions.

THE PHYSICAL CONTEXT OF THE NEGOTIATION

Where the negotiation takes place—the physical context for the communication—has an impact on the outcomes. For example, if the negotiation takes place by telephone or fax, the nonverbal messages have a diminished impact compared with face-to-face negotiation. Indeed, most negotiation involves meetings between parties. The host team for the negotiations has an advantage because the environment is under its control. The guest team doesn't have the same degree of control.

Site and Space

The hosts can determine what city and what building will hold the meetings. If it's the boardroom of the building where the host organization members work, all the resources of that organization are at the disposal of the host team—from photocopiers to telecommunications and from files to assistants. Therefore, the hosts have an advantage of *convenience*. Handheld organizers and cellular telephones are increasing the convenience of access to one's own office, but there are still advantages to being in one's own setting.

Whether the home negotiators work from an open office with a dozen others, or in a cramped space at the back of a second-story building, or in a meeting room with stiff-backed chairs lining the walls—whatever the space, it will be familiar to them. It will

Dr. Jehad al-Omari, a consultant with the British firm Canning, says that for him, an Arab, an agenda is a very Western thing that is an effort by Westerners to compensate for their short and limited memories. Agendas seem to him to be impersonal, linear, and rigid. They may lead to confrontations. He prefers the flexibility of being able to take things off the table if the time doesn't seem right and to avoid potential confrontations. He likes to be able to surprise his counterpart and to spend time getting to know him.

"As a high-context person, I do not like the Western reductionist approach that tries to do one thing at a time, it is all so monochronic . . . What I like is to be able to approach the meeting in a holistic way, to spend some time discussing everything and nothing, to get the feel of my counterpart, his mood and temperament, his eagerness and readiness, before I launch into business."[11]

not be familiar to the visitors. The visitors will be getting used to an unexpected environment, and this can distract them from their negotiating goals. The visiting team may experience some *culture shock* that could be greater the longer they stay.

Schedule and Agenda

Jet lag can make the visiting team unable to perform well on the hosts' schedule. People whose internal clock says it's midnight find it difficult to stay alert even if the clock on the wall says it's 11 a.m. Russians, for example, have been known to conduct very long sessions at a time that is uncomfortable for a visiting team suffering from jet lag.

Control of the schedule also often carries over to control of the negotiating agenda. For example, hosts may suggest postponing certain discussions until guests are more rested, with the result that the hosts control the order in which issues are addressed while giving the appearance of concern for the guests' comfort. The order of the items discussed on the agenda can have an impact on the outcome. If the two sides agree to one principle or goal, then subsequent points may be presented as simply subsidiary to what has already been agreed. If the decision has been made to use a particular supply source of a raw material in a joint-venture manufacturing project, then the inclusion of a member of the supply organization on the board may seem a logical subsequent decision. But if the issue of membership on the board were addressed *first*, the decision might be different.

The power of the keeper of the agenda is considerable, determining when meetings take place and what amount of time is allotted to discuss which issues. An issue that isn't on the agenda may never be discussed. The visiting team has to be alert to its responsibility to participate in setting the agenda.

Negotiators often also operate from a "hidden agenda" that is not shared with the other side. The "open agenda" contains the agreed items for discussion, while the "hidden agenda" is the priorities a team has agreed upon privately.

Arab negotiators may have different ideas about how much sharing of priorities they are willing to do compared with, say, British negotiators.

Use of Time

The use of time is related to the agenda. Monochronic cultures see time as moving through the agenda in a linear pattern and excluding whatever is not scheduled. Polychronic cultures see time as allowing simultaneous activities that take as long as they need to, even if that means bending the schedule, and including whatever needs attention. When negotiators from monochronic cultures face polychronic negotiators, the guests have the greater responsibility to accommodate to the hosts.

Russians often use time to their advantage as part of the nonverbal communication in negotiations. For instance, they may delay negotiations in order to make the other side anxious. This behavior toward North Americans, for instance, is based on two assumptions: Americans "regard compromise as both desirable and inevitable, and . . . Americans feel frustration and failure when agreements are not reached promptly."[12]

Negotiators from the United States are well known for their impatience. Timothy Bennett, a United States trade negotiator to Mexico, characterizes his countrymen and countrywomen as thinking that some solution is better than no solution, which leads them to compromise more than their Mexican counterparts.[13] Decades of negotiations have taught the Japanese that Westerners, especially delegates from the United States, are not patient. If the Japanese prolong the negotiations sufficiently, the Westerners will probably agree to whatever the Japanese want. In Japan, however, to take time is to show maturity and wisdom. Haste shows poor judgment and lack of genuine commitment. Foreign negotiators who go to the Middle East often complain that they don't get meetings. Foreign negotiators who go to Latin America complain that they have to wait. In Asia, foreign negotiators complain they do too much sight-seeing and not enough negotiating. In the United States, foreign negotiators often feel rushed.

Host Hospitality

"[In Hungary] we drink *palinka*, a plum or cherry brandy. It's 200 proof. When we start, the Americans are already drunk. The Hungarians aren't. We're seasoned. In Hungary, the Hungarians use this. They try to influence Americans with good drink to sign a favorable contract. It's an instrument to oil the wheels.". . . A foreign man who can't hold his liquor is probably discarded as a potential business associate . . . [It is] reason to break off negotiations.[14]

Most negotiating involves some socializing. This may be a way to initiate the negotiations and establish some advantage for the host. Sometimes when negotiations are stuck, a meal together or an evening out can be a good strategy for refocusing the agenda. Socializing is often done at the end, after negotiations have been concluded favorably. The Canwall team was treated to a farewell banquet; in China, as in other Asian countries such as Korea and Vietnam, the toasts that are made at banquets carry messages about what items are particularly important to those negotiators.[15] In all cultures, socializing provides an opportunity to get to know the other party better and build relationships with its members. However, the food, beverages, and beds in which visitors sleep may be unfamiliar. With jet lag and unfamiliar food may come digestive and sleep disorders, and the visiting team may suffer a loss of *physical well-being*.

COMMUNICATION AND STYLE OF NEGOTIATING

Negotiation is a special communication task that uses special verbal and nonverbal skills. We will now look at other factors in communication between sides.

Differences in Focus

Focus may be positive or negative, explicit or implicit, general or specific. Cultures that emphasize communication as a tool for articulating specific goals in order to accomplish them tend to look upon negotiations as a series of points to "settle." Their language in negotiations is explicit and zeros in on what has yet to be agreed. These explicit statements may in fact be questions and emphasize negative points of disagreement, such as, "What do you still not like about this detail of product design?" Americans prefer this direct approach because their aim is to clarify and resolve an issue.

But cultures that use communication to encourage harmony, preserve face, and develop long-term relationships are not comfortable with direct and explicit talk. In Japan, for instance, getting straight to some point about which agreement has yet to be reached may result in confrontation and emotions—even anger. Someone may lose face. The Japanese,

A recent study of negotiation between companies in New Zealand and Argentina asked businesspeople to rate the importance of four factors in negotiation: communication, dependability (of the other party), customer orientation, and cultural sensitivity.16 Cultural sensitivity was rated as least important by the respondents. Communication was the most important factor.

At first glance, this seems to contradict what this book is saying: that culture matters. However, the study goes on to report that the researchers broke down communication into four dimensions: friendliness, congeniality, keeping to time, and punctuality. Yet all these dimensions are *determined by* culture. What defines "friendliness" varies by culture, especially friendliness on first face-to-face contact. Is it friendly to shake hands or not? To greet visitors standing or to go to the street door to escort them in? What constitutes "congeniality"? Smiling, maintaining harmony and avoiding confrontations, emphasizing the positives, trying to cooperate—all are driven by culture, and all play a part in the enactment of culturally appropriate behavior. Issues of time have already been discussed here as culturally defined. So in this study, "communication" was another way of talking about culture's influence on negotiation.

like negotiators from other Asian cultures, prefer to emphasize the positive points of agreement. They begin with general terms and seek agreement from the other side about general goals. Then regardless of the remaining details, the general agreement holds the two sides together in a relationship. They do not ask—and do not enjoy being asked—pointed questions. They want to develop relationships because once a relationship exists, each side has an obligation to consider the needs of the other, so the issue resolves itself.

The Chinese military strategist and philosopher, Sun Tzu (pronounced "swin zuh"), writing in the third century BC, described the inexhaustibility of indirect tactics as being as unending as the rivers and as recurring as the seasons.[17] Potential conflicts can be diffused by indirectness. In more modern times, indirect "many-layered" negotiation with the Chinese has been compared to

> courtyards in the Forbidden City, each leading to a deeper recess distinguished from the others only by slight changes in proportion, with ultimate meaning residing in a totality that only long reflection can grasp.[18]

The metaphor of many-layered courtyards is an apt one to describe the way the negotiations proceed.

The approach that focuses on particulars, especially unresolved ones, is typically Western. Negotiators look at the unsettled issues and one by one address them. That approach is logical for the Western problem-solving mind. But it isn't shared by all cultures. In Asia, unresolved issues are part of the whole web of the relationship being woven by the negotiation process. A simultaneous, not sequential, approach means the negotiators look at unresolved issues as potentially resolved because of the developing relationship between the two sides.

Businesspeople from Western cultures need to remember that Japanese, Chinese, and most other Asians dislike confrontation and will not argue when they feel they are right. Attacks on statements are the same as attacks on the people making the statements. Japanese and Chinese and other Asians need to remember that businesspeople in Western cultures prefer directness and the airing of different opinions, and to a large degree consider words apart from the people who produce them. When words are attacked, persons are not necessarily attacked also.

Honor

Group membership, when it is highly valued, can affect negotiations in a number of ways. Negotiators whose allegiance is to a family group, such as the ruling household of some

Arab countries, or to a nation, such as Korea, may be motivated to gain the best advantage for the honor of their group. The fact that something bigger than the individual seems to be at stake can make a negotiating team less flexible.

On the other hand, negotiators who are motivated by a desire to uphold their individual reputations and records can also be inflexible about backing down. The key is to understand what motivates your counterparts. Then you can accommodate the needs of the other side. If your counterparts are motivated to succeed for the honor of the group, then you need to send messages that show you understand. Your own group membership will be important to emphasize. In either case, words that provoke a defense of honor can be the wrong words to use.

Not backing down is related to a team's decision-making process. If it is a consensus-based process, then the team's position will have been determined by lengthy discussions in the group before the negotiations take place. This makes the team less able to change its position spontaneously. The team members have to go back and consult the others in the group before they can agree to changes in their initial position. If individuals have authority to make decisions, the team's position may be flexible and open to change.

Verbal Communication Style

Verbal communication styles vary across cultures. Some negotiating teams prefer directness and use explicit words, while other teams prefer indirectness and use circumlocutions. For example, one side may say, "Our objective in this investment phase of our agreement is to achieve cost neutrality." The other side may word the same idea this way: "Our consulting services to help you set up the new operation will be free of charge, but you will pay our expenses." The terms "investment phase" and "cost neutrality" may not have meaning for the team that is listening for explicit wording, and an agreement may not be reached because the team didn't hear those explicit words. Misunderstandings can result from different preferences for wording, compounding difficulties already present when one side or both are speaking a language in which they are not fluent.

Form

Form is very important in high-context cultures, and nowhere more so than in negotiation sessions. In Arab cultures, for example, sessions begin with small talk, and communication is indirect. In some situations, negotiators may sit on cushions on carpets, not on furniture. In other situations, the negotiations may take place in a restaurant or club owned by someone other than the negotiators. Visitors will be offered hospitality, such as a small cup of strong coffee, and the offer should not be refused. Proper respect is due older members of the Arab team, and that means not using too much familiarity. Visitors should use titles to address people and should not ask about female family members. (If you ask how many children a businessman has, he may give you the number of his male children.)

In Russia, negotiators must follow the protocol of correctly using Russians' names. This means using the full name: the given name, the patronymic or father's name, and the family name. Proper respect is shown when all three names are used to refer to someone. This may require a bit of effort on the part of a foreigner who is unfamiliar with the name system. The names change, depending upon whether the person is male or female: Alexei Fyodorovitch Melnikov is the son of Fyodor; his married sister is Irina Fyodorovna Dunayeva. A naming system that incorporates one's mother's family name is used by Mexicans and other Latin Americans to varying degrees.

Danes, by comparison, use informal address, speaking to each other with the familiar pronoun *du*. They follow the *Jantelov*, the "Law of Jante," in social interactions. This egalitarian principle says one shouldn't try to be "above" someone else. Modest about putting themselves forward, Danes are not hierarchical, and they observe little protocol in negotiation situations. However, they are monochronic and expect punctuality. Negotiations with Danes proceed without interruption.[19] Denmark provides a contrast with Arab, Asian, and Latin cultures, and points out how important it is to know the culture on the other side of the negotiating table.

New Zealanders of British descent are keenly aware of avoiding being "tall poppies." They learn from an early age that someone who stands above the others because of self-promotion will be ostracized. The "tall poppy syndrome" comes from the saying that in the field, the tall poppies are mowed down by the farmer's equipment; their bright heads are cut off if they have grown too high. Lower-growing poppies retain their blooms.

Emotion

In some high-context cultures, public display of emotion is a sign of immaturity and a potential cause of shame to the group. Japanese negotiators will close their eyes, or look down, or rest their heads against their hands and shade their eyes in order to conceal an emotion such as anger. Similarly, Thais have learned to keep potentially disruptive emotions from showing on their faces. Koreans, Taiwanese, and other Asians along with Japanese and Thais have earned the descriptor *inscrutable* from Westerners because of their learned cultural practice of avoiding a facial display of strong and disruptive emotion. High-context cultures value harmony in human encounters, and their members avoid sending any nonverbal messages that could destroy harmony. Other high-context cultures, for example in the Middle East, put a high priority on displays of emotion (although not anger) to emphasize the sincerity of the position being put forward.

In low-context cultures, the deliberate concealment of emotion is considered to be insincere. Members of low-context cultures have learned a large vocabulary of facial expressions that signal the emotions a speaker feels. When they see none of the expected indicators of emotion on the faces of negotiators on the opposite side of the table, they assume that an emotion is not present. If this assumption is discovered to be wrong and the speaker is indeed feeling an emotion such as anger, the members of the low-context culture feel deceived.

Silence

Similarly, silence as a nonverbal communication tool can be very effective in negotiations. In low-context cultures where ideas are explicitly encoded into words and unspoken ideas are more difficult to respond to, silence makes negotiators uneasy. Silence often means unhappiness in low-context cultures. Even when no message about unhappiness is intended, silence in low-context cultures indicates a rupture has occurred, a break in the process of communicating. For these reasons, negotiators from low-context cultures generally are uncomfortable with silence. They often feel responsible for starting a conversation or keeping it going.

Japanese speakers are comfortable with silence in negotiations and do not hurry to fill it up with speech. After a speaker from one side speaks, Japanese listeners pause in silence to reflect on what has been said and consider the speaker's feelings and point of view. This is how Japanese show consideration for others in oral interpersonal communication. Similarly, to interrupt a negotiator who is speaking is to show disrespect. Because of this protocol—and the Japanese value of silence—negotiators with Japanese counterparts must be careful not to speak too hastily or too much.

The Phases of Negotiation

The foregoing aspects of communication style are employed in specific phases of negotiation. Exchanges proceed according to four phases of negotiation in all cultures;[20] the emphasis and the time spent on any one phase are what differ:

1. **Development of a relationship** with the other side
2. **Information exchange** about the topic under negotiation
3. **Persuasion**
4. **Concessions and agreement**

Some see the process as involving as many as seven steps.

1. *Preparation*. This precedes the first step above. As we will see, preparation is an important key for successful negotiation.
2. *Building the relationship*. This corresponds to the first step.
3. *Exchanging information/first offer*. This corresponds to the second step.
4. *Persuasion*. This corresponds to Step 3.
5. *Concessions*. Step 4.
6. *Agreement*. Step 4.
7. *Implementation*. This follows the agreement, and points to the fact that many cultures, such as Japanese and Chinese, use a holistic approach to negotiation. Nothing is ever closed until the agreement is signed, and even then some issues may be reopened.

In a holistic negotiation, managers from the United States negotiating with the Japanese, for instance, may think they have decided a key point, only to find the Japanese bring that point up again when they are addressing something else in the negotiations. Westerners approach matters to be negotiated in a more linear way, going through the points sequentially and checking them off as they are settled. Easterners approach the items as discussion points within the context of the relationship they have formed with the other side. The relationship is what makes agreement possible. If a better solution arises for both sides following the negotiation of a point, they do not hesitate to revisit the item and offer a different solution.

THE DEVELOPMENT OF A RELATIONSHIP

Cultural priorities differ about how much time is spent on each phase; for example, Chinese spend much longer on phases 1 and 2, while Canadians want to get to phase 3 more quickly.

In the first phase, where the relationship between negotiating teams is being established, trust is the critical factor. In cultures where relationships have high priority, time may be spent in nonbusiness activities so the negotiators can get to know each other. Sight-seeing and a welcome banquet are two typical activities in Chinese business interactions with foreigners. In Argentina, the visiting team may be treated to an elaborate cocktail party in someone's home or to a barbecue, called a *parrilla*, in a home or restaurant; again, at the successful conclusion of negotiations, the teams may enjoy a celebratory meal, usually less formal in dress.

One way to establish a relationship is to identify the common goal both sides have in reaching an agreement. Once the desire or need for the other side to come to an agreement is on the table—in words—along with your desire, you can both refer openly to the common goal.

In order to develop trust, you need to have openness in your communication and to experience openness from the other side. This usually involves some gentle questioning by each side to see how willing the others are to reveal themselves. Often, the answers are already known to the questioners, and the probes are not so much for gathering information as for testing the openness of the other side. Usually each side displays apparent candor in these exchanges; whether it can be trusted or not is what each side has to determine.

Face is an important consideration in developing a relationship with someone from a high-context culture, especially someone from Asia.

Face may be lost as a result of many developments: a premature or overeager overture that is rebuffed by one's opponent; exposure to personal insult, in the form of either a hurtful remark or disregard for one's status; being forced to give up a cherished value or to make a concession that will be viewed by the domestic audience as unnecessary; a snub;

failure to achieve predetermined goals; the revelation of personal inadequacy; damage to a valued relationship. The list is endless, for in the give-and-take of a complicated negotiation on a loaded subject, anything can happen.[21]

Since face can be lost even without the awareness of the other party, negotiators need to take care. Asking questions that seem designed to expose weakness, or making comments that assume familiarity, or giving responses with the wrong degree of coolness can all lead to loss of face for the other party and, with it, loss of trust.

INFORMATION EXCHANGE ABOUT THE TOPIC UNDER NEGOTIATION

Frank disclosure often can work in your favor and generate trust. For example, if the negotiators from the Canwall company had said, "We're very glad to be talking with you about a sale of our product because we have a long-term interest in business with China," their Chinese counterparts would likely have considered this a frank admission of Canwall's aims. You need to disclose at least some of your positions. You also need to be able to believe what the other side is telling you.

One way to obtain information is to ask questions rather than wait for disclosure. According to Richard Mead,[22] you can ask questions

1. To determine common ground
2. To clarify information
3. To call bluffs
4. To show you are listening
5. To show your interest
6. To control the direction of the discussion
7. To broach potentially controversial issues (rather than by statement)

Items 1, 4, and 5 particularly have to do with developing relationships; item 2 has to do with understanding facts; items 3, 6, and 7 have to do with managing the negotiation process.

Asking questions can be problematic, however. In order not to seem overly aggressive, you may need to "frame" your questions. Framing means putting a frame of explanatory language around a request that does not change the meaning but makes it less aggressive: "I hope you don't mind my asking for your unit price, but our estimates were much higher and our head office will ask why we were so far off." The frame softens what could be a very hard-nosed question: "Where did you get that unit price?"

Another problem with asking *why* questions if you expect a *cause* answer is that in some cultures the typical response is not a cause but an explanation of a pattern—an organizational structure, or market consumption, or an economic policy, for instance.

Let's assume you want to negotiate a purchase from a supplier from another culture. You'll need to ask about technical information, price, discounts, quantity, shipping dates, insurance, payment method, shipping method, repeat orders, and quality control. You'll ask questions about all those items, and each is potentially an issue to be negotiated. As you ask questions, you are refining your idea about the importance to the other side of reaching an agreement and what the other side's *best alternative to a negotiated agreement* (BATNA) is. You are discovering what items the other team is willing to yield on and what items the other team is inflexible about.

PERSUASION

This brings us to the third communication phase: persuasion. By this point, you have established what you need to focus on in order to reach an agreement. In other words, you have a clear idea where the conflicts lie, as well as the concord. Now you will attempt to persuade your counterparts to accept a settlement that ensures you what you need and perhaps more. They will do the same.

The language of persuasion varies among cultures, You can employ the language strategy of inclusiveness for persuasion. For example, if the individual needs of your counterparts are to appear tough and persistent because those are cultural values that drive individual behavior, you can avoid using language that forces them to back down. Use inclusive language such as *together we can . . .* rather than exclusive language such as *you'll have to accept . . .* and *we absolutely require . . .* Avoid *I*-centered messages and *must, should,* and *ought* messages. In other words, use *you-viewpoint* messages and indicate you understand the others' point of view. Encourage your counterparts to focus on what they can gain, not what they may have to give up.

Differences in negotiation tactics between low-context cultures and high-context cultures are shown in Figure 10.1.

Obviously, the tactics used by low-context cultures will not work in high-context cultures. For example, many cultures are not persuaded by objective facts. Silence may signal unhappiness to the other side or may be understood as a comfortable pause during which you ponder and meditate. Some disagreement is inevitable, since that is why you are at a negotiating table, but how it is communicated varies culturally. Threats, personal attacks, insistence, and being emotional are all subject to cultural priorities.

When members of low-context cultures communicate with members of high-context cultures, they need to be especially aware of the cultural context of communication: concerns for harmony, for status, and for showing respect. When members of high-context cultures communicate with members of low-context cultures, they need to pay special attention to the words and what the words actually say, not to what can be implied or inferred in the words.

Arabic-speaking businesspeople need to remember that low-context cultures attach face-value meanings to words, analyze the meanings, and don't usually discount any words as mere rhetoric. Businesspeople from low-context cultures need to remember that members of Arabic-speaking cultures enjoy the way words, by their dancing and heaped up phrases and sheer volume, can affect people and that literal, face-value meanings may not be intended.

People from cultures that prefer explicit communication that is direct and to the point tend to persuade with facts. This is true of businesses in the United States, for example, where arguments that are based on fact have greater credibility than arguments that are based on opinion or inference. Facts just *are;* they do not need to be proven. So strong is the attitude that facts count that using a number of facts often seems to make an argument irrefutable. Statistics can make a business decision seem sound. But statistics can be used to say anything. Of course, people can also be mistaken and get facts wrong.

FIGURE 10.1

Low-Context and High-Context Negotiation Tactics

Low-Context Negotiation Tactics	High-Context Negotiation Tactics
• Supporting argument with factual data.	• Supporting argument with personal connections.
• Offering counterproposals.	• Offering counterproposals.
• Silence.	• Silence.
• Disagreeing.	• Suggesting additional items.
• Threatening the opposing side.	• Referring to precedent.
• Attacking opponents' characters.	• Deferring to superiors.
• Avoiding certain issues.	• Avoiding certain issues.
• Expressing emotion.	• Avoiding conflict.
• Insisting on a final position.	• Remaining open and flexible.
• Making a final offer.	• Revisiting and reopening items previously negotiated.

Some prefer arguments based on inference, which is a conclusion based on fact but not proven. Inferences are assumptions. Some believe inferences generated from facts are more powerful than the facts themselves. When a negotiator suggests that the plan her opposite party has to create new jobs will actually threaten the environment, the negotiator is inferring consequences.

Inferred consequences are the stuff of advertisements. Ads infer that a consumer will benefit in some way by purchasing the advertised goods. For example, drinking a certain beer will connect you to a more glamorous social circle; driving a certain car will put you in the company of professional racing drivers; using a certain credit card will enable you to join in fun international travel. Your response to these appeals is emotional: desire or perhaps disgust (the advertisers hope it's desire).

Asian negotiators often use inference when they refer to history. Asians, Europeans, Latin Americans, Middle Easterners, and Africans tend to take a long view of current activity, placing it in the context of a history reaching back far, but still having a very real meaning for the present. This enables them to take a long view of the future as well. Americans, Canadians, New Zealanders, Australians, most Argentines, and others have a short history, and even that seems remote and unconnected to the present. They often could use their historical contacts as a persuasive tool but instead overlook them.

Others prefer arguments based on opinion. Opinions cannot be proven to be true or false. They are usually also emotional. For some, emotion means genuine involvement on the part of the persuader. Without emotion, an argument lacks heart and conviction and is simply cold and impersonal.

Obviously, when someone who shuns emotion in favor of facts encounters another person who prefers emotion and finds facts alone unconvincing, the result can be miscommunication that results in a failure to reach an agreement. Some observers have noted this problem in Arab–Israeli negotiations: Arabs prefer argument based on a mixture of opinion and emotion with some fact and inference; Israelis prefer an argument based on fact and inference with little opinion and emotion.

The sequence in which items are discussed is often a critical communication factor in negotiations. Research has shown that skilled Western negotiators are more flexible in the sequence in which they communicate about factors than average Western negotiators who stick to a planned sequence.[23] The average negotiator treats items independently, while the skilled negotiator is able to link items. This is called "enlarging the pie"; the negotiator adds issues so the pie is larger, allowing everyone to have a larger piece.

Also, skilled negotiators make more frequent reference to long-term concerns than average negotiators. The negotiator who appears to be after a short-term, in-and-out business deal is less likely to succeed than the negotiator who makes reference to long-term goals.

CONCESSION AND AGREEMENT

Finally, the negotiators' communication task turns to concession and agreement. When making a concession, skilled negotiators link that to a counterconcession, using "if" language: "We'll accept your shipment dates if you'll agree to a discount on future orders." Many experienced negotiators warn that you can't come back and ask for a counterconcession after a concession has been granted to the other side and the discussion has moved on to another issue. Once you agree without conditions or "ifs," the issue is settled. You attempt to reopen it at the risk of losing what agreements—and trust—you have already gained.

Sometimes the final agreement arrives more quickly than you expect. Many Chinese negotiations, for example, consist of probing the other side's position, testing for firmness and the other side's final position. Then, suddenly, you may find the Chinese side offers a final agreement that solves many of the issues raised without the need to haggle and bargain or persuade. When this is the case, it probably isn't a good idea to offer too many counterproposals or alternatives, because that weakens your position. However, advice

Even with the best motives and the most careful preparation, negotiators who ignore the other culture's priorities can put a foot wrong. In 1983, an article in the *Harvard Business Review* outlined what the authors called the "American John Wayne" style of negotiating, which still has relevance today.[24] Here is a summary.

1. **I Can Go It Alone.** Many U.S. executives seem to believe they can handle any negotiation situation by themselves, even when they are outnumbered in negotiation situations.

2. **Just call me John.** Americans value informality and equality in human relationships. They try to make people feel comfortable by playing down class distinctions.

3. **Pardon My French.** Americans aren't very talented at speaking foreign languages.

4. **Check with the Home Office?** American negotiators get upset when halfway through a negotiation the other side says, "I'll have to check with the home office." The implication is that the decision makers are not present.

5. **Get to the Point.** Americans don't like to beat around the bush and want to get to the heart of the matter quickly.

6. **Lay Your Cards on the Table.** Americans expect honest information at the bargaining table.

7. **Don't Just Sit There; Speak Up.** Americans don't deal well with silence during negotiations.

8. **Don't Take No for an Answer.** Persistence is highly valued by Americans and is part of the deeply ingrained competitive spirit that manifests itself in every aspect of American life.

9. **One Thing at a Time.** Americans usually attack a complex negotiation task sequentially—that is, they separate the issues and settle them one at a time.

10. **A Deal Is a Deal.** When Americans make an agreement and give their word, they expect to honor the agreement no matter what the circumstances.

11. **I Am What I Am.** Few Americans take pride in changing their minds, even in difficult circumstances. Americans also think it is "phony" to act differently in a negotiation with foreigners than they would act at home.

You can venture a guess about how successful these strategies would be in a high-context culture—or in a low-context culture. Cultural values of the United States that are evident are individual performance, desire to achieve an agreement, preference for informality and for communication in English, emphasis on direct and explicit communication, and unease with silence.

---

to Chinese negotiators is to hold back from commitment to unattractive points to see if the other side will offer counterproposals or if it is really firm. Western negotiators are known to be under pressure from their own cultural priorities. They want to achieve an agreement; in some cases, they seem to feel *any* agreement is better than no agreement. They can be impatient, but they also can be imaginative about solutions.

Some negotiating teams can live with an agreement that at least gives them the *appearance* of having done well. Cohen quotes an Egyptian proverb:

Make your harvest look big lest your enemies rejoice.[25]

The agreement has to *look* good as well as be good.

Some cultures are not interested in settling the negotiations in a way that terminates them. To these context-oriented cultures, the relationship between organizations is what makes negotiations and agreements possible. Each side has an obligation to nurture the relationship and keep it going. Signed agreements don't do that. Japanese negotiators, for example, prefer escape clauses in contracts—when contracts are necessary at all. Western negotiators are dismayed when their Japanese or Chinese counterparts begin making changes immediately after contracts are signed. But in Asian cultures the documents are far less important than is keeping the interdependent, interwoven organizations in a good relationship.

Charles Sirois is a Canadian telecom entrepreneur whom a Canadian magazine article once labeled "the next master of the universe." His company, TIW, led by Bruno Ducharme, is a global mobile communications company with investments in Romania, the Czech Republic, India, and Western Europe. In 1995, Sirois had invested in telecommunications in Brazil in partnership with Daniel Dantas, a brilliant financier in Brazil who ran an investment banking company called Banco Opportunity SA.

In 1998, the Brazilian government began to sell off its telecommunications companies to private owners. TIW and Opportunity, led by Dantas, joined with a third party, a group of Brazilian pension funds, to form a consortium called Telpart. In turn, it bought two cellular phone companies formerly owned by the government, with a total of nearly two million customers.

But while the negotiations were optimistic and the Canadians went public about the trust everyone showed, and all three parties concurred in a nonbinding Memorandum of Understanding, the three never wrote a formal shareholder agreement. On the basis of trust, TIW had put about U.S. $266 million into the Telpart consortium, acquiring 49 percent of it.

Two weeks after the consortium was formed, Dantas began to change the ownership balance. He persuaded the third party, the pension funds, to join with Opportunity and create another company (Newtel) that would own 51 percent of Telpart. TIW was subsequently a minority, not majority, partner. TIW agreed to the new structure on the condition a formal agreement would be written to assure that TIW shared control of Telpart.

After 18 months of negotiation no agreement was produced. Meanwhile, Dantas had begun appointing directors and dictating policy for Telpart and controlling what Telpart did and did not do. TIW took Dantas and Newtel to court. In fact, about 20 lawsuits ensued, and nasty public allegations flew on both sides before Sirois finally pulled TIW out of Brazil in 2003, selling assets that had cost U.S. $266 million five years earlier for less than U.S. $50 million.26 The agreement made on trust and handshakes was unenforceable when one player changed the rules. Without a written agreement, TIW could not win in court.

Negotiators from the United States are keen to sign agreements. Contracts are firm and go a long way toward eliminating ambiguities and misunderstandings. They and other low-context negotiators see unwritten and informal agreements as unenforceable. They may allow the other side to conceal something; low-context cultures give openness high priority.

It is important for negotiators to understand their counterparts and balance the need for enforceable agreements on the one hand with the need for nurturing trusting relationships on the other. Agreements do not all look alike. *Time* magazine, nearly two decades ago, ran this statement:

> The successful negotiation between Japanese and Western businessmen usually ends up looking very much like one between two Japanese.[27]

That is still true today. Sensitivity to the other culture, and satisfying the needs of your own are both needed in the 21st century.

CHAPTER SUMMARY

This chapter has shown how cultural priorities affect specific communication tasks, in this case the task of business negotiations.

- The experience of Canwall in China illustrates cultural priorities and shows an outcome that was not what the Canadians had expected.
- What really happened involved the way culture affects communication. Chinese cultural dimensions include the following: *relationships*; expectations about *time* and efficiency; the way *obligation* is perceived; the value of *harmony*; the method of *learning*; the performance of tasks *simultaneously*; a preference for protocol and *form*, *seniority*, and *hierarchy*; *mediated access* to authority; *interdependence*; and *tolerance of uncertainty*.
- *Expectations for outcomes* is one way cultures differ at the negotiating table. Cultures may have different goals, different views of advantage or disadvantage, and a preference for one of the outcomes of negotiation: win–lose, win–win, or stalemate.
- *The makeup of the negotiating teams may also differ.* They might include
  - Members with high status
  - Members with special expertise
  - A translator
- *Physical aspects of the negotiations* also can affect the outcomes. Such aspects include
  - Site and space
  - Schedule and agenda
  - Use of time
  - Host hospitality
- *By far the most important differences are in communication styles:*
  - Verbal communication style may be more explicit and direct or more roundabout and indirect. Some circumlocutions (such as "cost-neutral" in English) may not be understood by a team with limited English language.
  - The focus may be on what has already been agreed or on what remains in dispute. Some teams negotiate for the honor of their country or firm.
  - Some teams prefer the observance of more form and specific protocol than others. Some show emotion and even make a deliberate display of emotion, while others show little.
  - Some teams use silence, while others are uncomfortable with silence.
- *Negotiation has four phases:*
  - Development of a relationship with the other side
  - Exchange of information and positions
  - Persuasion and argumentation
  - Concessions and agreement

Notes

1. William Zartman and Maureen Berman, quoted in Raymond Cohen, *Negotiating Across Cultures* (Washington, DC: United States Institute of Peace, 1991), pp. 16–17.

2. Geert Hofstede, *Cultures and Organizations* (New York: McGraw-Hill, 1991), p. 225.

3. Cohen, pp. 31–32.

4. Robert T. Moran and William G. Stripp, *Dynamics of Successful International Business Negotiations* (Houston: Gulf, 1991), p. 84.

5. Richard Mead, *Cross-Cultural Management Communication* (New York: John Wiley and Sons, 1990), p. 203.

6. Yale Richmond, *From Nyet to Da: Understanding the Russians* (Yarmouth, ME: Intercultural Press, 1992), p. 141.

7. Moran and Stripp, p. 77.

8. Ibid., p. 84.

9. Ibid.

10. Tom Getman, "World Vision," *The MacNeil/Lehrer News-Hour*, broadcast June 7, 1993, about Somalia.

11. John Mattock, ed., *Cross-Cultural Communication* (London: Kogan Page, 2003), p. 120.

12. Moran and Stripp, p. 168.

13. Cohen, p. 89.

14. Diane Zior Wilhelm, "A Cross-Cultural Analysis of Drinking Behavior within the Context of International Business." In *Anthropology in International Business*, Studies in Third World Societies, no. 28, Hendrick Serrie, guest ed. (Williamsburg, VA: Department of Anthropology, College of William and Mary, 1986), pp. 73–88.

15. Linda Beamer, "Toasts: Rhetoric and Ritual in Business Negotiation in Confucian Cultures," *Business Forum* (1994), pp. 22–25.

16. Richard Buchanan, Ron Garland, and Mark Armstrong, "Mañana and Manners May Not Be Enough! The Cultural Interface of New Zealand and Argentinean Negotiating Preferences," *Marketing* Bulletin, 13, no. 1, http://marketing-bulletin.massey.ac.nz/article13/Manana.asp (retrieved March 17, 2003).

17. Sun Tzu, *Art of War* (S. B. Griffith, Trans.) (New York: Oxford University Press, 1984), (original work published 256 BC).

18. February 21, 1972, *The White House Years*, pp. 1061–1062; quoted in Cohen, p. 123.

19. Richard R. Gesteland, *Cross-Cultural Business Behavior* (Copenhagen: Copenhagen School of Business Press, 2002), pp. 289–290.

20. Graham and Herberger, quoted by Mead, p. 189.

21. Cohen, p. 56.

22. Mead, pp. 196–197.

23. N. Rackham, "The Behavior of Successful Negotiators (Huthwaite Research Group Reports)." In *International Negotiations: A Training Program for Corporate Executives and Diplomats*, E. Raider, ed. (Brooklyn, NY: Ellen Raider International, 1976), pp. 196–197.

24. Philip R. Harris and Robert T. Moran, *Managing Cultural Differences*, 2nd ed. (Houston: Gulf, 1987), p. 59, boldface added.

25. Cohen, p. 131.

26. Tyler Hamilton, "Retreat from Brazil," *Toronto Star*, April 5, 2003, Section D, p. 1, (retrieved from Lexis-Nexis database on May 27, 2003).

27. Robert T. Moran, *Getting Your Yen's Worth: Negotiating with the Japanese* (Houston: Gulf, 1985), p. 67.

READING ONE

The Negotiation Checklist

Tony Simons and Thomas M. Tripp

Preparation increases your chance of success, whether in combat, sports, or negotiations. The well-prepared negotiator knows the playing field and the players, is seldom surprised, and can promptly capitalize on opportunities. This article offers a tool for use in effectively negotiating important transactions and disputes.

Making deals is a key part of being effective in business. Managers and executives negotiate constantly over issues as varied as hiring decisions and purchases, corporate resource allocations, and labor contracts. One could argue that the American system of government is based on an ongoing process of negotiation, which is sometimes successful and sometimes not.

The "negotiation checklist" that we present in this article is a systematic way to make sure you are well-prepared before you walk into your next negotiation. It is based on proven principles of negotiation that are taught at several of North America's top business schools. The techniques we describe apply whether you are getting ready for a labor negotiation, a negotiation with a supplier, or a negotiation with a customer. This checklist is not a formula for easy success in negotiations. Rather, it is a methodical approach that requires significant work. The amount of time and effort you spend answering the questions should depend on the importance of the negotiation and on the resources you have available. The payoff for your efforts emerges from the confidence and information that you gain from preparation.

The Negotiation Checklist

The negotiation checklist (see page 266) is a guide for thinking about an important, upcoming negotiation. The pages that follow describe and explain the items on the list.

A. About You

1. What Is Your Overall Goal?
Start with the big picture. What basic need will an agreement address? Why are you talking to this person or this company? What do you hope to accomplish? Understanding your main goal helps put all the other aspects of the negotiation into perspective. Most people begin and end their negotiation planning by determining their overall goal. We suggest that it is just the beginning.

2. What Are the Issues?
What specific issues must be negotiated for the final outcome or agreement to meet your overall goal? For example, if the overall goal is to book a successful convention, what assurances, services, and constraints will be involved? Price may be an obvious component, but it is worthwhile to consider other items, too—items that might make the agreement much more attractive both to yourself and to the other side. Delivery schedules, duration of contract, product or service upgrades, cancellation clauses, contingency plans, transportation services, complimentary room nights, and many other options all have some value to those negotiating a contract. Such side issues may be researched and introduced as part of a food contract, conference booking, or union contract that you are preparing to negotiate.

Consider also whether any of the issues you have considered might be broken down into multiple components or subissues. For the conference-booking negotiation, for example, you might normally consider the room-block guarantee as a single item (i.e., so many rooms reserved until such-and-such a date). In fact, breaking the room reservations down by percentages and multiple deadlines (e.g., 50 percent by one date, 75 percent by another date) might open avenues for mutually beneficial arrangements.

You should anticipate as many issues as possible for the negotiation. By doing so, you will be better informed and thus feel comfortable and confident when negotiating. Also, the more issues you can introduce, the more likely it becomes that creative solutions will arise, as those are often built by packaging or trading off multiple issues. Creative solutions often make it easier to discover an agreement that both parties like.

By adding items to the negotiations agenda, you increase your chance of discovering some issues that you value more than the other party, and discovering other issues that the other party values more than you. Trading off such differently valued issues dramatically increases the value of the agreement to you without costing the other party. Moreover, if you know what issues the other party highly values that you value less, you can use those issues to get concessions on issues that are important to you.

Imagine that you are a food and beverage director of a hotel seeking a dry-goods supplier and that you have written a request for bids from potential vendors. You have considered your storage capacity and specified every-other-week delivery in your request for bids. Now suppose you receive a bid from Alpha Dry Goods, which has another customer in town to whom they deliver once every three weeks. Alpha's quote for biweekly delivery might be mediocre, but it turns out that they could save you substantial money on triweekly delivery. They could save you so much money, in fact, that you consider changing your storage arrangement to accommodate their every-three-weeks delivery schedule. If you had been unwilling to negotiate the delivery schedule, you might never have discovered that opportunity. By adding delivery schedule to the agenda, you were able to discover an issue that improved the business potential for both parties. In this example, you are able to secure a lower overall price in return for a concession on delivery schedule.

In general, the more issues you can put on the table (within reason), the better off you are.[1]

Another reason to consider and discuss many issues in a negotiation is that it minimizes the chance of misunderstandings in the final contract. For any issue that is not discussed, the parties risk the possibility of making different assumptions. For example, the "standard frills" that accompany a banquet may not be known by the person purchasing the banquet.

Once you agree that it's a good idea to discuss many issues, how should you determine how many and which ones? For starters, check with your executive committee or association members. Draw also on outside resources. For example, call some friends and colleagues who have conducted similar negotiations and ask them about what issues they put on the table. Library research and obtaining experts' opinions may be helpful, too. Lawyers can be a marvelous source of ideas about which issues to place on the table, especially for a labor negotiation. Be prepared

Negotiation Checklist: A systematic way to ensure you are well-prepared before your next negotiation

☑ *Item accomplished*

A. About You

❑ 1. What is your overall goal?

❑ 2. What are the issues?

❑ 3. How important is each issue to you?

Develop a scoring system for evaluating offers:

❑ *(a)* List all of the issues of importance from step 2.

❑ *(b)* Rank-order all of the issues.

❑ *(c)* Assign points to all the issues (assign weighted values based on a total of 100 points).

❑ *(d)* List the range of possible settlements for each issue. Your assessments of realistic, low, and high expectations should be grounded in industry norms and your best-case expectation.

❑ *(e)* Assign points to the possible outcomes that you identified for each issue.

❑ *(f)* Double-check the accuracy of your scoring system.

❑ *(g)* Use the scoring system to evaluate any offer that is on the table.

❑ 4. What is your "best alternative to a negotiated agreement" (BATNA)?

❑ 5. What is your resistance point (i.e., the worst agreement you are willing to accept before ending negotiations)? If your BATNA is vague, consider identifying the minimum terms you can possibly accept and beyond which you must recess to gather more information.

B. About the Other Side

❑ 1. How important is each issue to them (plus any new issues they added)?

❑ 2. What is their best alternative to negotiated agreement?

❑ 3. What is their resistance point?

❑ 4. Based on questions B.1, B.2, and B.3, what is your target?

C. The Situation

❑ 1. What deadlines exist? Who is more impatient?

❑ 2. What fairness norms or reference points apply?

❑ 3. What topics or questions do you want to avoid? How will you respond if they ask anyway?

D. The Relationship between the Parties

❑ 1. Will negotiations be repetitive? If so, what are the future consequences of each strategy, tactic, or action you are considering?

❑ 2. ❑ *(a)* Can you trust the other party? What do you know about them?

❑ *(b)* Does the other party trust you?

❑ 3. What do you know of the other party's styles and tactics?

❑ 4. What are the limits to the other party's authority?

❑ 5. Consult in advance with the other party about the agenda.

to include all reasonable and relevant issues that are important to you, even if they are not important to the other party.

You can also call the people with whom you plan to negotiate to ask them what issues they expect to discuss and to share your plans. This kind of conversation will begin the negotiation as a cooperative process and should minimize any delays caused by either negotiator's needing to collect additional information, to get authority, or to figure out the value of issues they had not previously considered. As we discuss later, surprise is usually not conducive to effective negotiations.

3. How Important Is Each Issue to You?

Now that you have listed all the different issues that might be negotiated, you need to develop as precise a picture as possible of their relative importance. Which issues are most important to you and which are not particularly important? Knowing the answer to that question will help you answer the next: On which issues should you stand firm and on which issues can you afford to concede? In other words, what issues might you be willing to trade away?

Setting such priorities can be a complex task. To deal with the complexity of rating the importance of individual issues, we suggest you develop a system to keep track of all the issues without losing sight of the big picture. Many different kinds of systems are possible. The key requirement is that you list and prioritize issues so that no issue is left out when you structure and compare potential agreements. The system you use must allow you to readily determine how well each possible agreement addresses every issue. We offer one such scoring system for your use, as described next.[2]

We suggest developing a table that lists every issue in the negotiation. For each issue the table should list the possible range of settlements.[3] You will then assign points to each issue to reflect its relative priority and to every possible settlement of each issue to reflect the relative desirability of resolving the issue in that way. Such a table allows you to assess the value of any proposed agreement by adding up the points it generates. You can then accurately and quickly determine which of several complex agreements you prefer. Moreover, it can help you keep the big picture in mind as you discuss the details of your agreement. We describe additional benefits in the next few pages.

The first part of Exhibit 1 shows an example of a scoring system that a conference organizer might use to negotiate with a hotel representative. In that example, the issues on the negotiation table are the duration of the room-block reservation, the room rate to be charged, the number of complimentary rooms to be provided, and the late-cancellation policy.[4] The maximum number of points possible here is 100. (If the conference organizer gets 100

percent of what she wants, then she gets 100 points; if she gets none of the issues that are important to her, then she gets 0 points.) The organizer has said that keeping the specially priced block of rooms available to last-minute registrants up until the week before the conference is very important. Room rate is somewhat less critical, she says, but is still important. Complimentary rooms and the cancellation policy are also valued by her, but are less weighty than are the first two. Note that it is not critical for all the increments within an issue to be valued equally. The jump from a 21-day-out block reservation to a 14-day-out reservation, for example, is worth 20 points to the conference organizer, while the four-day jump from 14 days to 10 days is worth only two points. Such a difference in value carries an important message. The organizer is saying that it is *very* important to have at least a 14-day-out block reservation, and that any improvement over that would be nice but is not critical.

Constructing a detailed and accurate scoring system can mean considerable work (see the second column of Exhibit 1). However, the task can be worth the effort for several reasons. First, it allows you to compare any package of settlements that may make up an agreement. With large numbers of issues, it quickly becomes difficult to compare different packages without some kind of scoring system.

Second, having a scoring system can keep you analytically focused while keeping your emotions in check. If you force yourself to evaluate each proposal using a predetermined scoring system, you are less likely to lose sight of your original interest during the heat of the actual negotiations. Resist the temptation to revise your scoring system in midnegotiation.[5]

Third, a scoring system is a useful communication tool that gives you a format for soliciting detailed information about the priorities and goals of your boss, your company, or your constituency. Building an accurate scoring system can become the topic of prenegotiation meetings that will improve your chances of pleasing the people you represent.

4. What Is Your BATNA?

Before you begin a negotiation, you need to have a backup plan in case you fail to reach an agreement with the other party. Negotiation scholars refer to this backup plan as the Best Alternative to a Negotiated Agreement, or BATNA for short. Are you, for instance, negotiating with the only supplier in town, or do you already have several attractive bids in your pocket? Alternatives make all the difference.

Each side's BATNA is a key factor in determining negotiation power. The better your BATNA, the better an offer the other party must make to interest you in reaching an agreement. Your BATNA—what you get if you leave the table without an agreement—determines your willingness to accept an impasse, which in turn tells

EXHIBIT 1　Creating a Scoring System

The example shown is a scoring system such as a conference organizer might use.

Issue 1: *Block Reservation*

Maximum value: *40 points*

Rooms reserved until 7 days before conference	40 pts.
Rooms reserved until 10 days before conference	37 pts.
Rooms reserved until 14 days before conference	35 pts.
Rooms reserved until 21 days before conference	15 pts.
Rooms reserved until 30 days before conference	5 pts.
Rooms reserved until 31 days before conference	0 pts.

Issue 2: *Room Rate*

Maximum value: *25 points*

$95 per person single, $70 per person double	25 pts.
$105 per person single, $80 per person double	20 pts.
$115 per person single, $90 per person double	15 pts.
$125 per person single, $100 per person double	10 pts.
$135 per person single, $100 per person double	5 pts.
$145 per person single, $110 per person double	0 pts.

Issue 3: *Number of Complimentary Room Nights*

Maximum value: *20 points*

3 room nights per 100 booked	20 pts.
2 room nights per 100 booked	15 pts.
1 room night per 75 booked	10 pts.
1 room night per 100 booked	5 pts.
1 room night per 150 booked	0 pts.

Issue 4: *Late Cancellations*

Maximum value: *15 points*

No penalty up to 14 days before conference	15 pts.
No penalty up to 18 days before conference	9 pts.
No penalty up to 22 days before conference	3 pts.
No penalty up to 26 days before conference	0 pts.

Exhibit explanation: Develop a scoring system for evaluating offers.

To construct your own scoring system, we recommend that you use the following steps:

(a) List all issues of importance for the negotiation, from step 2 in the checklist.

(b) Rank-order all issues according to their value to you. Which is the most important? Next? Last?

(c) Assign points to the issues. The highest-ranked issue gets the most points and the lowest-ranked issue gets the fewest points. The sum of maximum points across all issues should be 100. The purpose of this step is to improve upon the simple rank ordering in step *b* by reflecting the size of the difference between adjacently ranked issues (i.e., how much more important the first issue is than the second, the second issue than the third, and so forth). At 40 points, room-block reservation is worth almost twice as much as the next most important issue, room rate. The number of complimentary rooms and room-cancellation policy are slightly less important than room rate.

(d) List the range of possible settlements for each issue. Identify these ranges using industry or local norms or your best assessments of realistic, high, and low expectations. It may be the case that the longest block-reservation policy in the industry is 30 days. This figure establishes a realistic low boundary. Since a seven-day-out guarantee for block reservation is possible but rare, it establishes a challenging high boundary to which one can aspire.

(e) Assign points to the possible outcomes that you identified for each issue. Give the maximum number of points to your preferred settlement for that issue, and assign zero points to any settlement that is least acceptable. Now rank and assign points to the possible settlements in between the best and the worst. Consider that the point values might increase dramatically between certain adjacent pairs of settlements in the range, or might just barely increase. The most important thing to remember about assigning points is that the assignment should reflect what is important to you.

(f) Double-check your scoring system. In completing steps *a* through *e* you undoubtedly will make a few capricious choices based on "gut feeling." For example, you may be so focused on the room-block issue that the points assigned to the other issues could be changed by five points either way without affecting your stance. The point is to make sure your scoring system accurately reflects the important issues and highlights the critical plateaus. To check your numbers, compose three to five completely different hypothetical agreements. Each agreement should emphasize different issues. For example, one agreement might offer a cheap room rate but a short no-penalty cancellation period, while another agreement offers high room rates but a long no-penalty cancellation period. Compare the different agreements on the basis of points and intuitive value. The prospective agreement that has the best "gut feel" should also have the most points. If not, you need to tinker with the values you assigned in steps *a* through *e* or reconsider your priorities.

(g) Use the scoring system to assess any offer that is on the table. You should work toward obtaining the highest-scoring agreement that the other party allows.

you how hard you can press for a favorable agreement. You can negotiate hard for a job if you already have a few offers in your pocket. The better your BATNA, the more you can demand.

Having a clear BATNA helps protect you from accepting a deal that you would be better off not taking. Often people get caught up in the negotiation process and accept a contract they should have rejected. Knowing your BATNA can keep you from accepting an agreement that would make you worse off than you were before you started negotiating.

Having identified your BATNA, calculate its value based on the scoring system you developed for step 3. That is, if the other party were to make an offer that was identical to your BATNA, how many points would that offer achieve under your scoring system? Use that score as a reference point to identify those agreements that are worth less to you than your BATNA.

Even if it is difficult to assign a score to your BATNA because it is qualitatively different from the deal under negotiation or because it involves risk or uncertainty, you should nevertheless assign it a rough score for comparison purposes.

5. What Is Your Resistance Point?

Your resistance point is the worst agreement you are willing to accept before ending negotiations and resorting to your BATNA. The resistance point is the point at which you decide to walk away from the table for good, and the BATNA is where you're headed when you take that walk.

You should choose your resistance point based primarily on how good your BATNA is. If your BATNA is great, you shouldn't accept anything less than a great offer; if your BATNA is poor, you may have to be willing to accept a meager final offer. Don't forget to factor into your resistance point the switching cost and the risk of the unknown that you would be taking if your BATNA involves changing suppliers.

To illustrate the effect of switching costs, put yourself in the "buying" position of the conference organizer described in Exhibit 1. Suppose the hotel you used last year has already offered to book your conference for $100 a night single occupancy, with a 10-day-out block-reservation clause. If another hotel wants your business, you need to determine your BATNA and decide the margin by which the new hotel must beat the existing agreement—say, five dollars a night—to justify the risk of switching. Conversely, if you are the hotel sales representative in this deal, you have to determine the risks you accept for this new business—namely, that the association might fail to deliver the promised room-nights and the opportunity cost of displacing any existing business. Your BATNA as a hotel sales representative is the probability of your booking the rooms that the conference

would otherwise occupy at a given rate, adjusted by the effort (labor and expenses) it will take to book them.

The resistance point is meant to encompass all the issues at the same time rather than each issue independently. If you set a resistance point for each issue under consideration, you sacrifice your strategic flexibility. Your BATNA might include a room rate of, say, $100 a night. If you set a resistance point for room rate, rather than for the agreement as a whole, then you might walk away from what is, in fact, an attractive offer—for example, a $105 per night rate that includes more amenities and a better booking policy than your BATNA. So there should be just one resistance point and not a collection of them. The resistance point should be set just slightly better than your BATNA. Numerically, it will be the sum of the points from your scoring system that represents your minimum requirements for all the issues being negotiated.

Being aware of the resistance point is useful in negotiations. It converts a good BATNA into a powerful negotiating stance. Unless you have previously decided how far you can be pushed, you are vulnerable to being pushed below your BATNA, and thereby may accept an agreement that is worse for you than no agreement at all. The more precise your resistance point, the better.

It may seem awkward to apply a precise resistance point, particularly if your BATNA is vague or not strong. In such circumstances, you might consider setting a "tripwire" or a temporary resistance point. Set it slightly above your actual resistance point; the tripwire then gives you the chance to suspend negotiations for further consultation with your team. For example, imagine that you are booking the conference as discussed earlier. Your members have expressed a slight preference for exploring new places, and so you are negotiating with a new hotel. You are willing to pay more for a new location, but you are not sure exactly how much more your membership will accept. You know that members will balk at an exorbitant room rate. Your BATNA is to stay at the same hotel as last year and face an uncertain amount of members' disappointment. To deal with the uncertainty, you can set a tripwire. If you are comfortable signing a contract that entails a $10-a-night increase, but if you are unable to secure a rate that low or better, the tripwire tells you that you should check with your membership before you make a commitment. You have, in effect, built a "safety zone" around an uncertain BATNA.

B. About the Other Side

Good negotiators seek to understand the other party's needs and limits almost as well as they know their own. Such negotiators might be able to accomplish this understanding before the negotiations begin, or early in the negotiation process. Obviously, the final agreement will reflect not only your own preferences and BATNA, but the other party's as well. Thus it is useful to ask the same questions about the other party as you ask about yourself.

1. How Important Is Each Issue to Them (Plus Any New Issues They Added)?

Consider and attempt to estimate the other party's priorities. What trade-offs can you offer that enhance the agreement's value for both sides, or that might be neutral for the other side but a boon for you? If your counterpart had a scoring system like yours, what do you think it would look like? Call people who might have information or insight into the other party's priorities. Build a scoring system like your own that estimates their priorities, and use it to design some potential trade-offs.

As the negotiation proceeds, try to test, correct, and complete your picture of the other party's scoring system. Try to fill out your understanding of what that scoring system might look like if one existed. Gather more information during the negotiations by asking direct questions about priorities, and also by judging the other negotiator's responses to your different offers and proposed trade-offs.

You might also want to probe whether there are any issues about which the other side will completely refuse to negotiate. Such a refusal might simply be a ploy, or it might be a genuine constraint on the way it does business.

2. What Is the Other Side's BATNA?

What are your counterpart's alternatives to doing business with you? How much do you think she or he values those alternatives? How badly does this company want to do business with you? Realize that the other party will probably accept an agreement only if it improves on her or his BATNA.

The other side's BATNA contains key information about how far you can push those negotiators before they walk away. If you are selling, the buyers' BATNA should determine the maximum price they would be willing to pay for your services or product. If you are buying, it should determine the lowest price at which they will sell. If you are booking a hotel conference in Hawaii in December, the hotel representative, who has a waiting list of customers, has a much stronger BATNA than the same representative has in July. If you are absolutely certain of the other side's BATNA, and if you propose an agreement that is just a little more attractive than the other side's BATNA, then those negotiators might accept your proposal.

3. What Is the Other Side's Resistance Point, If Any?

Given your assessment of the other party's BATNA, you can estimate the least favorable deal for which the other party might settle. We say "might" because the other party may not have considered his or her resistance point. We have found, though, that it is wise to assume the other

party is well prepared. If you know the other party's resistance point, as noted earlier, you can push for an agreement that barely exceeds it. This kind of lowball deal is often better for you than an "equitable" deal, though not always.

If you are the type of negotiator who prefers amiable negotiation tactics over lowballing, then you still may want to know the other side's resistance point for two reasons. First, the other party may try to lowball you. Knowing the party's resistance point will give you the information and confidence to counter a lowball tactic. Second, many negotiators consider a fair deal to be one that falls halfway between the two parties' resistance points. To find the halfway point, you need to know both resistance points. Since experienced negotiators consider their true resistance point to be confidential information, you will most likely have to make a best guess about how far you can push the other party before seriously risking impasse or generating ill will.

Openly asking for the other party's resistance point carries risks. The other party might lie and therefore be forced to take an uncompromising stance to avoid disclosing that misrepresentation. Or if the other party honestly reveals his or her resistance point to you, that negotiator may expect you to reveal your resistance point, too. At this point, you have two choices. One, you reveal your resistance point and open yourself to being lowballed or, at best, to being offered an agreement that reaches no farther than the halfway point between the two resistance points. Two, if you don't reveal your resistance point, you may violate the norm of reciprocity.

4. What Is Your Target?

You set your target based on what you know about the other side. By this point, you should know what is the least favorable agreement that you will accept, and you have estimated the other side's least favorable, acceptable agreement. Now consider the most favorable agreement for you. This is your upper limit—the top of your range. If you focus primarily on your resistance point, which is the bottom of your range, you are unlikely to secure an agreement that is far superior to that resistance point.

To properly set your target, you must consider the bargaining zone, and to do that you have to sum up the other side's situation. The bargaining zone is the range between the two parties' resistance points, comprising the range of mutually acceptable agreements.

C. The Situation

By this point you have drawn up a fairly accurate picture of the issues and the priorities that constitute the negotiations. Here are some additional contextual factors to consider to help you maximize your advantages and minimize your risk of making mistakes.

1. What Deadlines Exist? Who Is More Impatient?

The negotiator who feels a greater sense of urgency will often make rapid concessions in an effort to secure a deal quickly. Many Western cultures have a quick-paced approach to negotiations. When paired with negotiators from cultures that negotiate deliberately (e.g., Japan, India), quick negotiators risk getting unfavorable agreements. A good way to slow down your pace is to avoid negotiating under a close deadline. Flexibility with regard to time can be a negotiating strength.

2. What Fairness Norms or Reference Points Apply?

Negotiations often involve a discussion of what might constitute a "fair deal." In fact, some experts recommend the approach of always negotiating over the "principle" or standard that you will use to assess fairness before getting down to details and numbers. The abstract discussion may be less threatening or emotionally charged than the details, and may result in a more cooperative tone and outcome for the negotiation.

Recognize, however, that there are many valid ways to determine fairness, and each negotiator will often choose the fairness norm that most favors his or her position. Both parties know that the other is doing this; just the same, each party expects the other to justify an offer as fair by showing how an offer complies with some fairness norm. Because offers that are unaccompanied by a fairness argument will rarely be accepted, you should consider alternative norms of fairness for each negotiation. Ask yourself, which ones justify your demands and which ones defeat them? Which ones best reflect your conscience?

An associate of one of the authors, for example, faced a salary negotiation upon considering a new job. The potential employer stated an intent to pay "market value" and thought it fair to define market value as the salary that other starting local faculty members were paid. The job seeker, on the other hand, judged that as unfair and argued that market value should be defined as the salary paid to starting management faculty members at comparable nationally ranked universities. The candidate thereby successfully redefined "market value" by describing the salaries drawn by other graduates of his program who took management faculty jobs. Since the employer had already agreed to pay market value, the employer found itself making concessions to do the fair thing of acting consistently with its own stated principles.

That example shows how a negotiation often hinges on a discussion of fairness. Prepare for each negotiation by considering alternative norms of fairness.

3. What Topics or Questions Do You Want to Avoid? How Will You Respond If the Other Side Asks Anyway?

You might find yourself in a position where there is something that you do not want the other negotiator to know. Your BATNA may be weak, for instance. Good negotiators plan in advance how to respond to questions they do not want to answer. Prepare an answer that is in no way dishonest but does not expose your weaknesses. Preparation means rehearsing your answer until you can deliver it smoothly, just as if you were practicing for a play. If you do not prepare and practice your answers to dreaded questions, then you risk an awkward pause or gesture that will tip off the other negotiator to a potential weakness. Awkward gestures might even cause the other party to believe you are lying when you are not. We suggest preparation so that you avoid looking like a liar when you tell the truth but choose not to reveal confidential information. If there are things you do not want to discuss, prepare your deflections in advance and polish them until they are seamless.

D. The Relationship between the Parties

1. Are the Negotiations Part of a Continuing Series? If So, What Are the Future Consequences of Each Strategy, Tactic, or Action You Are Considering?

Consider whether you expect or want to continue a business relationship with the party across the table. If the answer is yes, then you probably want to be careful about using negotiation tactics that the other side might perceive as bullying, insulting, or manipulative. Extracting those last few additional concessions out of the other party is usually not worth the loss of goodwill.

The fact that you plan to do business with the other party in the future offers a few freedoms as well as restrictions. The trust and goodwill that you develop in the current deal may have a payoff for the next time. Also, if you can safely assume that the other party wants a relationship with you, then you can worry less about them negotiating in bad faith. Trust facilitates successful negotiations much more than does paranoia.

2. Can You Trust the Other Party? What Do You Know About Them?

Call around to inquire how this company conducts negotiation. How much you trust the other party will influence your negotiation style. To find the trade-offs and creative solutions that ensure that everyone gets a fair deal, you have to share information about your needs and priorities. Unfortunately, though, sharing your information makes you vulnerable to an unscrupulous negotiator across the table. Untrustworthy opponents can ascertain your priorities before you know theirs and use this knowledge to gain maximum concessions from you. They might also lie about their own priorities.

The extent to which you trust the other party should determine your approach to sharing and collecting information. A series of small information "trades" is a good way to build mutual trust without opening either side to exploitation. A second approach to gathering data when you do not trust or know the other party well is to offer multiple proposals and see which ones the other side prefers. Be careful in this approach, however, as you must be willing to live with all the proposals you offer. It is considered a breach of faith if you propose an offer (for any reason) but have no intention of carrying through with the deal even if the other party says OK.

If you already know and trust the other party, your task is much easier. In such cases negotiations can involve an extensive exchange of information about interests and priorities.

3. What Do You Know of the Other Party's Styles and Tactics?

Different negotiators have different personal or cultural preferences. You are likely to secure the best deal and have the most positive interaction if you learn about their style in advance and try to accommodate it.

We have observed three types of negotiators. One type prefers to ease into the issue at hand after some personal contact. Once that negotiator is at ease with you as a person, she or he will be comfortable revealing information afterward.

Another type of negotiator prefers a direct approach and eschews disclosure and creative problem solving. Such a negotiator requires a competitive approach to the interaction.

The third type of negotiator enters the process having carefully computed and decided what is the best deal—and makes that offer up front and announces that it is nonnegotiable. Having already made up his or her mind about what the agreement must be, this negotiator will likely become impatient and annoyed at any attempt at give-and-take. If you know that the person you face prefers to do business this way, recognize that it is probably not a ploy. Simply assess the offer to see if it beats your BATNA. If it does, take it. If it does not, then politely refuse.

Some negotiators use either of two common gambits. One is to return from a break with a request for just one more concession that can seal the deal. This tactic, known as "taking a second bite of the apple," is common among car dealers. The appropriate response is to suggest that if the other party would like to reopen negotiations, you are willing to reopen them, too—but on all the issues, not just one.

"Good cop, bad cop" is a tactic whereby the person with whom you negotiate plays the role of "wanting" to meet all your needs, but "demands" are being made by someone who is higher up and usually absent from the actual negotiation (e.g., the sales manager). One response to this approach is to take a break to reassess the other side's stance compared to your tripwire. Another is to insist on speaking directly with the final decision maker.

4. What Are the Limits to the Other Party's Authority?

Establish early the level of authority held by your counterpart. Most negotiators, unless they are the CEOs of their companies, are authorized to negotiate only certain specified issues and within certain ranges. Determine whether you are negotiating with the right person, or whether far more latitude in generating resolutions might be available if you negotiated with someone else.

5. Consult in Advance with the Other Party about the Agenda.

As we stated earlier, consider calling the other party beforehand to share what issues you plan to discuss and to ask what issues the other party might raise. In general, holding back information is counterproductive, and introducing unexpected issues generally delays the proceedings.

Although good negotiators often get creative in their approach to the issues, this creativity must be well grounded in an understanding of the issues and of both parties' priorities. A well-prepared negotiator has considered these factors in depth, and has also considered the past and future context of the business relationship between the parties. It has been said that no plan survives contact with the enemy—but it remains true that the shrewd general will have memorized the terrain and analyzed the strengths and weaknesses of both sides before an engagement. Fortune favors the prepared mind.

Notes

1. There is some risk of overwhelming oneself—and one's negotiation partner—with too many issues. We suggest a combination of moderation in adding issues with an effective system of note taking and organization.

2. Any method that serves as a mnemonic device to track and evaluate multiple issues and deals may work. The one we describe is one that has received much attention in negotiation courses and research. See D. A. Lax and J. K.

Sebenius, *The Manager as Negotiator* (New York: Free Press, 1986).

3. Several negotiation sessions may take place before you can identify all the issues and the range of possible resolutions for those issues. However, we recommend that you list in advance as many issues as you know about and then update the table between negotiation sessions to include additional issues and settlements.

4. Note that we have simplified the issues of such a negotiation for expository purposes. Additional issues might include cancellation clauses, airport transportation, continental breakfasts, function space, additional events or amenities, and so on.

5. In the interest of maintaining your original goals, do not adjust your scoring system while in the middle of discussion with the other party. During negotiations you may hear things that suggest your original preferences and priorities may be in error. Such new information might be valid, or it might simply be the other negotiator's effort to mislead you. There are a bad way and a good way to deal with the uncertainty such rhetoric may cause you. The bad way is to lose confidence in the accuracy of your scoring system, throw it out, and continue to negotiate. The good way is to take a break and verify the information as both true and relevant to your preferences. If it is, during that break adjust your scoring system to reflect the new information and restart negotiations with the new scoring system.

READING TWO

Negotiation and Culture: A Framework

Jeanne M. Brett

At the height of foreign investment in Russia, BP PLC spent $484 million to buy 10 percent of Sidanko, one of the five largest Russian oil companies. Eighteen months later, BP was enmeshed in a bankruptcy proceeding and takeover fight that resulted in the loss of BP's investment. What went wrong with this deal? In the race to have a foothold in an emerging market, BP apparently overlooked negotiating fundamentals and cultural issues. A young pro-Western banker with excellent political connections ran Sidanko. He had taken the company private for $470 million, only slightly less than what BP paid for 10 percent ownership, 20 percent voting rights, and a few senior management positions. BP clearly wanted access to Sidanko's oil fields but unfortunately did not negotiate enough leverage to take over the direction of the company and make it profitable. According to one commentator who follows foreign investment in Russia, the BP executives' instructions were not carried out either because Russian management culturally would not do so or because Russian management was getting orders from somewhere else.[1] BP ended up facing off with a recalcitrant creditor who owned part of Sidanko's $450 million in outstanding debt and wanted the oil fields itself.

Culture is often the culprit when deals that cross national borders, like the one between BP and Sidanko, lead to disputes and unanticipated costs. This chapter lays the groundwork for understanding how culture affects negotiation. It begins by describing negotiation fundamentals, those elements of negotiation that are the same across cultures. It then describes culture and explains how culture affects negotiations.

Negotiation Fundamentals

When you ask people all over the world what comes to mind when you say *negotiation*, most describe some sort of a market in which two people exchange a series of offers. Implicit in their answer is the assumption that a deal is in the making, that the two are speaking directly (though the medium may be electronic), and that they are bargaining to divide a fixed pie of resources. Yet negotiations are not limited to direct deal making over fixed resources. In all cultures, people negotiate to resolve disputes and to make decisions in teams. When negotiators reach agreement, resources are always distributed, but the amount of resources available for distribution is not necessarily fixed. Fundamental to negotiation are the circumstances in which people negotiate and the types of agreements they reach.

Types of Negotiations

All types of negotiations occur because people perceive that their goals are incompatible. When people see themselves as interdependent (or potentially so) but in *conflict*,

Source: Jeanne M. Brett, *Negotiating Globally* (San Francisco: Jossey-Bass, 2001).

they naturally negotiate to try to deal with the conflict. Negotiators from BP trying to buy Sidanko wanted to pay as little as possible. Negotiators from Sidanko trying to raise capital by selling a stake to a foreign oil company wanted to gain as much as possible. Their *deal-making negotiations* sought terms that were better than either party could negotiate elsewhere despite their conflicting goals. Conflict is frequently the subtext when groups or teams are trying to make decisions. BP placed managers in top executive positions at Sidanko, but these managers did not have sufficient leverage to influence *decision-making negotiations* at the top. When BP realized that its goals were not being met, it made a series *of claims* for more management control. When its claims were rejected, *dispute resolution negotiations* ensued. Deal-making, decision-making, and dispute resolution negotiations occur in all cultures. However, because culture affects how negotiators reach deals, resolve disputes, and make decisions, it also affects their agreements.

Distributive and Integrative Agreements

Negotiation is about claiming *value*: how much of a set of resources you are going to get and how much the other party gets. Successful *value-claiming negotiation* leads to a distributive outcome that divides a fixed set of resources such that your interests or the needs underlying your positions are met. But negotiation can also be about creating value: how you and the other party can increase the resources available to divide. Successful *value-creating negotiation* leads to an agreement that is both integrative and distributive, one that divides an enhanced set of resources.

The concept of *integrative agreements*, much less how to reach them, is not intuitive. To create value takes transforming what appears to be a fixed set of resources into a set of resources that are differentially valued by the negotiators and then distributing resources to the negotiators who value them the most.

There may be opportunities to create value in even the simplest of negotiations. While living in a small village in France, my husband and I offered to organize a traditional Halloween party for the 30 children in the local grade school. Our children had told their French friends about making jack-o'-lanterns (pumpkins are hollowed out, a face is carved, and a lighted candle is placed inside). My job was to purchase enough pumpkins for 30 children to carve. I had difficulty locating any pumpkins but finally found a roadside stand outside a small house with some for sale. I counted; there were exactly 30. I knocked on the door, and a woman came out. I told her I wanted to buy the pumpkins and asked the price. She named a reasonable figure, and I said, "Fine, I'll take all of them." "Oh, no," she replied, "I cannot sell you all of them." I immediately had visions of making jack-o'-lanterns with pumpkin

halves, holding a lottery to determine which children got to carve and which got to take home a jack-o'-lantern, carving melons instead . . . But then I thought, wait a minute, you're supposed to know something about negotiation. So I asked, "Why won't you sell me all the pumpkins?" She answered, "If I sell all of them to you, I won't have any seeds to plant next year." I asked her if having the seeds by November 1 would allow sufficient time for planting. She said it would and sold me all the pumpkins on the condition that I return the seeds on November 1, which I did.

Madame Petit and I negotiated an integrative agreement. We created value by my asking and her answering truthfully a series of questions that led us to separate the pumpkins and the seeds. There are two sources of integrative potential in negotiations: differences in negotiators' *preferences* and compatibility of preferences. Madame Petit had a stronger preference for the seeds and I for the rind of the pumpkins. Madame Petit did not need the seeds immediately and I did not want to give them to her right away. Our interests on the timing issue were compatible. Our integrative negotiation took advantage of our different uses for the pumpkins and our compatible time frame.

Had I accepted Madame Petit's refusal to sell me all the pumpkins, our agreement would have been distributive. I would have bought as many pumpkins as she would sell, and she would have kept as many as she needed for seeds. Neither of our interests would have been as fully satisfied as they were with the integrative agreement. With the integrative agreement, Madame Petit gained more money by selling me all the pumpkins, and she gained all the seeds. I gained all the pumpkins I needed so that every child could make a jack-o'-lantern.

Had I stood on principle, refusing to buy any pumpkins if I could not buy all of them, we would have reached an *impasse*. I thought my best alternative, if I could not buy pumpkins, was to have the children carve melons, a messier prospect at best. Madame Petit's alternative was to interrupt her housework repeatedly to get rid of her stock of pumpkins.

Note that our integrative agreement over the pumpkins was also distributive. Madame Petit got all of the seeds *and* her full asking price; I got all of the pumpkins. In fact, all integrative agreements also distribute value.

This is one important reason to integrate: Negotiators who integrate have more value available to distribute and are therefore more likely to claim what they want. A second important reason to integrate is that negotiators who integrate are sometimes able to structure an agreement when otherwise there would be none. Impasses normally occur when a seller asks more than a buyer can pay. However, if the seller learns why the buyer cannot pay the asking price or the buyer learns why the asking price is so high, the negotiators may be able to structure the deal—

for example, with creative financing or with nonfinancial compensation that corresponds to both parties' interests.

The term *integrative* is frequently used with a great deal of imprecision to mean an agreement that is mutually satisfactory. Mutual satisfaction, however, is an evaluation of an agreement, not a type of agreement. Negotiators who have failed to look for or find an integrative agreement may be quite satisfied with a distributive agreement. For example, if I were only able to buy 26 pumpkins and evaluated that outcome against the alternative of carving melons, I might have been satisfied. Madame Petit, who had no intention of selling all her pumpkins anyway, would also have been satisfied. Distribution and integration have to do with the amount of resources, not with the evaluation of them.

When I tell the pumpkin story in class, someone invariably suggests that I did not get such a great deal because I did not negotiate a discount for buying all the pumpkins. It is possible that had I pushed for a better price, I might have gotten one. Yet I did not for several reasons. First, I knew that haggling over price is not common in the open-air food markets in that part of France. Second, I was concerned that if I did haggle, Madame Petit might refuse to sell me any pumpkins, and my melon alternative was not particularly attractive. Third, I thought it possible that the school might want to continue the Halloween tradition and I might have future interactions with Madame Petit. My poor alternative and my concern for the relationship affected my distributive outcome. In the negotiation literature, especially the cross-cultural literature, the relationship is sometimes represented as an outcome. Yet as the example illustrates, relationship is an issue in negotiation and can be one element of a distributive or an integrative agreement.

Negotiation Fundamentals Affected by Culture: Interests, Priorities, and Strategies

All negotiators have interests and priorities, and all negotiators have strategies. *Interests* are the needs or reasons underlying the negotiator's positions. *Priorities* reflect the relative importance of various interests or positions. My interest in the negotiation with Madame Petit was having a pumpkin for each child. As we negotiated, we realized that we had different priorities: hers was for seeds and mine for the rind. A negotiation *strategy* is an integrated set of behaviors chosen because they are thought to be the means of accomplishing the goal of negotiating. My strategy negotiating with Madame Petit included confronting her directly and asking for information. I could have sent a third party, but I did not. I also refrained from using *influence* because my alternative was so poor.

Negotiators' interests, priorities, and use of strategies are affected by culture. So it is useful to have an understanding of culture before considering how and why culture affects interests, priorities, and strategies.

Culture and Negotiation

Culture is the unique character of a social group.[2] Cultures consist of psychological elements, the values and norms shared by members of a group, as well as social structural elements: the economic, social, political, and religious institutions that are the context for social interaction.[3] Cultural *values* direct attention to what issues are more and less important and influence negotiators' interests and priorities. Cultural *norms* define what behaviors are appropriate and inappropriate in negotiation and influence negotiators' strategies. Cultural *institutions* preserve and promote values and norms. Cultural values, norms, and *ideologies* serve as shared standards for interpreting situations (this is a negotiation, therefore I ought to . . .) and the behavior of others (she threatened me, therefore I should . . .).[4]

When two parties negotiate, both bring culture to the table with their interests and priorities and their negotiation strategies. Exhibit 10.1 illustrates how culture affects negotiation. It shows culture affecting the interests and priorities that underlie negotiators' positions on the issues. That is, culture may affect why the negotiators have taken the position they have or why one issue is of higher priority than another is. The fit between negotiators' priorities and interests is what generates the potential for an integrative agreement.

Culture may also affect the strategies that the negotiators bring to the table—for example, the way they go about negotiating, whether they confront directly or indirectly, their motivations, and the way they use information and influence. Exhibit 1 shows that negotiators' strategies cause patterns of interaction in negotiation. Those interaction patterns can be functional and facilitate integrative agreements, or they may be dysfunctional and lead to suboptimal agreements in which integrative potential is left on the table.

Effects of Culture on Interests and Priorities

Cultural values may reveal the interests underlying negotiators' positions. Negotiators from cultures that value tradition over change, for example, may be less enthusiastic about economic development that threatens valued ways of life than negotiators from cultures that value change and development. This was the situation in which Disney found itself after purchasing a large tract of land south of Paris to construct EuroDisney. Although EuroDisney promised jobs and economic development to an area that had high unemployment and few nonfarm jobs for youth, the local populace valued its traditional agricultural lifestyle. EuroDisney management, with its

EXHIBIT 1

How Culture Affects Negotiation

Source: J. M. Brett, "Culture and Negotiation," *International Journal of Psychology* 35 (2000), p. 102. Reprinted with the kind permission of the International Union of Psychological Science (IUPSYS).

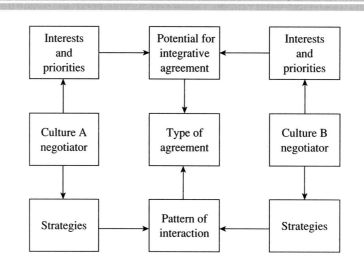

American values for economic development, had difficulty reconciling the local population's preferences for tradition over development.

The example also points out that the same values that generate cultural differences in preferences may also act as cultural blinders. Negotiators from one culture, expecting preferences to be compatible, cannot understand the rationality of negotiators from another culture whose views on the same issue are at odds with their own.[5] It is generally unwise in negotiation to label the other party as irrational. Such labeling encourages persuasion to get the other party to adopt your view of the situation and distributive outcomes, rather than the search for differences and the *trade-offs* that are the foundation of integrative agreements. There is opportunity for integration in differences. Instead of trying to persuade local French farmers that they should want to give up their traditional way of life, Disney had the opportunity to seek ways to preserve the traditions in the agrarian community in return for the community's support of the new park.

How Culture Affects Negotiation Strategies

When people negotiate, their behaviors are strategic and their strategies may be culturally based. This means that negotiators in one culture are more likely to enact a strategy with one set of behaviors and negotiators from another culture are more likely to enact that same strategy with another set of behaviors. Not only are there differences in strategic behavior between cultures, but there are also differences within cultures and overlap between cultures, with the result that some members of a culture may negotiate less like their own cultural prototype and more like the *prototype* of another culture.

Exhibit 2 shows the distribution of a negotiation strategy in two different cultures. The horizontal axis shows the level of strategic behaviors, ranging from low to high. The vertical axis shows frequency in terms of proportions of cultural members who exhibit different strategic behaviors. The normal curves drawn for cultures A and B indicate that the two cultures' prototypes are quite different but there is variability within each culture. Some members' behaviors are more and some less similar to the cultural prototype. There is also some overlap between the two cultures such that Smith from culture A behaves more like the prototype for culture B than the prototype for his own culture and vice versa for Chen from culture B.

EXHIBIT 2   Cultural Prototypes, Variability, and Overlap

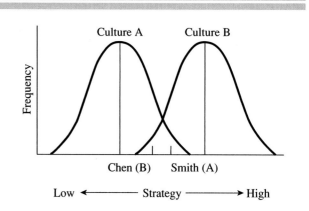

Negotiation strategies are linked with culture because cultures evolve norms to facilitate social interaction. Norms are functional because they reduce the number of choices a person has to make about how to behave and because they provide expectations about how others in the culture will behave. Functional norms become institutionalized, meaning that most people use them and new members of the culture learn them because they make social interaction efficient. Our research indicates that there is a range of behaviors available for negotiators to use when enacting confrontation, information, influence, and motivation strategies and that culture has an impact on what behaviors negotiators use. Exhibit 3 summarizes these strategies and the alternative behaviors that negotiators can use to enact them.

Confrontation

Negotiations are not always direct verbal interactions between principals. Sometimes the verbal message is indirect. A U.S. company had a contract from a German buyer to sell bicycles produced in China. When the first shipment was ready, there was a problem. The bikes rattled. The U.S. buyer did not want to accept the shipment, knowing that with the rattle, they would not be acceptable to the German customer, whose high-end market niche was dominated by bikes that were whisper-quiet. What to do? In the U.S. culture, the normal approach would be to tell the manufacturer that the rattling bikes were unacceptable and that the problem had to be fixed. In China, such a direct *confrontation* would be extremely rude and cause much loss of face. Knowing this, the U.S. manager went to the Chinese plant, inspected the bicycles, rode a few, and asked about the rattle. "Is this rattle normal? Do all the bikes rattle? Do you think the German buyer will think there is something wrong with the bike if it rattles?" Then he left. The next shipment of bikes had no rattles.

Sometimes nonverbal behavior sends the message. An Asian woman, a new member of a multicultural team I was observing, was participating in discussion at a low level until an issue arose that involved her part of the organization and on which she had clearly been briefed.

She spoke clearly and forcefully about the problems the team's plans would cause in her area. The rest of the team listened politely, asked no questions, and went ahead with the plan. Her response was to withdraw and stop participating altogether. Unfortunately, the rest of the team was not attuned to her nonverbal behavior.

At other times, instead of direct confrontation, a third party gets involved. When a U.S. manager in a U.S.–Chinese joint venture did not receive the information he was expecting in a report, he asked the Chinese woman responsible for the report for a meeting to discuss his needs. She politely put him off. A day later, he was called into her manager's office and told that there was no problem with the report, the report had the information it always had, and the report could not be changed.

People from different cultures vary in their preferences for direct verbal confrontation in negotiation. Some who are comfortable negotiating deals face-to-face are not comfortable engaging in face-to-face confrontation over a dispute or in a team meeting. Global negotiators need to understand how to confront directly and indirectly.

Motivation

Motivation is all about negotiators' interests. Negotiators may be concerned about *self-interests*, about the interests of the other party at the table, or about *collective interests* that extend beyond the immediate negotiation table. My negotiation with Madame Petit was motivated by self-interests and *other interests*—mine with the pumpkins, hers with the seeds. Collective interests did not really enter into the negotiation. The children might have been just as happy carving melons! However, in some negotiations, collective interests are very important. For example, when the French automaker Renault bought a large stake in Nissan in 1999, business commentators predicted that the measures required to make Nissan profitable—plant closings, lay offs, winnowing of suppliers—would be extremely difficult to accomplish. Japanese companies traditionally feel responsible for their employees and to the communities in which their plants are located. Laying off employees, closing plants, and generating competition

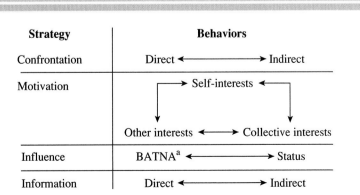

EXHIBIT 3

Cultural Prototypes, Variability, and Overlap

[a]Best alternative to a negotiated agreement.

Strategy	Behaviors
Confrontation	Direct ←——→ Indirect
Motivation	Self-interests; Other interests ←——→ Collective interests
Influence	BATNA[a] ←——→ Status
Information	Direct ←——→ Indirect

among suppliers is not a normative business practice in Japan, where collective interests dominate.

The relative importance of negotiators' self-interests, other interests, and collective interests vary by culture. Negotiators from some cultures are much more concerned with self-interests; negotiators from other cultures pay as much attention to the interests of others as to their own; and negotiators from still other cultures take the interests of the collective into account when setting priorities and deciding whether to accept a proposal or continue negotiating. Global negotiators need to be sensitive to cultural differences in negotiators' goals and motivation and in negotiators' interests.

Influence

Power is the ability to influence the other party to accede to your wishes.[6] There are many different bases of power in social interaction,[7] but two, BATNAs and fairness standards, seem to be particularly important for negotiation and to be relied on differently in different cultures.

BATNA stands for the *best alternative to a negotiated agreement*.[8] The worse a negotiator's BATNA, the more dependent the negotiator is on reaching an agreement and the less powerful in terms of extracting concessions. My BATNA in negotiating with Madame Petit was buying melons—not very good. I could hardly have influenced her to sell me all her pumpkins by threatening to go elsewhere and buy melons!

Fairness standards are decision rules, wrapped in a veneer of justice. The rule might be precedent, it might be contract or law, or it might be social status (for example, age or experience) or social ideology (for example, equity, equality, or need). I could have proposed need as a fair standard to try to convince Madame Petit to sell me all her pumpkins. However, she had needs too, and this illustrates the problem with fair standards as influence strategies: There are almost always competing standards, even within a culture.

Across cultures, differences in ideology are likely to make it difficult to agree on a fairness standard. For example, ideology is at the heart of the long-standing "banana wars" between the United States and the European Union (EU). The fair standard that applies is the open markets standard that both parties have agreed to as members of the World Trade Organization (WTO). Yet France, an EU and WTO member, effectively blocked the importation of bananas from U.S. companies by imposing tariffs, making U.S. bananas more expensive than bananas from former French colonies whose economies in the near term depend on bananas. French ideology has a social welfare slant that extends to its former colonies. U.S. ideology is more capitalistic.[9]

The relative importance of BATNAs versus fairness standards, especially standards based on social status, as a basis of power in negotiations varies by culture. The

relative frequency of use of influence tactics also varies by culture.

Information

Information is the currency of negotiation. Information about BATNAs, status, and other fair standards affects distributive agreements. Information about interests and priorities affects integrative agreements. When negotiators do not understand the information conveyed by the other party, integrative potential is almost always left on the table, and sometimes negotiations end in impasse.

Consider the inauspicious opening in the following negotiation. A U.S. negotiator on his first trip to Japan was confused by the formal opening meeting, which his Japanese hosts filled with a recitation of the history of their company, a story about the founder, and a litany about their product. After the meeting, the U.S. negotiator turned to his local representative and said, "What was that all about? Do they think I would arrive so unprepared as not to know about their company and their product? I want to buy their product. Why are they treating me as though I've never heard of it or their company? All the information they conveyed this afternoon is readily available in the marketplace, and I already know it." The local representative explained that the Japanese negotiators were attempting to convey information, albeit indirectly, about the status of their company and the product. The U.S. negotiator, fully aware of the Japanese company's status, was eager to get down to direct negotiations.

Culture affects whether information is conveyed directly, with meaning on the surface of the communication, or indirectly, with meaning conveyed within the context of the message. Culture also affects whether information is conveyed at all.

Why Culture Affects Negotiation Strategy

The behaviors that negotiators from a culture characteristically use to enact a negotiation strategy are related to other features of that culture, including its values, norms for social interaction other than negotiation, and ideologies. Three widely studied features of culture seem to be related to the variability in negotiation strategy across cultures: the cultural values of individualism versus collectivism and egalitarianism versus hierarchy, and the low- versus high-context norm for communication.

Individualism versus Collectivism

The most widely studied cultural value, *individualism* versus *collectivism*, distinguishes between cultures that place individuals' needs above collective needs and cultures that place the needs of the collective above the needs of individuals.[10] In individualist cultures, norms promote the autonomy of the individual. Social and economic institutions reward individual accomplishments. Legal institutions protect individual rights. In collectivist cultures, norms promote the interdependence of individuals by emphasizing social obligation. Social and economic institutions reward classes of people rather than individuals. Legal institutions support collective interests above individual rights.

The way a society treats people affects how they construe themselves and how they interact. People in all cultures distinguish between *in-groups*, of which they are members, and *out-groups*, of which they are not.[11] In individualist cultures, self-identity is likely to consist of attributes that are independent of in-group membership.[12] A negotiator from an individualist culture might say, "I am tall; I am intelligent; I have a sense of humor." In collectivist cultures, self-identity is likely to be interdependent with in-group membership. A negotiator from a collectivist culture might say, "I am a wife, mother, and daughter; I am a Kellogg faculty member."

Two researchers, Geert Hofstede and Shalom Schwartz, have measured social values in many cultures.[13] They used questionnaires and classified cultures by differences in average scores. Exhibit 4 summarizes Hofstede's classification of individualist and collectivist cultures, ranked in each category in decreasing order of individualism.

Members of individualist and collectivist cultures differ in many ways. Exhibit 5 suggests that both confrontational and motivational behaviors may stem from this cultural value.

Reluctance to confront directly in a negotiation may stem from the emphasis on cooperation in collectivist cultures.[14] Confronting—for example, telling the bicycle maker that the rattles indicated unacceptable quality—signals a lack of respect for an individual with whom you have a relationship.[15] An indirect approach is thought to be relationship-preserving.[16]

Negotiators' motivational orientations may also stem from their culture's values for individualism versus collectivism. This cultural value reflects a society's goal orientation.[17] Individualist cultures emphasize self-interests. Collectivist cultures emphasize collective interests.

Egalitarianism versus Hierarchy

The second most widely studied cultural value distinguishes *hierarchical cultures*, which emphasize differentiated social status, from *egalitarian cultures*, which do not. In hierarchical cultures, social status implies social power. Social inferiors are expected to defer to social superiors, who in return for the power and privilege conferred on them by right of their status have an obligation to look out for the well-being of low-status people.[18]

Hofstede and Schwartz have also classified cultures on this dimension, which Hofstede calls "power distance." High-power-distance cultures are hierarchical ones where social status is differentiated into ranks. Exhibit 6 summarizes Schwartz's classification of egalitarian and hierarchical cultures, ranked in descending order of egalitarian and hierarchical commitment.

Individualist Cultures	Intermediate Cultures	Collectivist Cultures
United States	Austria	Brazil
Australia	Israel	Turkey
Great Britain	Spain	Greece
Canada	India	Philippines
Netherlands	Japan	Mexico
New Zealand	Argentina	Portugal
Italy	Iran	Hong Kong
Belgium		Chile
Denmark		Singapore
Sweden		Thailand
France		Taiwan
Ireland		Peru
Norway		Pakistan
Switzerland		Colombia
Germany		Venezuela
Finland		

EXHIBIT 4

Individualist and Collectivist Cultures

Source: G. Hofstede, *Culture's Consequences: International Differences in Work-Related Values* (Thousand Oaks, CA: Sage, 1980), p. 158, copyright © 1980 by Sage. Reprinted by permission of Sage Publications, Inc.

EXHIBIT 5   Individualism–Collectivism and Negotiation Strategy

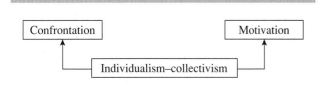

EXHIBIT 6   Egalitarian and Hierarchical Cultures

Egalitarian Cultures	Hierarchical Cultures
Portugal	Thailand
Italy	China
Spain	Turkey
Denmark	Zimbabwe
France	Japan
Netherlands	Taiwan
Germany	Hong Kong
Greece	Singapore
Finland	Brazil
Switzerland	Poland
New Zealand	Malaysia
Turkey	Hungary
United States	United States
Mexico	New Zealand
Australia	Australia
Brazil	Mexico
Israel	Germany
Hong Kong	Netherlands
Poland	Switzerland
Singapore	France
Japan	Portugal
Taiwan	Spain
Malaysia	Finland
China	Greece
Zimbabwe	Denmark
Slovenia	Slovenia
Thailand	Italy

Source: S. Schwartz, "Beyond Individualism/Collectivism: New Cultural Dimensions of Values," in H. C. Triandis, U. Kim, and G. Yoon (eds.), *Individualism and Collectivism* (London: Sage, 1994), pp. 113–14, copyright © 1994 by Sage. Reprinted by permission of Sage Publications, Inc.

Members of egalitarian and hierarchical cultures may have rather distinct confrontational styles. They may also use influence differently. Exhibit 7 suggests that both confrontational and influence behaviors may be related to this cultural value.

People in hierarchical cultures may be reluctant to confront directly in negotiation because confrontation implies a lack of respect for social status and may threaten social structures. The norm in such a culture is not to challenge higher-status members. When conflict does occur, it is more likely to be handled by a social superior than by direct confrontation.[19] When a higher-status third party gets involved in a dispute, that party's decision reinforces his authority without necessarily conferring differential status on the contestants, as a negotiation that one party lost and the other won would do. In an egalitarian culture, differentiated status due to success in direct negotiations is not likely to translate into permanent changes in social status because there are few avenues for setting precedents in egalitarian cultures.

Negotiators from hierarchical and egalitarian cultures may use influence rather differently if their views of power in negotiation reflect the way power is construed in their cultures. In egalitarian cultures, power is transitory and situational; in hierarchical cultures, power is long-term and general. The concept of BATNA fits well with the conceptualization of power in egalitarian cultures. BATNAs are situational and flexible. If a negotiator is unhappy with his BATNA, he may be able to improve it. Power as status fits well with the conceptualization of power in hierarchical cultures. Status-based power should endure over time and across situations.[20]

The reliance on a status-based interpretation of power can be seen in Japanese commercial relationships in the 1960s and the 1980s. Japan is a hierarchical culture. In the 1960s, when Japanese automobile companies were trying to break into the U.S. market, they sold their cars at a very low margin. Presumably, they viewed themselves as having lower status than the American carmakers, and that status dictated that they could not charge the same high prices for their cars as the higher-status Americans. When the Japanese economy was booming in the 1980s, Japan's self-image of its economic status improved, and Japanese companies paid top dollar, bidding and winning against American companies for commercial real estate and private companies.

These events can be interpreted, as indeed they were in the U.S. press, from an in-group versus out-group perspective. Japan is a collectivist culture. Negotiators from collectivist cultures are said to deal with in-group members cooperatively and out-group members competitively. Japanese commercial behavior in both the 1960s and the 1980s was motivated by competition. This explanation based on competitiveness due to collectivism may be correct, but it is simplistic. Selling at

EXHIBIT 7 Egalitarianism–Hierarchy and Negotiation Strategy

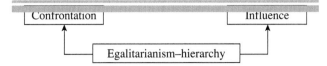

or below margin, as the Japanese automakers did in the 1960s, does not make a lot of competitive sense because it does not build market share when competitors drop their prices too. (Japanese market share for automobiles in the United States was ultimately built on quality, not on price.) Paying significant premiums when you are the powerful buyer in the market and presumably have many options for investment also does not make competitive sense. An explanation based on hierarchy and the status of the Japanese in the marketplace in the 1960s and the 1980s provides additional insight into the behavior of Japanese negotiators.

Low-Context versus High-Context Communications

People in low-context cultures prefer to communicate directly. Meaning is on the surface of the message. Information is explicit, without nuance, and relatively context-free. People in high-context cultures prefer to communicate indirectly. Meaning is embedded in the context of the message and must be inferred to be understood.

Exhibit 8 identifies national cultures according to whether high- or low-context communication is normative.[21] In general, high-context cultures are those in which people have extensive information networks among family, friends, colleagues, and clients and are involved in close personal relationships.

Negotiators from low- and high-context cultures may have rather distinct confrontational styles. They may also use information differently. Exhibit 9 suggests that both confrontational and information-sharing behaviors may be influenced by this cultural value.

EXHIBIT 8 Low- and High-Context Cultures

Low-Context Cultures	High-Context Cultures
Germany	Arab cultures
Scandinavian cultures	France
Switzerland	Japan
United States	Mediterranean cultures
	Russia

Source: E. T. Hall and M. R. Hall, *Understanding Cultural Differences* (Yarmouth, ME: Intercultural Press, 1990), pp. 7–8, 23.

The Western manager in the rattling bicycles story was using high-context communication. He expected his Chinese counter-part to infer from his calling attention to the rattle that the bicycles needed to be repaired. He was neither confronting directly nor communicating directly. The Asian manager on the multicultural team was showing her displeasure at being ignored by in turn ignoring the team for the rest of the meeting. Her behavior was a form of indirect confrontation and communication. The Chinese manager in the joint venture confronted and communicated indirectly by having a third party, who just happened to be the boss, communicate the refusal.

Culture and Negotiation Strategy: A Complex Link

It would be helpful if the relationships between negotiation strategies and other features of a culture were strong and straightforward. The research to date indicates quite clearly that this is not the case. The link between cultural values and cultural ideology and negotiation strategies is complex.

A look back at Exhibit 2 reveals two reasons why this link between features of a culture and negotiators' strategy is not straightforward: Not all members of a culture behave like the cultural prototype, and cultural profiles overlap.

Another reason for the complex relationship between culture and negotiation strategy is that cultures are not composed of single features. Cultures have profiles of features. Single cultural features may be more or less important, depending on the profile in which they are embedded. Given the state of the research, we can make at most general statements about single cultural features and negotiation strategy.

Yet another reason why negotiation strategy is not perfectly related to other features of a culture is that cultural norms for negotiation may be cued more strongly in some situations than others.[22] For example, members of a multicultural team may act more in accordance with their national cultural norms when they report to local superiors. When they report to a senior manager at corporate headquarters, they may act more in accordance with corporate norms.

EXHIBIT 9 Low- and High-Context Communication and Negotiation Strategy

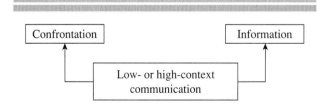

Finally, there is the influence of the strategies of the other negotiators at the table. Negotiators are quite likely to reciprocate each other's strategies.[23] When all negotiators are from the same culture, reciprocity reinforces culturally normative negotiation behaviors. When negotiators are from different cultures, reciprocity may help negotiators adjust their strategies to each other.[24]

Given all of these caveats, it is not unreasonable to wonder why we should study culture and negotiation strategy at all. The answer is that there are cultural differences in the behaviors negotiators use to enact a strategy. Anticipating these differences helps negotiators make sense of them and adjust their own behaviors to reinforce or to block the other party's strategy. However, the global negotiator needs to be aware of several important points:

- Research is only beginning to profile the characteristic negotiation strategies of different cultures. There may be important strategic differences between cultures in addition to the motivational, influence, information, and confrontational strategies discussed here. Many cultures have not yet been thoroughly studied.

- Individual cultural members may not act like the cultural prototype, especially in particular situations. The cultural typologies based on individualism–collectivism, egalitarianism–hierarchy, and low- or high-context communication may not characterize the negotiators you are dealing with.

- A negotiator's strategy is not immutable; negotiators adjust their strategies to accommodate one another.

There is a risk in knowing too much about the other party's culture and assuming that he will act according to the cultural prototype. Excellent cross-cultural negotiators proceed slowly, testing their assumptions about what strategy will be effective with the other party. They are willing to adjust their use of negotiation strategy to achieve their goals but not compromise on their goals.

Notes

1. N. Banerjee, "BP's Losses in Russia Seen as a Warning for Investors," *International Herald Tribune*, Aug. 13–14, 1999, pp. 9, 13.

2. Individuals are members of many different cultural groups in addition to their nation–state. Furthermore, cultural subgroups are embedded within nation–state cultural groups. This all gets rather confusing. So when doing cultural research, it is imperative to identify the type of group you are studying. In our studies, negotiators bring their individual differences to the table; they bring their employer's culture to the table, the culture of their ethnic group, and their national culture. We are interested only in the cultures of nation–states, and those cultures are relevant only if there are systematic differences between them. This requirement is a reasonably high hurdle for the research. If there are no differences between national cultural groups, then there is no basis for drawing cultural inferences.

3. A. L. Lytle, J. M. Brett, Z. I. Barsness, C. H. Tinsley, and M. Janssens, "A Paradigm for Confirmatory Cross-Cultural Research in Organizational Behavior," in L. L. Cummings and B. M. Staw (eds.), *Research in Organizational Behavior* (Greenwich, CT: JAI Press, 1995).

4. S. T. Fiske and S. E. Taylor, *Social Cognition* (New York: McGraw-Hill, 1991).

5. U.S. companies apparently do not learn well from each other's experiences. Mondavi Vineyards announced in May 2000 that it was planning to lease a forested hillside above Aniane, near Montpellier, to produce France's first foreign-owned *vin de terroir*. Mondavi expected Aniane's 2,120 inhabitants to be pleased that this fine American company would be pumping $8 million into the local economy over the next 10 years. Instead, villagers protested the destruction of the communal forest where they hunt wild boar: V. Walt, "French Village Unwilling to Welcome Mondavi," *International Herald Tribune*, July 20, 2000, p. 11.

6. Ury, Brett, and Goldberg, *Getting Disputes Resolved*.

7. J. French and B. Raven, "The Bases of Social Power," in D. Cartwright (ed.), *Studies in Social Power* (Ann Arbor, MI: Institute for Social Research, 1959).

8. R. Fisher, W. Ury, B. Patton, *Getting to Yes* (New York: Penguin, 1991).

9. Office of the U.S. Trade Representative, "USTR Kantor Makes Preliminary Decision That EU Banana Regime Harms U.S. Interests" (press release), Jan. 9, 1999.

10. G. Hofstede, *Culture's Consequences: International Differences in Work-Related Values* (Thousand Oaks, CA: Sage, 1980); S. Schwartz, "Beyond Individualism/Collectivism:

New Cultural Dimensions of Values," in H. C. Triandis, U. Kim, and G. Yoon (eds.), *Individualism and Collectivism* (London: Sage, 1994); H. C. Triandis, *Individualism and Collectivism* (Boulder, CO: Westview Press, 1995).

11. J. C. Turner, *Rediscovering the Social Group: A Self-Categorization Theory* (Cambridge: Blackwell, 1987).

12. Triandis, *Individualism and Collectivism.*

13. Hofstede, *Culture's Consequences;* Schwartz, "Beyond Individualism/Collectivism."

14. W. B. Gudykunst, G. Gao, K. L. Schmidt, T. Nishida, M. H. Bond, K. Leung, G. Wang, and R. A. Barraclough, "The Influence of Individualism–Collectivism, Self-Monitoring, and Predicted Outcome Value on Communication in Ingroup and Outgroup Relationships," *Journal of Cross-Cultural Psychology,* 23 (1992), pp. 196–213.

15. A more technical and psychologically insightful explanation for why negotiators from collectivist cultures are reluctant to use confrontation focuses on the importance of in-groups in these cultures. In-groups provide social identity to their members. In a collectivist culture, group-based social identity is very important because individual needs and values are subordinate to collective needs and values. People do not want to risk ostracism from in-groups that confer identity and social benefits. For this reason, cooperation and harmony with in-group members is emphasized. Confronting a member of an in-group signals a lack of respect for that person, and for yourself, since you are both members of the same social identity group: Turner, *Rediscovering the Social Group.*

16. As a member of a Western culture, I admit that I find it difficult to understand how being told no indirectly by the boss is going to preserve my relationship with my peer, whom I originally asked for something and who did not respond to that request. Some things about culture you just have to accept, and one of them seems to be that in some cultures, involving the boss (indirect confrontation) is seen as a way of preserving the peer relationship and in others it is not. Recognizing the difference does not mean that you have to accept it as your own way of interpreting the situation, just that there is another way to frame the same situation that is legitimate in other cultures.

17. Schwartz, "Beyond Individualism/Collectivism."

18. K. Leung, "Negotiation and Reward Allocations across Cultures," in P. C. Earley, M. Erez, and Associates, *New Perspectives on International/Industrial Organizational Psychology* (San Francisco: Jossey-Bass, 1997).

19. Leung, "Negotiation and Reward Allocations across Cultures."

20. J. M. Brett and T. Okumura, "Inter- and Intra-Cultural Negotiation: U.S. and Japanese Negotiators," *Academy of Management Journal* 41 (1998), pp. 495–510.

21. E. T. Hall and M. R. Hall, *Understanding Cultural Differences* (Yarmouth, ME: Intercultural Press, 1990). See also M. Rajan and J. Graham, "Nobody's Grandfather Was a Merchant: Understanding the Soviet Commercial Negotiation Process and Style," *California Management Review,* Spring 1991, pp. 40–57.

22. Leung, "Negotiation and Reward Allocations across Cultures"; M. W. Morris, K. Leung, D. Ames, and B. Lickel, "Views from the Inside and Outside: Integrating Emic and Etic Insights about Culture and Justice Judgments," *Academy of Management Review* 24 (1999), pp. 781–96.

23. J. M. Brett, D. L. Shapiro, and A. L. Lytle, "Breaking the Bonds of Reciprocity in Negotiations," *Academy of Management Journal* 41 (1998), pp. 410–24; W. L. Adair, "Reciprocity in the Global Market," unpublished doctoral dissertation, Department of Management and Organizations, Northwestern University, 2000.

24. Adair, "Reciprocity in the Global Market."

Intercultural Dynamics in the International Company

11

LEARNING OBJECTIVES

After completing this chapter, you should be able to:

 LO¹ Understand the importance of corporate cultural in acquisition and mergers

LO² Become aware of the process of intercultural business communication

LO³ How to manage multicultural diverse global teams

On May 7, 1998, Daimler-Benz AG and Chrysler stunned the world by announcing that they had agreed to merge the two companies. There had been rumors for some time, yet when the news came, it made headlines. This was the first mega-merger of two big international companies, and it would make DaimlerChrysler the fifth-largest maker of cars and light trucks in the world.

Juergen Schrempp, chief executive officer (CEO) of Daimler-Benz, and Robert Eaton, CEO of Chrysler, had met at Chrysler's headquarters on January 12, 1998, to explore possible cooperation. That meeting, which lasted just 17 minutes, resulted in a decision to merge the two companies. The two CEOs met a number of times in Germany, London, New York, and South Africa in the following months, but their meetings were always kept secret. They never appeared together in public, and only a few trusted executives knew about the talks. In fact, each person who was told about the talks also was told that so far no information had leaked to the outside; therefore, any leaks in the future could be traced very easily and be punished accordingly. The threat worked, and everyone kept quiet.

When the merger was announced, Eaton and Schrempp hailed it as a "merger of equals." They were to be co-chairs for three years. After that, Eaton would step down and Schrempp would become the sole CEO. There would be headquarters both in Auburn Hills, Michigan, and in Stuttgart, Germany. The company language would be English. Economies of scale and the sharing of technology and other information would result in huge savings—$400 million in the first year alone—and higher profits. Daimler would contribute engineering know-how, and Chrysler would contribute creativity and marketing savvy.

The merger was made official on November 17, 1998. On that day, Eaton and Schrempp together rang the opening bell on Wall Street. In Stuttgart, employees celebrated with an American-style party that included turkey. In Auburn Hills, Chrysler employees ate potato salad and sauerkraut. Each member of the integration teams received half a share of stock in the new company.

From the very beginning, the merger required a reconciliation not only of big issues but also of seemingly unimportant points. For example, a committee had to sit down and decide whether a brochure encouraging employees to accept global assignments should have the shape of a globe or a rectangle. The choice of color was another stumbling block. After several months of regular meetings the committee finally decided on the globe shape, but the color was still unresolved. Ultimately, the group agreed on yellow and blue. The Germans immediately thought of Lufthansa Airlines, and the Americans, all from the Detroit area, thought of the University of Michigan.

The negotiations for expatriate pay were tough as well. American expatriates are used to lavish compensation packages, much larger than what their German counterparts were used to. The Germans were used to long vacations. The proposal that finally was hammered out included the following: Expatriates from Germany and the United States would stay on the home-country payroll and would be paid in the home-country currency. That meant no more special pay packages. The Americans were used to a three-month lump sum at the beginning of an expatriate assignment to cover costs; the Germans wanted none of that. The two sides finally compromised on one month's pay. The company offered to pay for housing in the new location and upkeep of the expatriate's house in his or her old location, including snow removal and lawn care. Expatriates from both countries would be given 25 days of vacation and a plane trip home for themselves and their families once a year. The company offered to help spouses find employment in the new location. German expatriates in the United States would get Chrysler automobiles at discount rates; American expatriates in Germany would get Mercedes vehicles at discount rates.

None of those issues dealt with the company product, marketing strategies, or customer relations. At times, the discussions went nowhere. Compromises frequently left both sides disappointed.

Less than two years after the merger, the company bought a controlling share of Mitsubishi. Now there were three corporations and three national cultures involved. Chrysler had had an unsuccessful joint venture with Mitsubishi in 1980, when together they built an automobile assembly plant in Normal, Illinois. Ultimately, that joint venture was dissolved, to some extent at least because of different approaches to doing business. In the joint venture, Chrysler had been the junior partner; Japanese headquarters had the ultimate say on most issues. In the new formation, Chrysler was aligned with the majority merger partner, Daimler; however, the earlier relationship between Chrysler and Mitsubishi did not seem to affect the ties to DaimlerChrysler.

Mitsubishi was in trouble when DaimlerChrysler acquired the majority interest; it had lost money in 2000, and the Japanese were deeply unhappy at the measures taken by DaimlerChrysler to bring it back to profitable figures, including firing many of the top executives at Mitsubishi.

Schrempp and Eaton had emphasized the potential savings and economies of scale that the merger of Daimler and Chrysler would create. On that expectation, the stock rose to a high of $108. When reports of culture clashes between Auburn Hills and Stuttgart began to emerge, sales problems and production issues made headlines, and the stock dropped to a low of $26.

Since then, the road for the merger has been rather bumpy, and to date the expected savings and market growth have not materialized. Daimler had been seen as the stronger partner that would pull Chrysler along; however, under Zetsche, who had worked for Daimler in Stuttgart, Chrysler stabilized while Daimler ran into problems. Among other things, the Smart became a drag on the profitability of Daimler. The Smart is a sub-compact car that was designed for city traffic. It is easy to park because it takes up very little space. In congested European cities, this was seen as a huge advantage. However, the Smart is expensive. Production was plagued by quality issues, and the Smart never quite attracted enough people to make it profitable.

At the same time, Mitsubishi Motors ran into major problems as well. The company had covered up defects in its cars over several years. Quality problems led to financial problems, and the question was whether DaimlerChrysler would support Mitsubishi financially. This would be a further drag on the profitability of DaimlerChrysler. Mitsubishi Motors is one company in the Mitsubishi Keiretsu, a conglomerate of companies that traditionally would help each other in case of problems. The companies composing the Mitsubishi Keiretsu are Mitsubishi Bank, Mitsubishi Corp., Kirin Brewery, Mitsubishi Rayon, Mitsubishi Electric, Mitsubishi Heavy Industries, and Mitsubishi Motors. Traditionally, all companies in the *keiretsu* would do business with each other whenever possible. Each *keiretsu* has a bank at its center, and all companies in the *keiretsu* use this bank for their financial and banking needs.

The question was whether the Mitsubishi Keiretsu would bail out a company that was controlled by a foreign firm. When DaimlerChrysler bought a controlling share of Mitsubishi Motors, this was seen as proof that the traditional *keiretsu* was breaking apart. As the crisis deepened in the spring of 2004, DaimlerChrysler decided not to put more money into Mitsubishi Motors.[1] Ultimately, the *keiretsu* followed tradition and bailed Mitsubishi Motors out. As a result, DaimlerChrysler's shares in Mitsubishi Motors fell to 22 percent.[2] In November, 2005, DaimlerChrysler sold its remaining shares of Mitsubishi Motors to Goldman Sachs.[3]

For 2005, DaimlerChrysler posted an 84 percent rise in income, but most of that came from the financial service area of the company rather than the production side. While Chrysler announced a profit for 2005, sales slumped as high gasoline prices scared buyers away from trucks and SUVs. The Mercedes division posted a loss of 505 million euros for 2005, its first annual loss in over ten years. In addition, Mercedes announced layoffs for 8,500 employees and a restructuring of the unprofitable Smart division.[4] At the end of 2005, Schrempp, the CEO of DaimlerChrysler announced that he would step down. The Board of Directors had voiced doubts about Schrempp's continuing effectiveness. Zetsche who had turned Chrysler around, followed Schrempp as the new CEO. In March 2006, the stock traded at $46, up from the low of $26 but only a shadow of the height of $108 at the excitement over the merger.

You are now equipped to identify cultural issues in international business ventures. You also know that when you read a newspaper or watch a television program, there is no signal that flashes to let you know: "Here is a particular cultural problem—pay attention," or "In Japan, the traditional corporate structure is based on seniority and group cohesiveness, which in turn are related to a high-context society. The Japanese function on a base of relationships that is developed over a long period. Change therefore is slow, and individuals should fit into the group rather than stick out." Since this cultural signal is not flashing, many people believe culture is not relevant. However, when you talk to expatriates and other businesspeople who are active in international business, they will tell you that an understanding of culture is one of the greatest contributors to success, while lack of understanding is one of the greatest contributors to failure.

You have the framework for learning the *why* of other cultures. You also know how to apply cultural understanding to writing correspondence and negotiation. It is now up to you to put this knowledge to use. In this chapter, we will apply this knowledge by discussing the merger of Daimler-Benz AG and Chrysler Corp. into DaimlerChrysler. In the process, we will:

- Identify cultural issues that affected the merger.
- Examine the role of intercultural business communication as a strategic tool for success.

In the Appendix at the end of the chapter, we give you two additional cases for practice. Good luck in this adventure that is just beginning.

Cultural Issues in the DaimlerChrysler Merger

Before we discuss the cultural issues that surfaced in the merger, we present an overview of the history of the two companies.

PREPARATION AND TRAINING

It was one thing to announce the merger; it was an entirely different thing to make the merger work. Three international accounting firms, four investment banks, and six corporate law partnerships worked on the merger. Clearly, both sides focused on financial, regulatory, legal, and business issues. As we will see, those issues played a major role; however, the merger almost was derailed over cultural issues.

To deal with internal merger issues, the company appointed 28 integration teams that set out to mesh the two corporations. The integration teams started their work in 1998 and officially finished in 1999; however, in a global company, integration is an ongoing task. The members received some intercultural training, but they complained that the training was not very helpful and got stuck in stereotypes. For example, the Germans were told that Americans are superficial and that an invitation does not mean anything. When a German executive came to Auburn Hills, he therefore booked a hotel room even though his American counterpart had invited him to stay at his house. He was very

THE HISTORY OF CHRYSLER

Chrysler started when Maxwell Motors became Chrysler Corp. in 1925, with Walter Chrysler as the president. In subsequent years, Chrysler bought Dodge and produced De Soto, Plymouth, and Chrysler cars. During World War II Chrysler produced tanks and combat vehicles. After the war, Chrysler became best known for big powerful cars, but with the Arab oil embargo in the 1970s, it ran into trouble. Consumers wanted smaller, fuel-efficient cars, and Chrysler could not deliver. Lee Iacocca became president of Chrysler in 1978. When the company faced bankruptcy, Iacocca was able to secure federal loan guarantees of $1.5 billion. Under Iacocca's leadership, Chrysler thrived and was able to repay the loans seven years ahead of schedule. In the 1980s, Chrysler's fortunes soared with the introduction of the minivan. Chrysler and Mitsubishi Motors started a joint venture in the mid-1980s under the name Diamond Star Motors Corp. In 1987, Chrysler bought the Jeep brand, thereby adding another popular vehicle to the Chrysler lineup. The cooperation with Mitsubishi ended in 1991, and Iacocca stepped down in 1992.

Chrysler, the smallest of the Big Three car companies (General Motors and Ford are the other two), was best known for its creativity and ability to overcome obstacles. Under Eaton, Iacocca's successor, Chrysler made significant progress in quality and efficiency, and the company became the world leader in profitability per vehicle.

HISTORY OF DAIMLER-BENZ

Daimler and Benz merged in 1926 to become Daimler-Benz AG. The company is best known for the Mercedes car, named after the daughter of a race car driver who ordered 30 cars with the stipulation that they be named Mercedes. During World War II, Daimler-Benz became a leading arms maker for Hitler, and it used slave laborers during that time. In the 1990s, the company paid huge sums of money as compensation and published a book about its role in World War II. In 1997, it had revenues of $70 billion. It employed 300,000 workers worldwide. More than two-thirds of its revenue came from outside Germany, and in the 1990s the company built plants in the United States and France.

In the 1980s, Reuter, the CEO, started on a path of diversification; however, when the company started losing money, Schrempp ousted Reuter and took over. He reversed the diversification efforts and went back to Daimler-Benz's core business: luxury cars and big trucks.

surprised that the American not only picked him up personally at the airport but actually took him to his home. The Americans had been told that Germans are stiff and that form and politeness are crucial: "Never, never greet a German with your hands in your pocket if you want to be taken seriously." When the Americans met the Germans in Stuttgart, they were surprised that quite a few of the Germans had their hands in their pockets.[5]

It seems that most of the training focused on cultural stereotypes and aspects that can be observed rather than the underlying reasons for behavior. The resulting stereotypes did not foster a systematic approach to studying and observing other cultures. Both German and American employees of DaimlerChrysler were frustrated because they did not learn *why* Germans or Americans behave as they do. Since many employees from the other side did not behave as the trainer had said they would, both Americans and Germans concluded that the training was not helpful. However, effective cultural training could have helped them understand a number of business and management practices that slowed the merger process.

ATTITUDES TOWARD MANAGEMENT

There were numerous cultural differences that the training did not address at all. The Germans came to meetings with thick folders and a detailed agenda. They prepared very detailed minutes of every meeting, whereas the Americans preferred free-flowing discussions and wanted agendas as general guidelines. The Germans wanted detailed summaries of previous meetings at the beginning of every session; the Americans wanted none of that.

After studying the role of culture in international business communication, you know that the German attitude toward meetings and agendas is related to a dislike for uncertainty. Agendas provide order and minimize the risk that something unexpected will happen. Americans, who are generally more willing to accept uncertainty, prefer a more flexible approach.

As the case at the beginning of the chapter pointed out, a decision was made to make English the official company language. The Americans who would deal with Germans on a regular basis were relieved because there was no need to learn the German language. When John Craig and Daniel Wilson went to their first meeting in Stuttgart, they were in for a surprise. During the official meeting everyone spoke English; however, as soon as the meeting was officially over, all the Germans switched to German. John and Daniel did not understand a word and decided that a few German lessons might be helpful after all.

The Americans were worried that the Germans would discuss the important points in German and leave the Americans out of the process of the discussions. The Germans, who spoke very good English, nevertheless were worried that their English might not be good enough to get all the nuances of the language.

The two sides also had to come to terms with different approaches to formality. The German members of the integration team called each other *Mr.*, using last names. The Americans, being used to first names, thought the Germans were stiff and unfriendly. The issue did not disappear when the Germans agreed to use first names because in German there is also the distinction between the informal *you* (*Du*) and the formal *you* (*Sie*). Typically, the informal *you* is used with persons one knows well. At the workplace, first names and *Du* hardly ever are used. The Germans tried the awkward combination of *Sie* and first names when the Americans were around. Gradually the Germans eased up and used first names with *Du* on a more regular basis.

The corporate cultures were very different as well. At Chrysler, executives ate in the executive dining room; in Stuttgart, executives ate in the same cafeteria with the workers even though generally Germans are more formal than Americans. In contrast, the Americans did not use titles, whereas in Stuttgart titles were important. Almost all top managers at Daimler had international experience. In fact, international assignments were considered a must on the way to the top. They had been in South Africa, South America, North America, and all over Europe. Also, they all spoke English and frequently a second foreign language. At Chrysler, in contrast, almost nobody even had a passport, and nobody at the top spoke a foreign language.

The majority of upper management at Daimler-Benz had been with the company for a long time. Schrempp, for example, had started his career as an apprentice at Daimler. Most managers had a technical and/or engineering background. As a result, they focused on technical designs and technical quality. Typically, engineers at Daimler decided what a new car would look like. It was almost unheard of to collect information relating to design from consumers. After all, the crucial aspect was technical perfection. Driving was a serious business; there was no place in cars for cup holders, for example. Chrysler managers, by contrast, came from a variety of backgrounds, including marketing and finance. Although some had been at Chrysler for a number of years, many had gained experience at other automobile companies or even in other industries before joining Chrysler.

The different approaches to cars and their design had an impact on views of corporate reputation. At the beginning, there had been talk of sharing technology and platforms. However, Daimler engineers were concerned about giving their first-class technology to a mass-market car company. Purchasing was to be consolidated, but it turned out that the differences were so huge that little consolidation would be possible.

ATTITUDES TOWARD COMPENSATION

In the summer of 1998, the German magazine *Stern* ran an article comparing the pay of a Daimler employee and that of a Chrysler employee. The article showed pictures of the houses of employees and talked about their vacations, hobbies, and work schedules. It also compared the pay of two supervisors, both before and after taxes.[6]

The German employees knew that they were among the highest-paid workers in the world. There was some fear that the merger would have a negative impact on German pay. By showing that the two supervisors in the story had comparable pay packages, the article helped reduce or eliminate that concern. It was interesting to note, however, that the German and American supervisors had very different priorities for spending their money. The German employee spent much of his money on his house, garden, and furnishings. The American employee also had a nice house but spent most of his disposable income on short vacations and eating out.

The difference in pay at the employee and supervisor levels might not have been that great; however, this was not true at the expatriate level. Daimler saw an expatriate assignment as a regular and required step on the ladder to the top. Expatriate packages therefore were small by American standards. However, on international flights, Daimler executives went first class. At Chrysler, only a few top executives were allowed to go first class, but compensation for foreign assignments was lavish by German standards. As the case at the beginning of this chapter pointed out, expatriate compensation became a big issue in the merger process. Ultimately, both sides gave a little. The attitude toward expatriate pay speaks volumes about attitudes toward international business. At Daimler, international experience was considered a prerequisite for success, whereas at Chrysler it was considered something unique that merited special compensation.

The difference in compensation, however, was most pronounced at the executive level, particularly for the CEO. At the time of the merger, Eaton received about $11 million a year, including stock options. Schrempp, by contrast, received about $2 million. In fact, the top ten people at Daimler-Benz made $11.3 million together, about the same as Eaton made by himself. In addition, under German law, individual executive pay does not have to be disclosed. Publication of the aggregate pay of the top earners is sufficient. Under American law, however, individual compensation must be disclosed. Rumors in Germany were flying that Schrempp's main goal for the merger was to receive an American-style salary under German disclosure laws.

Since the merger of Daimler and Chrysler, compensation for German CEOs and upper management has gone up considerably. As a result, employees, stockholders, and the public are increasingly asking for more transparency and more disclosure of executive pay. While some changes have occurred, the debate is ongoing with no clear solution in sight.

REGULATORY ISSUES

Because of government regulations, the new company was incorporated in Germany. That had some unintended consequences. Since DaimlerChrysler was incorporated under German law, the Standard & Poor's (S&P's) 500 no longer listed the company. Under existing law, U.S. pension funds no longer were allowed to invest in the company. The pension funds therefore sold their holdings in Chrysler.

DaimlerChrysler stock was listed on 12 international stock markets, becoming the first truly international stock. It was traded around the world in local currencies rather than as repository receipts. When traded as repository receipts, shares are deposited in the bank and then dollar-denominated receipts are issued against them. The rate of currency fluctuation therefore always plays a role in trading. With the trading of common shares in the local currencies, the conversion cost can be avoided. The shares can be traded at 12 different stock markets without incurring conversion costs.

Under German law, labor and banks sit on the board to look at the long-term health of the firm. Since the bank is not going to sell the stock, it is not that concerned when a stock goes down as long as the company seems to be healthy in the long run. American investors, in contrast, look for returns and fast results. As a result, American investors follow the stock market very closely and require explanations when a stock goes down.

When Schrempp became CEO, he asked the board members of Daimler what the Daimler stock price was. Only one of the members gave an answer, and his estimate was not close to the actual price. None of the others even ventured a guess. In the American context, it would be unethical and irresponsible for a board member not to have the latest information on a company's stock price.

Germany requires two financial reports a year, whereas the United States requires four quarterly reports each year on a timely basis. Usually, U.S. corporations announce expected results two weeks before the end of the quarter and actual figures right at the end of the quarter. Since American investors want fast and timely information, they would not accept two reports per year as sufficient information. The timing of reports and announcements created a problem as well. For example, Stuttgart would make announcements in the morning, when it was still night in the United States. By the time the Americans got the information, it was old news. The time lag became a big issue and was seen as proof that the Germans were excluding the Americans intentionally in an effort to gain total control.

REPORTS ON THE MERGER

In this section, we will look at attitudes toward the merger over time as reported in the media. As you will see, those attitudes varied.

Throughout 1998, views of the merger were generally positive even though cautionary voices spoke as well. From the beginning, there was concern that the merger was not a merger of equals but a takeover of Chrysler by Daimler. There also were articles in the business press in both countries warning of major culture clashes, but most of those articles talked in general terms rather than giving specifics.

That changed fairly dramatically in 1999. Increasingly, reports were critical of the slow speed of integration. For example, it took 25 percent of 300 managers' time to work out the details of the merger, time that those managers did not spend producing and selling cars. Schrempp came under criticism as well. He was seen as tyrannical and dictatorial by the American public and by Chrysler employees in Detroit, where he was firing executives at Chrysler to gain complete control. The board of directors, which had started out with an almost even split between American and German members, increasingly looked German. By October 1999, the board had eight Germans and five Americans.

Critics charged that there was a war of cultures and that Schrempp was not able to build a new culture. Rather than the promised merger of equals, Chrysler was organized as an American subsidiary of Daimler. Some voices went so far as to recommend dissolving the merger.[7]

By fall 2000, the stock had dropped from a high of $108 to $45. Forecasts were gloomy, and Chrysler had run into serious problems. Sixty percent of the value of the stock had been wiped out since its high. Eaton had left before his three years as Co-CEO were up, and his replacement, Holden, was fired by Schrempp, who sent his own person, Zetsche, to Auburn Hills in the United States. Critics talked of a cultural drama of Shakespearean proportions and the selling of an American icon to dictatorial and power-hungry Germans.[8]

Morale at Chrysler took a nosedive. Suppliers were unhappy when Zetsche, in an attempt to cut costs, asked them to lower their prices. Gradually, there was a realization that Chrysler's problems were not all of Schrempp's making. The company had been headed for trouble before the merger. Some people felt that Eaton had known about it and was glad to get out of a potential mess. He took his money and left.

Up to that point Schrempp had been criticized for being high-handed. Now he also was criticized for not being decisive enough and not moving fast enough. The merger had been mismanaged, and the intercultural communication was disastrous. Know-it-all Germans had been greedy for Chrysler's distribution system and marketing ability. But it was clear now that there seemed to be irreconcilable differences in marketing and engineering philosophies.

The conclusion at the end of 2000 was that the merger had failed miserably, that there was no synergy, and that the cultures were too different to be able to work together.

While DaimlerChrysler was still trying to merge as one company, Schrempp bought a controlling share of 34 percent of Mitsubishi Motors, arguing that the company needed a presence in Asia if it wanted to be global player. Earlier, he had toyed with the idea of buying Nissan, but Renault took that company.

In May 2001, after DaimlerChrysler had bought a controlling share of Mitsubishi, Mitsubishi, one of the smallest Japanese automakers, reported U.S.$750 million in pretax losses on sales of U.S.$31 billion for the year 2000. Mitsubishi sales had dropped 17 percent in the first part of the year. Quality problems, lack of a clear production focus, and a cash crunch had contributed to the problem. Schrempp had known about the problems at Mitsubishi when he bought parts of the company. He had sent Rolf Eckrodt to Japan to reverse the fortunes of Mitsubishi Motors. Eckrodt had a tough task ahead when he arrived at Mitsubishi Motors in Japan in January 2001.

Eckrodt had experience in restructuring ailing carmakers. In particular, he had been the key player in restructuring Daimler's subsidiary in Brazil, where he had earned a reputation for being ruthless in laying off workers and reorganizing the company. The Japanese, aware of his tough style, were apprehensive when he arrived and made it clear that they were not just going to take orders from Germany. Sonobe, Mitsubishi Motor's CEO, was no pushover. He had been responsible for Mitsubishi's turnaround in the United States, and he felt that he could do the same for the parent company in Japan. When Eckrodt first arrived in Japan, he and Sonobe had long talks about the best strategy for solving the problems. They were going to work together; however, when Mitsubishi had to recall 1.36 million cars because of quality defects, Eckrodt decided that the time had come to act decisively.

In March 2001, Eckrodt replaced five Japanese top executives with Germans. The Japanese were stunned, particularly since four of the Germans were under 40 years of age. He then decided to cut costs, lay off 9,500 workers, sever ties with one-third of the suppliers, and reduce the number of automobile models on the production line.[9]

In March 2002, Eckrodt ousted Sonobe as CEO of Mitsubishi Motors and took the job himself. In the same month, the company announced that Mitsubishi Motors had returned to profitability, made steady progress in its turnaround efforts, and surpassed the targets set for cost reduction. The company was determined to accelerate the turnaround plan on the basis of the positive results.[10] The Japanese had mixed reactions. Some saw the changes as a violation of fundamental cultural values that value lifetime employment and seniority. Others saw the changes as necessary if the Japanese company was to survive. Most of the Japanese agreed that the changes could not have been made by a Japanese manager.

As the opening case in this chapter mentioned, the union between DaimlerChrysler and Mitsubishi was dissolved in 2005. The Japanese Mitsubishi Keiretsu circled the wagons and supported its own member when DaimlerChrysler refused to put more money into Mitsubishi Motors.

When the merger of Daimler and Chrysler was first announced, newspapers, magazines, television, and radio ran numerous stories about this new company. Since then, the news has become much quieter. Today, the stories no longer celebrate the "sexy" global merger but concentrate more on the problems.

The stock, as has been pointed out in the opening case, has been on a rollercoaster. After an all-time high of $108, it slumped to a low of $26 and finally recovered to $46 in 2006, but the stock price is not just a result of the merger issues, it also has to be seen in the context of the general pattern of the stock market since 2000. Some manufacturing processes in DaimlerChrysler have merged successfully, and production managers from the two companies are more comfortable with each other, understand and speak the same language and build on each other's strengths. Zetsche, who had been greeted in Auburn Hills with great suspicion, seemed to fit in after all. Even Yokich, the boss of the United Auto Workers labor union, liked him in spite of the fact that 26,000 hourly and 6,000 salaried jobs had been lost. Gradually, Zetsche seemed to turn Chrysler around. At the same time, Schrempp lost his power. Layoffs in Stuttgart did not help. As pointed out earlier, Zetsche replaced Schrempp, but to the very end Schrempp stood by the merger and insisted that it will be very successful in spite of any current difficulties.

Intercultural Business Communication as a Strategic Tool for Success

As the DaimlerChrysler case illustrates, businesspeople are members of their national cultures. Eaton, CEO of Chrysler, and Schrempp, CEO of Daimler, brought their cultures to the negotiation table, and so did the members of the integration teams. In addition, they brought their respective corporate cultures, which are influenced by the national culture. The two corporate cultures also are embedded in the culture of the automobile industry. The web of cultural connections goes all the way down to the line workers in the two companies. A worker on the assembly line may not always be aware of the cultural context, but the influence is there nevertheless. One of the biggest tasks is to bridge the culture gap so that work teams can focus on business tasks.

All international companies face cultural issues, particularly in mergers and joint ventures. To build on the potential synergies of cultural diversity, companies need to

- Create awareness of the process of intercultural business communication and understand ways to communicate about culture and to communicate by using culture.
- Develop an understanding of the dynamics of culturally diverse groups.
- Place the communication process and the dynamics of diverse teams in the context of corporate strategy.

THE PROCESS OF INTERCULTURAL BUSINESS COMMUNICATION

Intercultural business communication has three parts, as illustrated in Figure 11.1: cultural strategy, business strategy, and communication strategy.[11] The list of variables in each circle is not complete. You may think of additional aspects that influence each circle, but the variables listed are the major ones. A company may have influence over some of those aspects, whereas others are beyond its control.

For example, national laws concerning mergers, government regulations concerning the listing of foreign companies and stocks, and reporting regulations affect the business strategy but are beyond the direct influence of a company. The company has to understand the rules and regulations to avoid violating them, but it cannot change them. They are a given. DaimlerChrysler had to comply with German reporting rules. Even if American investors want more information, the company is not bound by their requests. Daimler-Chrysler may agree that four quarterly reports are good for investor relations but may decide that two reports provide all the necessary information.

The particular business strategy a company develops also is influenced by the competition the firm faces and the position of its products. For example, Daimler wanted to get a foothold in the broader automobile market in addition to the luxury market. It hoped to do that by joining with a company like Chrysler. Schrempp furthermore hoped that a broader product line with lower-cost products would help the company's expansion into Asia. Eaton saw international expansion as a way to stay competitive. Daimler offered an opportunity for Chrysler to become a player in Europe, with Daimler's high-quality products that appealed to a luxury market.

At the time of the merger, both companies seemed to be in sound financial positions. Their practices were different, as we discussed earlier, and so were their corporate cultures, but both sides thought that those differences would not present major obstacles. Overall, the two companies seemed to be a good fit for a merger.

FIGURE 11.1 Intercultural Business Communication Strategy

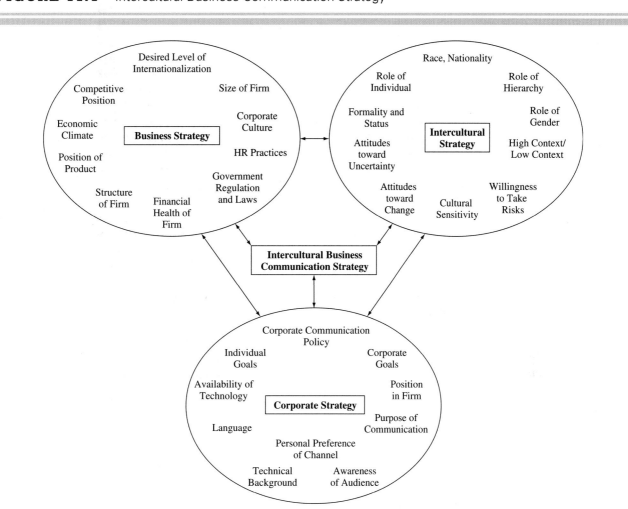

In the circle identifying intercultural strategy in Figure 11.1, we list ten variables. You have learned about cultural attitudes relating to hierarchy, change, risk, and the individual versus the group, among many others. The DaimlerChrysler case shows that the Germans and the Americans had different cultural priorities. When Mitsubishi joined the mix, the cultural factors became even more complex. The cultural differences find expression in the role of rules and formalities and views on risk and uncertainty, the promotion of women, and communication styles. In addition to national culture, there are other cultural variables, such as corporate culture and professional culture. Different professions have different cultures. For example, accountants have a different culture than do human resources (HR) managers. To some extent those cultures overlap, but they are also distinct.

The third circle focuses on communication strategy. The particular communication strategy is influenced by ten factors that we have discussed throughout this book.

The dynamics of communication in a company are shaped by the people in the firm. Managers develop policies and standards on corporate communication, but within that framework individuals can develop their own styles and preferences as long as they stay within corporate guidelines. In the DaimlerChrysler situation, members of the integration teams were not allowed to communicate with anybody outside the team, and communication between teams was heavily regulated as well. Confidentiality was seen as crucial so that team members would not be influenced by outside pressure groups. However, outside the specific issues of the merger process, both American and German companies are more transparent than Japanese companies. American companies are the most transparent. Legislation enforces rules on corporate reporting and communication with all stakeholders. German firms are less transparent, as reporting requirements for executive pay illustrate. Japanese firms are the least transparent in this group. Also, when Mitsubishi Motors ran into serious problems, the *keiretsu* stepped in to support one of its own members.

Frequently, the communication process is depicted in the model illustrated in Figure 11.2, which identifies a sender, a message, and a receiver of the message. A feedback loop indicates that communication is an interactive two-way process. However, the model does not provide details of the complexity of the relationships between people, businesses, and cultures. It merely shows that there are at least two parties involved.

In the case of the merger of Daimler and Chrysler, the model should show that representatives from Daimler and Chrysler discussed the merger; however, there is nothing in the traditional model that specifically relates the process to business or deals with group dynamics. Since we cannot enter the mind of a person we are communicating with, we ultimately communicate with our schema of that person. Now imagine this process involving not just two people but a group of ten people who all bring their own cultures to the business at hand. The potential conflict between reality and perception is multiplied. The approaches to solving conflicts, establishing goals, and collecting information, to name just a few regular business tasks, combine to become a huge endeavor. In the case of Daimler-Chrysler, the situation becomes even more difficult because the players of the integration teams are expected to step outside their own cultural orientations and create a new company with a new culture that fits into both the German and the American national culture.

Frequently, businesses sidestep a discussion of the communication process and focus on the way a business strategy affects corporate goals, work units, and individual employees (see Figure 11.3). This model shows as a corporate strategy that Daimler and Chrysler have decided to merge. At the upper-management level, the goals for the merger are spelled out, such as economies of scale in production, access to new markets, and greater international competitiveness. The specific business units and the individuals in these units will work out the details. However, we do not learn anything from this model about the interaction of people or the cultural variables of the interaction. In this case, it seems at times that the CEOs thought they could simply decree the merger by saying that it would be done because that was the strategy. But the case also makes it clear that this approach does not work unless business strategy and intercultural business communication are connected.

For an international businessperson, it is the interaction of the three circles in Figure 11.1 that is the exciting part. Throughout this book, we have shown the connections between those three variables. When Juergen Schrempp from Stuttgart, Germany, and Robert Eaton from Auburn Hills, Michigan, discussed a possible merger of their companies, they brought their cultural backgrounds with them, but in the process of discussion they also started the potential growth of a new culture. They took something from both environments and hoped to create something new. In that effort, both Schrempp and Eaton needed to understand how businesses function in the other country; they needed to understand the relationship between culture and business and needed to understand the dynamics of communication in both cultures. They needed to understand their own national and corporate cultures and where differences could be significant. The same process is at work when a joint venture is formed.

FIGURE 11.2

A Traditional
Communication Model

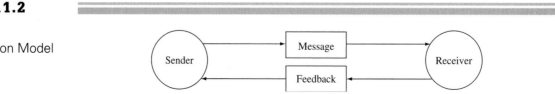

As the three variables interact, a new construct, an intercultural business communication strategy, emerges.[12] In intercultural business, communication means that we have to be aware of the role of each circle. At DaimlerChrysler, for example, the participants in the merger negotiation had to look at the strategic goals of the two companies, the cultural environments of both companies, and the communication practices of both companies. Building upon that background, they then could start to develop an intercultural strategy to achieve the goals of the merger.

As the case has illustrated, the two companies came from different realities in all three circles. Germans and Americans both lean toward egalitarianism rather than hierarchy. Germans tend to use titles, and protocol is important, but advancement tends to be based on skills and merit. However, they are very different when it comes to acceptance of uncertainty and the role of the individual versus the group. Americans have an orientation toward individuality and are willing to tolerate uncertainty to a much greater degree than Germans are. Germans therefore want tight rules and regulations and formalized work processes.[13] A background in a technical field such as engineering, and an academic titles guarantees that a person is an expert and has the background to do the job. This view is reflected in the corporate officers. Of the nine officers in 2006, one was Canadian, two were from the United States, and six were Germans. Among the six German executives, three had doctorates. Americans are less impressed with academic titles. It is noteworthy that there are no women in top management or on the Supervisory Board. In the initial merger negotiations, the Americans at times felt like unsophisticated country cousins. As the case points out, hardly anyone at Chrysler had a passport, and although the executives had college degrees, nobody had a doctorate.

Because of their dislike of uncertainty, Germans rely on form. From an American point of view they appear stiff. Americans, in contrast, appear insincere in their informality. The German executive arriving in Auburn Hills thought that the invitation to stay at the American's home was a mere figure of speech without any meaning. Zetsche, however, had work experience in America. He knew how to read signals more effectively and made it a point to adapt to American informality, a move that helped his acceptance in Detroit. For example, he joined civic organizations and mingled socially at community affairs. The case also illustrates the problems of stereotyping and focusing on the visible how-to culture. It seems that much of the training did not go beyond a list of dos and don'ts. The participants were not taught to look behind the façade and become familiar with the backstage culture, or the *why* of the culture.

In the beginning, the differences almost derailed the merger, and it took time to see the synergy that could result from cooperation. Even now, the work is not done. It probably never will be completed. As the environments change, the intercultural business communication strategy will change as well. When Zetsche came to Detroit, Chrysler was in bad shape. He had to develop a strategy that fit that particular situation. Although he left no doubt that he was the boss, he also worked to establish his credibility and gain the trust of the American workers. Zetsche proved that he could adapt his communication strategy. He listened to the people around him, and he observed the communication process and practices. Schrempp, on the other hand, has been widely criticized for not being able to adapt to the changing communication dynamics around him. In the beginning, Schrempp was hailed as a great and decisive leader, but increasingly his critics pointed out that he did not listen and could not see that his style might alienate employees, the public, and the Board of Directors. Zetsche had better intercultural communication knowledge and skills, and the ability to implement them.

The news reports of the merger tended to concentrate on the key players, but it is clear that much of the work had to be done by people below the executive level. Employees at both Daimler and Chrysler worked on the merger. They worked within their companies and then in joint teams. Before Daimler's and Chrysler's cultures had truly merged, Schrempp had brought in Mitsubishi, and a third and very different culture became part of the company. We have discussed how Figure 12.1 models the German–U.S. interaction; consider how it models the German–U.S.–Japanese interaction.

FIGURE 12.3

Strategy Model

Corporate Strategy

↓

Corporate Goals

↓

Unit Goals

↓

Individual Goals

DYNAMICS OF CULTURALLY DIVERSE TEAMS

In an era of globalization, most people work in an environment of cultural diversity. Increasingly, companies rely on teamwork, arguing that diverse teams make better decisions than do homogeneous teams; however, better performance does not come automatically. Culturally diverse teams face many challenges.

As you have learned, people from different cultures have different approaches to making decisions, solving problems, and negotiating deals. They view the world differently. Westerners tend to have a linear view of the world with an either-or approach, whereas Asians have a more holistic world view that is inclusive of contradictions. Although the top executives at both Daimler and Chrysler were either German or American, the employees and managers had a variety of backgrounds. Daimler employs many Turks and people from Eastern Europe. Chrysler in many ways reflects the cultural diversity of the American population at large. You can see similar situations in almost all major corporations around the world. For example, in one Swiss multinational company, all work teams are culturally diverse. In a team of ten people, it is not uncommon to have four or five nationalities represented. Even if the majority of the team members are Swiss, the cultural diversity still can be a major issue. The Swiss Germans, Swiss French, and Swiss Italians all come from different orientations and speak different languages. The cultural and communication dynamics in such groups are complex and at times confusing.

To harness the potential of culturally diverse groups, businesses need to spend time developing those groups by creating cultural awareness, understanding, and respect. The material in this book is at the heart of that process.

As you probably know from your own experiences in group projects, groups do not become productive automatically. It can be a long process. For example, it took months for the team at DaimlerChrysler to develop a brochure for expatriation strategies. It has been nearly a decade since the merger, and the two entities still are not one cohesive unit. It seems that they are getting closer, but they don't always speak with one voice. During the entire time of the merger, some people argued that the integration teams were not working fast enough whereas others argued they were not taking enough care to work out important details. It was almost a no-win situation. On the surface, the team-building phase is not always productive. Talking about building a cohesive team seems to get nowhere. Critics, for example, charged that managers were wasting 25 percent of their time on integration aspects rather than building and selling cars. From that viewpoint, bringing together culturally diverse teams takes attention away from the actual business task.

Most managers have not received training in developing culturally diverse teams that communicate effectively; they do not see culture as a variable that has a huge impact on business functions. It may be a nice add-on but is not a crucial element in success. This view is exemplified by the attitude that a good manager is a good manager anywhere. Goal orientation and focusing on the task at hand are seen as the ingredients that guarantee success. In the case of DaimlerChrysler, this became clear when German managers thought that an American company could be run the same way as a German company and the Chrysler people thought that they certainly could not learn anything from a foreign manager. In fact, the perception by each side that its way was the right way contributed to many of the problems at the start of the merger. Both sides may have paid lip service to understanding cultural differences, but deep down both "knew" that they were right.

With this view, a manager usually assembles a team and gives a charge to the team. Particularly in low-context cultures, a manager may expect the team to focus on the task at hand and not get "personal." The belief is that a rational and analytical discussion, culturally value-free, will get the fastest and best results. In the DaimlerChrysler case, both companies are Western companies, yet they faced huge problems in their discussions. If companies from very diverse cultures are involved, the approaches to task orientation and problem solving will be even more different.

Not all culturally diverse teams are the same. We can identify destroyer teams, equalizer teams, and creator teams.[14] In the extreme, the destroyers will argue that nothing is possible and that there is no way to cooperate. In the beginning of the DaimlerChrysler merger, for example, there had been talk about synergies in the areas of sharing technology, automobile parts, and marketing. Destroyers on both sides of the Atlantic, however, argued against this. Daimler did not want to risk its reputation of luxury and high quality by putting its parts into "cheap" cars, and Chrysler did not want to contribute its marketing knowledge. As a result, both sides blocked the team effort and thus the intercultural integration efforts.

The equalizers are more difficult to spot because everything they do seems to go according to schedule and plan. They work together and make decisions. However, the decisions may come too fast, and then the team does not build on the unique opportunities and different viewpoints that the team members bring to the table. Typically, equalizer groups say: "There is nothing to this culture bit. It is hugely overblown. We are all people with the same interests, and we all agree." After the first few months, some managers at DaimlerChrysler felt that the two sides were working together just fine. They said the cultural differences had been exaggerated. Perhaps a few had different ideas, but overall there was no problem. By not admitting that there are differences, equalizer teams never openly face their differences and build on their different expertise. They tend to be satisfied with mediocrity.

Creator teams take the time to work through their differences, a time-consuming process but one that is well worth the effort in the long run. Creator teams, as authors DiStefano and Maznevski argue, go through several stages.[15] Culturally diverse teams in an international business environment face additional challenges and therefore go through additional stages (see Figure 11.4).

Creating Self-Awareness

At the beginning, team members need to become aware of their own cultural priorities. Since a culture is normal to a native of that culture, few people consciously develop critical self-understanding. Frequently, the development of self-awareness is undervalued because it is assumed that people know their own priorities and cultural inclinations. However, a lack of self-awareness can hinder a solid understanding of the cultural priorities of the other group members.[16] Conscious self-awareness also can help identify and overcome one's self-reference criterion, in which a person judges somebody else on the basis of his or her own cultural priorities.

Members of the integration teams at DaimlerChrysler needed to develop a conscious understanding of their own cultural priorities by asking questions such as the following: What does it mean to be a manager at Chrysler? What are the values of a manager at Daimler-Benz? How do my personal values fit into this corporate setting? What is important to me? How do we make decisions?

Mapping Differences

In the second stage, group members map their differences. They literally plot the intensity of their cultural priorities on a piece of paper and compare the orientations of the various group members. This is a graphic illustration of where team members stand in relation to values. For example, one team member may value hierarchy, whereas another may dislike hierarchy very strongly. It may be helpful if each team member enters his or her own value positions on the chart.

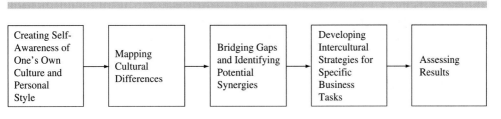

FIGURE 11.4

Stages in the Building of Culturally Diverse Teams

FIGURE 11.5

Mapping Differences

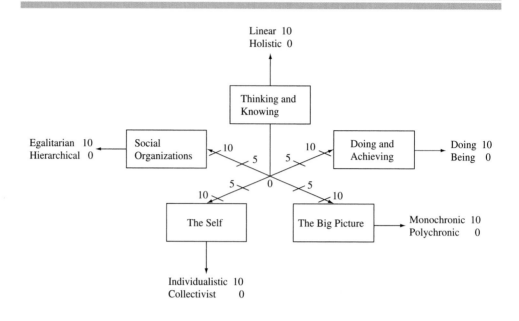

The chart resembles the spokes of a wheel (see Figure 11.5).

For each of those categories, we discussed several questions. Ideally, we would include each question in the mapping diagram, but the amount of detail would get confusing. Therefore, it might be more useful to select one or two of the questions that are most relevant to the task at hand. For the integration teams at DaimlerChrysler, we could decide on the following questions for each of the categories:

- Thinking and Knowing
  - How do people learn, from authoritative sources or from hands-on experience?
  - In what patterns do people reason?
- Doing and Achieving
  - Is uncertainty avoided or tolerated?
  - Are rules bent or observed?
  - Are results or relationships more important?
- The Big Picture
  - How is time understood?
  - Are tasks done sequentially or simultaneously?
  - Is change positive or negative?
  - Who is in control of events, people or deities?
- The Self
  - Is the basic unit of society the individual or the collective?
  - Is seniority valued or discounted?
  - How important is form?
- Social Organizations
  - Is group membership temporary or permanent?
  - Are social organizational patterns horizontal or hierarchical?

If we include the two or three questions for each spoke, the diagram will look like Figure 11.6.

For each question, team members can now enter their priorities on a scale from 1 to 10. The individual ratings carry a subjective judgment of a team member's priorities, but the completed diagram will indicate priorities and differences among the team members.

FIGURE 11.6

Mapping Questions

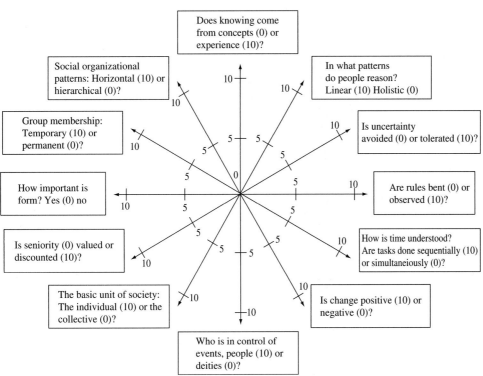

It is interesting to note that the emphasis on laying out differences may be acceptable in low-context cultures. High-context cultures, however, may be much more reluctant to identify differences explicitly. As we have pointed out repeatedly, we all bring our cultures with us, and the researchers who established these steps come from a low-context environment. It makes sense in low-context cultures to state differences explicitly. If the discussion involves low- and high-context cultures, this approach may not be acceptable. The members may want to find a more subtle way to identify different cultural priorities.

Bridging Gaps and Identifying Synergies

After the differences have been mapped, group members are ready to bridge the gaps. In this stage, they acknowledge their differences. The bridging is an important step in the establishment of cultural synergy because it entails building on the strengths that the various cultures represent.[17] The DaimlerChrysler teams at this stage verbalized their differences and acknowledged them publicly. For example, both sides openly acknowledged that they approached expatriation differently. As we discussed earlier, at Daimler, expatriation was a regular step in career advancement, whereas at Chrysler it was seen as a special assignment.

In this stage, team members don't yet have a way to overcome the differences, but they know where the issues are. In the beginning of the merger process, there was a lot of talk about sharing technology and platforms. If both sides had gone through a team development program, they would have been able to see that their approaches to technology, sharing information, and the importance of corporate reputation management were different. They could have worked on overcoming the obstacles much earlier if they had not pretended that there was no problem.

Developing Strategies

At this point, team members are ready to integrate their knowledge, approaches, and backgrounds, and develop an intercultural business communication strategy that will build on the strengths of the members and is aligned with organizational strategies and goals.

Team members at DaimlerChrysler at this stage would develop a detailed strategy for cooperation and integration. Ideally, the team now speaks with one voice, but only after all the differences have been explored and assessed. Because the viewpoints on sharing technology were different, they would have developed a strategy for determining areas for cooperation and integration and developed specific plans for reaching the goals. For example, they could have decided to develop a timeline for evaluating proposals for sharing technology and evaluating joint research projects.

Assessing Results

Throughout the entire team-building process, teams assess their progress, and at the end the members assess the results. The assessment also is done by the managers who formed the group. Management, in conjunction with the group, collects the process knowledge that has been gained. It stores that knowledge to have it ready for retrieval for future use.[18]

As the managers of DaimlerChrysler went through this process, they learned from past experiences and were able to anticipate responses from the other side. Over time, the process should be less time-consuming, but it should never be automatic. As soon as it becomes automatic, there is a danger of equalizing rather than maximizing the potential.

CULTURE IN THE CONTEXT OF CORPORATE STRATEGY

After examining the process of creating effective culturally diverse teams, we are ready to place the team process in the context of the organization as a whole. After all, group work is not an end in itself. The people at Daimler and Chrysler did not meet to perfect group dynamics or group processes. They had a specific business goal: to bring two different companies together and shape them into one unit. Teamwork has to be seen against that background. Figure 11.7 illustrates the interaction between the business strategy and the intercultural business communication work of the various players. In the model, two members come from culture A, two from culture B, and one from culture C.

The model is recursive, meaning that at any stage participants will verify that they are on track and that their activities are contributing to the reaching of the identified goals. If the activities do not contribute, the participants either realign the activities or reexamine the strategies and the stated goals. By integrating the team and group activities into the broader context of the organization, the model overcomes a major shortcoming of the conventional communication model.

The model separates activities into discrete steps; however, some of the steps can occur simultaneously. Before the multicultural group can start its work, the organization must have a clear strategy in place and identify the organizational goals to which the multicultural group will contribute. After the strategy and the goals have been identified, the organization needs to identify the skills that the participants should bring to the task so that they can work effectively and efficiently. The types of skills depend on the goals at hand. As a result, different goals may require different skills. Once the desirable skills have been identified, managers can go to the next step and select the players or group members who have the necessary mix of skills and attributes.

The process depicted in Figure 11.7 is simplified insofar as it shows only one culturally diverse group in one company. An example is a culturally diverse team at Caterpillar (CAT), a United States company. Its global marketing division develops marketing strategies for many different markets. To ensure that the diverse markets have input, CAT appoints employees from a variety of cultural backgrounds to the team; however, all team members are CAT employees. In that sense, they all work towards the same goal.

Today, all international businesses and many domestic businesses have culturally diverse teams. For example, teams in United States–based companies have members who are European-American, Latino-American, African-American, Asian-American, and many

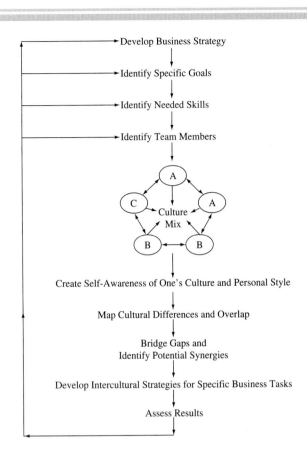

FIGURE 11.7

Intercultural Teams and Business Strategy: Process Involving One Diverse Team in One Company

Note: A, B and C stand for different cultures.

other combinations. In many European companies, the team members in a particular company may be German, French, Scandinavian, Italian, Turkish, Algerian, Dutch, and Polish. For those teams to be effective and add value to the company, they need to become creator teams.

In international business, however, we typically deal with several companies and many intercultural teams. This process is illustrated in Figure 11.8.

When two international companies enter negotiations as buyers or sellers of goods, they work together for a specific purpose but remain distinctly separate companies. The negotiation for the wallpaper contract between a Canadian company and a Chinese company falls into this category. The two sides came together for one particular project, but there were no plans to unite the companies. The two sides evaluated their international interaction against their own goals and objectives. The Chinese ultimately decided that a contract with the Canadians would not be in their interest and discontinued the talks.

In other instances, a relationship may be formed and go on for many years—for example, the company may use the same supplier over a long period, or the company may negotiate with many different groups and any relationship may be for just one specific project.

Most international companies work with local businesses and other international firms but keep their own identity. For example, Nestlé has subsidiaries around the world. The firm regularly needs to work with suppliers, interest groups, and governments in many different countries, and many of those groups have a culturally heterogeneous workforce. Nestlé works with those groups, but it keeps its own identity. Cooperative efforts would resemble the dynamics depicted in Figure 11.8.

When two companies decide to form a joint venture or explore the possibility of a merger, their beginning discussions may resemble what is depicted in Figure 11.8. At this stage, they explore possibilities for closer cooperation, but they still evaluate any proposal on the basis of their own goals. When Daimler and Chrysler first started their

FIGURE 11.8

Intercultural Teams and
Business Strategy:
Process Involving Two
Companies

Note: The letters in the circles
identify different cultures. In the
diagram each team has a member
from culture C. For example, a
team representing a Japanese
company and a team representing a Swiss company might both
have a member from the
Netherlands.

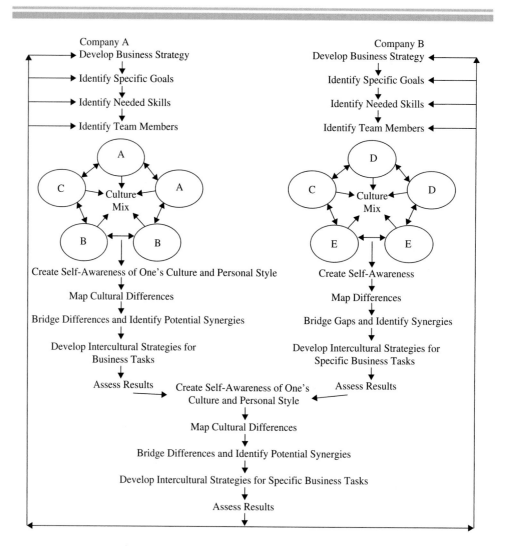

discussions for a merger, their interaction probably looked similar to what is depicted in
Figure 11.8. Two distinct companies planned to come together with players from different
backgrounds. There was diversity within and between groups. The goal was to see how
a merger would fit into the strategy of either company. Teams from both companies also
would work together and provide feedback to their respective companies in Detroit and
Stuttgart.

Once the merger was finalized, however, the picture changed. At this stage, there was
one company with culturally diverse teams. It no longer was a question of whether the
two sides wanted to cooperate; they had to cooperate if the merger were to be successful.
Chrysler and Daimler now had the same goals, and it became the task of the integration
teams to help develop cultural synergies. This situation is illustrated in Figure 11.9.

Some people argue that Schrempp and Eaton decided to merge before both sides had
thoroughly evaluated the issues involved in a merger and that many of the problems that
surfaced after the merger had been formed could have been avoided if the merger had
been prepared more thoroughly.

However, once the merger had been agreed on, DaimlerChrysler had one corporate
strategy. But as the case illustrates, the announcement of a merger does not eliminate
the need for intercultural integration. In fact, it became even more crucial because now
both sides had to work together; they could not walk away from each other. Furthermore,
intercultural communication was no longer an isolated occurrence but a daily reality. The

FIGURE 11.9

Intercultural Teams and
Business Strategy:
Process after a Merger

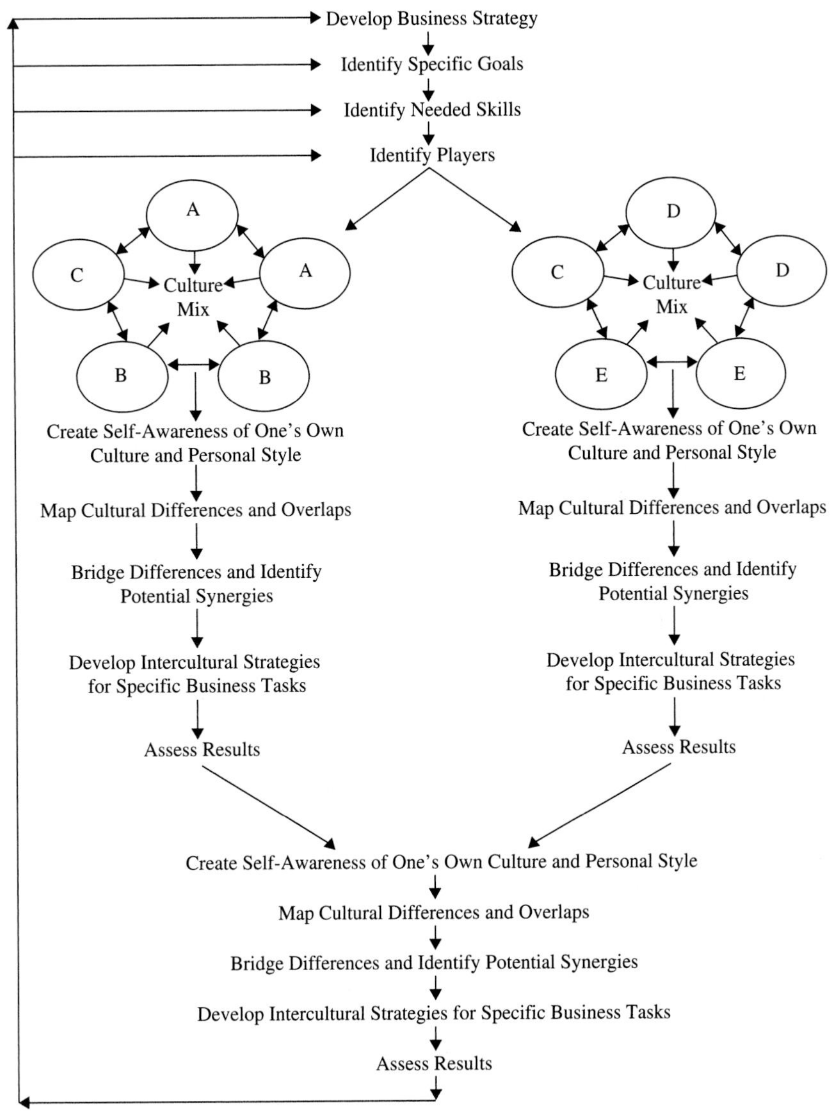

Develop Business Strategy
↓
Identify Specific Goals
↓
Identify Needed Skills
↓
Identify Players

Culture Mix (A, A, B, B, C)
Culture Mix (D, D, E, E, C)

Create Self-Awareness of One's Own
Culture and Personal Style
↓
Map Cultural Differences and Overlaps
↓
Bridge Differences and Identify
Potential Synergies
↓
Develop Intercultural Strategies
for Specific Business Tasks
↓
Assess Results

Create Self-Awareness of One's Own
Culture and Personal Style
↓
Map Cultural Differences and Overlaps
↓
Bridge Differences and Identify
Potential Synergies
↓
Develop Intercultural Strategies
for Specific Business Tasks
↓
Assess Results

Create Self-Awareness of One's Own Culture and Personal Style
↓
Map Cultural Differences and Overlaps
↓
Bridge Differences and Identify Potential Synergies
↓
Develop Intercultural Strategies for Specific Business Tasks
↓
Assess Results

difference is that under the merger the culturally diverse teams do not represent different companies but different entities within the same company.

Now we have one company with different players and groups, but all the groups strive to achieve the same corporate goals. You can see that it may take a long time before any merger gets to this point, and DaimlerChrysler is no exception. Successful international companies are able to build on the cultural diversity of their employees. In the process, they frequently build strong corporate cultures. The corporate culture does not eliminate the cultural backgrounds of the players, but it does facilitate the overcoming of one's self-reference criterion in view of the overall corporate goal and mission.

APPLYING YOUR CULTURAL KNOWLEDGE TO BUSINESS SITUATIONS

Understanding how cultural priorities can facilitate communication and make international business more productive is essential. An understanding of the relationship between effective intercultural business communication, the dynamics of culturally diverse groups, and the overall business strategy will prepare you to become a player in an exciting global environment.

In the Appendix, there are two more cases that give you an opportunity to apply cultural principles to international business situations. It will be helpful if you consider the cultural aspects, the specific business communication tasks, and the impact of culture on legal systems and organizational structures as you explore solutions to the problems at hand.

CHAPTER SUMMARY

This chapter applied the principles of intercultural communication in the global workplace to the case of DaimlerChrysler. Since there is no red flag indicating cultural problems in international business, it takes some practice to identify cultural issues. This chapter has given you the opportunity to examine a real case in view of what you have learned.

- After the presentation of the case, we identified the major cultural hurdles that DaimlerChrysler needed to overcome to be successful. The two sides had different approaches to dealing with uncertainty, the role of formality, conducting meetings, and compensation.
- We discussed the variables of the intercultural business communication process: the intercultural strategy, the business strategy, and the communication strategy. The interaction of these three variables creates new synergies that help establish an intercultural business communication strategy.

- As companies increasingly rely on teamwork, an understanding of the dynamics of culturally diverse teams is necessary. We identified the stages in developing teams that can take advantage of diverse viewpoints within the groups: self-awareness, mapping of differences, bridging gaps and identifying synergies, developing communication strategies, and assessing the results of teamwork.

- Teams function in the context of corporate strategies and goals. We examined the way teams fit into the corporate process and identified three situations: diverse teams within one company, diverse teams in two different companies that are working together but keep their own identity, and diverse teams in two companies that have merged or formed a joint venture.

Notes

1. "DaimlerChrysler Dumps Mitsubishi," BBC News, April 23, 2004.
2. Fuso Press Release, "Mitsubishi Fuso: Top Management Change Effective End of June 2005."
3. DaimlerChrysler Press Release, May 31, 2005.
4. Stephen Power, "Daimler Net Soars 84%, Lifted by Financial Arm," *The Wall Street Journal*, February 17, 2006, p. A3.
5. Peter Schneider, "Scenes from a Marriage," *New York Times Magazine*, August 12, 2001, pp. 44–48.
6. *Stern*, May 15, 1998.
7. *Forbes*, May 31, 1999.
8. *Ward's Automotive*, July 2000.
9. Chester Dawson, Jeff Green, Larry Armstrong, Christine Tierney, and Jonathan Wheatley, "Mr. Fix-It," *Business-Week*, May 14, 2001, pp. 26–27.

10. DaimlerChrysler Top Stories, "Mitsubishi Motors Announced Return to Profitability: Mitsubishi Motors FY 2001 Business Results and FY2002 Forecast," http://www.daimlerchrysler.com/ index_g.htm, (retrieved June 21, 2003).

11. Iris Varner, "The Theoretical Foundation for Intercultural Business Communication: A Conceptual Model," *Journal of Business Communication,* 37, no. 1 (2000), pp. 39–57.

12. J. M. Perkins, "Communication in a Global, Multicultural Corporation: Other Metaphors and Strategies." In *Exploring the Rhetoric of International Professional Communication,* C. R. Lovitt and D. Goswami, eds. (New York: Baywood Publishing, 1999), pp. 17–38.

13. Geert Hofstede, *Culture's Consequences,* 2nd ed. (Thousand Oaks, CA: Sage Publications, 2001).

14. Joseph DiStefano and Martha Maznevski, "Creating Value with Diverse Teams in Global Management," *Organizational Dynamics,* 29, no. 1 (2000), pp. 45–63.

15. Ibid.

16. J. Gresser, "Breaking the Japanese Negotiation Code: What European and American Managers Must Do to Win," *European Management Journal,* 10, no. 3 (1992), pp. 286–293.

17. J. M. George, G. R. Jones, and J. A. Gonzales, "The Role of Affect in Cross-Cultural Negotiations," *Journal of International Business Studies,* 29, no. 4 (1998), pp. 749–772; P. Guptara, "The Impact of Culture on International Negotiation," *European Business Review,* 92, no. 2 (1992), pp. xi–xii; Y. Paik and R. L. Tung, "Negotiation with East Asians: How to Attain 'Win-Win' Outcomes," *Management International Review,* 39, no. 2 (1999), pp. 103–122.

18. Teresa Palmer and Iris Varner, "Integrating Knowledge Management into HRD to Improve the Expatriate Process." In *Proceedings of the HRD Academy National Convention,* P. Kuchinke, ed. (Academy of Human Resource Development, 2000), pp. 921–926.

APPENDIX

Case 1: What Else Can Go Wrong?[1]

Joe Van West, President of Appliances Unlimited in Mexico, was thinking about his arrival in Mexico City and his life during the last six months as he was sitting in his office. He remembered getting the phone call late one evening while sitting in front of the TV in his house in Taipei, Taiwan, where he was Operations Manager of the local subsidiary of Appliances Unlimited, a Belgian firm. The phone call was to tell him that Mr. Brian Hodges, the President of the Mexican subsidiary of Appliances Unlimited, had had a major heart attack and would retire immediately. Mr. Van West had met Mr. Hodges several times at meetings, but he did not know him very well. The caller, his friend at headquarters, Stijn Verckens, indicated that management at headquarters was looking for a speedy replacement for Hodges, and that Joe Van West should talk to the President of the International Division at Headquarters immediately. Van West had always wanted to run a subsidiary. It would be a great opportunity, and he did tell Verckens that he would think about it.

Van West had gotten excellent reviews for his work as Operations Manager in Taipei. He was ready for the next step. He had hoped that there would be an opportunity in Canada or the United States, but he, an American citizen, and his wife, a native of Belgium, had decided a number of years ago that they would go wherever the opportunity presented itself. Van West talked to several people at headquarters, including the president for International. He applied for the job in Mexico, and was excited when he got the appointment. Being president of a subsidiary in a major market like Mexico was a big promotion and also financially rewarding. He looked forward to the new assignment.

When Van West arrived, he met with all the major players at the plant. He listened carefully and asked lots of questions about production, marketing, and sales. He sent e-mails to headquarters as well as had lengthy conversations on the phone with executives there. He went to Brussels twice to discuss the plans for the plant in Mexico.

By all accounts, his family had adjusted well. Antonio Hernandez, the Vice President for Manufacturing, had been wonderful in helping his family get settled. Mr. Hernandez and his wife had introduced Van West and his wife to one of the best clubs in the city, as well as many influential families in business and politics. The two women had become good friends. Mrs. Hernandez had helped with the everyday orientation, which consisted of things like shopping, schools, and household personnel. Mrs. Van West was grateful for all the assistance. The adjustment to Mexico City had been so much easier than the one to Taipei a few years earlier.

Everything had started so well that Van West had a hard time figuring out just what had gone wrong. Now he was facing major production problems, and the threat of a strike! Looking back, he could see the signs of problems building, but when they first appeared they had not seemed like major issues. Well, he had to get a handle on this, or he might as well pack his bags and look for another job. He reviewed each problem in turn.

Production Issues

The plant in Mexico manufactured small household appliances, such as toasters, electric irons, blenders, and coffee machines. In addition, the factory produced parts for washing machines to be assembled by the subsidiary of an American multinational company. The small appliances were mostly for the domestic market, while the washing machines were both for the domestic market and for export, mainly to other NAFTA countries. Over the last two years, the production lines had been upgraded to make use of the latest manufacturing technology. Projections called for future expansions and increasing profits.

A few weeks ago Van West had received a phone call from the production manager of the American subsidiary manufacturing the washing machines. He voiced concern over the quality and the delivery schedule of the washing machine parts. The number of defective parts had increased considerably over the last three months, and five times the parts had been delivered late enough to affect production schedules for the washing machines.

Van West had talked to Hernandez about the issue, but Hernandez did not seem to think it was a big deal. Just the same, he promised to look into it. Even with Hernandez's reassurances, Van West was concerned, and he started checking a bit on his own. He went to the factory floor. In the past, he had never gone by himself; Hernandez had always been with him. Van West felt a bit uncomfortable and intimidated. His Spanish was limited; he had had three years in high school, and although he had started taking private lessons after his arrival in Mexico, it was slow going and he was self-conscious about making mistakes. The line supervisor, Duarte Gonzales spoke enough English to lead him around.

Gonzales mentioned some difficulties with some of the new machines and the reasons they had broken down several times. He also indicated that some of the newer employees were different and not as dedicated as the long-time employees. Gonzales did not talk about Hernandez, but Van West picked up that their relationship was a bit tense. He grew concerned that Hernandez had never mentioned any of these problems, and he decided to talk to Hernandez again to emphasize the importance of quality and timeliness of delivery.

He phoned Hernandez, who was out to lunch and would not be back until the next day. As he was walking back to his office, it occurred to Van West that Hernandez was gone frequently. He had never paid much attention to this before but decided to keep a closer watch on Hernandez in the future. When Van West talked to Hernandez the next day, Hernandez brushed the issue with the washing machine parts aside. Gonzales was exaggerating the problems. Sure, there had been some problems in the past, but nothing to worry about. Things would be just fine. However, he also pointed out that Van West would have to make some concessions to local work attitudes. He said: "You know things are looser here. You just cannot expect the same performance you are used to. Take it easy; everything will be fine. Just don't worry. Leave it to me. I know how to take care of things."

Hernandez came from a distinguished Mexican family. His grandfather had been a prominent surgeon, and his father was a well-known lawyer. Hernandez himself had gone to the best schools in Mexico and had received an MBA from the University of Michigan. He knew everyone of importance in the business circles of Mexico City. But Van West was increasingly concerned about his nonchalant attitude towards day-to-day affairs at the plant. At the same time, he did not know how to best approach Hernandez. Their close social contacts made it difficult to criticize his performance. Van West was also wondering how involved and how knowledgeable Hernandez was about the production process and the new technology.

In the following weeks, Van West went several times to the factory floor when Hernandez was absent. He started to get a clearer picture of the production issues even though his limited Spanish slowed the discussions with Gonzales and the line supervisor.

After Van West had first arrived in Mexico and received a thorough briefing, he had asked Hernandez to deal with the day-to-day issues until he was settled and comfortable. He had shared his management philosophy with the management at the plant: to delegate as much as possible and include employees in the decision-making process. He felt that he could use his expertise and talents best by paying attention to the big issues. Everyone had agreed with him and thought that this was a good approach.

Worker Unrest

As Van West was contemplating what to do, Vincente Garcia, in charge of Human Resources, came to inform him that the workers were getting agitated and had started to meet in small groups to discuss their opposition to the implementation of new computer programs to monitor the quality of output, evaluate production costs, and track efficiency. While the updating of production equipment over the past few years had improved the quantity of output, cost overruns had remained a problem. Furthermore, efficiency levels and quality of output had not improved as much with the new equipment as headquarters had hoped. As a result, headquarters had been pushing for the installation of state-of-the-art computer systems to monitor all phases of operations.

Van West's predecessor had not been very familiar with computer programs. In fact, he had been very apprehensive about all the software and programs headquarters had been pushing. Finally, a year ago, headquarters had sent an expert to supervise the installation and implementation of the latest technology. Hodges had announced that Jones would be at the plant for a while and that he would work on installing technology to track performance. Frank Jones, the technician, was in his thirties. He certainly knew his stuff and was happiest when he could talk about computer technology. He had little direct contact with the workers. Whenever he had to talk to employees, he would go through the Vice President for Manufacturing. If Hernandez was not available, he would talk to Gonzalez.

Hodges had not paid any attention to Jones. When Van West arrived, he was briefed about the technology update, but with everything else going on, he had not taken the time to familiarize himself with any of the details. Things seemed to run just fine. Jones indicated that the system would soon be ready for testing and fully operational in a few more weeks. However, as employees learned a bit more about what Jones was doing, they grew concerned and uneasy. Some of the senior workers talked to Raoul Cortez, who worked with Jones, about their concerns and the new system. Cortez hinted that the new system could certainly be programmed to identify specific production problems and track individual work performance. Jones was not aware of the workers' concerns and their talks with Cortez. When an article in a local newspaper discussed layoffs after the introduction of new technology at another plant, the employees at Appliances Unlimited became very alarmed. They were not going to sit there and wait to lose their jobs. Several of the leaders were talking of forming a union and perhaps even calling a strike. Van West was not familiar with the Mexican union process and union legislation, but any disruption sounded terrible.

Thinking about the possible strike, Van West was in disbelief. He had been told that the workers at the plant were happy and dedicated. Nobody had ever talked about a union, at least not in public. Labor relations had been good, and Appliances Unlimited was known for excellent pay and benefits. A shutdown at this point would seriously affect delivery contracts. It would also affect negotiations with new clients.

Van West knew he had to do something. But what? He decided to call a meeting to discuss options. He asked the following people to attend a meeting the next morn-ing at 9 a.m.: Hernandez, Gonzales, Garcia, Jones, Cortez, and Sanchez.

Case Discussion Questions

In your discussion you may want to examine the following questions. Look at them in light of the cultural knowledge you have gained.

- What are the underlying cultural issues contributing to the problems?
- What should Van West have done when he first came to Mexico?
- How should Van West deal with Hernandez? Address the role of the boss in Mexican culture. Address the relationship between superiors and subordinates.
- How can Van West deal with the labor issue? How does this relate to attitudes towards change, the relationship between the individual and the group, and hierarchy?

Case 2: Hana, a Joint Venture Between Health Snacks and Toka Foods[2]

When Health Snacks and Toka Foods formed a joint venture four years ago, the future looked very promising. Health Snacks was looking for opportunities to enter the Japanese market, and Toka Foods was well positioned in Japan to facilitate that process. Toka Foods, on the other hand, was interested in gaining access to new technology. Since Health Snacks was a leader in the adaptation of new technology to business processes, the joint venture seemed ideal. At the time the joint venture was established, executives both from Health Snacks and Toka Foods had spent many hours hammering out an agreement that would help both sides realize their objectives.

Each side was excited about the new opportunities; however, after the first six months, several disagreements surfaced regarding the management of the joint venture. One of the issues was who should get copies of written communication regarding production schedules and marketing plans. The Americans felt that they were not sufficiently included in discussions relating to the joint venture. The Japanese managers, on the other hand, were frustrated with the number of requests for reports from the American side.

At first, these disagreements seemed rather superficial, but as time went by, both sides became increasingly unhappy and started to blame each other for any difficulties.

Health Snacks had tried to solve the problems via electronic communication, faxes and e-mails. They even had organized a teleconference to meet "face-to-face" so that each side could hear the other's viewpoint, but the problems remained. After much soul-searching, Ron Carter decided it was time to fly to Nagoya and face the problems head-on.

Mr. Carter had joined Health Snacks as President of International Operations only nine months ago. In this position, he also served as vice president for the joint venture with Toka Foods. He had received a thorough briefing at the time and had also studied the history of the joint venture on his own. He had been an expatriate in Australia and France managing international subsidiaries in both countries. He was 40 years old and was expected to have a bright future.

Health Snacks was a major manufacturer of convenience foods and health food products. The company had registered several patents for extending shelf life while maintaining quality. The company had sales of roughly $3 billion and had subsidiaries in 30 countries around the globe. In the last year, roughly 34 percent of corporate sales had come from international sales. Tim Davis, President for International Operations at Health Snacks, and Mr. Carter's predecessor, was given the task of exploring the expansion into the Japanese market.

Health Snacks had never had any major presence in Japan; however, top executives believed that Japanese consumers were increasingly interested in convenience foods and health foods. Many Japanese still went shopping for food daily, but the number of people making weekly food purchases was increasing. Toka Foods, a traditional food processor, had attempted to move into this market but ultimately decided that it lacked the processing and packaging technology, as well as the quality control to establish a major presence. As a result, Toka Foods started looking around for a potential partner. In the beginning, Health Snacks and Toka Foods had explored licensing agreements. Toka Foods, in particular, was interested in getting a license for using Health Snacks's processing and packaging technology. Health Snacks, however, felt that a joint venture would provide better opportunities for their establishing a presence in the Japanese market. Upper management knew that the Japanese market was difficult to enter, and they hoped that they would not have to develop an entire distribution system.

The negotiations had been very difficult and took much longer than executives from Health Snacks had anticipated. The Japanese were slow and deliberate in their approach to the negotiation. Everything seemed to take a long time, and once the Japanese side had made up its mind on a point, it was difficult to agree on any changes. Everything had to go back and be rediscussed by Japanese executives.

The composition of the negotiation team also became an issue. Based on initial contacts, Health Snacks knew that Toka Foods was interested in technical details. To speed up the process and provide technical details, Health Snacks had initially sent an engineer from production and one from packaging, both in their early thirties with no international experience. The two engineers took detailed reports, diagrams, and illustrations with them. They knew the technology inside out, but the Japanese, while asking many questions, did not move towards any agreement. When the two engineers from Health Snacks could not answer questions relating to projections of production and sales, the Japanese became impatient. The two engineers found the talks tiring, and sitting across from a team of eight Japanese managers was intimidating and exhausting. Furthermore, the Japanese repeatedly asked the same questions. It was only after the President of the International Division at Health Snacks, Tim Davis, participated in the negotiations that progress was made. He visited several times, and an agreement was finally signed.

The final agreement had the following provisions: The ownership of the joint venture was equally divided. Toka Foods was to provide facilities for processing of food and packaging. The Japanese side was also to provide its marketing network and develop new marketing channels where necessary. Health Snacks was to provide the latest technology and assist with the production setup. The joint venture was to be called Hana, and products from the joint venture were to be marketed under the brand name, Hana.

The management of the joint venture posed some special issues as well. Given that the joint venture would be located in Japan, the contract specified that the joint venture would have a board of eight people, four from each partner; however, all employees working for the joint venture would come from Toka Foods. The joint venture would have a president and a vice president. The president was to be Japanese, nominated by Toka Foods but subject to approval by the entire board. The Vice President of International Operations at Health Snacks would serve as the American vice president for the venture. Health Snacks would send a Health Snacks executive to serve as Technical Director and board member. This person would be the only American posted full-time to the joint venture in Japan.

The Board Composition Was as Follows

Health Snack representatives: the CEO of the parent company, the CFO of the parent company, the President of International Operations and Vice President of the joint venture, and the Technical Director.

Toka representatives: the CEO of Toka, the Vice President of Production of Toka, the President of the joint venture, and the CFO of the joint venture.

The establishment of the first board and the selection of president, vice president, and technical director had not posed any problems, and everything seemed to go according to schedule.

About ten months ago, Mr. Carter's predecessor left the company and Mr. Carter was hired to fill his place. Shortly after Mr. Carter assumed his position at Health Snacks, the Japanese president of the joint venture, Mr. Hyashida, died at the age of 63. Mr. Carter was waiting to discuss possible successors with Toka Foods's President, Mr. Sony, when he received an e-mail from Mr. Sony informing him that the Japanese had nominated Mr. Hiromitsu Ota for the position. Mr. Carter was upset because he had expected that even though the Japanese could select their nominee, they would have consulted him before making the nomination public. More importantly, Mr. Carter did not think that Mr. Ota was the right person for the position. His judgment was reenforced when he discussed the issue with Mr. Russell, the technical director and board member, of the joint venture in Japan.

Mr. Ota had joined Toka Foods right after graduating from Waseda University 35 years earlier. For the past 20 years, he had held staff positions at Toka Foods. He was manager of administrative services at a major company plant and after that was personnel manager at headquarters. In the latter position, he joined the board of directors at Toka Foods. Currently, he was general manager of several staff departments. Mr. Carter simply was at a loss as to why Mr. Sony would nominate someone without line experience for the position of president of the joint venture.

Mr. Russell filled him in on traditional Japanese corporate practices, and it began to dawn on Mr. Carter that he had little understanding of the management of Japanese corporations. Many of the major companies still practice a form of lifetime employment. With economic difficulties, increased competition from abroad, and increasing foreign ownership of Japanese corporations, the practice is not as common as it once was; however, lifetime employment is still seen as the ideal, particularly when it comes to older employees. Under lifetime employment, employees, almost all males, are recruited right out of college. They move slowly up the corporate ladder until the age of about 60. At that stage, most people retire and only selected people move into executive positions. Competence and performance play a role in the promotion to upper management and executive level positions, but seniority is a major factor throughout. Even though under Japanese law board members are elected by shareholders for two-year terms, in reality they are appointed by the president of the company and/or the chairman of the board. Frequently, a seat on the board is a reward for loyal and faithful company service rather than exceptional performance. Board membership is typically rotated every two years to make room for more junior managers; however, at that time of scheduled rotation, many board members, targeted for leaving the board, are still quite young and not ready to retire. Therefore, it is quite common to appoint outgoing board members who have no chance of further promotion at the company to positions in subsidiaries, affiliated companies, or joint ventures. It became clear to Mr. Carter that Mr. Ota was not going to be promoted to President of Toka Foods and would, therefore, be rotated off the board. He had served Toka Foods loyally and with great dedication but was considered unsuitable by the company to occupy the top positions. However, he was considered appropriate for president of the joint venture.

Mr. Carter was upset. He wanted the best person for the job and was convinced that other candidates were available. In fact, he had met Mr. Katsuki from Toka Foods only a couple of months ago in Chicago. He seemed to have the qualities that Mr. Carter was looking for and expecting in the president for the joint venture.

After talking to Mr. Russell, he informed Mr. Sony that he objected to Mr. Ota. At the same time, he proposed Mr. Katsuki for the position and gave his reasons for his choice. Mr. Katsuki was 48 years old and had been with Toka Foods during his entire career. Currently, Mr. Katsuki was the marketing director for the joint venture. He had made quite an impression at Health Snacks headquarters in Chicago. He spoke excellent English and seemed to have the characteristics and the energy for moving the joint venture forward. Mr. Katsuki seemed to be straightforward in his communication and very dynamic compared to many of the other Japanese Mr. Carter had met.

As Mr. Carter reflected on the joint venture, he came to the conclusion that the joint venture was run almost exclusively as a Japanese corporation. The American side had little input, and Mr. Carter felt that Health Snacks was increasingly marginalized. In addition, it always took weeks before he received responses to inquiries, and he was convinced that the management needed to be more responsive to queries from the American side. He realized that the time difference and language issues posed a hurdle to communication; it was all the more reason to get someone like Mr. Katsuki who could relate to the American side. He carefully worded his opposition to Mr. Ota and his suggestion of Mr. Katsuki. Only after he was convinced that the message was tactful, courteous, and constructive and had gone through several revisions, did he send it off. He was, therefore, rather surprised when he received a letter from Mr. Sony totally rejecting his suggestions. Mr. Sony was polite but made it quite clear that Toka Foods had carefully considered all options and that Mr. Ota was the right person, and Mr. Katsuki was out of the question. He further explained that a promotion for Mr. Katsuki would be totally unacceptable and would ruin Mr. Katsuki's career. In his letter, Mr. Sony gave no explanation as to why the appointment of Mr. Katsuki would ruin his career. When Mr. Carter asked Mr. Russell for more information, Mr. Russell talked about traditional Japanese management practices that would be next to impossible to change.

Mr. Carter was wondering how things could have progressed to such a state without Mr. Russell's informing him about the discussions at the joint venture. How effective was Mr. Russell in his job, and how well did he understand the Japanese and Japanese practices? Mr. Carter had assumed that Mr. Russell was well integrated into the running of the joint venture and actively participated in the discussion of management issues.

When Health Snacks was hiring a technical director, the company had looked for someone with Japanese experience and language ability. Such a person, however, was difficult to find, and Mr. Russell had been a compromise candidate. He spoke some Japanese and had been a student at a Japanese university 15 years earlier. From comments by the Japanese, Mr. Carter figured that Mr. Russell's Japanese language ability was rather limited. Furthermore, he did not seem to have established a close working relationship with the Japanese managers of the venture. Mr. Russell had his family with him in Japan, his wife and two teenage sons. He preferred to spend evenings and weekends with his family rather than to go out with colleagues. In fact, he found the evening entertainments and visits to bars unproductive and exhausting.

Mr. Sony was not looking forward to Mr. Carter's visit. He hated confrontations and was worried that the meeting would not be very pleasant. He had not met Mr. Carter before. He never did understand why American companies were hiring top people from the outside. The frequent changes in personnel were rather unsettling to him. It seemed to him that he had to adjust to new faces all the time. He also was not quite sure how much Mr. Carter understood about Japanese management practices. And the message from Mr. Carter concerning the nomination of Mr. Katsuki added to his suspicions.

Mr. Sony was convinced that Mr. Ota was the best and most appropriate person for the position in the joint venture. He was owed the position for his loyal and dedicated service. Given that several new board members needed to be appointed, a reappointment of Mr. Ota to the board was not a viable option. Mr. Sony was well aware that Mr. Ota was not a dynamic person or visionary manager, but he got along with people and always put the company first in all his business dealings. Therefore, the position of president of the joint venture was suitable and appropriate. He could see why Americans might not think so, but the president had to function in a Japanese environment and have the appropriate stature and seniority to represent the company well. In the Japanese environment, it was not necessary to have a strong leader or enthusiastic promoter. Someone who could build consensus and move the entire group along was much more important, and Mr. Ota had a proven track record in that area.

Clearly, Mr. Sony thought that Mr. Carter had no knowledge of Japanese business practices. If he did, he would have never even suggested Mr. Katsuki. Sure, Mr. Katsuki was dynamic, and he would have a bright future particularly with the internationalization of businesses. However, to promote him now would ruin his career forever. He would not be accepted by his peers, and his seniors would deeply resent his promotion over them. The only way to guarantee Mr. Katsuki's ultimate success would be for him to take his time and move up the ladder slowly.

As he was thinking the joint venture over, he was also focusing on Mr. Russell. What did Mr. Russell do to represent the Japanese viewpoint in Chicago? In fact, he had not seen much of Mr. Russell lately. Communication was difficult because he had a hard time understanding Mr. Russell when he spoke Japanese, and he himself did not speak very fluent English. It also occurred to him that Mr. Russell had not attended many of the social functions and had rarely participated in weekend outings and golf games. He just did not seem to be part of the joint venture family. Perhaps the joint venture had not been such a good idea after all.

As the plane was getting closer to Nagoya, Mr. Carter was wondering whether it was all worth it. Mr. Sony had very similar thoughts as he was preparing to meet Mr. Carter.

Case Discussion Questions

Consider the following questions in your discussion of the case and pay special attention to the cultural dimensions.

- What are the underlying cultural issues?
- What could both sides have done to avoid the current problems?
- Given that there is a problem, what can/should both sides do to overcome the problems?

Can the joint venture be saved?

Notes

1. The case is an update and adaptation by Iris Varner of: J. B. Schnapp, "Crisis in Caribia," *Harvard Business Review* (November–December 1968).

2. This case is an update and adaptation by Iris Varner of the Showa case, which is published by the President and Fellows of Harvard College.

READING ONE

Intercultural Negotiation in International Business

Jeswald W. Salacuse

Introduction

Although negotiating a purely domestic business deal and negotiating an international transaction have much in common, the factor that is almost always present in an international negotiation and generally absent from a domestic negotiation is a difference in culture among the parties. In international business, transactions not only cross borders, they also cross cultures. Culture profoundly influences how people think, communicate, and behave, and it also affects the kinds of deals they make and the way they make them. Differences in culture among business executives (for example, between a Chinese public-sector plant manager in Shanghai and an American division head of a family company in Cleveland) can therefore create barriers that impede or completely stymie the negotiating process. The purpose of this article is to examine the effect of differences in culture on international business negotiations and to suggest ways to overcome problems encountered in intercultural dealings.

The Nature of Culture

Definitions of culture are as numerous and often as vague as definitions of negotiation itself (Moran and Stripp 1991, pp. 43–56; Zartman 1993, p. 19). Some scholars would confine the concept of culture to the realm of ideas, feeling, and thoughts. For example, one working definition offered by two negotiation experts is that

"Culture is a set of shared and enduring meanings, values, and beliefs that characterize national, ethnic, and other groups and orient their behavior" (Faure and Sjostedt 1993, p. 3). Others would have culture also encompass behavior patterns and institutions common to a given group or community. E. Adamson Hoebel, a noted anthropologist, defined culture as "the integrated system of learned behavior patterns which are characteristic of the members of a society and which are not the result of biological inheritance" (Hoebel 1972, p. 7). While the essence of culture may reside in the mind, it must be pointed out that persons gain their understanding of their and others' cultures primarily, if not exclusively, from observing the behavior and institutions of a particular group.

For purposes of this paper, culture is defined as the socially transmitted behavior patterns, norms, beliefs, and values of a given community (Salacuse 1991, p. 45). Persons from that community use the elements of their culture to interpret their surroundings and guide their interactions with other persons. So when an executive from a corporation in Dallas, Texas, sits down to negotiate a business deal with a manager from a Houston company, the two negotiators rely on their common culture to interpret each other's statements and actions. But when persons from two different cultures—for example an executive from Texas and a manager from Japan—meet for the first time, they usually do not share a common pool of information and assumptions to interpret each others'

Source: Reprinted from Jeswald W. Salacuse, "Intercultural Negotiation in International Business," *Group Decision and Negotiation,* vol. 8, pp. 217–36, © 1999 Kluwer Academic/Plenum Publishers.

statements, actions, and intentions. Culture can therefore be seen as a language, a "silent language" which the parties need in addition to the language they are speaking if they are truly to communicate and arrive at a genuine understanding (Hall 1959). Like any language, the elements of culture form a system, which has been variously characterized as a "system for creating, sending, storing, and processing information" (Hall and Hall 1990, p. 179) and a "group problem-solving tool that enables individuals to survive in a particular environment" (Moran and Stripp 1991, p. 43). Culture serves as a kind of glue—a social adhesive—that binds a group of people together and gives them a distinct identity as a community. It may also give them a sense that they are a community different and separate from other communities.

This article is concerned primarily with national cultures, cultures identified with a particular country. But culture and nationality are not always the same thing. Within Nigeria, for example, the culture of the Ibos of the largely Christian southeastern part of the country and the Hausas of the mainly Muslim north are different and distinct. Similarly, individual corporations and professions may have their own distinct organizational or professional cultures whose norms and behavior patterns may predominate in certain respects over the ethnic or national cultures of their professions' members. For example, a continuing concern in the current wave of mergers and acquisitions in the United States is the problem of blending the cultures of two organizations, such as Morgan Stanley and Dean Witter, after the deal has been signed (Lublin and O'Brian, 1997). But while cultural values, attitudes, and behavior patterns may appear permanently embedded in a group, particularly in the context of an encounter between two different cultures, in fact culture is dynamic. It is constantly changing (Bohannan 1995).

And finally, in considering the role of culture in international business negotiation and relationships, it is important to remember that the world has a staggering diversity of cultures. For example, while certain observers speak of "Asian culture" as if it were a homogeneous set of values, beliefs, and behavior patterns followed by all Asians (Mahbubani 1995), in reality Asia has many different and distinct cultures from India to Laos, from Korea to Indonesia. Each has its own values and practices that may differ markedly from those prevailing in another country—or indeed in another part of the same country. The negotiating style of Koreans, for example, is not the same as that of the Lao. And even within countries that from outward appearances seem to have a fairly uniform cultural identity, like the French and the Germans, significant differences may nonetheless exist between regions—such as the difference between the business community in Paris and that of the *midi* in southern France.

The Elements of Culture

One may conceive of the four cultural elements mentioned in the previous definition—behavior, attitudes, norms, and values—as forming a series of concentric circles, like the layers of an onion, illustrated by Exhibit 1.

The process of understanding the culture of a counterpart in a negotiation is similar to peeling an onion. The outermost layer of the onion is behavior, the words and actions of one's counterpart. It is this layer which a negotiator first perceives in an intercultural negotiation. A second inner layer consists of attitudes of persons from that culture toward specific events and phenomena—for example, attitudes about beginning meetings punctually or the appropriate format of presentations. Attitudes may become evident to a counterpart in an intercultural negotiation only after protracted discussions. Next are norms, the rules to be followed in specific situations. Here, for example, a negotiator may come to realize that his or her counterpart's seemly rigid insistence on punctuality is not merely a personal idiosyncrasy but is based on a firm rule derived from his or her culture.

The innermost layer—the core—consists of values. Norms about the way meetings are conducted, representatives chosen, or persons rewarded are usually based on certain values that are important to that culture. Such differences in values are often the most difficult for negotiators to detect and understand. Indeed, the parties to an international negotiation may discover their value differences only after they have signed the contract and begun to work together. Such differences in cultural values between partners in an international joint venture, for example, may lead to severe conflict and ultimately the failure of their enterprise, a factor that may explain why many international ventures have a short life.

In their valuable book *The Seven Cultures of Capitalism*, based on extensive survey research among thousands of executives from throughout the world, Hampden-Turner and Trompenaars (1993) found sharp differences that could be explained only by different cultural values

EXHIBIT 1   Culture as an Onion

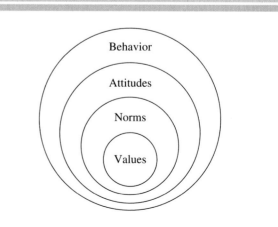

to such basic management tasks as group decision making, hiring, rewarding employees, and making and applying rules. For example, with respect to group decision making, wide variations among cultural groups existed in answering the following question:

> What is the better way to choose a person to represent a group?
>
> **A.** All members of the group should meet and discuss candidates until almost everybody agrees on the same person; or
>
> **B.** The group members should meet, nominate persons, vote, and choose the person with a majority of the votes even if several people are against the person.

In this question, according to the authors, the values of adversarial democracy and consensual democracy were in tension. While 84.4 percent of the Japanese opted for Answer A (consensual democracy), only 37.7 percent of the Americans did so. It is interesting to note that there were differences among Asians on this question. For example, unlike the Japanese, only 39.4 percent of the Singaporeans chose Answer A, exhibiting an aversion to consensual democracy that is perhaps reflected in Singapore's authoritarian political system. One can imagine that this difference in cultural values about decision making between Japanese and American executives in a joint venture might lead to serious conflict between the joint venture partners. Other kinds of value conflicts may arise, for example, between individualism prized by Americans and communitarianism embodied in many Asian cultures; about whether in hiring an employee it is more important to consider individual talent or the ability to fit into the organization; or about whether to reward persons on the basis of group performance or by individual achievement only.

Differences in cultural values can present themselves in international business transactions and relationships time after time and day after day, and they may ultimately turn what appeared to be a harmonious negotiation or business relationship into a continuing source of conflict between the parties. Once the conflict surfaces, it may be exacerbated by the way the parties try to cope with it. One unfortunate tendency is for each of the parties to extol their own cultural values but to denigrate those of their business or negotiating partner. For example, Americans, with their high store on individualism, will tend to see their value system positively: as for individual rights and human freedom, as putting the individual above the tyranny of the group, as knowing that a group prospers only when individuals prosper, and as efficient. Persons coming from cultures where communitarian values are prized will see themselves as unselfish, humane, for group interests and rights, and knowing that individuals prosper only when the group prospers. Yet Americans, when confronted with a communitarian culture, may tend to ascribe to it only

negative characteristics. So Americans, reacting to Japanese values in a decision to retain a 15-year employee whose performance has declined, might consider their Japanese counterparts as tolerant of freeloaders, giving in to the tyranny of the group, weak, and inefficient. On the other hand, the Japanese would probably characterize the Americans as ignoring the contributions and needs of the group, lacking in loyalty, inhumane, and selfish.

It is important therefore for business executives in a negotiation to understand the values inherent in the culture of their counterparts and not to characterize those values in a negative way.

The Effect of Cultural Differences on Negotiation

Differences in culture between deal makers can obstruct negotiations in many ways. First, they can create misunderstandings in communication. If one American executive responds to another American's proposal by saying, "That's difficult," the response, interpreted against American culture and business practice, probably means that the door is still open for further discussion, that perhaps the other side should sweeten its offer. In some other cultures, for example in Asia, persons may be reluctant to say a direct and emphatic no, even when that is their intent. So when a Japanese negotiator, in response to a proposal, says, "That is difficult," he is clearly indicating that the proposal is unacceptable. "It is difficult" means "no" to the Japanese, but to the American it means "maybe."

Second, cultural differences create difficulties not only in understanding words, but also in interpreting actions. For example, most Westerners expect a prompt answer when they make a statement or ask a question. Japanese, on the other hand, tend to take longer to respond. As a result, negotiations with Japanese are sometimes punctuated with periods of silence that seem excruciating to an American. For the Japanese, the period of silence is normal, an appropriate time to reflect on what has been said. The fact that they may not be speaking in their native language lengthens even more the time needed to respond.

From their own cultural perspective, Americans may interpret Japanese silence as rudeness, lack of understanding, or a cunning tactic to get the Americans to reveal themselves. Rather than wait for a response, the American tendency is to fill the void with words by asking questions, offering further explanations, or merely repeating what they have already said. This response to silence may confuse the Japanese, who are made to feel that they are being bombarded by questions and proposals without being given adequate time to respond to any of them.

On the other hand, Latin Americans, who place a high value on verbal agility, have a tendency to respond quickly. Indeed, they may answer a point once they have understood it even though the other side has not finished speaking. While inexperienced American negotiators are sometimes confused by Japanese delays in responding, they can become equally agitated in negotiations with Brazilians by what Americans consider constant interruptions.

Third, cultural considerations also influence the form and substance of the deal you are trying to make. For example, in many parts of the Muslim world, where Islamic law prohibits the taking of interest on loans, one may need to restructure or relabel finance charges in a deal as "administrative fees" in order to gain acceptance at the negotiating table. More substantively, differences in culture will invariably require changes in products, management systems, and personnel practices. For example, in Thailand, the relationship between manager and employee is more hierarchical than it is in the United States. Workers are motivated by a desire to please the manager, but they in turn expect and want their managers to sense their personal problems and be ready to help with them. In other cultures, such as in Australia, employees neither expect nor want managers to become involved with employees' personal problems. Thus an Australian project in Thailand would need to change its concept of employee relations because of the local culture (Hughes and Sheehan 1993).

And finally, culture can influence "negotiating style," the way persons from different cultures conduct themselves in negotiating sessions. Research indicates fairly clearly that negotiation practices differ from culture to culture (Weiss 1994, p. 51). Indeed, culture may influence how persons conceive of the very nature and function of negotiation itself. Studies of negotiating styles are abundant (e.g., Binnendijk 1987; Fisher 1980; Graham et al. 1988; Campbell et al. 1988). Some seek to focus on describing and analyzing the negotiating styles of particular groups. Indeed, the practitioner's fascination with cultural negotiating styles seems to have spawned a distinct literary genre: the "Negotiating with . . ." literature. Numerous books and articles bearing such titles as "Negotiating with the Japanese," "Negotiating with the Arabs," and "Negotiating with the Chinese" seek to lead the novice through the intricacies of negotiating in specific cultures (for a bibliography of such literature, see Salacuse 1991, pp. 174–83). Another approach to studying negotiating style is cross-cultural and comparative. It seeks to identify certain basic elements in negotiating style and to determine how they are reflected in various cultures. It is this approach which the next part of this article will adopt.

Culture and Negotiating Styles: Ten Factors in Deal Making

The great diversity of the world's cultures makes it impossible for any negotiator, no matter how skilled and experienced, to understand fully all the cultures that he

or she may encounter. How then should an executive prepare to cope with culture in making deals in Singapore this week and Seoul the next? One approach is to identify important areas where cultural differences may arise during the negotiation process. A knowledge of those factors may help an international business negotiator to understand a counterpart and to anticipate possible misunderstandings. Toward this end, scholars have developed a variety of frameworks and checklists that may be applied cross-culturally (e.g., Weiss 1985; Moran and Stripp 1991; Salacuse 1991). Based on a review of the literature as well as interviews with practitioners, the author, in an earlier work (Salacuse 1991), identified 10 factors that seemed to be the most problematic. These 10 factors, each of which consisted of two poles, were (1) negotiating goals (contract or relationship?); (2) attitudes to the negotiating process (win–win or win–lose?); (3) personal styles (formal or informal?); (4) styles of communication (direct or indirect?); (5) time sensitivity (high or low?); (6) emotionalism (high or low?); (7) agreement form (specific or general?); (8) agreement-building process (bottom up or top down?); (9) negotiating team organization (one leader or consensus?); and (10) risk taking (high or low?). Negotiating styles, like personalities, display a wide range of variation. The 10 negotiating traits listed here can be placed on a spectrum or continuum as illustrated in Exhibit 2.

The purpose of the matrix in Exhibit 2 is to identify specific negotiating traits affected by culture and to show the possible variation that each trait or factor may take. With this knowledge, an international business negotiator may be able to understand better the negotiating styles and approaches of his counterparts from other cultures. Equally important, it may help negotiators determine how their own styles appear to those same counterparts on the other side of the bargaining table.

EXHIBIT 2   The Impact of Culture on Negotiation

Trait	
Goal	Contract ↔ Relationship
Attitudes	Win–lose ↔ Win–win
Personal styles	Informal ↔ Formal
Communications	Direct ↔ Indirect
Time sensitivity	High ↔ Low
Emotionalism	High ↔ Low
Agreement form	Specific ↔ General
Agreement building	Bottom up ↔ Top down
Team organization	One leader ↔ Consensus
Risk taking	High ↔ Low

In order to test this approach to understanding negotiating style, the matrix was translated into a survey questionnaire and administered to 310 business executives, lawyers, and graduate business students (many of whom had substantial work experience) from all continents at various sites in North America, Latin America, and Europe. The respondents came from 12 countries: the United States, the United Kingdom, France, Germany, Spain, Mexico, Argentina, Brazil, Nigeria, India, China, and Japan. After receiving an explanation of the matrix and questionnaire, respondents were asked to rate their own attitudes anonymously toward each of these negotiating traits on a five-point scale. In general, as will be seen, the survey revealed significant correlations between the respondents' assessment of certain traits of their negotiating styles and the national cultures from which they came.

The results of the survey must be read with several caveats. First, the answers that the respondents gave reflected only how they saw themselves (or would like others to see them) rather than their negotiating styles and behavior in actual negotiations. The results can be read only as indicating a certain predisposition of individual cultures toward certain factors affecting the negotiation process. Second, negotiating style in a given negotiation may be influenced by numerous factors besides culture, including personality, bureaucracy, business experience, and the nature of the transactions under negotiation. For example, an executive who is predisposed to approach a business negotiation as a problem-solving, integrative process (win–win) may behave in a distributive, confrontational way (win–lose) when confronted by a hostile counterpart at the negotiating table. Third, all the respondents spoke English, completed the survey in English, had substantial international experience, and were participating in graduate university education or advanced executive seminars, also conducted in the English language. As a result, they may not be representative of most business executives in their cultures. On the other hand, they are fairly representative of the kinds of persons who conduct international negotiations on behalf of companies. Fourth, the meaning of key terms in the survey, such as *direct, indirect, risk, general,* and *specific,* were not strictly defined but instead were interpreted by each respondent according to his or her own subjective interpretation, a factor obviously influenced by culture. Fifth, both the size of the sample and the number of cultures surveyed were limited.

Negotiating Goal: Contract or Relationship?

Different cultures may view the very purpose of a business negotiation differently. For many American executives, the goal of a business negotiation, first and foremost, is often to arrive at a signed contract between the parties. Americans consider a signed contract as a definitive set of rights and duties that strictly binds the two sides, an attitude succinctly summed up in the statement "a deal is a deal."

Japanese, Chinese, and other cultural groups in Asia, it is said, often consider that the goal of a negotiation is not a signed contract, but the creation of a relationship between the two sides (e.g., Pye 1982). Although the written contract describes the relationship, the essence of the deal is the relationship itself. For Americans, signing a contract is closing a deal; for many Asians, signing a contract might more appropriately be called opening a relationship. This difference in view may explain why Asians tend to give more time and effort to prenegotiation, while Americans want to rush through this first phase in deal making. The activities of prenegotiation, whereby the parties seek to get to know one another thoroughly, are a crucial foundation for a good business relationship. They may seem less important when the goal is merely a contract.

The results of the survey showed significant differences among the cultures surveyed with respect to the negotiating goals of contract and relationship. Thus only 26 percent of the Spanish respondents claimed that their primary goal in a negotiation was a relationship compared to 66 percent of the Indians. On the other hand, the preference for a relationship was not as pronounced among the Chinese (54.5 percent) as one might have expected from the literature, and the Japanese appeared almost evenly divided on the question, with a slight preference for a contract as a negotiating goal. Table 1 summarizes the survey results on this issue.

Negotiating Attitude: Win–Lose or Win–Win?

Because of differences in culture or personality, or both, businesspersons appear to approach deal making with one of two basic attitudes: that a negotiation is either a process in which both can gain (win–win) or a struggle in which of necessity, one side wins and the other side loses (win–lose). Win–win negotiators see deal making as a collaborative and problem-solving process; win–lose negotiators see it as confrontational. In a reflection of

TABLE 1   Goal: Contract or Relationship?

Contract:	Spn.	Fr.	Braz.	Jpn.	USA	Ger.	UK	Nig.	Arg.	Chi.	Mex.	Ind.
Percentage:	73.7	70	66.7	54.5	53.7	54.5	47.1	46.7	46.2	45.5	41.7	33.3

this dichotomy, negotiation scholars have concluded that these approaches represented two basic paradigms of the negotiation process: (1) distributive bargaining (i.e., win–lose) and (2) integrative bargaining or problem solving (i.e., win–win) (e.g., Hoppman 1995; Lewicki et al. 1993). In the former situation, the parties see their goals as incompatible, while in the latter they consider themselves to have compatible goals.

For example, developing country officials often view negotiations with multinational corporations as win–lose competitions. In negotiating investment contracts, they often consider profits earned by the investor as automatic losses to the host country. As a result, they may focus their efforts in the negotiation fixedly on limiting investor profit in contrast to discovering how to maximize benefits from the project for both the investor and the country. It is interesting to note that those same officials might approach negotiations in their home villages with members of their ethnic group or clans on a win–win basis.

The survey conducted by the author found wide differences among the cultures represented in the survey on this question. Whereas 100 percent of the Japanese viewed business negotiation as a win–win process, only 36.8 percent of the Spanish were so inclined. The Chinese and Indians, the other two Asian cultures represented in the survey, also claimed that negotiation was for them win–win, and the French, alone among Europeans, took a similarly pronounced position on the question. Table 2 summarizes the results of all groups surveyed with respect to this attitude toward negotiation.

Personal Style: Informal or Formal?

Personal style concerns the way a negotiator talks to others, uses titles, dresses, speaks, and interacts with other persons. Culture strongly influences the personal style of negotiators. It has been observed, for example, that Germans have a more formal style than Americans (Hall and Hall 1990, p. 48). A negotiator with a formal style insists on addressing counterparts by their titles, avoids personal anecdotes, and refrains from questions touching on the private or family life of members of the other negotiating team. An informal-style negotiator tries to start the discussion on a first-name basis, quickly seeks to develop a personal, friendly relationship with the other team, and may take off his jacket and roll up his sleeves when deal making begins in earnest. Each culture has its own formalities, which have special meaning within that culture. They are another means of communication among the persons sharing that culture, another form of adhesive that binds them together as a community. Negotiators in foreign cultures must respect appropriate formalities. As a general rule, it is always safer to adopt a formal posture and move to an informal stance, if the situation warrants it, than to assume an informal style too quickly.

On the other hand, an encounter between negotiators having different personal styles can sometimes lead to conflict that impedes a negotiation. For an American or an Australian, calling someone by his or her first name is an act of friendship and therefore a good thing. For a Japanese or an Egyptian, the use of the first name at a first meeting is an act of disrespect and therefore a bad thing.

Except for the Nigerians, a majority of the respondents within each of the 12 groups surveyed claimed to have an informal negotiating style; however, the strength of this view varied considerably. While nearly 83 percent of the Americans considered themselves to have an informal negotiating style, only 54 percent of the Chinese, 52 percent of the Spanish, and 58 percent of the Mexicans were similarly inclined. Among the four European national cultures surveyed, the French were the strongest in claiming an informal style. Although both the Germans and Japanese have a reputation for formality, only slightly more than one-quarter of the respondents in these two groups believed they had a formal negotiating style. Differences in cultures with respect to the meaning of the terms *formal* and *informal* may have influenced this result. The survey's findings on this negotiating trait are summarized in Table 3.

Communication: Direct or Indirect?

Methods of communication vary among cultures. Some place emphasis on direct and simple methods of communication; others rely heavily on indirect and complex

TABLE 2 Negotiating Attitude: Win–Win or Win–Lose?

Win–Win:	Jpn.	Chi.	Arg.	Fr.	Ind.	USA	UK	Mex.	Ger.	Nig.	Braz.	Sp.
Percentage:	100	81.8	80.8	80	77.8	70.7	58.8	50	54.5	46.7	44.4	36.8

TABLE 3 Personal Style: Formal or Informal?

Formal:	Nig.	Spn.	Chi.	Mex.	UK	Arg.	Ger.	Jpn.	Ind.	Braz.	Fr.	USA
Percentage:	53	47.4	45.5	41.7	35.3	34.6	27.3	27.3	22.2	22.2	20	17.1

methods. It has been observed, for example, that whereas Germans and Americans are direct, the French and the Japanese are indirect (Hall and Hall 1990, p. 102). Persons with an indirect style of communication often make assumptions about the level of knowledge possessed by their counterparts and to a significant extent communicate with oblique references, circumlocutions, vague allusions, figurative forms of speech, facial expressions, gestures, and other kinds of body language. In a culture that values directness such as the American or the Israeli, one can expect to receive a clear and definite response to proposals and questions. In cultures that rely on indirect communication, such as the Japanese, reaction to proposals may be gained by interpreting seemingly indefinite comments, gestures, and other signs.

The confrontation of these styles of communication in the same negotiation can lead to friction. For example, the indirect ways Japanese negotiators express disapproval have often led foreign business executives to believe that their proposals were still under consideration when they had in fact been rejected by the Japanese side. In the Camp David negotiations, the Israeli preference for direct forms of communication and the Egyptian tendency to favor indirect forms sometimes exacerbated relations between the two sides. The Egyptians interpreted Israeli directness as aggressiveness and, therefore, an insult. The Israelis viewed Egyptian indirectness with impatience and suspected them of insincerity, of not saying what they meant.

In the survey, respondents in all cultural groups by a high margin claimed to have a direct form of communication. Here too the organizational culture of the participants and their international experience may have strongly influenced their responses to the questionnaire. It is worth noting, however, that the two cultural groups with the largest percentage of persons claiming an indirect style were the Japanese and the French. Table 4 summarizes the results on this issue.

Sensitivity to Time: High or Low?

Discussions of national negotiating styles invariably treat a particular culture's attitudes toward time. So it is said that Germans are always punctual, Latins are habitually late, Japanese negotiate slowly, and Americans are quick to make a deal. Commentators sometimes claim that some cultures "value" time more than others, but this may not be an accurate characterization of the situ-

ation. Rather they may value differently the amount of time devoted to and measured against the goal pursued. For Americans, the deal is a signed contract and "time is money," so they want to make a deal quickly. Americans therefore try to reduce formalities to a minimum and get down to business quickly. Japanese and other Asians, whose goal is to create a relationship rather than simply sign a contract, will need to invest time in the negotiating process so that the parties can get to know one another well and determine whether they wish to embark on a long-term relationship. They may view aggressive attempts to shorten the negotiating time with suspicion as efforts to hide something.

As a general rule, Asians tend to devote more time and attention to the prenegotiation phase of deal making than do Americans. Whereas American executives and lawyers generally want to "dispense with the preliminaries" and "to get down to cases," most Asians view prenegotiation as an essential foundation to any business relationship; consequently, they recognize the need to conduct prenegotiation with care before actually making a decision to undertake substantive negotiations of a deal. One of the consequences of this difference in approach is that Americans sometimes assume that discussions with Asian counterparts have passed from prenegotiation to a subsequent stage when in fact they have not because the Asians have not yet decided to undertake substantive negotiations. This type of misunderstanding can lead to suspicions of bad faith, resulting ultimately in total failure of the talks. Negotiators need to be sure that they and their counterparts are always in the same phase of the deal-making process. One way of making sure is by using written agendas, memoranda, and letters of intent to mark the various phases.

The survey did not reveal significant divergences with respect to time. A majority of the respondents from all cultural groups surveyed claimed to have a high sensitivity to time; however, the strength of the minority view on this question varied considerably among the groups. The Indians, French, and Germans included a substantial percentage of respondents asserting a low sensitivity to time. Table 5 summarizes the results.

These survey results on this question could have been affected by the organizational cultures of the respondents, as well as by variations in the way that respondents interpreted the term *time sensitivity*. Cultural discussions about time in negotiations often refer to two elements: promptness is meeting deadlines and the amount of time

TABLE 4 Communication: Direct or Indirect?

Indirect:	Jpn.	Fr.	Chi.	UK	Braz.	Ind.	Ger.	USA	Arg.	Spn.	Mex.	Nig.
Percentage:	27.3	20	18.2	11.8	11.1	11.1	9.1	4.9	3.8	0	0	0

TABLE 5 Sensitivity to Time: High or Low?

Low:	Ind.	Fr.	Ger.	Mex.	Spn.	Arg.	US	Jpn.	Chi.	Nig.	UK	Braz.
Percentage:	44.4	40	36.4	33.3	21.1	15.4	14.6	9.1	9.1	6.7	5.9	0

devoted to a negotiation. Thus Germans, it has been observed, are highly time sensitive with regard to promptness but less so with respect to their willingness to devote large amounts of time to a negotiation (Hall and Hall 1990, p. 37). Thus they are punctual (high time sensitivity) but slow to negotiate and make decisions (low time sensitivity).

Emotionalism: High or Low?

Accounts of negotiating behavior in other cultures almost always point to a particular group's tendency or lack thereof to act emotionally. According to the stereotype, Latin Americans show their emotions at the negotiating table, while Japanese and many other Asians hide their feelings. Obviously, individual personality plays a role here. There are passive Latins and hotheaded Japanese. Nonetheless, various cultures have different rules as to the appropriateness and form of displaying emotions, and these rules are brought to the negotiating table as well.

In the survey conducted by the author, Latin Americans and the Spanish were the cultural groups that ranked themselves highest with respect to emotionalism in a clearly statistically significant fashion. Among Europeans, the Germans and English ranked as least emotional, while among Asians the Japanese held that position, but to a lesser degree than the two European groups. Table 6 summarizes the results with regard to emotionalism.

Form of Agreement: General or Specific?

Cultural factors also influence the form of the written agreement that parties try to make. Generally, Americans prefer very detailed contracts that attempt to anticipate all possible circumstances and eventualities, no matter how unlikely. Why? Because the "deal" is the contract itself, and one must refer to the contract to handle new situations that may arise in the future. Other cultures, such as the Chinese, prefer a contract in the form of general principles rather than detailed rules. Why? Because it is claimed that the essence of the deal is the relationship between the parties. If unexpected circumstances arise, the parties should look to their relationship, not the contract, to solve the problem. So in some cases, a

Chinese may interpret the American drive to stipulate all contingencies as evidence of lack of confidence in the stability of the underlying relationship.

Some practitioners argue that differences over the form of an agreement are caused more by unequal bargaining power than by culture. In a situation of unequal bargaining power, the stronger party usually seeks a detailed agreement to "lock up the deal" in all its possible dimensions, while the weaker party prefers a general agreement to give it room to "wiggle out" of adverse circumstances that are bound to occur. So a Chinese commune as the weaker party in a negotiation with a multinational corporation will seek a general agreement as a way of protecting itself against an uncertain future. According to this view, it is context, not culture, that determines this negotiating trait.

The survey showed that a majority of respondents in each cultural group preferred specific agreements over general agreements. This result may be attributed in part to the relatively large number of lawyers among the respondents, as well as to the fact that multinational corporate practice favors specific agreements and many of the respondents, regardless of nationality, had experience with such firms. The survey responses on this point may have been a case where professional or organizational culture dominated over national cultural traits. On the other hand, the degree of intensity of responses on the question varied considerably among cultural groups. While only 11 percent of the British favored general agreements, 45.5 percent of the Japanese and of the Germans claimed to do so. Table 7 sets out the survey results with respect to agreement form.

Building an Agreement: Bottom Up or Top Down?

Related to the form of the agreement is the question of whether negotiating a business deal is an inductive or a deductive process. Does it start from agreement on general principles and proceed to specific items, or does it begin with agreement on specifics, such as price, delivery date, and product quality, the sum total of which becomes the contract? Different cultures tend to emphasize one approach over the other.

TABLE 6 Emotionalism: High or Low?

Low:	Ger.	UK	Jpn.	Ind.	Fr.	Nig.	USA	Chi.	Spn.	Mex.	Arg.	Braz.
Percentage:	63.6	52.9	45.5	44.4	40	40	36.6	27.3	21.1	16.7	15.4	11.1

TABLE 7   Agreement Form: General or Specific?

General:	Jpn.	Ger.	Ind.	Fr.	Chi.	Arg.	Braz.	USA	Nig.	Mex.	Spn	UK
Percentage:	45.5	45.4	44.4	30	27.3	26.9	22.2	22	20	16.7	15.8	11.8

Some observers believe that the French prefer to begin with agreement on general principles, while Americans tend to seek agreement first on specifics. For Americans, negotiating a deal is basically making a series of compromises and trade-offs on a long list of particulars. For the French, the essence is to agree on basic principles that will guide and indeed determine the negotiation process afterward. The agreed-upon general principles become the framework, the skeleton, upon which the contract is built.

A further difference in negotiating style is seen in the dichotomy between "the building-down approach" and the "building-up approach." In the building-down approach, the negotiator begins by presenting the maximum deal if the other side accepts all the stated conditions. In the building-up approach, one side begins by proposing a minimum deal that can be broadened and increased as the other party accepts additional conditions. According to many observers, Americans tend to favor the building-down approach, while the Japanese tend to prefer the building-up style of negotiating a contract.

The survey did not reveal significant cultural trends on this issue among Americans, Germans, and Nigerians, since the respondents from these three groups were relatively evenly divided on the question. On the other hand, the French, Argentineans, and Indians tended to view deal making as a top-down (deductive) process, while Japanese, Mexicans, and Brazilians tended to see it as a bottom-up (inductive) process. Table 8 summarizes the results on the question.

Team Organization: One Leader or Group Consensus?

In any international business negotiation, it is important to know how the other side is organized, who has the authority to make commitments, and how decisions are made. Culture is one important factor that affects how executives and lawyers organize themselves to negotiate a deal. Some cultures emphasize the individual while others stress the group. These values may influence the organization of each side to a negotiation. One extreme is the negotiating team with a supreme leader who has complete authority to decide all matters. Many American teams tend to follow this approach, which has been labeled the "John Wayne style of negotiations" (Graham and Herberger 1983, p. 160). Other cultures, notably the Japanese, stress team negotiation and consensus decision making. When you negotiate with such a team, it may not be apparent who is the leader and who has authority to commit the side. In the first type, the negotiating team is usually small; in the second it is often large. For example, in negotiations in China on a major deal, it would not be uncommon for the Americans to arrive at the table with 3 persons and for the Chinese to show up with 10. Similarly, the one-leader team is usually prepared to make commitments and decisions more quickly than a negotiating team organized on the basis of consensus. As a result, the consensus type of organization usually takes more time to negotiate a deal.

The survey on negotiating styles revealed differences in preference among respondents, depending on culture. The group with the strongest preference for a consensus organization were the French. French individualism has been noted in many studies (Hall and Hall 1990), and perhaps a consensus arrangement in French eyes is the best way to protect that individualism. Despite the Japanese reputation for consensus arrangements, only 45 percent of the Japanese respondents claimed to prefer a negotiating team based on consensus. The Brazilians, the Chinese, and Mexicans, to a far greater degree than any other groups, preferred one-person leadership, a reflection perhaps of the political traditions in those countries. The results of the survey on this point are summarized in Table 9.

Risk Taking: High or Low?

Research supports the conclusion that certain cultures are more risk averse than others (Hofstede 1980). In deal making, the culture of the negotiators can affect the willingness of one side to take "risks" in the negotiation—to divulge information, try new approaches, or tolerate uncertainties in a proposed course of action. A negotiator who senses that the other side is risk averse needs to focus efforts on proposing rules and mechanisms that will reduce the apparent risks in the deal for them.

TABLE 8   Building an Agreement: Bottom Up or Top Down?

Top down:	Ind.	Arg.	Fr.	UK	Chi.	Ger.	USA	Nig.	Spn.	Jpn.	Braz.	Mex.
Percentage:	66.7	61.5	60	58.8	54.5	54.5	53.7	53.3	52.6	36.4	33.3	33.3

TABLE 9

Team Organization: One Leader or Consensus?

One Leader:	Braz.	Chi.	Mex.	UK	USA	Spn.	Arg.	Ger.	Jpn.	Ind.	Nig.	Fr.
Percentage:	100	90.9	90.9	64.7	63.4	57.7	57.7	54.5	54.5	44.4	40	40

The Japanese, with their emphasis on requiring large amounts of information and their intricate group decision-making process, tend to be risk averse, a fact affirmed by the author's survey, which found Japanese respondents to be the most risk averse of all countries covered in the survey. Americans in the survey, by comparison, considered themselves to be risk takers, but an even higher percentage of French, British, and Indians claimed to be risk takers. Table 10 summarizes the survey results with respect to risk.

Coping with Culture

In view of the importance of cultural differences in international business negotiations, how should negotiators seek to cope with them? The following are a few simple rules.

Rule 1: Learn the Other Side's Culture

In any international business dealing, it is important for a negotiator to learn something about the other side's culture. The degree to which such learning takes place depends on a number of factors, including the nature and importance of the transaction, the experience of the negotiators, the time available for learning, and the similarities or lack thereof between the cultures represented in the negotiation. For example, the negotiation of a simple, one-time export sale may demand less cultural knowledge than the negotiation of a long-term strategic alliance, which may require the parties to audit each other's culture as well as their financial assets.

Ideally, learning another's culture can require several years of study, mastery of a foreign language, and prolonged residence in the country of that culture. An American faced with the task of negotiating a strategic alliance with a Thai company in Bangkok in two weeks' time cannot, of course, master Thai culture that fast. At best, he or she can learn enough to cope with some of the principal effects that Thai culture may have on making the deal. Important sources of information on Thai cul-

ture would include histories of the country, consultation with persons having business experience in the country, local lawyers and consultants, anthropological and ethnographic studies, reports on the current political situation, and accounts, if any, on negotiating with the Thais. As Weiss quite correctly points out, the degree of a negotiator's cultural knowledge will influence strategies and tactics during the negotiation (Weiss 1994, p. 53). For example, a person with strong familiarity with the counterpart's language and culture may use the negotiation style and approach of his counterpart's culture, while a person with less familiarity may choose, as a strategy, to employ an agent or mediator from that culture to assist in the negotiations.

As international business transactions increasingly take the form of long-term relationships—what Gomes-Casseres (1996) has termed the "alliance revolution"—it is equally important to recognize that cultural learning continues long after the contract is signed. In effect, the dynamics of such long-term relationships between the parties are very much a continuing negotiation as the alliance partners shape the rules and practices of their business relationship.

Rule 2: Don't Stereotype

If rule one in international negotiation is "know the other side's culture," rule two is "avoid overreliance on that knowledge." As the survey indicates, not all Japanese evade giving a direct negative answer. Not all Germans will tell a counterpart specifically what they think of a proposal. In short, the negotiator who enters a foreign culture should be careful not to allow cultural stereotypes to determine his or her relations with local businesspersons. Foreign business executives and lawyers will be offended if they feel their counterparts are not treating them as individuals, but rather as cultural robots. In addition to giving offense, cultural stereotypes can be misleading. Many times the other side simply does not run true to the negotiating form suggested by books, articles, and consultants. The reason, of course, is that

TABLE 10   Risk Taking: High or Low?

Low:	Fr.	Ind.	UK	Chi.	USA	Nig.	Arg.	Ger.	Braz.	Mex.	Spn.	Jpn.
Percentage:	90	88.9	88.2	81.8	78	73.3	73.1	72	55.6	50	47.4	18.2

other forces besides culture may influence a person's negotiating behavior. Specifically, these forces may include the negotiator's personality, the organization he or she represents, and the context of the particular negotiation in question.

Rule 3: Find Ways to Bridge the Culture Gap

Generally, executives and lawyers who confront a culture different from their own in a negotiation tend to view it in one of three ways: as an obstacle, a weapon, or a fortress (Salacuse 1993). At the operational level, cultural differences are hardly ever seen as positive.

The conventional view among most American executives is that cultural differences are an obstacle to agreement and effective joint action. They therefore search for ways to overcome the obstacle. But a different culture in a business setting can become more than an obstacle; it can be seen as a weapon, particularly when a dominant party tries to impose its culture on the other side. For example, American lawyers' insistence on structuring a transaction "the way we do it in the United States" may be considered by their foreign counterparts as the use of American culture as a weapon.

Faced with a culture that it perceives as a weapon, a party to a business deal may become defensive and try to use its own culture as a fortress to protect itself from what it perceives as a cultural onslaught. The Japanese have often adopted this approach when confronted with American demands to open their markets. France's drive to limit the use of English in advertising is a defensive response to what it considered to be the weapon of "Anglo-Saxon" culture.

It may be helpful to try to think of cultural differences in yet another way. Differences in cultures tend to isolate individuals and groups from each other. In short, cultural differences create a gap between persons and organizations. Often the action that people take when confronted with cultural differences serves only to widen the gap—as, for example, when one side denigrates the other side's cultural practices.

Remembering the words of the English poet Philip Larkin, "Always it is by bridges that we live," effective international business negotiators should seek to find ways to bridge the gap caused by cultural difference. One way to build that bridge is by using culture itself. If culture is indeed the glue that binds together a particular group of people, the creative use of culture between persons of different cultures is often a way to link those on opposite sides of the culture gap. Basically, there are four types of cultural bridge building that one may consider when confronted with a culture gap in a negotiation:

1. *Bridge the gap using the other side's culture:* One technique for bridging the gap is for a negotiator or manager to try to assume some or all of the cultural values and characteristics of the foreign persons with whom he or she is dealing. In international business, negotiators often try to use or identify with the other side's culture in order to build a relationship. For example, when President Sadat of Egypt negotiated with Sudanese officials, he always made a point of telling them that his mother had been born in the Sudan. He was thus using a common cultural thread to build a relationship with his counterparts. In effect, he was saying, "Like you, I am Sudanese, so we have common cultural ties. I understand you and I value your culture. Therefore you can trust me." Similarly, an African American managing a joint venture in Nigeria stressed his African heritage to build relationships with Nigerian counterparts. And an Italian American negotiating a sales contract in Rome emphasized his Italian background as a way of bridging the cultural gap that he perceived.

2. *Bridge the gap using your own culture:* A second general approach to bridging the culture gap is to persuade or induce the other side to adopt elements of your culture. To implement this approach successfully requires time and education. For example, in order to give a common culture to a joint venture, an American partner incurred significant cost by sending executives of its foreign partner to schools and executive training programs in the United States and then assigning them for short periods to the U.S. partner's own operations.

3. *Bridge with some combination of both cultures:* A third approach to dealing with the culture gap is to build a bridge using elements from cultures of both sides. In effect, cultural bridging takes place on both sides of the gap and, with luck, results in the construction of a solid integrated structure. The challenge in this approach is to identify the most important elements of each culture and to find ways of blending them into a consistent, harmonious whole that will allow business to be done effectively. Sometimes a third person in the form of mediator or consultant can help in the process.

4. *Bridge with a third culture:* A final method of dealing with the culture gap is to build a bridge by relying on a third culture that belongs to neither of the parties. Thus, for example, in a difficult negotiation between an American executive and a Chinese manager, both discovered that they had a great appreciation of French culture since they had both studied in France in their youth. They began to converse in French, and

their common love of France enabled them to build a strong personal relationship. They used a third culture to bridge the cultural gap between China and America. Similarly, negotiators from two different national cultures may use elements of their common professional cultures, as lawyers or as engineers, to bridge the gap between them.

Conclusion

Cultural bridging, like bridge construction, requires the cooperation of the parties at both ends of the divide. No negotiator will permit a bridge to be built if he or she feels threatened or sees the bridge as a long-term danger to security. Consequently, negotiators who want to build a bridge across the cultural divide to their counterpart must be concerned to strengthen the other side's sense of security, not weaken it as happens all too often in international business relationships.

References

Binnendijk, H. (ed.). (1987). *National Negotiating Styles*. Washington, DC: U.S. Department of State.

Bohannan, P. (1995). *How Culture Works*. New York: Free Press.

Campbell, N. C. G., et al. (1998). "Marketing Negotiations in France, Germany, the United Kingdom, and the United States," *Journal of Marketing* 52, pp. 49–62.

Faure, G. O., and G. Sjostedt. (1993). "Culture and Negotiation: An Introduction," in G.O. Faure and J. Z. Rubin (eds.), *Culture and Negotiation*. Newbury Park, CA: Sage Publications.

Fisher, G. (1980). *International Negotiation: A Cross-Cultural Perspective*. Yarmouth, ME: Intercultural Press.

Gomes-Casseres, B. (1996). *The Alliance Revolution*. Cambridge, MA: Harvard University Press.

Graham, J. L., et al. (1988). "Buyer–Seller Negotiations around the Pacific Rim: Differences in Fundamental Exchange Processes," *Journal of Consumer Research* 15, pp. 48–54.

Graham J. L., and R. A. Herberger. (1983). "Negotiators Abroad—Don't Shoot from the Hip: Cross-Cultural Busi-

ness Negotiations," *Harvard Business Review* 61, pp. 160–83.

Hall, E. T. (1959). *The Silent Language*. New York: Doubleday.

Hall, E. T., and M. Reed Hall. (1990). *Understanding Cultural Differences*. Yarmouth, ME: Intercultural Press.

Hampden-Turner, C., and A. Trompenaars. (1993). *The Seven Cultures of Capitalism*. New York: Doubleday.

Hoebel, E. A. (1972). *Anthropology: The Study of Man* (4th ed.) New York: McGraw-Hill.

Hofstede, G. (1980). *Culture's Consequences: International Differences in Work-Related Values*. Newbury Park, CA: Sage Publications.

Hoppman, T. (1995). "Two Paradigms of Negotiation: Bargaining and Problem Solving," *Annals, AAPSS* 542, pp. 24–47.

Hughes, P., and B. Sheehan. (1993). "Business Cultures: The Transfer of Managerial Policies and Practices from One Culture to Another," *Business and the Contemporary World* 5, pp. 153–70.

Lewicki, R., et al. (1993). *Negotiation—Readings, Exercises, and Cases*. Burr Ridge, IL: McGraw-Hill.

Lublin, J. S., and B. O'Brian. (1997). "Merged Firms Often Face Culture Clash," *The Wall Street Journal*, February 14, 1997, p. A9A.

Mahbubani, K. (1995). "The Pacific Way," *Foreign Affairs* 74, pp. 100–11.

Moran, R. T., and W. G. Stripp. (1991). *Successful International Business Negotiations*. Houston: Gulf Publishing Company.

Pye, L. (1982). *Chinese Negotiating Style*. Cambridge, MA: Oelgeschlager, Gunn and Hain.

Salacuse, J. W. (1991). *Making Global Deals—Negotiating in the International Market Place*. Boston: Houghton Mifflin.

Salacuse, J. W. (1993). "Implications for Practitioners," in G. O. Faure and J. Z. Rubin (eds.), *Culture and Negotiation*. Newbury Park, CA: Sage Publications.

Weiss, S. E. (1994). "Negotiating with Romans," (parts 1 and 2), *Sloan Management Review* 35, pp. 51, 85.

Zartman, I. W. (1993). "A Skeptic's View," in G. O. Faure and J. Z. Rubin (eds.), *Culture and Negotiation*. Newbury Park, CA: Sage Publications.

READING TWO

American Strengths and Weaknesses

Tommy T. B. Koh

American Strengths and Qualities

Two caveats are appropriate for any discussion of national negotiating styles. First, there may not necessarily be a definable negotiating style for each country or people. Good and effective negotiators, irrespective of their national or cultural background, have certain common skills. Second, although it is probably possible to say impressionistically that the American people possess certain character and personality traits, there are many exceptions to the rule, and a person's negotiating style is inevitably affected by his character, temperament, and attitude toward people.

American negotiators have many strengths and qualities. If distance makes the heart grow fonder, my perception of Americans may be unrealistically favorable and idealized, since Singapore is located 12,000 miles away from the United States.

First, U.S. negotiators are usually well prepared. They arrive at negotiations with their homework completed, and they are armed with facts, figures, maps, and charts. They usually know what their national interests are and what their negotiating objectives are. This is not always the case among Third World negotiators.

Second, American negotiators tend to speak clearly and plainly. As someone who was educated in the Anglo-Saxon legal tradition, I regard this as a virtue, not a liability. However, the American preference for plain speaking can sometimes cause unintended offense to other negotiators whose national culture prefers indirectness, subtlety, and avoidance of confrontation. There are, of course, exceptions to this rule.

Third, U.S. negotiators tend to be more pragmatic than doctrinaire. They focus on advancing their country's interests rather than principles that they cherish. The Reagan administration, however, was a clear exception to this rule, and at the Third U.N. Conference on the Law of the Sea decided, for rational and arguable reasons, that principles were more important than interests.

Fourth, American negotiators generally do not regard negotiations as a zero-sum game. A good U.S. negotiator is even prepared to put himself in the place of his negotiating adversary. A good U.S. negotiator is prepared to admit that his adversary, like himself, has certain irreducible, minimum national interests. A good U.S. negotiator is prepared to engage in a process of give and take, and he believes that the successful outcome of a negotiation is not one in which he wins everything and his adversary loses everything, but rather one in which there is a mutuality of benefits and losses, in which each side has a stake in honoring and maintaining the agreement.

Fifth, a U.S. negotiator's opening position is never his final position. He expects his opponent to make a counterproposal or a counteroffer. He is anxious to reach an agreement and will, therefore, make concessions to his opponent, expecting—not unreasonably—that his adversary will behave in like manner. Americans are sometimes completely exasperated at international forums when their adversaries do not behave as they do.

Sixth, the American people are very candid and straightforward, and this is reflected in their negotiating style. Americans are not usually perceived as cunning or devious. In only one incident have I found American negotiators to be devious, and that was shocking. This incident occurred in July 1981 when the United Nations sponsored an international conference on Cambodia. The conference was initiated by the ASEAN (Association of Southeast Asian Nations) countries, which proposed a framework for the resolution of the Cambodian situation. All Cambodian factions were invited to participate in the conference, including, of course, the Khmer Rouge. Vietnam was invited, but boycotted the meeting. At the conference General Alexander Haig, then U.S. Secretary of State, staged a dramatic walkout, accompanied by the entire U.S. delegation, when the Khmer Rouge leader approached the rostrum to speak. The picture of this walkout appeared on the front page of *The New York Times*.

On a subsequent day, the ASEAN countries and the People's Republic of China (PRC) were locked in a ferocious confrontation over the future role of the Khmer Rouge in any postsettlement Cambodia. The ASEAN countries argued that in light of the massacres and atrocities that the Khmer Rouge had committed, it would

Source: Reprinted from *International Negotiation* 1 (1996), pp. 313–17. Used with permission

be morally and legally impermissible to allow them to return to power. We demanded a public election to be organized and supervised by the United Nations. To ensure free elections, we insisted that all armed elements be disarmed or sequestered in camp. The Chinese fought against all these points. The negotiating group was composed of 25 delegations, but the dynamics of the discussions revolved around the PRC, the ASEAN countries, and Pakistan as a middleman. Pakistan, however, was not an honest broker and basically submitted a series of amendments to dilute the ASEAN position. I assumed that Pakistan, because of its proximity to the PRC, was "fronting" for the Chinese, and was shocked to learn later that they were actually fronting for the Americans. Although the American delegation had publicly walked out of the negotiations, they were privately supporting China for geostrategic reasons. This is the only example of devious behavior by American negotiators of which I am aware, but I will remember it.

Weaknesses and Idiosyncrasies

One problem in negotiating with Americans is that American delegations usually suffer from serious interagency rivalries. During the U.N. Law of the Sea Conference the American delegation met every morning, and sometimes their internal meetings lasted longer than the other meetings in the conference.

A second problem in negotiating with the United States is the separation of power between the administration and the Congress. One has to be very careful if one is negotiating an agreement that is subject to ratification by the U.S. Senate. It is important to always keep in touch with U.S. senators as the negotiating process continues in order to obtain their independent inputs, be aware of their sensitivities, and recognize vested domestic interests and blocking constituencies.

A third special characteristic is the influence of the U.S. private sector and private interest groups on negotiations. During the Law of the Sea Conference I made it a point to meet not only with the official U.S. delegation and members of the Congress, but also to meet with representatives from the seabed mining industry, the petroleum industry, the fishing industry, the marine scientific community, the environmental lobby, and individuals who have an affection for marine mammals. The reality of political life in America is that even one of these many lobbies can block ratification of a treaty. Foreign negotiators must understand the domestic political process in the United States and must, in some way, interfere in American internal affairs to ensure the success of their mission.

A fourth problem—the role of U.S. media—is a problem more for U.S. negotiators than for their counterparts. This is a problem because somehow the good nature of Americans and their propensity to candor makes it very difficult even for negotiators to keep confidences. And in the midst of a sensitive negotiation it is sometimes very counterproductive for the media to report on issues that are under negotiation. In a speech to the House Foreign Affairs Committee, Secretary of State George Shultz recounted with great frustration an occasion when the United State and U.S.S.R. were engaged in bilateral negotiations. The negotiation had reached a critical point, and he had that day drafted a cable giving his final instructions. He said he found to his horror at breakfast the next morning that *The New York Times* had reported the content of his cable. Members of the U.S. media should be asked whether they should exercise more discretion and self-restraint. Do they not feel an allegiance as American citizens to the advancement and protection of American national interests? Should not the right of the public to know and the freedom of the press sometimes be modulated by competing and larger interests? The extent to which the United States exposes its flank makes it easier for others to win at the negotiating table.

A fifth weakness is impatience. Americans suffer from an "instant-coffee complex." They do not have time, as Europeans and Asians do, to buy coffee beans, grind them every day, brew the coffee, enjoy the aroma, and savor every sip. Americans are always in a rush and are extremely frustrated when there is a lack of progress. Americans are result-oriented. Jeane Kirkpatrick had a shock several years ago when she visited the ASEAN capitals and met the foreign ministers of the six ASEAN countries. To each she asked, "Do you think there are prospects for settling the Cambodian conflict?" All six ASEAN foreign ministers said yes. She said, "Do you think it will be soon?" They all said, "Oh yes, very soon." She said, "Well, how soon?" They said, "Oh, about five years' time." She was shocked because to an American five years' time is certainly not soon.

A sixth weakness is cultural insensitivity. Everyone is guilty of this, not only Americans. Everyone assumes that others have similar cultures, customs, and manners. Singaporeans are "the barbarians of Southeast Asia." We are "the least sensitive and least subtle people in the region." But if one is a professional negotiator, then part of the preparation for an effective negotiation is to learn enough about the culture of one's adversary to at least avoid simple errors of behavior, attribution, and body language.

Finally, it is surprising that in many recent multilateral forums the United States has been represented by amateur rather than professional negotiators. Given that the United States is so rich in human resources and has a foreign service studded by superstars, it is amazing how inadequately the United States is represented at important international negotiations.

Conclusion

In conclusion, a good negotiator, whether an Indian, an American, a Canadian, English, Ghanian, or whoever, is a person with certain definable skills, aptitudes, and temperaments. His character and personality have an impact on his effectiveness. Some American negotiators put people off; others readily win people's confidence. In choosing a negotiator, select someone who does not bristle like a porcupine but who can win the trust and confidence of his negotiating partners. What are these qualities that attract people's confidence and trust? These are moral qualities, qualities of leadership. If a negotiator is a leader, a person who acquires a reputation for competence, reliability, and trustworthiness, then others will trust him with leadership roles. The word *charisma* is not useful because it does not accurately portray the quality that bestows leadership on certain negotiators and not others. Henry Kissinger is not charismatic; he is dominating and impassive and has an exceptional intellect and a monotonous voice. In 1976, when the Law of Sea Conference was deadlocked between industrialized and developing countries, Kissinger, who was then secretary of state and had no background in the law of the sea and knew nothing about seabed mining, spent one morning in New York meeting with the U.S. delegation. In the afternoon he met with other leaders of the Group of 77, and by the end of the day presented an innovative scheme for reconciling the competing ambitions and claims of the different countries.

There probably is an American negotiating style, and this partakes of the qualities, attitudes, customs, conventions, and reflexes that have come down through U.S. history, culture, and political institutions. On the whole, American negotiators have very positive qualities, being well prepared, reasonable, competent, and honorable. Even more than this, some, like Elliott Richardson, will take it upon themselves to be an honest broker and help to settle a conflict between two other groups in which they are a totally disinterested party. This graciousness and willingness to help are positive attributes as well.

Creating Productive Interpersonal Relationships

LEARNING OBJECTIVES

After completing this chapter, you should be able to:

 Appreciate *the importance of good interpersonal relations at work.*

 Understand *the importance of emotional intelligence.*

 Appreciate *the impact of personality differences on relationships.*

 Assess *interaction climates.*

 Recognize *differences in self-disclosure.*

 Deal *effectively with male/female differences in work behaviors.*

Understand *the importance of ethics in interpersonal relations.*

Get along better *with people with different interpersonal styles.*

Charm Schools for Managers: Improving Interpersonal Skills

On the grounds of Arthur Andersen & Co.'s headquarters outside Chicago, a senior executive jumps off a flagpole and onto a trapeze. Colleagues pass a bucket of water between two nearby trees. Others try to scale a wall. This is no company circus; the antics are part of a program at the accounting firm to teach employees interpersonal skills. Jumping from the pole teaches confidence; passing the bucket and scaling the wall teach teamwork. The firm also trains its employees in skills such as running meetings and listening to others.

Arthur Andersen is one of the many companies placing a new emphasis on "people skills" for managers and executives. In the past, even ornery managers could succeed just by knowing the business. But increasingly, managers with "people conflicts" are being sent to school to learn how to relate better to others. "Pure technical knowledge is only going to get you to a point," said Lawrence A. Weinbach, Arthur Andersen's chief executive (now CEO of Unisys). "Beyond that, interpersonal skills become critical."

The Center for Creative Leadership in Greensboro, North Carolina, estimates that half of all managers have some type of difficulty with people. But discovering such a weakness in a so-called charm school can be humbling. The training doesn't always work, of course. Randall P. White, director of the Center for Creative Leadership's Executive Development Program, estimates that although 10 to 15 percent of the participants in his program are highly receptive and change dramatically, an equal amount are hopeless. Some sit in the back of the room and tell counselors they were "forced" to attend and have no problems. When confronted with poor reviews, one manager claimed he was a good manager but all his workers were stupid.

When Richard S. Herlich was promoted to director of marketing for an American Cyanamid Co. division, he saw himself as an enlightened manager. He delegated responsibility, encouraging subordinates to set their own deadlines. "I thought that I had the perfect style," he says. But then he attended the Center's weeklong Leadership Development Program. In surveys that his peers, subordinates, and superiors answered before the course, he found that he was too trusting, aloof, and a poor communicator. The diagnosis was confirmed in role playing games by feedback from the other participants. "I was devastated," Herlich says.

When he went back to work, he held a meeting to discuss his problem with his 15 subordinates, who said his aloofness was intimidating. So he became more involved in their work and learned to set deadlines; projects that had taken six to seven months were done in three.

Bethlehem Steel Corp. plant manager Robert Siddall had just the opposite problem. An aggressive and sometimes abrasive leader, he got into damaging clashes with the labor union head, and many of his 170 workers came to view him as dictatorial. "I'm very strong technically," he says, but "I really didn't fit in well on an interactive basis." Instructors taught Siddall to act like a "coach" and to try to listen to and respect other points of view.

He says he gets along with the union leader now. His performance ratings have improved, and his workers now refer to the "old Bob" and the "new Bob." "If I start screaming and yelling, they say, 'old Bob, old Bob,' " he says. "We have a lot more fun together." He also believes he's back on track for a promotion.

In the new information era, interpersonal communication is a valuable business tool. Understanding different mindsets, technical backgrounds, and cultural perspectives is more crucial than ever for managers today and in the future. To deal effectively with diversity, managers have to be flexible in how they relate to people from different cultures and backgrounds. No one's personal set of behavioral rules will prevail intact in organizations designed to incorporate diversity and still provide a common integrating culture that promotes the organization's goals.

To make organizations with diverse work forces viable and to be effective leaders, managers need to learn a new respect for differences. As Arthur Andersen's chief executive said in the opening vignette, pure technical knowledge will only get you so far; beyond that, interpersonal skills become critical. According to R. Roosevelt Thomas, Jr., executive director of the American Institute for Managing Diversity at Atlanta's Morehouse College, "This is no longer simply a question of common decency. It is a question of business survival."[1]

And how well are American managers equipped to deal with diverse work forces? Probably not nearly as well as required. Consequently, many managers are being sent to "charm schools" like those described in the opening vignette. This chapter discusses concepts and skills necessary for successfully managing interpersonal relations with different types of people in organizations.

🌐 What Influences Interpersonal Relations?

A recent Gallup survey of executives investigated the biggest challenges management will face by the year 2000. The foremost finding was the importance they placed on interpersonal and communication skills.[2] Possessing interpersonal skills was noted more often than any other response by senior and middle-level executives as a sign that a recent hire had potential to develop into a senior-level executive. A corresponding finding of this and other studies is that, although interpersonal skills are determined to be essential for management development, they are named more often than any other management skill by recent hires as the attribute least emphasized in university and development programs.[3]

Most work either requires or encourages interaction among individuals. The more a job requires two people to work together, the more important becomes the nature of the relationship between them. "There are lots of brilliant people who can't relate with others," says Robert LoPresto, an executive recruiter. "We replace that kind of person every day."[4] Even where interaction is only peripheral to the task, relationships can still be a source of satisfaction or frustration and affect the total work effort in many ways. Good interpersonal relations support the work effort; bad ones inhibit it.[5] This can be especially true in international situations, as the World Watch box illustrates.

It can be very frustrating trying to figure out all the possible reasons people do or don't get along well together. You have already been introduced in previous chapters to some concepts that can help you understand what contributes to interpersonal differences in perception, motivation, and communication. This chapter focuses on emotional intelligence, personal, behavioral, and situational factors that can create difficulties in relationships. Strategies for effectively managing interpersonal relationships are also described.

EMOTIONAL INTELLIGENCE

Emotional intelligence (EQ) is very different from the common intelligence measure IQ. While IQ measures intellectual ability, EQ focuses on interpersonal and communication skills. Emotional competence includes a large number of attributes such as self-awareness, impulse control, persistence, confidence, self-motivation, empathy, social deftness, trustworthiness, adaptability, and the ability to work collaboratively.[6]

In today's business world, the importance of EQ is overriding sheer intellectual ability for many managers and high-level personnel. The more people with whom one must

WORLD WATCH

Rule Number 1: Don't Diss the Locals

When deciding whom to assign to an important foreign client, many companies select employees who are aces at technical matters or have an outstanding record in management. A recent study by Prudential Relocation Intercultural Services, a subsidiary of Prudential Insurance, discovered a number of horror stories about such selection criteria. One company sent an evangelical Christian to Saudi Arabia where he offended locals by setting up a Bible group and got booted out of the country. An American oil company transferred an executive to Peru where he told jokes deriding the natives' industriousness and excluded them from his parties. Indigenous employees complained to government officials who canceled the company's oil concession. American multinational companies admit that about 90 percent of their overseas placements are mistakes primarily due to their employees' failures to adjust properly to a new culture.

Prudential's survey of 72 personnel managers working at multinationals found that 35 percent agreed that the best trait for overseas success was cultural adaptability, which includes patience, flexibility, and tolerance for others' beliefs. Only 22 percent of the respondents listed technical or managerial skills.

Fortunately, there are a variety of training techniques available to prepare people better for intercultural work. They include (1) reading programs to expose people to the country's sociopolitical history, geography, economics, and cultural institutions; (2) cultural assimilators who expose trainees to specific incidents critical to successful interaction with a target culture; (3) language preparation; (4) sensitivity training to increase people's self-awareness; and (5) exposing trainees to minicultures within their own country during short field exercises.

Sources: "Rule Number 1: Don't Diss the Locals," *Business Week* (May 15, 1995), p. 8; and P. Christopher Earley, "Intercultural Training for Managers: A Comparison of Documentary and Interpersonal Methods," *Academy of Management Journal* 30 (August 1987), pp. 685–698.

interact, the more important interpersonal and communication skills become. Think of a manager who must lead a project team of diverse people. That manager may possess all the technical knowledge sufficient to complete tasks. However, it is of extreme importance for the team's success that the manager be able to lead, understand and "connect with people," and know how to conduct himself or herself in both positive and negative situations. A recent study of what characteristics corporations are seeking in MBA candidates completed by the U.S. Department of Labor revealed that the three most desirable traits are communication skills, interpersonal skills, and initiative.[7] All three of these traits are part of one's emotional intelligence.

Although it is important to understand what emotional intelligence is, it is more important to understand how one can continually improve one's interpersonal skills. As one ascends into higher management positions, the degree of interaction with other people increases. Additionally, the ability to lead and obtain a consensus increases dramatically. While technical skills and fundamental business skills are important and serve as a decision basis, one's ability to articulate ideas and build rapport and trust will be of increasing importance. A manager's success will largely be dependent upon his or her interpersonal skills, hence emotional intelligence. See the Technology Transformation box on the importance of interpersonal skills in a technology environment. To get an estimate of your own EQ, complete the "What's Your Emotional Intelligence at Work?" inventory in the Your Turn exercise.

Managers who are attuned to their own feelings and the feelings of others can use their understanding to enhance the performance of themselves and others in their organizations. The five basic components of emotional intelligence most important for managers are discussed below.[8] Review the following discussion of the five components of emotional intelligence, and think about what you might do to develop those areas where you scored low.

Success at High-Technology Jobs from Interpersonal Skills

Success at information technology (IT) jobs in the past depended upon one's pure technical skills (e.g., programming, network design, hardware). While these skills are continuing to increase in value, the success for IT personnel in the future will lie more in their interpersonal skills than pure technical abilities. A recent research study conducted by OfficeTeam (a staffing service company with 200 locations worldwide) found that the skills in demand for IT professionals are the "soft skills," or "people skills." These skills include listening, public speaking, persuasiveness, leadership, and positive interpersonal relationship skills, all aspects of emotional intelligence. While technical skills are still important, one's career success will depend more and more on these softer skills.

A challenge for IT firms today and into the future is recruiting. Traditionally, IT recruiting takes into account solely technical skills. Now, IT managers are adjusting their recruiting techniques to properly evaluate the softer skills. It is felt by many IT managers that the technical skills can be taught to someone who already possesses strong interpersonal skills. Teamwork will be a vital skill since, according to a study by RHI Consulting, roughly 60 percent of all IT projects will be team based. Therefore, one's people skills, or interpersonal skills, will dictate future success.

Sources: "The Challenges Facing Workers in the Future," *HR Focus* (August 1999), p. 6; and Howard Solomon, "Soft Skills Key to IT Success, Execs Say," *Computing Canada* (July 23, 1999), pp. 1–2.

Self-Awareness

This is the basis for all the other components of emotional intelligence. Self-awareness means being aware of what you are feeling, being conscious of the emotions within yourself. People who are in touch with their emotions are better able to guide their own lives. Managers need to be in touch with their emotions in order to interact effectively and appreciate emotions in others. Managers with high levels of self-awareness learn to trust their "gut feelings" and realize that these feelings can provide useful information about difficult decisions. Answers are not always clear about who is at fault when problems arise or when to let an employee go, reorganize a business, or revise job responsibilities. In these situations, managers have to rely on their own feelings and intuition.

Managing Emotions

The second key component of emotional intelligence is managing emotions. Operationally this means the manager is able to balance his or her own moods so that worry, anxiety, fear, or anger do not get in the way of what needs to be done. Managers who can manage their emotions perform better because they are able to think clearly. Managing emotions does not mean suppressing or denying them but understanding them and using that understanding to deal with situations productively.[10] Managers should first recognize a mood or feeling, think about what it means and how it affects them, and then choose how to act.

Motivating Oneself

This is the ability to be hopeful and optimistic despite obstacles, setbacks, or even outright failure. This ability is crucial for pursuing long-term goals in life or in business. A classic example of this occurred when the MetLife insurance company hired a special

Your Turn

What's Your Emotional Intelligence at Work?[9]

For each item below, rate how well you are able to display the ability described. Before responding, try to think of actual situations in which you have had the opportunity to use the ability.

	Very Low Ability		Moderate Ability		Very High Ability
1. Associate different internal physiological cues with different emotions.	1	2	3	4	5
2. Relax when under pressure in situations.	1	2	3	4	5
3. "Gear up" at will for a task.	1	2	3	4	5
4. Know the impact that your behavior has on others.	1	2	3	4	5
5. Initiate successful resolution of conflict with others.	1	2	3	4	5
6. Calm yourself quickly when angry.	1	2	3	4	5
7. Know when you are becoming angry.	1	2	3	4	5
8. Regroup quickly after a setback.	1	2	3	4	5
9. Recognize when others are distressed.	1	2	3	4	5
10. Build consensus with others.	1	2	3	4	5
11. Know what senses you are currently using.	1	2	3	4	5
12. Use internal "talk" to change your emotional state.	1	2	3	4	5
13. Produce motivation when doing uninteresting work.	1	2	3	4	5
14. Help others manage their emotions.	1	2	3	4	5
15. Make others feel good.	1	2	3	4	5
16. Identify when you experience mood shifts.	1	2	3	4	5
17. Stay calm when you are the target of anger from others.	1	2	3	4	5
18. Stop or change an ineffective habit.	1	2	3	4	5
19. Show empathy to others.	1	2	3	4	5
20. Provide advice and emotional support to others as needed.	1	2	3	4	5
21. Know when you become defensive.	1	2	3	4	5
22. Know when you are thinking negatively and head it off.	1	2	3	4	5
23. Follow your words with actions.	1	2	3	4	5
24. Engage in intimate conversations with others.	1	2	3	4	5
25. Accurately reflect people's feelings back to them.	1	2	3	4	5

(continued)

Scoring: Sum your responses to the 25 questions to obtain your overall emotional intelligence score. Your score for *self-awareness* is the total of questions 1, 6, 11, 16, and 21. Your score for *managing emotions* is the total of questions 2, 7, 12, 17, and 22. Your score for *motivating oneself* is the sum of questions 3, 8, 13, 18, and 23. Your score for *empathy* is the sum of questions 4, 9, 14, 19, and 24. Your score for *social skill* is the sum of questions 5, 10, 15, 20, and 25.

Interpretation: This questionnaire provides an indication of your emotional intelligence. If you received a total score of 100 or more, you have high emotional intelligence. A score from 50 to 100 means you have a good platform of emotional intelligence from which to develop your managerial capability. A score below 50 indicates that you realize that you are probably below average in emotional intelligence. For each of the five components of emotional intelligence—self-awareness, managing emotions, motivating oneself, empathy, and social skill—a score above 20 is considered high, while a score below 10 would be considered low.

group of job applicants who tested high on optimism but failed the normal sales aptitude test. Compared to salespeople who passed the regular aptitude test but scored high on pessimism, the "optimistic" group made 21 percent more sales in their first year and 57 percent more in the second.[11]

Empathy

The fourth component is empathy, which means being able to put yourself in someone else's shoes, to recognize what others are feeling without them needing to tell you. Most of the time people don't tell us what they feel in words but rather in tone of voice, body language, and facial expression. Empathy is built from self-awareness; being attuned to one's own emotions makes it easier to read and understand the feelings of others.

Social Skill

The ability to connect to others, build positive relationships, respond to the emotions of others, and influence others is the final component of emotional intelligence. Managers need social skills to understand interpersonal relationships, handle disagreements, resolve conflicts, and pull people together for a common purpose.

THE A-B MODEL[12]

The A-B model in Figure 12.1 illustrates the chain of rapid events that occur between two interacting people. Both parties have *needs* they want to satisfy and sets of *values* indicating the most desirable ways of doing so. Sometimes needs are satisfied through defense mechanisms that protect established self-concepts and frames of reference regardless of their current appropriateness. Based on past experiences, both people also make *assumptions* about the nature of the other and of the particular kind of situation they are in (e.g., competitive or cooperative). Each person develops positive or negative *feelings* that contribute to enhanced or diminished *perceptions* of self, the other, and the current situation. These perceptions contribute to *evaluations* of the other person in this situation and lead to the formulation of *intentions* to interact in specific ways to accomplish personal objectives. The *consequences* of that behavior and subsequent *interactions* generate new input for another loop of reactions.

Relationships tend to be *reciprocal* in nature, meaning that one person will most often treat another the same way he or she is, or expects to be, treated by that person. In enduring productive relationships, people expect positive **reciprocity**—an exchange of benefits in their interpersonal transactions. For example, physical and mental efforts may

FIGURE 12.1

A-B Model of
Interpersonal Behavior

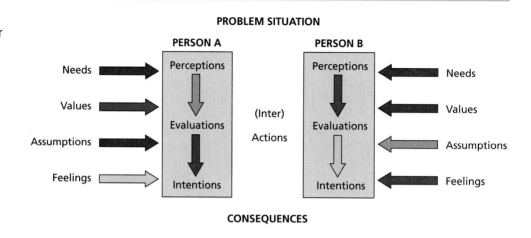

be "traded" for dollars or recognition. Help and kindness may be exchanged for affection and respect. The exchange need not be equal, but unless it is perceived as fair by both parties, tension likely will rise.

On the other hand, if A assumes that B perceives him or her negatively, A may feel diminished, causing him or her to perceive B negatively and interact with B accordingly. Even if A's first assumption was incorrect, his or her subsequent behavior may make this incorrect assumption come true and a negatively reciprocal relationship may emerge. Many times the stage is set for a particular type of reciprocity by various personality factors or preexisting interaction climates.

PERSONALITY FACTORS

When trying to understand your feelings and behaviors, it helps to be aware that how you think and feel about yourself and others may be very unlike how they think and feel about themselves and you. These different evaluations and reactions depend on each individual's self-concept, frame of reference, defenses, interpersonal relationship needs, and feelings.

Self-Concept

Starting with messages from parents, which are later reinforced by significant others, you learn to view and evaluate yourself in a certain way. The identity and evaluation of yourself that you come to accept is your **self-concept**, which may be anything from essentially positive ("I am worthwhile") to negative ("I am worthless"). You protect yourself from any attempts to change your self-concept, even if your view of yourself is a painful one. Even if not ideal, your self-concept allows you to cope, and it's safer to hold on to something known than to let go and take the risk of something new. Yet feedback occurs and learning takes place, causing you to choose between the need to know and the fear of knowing about yourself, especially if the knowledge may force you to change your self-concept.

Through observation and interaction, you learn what significant others think is important. These messages about how you "ought" to feel and behave become your guiding values for later interactions. You also learn what you "ought" to want to achieve, such as graduation from college or freedom from responsibility. Finally, you learn certain techniques that are acceptable to your significant others to gain their approval. These beliefs about what behaviors, feelings, goals, and techniques are desirable become internalized into your **value system**.

Personal Frame of Reference

Your self-concept and perceptions of other people and things develop into a **personal frame of reference** for perceiving and interpreting experiences. Two people with different frames of reference may do very different things in the same situation to try and satisfy the same needs. For example, two students in a highly interactive seminar may perceive the emphasis on participation very differently. One who has been praised for contributing in classes in the past may feel comfortable and view the situation as potentially rewarding. The other, who has had past class contributions rejected and ridiculed, however, may see the class as very threatening. Consequently, to protect and enhance their self-concepts, these two students are likely to behave in opposite ways in the seminar.

Frames of reference are abstractions of reality, and everyone sees reality differently because of different needs and past experiences. Furthermore, new experiences and changing needs keep the reality changing somewhat. It is very difficult to understand how others perceive their world, especially since we tend to filter their behavior through our own unique frame of reference. Our actions are logical to us given our frame of reference, but so are other people's different behaviors to them, even though they don't make sense to us because of their alternate perception of the situation.

Cultural backgrounds are a frequent source of different frames of reference. Paul Nolan is director of corporate training for the Lincoln Savings Bank in New York, which has a diverse employee mix including young and old men and women who are Hispanic, Chinese, East Indian, African-American, and Italian-American. After going through a number of multicultural training sessions, he believes that he is a better manager. "I've always seen life through white, male eyes," says Nolan. "Even now, when I speak to white males, I'm very structured, very aggressive, succinct. But if I were talking to a Chinese person, I'd ask open-ended questions, such as 'Tell me what you think about this' instead of 'This is what I think.' I've learned that others can perceive me as 'this white man telling me what to do'. " Nolan's new, more flexible approach has dramatically increased the participation rate of minorities on the staff.[13] The Dynamics of Diversity box illustrates how corporations that have been thought to be managed by "the old boys network" are responding to the need for cultural diversity.

To understand others, you need to understand their frames of reference without judging them in terms of your own values. This does not mean that you must accept for yourself the means they are using to satisfy their needs. Nor should you expect others to always accept your own behavior as the most satisfying for them. But you can benefit from continuously exploring with others your own perception of reality compared to theirs. Failure to be accepting and understanding can cause defensiveness, inhibit personal growth, and cause conflicts.

Defensiveness

One response to an interpersonal encounter that threatens your self-concept or frame of reference is to apply one or more psychological defenses. A **defense** is a cognitive distortion that protects the self-concept from being diminished. Defensiveness occurs when you protect yourself by denying, excusing, or rationalizing your actions to protect your self-concept against the threat of being damaged by failure, guilt, shame, or fear.

All defense mechanisms involve a degree of distortion of the true relationships between the individual and external reality. Although defense mechanisms provide some relief from tension and anxiety, they do not satisfy underlying needs. Individuals learn defense mechanisms at an early age and continue to use those that have worked for them in the past. Defense mechanisms affect the way individuals relate to each other and the way they understand and adapt to their relationships.[14] Some of the more common defenses are summarized in Figure 12.2 on page 338.

Defenses alleviate painful feelings, but they fail to deal with the causes of the problem. If overused, defenses can be dysfunctional because they inhibit individual growth and interactions with others. Defensiveness may distort ideas, obscure solutions, or hinder interpersonal communication. Individuals can respond nondefensively by acknowledging and accepting the threatening event and then attempting to cope with it by eliminating or moderating their behavior. One way to avoid your own defensive behavior is to

DYNAMICS OF DIVERSITY

Diversity Challenges in the "All Boys Clubs"

Cultural diversity became a corporate "tag phrase" in the 1990s. Companies struggled to manage the changing demographics of the work force. More and more women and minority group members received college degrees, and as these groups ascended the corporate ladder, corporate management was forced to change. Particularly, upper management levels faced new challenges as the familiar "old boys" world and network was disappearing.

The Chevron Company of yesterday was an all too familiar scene—white, Anglo-Saxon males in pinstripe three-piece suits dominated the halls of management. It was not a place where you would find a person wearing a turban. However, that is exactly what Jeet Bindra was wearing when he took over as President of Chevron Pipeline Company. Although extremely competent, questions remain about how cultural differences will impact Jeet's effectiveness in leading other all white male teams of the $2 billion Caspian Pipeline Consortium. How will the public perceive Jeet, and hence Chevron, when Jeet travels to corporate locations such as Texas and Mississippi as the top representative of the management committee?

When Amoco conducted a worldwide survey of its employees in 1988, management expected to find the impression of a well-run organization. However, the survey confirmed reality: white males who spent their entire career with Amoco were largely directing the corporation. Women and minority groups, who were typically difficult to attract into the oil industry, were not present, especially in management. As a result of the survey, Amoco launched an initiative to diversify its work force and improve organizational deficiencies. When a follow-up 1996 survey was conducted, the results found that now 80 percent of its work force felt that Amoco was a good place to work.

Deborah Sawyer is really cleaning up in the toxic and hazardous waste management industry. In a field where one rarely finds women, it is even more difficult to find a black woman. Deborah has built her Environmental Design International company into a $2.7 million enterprise with 40 employees. In a primarily male dominated business, Deborah still has to overcome the perception of being a "nice girl in a boy's world." She still has trouble recruiting other black female engineers, but the business continues to grow. Already with four offices in the midwest, her plans are to expand internationally to France and Italy.

Sources: Paul Watson, "Diversity Challenge," *People Management* (May 1997), pp. 30–32; Jeet S. Bindra, "Not Nirvana . . . Yet," *Across the Board* 35, Issue 10, (November/December 1998), pp. 14–15; and Marty Jackson "Dollars in Dirt," *Black Enterprise* (June 1997), pp. 42–46.

---

acknowledge what is being said as at least partially true. If you are frequently late, for example, and someone criticizes you for it, you could simply acknowledge, "Yes, I often am late" as opposed to trying to convince the other that you're really not always late or that there are always good reasons why you are late.

One way to reduce another person's defensiveness is to use active listening. This means using verbal and nonverbal responses to show that you are listening nonjudgmentally to truly understand the other person. By reflecting back your perception of the other's concerns in a nonjudgmental way, he or she may feel safe and understood enough to reduce defenses.

Interpersonal Relationship Needs

William Schutz contends that people have three dominant interpersonal needs.[15] The first is *inclusion*—the need to establish and maintain relationships with other people. Inclusion concerns balancing the desire to be part of a group against the desire for solitude. The second is *control*—the need to maintain a satisfactory balance of power and influence in relationships. Control concerns trade-offs between the desires for structure and authority versus the desire for freedom. Finally, there is the need for *affection*—the need to form

FIGURE 12.2   Common Defense Mechanisms

Defense	Psychological Process	Illustration
Rationalization "Everybody does it."	Justifying behaviors and feelings that are undesirable by providing explanations that make them acceptable.	You pad your expense account because "everybody does it."
Repression "Motivated forgetting."	"Forgetting" painful and frustrating events by unconsciously putting them out of your memory.	You "forget" to tell the boss about an embarrassing error you made because you feel guilty.
Reaction-Formation "Methinks the lady doth protest too much."	Repressing unacceptable urges and exhibiting the opposite attitudes and behaviors.	The manager who represses the desire to have an affair with his secretary crusades against such activities.
Projection "It's all your fault."	Protecting yourself from awareness of your own undesirable traits or feelings by attributing them to others.	In a crisis, the manager tells employees not to panic to hide his own undesirable feelings of panic.
Regression "Disneyland, here I come."	Responding to frustration by reverting to earlier and less mature forms of behavior; attempting to go back to a more comfortable time.	A manager who cannot get approval for an additional secretary begins typing, filing, and doing other activities more appropriate for subordinates.
Displacement "Kick the dog who bites the cat."	Redirecting pent-up emotions toward persons other than the primary source of the emotion.	You roughly reject a simple request from a subordinate after receiving a rebuff from the boss.
Compensation "Tit for tat."	Engaging in a substitute behavior to make up for a feeling of inadequacy.	A manager who is not advancing professionally works very hard on volunteer activities.
Denial "It ain't true."	Refusing to absorb threatening information.	You are unwilling to accept that others see you as hostile when you are pressed for time.
Withdrawal "If I'm not here, I don't have to deal with it."	Physically or mentally leaving a situation that produces anxiety, conflict, or frustration.	A person's idea is rejected by a committee, so he either is absent from future meetings or fails to participate.
Resignation "If I got to do it, I got to do it, but not too well."	Withholding any sense of emotional or personal involvement in an unpleasant situation.	An employee who hasn't received praise no longer cares whether or not he does a good job.
Conversion "It makes me hurt so bad."	Transforming emotional conflicts into physical symptoms.	A salesman about to meet with a client who is anticipated to say no experiences a headache.
Counterdependence "You can't make me."	Suppressing feelings of dependence and expressing hostile independence.	A boss feeling confused and lost rudely rejects help from subordinates.
Aggression "The best defense is a good offense."	Instigating a hostile attack on another because you are frustrated or uncomfortable.	A manager makes a sarcastic remark to an employee who has just made a minor error.

Sources: Adapted from Timothy W. Costello and Sheldon S. Zalkind, *Psychology in Administration: A Research Orientation* (1963), pp. 148–149. Reprinted by permission of Prentice Hall, Inc., Upper Saddle River, NJ. D. I. Costley and R. Todd, *Human Relations in Organizations* (St. Paul, MN: West Publishing, 1987), pp. 232–235.

close and personal relationships with others. Affection concerns balancing desires for warmth and commitment against those for maintaining distance and independence.

Each of these three needs has two subdimensions—the *expressed* desire to give, or impose the need on others, and the *wanted* desire to receive the need from others; for example, the need to invite or include others in our activities, and the need to be invited and included in others' activities. These three interpersonal needs and their two subdimensions

Your Turn
What Are Your Relationship Needs?

Instructions: Allocate between 0 and 9 points to indicate the degree to which each of the following six questions applies to you. Place the number of the answer at the left of the statement.

_____ 1. I like to invite people to join social activities.

_____ 2. I feel badly when other people do things without inviting me to join them.

_____ 3. I try to have other people do things the way I want them done.

_____ 4. Other peoples' preferences strongly influence my behavior.

_____ 5. I try to develop close personal relationships with people.

_____ 6. I like people to act close and personal toward me.

_____ **Total Points**

Scoring: Add up the number of points for the six questions to determine your total interpersonal needs score. Your score will fall somewhere between 0 and 54. The point allocations to each of the six questions provides the relative strengths of your interpersonal needs as follows: 1—expressed inclusion; 2—wanted inclusion; and 3—expressed control; 4—wanted control; 5—expressed affection; and 6—wanted affection. You can write these in the boxes in Figure 12.3 to visually depict the relative strengths of your interpersonal needs.

Interpretation: There is no "right" score. The value of this information is that it lets you know the relative strength of your own interpersonal needs. The average person, according to national studies, has a total score of 29.16 Your highest scores on individual questions indicate which interpersonal needs are least satisfied and probably dominate your relationships with others.

Source: Developed by Phillip L. Hunsaker for class discussion, University of San Diego, 1995.

are illustrated in Figure 12.3. Complete the Your Turn exercise to determine the relative strengths of your interpersonal needs.

If you have strong interpersonal needs, you desire to interact with others and are probably outgoing and gregarious. If you have low interpersonal needs, you don't mind being alone and are more reserved around others. Typically, marketing and human resource majors in business schools have stronger interpersonal needs than accounting and systems analysis students.[17] This indicates that students with higher interpersonal needs tend to select people-oriented careers and vice versa. The findings do not necessarily predict success as a manager, however, because that depends to a large degree on the types of work and people you are supervising.

The degree of need compatibility between two or more people can make the difference between a happy and productive team and a dissatisfied and ineffective one. If one person has a high need to express dominance and control, and another had a high need to receive direction, they are likely to get along well. On the other hand, if they both have high needs to express dominance and low needs to receive it, conflict is probable. The key is whether the important needs of each person are complementary and to what degree they are satisfied in the relationship. Compatible individuals usually like each other more and work better together.[18] Awareness of differences in interpersonal needs can help

FIGURE 12.3   Fundamental Interpersonal Relationship Orientations

Behaviors	Interpersonal Needs		
	Inclusion	**Control**	**Affection**
Expressed toward others	I want others to join me	I take charge and influence others	I get close to others
Wanted from others	I want others to include me	I want others to lead me	I want others to get close to me

you adapt your own behaviors to let others satisfy their needs, which can enhance your relationships with them.[19]

Feelings

People continually experience feelings about themselves and others, but many have not learned to accept and use feelings constructively. How you express feelings is a frequent source of difficulty in interpersonal relationships. Problems arise not because emotions are present, but because they are not used well. Rather than express them constructively, people often deny or ignore their own and others' feelings in an attempt to avoid rejection or struggle for control.

For example, you may have experienced immediate rapport or dislike toward someone you just met. What you are feeling has to do with things about the other person and yourself that you are only unconsciously aware of.[20] Immediate liking for a person you have just met is often caused by seeing in them things you like in yourself, or traits you would like to have but don't, like charm or humor.

It's the negative reactions that can cause you the most problems, however, especially if they are directed at a person you will be interacting with for a long time, like your boss or a co-worker. Therefore, it is important to try to understand what caused your reaction and why. It may be that the other person has characteristics that remind you of someone in the past who brought you pain. Or, it might be that the person triggers awareness of your "shadow self," that is, parts of yourself that you are not aware of because you don't like them. Being egotistical, wimpy, or aggressive may be behaviors you repress in yourself, and seeing someone else who dares to act in these ways can cause negative reactions.

Maintaining a productive relationship requires that you first look at yourself to understand what it is about you that's causing the negative feelings. You may then see that it is not really the other person you don't like, but a particular characteristic that you also have yourself. Then you may be able to overlook the characteristic in the other, as you do in yourself. If self-analysis isn't enough, it can be helpful to tactfully express personal feelings so that you and the other party can try to work out potential difficulties in a productive way.[21]

INTERACTION SETTING

Often, what appear to be personality changes may just be two people's varying responses to different and incompatible job requirements. This frequently happens when people work in different parts of the organization, under different organizational cultures, for different bosses, and in different jobs that make different demands.

Job Requirements

Job requirements determine how psychologically close or distant two people need to be to perform their work. The depth of interpersonal relationships required by a job depends on how complex the task is, whether the people involved possess different kinds of expertise, the frequency of interaction in the job, and the degree of certainty with which job outcomes can be predicted.[22]

Photodisc

For minority entrepreneurs, interpersonal skills are vitally important for bringing new business and ideas to their companies. A major obstacle to business between white-owned and minority-owned business is that owners do not know one another professionally or personally. By forming friendships based on openness and trust, satisfaction and productivity can improve.

Work situations that are simple and familiar to both workers, don't require strong feelings, demand little interaction, and have a high certainty of outcomes call for minimal task relationships. Complex situations that require different knowledge from each person, high trust, much interaction, and have an uncertain outcome call for more intense interpersonal relationships closer to colleagueship.[23] An example of a minimal task relationship would be an operating room nurse and a surgeon, whose only required exchange regards information about the patient's welfare and the surgeon's need for instruments. Colleagueship requires that people collaborate in a complex task situation demanding trust and mutual support, like when two police detectives are attempting to arrest an armed criminal.

Organizational Culture

The organization's culture influences the general nature of employee relationships. People take cues from the culture they work in and usually respond to what they perceive as general expectations. Some cultures discourage intimacy and only allow distant, impersonal relationships. The more culture fosters competitiveness, aggressiveness, and hostility, the greater the likelihood that people will be cautious and on guard with each other. Other cultures encourage familylike closeness. The more sociable and personal the culture, the more people are likely to share nonwork information and feelings.[24] Different interaction patterns can be distinguished by four primary factors:[25]

- *Openness* is the degree to which participants share their thoughts and feelings with others.
- *Trust* is the degree to which you believe someone else is honest and supportive.
- *Owning* refers to taking responsibility for a problem to which you are a contributor versus blaming someone else.
- *Risk to experiment* is the degree to which you are punished for trying something new, especially if it fails, versus doing things in safe, approved-of ways.

In **regenerative interaction patterns**, people are open with each other, which develops trust and promotes rapport and intimacy. This is a "win-win" relationship where people are "for each other"; they want to help each other grow and consequently cooperate for their mutual benefit. Owning is high because people want to understand each other and learn from mistakes. The risk associated with trying new behaviors is low because trust and goodwill promote constant growth and improvement. If there are problems in a regenerative relationship, the parties try to understand and learn from past mistakes in order to develop an even more satisfying and productive relationship.

In **degenerative interaction patterns**, on the other hand, any problems that develop result in blaming others, defensiveness, lack of trust, and decreased openness. In such a "win-lose" relationship, lack of trust leads to a reduction of openness, risking new behaviors that may fail, and owning up to past mistakes, because all of these can make you more vulnerable. Most people try to escape degenerative climates if they want to grow and relate productively with others. If they stay, it is usually because of a high need for power and dominance or a very low self-esteem and high insecurity.

Trust Levels

Trust is a key ingredient in any win-win relationship, whether personal or business. **Trust** exists whenever you choose to let yourself be dependent on another person whose future behavior can affect your well-being. Trust occurs to the degree that you are aware that

Building Productive Interpersonal Relationships through Trust at ServiceMaster

Phil Myers was working nights as a janitor in an operating room in Indianapolis when his meticulous work attracted the attention of his supervisor, Chris Kinman. Kinman began to give Myers more responsibility until six or seven months later he promoted Myers to the position of evening supervisor.

Shortly after he became a supervisor, Myers was put to the test. He discovered that a friend had left his shift fifteen minutes early but signed out at the normal time. "Now I had my first major, major situation," says Myers. "Number one, I had somebody here who was breaking a major time compliance rule. And, I had a person that I worked with for a year, who was my friend, and now . . . he was reporting to me." Myers turned to Kinman, who coached and tested but never directed him. Kinman's coaching was firm, fair and friendly." He was not saying, "Go terminate him. That's what you have to do." Chris became a mirror to me, he held it up, and I had to say, "What's the right thing to do?" . . . He took me through a process of review of my options and what was required to do the right thing. When I decided, Chris said, "Go for it. If you need any help let me know. If you need me to be with you, let me know." Myers met with the employee alone, and after reviewing the event with him, decided he had to let him go because it was a serious violation of ServiceMaster's values of honesty and the sanctity of work.

While confronting a values transgression in one service worker may seem like a small deal, interactions like this are where the rubber meets the road. Values are only as good as their embodiment by every employee all the time. And it is people like Phil Myers who handle situations like this every day that make the difference at ServiceMaster. On the front lines, these decisions can be even tougher than those made in the executive suite. When a top executive fires another executive, he knows that the person is probably going to get 18 months' salary as severance and is sitting on millions in stock. Supervisors like Myers are dealing with people in much more tenuous circumstances. Of his experience with the worker in Indianapolis, Myers, who now manages a ServiceMaster account at a hospital on Chicago's West Side, remarks, "I think it set the structure for discipline in my career. It was one of the major things because it was so serious. My thoughts were, 'Sam may no longer have an income.' But it was the fairest thing to do."

Myers has faced many more tests in leading three turnaround situations, two of which involved the pending loss of a big customer. In these situations, Myers says he has relied heavily on the ServiceMaster values to bring in the business result. The key to each of his successful turnarounds, he says, was honesty, teaching, and respect for the workers. The workers are usually scared, says Myers, "that you're going to come in and all of a sudden people are going to get hatcheted. . . . [So] you go through the course of nurturing with people to get them to trust you, to have confidence in you and to give them some of our mission and corporate culture."

Source: Noel M. Tichy, *The Leadership Engine* (New York: Harper Business, 1997), pp. 112–113. Copyright 1997 by Noel M. Tichy. Reprinted by permission of HarperCollins Publishers, Inc.

---

another's behavior can benefit or harm you, and you feel confident that the other person will act to benefit you.[26] An example of trust occurs when a working mother leaves her baby at a day-care center. She is aware that her choice could lead to harmful or beneficial consequences and feels relatively confident that the staff will behave to bring about beneficial consequences.

Relationships do not grow and develop until individuals trust each other. Trust is learned from past interactions with another. Trust is earned as the parties self-disclose personal information and learn that they will not be hurt by making themselves vulnerable to each other. Increased trust leads to the sharing of more personal information between the parties, which enhances regenerative interaction patterns and contributes to improved problem solving and productivity.[27] Read the Eye on Ethics box to see how trust contributes to successful interpersonal relations at ServiceMaster.

Whenever trust is broken, the relationship suffers. The damage may be temporary or permanent, depending on the nature of the relationship. The way Richard Nixon handled the Watergate scandal by denying responsibility and withholding information, for example, cost him the trust of the American people and the possibility of a second term in office.[28]

In his best-selling book, *The 7 Habits of Highly Effective People*, Stephen Covey uses the metaphor of an "emotional bank account" to describe the amount of trust that has been built up in a relationship.[29] To Covey, trust refers to the overall feeling of safeness that you have with another person. You make "deposits" into an emotional bank account with another person through kindness, honesty, and keeping commitments. These acts build up a reserve trust account that promotes confidence in you even if your communication is sometimes ambiguous or you make an occasional mistake. But, if you show disrespect, fail to honor commitments, or take advantage of the other person, your trust account becomes depleted. The relationship then becomes degenerative, with hostility and defensiveness making it difficult to build up trust again.

Covey suggests six major deposits to build up emotional bank accounts:[30]

- *Understand and honor other peoples' needs and priorities*, which may be very different than our own.
- *Attend to little things*, like showing kindness and being courteous, because they make big positive deposits in relationships.
- *Keep commitments*. Breaking a promise can be a massive withdrawal that may prevent future deposits because people won't believe you.
- *Clarify expectations* so that others don't feel cheated or violated if you don't behave in ways that they assumed you knew they desired, even though they never overtly told you.
- *Show personal integrity* by keeping promises, being honest, fulfilling expectations, and being loyal to all people equally, including those not present.
- *Apologize sincerely when you make a withdrawal*, without rationalizing or trying to shift some of the blame to the other.

As trust builds in our emotional bank account, it becomes the foundation of regenerative relationships with others. People learn to put all their cards on the table to deal with issues and solve problems without wasting energy focused on differences in personality or position. Without trust, you lack the credibility and safety for open communication, creativity, problem solving, or mutual learning.

Why Do People Have Different Styles of Relating?

When interacting with others, sometimes you get the reactions you want, but other times you don't. Your **interpersonal effectiveness** is the degree to which the consequences of your behavior match your intentions. You can improve interpersonal effectiveness by disclosing your intentions, receiving feedback on your behavior, and modifying your behavior until it has the consequences you intend it to have.[31] Important aspects of your behavior to be aware of include your self-presentation, orientation toward others, behavioral style, ethics, and reactions to people who differ in gender or ethnic background.

DIFFERENCES IN SELF-DISCLOSURE

How well do other people know you? Are you easy to get to know? Do you feel free to tell others what you feel and think? In order to know you and be involved with you, I must know who you are and what you need. For that to happen, you must **self-disclose** how you perceive, think, and feel about the present situation, along with any relevant information from your past. Without self-disclosure, you cannot form a meaningful relationship with another person.

The Johari Window

The **Johari window**,[32] diagrammed in Figure 12.4, is a model of the different degrees of openness between two people. It is based on the degrees of self-disclosure and solicitation of feedback when sharing information with another person. The model presents four windowpanes of awareness of others and ourselves.

In the *open area*, information is disclosed and known by both parties; mutually shared perceptions confirm both parties' frames of reference. In the *hidden area* lie things that you are aware of but do not share because you may be afraid that others will think less of you, use the information to their advantage, or chastise you because they may hurt the other's feelings. The *blind area* encompasses certain things about you that are apparent to others but not to yourself, either because no one has ever told you or because you defensively block them out. Blind spots, however, make you less effective in interactions with others. A certain team member may be terrible at running meetings, for example, but may not know it because no one has given her any feedback. Finally, in the *unknown area* lie repressed fears and needs or potential that neither you nor the other are aware of.

Different Styles of Self-Disclosure[33]

In important intimate and trusting relationships, aboveboard behavior is called for and people self-disclose freely with each other. This is the *transparent style* of interacting illustrated in Figure 12.5, characterized by the large "open" area. Transparent styles are appropriate for significant relationships in regenerative climates. They would not be appropriate with casual acquaintances, in competitive situations, or where trust and goodwill have not been established.

A person with a relatively large "hidden" area uses an *interviewer style* because this person asks a lot of questions when soliciting feedback but does not self-disclose to others. Consequently, others have a difficult time knowing how the person feels or what she wants. After a while, people can become irritated at continually being asked to open up and share things without any reciprocation from the interviewer. They may become suspicious about how the information will be used and may begin to shut down on the quantity and quality of information they are willing to share.

People with large "blind" areas give a lot of feedback but solicit very little from others. People with this *bull-in-the-china-shop style* frequently tell others what they think and feel and where they stand on issues, but they are insensitive to feedback from others. Since they do not "hear" what others say to and about them, they do not know how they come across and what impact their behavior has on others.

A person with a large "unknown" area does not know much about himself—nor do others. He may be the silent observer type, who neither gives nor asks for feedback. This is the *turtle*, who carries an imaginary shell around him that insulates him from others. People have a hard time knowing where he stands or where they stand with him.

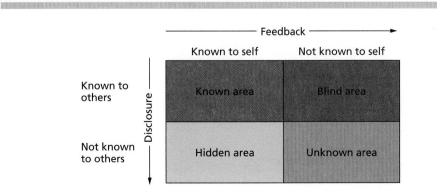

FIGURE 12.4

Johari Window

Source: From *Group Processes: An Introduction to Group Dynamics, Third Edition,* by Joseph Luft. Copyright 1984 by Mayfield Publishing Company. Reprinted by permission of the publisher.

FIGURE 12.5

Different Self-Disclosure Styles

Source: Reprinted from *Group Process: An Introduction to Group Dynamics*, Third Edition, by Joseph Luft. Copyright 1984 by Mayfield Publishing Company. Reprinted by permission of the publisher.

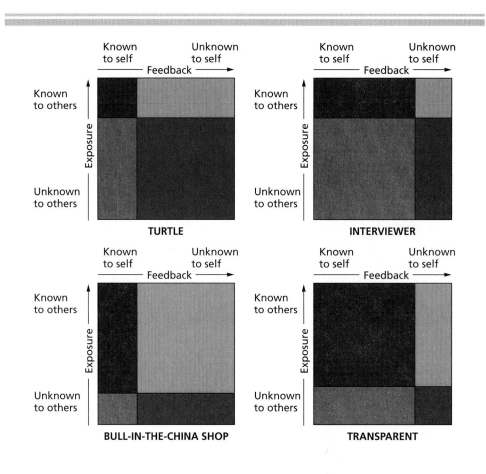

Managing Openness: Guidelines for Self-Disclosure[34]

Because openness is risky—having both potential costs and rewards—it can be difficult to decide how open to be and with whom. Sharing your feelings and needs with others can build strong relationships in which you feel understood and cared about and have your needs satisfied. With the wrong parties, however, your openness could be used against you. With closed behavior, you don't risk rejection nor being taken advantage of, but you

When G. Rives Neblett took over Shelby Die Casting in Mississippi, he organized workers into teams and changed the company's degenerative climate to a regenerative one. Initially there was turmoil while they learned to conduct meetings democratically and managers learned not to dominate. This resulted in a trusting climate where teams worked cooperatively, pinpointing problems and working to solve them.

incur the costs of possibly not satisfying your needs and goals. It is difficult to establish meaningful relationships if you don't let yourself be known to significant others. Either too much or too little openness can be dysfunctional in different types of interpersonal relationships.

Managing your openness means choosing when and how to be more open and authentic in your relationships with others. It means thinking before acting. In choosing how open to be in any situation, consider your own motives, the probable effects of your remarks on the other, and the recipient's readiness to hear your views. This includes an assessment of the degree of trust between you to determine if self-disclosure would be too risky.[35] In mature relationships, for example, the bonds of trust between parties causes them to assume that the other will not use disclosed personal information in ways that risk negative consequences.

DIFFERENT BEHAVIORAL STYLES[36]

Many times two people who cannot get along with one another (whether they be peers or boss and subordinate) have no difficulty interrelating with other people. Sometimes these differences can be accounted for by different frames of reference, needs, goals, or self-presentation styles. Often they occur, however, because people have different preferred ways of being treated by others. If two people's preferred ways of interacting don't match, there is a high likelihood of conflict and tension.

A person's **behavioral style** is his or her habitual way of interacting with other people. It can be determined by examining two dimensions. *Responsiveness* is a person's degree of readiness to show emotions and develop relationships. *Assertiveness* refers to the amount of control a person tries to exercise over other people. Figure 12.6 summarizes the four primary behavioral styles determined by different levels of responsiveness and assertiveness.

People with different behavioral styles often irritate each other and have incompatible work methods. A key interpersonal skill is knowing how to adapt your own behavioral style to others' in order to avoid alienation. This is practicing *behavioral flexibility*: treating others the way they want to be treated. American corporations are realizing the importance of being more considerate of others and are sending their managers to "charm schools," as described in the opening vignette. But before you polish your charm, you need to understand your own behavioral style and be able to determine that of others.

The Expressive Style

Expressives are animated, intuitive, and lively, but they can also be manipulative, impetuous, and excitable. They are fast paced, make spontaneous decisions, and are not very concerned about facts and details. They thrive on involvement for others. They are very verbal and good at influencing and persuading. They are the cheerleaders: "I can, you can, we can make a difference." They like to be recognized.

Expressives are very emotional and are relatively comfortable sharing their own feelings and hearing about the feelings of others. To maintain productive relationships with them, it helps not to hurry a discussion and to be entertaining. When striving for an agreement with an expressive, make sure that you both fully understand all the details and summarize everything in writing so it won't be forgotten.

The Driving Style

Drivers are highly assertive but not very responsive. They are firm with others and make decisions rapidly. They are oriented toward productivity and concerned with bottom-line results, so drivers can be stubborn, impatient, and tough minded. Drivers strive to dominate and control people to achieve their tasks.

Drivers like expressing and reacting to tough emotions, but are uncomfortable either receiving or expressing tender feelings. You can maintain a productive relationship with a driver if you are precise, efficient, and well organized. You should keep the relationship

FIGURE 12.6   Characteristics of the Four Behavioral Styles

High Responsiveness

Amiable Style

Slow at taking action and making decisions

Likes close, personal relationships

Dislikes interpersonal conflict

Supports and "actively" listens to others

Weak at goal setting and self-direction

Has excellent ability to gain support from others

Works slowly and cohesively with others

Seeks security and belongingness

Good counseling skills

Expressive Style

Spontaneous actions and decisions

Likes involvement

Dislikes being alone

Exaggerates and generalizes

Tends to dream and get others caught up in the dream

Jumps from one activity to another

Works quickly and excitingly with others

Seeks esteem and belongingness

Good persuasive skills

Low Assertiveness ←——————→ **High Assertiveness**

Analytical Style

Cautious actions and decisions

Likes organization and structure

Dislikes involvement with others

Asks many questions and wants specific details

Prefers objective, task-oriented, intellectual work environment

Wants to be right and therefore relies heavily on data collection

Works slowly and precisely alone

Seeks security and self-actualization

Good problem-solving skills

Driver Style

Firm actions and decisions

Likes control

Dislikes inaction

Prefers maximum freedom to manage self and others

Cool and independent; competitive with others

Low tolerance for feelings, attitudes, and advice of others

Works quickly and impressively alone

Seeks esteem and self-actualization

Good administrative skills

Low Responsiveness

Source: P. L. Hunsaker and A. J. Alessandra, *The Art of Managing People* (New York: Simon & Schuster, 1986), p. 36. Copyright © 1980 by Phillip L. Hunsaker and Anthony J. Alessandra. Reprinted by permission of Simon & Schuster, Inc.

businesslike. To influence a driver in the direction you desire, provide options you are comfortable with, but let the driver make a decision.

The Analytical Style

Analyticals are not very assertive or responsive. They are persistent, systematic problem solvers who sometimes appear aloof, picky, and critical. They need to be right, which can lead them to rely too heavily on data. In their search for perfection, their actions and decisions tend to be extremely cautious. They do not shoot from the hip, they avoid being confrontational, and think before they speak.

Analyticals suppress their feelings because they are uncomfortable with any type of emotion. To get along with an analytical, try to be systematic, organized, and prepared. Analyticals require solid, tangible, and factual evidence. Do not use gimmicks or push them for a fast decision. Take time to explain the alternatives and the advantages and disadvantages of your recommendations.

The Amiable Style

Amiables are very responsive, but unassertive, causing them to be supportive and reliable. Sometimes they appear to be complaining, soft hearted, and acquiescent. They are slow to take action and want to know how other people feel about a decision before they commit themselves. Amiables dislike interpersonal conflict so much that they often tell others what they think others want to hear rather than what is really on their minds.

Amiables like expressing and receiving tender feelings of warmth and support, but abhor tough emotions like anger or hostility. They are good team players and have no trouble recognizing the person in charge, unlike drivers, who always act as if they are the boss. To get along with amiables, support their feelings and show personal interest in them. Move along in an informal manner and show the amiable that you are "actively listening."

MALE/FEMALE DIFFERENCES

No one denies that males and females are different. Because of these differences, most people interact differently with same-sex than with different-sex communicators. Some of the most common sexual differences in interpersonal relationships concern communication styles, relating strengths, interaction preferences, and social-sexual behavior.

Relating Strengths

Different interacting psychological and social forces place women's early development in a context of *communion*, emphasizing expressiveness, connection, and relatedness, whereas men's early development occurs in a context of *agency*, emphasizing independence, autonomy, and instrumentality. This early emphasis on relatedness and connection causes

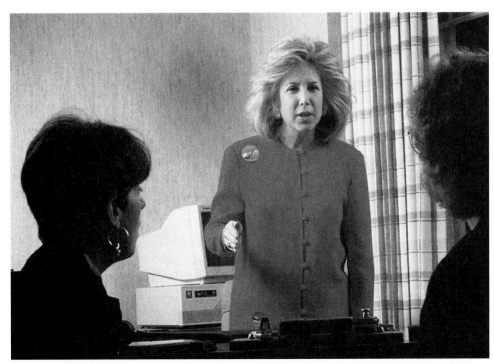

© 1992 John Zich

Because of differences in male/female communication behaviors, Chicago attorney Laurel G. Bellows advises women in business to learn two styles of negotiating: nonpositional and confrontational. She suggests that female traits such as building relationships and being creative work well in nonpositional negotiations—situations in which parties use creative and cooperative methods to reach agreements helpful to both sides. In confrontational negotiations, women must realize it is okay to be adversarial and argue with the other parties—typical traits that men learn as young boys playing sports.

women to develop, more highly than men, the qualities of vulnerability, empathy, and an ability to empower and enable others.[37]

Men are socialized to deny feeling vulnerable and are encouraged to strive for self-reliance, strength, and independence, while women are expected to attend to their own and others' feelings and connect emotionally with others. By being better able to comfortably recognize and respond to feelings of self-doubt, inadequacy, and vulnerability, women are better able to nonjudgmentally address weaknesses in themselves and others, which are preconditions to personal growth, healthy interdependence, and helping others.

Women learn to listen with empathy and to be responsive and sensitive to others' emotions. Men, on the other hand, are encouraged to be rational and strong and to deny feelings in order to maintain rationality and control. Women's stronger empathy is thought to be valuable in maintaining collaborative, growth-enhancing relationships.

Finally, women grow up expecting a two-directional pattern of relational growth, where contributing to the development of others will increase their feelings of effectiveness and competence and where others will be motivated to reciprocate. This is opposed to men's early training, which emphasizes independence and competitiveness. Consequently, women are more naturally adaptable to helping others at work in coaching or mentoring relationships.[38]

Interaction Preferences

Males and females differ in their reactions to authority figures and how they prefer to deal with conflict. These issues have grown in importance as more women have assumed positions of authority in organizations. In terms of supervisor preference, females tend to have more positive attitudes toward female managers than do males. They also perceive female managers as more competent than males perceive them.[39] Although female college students report that they would prefer a female boss upon graduating, more females with work experience prefer male supervisors.[40]

With respect to conflict, more female than male managers have been socialized to avoid confrontations altogether or to seek help in resolving them. More women than men settle for noninfluential roles rather than become involved in power struggles and conflicts. In contrast, many men have been taught to overemphasize power and strive for one-upmanship even when it is unnecessary or counterproductive.

Social-Sexual Behavior

Social-sexual behavior is any non-work-related behavior having a sexual component; it includes things like sexual harassment, flirting, and office romances. Analyses of office romances and sexual harassment have suggested that over half of all employees have received some kind of sexual overture from a co-worker of the other gender. About 10 percent of all women have actually quit a job because of sexual harassment,[41] which includes all unwelcome verbal or physical sexual advances.[42]

More than half of U.S. women executives say they have suffered sexual harassment, a problem reported by 70 percent of Japanese working women and 50 percent of women working in European countries. In addition, 15 percent of men in the United States say either female or male co-workers have harassed them. Harassment results in stress, absenteeism, productivity declines, turnover, and lawsuits, which cost companies an average of about $300 per employee per year. Solutions include raising awareness, providing training, and consistent enforcement of clearly communicated rules and penalties.[43]

The existence of genuine attraction between men and women in the workplace can't be ignored. When men and women work closely and intensely together, they often become attracted to each other even if they didn't intend it to happen. Sex goes to work with us every day, and we are naive if we assume that management can hand down an edict stating, "We'll have no attraction here." Since people do choose whether or not to act on these feelings, it is better to give people guidelines and help in managing attraction productively. Effectively managing sexual attraction in relationships involves learning to communicate directly, setting personal boundaries, and having a sense of ethics.[44]

Charm Schools for Managers—
A Second Look

Feedback from others at the "charm schools" described in the opening vignette enables managers to eliminate blind spots in their interpersonal styles. The word is out about how these charm schools help managers learn how to satisfy the interpersonal relationship needs of themselves and others; build trust with others; interact productively with different behavioral styles; deal effectively with male and female differences; and act ethically. So recently the U.S. Army has established its own version.

At the U.S. Army's annual Brigadier General Training Conference, the select few who are promoted from colonel are pushed to make a mental and emotional leap and consider the Army and their command in a new way. One lecturer at a recent conference told the new generals to get in touch with the "inner jerk" and work on losing that aspect of their personalities. Another warned that the "first deadly sin of the general officer is arrogance. Bask in the glow and get over it."

Much of the conference focuses on avoiding trouble and leading ethically and with heart. Lieutenant General John Keane, an infantry commander since 1966, stresses the importance of "leading from the front: to have empathy for soldiers on the front lines." "You've got to put yourself in harm's way to have moral authority," Keane says. "You must feel the horror they feel, the loneliness and despair they feel." Other sessions focus on problems such as sexual harassment, diversity issues, and improper use of power and privilege. New generals are advised to hone their social skills to interact effectively not only with insiders but with outsiders such as congresspeople and journalists.

On the final day, the group finally hears from four-star General Dennis Reimer, Army chief of staff, who has spent most of the conference observing from the back row. After encouraging the generals to maintain balance to avoid burning out themselves and their staffs, Reimer adds this piece of advice: "Get your own coffee. It keeps you humble."[45]

These examples demonstrate how many different types of organizations believe that emotional intelligence is related to effective leadership. A high level of self-awareness, combined with the ability to manage one's own emotions, enables managers to display self-confidence and earn the respect and trust of followers. In addition, the ability to manage or temporarily restrain one's emotions can enable a leader to objectively consider the needs of others over his or her own immediate feelings. Giving in to strong feelings of anger or depression, for example, may intensify a self-centered focus on one's own needs and limit the ability of the manager to understand the needs of others or see things from others' perspectives.

Furthermore, the emotional state of the manager impacts the entire group, department, or organization. Managers who are able to maintain balance and keep themselves motivated are positive role models to help motivate and inspire those around them. The energy level of the entire organization increases when managers are optimistic and hopeful. The ability to empathize with others and to manage interpersonal relationships also contributes to motivation and inspiration because it helps managers create feelings of unity and team spirit.

(continued)

Perhaps most importantly, emotional intelligence enables managers to recognize and respect followers as whole human beings with feelings, opinions, and ideas of their own. Empathy allows managers to treat followers as individuals with unique needs, abilities, and dreams. Empathic managers can use their social skills to help followers grow and develop, see and enhance their self-image and feelings of self-worth, and help meet their needs and achieve their personal goals.

As demonstrated in these applications of emotional intelligence, mastering interpersonal skills is often more critical for managerial success than IQ. Recent behavioral research indicates that people with high emotional intelligence, that is, self-awareness, empathy, impulse control, and social deftness, are stars in the workplace whose relationships flourish. Lack of emotional intelligence, on the other hand, can ruin relationships and sabotage careers. The good news is that emotional intelligence is not fixed at birth and it can be nurtured and strengthened in families, schools, and even the kind of executive training described in these vignettes.[46]

CHAPTER SUMMARY

Executives emphasize the critical importance of interpersonal skills in achieving organizational objectives and managerial success. A good starting place for improving your competence in interpersonal relations is to understand the personality factors that influence them. These include things like self-concept, frame of reference, defenses, feelings, and need compatibility. Successful managers and executives also know the importance of emotional intelligence. Emotional intelligence encompasses many specific factors; however, the ability to develop positive interpersonal relationships ranks high in skills desired for most firms. Additionally, it is important to recognize that emotional intelligence is not a fixed amount or number. Rather, emotional intelligence is something individuals can improve. Sometimes where interactions take place determines how effective they are. Job requirements determine the depth and range of possible interpersonal relationships. Some jobs require that people work closely together in tight quarters and with a high degree of interaction, while other jobs require only distant contact on relatively independent tasks. Another factor that determines how people interact emotionally is organizational culture. In some organizations, openness, trust, personal ownership, and the ability to take risks are cultural values. The prevalent organizational culture will dictate how people interact on an emotional level, influencing the level of trust and intimacy. Other factors affecting how people relate are their degrees of openness in sharing information, their preferred behavioral styles, their comfort level in expressing emotions, and their tendencies to deceive one another.

How much a person knows about themselves and how much they share with others impacts others' perceptions of these individuals. Some people know a lot about themselves but choose to disclose little, while others are just the opposite. People also exhibit different behavioral styles. Some people are very "driving," while others are expressive, analytical, or amiable in their style. Additionally, men and women have specific differences in relating strengths, interaction preferences, and reactions to social-sexual behavior.

Personal Skills Inventory

Since one of the biggest challenges managers face in the global work environment today is successfully managing interpersonal relations with different types of people in organizations, mastering interpersonal relations skills is of paramount importance. You can be more effective in developing and maintaining productive interpersonal relations if you remember to apply the following interpersonal skills.

1. **Focus on self-awareness.** Being aware of what you are feeling allows you to guide your own actions so that you can interact effectively with others. If you are able to recognize a mood or feeling, rather than suppressing or denying it, you can consider how it affects you. Then, instead of reacting spontaneously, you can choose how to act appropriately to maintain the relationship and get the results you want from others.

2. **Practice empathy.** Put yourself in the other person's shoes. What are his or her feelings, objectives, and past experiences? Try to see the situation from the other person's frame of reference.

3. **Be aware of defensiveness: Yours and others.** Defensiveness occurs when you protect yourself by denying, excusing, or rationalizing your actions to protect your self-concept against the threat of being damaged by failure, guilt, shame, or fear. The problem is that all defense mechanisms involve a degree of distortion of reality. So you need to be aware of your own and others' defense mechanisms. Then you can avoid doing things that promote defensiveness in others. You will also be better prepared to recognize and avoid defensive reactions in yourself.

4. **Determine interpersonal relationship needs and modify your behavior appropriately.** The degree of compatibility between two or more people's needs for inclusion, control, and affection can make the difference between a happy and productive team and a dissatisfied and ineffective one. First determine differences in interpersonal needs and then adapt your own behaviors to let others satisfy their needs. This consideration will enhance your relationships with them.

5. **Maintain regenerative interaction climates.** Try to always promote "win-win" relationships where people are motivated to help each other grow and cooperate for their mutual benefit. Stress owning responsibility for problems so that people want to understand each other and learn from mistakes. Make sure that risks associated with trying new behaviors are low so that people are free to be creative and innovative.

6. **Develop high trust levels.** You earn trust by encouraging others to make themselves vulnerable to you by self-disclosing personal information and learning that they will not be hurt by you when they do. To build trust with others, understand and honor their needs and priorities. Second, show kindness and be courteous. Third, keep your commitments. Fourth, clarify your expectations. Fifth, show personal integrity by keeping promises, being honest, fulfilling expectations. Sixth, apologize sincerely when you violate others' trust without rationalizing or trying to shift some of the blame.

7. **Self-disclose to others.** In order to know you and be involved with you, others need to know who you are and what you need. For that to happen, you have to share how you perceive, think, and feel. Without self-disclosure, you cannot form a meaningful relationship with another person.

8. **Solicit feedback from others.** To determine how you come across to others and learn about your interpersonal strengths and weaknesses, it is necessary to ask others to provide you with feedback. This won't happen automatically, especially from subordinates. So you need to request constructive feedback from significant others to improve your own effectiveness and your relationships with them.

9. **Practice behavioral flexibility.** Adapt your preferred style of interacting to meet the needs and preferences of others. By treating others the way they want to be treated you will avoid alienation and build positive relationships.

Key Terms and Concepts

behavioral style, *347*

defense, *337*

degenerative interaction patterns, *342*

emotional intelligence, *331*

interpersonal effectiveness, *344*

Johari window, *345*

personal frame of reference, *336*

reciprocity, *335*

regenerative interaction patterns, *342*

self-concept, *336*

self-disclose, *344*

trust, *342*

value system, *336*

Critical Thinking and Discussion Questions

1. Why are interpersonal relationships in the workplace important? What are some relationships you have had that affected your productivity and satisfaction positively? Negatively?

2. What is emotional intelligence? Do you feel you have a strong emotional intelligence? What steps can you take to strengthen your emotional intelligence?

3. What is your present self-concept? Describe times when you had a diminished self-concept and what caused it. Have you experienced an inflated self-concept? Describe what happened.

4. Describe a negative relationship you have had with someone in terms of the A-B model. Do the same for a positive relationship. What are the key differences between the factors in each situation?

5. Describe a relationship with someone in whom you place great trust. What conditions create and maintain that trust? Describe a relationship with someone in whom you place little trust and the conditions that created it. What are the differences between the trusting and distrusting relationships?

6. What is your behavioral style? How does it influence your relationships with other people at work, at school, and in your personal life? How can your knowledge of behavioral styles be applied to improve your relationships in these different settings?

7. What are the main relationship differences between females and males? Think of your most important relationship with a male and a female. How do the different relating preferences affect you specifically in these relationships?

8. Draw a Johari window with the four quadrants reflecting your personal degrees of self-disclosure and solicitation of feedback. How does your Johari window influence your relationships with others?

Personal Skills Exercise

Comparing Interpersonal Needs

Preparation   Complete the Your Turn exercise—*What Are Your Relationship Needs* assessment—presented earlier in this chapter. Then form discussion groups of three to six.

Time   30 to 60 minutes (depending on size of the discussion groups).

Activity   Share your scores with others in your small group and discuss the implications for your interpersonal relationships according to the following questions. (10 to 15 minutes for each student.)

1. Examine your scores on each need category as they relate to each other. Your highest scores indicate which interpersonal needs probably dominate your relationships with others. How well do these scores describe your interpersonal behavior in the various aspects of your life?

2. How do the other people in your group react to your scores in terms of how they experience you?

3. Examine how different you are relative to others on the six different interpersonal need scores. How are these differences perceived by others?

4. Your scores are also good indicators of how others are likely to react to you. Compare your scores to others in your group.

   a. Who are you compatible with, that is, one person wants what the other expresses?

   b. Who are you incompatible with, that is, one person expresses something another does not want, or both parties express the same thing (for example, if you have control, or neither wants something that is necessary, such as control)?

   c. What happens when two people emphasize the same need (for example, affection), as opposed to situations where they emphasize different needs (for example, control versus affection)?

5. Discuss the implications of your interpersonal needs for inclusion, control, and affection for you as a manager.

6. Reflect back on the previous discussion with your group members. Do you behave in ways that you want to change? Share the changes you propose and see how others react.

Team Exercise

Getting to Know You: Connecting by Rubber Bands

Preparation   Requires a room with space to move about freely.

Time   35 to 40 minutes.

Activity 1   All members of the class stand up and silently mill around greeting each other nonverbally. After you have greeted everyone (about 3 minutes) you nonverbally choose a partner for activity 2.

Activity 2   Stand about 2 feet apart facing your partner. Put your hands out in front of you, almost touching the hands of your partner. Pretend that your hands are connected by rubber bands and that you are facing your partner in a mirror. Nonverbally move your hands around in a creative way (3 to 5 minutes).

Activity 3   Stay in your hand-mirroring position. Now pretend that your feet are also connected by rubber bands. Again, nonverbally move your hands and feet around. Be creative: See if you can move around the room, encounter other dyads, and so on (3 to 5 minutes).

Activity 4   With your partner, nonverbally choose another dyad. Sit down together and share what you learned about your partner from participating in activities 1, 2, and 3 with the other dyad. Rotate sharing until all are finished (10 minutes); then discuss the following questions in your group (15 minutes):

1. Who invited the other to be his or her partner? What did you learn about needs for including or being included about yourself and your partner?

2. What did you learn about your own and your partner's need for control from how your movements were initiated in the hand and feet mirroring?

3. Was there reciprocity with your partner, or did one person take charge?

4. What kind of behavioral style do you think your partner has from sharing this exercise with him or her?

5. What else did you learn about yourself and your partner?

CLOSING CASE

The Bill and Mary Show: Bendix to Morrison Knudsen[47]

Mary Cunningham was a hot topic at Bendix Corporation long before September 1980, when Bill Agee stood before more than 600 employees and denied that her rapid advancement had anything to do with "a personal relationship that we have." Cunningham joined the company in the previous June as executive assistant to the CEO, Bill Agee, after a three-hour interview in New York at the Waldorf-Astoria. "A meeting of kindred spirits," she said. Exactly one year later, Agee gave her a bigger title—vice president for corporate and public affairs. Three months after that came the promotion to vice president for strategic planning. Agee tried to confront the uproar that immediately followed by announcing to employees that his new vice president and he were "very, very good friends" but not romantically involved. The comment backfired, creating a national media furor so intense and so focused on Cunningham's youth, blond hair, and shapely figure that in the fall of 1980 the Bendix board of directors forced her resignation.

Inside Bendix, gossip about the relationship between Cunningham and Agee began to reach a crescendo after her June promotion, and all sorts of things helped keep the noise level up. A TV camera focusing on former President Gerald Ford at the Republican National Convention happened to find Agee and Cunningham sitting next to him. Some Bendix people suggested that Agee was less accessible than he had once been, and Cunningham's growing influence with him did not help to allay suspicions. She had called herself his "alter ego" and "most trusted confidante"; he said she was his "best friend." Then in August, Agee and his wife of 25 years divorced so quickly it surprised even top officials at Bendix.

Top corporate executives in the United States had been accused of almost everything imaginable except having romances with one another. But, what was one to think? Here were two young, attractive, unattached people working together, traveling together, even staying in the same two-bedroom suite at the Waldorf Towers. They had to be having an affair—and that would explain Cunningham's sprint up the ranks. Or was Cunningham, as Gail Sheehy portrayed her in a four-part newspaper series, a brilliant, idealistic corporate missionary destroyed by jealous cynics? Barbara Walters interviewed Cunningham, and feminist leaders like Gloria Steinem rallied to her defense asking if this meant that young, talented, attractive, ambitious, and personable female executives were permitted only slow climbs upward, lest they invite gossip?

Insisting that their relationship had been platonic until after she left Bendix, Agee and Cunningham married in June 1982. By then, Agee had converted to Catholicism and divorced his wife of 25 years. Cunningham's six-year marriage to Howard Gray, a black executive with American Express, was annulled. The same year, after resurfacing as a vice president at Seagram's, Cunningham acted as Agee's unpaid adviser during Bendix's attempted takeover of the Martin Marietta Corporation. But their ambitious plan collapsed when Bendix was swallowed by the Allied Corporation in a merger that cost hundreds of Bendix employees their jobs. The fiasco was blamed, in part, on the chair's young wife, the strategic planner.

The couple escaped to Cape Cod and started a small venture capital firm. In 1983, Mary Agee founded the Nurturing Network, a nonprofit organization that helps single working and college-age women with unplanned pregnancies. In 1988, Bill Agee was named CEO of the Morrison Knudsen Corporation in Boise, Idaho.

In 1994 Morrison Knudsen (MK) posted losses of $310 million and lurched toward bankruptcy. In February 1995, Bill Agee was ousted as MK stock fell from $30 a share to $5½; employees and retirees alike watched their futures evaporate. In February, too, Mary Agee resigned as executive director of the nonprofit Morrison Knudsen Foundation, a position critics say she used to benefit the Nurturing Network. Once more, the Agees were at the center of a corporate ethics controversy—and this one seemed no less vitriolic than the last.

The Boise community has not regretted the Agees' demise. It wasn't only the shareholders' losses and the hundreds of MK workers Bill Agee fired, but the fact that the Agees rubbed Boise the wrong way—almost from the start. So much so that after being excluded from the town's private clubs and most prestigious boards, the couple and their two children abruptly relocated three years ago to a $3.4 million estate in Pebble Beach, California. From that Pacific Coast setting, 600 miles away from their offices, Mary Agee managed her charity and Bill Agee ran MK by phone, fax, and FedEx, and from a $17 million corporate Falcon jet that peeved MKers dubbed "Mary's taxi."

Now, with more than a dozen lawsuits filed by shareholders, charging that Bill Agee and the MK board wasted assets and managed the company recklessly, Mary Agee's role is under legal as well as public scrutiny regarding the use of MK assets to benefit the Nurturing Network.

The lawyers are also eyeing the close relationship linking MK and its foundation with the Nurturing Network—a complex web of friendships, business interests, and moral commitments. In 1992, half the MK board members had wives on the Nurturing Network board, while Bill Agee served on both boards. "Once so many of the directors and their wives had joined with the Agees in . . . a moral crusade," the *New York Times* pointedly asked, "how likely was it that they would challenge Mr. Agee in the boardroom?"

Case Discussion Questions

1. Was Mary Cunningham/Agee unfairly victimized by a society suspicious that attractive women advance on their wiles, not their wits?

2. Is any 29-year-old fresh from business school, no matter how smart, qualified to be the chief planning executive of a multibillion-dollar corporation in the throes of a major restructuring?

3. Are the personal lives of Agee and Cunningham—or any other corporate officials—anybody's business?

4. Once such an embarrassing controversy surfaces, how should a corporation deal with it?

5. What ramifications do romantic relationships at work have for other organizational members and for organizational effectiveness in general?

6. What are the probable reasons people reacted as they did to the actions of Bill and Mary?

7. What mechanisms could organizations institute to avoid these kinds of problems?

8. What could Bill and Mary have done differently to avoid the negative outcomes?

WWW Exercise

Manager's Internet Tools

Web Tips: Emotional Intelligence on the World Wide Web The first part of this chapter examined the role and importance of emotional intelligence (EQ). Knowing the importance of EQ and an individual's understanding of his or her own EQ is not something to be taken lightly. As the business world increasingly becomes more competitive, the corporate search for the "best people" becomes a tighter and tighter race. Companies are now defining the best people as individuals who possess trustworthiness, integrity, honesty, leadership, and other qualities that build teamwork and strong interpersonal relationships. Sheer technical skills or IQ alone will not define success. Rather the ability to interact successfully with others and lead will define the best people.

General World Wide Web Search Exercise EQ.org (http://www.eq.org/) is a website established to further the understanding of what EQ is and the importance of EQ for success. This website contains some of the latest research articles written on emotional intelligence, definitions of emotional literacy, and suggestions for training to improve one's EQ. Check it out and find other sites using a search engine that deals with interpersonal relations.

1. From the EQ.org website, read some of the latest articles on EQ. What do these articles say or imply about the importance of EQ? How would you build these success factors into your work life?

Specific Website Exercise Q-Metrics (http://www.qmetricseq.com/) is a San Francisco–based international consulting firm specializing in developing and measuring human intelligence in the workplace. The firm works with organizations to help them better understand what human skills are present and how to further develop these skills to build leadership and competitive advantages. Their website provides further definitions of EQ and examples of how EQ is leading to more effective organizations through the creation of specific EQ competitive advantages.

2. According to a UCLA research study (listed on the Q-Metrics website), what percentage of leadership success is attributable to EQ versus IQ? What does this research imply for the future successful manager?

Video Case

Humor in the Workplace

Many of today's managers believe in the beneficial role of humor in the workplace. Humor can be injected into organizations in many ways—from hiring humor consultants at Price-Waterhouse to the Gang of Fun at Ben and Jerry's Ice Cream to humor rooms at Eastman-Kodak. Executives from each of these companies believe that interjecting fun into an often stressful work environment is an investment in their companies' human assets. Enabling employees to have fun at work can relieve stress and enhance creativity and productivity. These managers know that effective organizations start with effective people and that by employing a human resources development thrust, the investment in people ultimately results in better-quality products, improved processes, and enhanced organizational productivity. This approach is consistent with the assumptions of Theory Y, which assumes that workers are creative and motivated and need the proper organizational environment to thrive.

Does humor in the workplace always lead to greater productivity? Not necessarily. Managers should use the contingency approach to determine the circumstances under which the use of humor will lead to desired results. But, when workplace fun is used appropriately, even a group of Elvis impersonators can help to create an atmosphere of learning and creativity!

Video Case Discussion Questions

1. Is humor in the workplace appropriate in all situations? Use the contingency approach to support your point.

2. How might humor help organizations overcome problems associated with conflict and stress in the workplace?

3. Do you think human resource development strategies such as humor consultants, humor rooms, and "fun gangs" would have a positive impact on employee creativity? Why or why not?

Cases

TRYING TO DO BUSINESS IN MEXICO, GRINGO STYLE

Ted Dorman was looking forward to his new assignment as plant manager at a newly formed American-Mexican joint venture in Guadalajara, Mexico. The American company, Sterling Metal, produced hardware and decorative fixtures for furniture manufacturers in the United States and Mexico. The new joint venture was an attempt to lower labor costs by operating in Mexico.

Ted had worked at Sterling Metal since graduating from college with a degree in accounting. He had worked his way up in the company through accounting, and eventually shifted his career focus to production. Ted found the challenges of managing the production function very interesting, and he was successful in this area. His position at the new company, SterMexicana, would be a promotion for him, and he looked forward to the opportunity of building a new company.

Although Ted had not worked outside the United States before, he felt confident that his managerial abilities would transfer "south of the border." He and his wife enjoyed vacationing in Cancun and they both liked Mexican food, so the idea of spending a few years building a new company in Mexico appealed to him. Ted's wife, Kim was not as excited about the move, since she and their two small children would have to leave family and friends. Kim would also probably not be working in Mexico, as she had done in the United States.

Before the move, both Ted and Kim read travel books on Mexico and visited Guadalajara to select suitable housing. While Kim had reservations about the move, she felt that it would be a good opportunity for Ted and that she and the children would learn to adapt to their new surroundings. After all, she reasoned, they were only planning on living in Mexico for two years; just long enough for Ted to get the plant up and running and profitable. None of the Dorman's spoke Spanish fluently; however, Kim thought that she could get by, since she had taken three years of Spanish in high school. She had heard that Guadalajara was home to a large expatriate community, and that she could isolate herself and the children from Mexican culture if she felt the need. Ted would be working with English speakers mostly, and many people at the plant could do translating for him. A number of SterMexicana managers had been to the United States and were familiar with its culture. Ted and Kim concluded that cultural adaptation would not be difficult, and no matter how hard the assignment, its short duration was manageable.

When the family arrived in Guadalajara, Manuel Angel Menendez Mata met them at the airport. Manuel would be Ted's Mexican counterpart, acting in the official capacity of assistant plant manager, and unofficially as a cultural mentor. Ted and Kim were surprised by the warmth and friendliness of Manuel and his wife Adriana, and they felt very welcomed by their new Mexican friends. Over the next few days Manuel and Adriana helped the new expatriates get settled in and familiar with their new home. Ted appreciated the personal attention Manuel was giving him and his family; however, Ted was anxious to begin discussing the needs of the new business. It sometimes seemed to Ted that Manuel didn't care to discuss the business or that he was very excited about the new opportunity. Manuel seemed more interested in showing Ted and his family the city and discussing its history, politics, and culture.

Once the Dorman family had settled in, Ted was able to turn his attention toward the business. He had many matters to attend to, including a review of the preliminary work Manuel had done in securing the facility, hiring a work force, and establishing an organizational structure. Manuel explained what he had done and how it would work well. He predicted that the new plant would be fully functional in less than two weeks. Ted was very impressed with Manuel's work and looked forward to the opening of the plant.

During their many conversations, Ted felt that Manuel was very friendly and polite, but that he was a bit too formal and not very relaxed. Manuel wore a suit and tie, even when Ted told him that a more casual form of dress would be appropriate. Ted stated that he had no intention of ever wearing a tie the whole time he would be in Mexico. Manuel sometimes referred to Ted as "Mr. Dorman," even though Ted had instructed him to call him by his first name. During their meetings with outside business associates, Ted noticed that Manuel was even more formal. Manuel, who had visited the United States many times and spoke English very well, understood that Americans were more relaxed when it came to such matters, but he was not happy when Ted began to call him "Manny." Manuel was also unhappy with Ted's refusal to recognize his title, "Licenciado" (licensed one), and that he sometimes referred to him as Senor Mata.

Although things seemed to be progressing toward the opening of the plant, Ted began to worry that Manuel's estimate of when the plant would be functional was too optimistic. Manuel insisted that everything was on schedule and that there would be no problems. It did, however, become obvious as the days went by that the plant was not going to be ready, as Manuel had promised. Ted felt that he had been misled by

Manny and that he would have to explain to his superiors back in the U.S. why the plant was not going to open on schedule. Manuel finally admitted that some problems had developed with work permits, but he assured Ted that the plant would be operational in an additional week's time. The plant finally opened, five weeks past the scheduled date.

This delay had caused tension between Manuel and Ted, and Ted felt that he could not trust Manuel. Manuel felt that Ted was too impatient, and that he was not sensitive enough to the problems sometimes found in conducting business in Mexico. Manuel complained to a friend that Ted was trying to do business in Mexico, "gringo style." He offered as an example the failed attempt Ted had made to establish a business relationship with a new supplier. Manuel had arranged for a business lunch between Ted, himself, and representatives from a well- respected metals supplier. Manuel explained how Ted offended the Mexican businessmen by attempting to get down to business quickly. The supplier's representatives felt that Ted was too concerned about business matters, especially price, and that he was rushing to close a deal. They were also offended when Manuel offered to take the visiting businessmen on a tour of the city and show then some important cultural sites and Ted refused to come along. Ted later told Manuel that he felt that the suppliers were not really serious about getting SterMexicana's business, and that, if they wanted to do business with the company, they would have to send only one representative to his office with samples and a price list. Ted told Manuel that he would no longer spend hours discussing politics, sports, and history without any consideration given to the actual business deal.

The plant had been functioning for about six months without any serious problems when Ted received word from corporate headquarters that the plant needed to improve its efficiency. The quality of the product was considered acceptable, however, the American managers were disappointed with the productivity of the plant. Sterling's main incentive for investing in Mexico was the desire to reduce its labor costs and improve its overall operational efficiency. Ted worried that his career mobility was in serious jeopardy if he did not make major improvements. With this in mind, Ted began to look more carefully at Manuel's work.

From the beginning Ted had turned over to Manuel the day-to-day responsibility for running the plant, but he now felt that he would have to intervene and make some significant changes. After analyzing the situation Ted concluded that three major changes should be made. He proposed to Manuel that an incentive pay system be introduced, that a more participative approach to decision making be implemented, and that a number of workers be fired.

The productivity level of the plant was considered low by American standards, and Ted felt that there was simply no incentive for workers to do more than the minimum level of work. He proposed a pay-for-performance plan in which workers would essentially be paid on a piece-rate basis. The workers would also be given more responsibility for planning and organizing their work, and, in some cases, even planning their own schedules. Ted felt that a more flexible scheduling system would eliminate the excessive time off requested by many workers to handle family matters. Ted also created a list of the lowest-performing workers and instructed Manuel to fire all of them immediately. Since the unemployment rate was much higher in Mexico than in the United States, Ted reasoned that he would have no problem replacing the workers.

Manuel was stunned by what he was hearing from Ted. Manuel was upset, first, that Ted had chosen to invade his areas of responsibility, and he was further upset by Ted's recommendations. Manuel felt that Ted was being too aggressive and insensitive in labor relations matters, and that his recommendations would not be successful in Mexico. He told Ted that there would be problems with these proposed changes; however, Ted did not seem to want to listen.

Although Manuel did not agree with the recommendations, he did as Ted had instructed and began by firing some of the employees Ted had targeted as low performers. He then implemented the pay-for-performance plan and attempted to explain how it would work. Most workers felt confused by the complex, flexible working-hours plan, which involved basic quotas, a two-tiered pay system, and a time borrowing option, which could be used for personal time off, such as doctor's appointments. Manuel simplified the plan so that workers could go home when they had met their quota, or they could continue to work for additional compensation at a slightly lower per-unit rate. Ted felt that workers would be willing to work longer hours even at a reduced rate if their total compensation would rise. After all, he reasoned, "Mexico is a dirt-poor country and people really need money." Finally, Manuel told the plant supervisors about the plan to empower factory workers and allow them some of the decision-making authority that the supervisors had exercised in the past.

Ted had high hopes that his recommendations for change would produce significant improvements at SterMexicana. He was aware that Mexican culture was different from his; however, he felt that business activities were for the most part universal and that efficiency was not a cultural issue. Ted felt that the proposed changes would result in an immediate improvement in overall operating efficiency.

Slowly, however, Ted began to realize that problems were developing with his recommendations. The first problem he confronted was notification that severance pay would have to be paid to the employees he had recently fired. Ted was unaware, and Manuel did not mention, that Mexican law does not operate the same way as U.S. law, in which workers are considered to be hired at will and subject to at-will termination. Ted was also surprised to learn that not all the employees he had targeted for termination had, in fact, been fired. After investigating the situation further, he discovered that five of the employees whom he had instructed to be fired were still working for the company. Ted was shocked to learn that the five employees were close relatives of Manuel. When confronted with this fact, Manuel just shrugged his shoulders and told Ted that he could not bring himself to fire them.

Although Ted was upset with Manuel's insubordination, he was far more concerned with the lack of any productivity gains at the plant. He was told that most workers did complete their tasks more quickly under the incentive plan; however, they elected to go home rather than work additional hours for more money. Ted was confused by this behavior so he asked some of the supervisors to explain it. They didn't provide satisfactory answers so Ted decided that he should conduct interviews with the employees themselves. Working through an interpreter, Ted asked workers about their jobs and what he could do to make them more productive. He was frustrated by the lack of responses he was getting from the employees. When Ted probed more deeply he discovered that the supervisors had not implemented the participative management practices he had ordered.

Faced with poor operating results during the first year of operation, Ted wondered if the decision to take the job in Mexico had been a mistake. To make matters worse, Ted's family was very unhappy about living in Mexico. Ted had been working long hours at the plant and had basically discounted the complaints he had heard from his wife and children. At this point he began to feel that perhaps they were right in their frequent criticisms of Mexican culture. With over a year left in his assignment in Mexico Ted felt frustrated and wondered what he should do next.

Discussion Questions:

1. What mistakes did Ted make in his management of SterMexicana?
2. Is Manuel responsible for any of the difficulties presented in the case?
3. What should Ted do now to correct the situation?

Sources: R. Malat, <u>Passport Mexico</u>. San Rafael, CA: World Trade Press, 1996; P. Beamish, A. Morrison, and P. Rosenweig, <u>International Management</u>. Chicago: Irwin, 1997; R Sanyal, <u>International Management: A Strategic Perspective</u>. Upper Saddle River, NJ: Prentice Hall, 2001; J. Scarborough, <u>The Origins of Cultural Differences and Their Impact on Management</u>. Westport, CT: Quorum, 2001.

Case prepared by Charles A. Rarick

ED'S BIG CAREER MOVE

As his plane lands at the Santa Maria International Airport in San Jose, Costa Rica, Ed Moore reassures himself that he made the right decision in accepting his first international assignment in this Central American country. The new job will be a promotion, the first time Ed will be entirely responsible for an entire plant, and it will give him international experience, which he hopes to use to continue his advancement in the company.

Ed Moore has worked for his present employer, Jestin Apparel, for 16 years. Ed is viewed as a loyal employee and he prides himself on the fact that he has worked for Jestin longer than he has been married to his wife, Susan. Susan and their two children (Eddie, age 10, and Jessie, age 13) are not as enthusiastic about the idea of living in Turrialba, a rather isolated town about a two-hour drive from San Jose. Although Turrialba is in a beautiful area of the country and offers abundant hunting and fishing opportunities for Ed, Susan worries about the ability of the children to adapt to the isolation. In fact, since the children do not speak Spanish, it will be necessary for Eddie and Jessie to attend school in San Jose, which requires a long bus ride daily. Both Ed and Susan want their children to become "citizens of the world" and they both feel this opportunity may be good for personal development. Although the family vacationed in Europe once before, their international experience was very limited and none of the Moore family members speak another language.

Ed will be the new plant manager for the Costa Rican manufacturing facility of Jestin. This plant sews together pre-manufactured garments and exports the finished product back to the United States. The previous plant manager relocated to San Salvador to open a new, larger facility for Jestin. Most of the 230 employees are young females, although a number of young men and older women are also employed at the plant. The workers receive an hourly wage which is considerably higher than the average wage in Costa Rica. By most reports the workers are happy with their jobs at Jestin. Turnover at the plant is mainly due to young women getting married and starting a family, or young men moving to the capital for better wages.

Although the quality and efficiency of the plant are considered acceptable by management, Ed has been instructed to try and improve both areas. Ed is known as a rather tough manager, who feels that the best way to motivate employees is through a combined program of threats and incentives. Corporate management felt that Ed's somewhat autocratic style of management would be effective in Costa Rica.

Susan was employed in the United States as an assistant human resources manager, even though she had no formal training in that area. She enjoyed her job and she was hoping that she would be able to work in Costa Rica in a similar capacity. The Turrialba plant already had a bilingual HR manager who was familiar with Costa Rican labor laws and regulations; however, it was felt that perhaps Susan could first learn Spanish and then assist the HR manager. Ed's salary as plant manager will be more than their combined incomes in the United States, and the family will be provided with free housing, a maid, and company provided transportation. The family will live in extreme luxury by local standards.

As the plane touches down in San Jose, Ed remembers the trip the family made to Costa Rica three months earlier. The company had sent the family to Costa Rica to preview the country and to acquaint them with Costa Rican culture. The Moore's enjoyed the cultural tours and the whitewater rafting experiences, however; the children still protested against the move. Leaving friends in the United States is not easy, and they know that they will be giving up the comforts they have become accustomed to in the United States. Ed hopes the assignment will only be for a couple of years, although no plans have been made for his repatriation back to the United States.

As the plane comes to a halt at the gate, Susan looks at Ed and the worry in her face tells him that not all the Moore's are confident that the decision was a good one.

Discussion Questions:

1. What stress factors will Ed and his family likely encounter in this new assignment?
2. How significant a factor will family happiness be when it comes to Ed's success in this new job?
3. How do you think the Costa Rican employees will respond to Ed's management style?
4. Was Ed the best choice for the position? What criteria should be used in selecting expatriates?
5. What could Jestin do to increase the probability that this international assignment will be successful?

Case prepared by Charles A. Rarick.

AU REVOIR, MRS. WILLIAMSON

Margaret Williamson, age 50 has just returned to London from Paris, where she worked for the past six months as a marketing specialist for a British and French joint venture called EUROi. British computer manufacturer RoyalPC formed the joint venture with a French ISP called Internet du France (IDF). The two companies hope to capitalize on their particular strengths and grow a Pan-European Internet service. EUROi competes in Europe on the basis of price, and has positioned itself as an alternative ISP in an already crowded market. EUROi targets the 16 to 24 year-old market by offering programming that appeals to a more youthful market. The company also offers subscribers sizable discounts on Royal personal computers.

Margaret began her career at Royal fifteen years ago as a secretary. As a recently divorced mother of two, Margaret entered the work force for the first time and displayed a strong work ethic. Although she did not attend college, Margaret is a very intelligent individual and a quick learner. These traits did not go unnoticed at Royal, and she was promoted out of the secretary pool and placed into the Marketing Department. Margaret advanced in the department, gaining a reputation for handling difficult assignments. With a strong devotion to her children and her work, she chose not to remarry. With her children now grown she became interested in an international assignment.

Her colleagues viewed Margaret as an effective manager. She was seen as fair to all, conscientious, a good decision maker, and very loyal to the company. Because of her abilities, she was selected to act as marketing liaison between her company and the French partner in the newly formed joint venture.

Mrs. Williamson, as she prefers to be called, is a refined British lady. She possesses excellent manners and prides herself on her personal composure. Her ability to remain calm and level-headed in tense situations would be challenged when she moved to Paris for her new assignment.

Georges DuPont, age 35 is director of marketing for EUROi. DuPont, a graduate of the prestigious Ecole Nationale d' Administration, comes from an elite French family. Somewhat of a renegade, Georges refused to work in the family business after college. He instead, found employment in a number of computer-related businesses. DuPont became fascinated with the creative side of the computer and Internet business. He had been at IDF for four years, and was highly regarded as an effective manager and creative promoter. As marketing director of the joint venture, DuPont was given the responsibility of working with Williamson to find a way to increase revenue for EUROi. DuPont prides himself on his literary and artistic skills and enjoys engaging others in verbal debate.

From the start of their working relationship, problems surfaced between Margaret and Georges. At first, small personal habits of the two seemed to cause friction. Margaret often remarked that Georges never smiled at her, and Georges called Margaret's personality as "interesting as a bottle of cheap California wine." Over the early weeks of the relationship, the situation deteriorated further. Margaret was convinced that Georges was an incompetent and lazy manager. She felt that Georges was too autocratic and did not delegate enough responsibility to lower levels in the organization.

Margaret further complained to her superiors back in London that Georges frequently broke company policy, canceled meetings with little notice, took two-hour lunch breaks, and never admitted his mistakes. She felt that he did not respect her as an equal partner; in fact, she felt that he actually resented her help in promoting the joint venture.

To add more tension to the already strained relationship, Margaret learned that Georges (a married man) was having an affair with his secretary, Giselle. This fact came to light when Margaret found out that the two of them were going to a resort in the south of France for three weeks of vacation. Margaret was offended by Georges's lack of morality, which included his affair with Giselle as well as his advances to other women in the company.

Georges was equally unimpressed with Margaret. He felt that she was uneducated, insensitive, and too concerned with money and company regulations. Georges frequently joked to others about the way in which Margaret dressed. He felt that she had no taste in fashion, and that this alone made her abilities in the company suspect. Georges was unhappy that Margaret forced everyone to communicate with her in English. Although she spoke little French and Georges and most others spoke fluent English, he resented this, nevertheless. When Margaret requested that she be referred to as "Mrs. Williamson," Georges just rolled his eyes and muttered something in French that Margaret did not understand. He seldom used either her first or last name in conversations with her.

The workplace tensions continued for some time, with Georges and Margaret frequently disagreeing and complaining about each other. It was known throughout EUROi that the two did not get along, and their strained interactions were often the butt of jokes around the company.

Georges tried to avoid Margaret as much as possible, which put her in the awkward position of having to go through Giselle to communicate with him. Margaret did not like to deal with Giselle because of her "illicit" behavior with her boss.

The situation finally came to a head when a creative team was to be assembled to design a large advertising campaign for EUROi. Margaret had already developed a plan to assemble the team and empower them with the responsibility of creating a more youth-oriented advertising theme. Margaret had identified five people whom she felt would be best suited for the project. Her plan was to allow these people to work independent of management in creating a new series of advertisements. Margaret felt that a more creative approach to promotion was needed, and she wanted this team to develop a breakthrough design for the promotional strategy.

When Margaret approached Georges with her idea, he refused to accept it. He told Margaret that he felt the current campaign was effective, but admitted that he could see a need for some improvement. Georges recommended that he solicit the advice of a few key people and that he create the new ad design. After all, he was the director of marketing for the new company. Margaret tried to explain to Georges why her plan was better, and that a similar approach had been successful with RoyalPC. Georges just stared at the ceiling, smoking his cigarette. Margaret wasn't even sure if he was listening to her.

After a few weeks of attempting to convince Georges that her plan was better, Margaret decided that she needed help from London. She arranged for a video conference call to be held between London and Paris, in which she and some senior managers at Royal would discuss the issue further with Georges. Margaret sent an e-mail message to Georges, informing him of the conference but received no response. After two days, she asked Giselle if her boss knew of the proposed meeting and if he could attend. Giselle just smiled and responded that he could attend the meeting, if he desired to do so. Margaret sent a memo to Georges indicating the date and time of the conference call and emphasizing the importance of his presence at the meeting.

On the day of the meeting, Margaret searched for Georges. Even though the meeting wasn't for a few hours, she wanted to make sure he would attend, and she thought that perhaps she could even get him to change his mind before the call took place. Giselle told Margaret that he would be in the office soon and that she would remind him of the meeting.

As the 1:00 PM hour for the meeting approached, Margaret was frantic. She phoned Giselle and demanded to know where Georges was and when he would be in the conference room. Giselle responded that she didn't know where he was and that she really didn't care. When Giselle rudely hung up the phone, Margaret was convinced that Georges would not show up for the meeting. She decided, however, that she might be able to use this to her advantage.

The call from London came precisely at 1:00 PM, with just Margaret sitting in the Paris office. She explained to the people in London that Georges was not present and that she had no idea why he was not there. She went on to tell the London managers that she was not surprised by Georges's behavior; he continually expressed contempt for her, and he had an apparent disregard for the welfare of EUROi. Margaret went on for over 30 minutes detailing Georges's shortcomings, when suddenly he entered the room with three other EUROi employees. Georges apologized for his tardiness but explained that he and the others had been across town working with marketing personnel from a very popular magazine targeted toward the 16 to 24 age group in Europe. Georges was very excited about what this "team" had accomplished, and he wanted the London managers to know the details.

The video call went on for another hour with the three EUROi employees explaining with charts and figures how the association with the youth magazine would be beneficial to the company. They proposed new creative advertising designs and an association with the popular magazine. The team appeared to have been well prepared for the meeting. Georges, who spoke with great confidence and enthusiasm, directed the entire presentation. From the questions asked by the London managers, it was clear that they felt Georges's plan was superior to the one proposed by Margaret. When the presentation was completed they thanked Georges and his team and quickly approved the plan.

At that point Margaret rose from her chair, red-faced and very angry. She appeared at first barely able to speak, but when she began, she angrily accused Georges of undermining her authority. Margaret called Georges a "sneaky bastard," and for the next five minutes vented her frustration at Georges, who sat quietly staring at the ceiling, smoking his cigarette.

Finally the most senior London manager interrupted Margaret and politely asked if Georges and his team could leave the room for a moment. Georges got up and began to leave, but before he left he stopped, smiled at Margaret, and said, "au revoir, *Mrs*. Williamson."

Discussion Questions:

1.   What role does culture play in the interpersonal difficulties found in this case?
2.   Who is more to blame; Georges or Margaret; for these difficulties?
3.   What advice would you give a British expatriate going to France?

Sources: N. Joseph, <u>Passport France.</u> Novato, CA: World Trade Press, 1997; and J. Scarborough, <u>The Origins of Cultural Difference and Their Impact on Management.</u> Westport, CT: Quorum, 1998.

Case prepared by Charles A. Rarick

A NAÏVE SAHAB IN INDIA

It was the opportunity of a lifetime, or so Brian Moseley thought, as he accepted a managing director position for Aspen Automotive's new acquisition in India. Aspen Automotive was a supplier to American automobile manufacturers. The company supplied various component parts for the American automakers, and the recent acquisition of an Indian brake-pad company was seen as a keen strategic move for the company. The Bindi Brake Company was an established manufacturer of automotive brake pads that supplied a few European car companies with a high-quality product. Competition in this market is fierce, and Bindi experienced difficulty in recent years competing with American and Japanese firms. Aspen thought it could capitalize on the experience and low costs of production found in the New Delhi operation, and it sent Brian Moseley, an experienced automotive engineer, to India in order to "make the Indians efficient."

Brian and his family quickly adapted to India. Although many expatriates from developed countries experience overwhelming culture shock, the Moseleys' assimilated well into the expatriate community of New Delhi. With the help of personal assistants and children in private schools, the Moseleys' could separate themselves from most of the challenges of everyday life in urban India. Although they sometimes missed some of the luxuries they had taken for granted back in the United States, they enjoyed the standard of living they were experiencing as privileged expatriates in India. Brian knew that his job responsibilities were to turn around the newly acquired Indian operation, and that if he did this within two years, he would be promoted and moved back to U.S. He felt that this assignment could greatly advance his career.

Managers at Aspen's corporate headquarters felt that the introduction of certain Western managerial practices would be beneficial to Bindi and improve overall efficiency and profitability. Brian was selected to direct the organizational change effort because of his past record of accomplishments in the U.S. and abroad. He had been successful in the turnaround of troubled parts-manufacturing plants in Louisville, Kentucky, and Toledo, Ohio. Additionally, he had worked internationally in Canada, Mexico, and Brazil. Aspen felt that his M.B.A. in management from Michigan State, coupled with his previous domestic and international experience, made him a suitable person to direct the Indian productivity improvement strategy.

Although Bindi produced reasonably high-quality brake components, and labor costs were exceptionally low, the overall efficiency of the operation was considerably below that of other Aspen plants. Top management felt that if the Indian operation could match the level of efficiency of even the least efficient American plant, the acquisition would be a success. After an initial plant visit, top management concluded that the plant was crippled with bureaucracy and that there was no incentive for exceptional performance. Aspen managers observed what they felt were too many Bindi employees drinking tea and socializing instead of working at a brisk pace. They were also shocked to find that no Bindi employee ever received a performance review and that pay for performance was never even considered by past management. Bindi employees were seldom discharged, even when they were clearly not well suited to their jobs and performed poorly. Pay increases and other rewards were administered on the basis of seniority. Employees were often hired, not based on their abilities or potential, but because they were related to a current employee of Bindi. The number of sick days and personal days requested was well above the average of the other Aspen plants.

Brian was directed to make the India subsidiary more like the rest of the Aspen corporate family. For the first three months, Brian did little more than observe and learn about Bindi's current managerial practices. He spoke with managers and employees alike, and made mental notes of the conversations. Brian identified employees whom he felt should be replaced and employees whom he felt had the greatest potential for advancement. After this initial three-month investigation, Brian met with his senior managers at Bindi and proposed that they collectively formulate a turnaround strategy. All of Bindi's managers were Indians and most had been educated in Indian universities. One manager, Rajan Patel, had studied in London and received a postgraduate diploma from the University of London in economics. Brian felt that Rajan was one of the most promising candidates for advancement, and he hoped that Rajan would take the lead in structuring the change management program.

Although Brian had hoped that the Indian managers would formulate a plan for change among themselves, he increasingly became frustrated after a month when no one came forth to recommend a plan. Brian suggested to the group that they consider changes such as pay-for-performance programs, annual performance reviews, management by objectives, and perhaps a 360-degree performance appraisal program. In his view, if the group emphasized performance appraisal, many of Bindi's efficiencies would disappear. Brian believed that most of the employees had the potential for great improvement, and that all they needed was a better system of management. A more scientific and objective approach to management, coupled with a more participative approach, would succeed in increasing the efficiencies and ultimate success of Bindi.

Over the next several months, Brian became increasingly dissatisfied with the progress of the Indian managers in coming up with any constructive plan for changing Bindi's managerial practices. Highly frustrated, he sometimes angrily criticized members of his managerial team in front of their subordinates. The relationship between Brian and the managers became increasingly strained; he was being referred to behind his back as "sahab" or "big boss." A throwback to the British colonial days, this term was used in some instances to refer to a manager who had little understanding of Indian culture.

One of Brian's biggest critics was Rajan Patel. Rajan often criticized Brian's managerial style as being too direct and forceful. On at least one occasion, Rajan referred to Brian's tactics as "culturally imperialistic," asserting that Brian was too immature to be the managing director. He was concerned that Brian was trying to change India's culture to fit an American model of management. Although educated in the West, Rajan did not feel that Indian employees were receptive to many Western managerial practices, which ran counter to basic Indian cultural values. He openly questioned Brian and Aspen's approach to changing the corporate culture of the Bindi Brake Company.

After seven months in India, Brian decided that if change were to occur, he would have to be the one to initiate that change. He called his senior managers into his office one morning and told them of the following changes that were to be effective immediately. First, Brian announced that C.P. Rao would replace Prakash Nur, the assistant plant director and the most senior manager. Rao was a young engineer, educated at an American university, and a person who Brian felt would be best able to implement his vision of change at Bindi. Second, Brian announced that performance appraisals would begin immediately and that at least two employees in each work group would be eliminated in the interest of organizational efficiency. Third, a new plan of 360-degree feedback would be implemented: Subordinates would evaluate their superiors, and annual compensation increases would be contingent on these reviews. No annual increases in compensation would be automatic, and all raises would now be based on merit. Finally, all personal assistants (chaprasi) would be fired and their responsibilities assumed by the managers themselves. Even though the salary expense of the personal assistants was small, Brian felt that it created an unnecessary level of administration, and no other Aspen unit allowed such positions.

At first, the Indian managers seemed stunned by Brian's mandates. No one spoke, and a dead silence filled the room. When Brian asked for feedback on his "recommendations," the managers looked down at the table in front of them and said nothing. Prakash, who got up and left the room, broke the silence. Later, a few of the managers politely told Brian that the ideas were too bold and too sudden a change for Bindi. Brian angrily responded that the change was long overdue and that anyone who would not go along with the new plan should leave the company.

Much grumbling was heard at Bindi over the next few days, as the managers announced the changes. Brian learned that Prakash had resigned and that Rajan was telling everyone about his dissatisfaction with Brian's managerial style. Brian decided to talk individually with all the managers, starting with Rajan. The meeting was less than cordial, and ended with Brian's warning Rajan that he'd "better come on board soon" or he too would be replaced. During subsequent meetings with all the Indian managers, Brian tried to convince them of the urgency and necessity of these proposed changes. At times, it seemed as if they agreed with him and he felt that change would finally occur. After all, when asked directly, no one actually refused to implement the changes.

After a week in which no changes were taking place, Brian reasoned that it might take a little longer than he thought due to cultural constraints. However, he worried that Rajan might be trying to sabotage the change effort. Brian kept a close eye on Rajan, and one morning he was told that Rajan would not be in the office for a week because his brother was getting married in Bombay. Brian was suspicious, checked the personnel records, and discovered that Rajan did not have any brothers. He waited for Rajan to return and then asked him where he had been. Rajan replied that he had attended the wedding of his brother in Bombay. Brian, outraged by the lie, immediately fired him on the spot. Rajan left without a word to Brian.

Although things seemed to be a bit tense at Bindi, Brian told himself that change is difficult and that the long-term consequences would be good for Aspen, Bindi, and India. He continued to quiz the managers on their progress in carrying out the change efforts, and was told that all changes were being implemented, as he had instructed. But further investigation revealed that no changes were being made. Brian called for another meeting of his managers and was shocked to learn that a number of them had decided to quit rather than attend the meeting. Included in the group who resigned were C.P. Rao, whom Brian was convinced would be a leader in making his vision of change a reality at Bindi. Brian sat alone in his office, wondering if change would ever come to the Bindi Brake Company.

Discussion Questions:

1. Evaluate the managerial style of Brian Moseley and explain how it fits with Indian culture. Be specific in identifying any mistakes Brian made in managing Indian workers.
2. Rank the following principals and justify the ranking in terms of responsibility for the lack of change at the Bindi Brake Company: Brian, Rajan, Aspen, the Indian manager.
3. What could each of the above-named principals have done differently to avoid this situation?
4. What should Brian do now?

Case prepared by Charles A. Rarick

PAULA KOBE'S HARASSMENT IN BRAZIL

ABSTRACT

A recent MBA graduate lands her dream job in Sao Paulo working as a consultant in the Brazilian office of an American company. While she finds the job and country to be very interesting, unexpected challenges, mainly sexual harassment, make the assignment too difficult to handle. The case explores cross-cultural gender roles and legal issues in international assignments.

The thought of being assigned to Brazil fresh out of her MBA program was a dream come true for Paula Kobe. Paula had been offered a job with Behavioral Management Systems (BMS) upon graduation from Duke University, where she graduated with an MBA in management. It was her dream to work abroad, and she was especially excited about the offer made by BMS to work in Brazil as a consultant. Paula had studied for a year in Portugal as an undergraduate student and was almost fluent in Portuguese. The assignment in Sao Paulo seemed to an ideal situation. Unfortunately, the assignment presented challenges she had not expected.

Paula Kobe worked four years after earning her undergraduate degree in engineering before attending graduate school. With the failure of her marriage, Paula felt that it was a good time to change her life, and she was seeking something new and exciting. Behavioral Management Systems was headquartered in Atlanta and had offices in Mexico, Venezuela, Chile, and Brazil. The company specialized in providing management and teamwork consulting, and also provided some consulting services in quality management. Paula would be providing Brazilian firms advice on achieving ISO 9000 certification and in improving the quality of their manufacturing processes. Her engineering background, coupled with her management training, made for a good fit in this area of consulting.

A New Life in Sao Paulo

BMS had offered Paula an attractive compensation package, one that would allow her to live quite well as an expatriate in Brazil. She was able to rent a large, luxury apartment in an upscale part of town and hire a maid/cook, something she had never thought she could afford. While the job responsibilities were of interest to her, and the compensation was appealing, Paula did realize that she would be giving up contact with her friends and boyfriend back in the United States. Adjusting to the culture of Brazil was not especially difficult for Paula. She had traveled abroad quite a bit, including vacationing in Rio de Janeiro, and she was somewhat familiar with Brazilian culture. BMS had allowed Paula two weeks to become familiar with Sao Paulo and the company before giving her any significant responsibility. During her first two weeks Paula learned about company policy, Brazilian business, and made many calls back to the United States. She had planned for her boyfriend to visit her in Brazil every month, and she would fly back to the U.S. every month, reducing the time apart to only two weeks. With a maid and someone to cook her food, international television, and an interesting job, Paula felt good about being in Brazil.

Rafael Scarado

After two weeks of orientation and getting to know the company, Paula was ready to be assigned to her work area. She would be working in the Quality Improvement Division and she would be reporting to Rafael Scarado. Rafael was the head of the smallest of BMS's divisions and was responsible for Paula's training. Although Paula had studied quality management at Duke, BMS had a proprietary system that all new employees had to learn and implement.

When Paula first met Rafael she concluded that, while he was a very pleasant man, his orientation towards women was typical of most Brazilian men. Paula thought that Rafael was too forward towards her and that she would have to gradually train him in how to treat women. For example, when they first met, Rafael immediately asked Paula how old she was and when Paula responded that she was 29, Rafael patted her on the cheek and said "such a baby." Rafael's English was very good since he had studied for four years in the United States and worked in Canada. Rafael grew up poor in the old capital of Brazil, Salvador, and was fortunate enough to earn a soccer scholarship to a small midwestern college in Illinois. A chance encounter with a soccer coach from a small college in Illinois was only the beginning of Rafael's luck. After college, Rafael was offered a position by a trustee of the college to work for an affiliate of the trustee's company in Canada. Rafael had studied mathematics and business administration in college, and the trustee felt that this background would be helpful in creating a new quality management program at the Canadian facility. Rafael had been a star soccer player in college and was quite good with interpersonal relations. The trustee liked Rafael and had confidence in his abilities. Rafael worked in Canada for three years before returning to Brazil. In Canada, Rafael met his wife and now lives with her in Sao Paulo with their three children.

Uncomfortable Encounters

One of the first things that Paula told her friends back in the U.S. about her job was the fact that her boss, Rafael would greet her in the morning with a kiss on the cheek. Paula knew that this was not uncommon in Brazil, nevertheless, it made her uncomfortable. She wanted to tell Rafael that she did not want him to greet her this way but she worried that he might be offended and so decided to put up with it for the time being. Rafael provided good conversation for Paula and her friends when Paula called them to recount her experiences in Brazil. Her friends began calling Rafael her "Latin lover." It appeared to Paula that Rafael had a romantic interest in her because he would spend much time asking her about her personal life and staring into her eyes. These long stares also made Paula uncomfortable. It appeared to Paula that Rafael was a caring person and an understanding trainer, but she worried that his attention and concern may be more related to his romantic interest in her. She felt that if she offended Rafael that he might not be as helpful in her career development.

As time progressed the level of discomfort began to increase. In addition to the good morning kiss, Rafael would touch Paula from time to time when making a point. He would put his hands on her shoulders, touch her arm, brush her hair, and hold her hand. Paula became increasingly troubled by Rafael's actions and decided that she should find a way of letting him know that this behavior was not welcomed. At one point Paula asked Rafael if his wife knew about your flirting at the office. Rafael just laughed and responded, "She knows how romantic Brazilian men can be." Mentioning his wife did not seem to have much effect on Rafael's behavior, so Paula thought she might have to come up with another approach. She wasn't sure what that would be, but she put it aside as she planned for the upcoming visit of her boyfriend.

A Visitor from America

Although Paula had planned on returning to the United States every two weeks, this plan proved impractical. The time required for travel and her busy training schedule were not compatible. It was decided that Paula's boyfriend, Shane, would visit her. Rafael had agreed to give Paula an extended weekend so the "two lovers could make up for lost time." Paula appreciated the understanding of Rafael, and she also hoped that he would get the message that she was involved with someone else and not interested in his advances.

Shane arrived in Sao Paulo and Paula could not wait to see him and tell him about her new life in Brazil. She wanted to show him around the country but the limited amount of time Shane could stay prohibited that from happening. The two explored Sao Paulo and discussed their future together. Throughout the visit Paula did not give a thought to Rafael and the problems she was having with him. On the last night of Shane's visit Paula finally mentioned, "The guy who is training me seems to be in love with me." This statement caught Shane's attention and he pressed for more details. Paula explained what Rafael would do that made her uncomfortable and Shane insisted that she tell him to stop, or that she tell Rafael's superior about "the sexual harassment." Paula told Shane not to worry and that it was "no big deal." She told him that Brazil was different from the United States and that she could handle it. Although Shane was worried, he had confidence in Paula's judgment and the issue was not discussed further.

Short Skirts Make for Good Business

Paula returned to BMS refreshed from her short vacation and ready to complete her training. She was looking forward to actually working with clients and getting out into the field. When she saw Rafael on her first day back, he kissed her on the cheek and asked her how she enjoyed the weekend. She responded that it was wonderful and she mentioned Shane by name many times. Rafael told her that he was surprised that she looked so rested. When asked why, Rafael told her "surely the two lovers spent the entire nights making love." Paula was embarrassed and not sure what to say so, she decided to change the conversation to a work matter.

After another week, Paula was ready for her first assignment. She and Rafael would be visiting the offices of a medium-sized manufacturer in hopes of landing a quality improvement contract. Paula was excited about the upcoming visit and prepared her part of the presentation with great diligence. Rafael coached her on some parts of the presentation and she felt confident that she was ready to make what amounted to a sales call on the client.

During the presentation Rafael played a dominant role. It appeared that he wanted to make it clear that he was in charge of the presentation. Since it was Paula's first presentation for BMS, she allowed Rafael to do most of the talking, and to interrupt her during her presentation. The client seemed very interested in what BMS could do for his company in terms of team building and continuous improvement efforts. Paula felt as if the presentation was a success. No contract was signed that day, however, Paula felt that BMS had made a good impression and that surely they would get the contract.

On the way back to the office, Rafael told Paula that she did a good job and that he would be relaying that information back to management. She praised her presentation skills and complimented her preparation. Rafael told Paula that he was confident that if she had just worn a shorter skirt they would have signed a contract immediately with the prospective client. Paula laughed, assuming that this was just another one of Rafael's attempt at humor, but Rafael was not laughing. When she asked him if he was serious, he replied that he was very serious. Rafael told Paula that he watched the client look at her, and that since she was "a very beautiful woman," she should use this to her advantage. In Rafael's words "short skirts make for good business in Brazil." Paula could not believe what she was hearing. She felt that Rafael was trying to exploit her, and that he really didn't care that she had an MBA and a skill set that was useful to her job.

The drive back to the office was an uncomfortable one with Paula remaining silent most of the time. Later that evening, when Paula called her friends back in the U.S., she told them about the incident and that she felt that Rafael was only interested in "pimping her out." Her friends suggested that she bring a charge of sexual harassment against Rafael and the company. Paula wasn't sure what to do. She wondered what would happen to her career if she protested Rafael's action, and she wondered if what he was doing was illegal. Paula thought about her job, her apartment and maid, and her head was spinning. She went to sleep that night anxious and pondering her next move.

This case was prepared by Charles A. Rarick

HANS AND WOLFGANG EXPERIENCE AMERICAN CULTURE

ABSTRACT

Two German expatriates are assigned to a newly formed strategic alliance with a company in the United States. They experience difficulty with American culture and the culture of the organization. Although they achieve some success in their assignment, the two men leave the company a year early and return to Germany. The case explores possible areas of conflict between German and American culture.

In an effort to gain a competitive advantage in the increasingly competitive information technology (IT) marketplace, Business Software Solutions, Inc (BSS) of Lexington, Kentucky and ABBA Deutschland of Stuttgart, Germany decided to form a strategic alliance. Both firms felt as if they could gain from the partnership by combining the narrow expertise and competitive advantage they had developed in their fields. Business Software Solutions was founded by Jim Gibson, a former professor of engineering at the University of Kentucky who developed a number of business applications software packages in an era when few existed. The company grew rapidly, and was very profitable from its inception. From basic software development, BSS has expanded more into serving the IT needs of medium and large-sized companies. ABBA Deutschland is a large German multinational company with a specialization in satellites and data transmission. ABBA is considered one of Europe's leading information and communications companies, yet it lacks the software development capabilities it needs and must subcontract much of this important function. It was felt that the creation of a partnership between BSS and ABBA would be beneficial to both firms, but that the partnership should begin slowly.

The Germans Arrive

It was decided that two technical managers from Germany would be assigned to the Kentucky company for a period of two years. Hans Reinhardt and Wolfgang Reinhardt (not related) were chosen to work at BSS in Lexington to help develop the strategic alliance. It was hoped that the two-man team could learn about BSS's software development process and act as a liaison between the two firms. Both Hans and Wolfgang were software engineers who graduated from the same prestigious technical university in Germany with a degree in software engineering. They both also attended Stuttgart Institute of Management and Technology and earned advanced degrees in information systems and management. As part of their academic studies, the pair completed an extensive internship at Cisco Systems GmbH. Both men were single and looked forward to living in the United States for the two year assignment. The boyhood friends loved to travel and hoped to see more of the United States during their short stay in the United States.

BSS provided Hans and Wolfgang with a furnished apartment. Because the two of them wanted to live together, BSS felt that they could provide more upscale living facilities. The apartment was in a luxurious complex 20 minutes from BBS headquarters. The two men also decided to lease one automobile, and they decided on a 7 series BMW. It seemed like the two-year stay would be very enjoyable for the two of them.

Hans and Wolfgang immediately began to impress the people at BSS. They were quite motivated and appeared to be technically very competent. After only one week at BBS, Hans was able to suggest an improvement in a software design that would save BBS a considerable amount of money. The two men appeared eager to make a large contribution to the strategic alliance. While their part was mostly technical, they were also to report back to Germany on the progress of the partnership.

Most of the employees at BSS found the Germans interesting. While the city of Lexington was diverse (at least for Kentucky) due to the fact that the University of Kentucky was located there and attracted more foreign-born residents, not many Germans lived there. While the employees of BSS were interested in the two men, not everyone found them likable. Many employees reported to Sam Sherwin, Hans and Wolfgang's supervisor and a member of middle management, that the men were "kinda stuffy" and that they "keep to themselves too much." Some of their co-workers resented the fact that the two men keep the doors to their offices closed while they were inside working. It appeared that they did not want to interact much with others.

While everyone at BSS was on a first name basis, Hans and Wolfgang always introduced themselves as "Reinhardt." Since they both had the same last name, this created some confusion. The two were given nicknames by one of the employees and those nicknames caught on quickly. Hans was called "Hands" and Wolfgang was called "Wolfie." While the two Germans responded to the nicknames, it sometimes appeared that they did not appreciate their new American names. Most BSS employees found Hans and Wolfgang to be pleasant, but they were not quite as friendly as most of the employees, who, were mostly from central Kentucky.

Hans and Wolfgang were assigned to work on a project with three American engineers. The project was directly related to the work BSS had been doing for ABBA on a contract basis. The software application for an advanced personal data transmission system had presented the engineers at BSS with many difficulties. With the help of the German engineers, especially Hans, the team was able to overcome the most significant difficulties and move the project mostly towards closure.

Assigned to Colin

Sam decided that Hans' early success should be leveraged into a new project being directed by Colin Corum. Colin had just graduated from the University of Kentucky with a degree in computer science and he was very young, however, Sam believed that Colin showed great promise. He had made a significant amount of money while still a college student working as an independent contractor for some of the biggest names in software design. Although it was rumored that Colin had made over a million dollars while a college student, the fact that he was working at BSS made others think that he may not be wealthy. Colin was offered jobs at more prestigious companies, however he wanted to remain in Lexington and this limited his opportunities.

When Sam approached Hans with the idea that he work with Colin on another, bigger project, Hans suggested that he and Wolfgang both be assigned to the project. Although Sam felt that Wolfgang could be better used elsewhere, he agreed, reasoning that the two men were insecure living and working in a new country. Hans and Wolfgang did not have much respect for Colin. They had interacted with him briefly on the earlier assignment and felt that he was not capable of leading a team of engineers.

Although only a few years separated Colin from the Germans, Hans and Wolfgang felt that Colin was very immature. They would be reporting to him and he would be reporting on their progress to Sam. Although the men felt uncomfortable with this assignment, they nevertheless agreed to Sam's suggestion.

Colin was a very talented software engineer, but some of his personal habits were a bit unconventional. For example, he frequently brought his dog to the office with him, an office that looked more like a sports memorabilia store, featuring his favorite team – the University of Kentucky basketball team. The office was very cluttered and his personal appearance was less than professional, at least from the eyes of Hans and Wolfgang. The two German's felt that Colin was too young and immature to be in such a responsible position. They had great respect for Sam, so they tolerated the quirks of Colin and tried to work with him.

Colin referred to the two men by their newly acquired nicknames, as did most BSS employees. He seemed to have some respect for Hans, but paid little attention to Wolfgang. As the days and weeks went by, Wolfgang began to miss work sporadically, complaining about allergies and bad headaches. Colin didn't seem to mind that Wolfie wasn't around and assigned more work to Hans. Hans didn't seem to mind the additional workload and defended Wolfgang whenever Colin made negative comments about Wolfgang.

Cultural Differences

Sam would on occasion stop by to see how the expatriates were doing, and perhaps sensed that things weren't going too well. He invited Hans, Wolfgang, and Colin to join him at an Irish pub near work for dinner and a night of drinking. The evening went well, at first. Sam asked Hans and Wolfgang to talk about Germany and how their country was different from the United States. Hans and Wolfgang also talked about how ABBA was different from BSS. At first the Germans appeared to be somewhat tense, especially Wolfgang, but as time went on all four men became relaxed and joked about many things. As Wolfgang drank more beer he became bolder and began to provide a "German perspective on America." He told some jokes about Americans and explained how Germans respected Americans, but felt that they were not very cultured, were undisciplined, and did not take a world-view, and instead thought everything resolved around the United States. Wolfgang also complained about the lack of respect many Americans had for society. He explained for example that "someone with a punk automobile and very loud music invades the personal space of others." It appeared that Colin did not appreciate the cross-cultural analysis provided by Wolfgang and made some derogative comments about Nazi's and World War II. Although there was some tension at times, the beer flowed freely; the men laughed, and it appeared, left the pub on good terms.

After about six months at BSS, Hans asked Sam if the two men could take a few days off. He told Sam that he and Wolfgang had some friends in Florida and they wanted to visit them. Sam told Hans that he would have to check with Colin since he was the project manager. When asked, Colin refused to grant the time off. Colin told Hans that he was about to assign him a very important part of the project they were working on and that it was important that the team show early progress. He told Hans that "if Wolfie picked up some of the slack" the team would be making more progress. Besides, he said, BSS was receiving a number of orders for software development from ABBA that they had not anticipated, and the firm would need both of them to work extra hours to help with the new business. Hans mildly protested, but Colin would not budge on his decision. After a discussion with Wolfgang, the two men decided to approach Sam about the time off request. Sam reaffirmed the need for everyone to work more hours but agreed to talk with Colin. After a short time, Sam told Hans and Wolfgang that they could take a Friday off and have a three-day weekend. The Germans thanked Sam and began planning their trip. They drove the next weekend to Florida, picking up two speeding tickets, and arrived at work the following Monday exhausted, and less than friendly.

Problems Continue

Tensions between Colin and Wolfgang continued, and it was clear to everyone at BSS that the two did not like each other very much. Sam felt that Wolfgang was a hard worker, but that he was not as talented an engineer as Hans. His personality was more stoic, and he was very formal and didn't smile very much. Sam had told Colin to work with Wolfgang in improving their relationship because the partnership was very important to BSS, and Hans was needed in the coming months to handle projects which no one at BSS was capable of doing.

With increased business coming in, it was clear that BSS would need more software engineers. Sam decided that it might be a good time to have a meeting with Colin, Hans, and Wolfgang to discuss how things were going, and to see about the possibility of bringing more ABBA engineers to BSS. Sam had already decided to hire more American engineers, but he also wanted to get ABBA engineers involved in the projects. The meeting was scheduled for 1 PM and Hans and Wolfgang arrived promptly. Sam entered the meeting room a few minutes later and the three men began talking. Hans told Sam that in Germany it is customary for employees to take an entire month off from work during the summer months. Sam chuckled and said that maybe he should be assigned to ABBA for a while. By 1:15 PM Wolfgang was beginning to appear upset. He kept looking at his watch and said nothing. A few minutes later he told Sam that he didn't know if he could work any longer with Colin. When Sam asked why, Wolfgang proceeded to list the many concerns he had about the young manager. Wolfgang told Sam that Colin was immature, that he didn't respect the education and training of Hans and himself, and that Colin was intentionally giving him work that was not challenging and that he knew Wolfgang would dislike. Hans said nothing but appear not to disagree with what Wolfgang was saying. At that moment, Colin arrived for the meeting. He apologized for being late, and explained that he was on the telephone with an important customer.

Sam thought that it might be a good idea not to discuss the tension between Wolfgang and Colin at this time and proceeded to talk about the upcoming workload. He explained to the three men how work orders were increasing, and that BSS would need o hire more engineers. Sam asked if ABBA would be willing to send additional engineers to Lexington. Both German men felt that it would be possible, and also a good idea to bring in more Germans. Hans volunteered to contact ABBA and make an informal inquiry about this possibility. The meeting ended without any further discussion of the tensions between Colin and Wolfgang.

Things continued as usual at BSS. The workload increased and tensions were sometimes high between Wolfgang and Colin. The Germans tried to enjoy their time in Kentucky by taking road trips on the weekends and making new American friends. Two additional engineers would be coming from ABBA and Sam felt that this addition might help reduce some of the difficulties between Colin and Wolfgang. Sam also increased the pay of all members of the special project team headed by Colin due to their increased workload. He felt that this might also help in easing the strain experienced by all.

Goodbye to America

Upon the approach of their one-year anniversary at BSS, Hans and Wolfgang requested a meeting with Sam. He assumed that the men wanted to talk about the upcoming arrival of the two additional German expatriates. The meeting instead was about Hans and Wolfgang returning to Germany. Hans explained that he and Wolfgang were returning to Germany, but that they would stay two weeks after the new expatriates arrived to help them settle in and get use to their new surroundings. Sam was shocked and very disappointed. He had actually hoped that Hans, especially, would decide to stay even longer than the planned two years. The two men thanked Sam for allowing them to work for BSS and they told him that they had enjoyed their experiences in America, however, they were anxious to return to Germany. Sam asked if there was anything he could do to change their minds, but the Germans appeared not to be flexible on the issue. Sam shook their hands and said that he hoped that he would be able to visit them in Germany. As the men left his office, Sam sat, wondering how he was going to replace Hans, and if he should have managed the German engineers differently.

SOURCES

Crane, R. (2000). <u>European Business Cultures</u>. Essex: Pearson Educational, Limited.

Flamini, R. (1997). <u>Passport Germany</u>. San Rafael, CA: World Trade Press.

Scarborough, J. (2001). <u>The Origins of Cultural Differences and Their Impact on Management</u>. Westport, CT: Quorum Books.

This case was prepared by Charles A. Rarick.

ANNE BURN'S PERSONAL JIHAD

ABSTARCT

An American expatriate is assigned to work in a non-profit organization in Jordan that sought to promote Jordanian exports, especially those produced and sold by female entrepreneurs. She experienced difficulties as she attempted to promote the economic standing of women in Jordan, and became involved in organizational politics she did not understand.

Anne Burns, a forty-five year old American woman who started a number of businesses in the United States, was hired by a recently established non-profit organization called ExportJordan. Working with a grant from USAID, ExportJordan's mission was to further develop local businesses in Jordan in order to capitalize on the recently signed free trade agreement with the United States. Having just sold her last business, and having her two grown children out of the house, Anne and her husband, Don, decided to forgo their empty nest and strike out on a new adventure in the Middle East.

Anne and Don did not need to work since the businesses they had created, and sold, provided more than a comfortable living for them. Having many productive years ahead of them, they sought out a unique challenge. Jordan was to be that new challenge.

Jordan

Jordan is a constitutional monarchy based on heredity. Male descendants of the dynasty of King Abdullah bin al Hussein inherit the throne and rule the country without opposition. The country now called Jordan was created at the end of World War I when the League of Nations gave the territory to the United Kingdom to rule. The UK created a semi-autonomous jurisdiction called the Emirate of Transjordan. In 1946 Transjordan became an independent country and changed its name in 1950 to the Hashemite Kingdom of Jordan. The country is presently ruled by King Abdullah II, a western educated and progressive leader who has strong ties to the United States. King Abdullah has moved for a free press, democratic reform, and women's rights. King Abdullah's father ruled Jordan through much of its independence. As King Abdullah has moved for even more reforms than his father, both the United States and the European Union have rewarded Jordan with free trade agreements. Jordan is a member of the World Trade Organization. The close ties between Jordan and western nations, coupled with the King and his wife's desire to advance the status of women helped create ExportJordan. ExportJordan was charged with helping to create an entrepreneurial spirit among Jordan's female citizens, and to help them develop and export products. Currently Jordan is successful in exporting clothing, food products, phosphate, and some pharmaceuticals. With the new free trade agreements it was hoped that additional areas could be developed for export.

Trouble from the Start

It was a spirit of adventure and a genuine desire to help others that lead Anne and her husband to Jordan. They were both impressed with the young King and his views for leading his country into the 21st Century. They had hoped to find a cooperative environment, but that hope was somewhat challenged from the start.

When Anne arrived at the offices of ExportJordan for the first time, she met Hayat Maani. Hayat was a western educated young woman with passion. She was deeply concerned with the plight of women in her country and was involved in a number of social causes throughout Jordan. She welcomed Anne and gave her a tour of the offices, explaining what the organization did and what Anne's role would be in the new venture. Anne would work closely with Hayat in helping small businesses owned by Jordanian women to find international buyers for their products. The mission of ExportJordan was to promote all Jordanian products, but Anne would mainly be involved in helping female entrepreneurs. On the initial office tour and series of introduction, Anne met Jafar Faqir, a middle-aged man who worked in the export finance division of the organization. Hayat introduced Jafar to Anne. Jafar did not extend his hand when Anne initiated a handshake and she thought this a bit odd, but quickly forgot about it when Jafar asked her "how do you find Jordan." Anne explained that she had only been in the country a short time but that she was very impressed with the King and his approach to the advancement of women. The look on Jafar's face told Anne that he did not like her response. Hayat told Jafar that Anne would be responsible for promoting women entrepreneurs and Jafar told her to remember these words, "The eye cannot raise above the eyebrow." Hayat shouted to Jafar something in Arabic and Jafar left without saying another word. When Anne asked what had just happened, Hayat simply said that unfortunately not all Jordanian men were supportive of equality for women. Anne would find that this would not be her only negative encounter with Jafar.

The rest of the day went smoothly for Anne as she continued to meet more people associated with the organization. She noticed that all of the women in the offices wore a hejab or headscarf, except for Hayat. Anne noticed other interesting cultural dimensions, such as the common response "Inshallah" or God willing." Many of the people she met seemed very interested in her and asked many questions, such as how many children she and her husband had, especially boys. Anne and her husband had two girls and when she told this to one of her male colleagues, he responded with "Oh, I'm so sorry." Anne knew that it was going to be a very different and interesting experience living in the Middle East.

Progress Begins

Anne and Don settled into their life in Jordan and apart from the normal difficulties of living abroad, the couple didn't feel as if they experienced too much difficulty adjusting. Although there were no other Westerners at ExportJordan, Anne and Don met other American and British expatriates and enjoyed their company and they all enjoyed sharing their experiences living in Jordan. Don kept busy looking for business opportunities for himself and helping Anne with her assignment.

After two months it became clear to Anne that she was in need of an assistant to help her with the preliminary analytical work she was doing. Anne suggested to Hayat that Don be hired to help her. Hayat told her that she didn't think that would be possible, however, she would find someone else to help her. After a few days, Hayat introduced Anne to Karim Dabbas, a young Jordanian man who was hired as her assistant. Karim spoke English well, yet his youth and inexperience gave Anne some concern.

With the help of Karim, Anne completed her initial analysis and was ready to begin to do her fieldwork. Anne had planned on hosting seminars for women around Jordan explaining the possibilities of the export market and finding women with whom she could personally consult about their businesses. Karim would be helpful in the fieldwork, acting as both a driver and interpreter.

The first seminar was planned for Amman and was heavily promoted. Although Anne and Hayat had hoped for a very large audience, they were not unhappy with the few women who attended, because among the attendees were some good prospects for the export market. With Anne's expertise in creating business plans and her knowledge of the U.S. market, Anne and Hayat began helping three women who produced crafts which were felt had international appeal. Additional seminars were planned for other cities in Jordan in the future, and Anne was convinced that she would be able to make a contribution to ExportJordan.

Warnings from Jafar

During the next two weeks Anne and Karim worked with the three women from the seminar on their business plans and creating ways of making their products more appealing to the global marketplace. Anne had not seen Hayat for a few days but she and Karim were busy, and she really didn't need any help from Hayat at that time. One of the female entrepreneurs introduced Anne to two other women who were seeking help with their businesses and so Anne now had five clients to assist. With the increasing workload, Anne began to turn more responsibility over to Karim. Karim was not confident that he could do the work requested by Anne, but she tried to reassure him that he was capable and there would not be any problems.

Karim made slow progress and frequently asked Anne for help with his work. Anne became increasingly frustrated by the slow pace of Karim's work and his constant need for assurances. She developed a nickname for him, "worn sole," meaning that he was wearing out the bottom of his shoes running back and forth from his office to hers asking questions. His nickname appeared appropriate as well to her in that Karim was constantly worried and thus was developing a "worn soul." Karim took the puns in stride but, nevertheless, didn't seem to change his behavior.

One particular incident involving Karim produced difficulties for Anne. She was standing in the hallway talking to another ExportJordan employee when Karim came running down the hall, again looking for her. She mentioned to her coworker "here comes old worn sole again." She continued to tell the coworker about Karim's weaknesses and as she discussed these weaknesses she noticed that Jafar was near and listening. Anne and Jafar did not have much contact with each other, yet the relationship between the two was strained. When they passed in the hall

Jafar would not even look at Anne. After once again giving Karim clarification on his task, Anne turned to Jafar and asked him if he needed anything from her. He stared at her for what seemed like a very long time and then muttered, "Just remember this – the family knife does not cut." At this point Anne had had enough with Jafar and his sayings and so she decided to confront him. Jafar turned and went back to his office and Anne followed him. Anne asked Jafar, in a loud voice, "what is it with you and all of these bullshit sayings." Jafar's eyes got big as he pointed his finger towards her and told her that she should be very careful in her "American ways." With no intention of letting this go, Anne sat down in the chair in front of Jafar's desk and propped her feet up on his desk. She told Jafar to sit down, as they needed to talk. Jafar refused to sit down and asked her leave. Anne began to explain to Jafar that she was in Jordan to help the Jordanian people and that by helping women to develop their businesses she was helping all people in Jordan. It appeared to Anne that Jafar was not listening to a word she was saying. After a long silence Anne stood up and walked out of the office. As she was leaving Jafar said to her "Don't you want to know what happened to your friend, Hayat?" When she turned in surprise, Jafar closed and locked the door.

Anne hadn't seen Hayat for a number of days and was curious where she was but now she was concerned. Anne immediately found Karim and asked him if he knew where Hayat was, and he responded that he didn't. He also didn't know if she still worked at ExportJordan. Anne began to ask others in the offices if they knew what happened to Hayat, and it seemed that no one did. One of her colleagues, Mania told her that she thought that Hayat had been fired and that Jafar had something to do with it. Already upset with Jafar, Anne decided that it was time to confront him again. She went to his office and found the door unlocked this time. She barged in and demanded to know what he meant by his statement about Hayat and what happened to her. At first Jafar denied knowing much about the situation and told her that he was only in charge of financing arrangements and that he had no authority over Hayat. Anne losing her temper shouted to Jafar, "Goddamn it Jafar, tell me the truth about Hayat." At that moment it appeared that a calm had come over Jafar. He put his head down and stared at the floor. He then raised his head and told Anne that he wanted her to tell him about "the truth of America's plan to eliminate Palestine." Anne could see that this conversation was not going well and decided just to leave Jafar's office. Before she could go, Jafar approached her, stood very close, and looking into her eyes announced, "Muslim Brotherhood will prevail." Anne felt frightened and threatened as she left the office.

Meeting with the Director

Anne made it straight to her office and felt comfort there. She composed herself and began thinking about what she should do. The organizational structure of ExportJordan was very unstructured and Anne really did not have a supervisor. Hayat acted in some ways as her manager, however, Hayat really did not have formal authority over Anne, and Anne also was not sure whom Jafar reported to as well. Anne decided that perhaps she should schedule an appointment with Dr. Massimi, director of ExportJordan. She felt a bit uncomfortable approaching him directly, but since there really wasn't any formal organizational structure (at least that she knew), she reasoned that it would not be improper. She had met Dr. Massimi on a number of occasions and he appeared to be a very kind and understanding man. She hoped that a meeting with him would clear up what happened to Hayat and resolve the tensions with Jafar.

Anne asked Karim to call and schedule an appointment for her with Dr. Massimi. Karim appeared very nervous and didn't appear to want to talk. He said he would do it as soon as he returned from a meeting. Anne wasn't aware of any meeting involving Karim and he wasn't forthcoming about the details. Anne decided to do some work to get her mind off the Jafar incident. Later in the afternoon Anne came out of her office to check on Karim. He was nowhere to be found. Anne asked if anyone knew where Karim was and was told by one of her colleagues that he was with Jafar. Surprised by this information, Anne went back in her office and decided to call Dr. Massimi herself. Dr. Massimi answered the telephone directly and Anne told him that she needed to see him as soon as possible. He told her that she could come to his office immediately.

Anne entered the office and immediately asked Dr. Massimi what happened to Hayat. Dr. Massimi sat in his chair and without answering, asked her how she was enjoying Jordan. Anne told him that she liked most of the people but that she was having a problem with Jafar. At that moment an assistant brought a tray of tea into the office and offered a cup to Anne. She was too upset to drink tea, she told the assistant. Dr. Massimi took a cup and told Anne to take a cup and that it would calm her. Anne still refused the tea. As Dr. Massimi enjoyed his tea, Anne began to tell him about Jafar. He listened a bit and then asked Anne about her family. Anne told him that they were fine and then preceded to again explain her situation with Jafar. Dr. Massimi listened a bit more and then interrupted Anne again by telling her about his family and told her that his son was studying in the United States. He explained that his son had some difficulties adjusting to American culture. Anne told Dr. Massimi that she and her husband were adjusting well but that she was having problems with her job. Dr. Massimi then began telling a story about his first international job in Iran. He went into great detail about the problems he experienced. Anne listened but wondered if Dr. Massimi was just avoiding her questions.

Anne decided to take another approach. When Dr. Massimi finished his story, Anne told him how happy she was to be able to help Jordanian women and that she was hoping that she could be more successful in her job. Dr. Massimi told her that she was providing a very important service to Jordan and that her work was appreciated. When Anne started to mention Jafar again Dr. Massimi interrupted her to ask if she had visited Petra. When she said that she had planned a visit but had not yet had time, Dr. Massimi began to tell her the history of this ancient city and its importance. Visitors to the office interrupted the history lesson. Three men from the Jordanian Ministry of Tourism stopped by to see Dr. Massimi. He invited them in and introduced them to Anne. Dr. Massimi told the men that he was just talking about Petra and the four men began a discussion about tourist sites in Jordan, and more tea was brought in the office. The four men discussed many things, sometimes in Arabic and sometimes in English, as Anne sat looking at her watch. Getting impatient Anne got up and told Dr. Massimi that she would come back and talk to him "when he could give her his full attention."

Returning to her office, Anne decided that she should compose an email message to Dr. Massimi explaining what she was not able to explain in his office. She explained the situation with Jafar, asked for clarification on Hayat, and told him that she was confused by the structure of the organization.

As Anne was ready to leave for home she checked her email one last time. There was a response from Dr. Massimi. As she anxiously opened the message expecting to get clarification on all the issues, she was shocked to see the response was "Yes, Mrs. Burn, Jordan is a complex country." He did invite her to come to see him again so that they could discuss her situation. Anne muttered as she turned off her computer "What's the use." She set out for home with the intention of telling her husband that they should look for another opportunity, one not in the Middle East.

Sources

Kelly, R. (2003). <u>Countrywatch Jordan Report.</u>
Nydell, M. (2003). <u>Understanding Arabs</u>. Yarmouth, ME: International.
www. Countrywatch.com
www.odci/cia/publications/factbook/geos/jo.html
www.state.gov

This case was prepared by Charles A. Rarick.

STEW'S NIGERIAN BUSINESS TROUBLES

Sitting at the desk in his office in Atlanta, Stew Morrison was elated by the contents of an envelope that had recently arrived from Africa. The envelope contained a letter and supporting documentation from a contact Stew had established in Nigeria and was promising to provide many new customers for Stew's company. Stew Morrison was the CEO of a company called, e-Future; a company that specialized in the sale of education vouchers for the developing world. The letter from Nigeria indicated that a number of businesses, and the government of Nigeria were very interested in purchasing the education vouchers. The letter invited Stew to come to Nigeria and meet with these important prospective customers. Stew was confident that the business was finally beginning to turn around and he was excited about the prospects awaiting him in Nigeria.

E-FUTURE

Begun with limited capital from a few wealthy investors in 2002, e-Future was a company with a dream. That dream was to bring education to the developing world. Stew Morrison, a former professor of education, had developed the idea of offering a simple means for potential students to pay for higher education and technical training through the use of electronic vouchers. Individuals could purchase the vouchers themselves, or the vouchers could be purchased by governments for their citizens. It was also assumed that businesses may offer them as incentives to their employees. The vouchers could be used in a number of universities and technical schools in Africa, Asia, and in Latin America. In addition, an on-line university created by e-Future offered a number of courses and would accept the voucher as payment. The voucher concept reduced the cost of a course significantly, as universities and schools deeply discounted their tuition under the program. The business concept, first developed by Morrison found its way to Jay Nettlehouse, who in turn convinced other private investors to fund startup of the organization. Nettlehouse became Chairman of e-Future and continued to provide financial support for the company. While the private investors hoped to profit from the business, they also hoped that their money would be used to help develop the poorer countries of the world. Unfortunately, sales of the vouchers proved to be more difficult than anticipated. The company had yet to make a profit and the private investors had to make additional contributions to keep the business operational.

NIGERIA

While Stew had never to been on the African continent, he had no concerns with the upcoming trip to Nigeria. Doing some research Stew learned that Nigeria had gained its independent from Britain in 1960 and that political instability had ensued up until 1999 when a democratic government was established. He discovered that Nigeria is a diverse country with over 250 ethnic groups. The country is divided by religious identity with the north being mostly Muslim and the south being mostly Christian. The political boundaries of present day Nigeria came into being when the British gained control of the area in the late 1800's and established the area as a colony. During World War II, Nigerians fought with the British and shortly thereafter gained some autonomy, and a constitution. Stew learned from his investigations that democracy has not been the norm during Nigeria's short existence. Due to differing religious and ethnic identities, a series of coups and dictators had exercised power during most of Nigeria's history. With democracy once again in place, Stew felt that perhaps e-Future could help Nigeria in its nation building effort. Stew was encouraged by the fact that Nigeria is a leading supplier of crude oil to the world and is the most populated country in Africa with over 90 million inhabitants. Stew also was happy to learn that English was the official language of Nigeria. While Stew felt that Nigeria offered great promise to e-Future, he also had some concerns about the level of corruption found in the country. He had read that corruption was a problem, and that some foreigners had been victims of various scams.

BIMBOLA

When Stew arrived at the Lagos airport he was overwhelmed by the sights and sounds he was experiencing. The airport was very noisy and crowded and being tired from his long journey, he felt as if he was too confused to find his way past immigration and get his luggage. As he wandered towards the immigration area he saw a sign being held up by a rather small, middle-aged man. The sign read "Welcome Mr. Stew Morrison". When he approached the man with the sign he realized that it was his contact in Nigeria, Bimbola Ogunk. The two men exchanged greetings and Bimbola took Stew's handbag and escorted him towards immigration. When Stew asked Bimbola if he would have any trouble passing through immigration Bimbola told him not to worry. He reminded Stew that he had connections and asked if he had acquired a Nigerian visa.

Stew replied that he had not, as previously instructed by Bimbola, and Bimbola said "no problem." The two men proceeded to a separate line at the immigration stop and Bimbola told the official "this is my special friend." The official looked at Stew and waved the two through immigration. To Stew, it did appear that Bimbola had connections. Stew retrieved his luggage and the two men headed for the exit. Bimbola had arranged for Stew to stay at a hotel where he had further connections. Stew at that point just wanted to get to the hotel as quickly as possible and sleep. Unfortunately the traffic of Lagos would keep Stew from his room for another two hours. The two men chatted on the way to the hotel with Bimbola constantly reassuring Stew that he had connection in the government, and connections with education officials, and industry leaders. Stew would be meeting some of those officials later in the week, he was told. Bimbola also told Stew that he wanted to take him on a trip first; a trip he would "surely enjoy." Stew checked into his hotel to get some sleep.

Early the next morning the telephone in the hotel room rang and it was Bimbola. He told Stew that he was in the hotel lobby and ready to take him on a special tour. Stew arranged for a quick breakfast before leaving with Bimbola for a trip to Benin. The long trip, over 200 miles, allowed Stew the opportunity to get to know Bimbola better. The two men discussed many things, however, Bimbola seemed unable or unwilling to provide any details as to how he was going to arrange for the sale of large quantities of e-Future vouchers. He frequently told Stew not to worry and that he, Bimbola, would handle everything. When pressed, Bimbola told Stew that he had arranged for a meeting with Dr. Kema Agaguelu, Minister of Education and that she was very interested in the educational voucher system offered by Stew's company. While not much business was discussed on the trip to Benin, Stew did learn much about the ancient walled city and about the once great kingdom. He was grateful to Bimbola for taking him to see the impressive sights.

MEET DR. AGAGUELA

The entire day, and much of the night was taken up by the trip to Benin. Stew was feeling weary and anxious to return to his room for a good night's rest. Although exhausted, he hardly slept due to the differences in time zones. The following morning he awoke to the sound of the telephone ringing. It was Bimbola greeting him good morning. The two ate breakfast in the hotel restaurant and Bimbola explained to Stew that the meeting with Dr. Agaguela was going to take place that day, later in the afternoon. He told Stew that he should get his presentation material together to show the education minister. Bimbola explained that while the government offices were in the capital, Abuja, the Education Minister had an office in Lagos and that it would not be necessary to travel to the capital to meet her.

The traffic in Lagos was horrendous and it took hours to reach the government building. Bimbola escorted Stew up the flights of stairs in the rather stark building to meet the minister. They arrived on the fifth floor and entered an office void of any marking to find a middle-aged woman sitting behind a desk looking at some papers. Bimbola introduced her as the Minister of Education and Stew began to make a presentation on what his company could offer Nigeria. He went into great detail explaining how the government could advance higher education through the e-Future program, all the time Dr. Agaguelu listened and smiled. While she never asked any questions, she seemed very interested in what Stew had told her, and she thanked him for visiting. Bimbola told Stew that he had made a very good impression on her and that she would certainly be recommending that the government purchase a very large quantity of vouchers. Stew felt a bit uneasy about the meeting but he was encouraged by what Bimbola was telling him. Stew began to press Bimbola for more details on other contacts but Bimbola told him not to worry. Bimbola stated that it was time for Stew to purchase some gifts for his family back in America.

Bimbola took Stew to a large market for shopping. While Stew had no interest in shopping at this time, he felt it best not to insult his host. The market was unlike anything Stew had ever seen. A mix of food and household items, along with crafts and animal skins and skulls. The variety and unique nature of the market was overwhelming to Stew. He managed to purchase some craft items and a special type of woven cloth recommended by Bimbola. It was approaching dinnertime and Bimbola told Stew that he had arranged for Stew to meet his family that evening. Bimbola took Stew to a restaurant where Bimbola's wife and many adults were waiting. The group represented Bimbola's immediate family as well as members of his extended family. Although the group was rather large, Stew enjoyed his meal and the company of this quite lively group of people. One of the dinner items Stew especially enjoyed was jollof rice, a Nigerian specialty. He was impressed when told by one of Bimbola's brothers that Bimbola's grandmother had invented the national dish. Some of the previous apprehensions Stew felt about Bimbola were beginning to be eased. When the waiter brought the restaurant bill to Stew, the moment was a bit uneasy. The bill was quite high and he wasn't sure who was expected to pay, but he reasoned that he would pay the bill since Bimbola had been so kind in taking him to Benin as a cultural side trip. The evening ended well and it appeared to Stew that Bimbola's family had enjoyed the meal. Bimbola took Stew back to the hotel and told him to "expect great things tomorrow."

GREAT EXPECTATIONS

Once again it was a night without much sleep for Stew. He was dragging during the day and awake most of the night. He hoped that he would be able to soon adjust to the time difference and get a good night's sleep. He was also uneasy because he still was not able to call home and speak to his wife, as the hotel's international telephone line was not working. As the telephone rang in his room, Stew knew that it Bimbola and he was looking forward to those great expectations promised by Bimbola. Bimbola told Stew that he had very good news for him and to come down to the hotel restaurant and they would discuss it. Over breakfast Bimbola had a hard time containing his happiness. He finally told Stew that he had heard from the Minister of Education and that she was arranging for the government of Nigeria to make an initial purchase of $500,000US e-Future education vouchers. Stew was excited about the news and thanked Bimbola for helping to arrange the meeting that produced these results. Bimbola told Stew that all that was needed now were three things. First, Bimbola would need the bank account number of e-Future in order to wire the funds, secondly, Stew would need to make a small payment of $10,000US to the education minister for her help, and lastly, e-Future would need to pay Bimbola a $50,000US finder's fee. Stew was taken aback by these requests. He asked Bimbola to explain more but all that Bimbola would tell him was that this is the way business was conducted in Nigeria. Bimbola told Stew that unless he wanted to lose this large contract, he would need to meet those three conditions. Stew told Bimbola that he was not sure if he would be able to do what was requested and that he would have to check with someone back in Atlanta. Bimbola told Stew that time was critical and that if he waited, he would certainly lose the contact.

Without the matter being resolved, Bimbola proceeded to tell Stew that he was going to meet with very high-level industry officials who were interested in hearing about the education vouchers for use with their companies. They were going to meet for lunch and so Stew needed once again to gather his presentation material and come along for a ride across town. On the drive across town Bimbola explained how many Americans are surprised by the way business is done in Nigeria but that "once they realize this they are able to acquire very good contracts and earn much money." Bimbola told Stew that "Nigeria is a good place to do business."

A LONG LUNCH

At lunch, Stew met with four men who were introduced by Bimbola as the leaders of Nigeria's business community. One gentleman, Segun Adelaja was introduced as Prince Segun, head of the Nigerian National Petroleum Corporation. Each man gave Stew a business card indicating their association with various business groups in Nigeria. In addition to the oil industry, the men represented textiles, agriculture, and manufacturing. The six men ate lunch and discussed many things including their love of "football" but not much attention was directed towards business, or e-Future's product. Stew felt very tired and his patience was getting thin. He asked to speak to Bimbola alone and expressed his concerns with the lack of business substance. Bimbola explained that in Nigeria it was customary for people to get to know each other first before they discussed business. Bimbola told Stew that he would provide the opportunity for Stew to present his business ideas before the group left. After many hours of entertaining Bimbola finally told the group "Mr. Morrison has a plan that is of great value to each of you." Acting on this cue, Stew proceeded to tell the men how e-Future could help their industries, and Nigeria in general. The men seemed very interested and asked a number of questions. Stew felt encouraged and continued to discuss product features at great length. After more than five hours of eating, drinking, and discussing, Bimbola told the group that Mr. Morrison had to get back to his hotel and that that they should contact him, Bimbola, if they were interested in having their companies buy the vouchers. He told the group that he strongly recommended that they take advantage of this opportunity. Once again Stew was presented with a rather large bill from the restaurant.

Bimbola drove Stew back to his hotel and explained that these men represented the best opportunity for Stew to sell thousands of vouchers. He told Stew that millions of dollars were at stake and that it was necessary that Stew completely trust Bimbola to make the deals. All that would be required was for Stew give Bimbola his normal ten percent fee, along with a retainer of "a few thousand dollars, today." Stew felt as if he was being played by Bimbola and told him that he needed to rest before making any decisions. Stew felt that it was time to make a call to Jay Nettlehouse back in Atlanta. At the hotel Stew once again experienced difficulties making an international call. His frustration level was rising and he was unsure of what he should do. While he was worried that he might be taken advantage of by Bimbola, he didn't want to miss out on the opportunities that may emerge from the relationships Bimbola provided. Stew decided to try and find another way of calling America. Stew sat on his bed watching television, resting, worrying, and wondering what his next move should be.

AN OFFICIAL CONTRACT

When the telephone rang in his room Stew hoped that it would be someone from e-Future calling. It was Bimbola who told Stew that he was coming over to the hotel for dinner and that he was bringing Stew "something that would make him very happy." When pressed as to what the surprise was, Bimbola told him that it was a contract from the Nigerian government. Stew decided to rest a bit before dinner and was hopeful that perhaps something was finally developing.

Bimbola arrived for dinner with Stew and brought along Dr. Agaguelu who presented Stew with a three-page document. The document was a government contract for $500,000US and included many seals and official stamps. It had already been signed by the President of Nigeria and the Minister of Education. Dr. Agaguela explained that the government was receiving much oil revenue and that in an effort to develop support from the people of Nigeria, the President had decided to spend some of the money to expand the educational opportunities of its citizens. Bimbola explained that it was important that the contract be signed by Stew and that the necessary payments be made immediately. When Stew asked about how he could pay the necessary "fees" Bimbola told him that he could wire the funds into a bank account, or better yet, Stew "could get cash from his American Express card and be done with it." Bimbola stressed how important he and Dr. Agaguela were in getting this contract, and that many more could follow if Stew took care of them.

Sitting at the table, confused and totally exhausted, Stew wondered what he should do, as he looked at the smiling faces of Bimbola and Dr. Agaguela.

Discussion Questions:

1.   What mistakes did Stew Morrison make in his Nigerian business trip?
2.   Do you think Bimbola is trustworthy? Explain.
3.   What should Stew do now?

Sources: Blauer, E. and J. Laure. (2001). Nigeria. New York: Scholastic; Nnoromele, S. (2002). Nigeria. San Diego: Lucent; www.countrywatch.com

Case was prepared by Charles A. Rarick

Central Michigan University

Central Michigan University

At Central Michigan University, we are dedicated to the success of our students. This book is a prime example of that philosophy. The MSA program in conjunction with CMU Off-Campus Programs and McGraw-Hill has worked to create a single textbook for each of the core courses in the MSA program. Our goal: to get our students the most current and relevant information in the most cost effective format.

This dedication to ensuring our students' success continues with the many excellent services that are available to help you throughout your MSA program:

LIBRARY SERVICES

- Main campus students have direct access to CMU's excellent library system. More information on services offered can be found at http://library.cmich.edu.

- Off-Campus Programs and CMU Online students have access to librarians and document delivery services through CMU's nationally-recognized Off-Campus Library Services. Information is available at www.ocls.cmich.edu

WRITING CENTER

The CMU Writing Center provides assistance with any writing project from help with choosing a subject within the parameters set by your instructor to suggestions on polishing of final drafts.

On-campus students please go to www.chsbs.cmich.edu/writing_center.

Off-Campus and Online students go to www.cel.cmich.edu/student/writing-center.html

FINANCIAL AID

Our dedicated staff is ready to help you find the resources to finance your education.

On-campus students: www.financialaid.cmich.edu

Off-campus students: www.cel.cmich.edu/financial-aid

OFF-CAMPUS LIBRARY SERVICES

Access to library resources and services is provided to students enrolled through CMU's Off-Campus Programs and CMU Online by the **Off-Campus Library Services (OCLS)** department. Through OCLS, off-campus and online students have access to the full range of book, e-book, journal, and online resources owned by the CMU Library and the same library services available to on-campus students.

RESEARCH ASSISTANCE

OCLS librarians are available to:

- Provide direction to appropriate sources for your topic
- Identify proper terminology to effectively search the library's databases
- Give instruction in use of library resources and services
- Create lists of citations for relevant articles and books
- Provide assistance with citing sources www.ocls.cmich.edu

OCLS librarians are accessible via telephone, e-mail, Web form, and a chat interface.

DOCUMENT DELIVERY SERVICE

OCLS's document delivery service allows Off-Campus and CMU Online students to obtain books as well as copies of single book chapters, journal articles, sample MSA and EDU projects, and more. This service is provided at no charge and all requests are typically processed within a 24 – 48 hour period. If the item you seek is not owned by the CMU Library, the Document Delivery Office (DDO) can obtain a copy from another library.

The Off-Campus Library Services Web site is available at http://ocls.cmich.edu and offers many additional helpful resources including our hours of operation. On the site you will find librarian and DDO contact information, subject guides that offer specific lists of resources for a wide range of academic subjects, tutorials that explain how to use the resources of the library, a page that includes helpful writing and research resources, and links to other CMU sites that will be of use to you, such as the university's portal, Blackboard, and the CMU Writing Center. If you have any questions, be sure to let us know. We're here to help *you*.

Index